Infancy & Toddlerhood	Physical Development	Dynamic Systems View, (pp. 75–76)	Motor skills don't just happen; in order to develop motor skills, infants must perceive something in the environment that motivates them to act, then to use their perceptions to fine-tune their movements
	Language Development	Interactionist View, (p. 99)	Children are biologically prepared for language learning but must interact with others to learn it
		Chomsky's Universal Grammar, (p. 97)	Children are born with the ability to detect basic language features and rules; adults help children acquire language through child-directed speech
	Perceptual Development	Gibson's Ecological View, (pp. 80–81)	Perception brings people in contact with the environment to interact with it and adapt to it
	Cognitive Development	Piaget's Sensorimotor Stage, (pp. 17, 18, 88–90)	Infant organizes and coordinates sensations with physical movements; six substages: simple reflexes; first habits & primary circular reactions; secondary circular reactions; coordination of secondary circular reactions; tertiary circular reactions, novelty and curiosity; internalization of schemes
	Socioemotional Development	Chess & Thomas' Classification of Temperament, (pp. 106–107)	Three basic types of temperament in children: easy, difficult, and slow-to-warm-up
		Kagan's Behavioral Inhibition, (p. 106)	Focuses on differences between shy, subdued, timid children and sociable, extraverted, bold children
		Rothbart & Bates' Effortful Control, (p. 107)	Self-regulation is an important dimension of temperament
		Bowlby's Theory of Attachment, (pp. 112–114)	Infants and their primary caregivers are biologically predisposed to form attachments; Attachment forms gradually over four phases
		Erikson's Trust vs. Mistrust Stage, (pp. 16, 108)	Infants' sense of trust is the foundation for attachment and sets the stage for a lifelong expectation for how the world will be
		Ainsworth's Strange Situation, (p. 113)	Observational measure of infant attachment; based on how babies respond, they are securely attached to caregiver, or are classified as insecure avoidant, insecure resistant, or insecure disorganized
Early Childhood	Cognitive Development	Piaget's Preoperational Stage, (pp. 16, 17, 128–132)	Child represents the world symbolically and can't perform operations yet; two substages: symbolic function and intuitive thought
		Vygotsky's Social Constructivist, (p. 132)	Zone of proximal development, scaffolding; children use speech to solve tasks
		Information Processing, (pp. 135–138)	Child's ability to pay attention improves; control of attention and memory are essential to children's cognitive development
		Theory of Mind, (pp. 138–139)	Awareness of one's own mental processes and the mental processes of others
	Emotional and Personality Development	Erikson's Initiative vs. Guilt Stage, (pp. 16, 149)	Children use their cognitive, motor, perceptual and language skills to make things happen; children's actions may bring rewards or guilt
	Moral Development	Kohlberg's Heteronomous Morality, (pp. 153, 206)	Children obey because adults tell them to; moral decisions are based on fear of punishment
		Piaget's Stages of Morality, (p. 153)	Three stages: heteronomous morality, transition, autonomous morality.
	Gender	Social Role Theory of Gender, (pp. 154–155)	Gender differences result from differing roles for men and women.
		Social Cognitive Theory of Gender, (pp. 154–156)	Gender developed by observing and imitating what other people say and do, and through being rewarded and punished for gender-appropriate and gender inappropriate behavior.
		Gender Schema Theory, (p. 156)	Gender typing emerges as children gradually develop gender schemas of what is and isn't gender-appropriate in their culture.
	Parenting	Baumrind's Parenting Style, (p. 157)	Four parenting styles: authoritarian, authoritative, neglectful, indulgent; combinations of acceptance and responsiveness on the one hand and demand and control on the other.
Middle and Late Childhood	Cognitive	Piaget's Concrete Operational Stage, (pp. 182–184)	Children can perform concrete operations, seriation, transitivity, conservation, and classification.
		Information Processing, (pp. 184–187)	Children dramatically improve their ability to sustain and control attention; long-term memory increases, but short-term memory doesn't; children use mental imagery and elaboration strategies
		Fuzzy Trace Theory, (p. 186)	Two types of memory representations: verbatim memory trace and gist; older children's better memory is caused by extracting the gist of information.
	Intelligence	Sternberg's Triarchic Theory of Intelligence, (p. 189)	Three forms of intelligence: analytical, creative, and practical.
		Gardner's 8 Frames of Mind, (pp. 189–190)	Eight types of intelligence: verbal, mathematical, spatial, bodily-kinesthetic, musical, interpersonal, intrapersonal, naturalist.

Adolescence	**Socioemotional Development**	Erikson's Industry vs. Inferiority Stage, (pp. 16, 203–204)	When children are encouraged to follow inclinations to create, their sense of industry increases. If authority figures view these efforts negatively, children will feel inferior.
		Kohlberg's 3 Levels and 6 Stages of Moral Development, (pp. 205–209)	3 levels of moral thinking: preconventional, conventional, postconventional; 6 stages.
		Constructivist Approach to Learning, (p. 219)	Learner centered, emphasizes individuals actively constructing their knowledge and understanding; teacher is guide.
		Direct Instruction Approach to Learning, (p. 219)	Teacher centered, controlled, and directed; students spend time on learning tasks, teacher minimizes negative affect.
	Cognition	Piaget's Formal Operational Stage, (pp. 17, 18, 242–243)	Child can understand and reason logically about hypothetical events, and think about thinking; can use hypothetical deductive reasoning to solve problems.
		Elkand's Adolescent Egocentrism, (pp. 243–244)	Heightened self-consciousness; has 2 components: imaginary audience and personal fable.
		Information Processing, (p. 244–245)	Improvement in executive functioning leads to more effective learning and an improved ability to determine how to allocate attention.
	Socioemotional Development	Erikson's Identity vs. Identity Confusion Stage, (pp. 16, 252)	Adolescents search for their own identity by trying different roles and personalities to find where they fit in the world.
		Marcia's 4 Statuses of Identity, (pp. 252–253)	4 statuses in developing an identity: identity diffusion, identity foreclosure, identity moratorium, and identity achievement; status depends on presence or absence or a crisis or commitment to an identity.
Early Adulthood	**Cognitive Development**	Piaget's View, (p. 282)	Adolescent and adult thinking is very similar.
		Perry's View, (p. 282)	The absolutist, dualistic thinking of adolescence gives way to the reflective, relativistic thinking in adulthood.
		Postformal Thought, (pp. 282–283)	Understanding that correct answers to a problem can require reflective thinking, what's right varies depending on the situation, and the search for truth is ongoing.
	Socioemotional Development	Erikson's Intimacy vs. Isolation Stage, (pp. 16, 293)	3 types of love: passion, intimacy, and commitment; various combinations of these result in infatuation, affectionate love, fatuous love, and consummate love.
		Sternberg's Triangle of Love, (pp. 292–295)	3 types of love: passion, intimacy, and commitment; various combinations of these result in infatuation, affectionate love, fatuous love, and consummate love.
Middle Adulthood	**Cognitive Development**	Horn's Fluid and Crystallized Intelligence, (p. 313)	Fluid intelligence (ability to reason abstractly) declines while crystallized intelligence (accumulated info and verbal skills) increases.
		Information Processing, (pp. 315–316)	Perceptual speed declines, memory capacity becomes more limited if memory strategies aren't used; expertise increases.
	Socioemotional Development	Erikson's Generativity vs. Stagnation Stage, (pp. 16, 322–323)	Generativity is adults' need to leave legacies to the next generation; stagnation develops instead if individuals think they haven't done much for the next generation.
		Levinson's Seasons of a Man's Life, (p. 323–324)	Adulthood has 3 main stages which are surrounded by a transition period; specific tasks and challenges pertain to each stage.
		Contemporary Life Events Approach, (pp. 324–325)	Influence of a life event depends on the event itself, mediating variables, the life stage and sociohistoric context, and on the individual's take on the event and coping strategies.
		The Big 5 Personality Factors, (pp. 327, 364)	Important dimensions of personality: Openness to experience, conscientiousness, extraversion, agreeableness, and neuroticism.
		Cumulative Personality Model, (p. 329)	With time and age, people become more adept at interacting with their environment in ways that promote the stability of personality.
Late Adulthood	**Physical Development**	Cellular Clock Theory of Aging, (pp. 338–339)	As we age, our cells are less able to divide.
		Free-Radical Theory of Aging, (p. 339)	Cells' metabolism produces free radicals that damage DNA and other cellular structures.
		Hormonal Stress Theory of Aging, (p. 339)	Aging in the hormonal system can lower resilience to stress and increase disease.
	Socioemotional Development	Erikson's Integrity vs. Despair, (pp. 16, 361–362)	Reflecting on the past and either piecing together a positive review or concluding that one's life hasn't been well spent.
		Activity Theory, (p. 362)	The more active and involved older adults are, the more likely they are to be satisfied with their lives.
		Socioemotional Selectivity Theory, (pp. 362–363, 369)	Older adults are more selective about their social networks and spend more time with familiar individuals with whom they have rewarding relationships.
		Selective Optimization with Compensation Theory, (pp. 363–364)	Successful aging is related to 3 main factors: selection, optimization, and compensation.
Dying, and Grieving		Kübler-Ross' Stages of Dying, (pp. 378–379)	A dying person mentally and emotionally goes through 5 stages: denial and isolation, anger, bargaining, depression, and acceptance.

Essentials of Life-Span Development

SECOND EDITION

John W. Santrock

University of Texas at Dallas

McGraw Hill

Connect
Learn
Succeed™

Published by McGraw-Hill, an imprint of The McGraw-Hill Companies, Inc., 1221 Avenue of the Americas, New York, NY 10020. Copyright © 2012, 2008. All rights reserved. No part of this publication may be reproduced or distributed in any form or by any means, or stored in a database or retrieval system, without the prior written consent of The McGraw-Hill Companies, Inc., including, but not limited to, in any network or other electronic storage or transmission, or broadcast for distance learning.

This book is printed on acid-free paper.

1 2 3 4 5 6 7 8 9 0 QDB/QDB 9 8 7 6 5 4 3 2 1

ISBN: 978-0-07-353207-3
MHID: 0-07-353207-X

Executive Vice President, Editorial: *Michael Ryan*
Editorial Director: *Beth Mejia*
Publisher: *Mike Sugarman*
Executive Editor: *Krista Bettino*
Executive Marketing Manager: *Julia Flohr*
Director of Development: *Dawn Groundwater*
Senior Developmental Editor: *Judith Kromm*
Project Manager: *Holly Irish*
Production Editor: *Melanie Field*
Manuscript Editor: *Patricia Ohlenroth*
Text Designer: *Jeanne Calabrese*
Cover Designer: *Laurie Entringer*
Art Manager: *Robin Mouat*
Photo Research: *Jenifer Blankenship*
Production Supervisor: *Carol Bielski*
Composition: *10/12 Scala by Aptara®, Inc.*
Printing: *45# New Era Thin Plus, Quad Graphics*

Credits: The credits section for this book begins on page 463 and is considered an extension of the copyright page.

Library of Congress Cataloging-in-Publication Data

Santrock, John W.
    Essentials of life-span development / John Santrock. • 2nd ed.
        p. cm.
    Includes bibliographical references and index.
    ISBN-13: 978-0-07-353207-3 (alk. paper)
    ISBN-10: 0-07-353207-X (alk. paper)
    1. Developmental psychology. I. Title.
BF713.S256   2011
155•dc22

2010046825

The Internet addresses listed in the text were accurate at the time of publication. The inclusion of a Web site does not indicate an endorsement by the authors or McGraw-Hill, and McGraw-Hill does not guarantee the accuracy of the information presented at these sites.

With special appreciation to my wife, Mary Jo

About the Author

John Santrock with his grandchildren, Luke, Alex, and Jordan

John W. Santrock received his Ph.D. from the University of Minnesota in 1973. He taught at the University of Charleston and the University of Georgia before joining the Program in Psychology and Human Development at the University of Texas at Dallas, where he currently teaches a number of undergraduate courses and was given the University's Effective Teaching Award in 2006.

John has been a member of the editorial boards of *Child Development* and *Developmental Psychology*. His research on father custody is widely cited and used in expert witness testimony to promote flexibility and alternative considerations in custody disputes.

John also has authored these exceptional McGraw-Hill texts: *Children* (11th edition), *Adolescence* (12th edition), *Life-Span Development* (13th edition), *Topical Life-Span Development* (5th edition), and *Educational Psychology* (5th edition).

For many years, John was involved in tennis as a player, teaching professional, and coach of professional tennis players. He has been married for more than 35 years to his wife, Mary Jo, who is a realtor. He has two daughters—Tracy, and Jennifer, who is a medical sales specialist at Medtronic. Tracy recently completed the New York City Marathon, and Jennifer was in the top 100 ranked players on the Women's Professional Tennis Tour. He has one granddaughter, Jordan, age 19, and two grandsons, Alex, age 6, and Luke, age 4. In the last decade, John also has spent time painting expressionist art.

Brief Contents

Contents

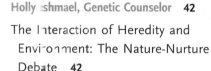

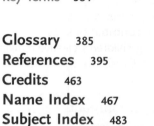
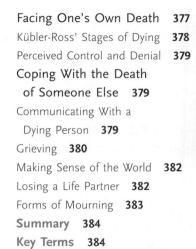

How Would You?

Health Care Professions

Family Studies Professions

Preface

The Essential Approach

In the view of many instructors who teach the life-span development course, the biggest challenge they face is covering all periods of human development within one academic term. My own teaching experience bears this out. I have had to skip over much of the material in a comprehensive life-span development text in order to focus on key topics and concepts that students find difficult and to fit in applications that are relevant to students' lives. I wrote *Essentials of Life-Span Development* to respond to the need for a shorter text that covers core content in a way that is meaningful to diverse students.

This second edition continues my commitment to a brief introduction to life-span development—with an exciting difference. Recognizing that most of today's students have grown up in a digital world, I take very seriously the need for communicating content in different ways, online as well as in print. Consequently, I'm enthusiastic about McGraw-Hill's new online assignment and assessment platform, *Connect Life-Span*, which incorporates this text and the captivating *Milestones* video modules. Together, these resources give students and instructors the essential coverage, applications, and course tools they need to tailor the life-span course to meet their specific needs.

The Essential Teaching and Learning Environment

Research shows that students today learn in multiple modalities. Not only do their work preferences tend to be more visual and more interactive, but their reading and study sessions often occur in short bursts. With shorter chapters and innovative interactive study modules, *Essentials of Life-Span Development* allows students to study whenever, wherever, and however they choose. Regardless of individual study habits, preparation, and approaches to the course, *Essentials* connects with students on a personal, individual basis and provides a road map for success in the course

For students to succeed in the life-span development course, instruction must be engaging and student friendly. To this end, all the resources of this edition of *Essentials* were developed to engage students and help them be successful. Two resources that are new to this edition are *Milestones* and *Connect*.

Milestones is an assessable video-based program that tracks human development through each major life stage. In *Milestones of Child Development*, students can watch an individual child as he or she approaches and achieves the major developmental milestones, or for a topical view, students can compare several children on a specific milestone. *Milestones* also includes gradable, multiple-choice assessments to check students' understanding of the concepts illustrated by the videos.

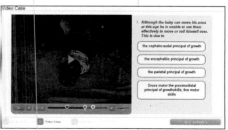

In *Milestones: Transitions,* students encounter adolescents and adults reflecting on critical points in their lives. Students learn firsthand about changing perspectives on key issues, such as body image, cognitive changes, and death and dying. *Milestones: Transitions* also provides students with a series of critical-thinking exercises, allowing them to examine the differences in attitudes that arise throughout the life span.

Connect Life-Span is designed to allow students to engage with the relevant course content at their own pace, using their mobile devices. By showing students what they know, this program helps them focus on learning what they don't know. Features of *Connect Life-Span* include:

- a powerful adaptive diagnostic tool—based on thousands of hours of research on faculty and student behavior and workflow—that assesses what a student has and has not mastered, as well as how much additional study time is needed

Adaptive diagnostic tool helps students know what they don't know.

- online assignments with immediate feedback
- the *Milestones* video program with assessment
- the ability to record class lectures that can be accessed by computer or a mobile device
- an interactive version of *Essentials of Life-Span Development* that dynamically engages students to improve learning and retention
- concise, visual snapshots of student performance
- tools that enable instructors to create and manage assignments online

For instructors, the benefits of going digital include autogradable assignments and the ability to evaluate each individual student's progress at a glance, identify struggling students before the first exam, and tailor lectures, assignments, and exams accordingly. These tools enable instructors to present course content in a way that helps students learn faster and prepare better for tests.

Essential Coverage

The challenge in writing *Essentials of Life-Span Development* was determining what comprises the core content of the course. With the help of consultants and instructors who responded to surveys and reviewed the content at different stages of development, I have been able to present all of the core topics, key ideas, and most important research in life-span development that students need to know in a brief fromat that stands on its own merits.

The 17 short chapters of *Essentials* are organized chronologically and cover all phases of the life span, from the prenatal period through late adulthood and death. Providing a broad overview of life-span development, this edition also gives particular attention to the theories and concepts that students seem to have difficulty mastering.

Essential Applications

Applied examples give students a sense that the field of life-span development has personal meaning for them. In this edition of *Essentials* are numerous real-life applications as well as research applications for each phase of the life-span.

In addition to applied examples, *Essentials of Life-Span Development* offers applications for students in a variety of majors and career paths.

- *How Would You . . . ?* questions. Given that students enrolled in the life-span course have diverse majors, *Essentials* includes applications that appeal to different interests. The most prevalent areas of specialization are education, human development and family studies, health professions, psychology, and social work. To engage these students and ensure that *Essentials* orients them to concepts that are key to their understanding of life-span development, I asked instructors specializing in these fields to contribute *How Would You . . . ?* questions for each chapter. Strategically placed in the margin next to relevant topics, these questions highlight the essential takeaway ideas for these students.

- *Careers in Life-Span Development.* This feature personalizes life-span development by describing an individual working in a career related to the chapter's focus. Chapter 2, for example, profiles Holly Ishmael, a genetic counselor. The feature describes Ms. Ishmael's education and work setting, includes a direct quote from Ms. Ishmael, discusses various employment options for genetic coun-

How Would You...?

As a social worker, how would you help a rejected child develop more positive relationships with peers?

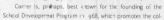

CAREERS IN LIFE-SPAN DEVELOPMENT

James Comer Child Psychiatrist

James Comer grew up in a low-income neighborhood in East Chicago, Indiana and credits his parents with leaving no doubt about the importance of education. He obtained a B.A. degree from Indiana University. He went on to obtain a medical degree from Howard University College of Medicine, a Master of Public Health degree from the University of Michigan School of Public Health, and psychiatry training at the Yale University School of Medicine's Child Study Center. He currently is the Maurice Falk Professor of Child Psychiatry at the Yale University Child Study Center and an associate dean at the Yale University Medical School. During his years at Yale, Comer has concentrated his career on promoting a focus on child development as a way of improving schools. His efforts in support of healthy development of young people are known internationally.

Comer is, perhaps, best known for the founding of the School Development Program in 1968, which promotes the col-

James Comer (*left*) is shown with some of the inner-city children who attend a school that became a better learning environment because of Comer's intervention.

laboration of parents, educators, and community to improve social, emotional, and academic outcomes for children.

selors, and provides resources for students who want to find out more about careers in genetic counseling.

New in This Edition

I have updated both the research and applied content significantly for this edition of *Essentials of Life-Span Development*. In addition to presenting the latest, most contemporary research in each period of human development, including more than 1,000 citations from 2009, 2010, and 2011 alone, I made the following revisions.

Chapter 1: Introduction

- Updated statistics on the percentage of U.S. children under age 18 living in poverty (Childstats.gov, 2009)
- Updated information about the Minnesota Family Investment Program (2009)
- New section, Connecting Biological, Cognitive, and Socioemotional Processes (Diamond, 2009; Diamond, Casey, & Munakata, 2011)
- New description of the rapidly emerging fields of developmental cognitive neuroscience and developmental social neuroscience to illustrate the interface of biological, cognitive, and socioemotional processes (Diamond, Casey, & Munakata, 2011)
- Expanded coverage of Bronfenbrenner's contributions (Gauvain & Parke, 2010)
- New Figure 1.10 summarizing major theories and issues in life-span development

Chapter 2: Biological Beginnings

- Expanded discussion of criticisms of evolutionary psychology
- Added material connecting the discussion of evolution and genetics
- New coverage of susceptibility (Paquette & others, 2010) and longevity genes (Bauer & others, 2010)
- New material on the concept of gene-gene interaction (Bapat & others, 2010; Chen & others, 2010)
- Description of epigenetic research on early experiences and effects on later behavior
- New section and coverage of the concept of genetic × environment (g × e) interaction (Goldman & others, 2010; Keers & others, 2010), including a recent study on the gene 5-HTTLPR (Caspers & others, 2009)
- New concluding paragraph on the interaction of heredity and environment
- New major section on brain development in the prenatal period (Nelson, 2011)
- New coverage of a link between maternal diabetes and obesity and the development of neural tube defects (Yazdy & others, 2010)
- Description of recent research on maternal smoking and inattention/hyperactivity in children (Knopik, 2009)
- New coverage of the offspring of diabetic mothers (Huda & others, 2010)
- Description of a study linking failure to take folic acid supplements in the first trimester of pregnancy with toddlers' behavioral problems (Roza & others, 2010)
- New discussion of a study on maternal depression and its link to negative prenatal and birth outcomes (Diego & others, 2009)
- Description of a study indicating positive benefits in CenteringPregnancy groups (Klima & others, 2009)
- Updated figures on the increase in preterm births in the United States (National Center for Health Statistics, 2009b)
- Significant updating of research on the role of progestin in preventing preterm births (da Fonseca & others, 2009; Norman & others, 2009)

- Discussion of a study on the percentage of women with postpartum depression who seek help (McGarry & others, 2009)
- Updated coverage of fathers' adjustment during the postpartum period (Dietz & others, 2009; Smith & Howard, 2008)
- Coverage of a research review of the interaction difficulties of depressed mothers and their infants (Field, 2010)

Chapter 3: Physical and Cognitive Development in Infancy

- New material on the most common sleep problem in infancy (The Hospital for Sick Children & others, 2010)
- Updated and expanded coverage of SIDS, including the role of the neurotransmitter serotonin and brain stem functioning (Kinney & others, 2009)
- Expanded coverage of breast feeding (Agency for Healthcare Research and Quality, 2007; Jansen, de Weerth, & Riksen-Walraven, 2008)
- Expanded discussion of the importance of practice in learning to walk (Adolph, 2010)
- New Figure 3.12 illustrating how eye tracking is used to study early visual ability in infants (Franchak & others, 2010)
- New section on infants' perception of occluded objects (Johnson, 2010a, b, c; Bertenthal & others, 2007)
- New section, Nature, Nurture, and Perceptual Development, that examines nativist and empiricist views of perception (Amso & Johnson, 2011; Johnson, 2010a, b, c; Slater & others, 2010)

- New section on perceptual-motor coupling (Kim & Johnson, 2011)
- Much expanded coverage of the nature/nurture issue in infant cognitive development and the key issues in this area of research
- New discussion of Elizabeth Spelke's (2004; Spelke & Kinzler, 2009) core knowledge approach to cognitive development, including criticism by Mark Johnson (2008)
- Expanded conclusion about the most difficult task facing researchers in determining the influence of nature and nurture on cognitive development (Aslin, 2009)
- New Figure 3.20, summarizing how long infants of different ages can remember information (Bauer, 2009)
- Expanded discussion of concept formation and categorization in infancy and new summary statement about an infant's remarkable degree of learning power (Diamond, Casey, & Munakata, 2011; Mandler 2009)
- Discussion of recent research on early gestures and SES disparities in child vocabulary at school entry (Rowe & Goldin-Meadow, 2009)
- New material on shared book reading and its benefits for infants and toddlers (DeLoache & Ganea, 2009)

Chapter 4: Socioemotional Development in Infancy

- Added commentary about the importance of the communication aspect of emotion in infancy (Campos, 2009)
- Expanded coverage of the onset of emotions in infancy (Kagan, 2010)
- New material on smiling in infancy (Campos, 2009; Messinger, 2008)
- Revised definition of temperament based on Campos (2009)
- Description of recent research on the interaction between temperament style and the type of child care young children experience (Pluess & Belsky, 2009)

- New material on the importance of considering the multiple temperament dimensions of children (Bates, 2008)
- New coverage of cultural variations in toddlers' mirror self-recognition (Thompson & Virmani, 2010)
- Inclusion of research on the early appearance of infants' conscious awareness of their bodies (Brownell & others, 2010)
- New section, Social Orientation and Understanding, that focuses on infants' social sophistication and insight
- Discussion of a study of maternal sensitive parenting and infant attachment security (Finger & others, 2009)
- Coverage of a meta-analysis linking three types of insecure attachment to externalizing problems (Fearon & others, 2010)
- Description of research indicating a genetic × environment interaction between disorganized attachment, the short version of the serotonin transporter gene, and a low level of maternal responsiveness (Spangler & others, 2009)
- Expanded discussion of fathers and mothers as caregivers
- New coverage of the father's role as a caregiver in the Aka pygmy culture (Hewlett, 2000; Hewlett & MacFarlan, 2010)
- Coverage of a recent NICHD study linking early nonrelative child care and adolescent development at age 15 (Vandell & others, 2010)
- Inclusion of the following important point about the NICHD SECC research: findings consistently show that family factors are considerably stronger and more consistent predictors of a wide variety of child outcomes than are child-care experiences (quality, quantity, type)

Chapter 5: Physical and Cognitive Development in Early Childhood

- Coverage of a national study on children's eating behavior and fat intake (Center for Science in the Public Interest, 2008)
- Inclusion of a study that found children's weight at five years of age was significantly related to their weight at nine years of age (Gardner & others, 2009)
- Discussion of a study on developmental changes in the percentage of overweight children from 4 to 11 years of age depending on whether they have lean or obese parents (Semmler & others, 2009)
- Description of a study of sedentary behavior and light to vigorous physical activity in preschool children (Brown & others, 2009)
- Updated information about the WIC program and young children's nutrition (Sekhobo & others, 2010)
- Coverage of a study linking young children's exposure to second-hand smoke to sleep problems (Yolton & others, 2010)
- Coverage of research on the effectiveness of the Tools of the Mind curriculum on self-regulatory and cognitive control skills in at-risk young children (Diamond & others, 2007)
- New material on using computer exercises to improve children's attention (Jaeggi, Berman, & Jonides, 2009; Tang & Posner, 2009)
- Discussion of a study linking children's attention problems at 54 months of age with a lower level of social skills in peer relations in the first and third grades (NICHD Early Child Care Research Network, 2009)
- Description of a study on young children's narrative ability and resistance to suggestion (Kulkofsky & Klemfuss, 2008)

- Expanded coverage of theory of mind, including a new section on individual differences
- Coverage of a study of key factors in young children's early literacy experiences in low-income families (Rodriquez & others, 2009)
- Inclusion of NAEYC's (2009) latest guidelines for developmentally appropriate practice
- Expanded discussion of the characteristics and goals of developmentally appropriate education (Barbarin & Miller, 2009)
- New discussion of the Early Head Start program (Administration for Children & Families, 2008)
- New coverage of the effects of Project Head Start on children's cognitive, language, and math skills and achievement (Hindman & others, 2010; Puma & others, 2010)

Chapter 6: Socioemotional Development in Early Childhood

- New coverage of Ross Thompson's (2009a) commentary on how current research on theory of mind and young children's social understanding challenges Piaget's egocentrism concept
- Description of recent research on young children's understanding of commitments to other people (Grafenhain & others, 2009)
- Discussion of a study linking young children's understanding of emotion with their prosocial behavior (Ensor, Spencer, & Hughes, 2010)
- Reorganization of the discussion of emotional development based on expert Susan Denham's recommendation
- Expanded discussion of advances in young children's understanding of emotions (Cole & others, 2009)
- Coverage of a meta-analysis indicating that emotion knowledge was positively linked to social competence in 3- to 5-year olds and negatively related to their internalizing and externalizing problems (Trentacosta & Fine, 2010)
- New material on the correlational nature of studies of parenting styles and children's development
- Expanded discussion of the effects of punishment on children
- New discussion of research on the use of mild physical punishment (Grusec, 2011)
- Updated statistics on child maltreatment in the United States (U.S. Department of Health and Human Services, 2008)
- New material on adolescent outcomes of child abuse and neglect (Wekerle & others, 2009)
- Discussion of a study linking child maltreatment with financial- and employment-related difficulties in adulthood (Zielinski, 2009)
- Coverage of a study linking coparenting to young children's effortful control (Karreman & others, 2008)
- New material on E. Mark Cummings and his colleagues' view of children's emotional insecurity and interparental conflict (Cummings & Davies, 2010)
- Enhanced discussion of why pretend play is an important aspect of early childhood development (Coplan & Arbeau 2009)
- Coverage of recent research indicating that pretend play increases young children's self-regulation (Diamond & others, 2007)
- Expanded and updated material on social play as the main context for most young children's interactions with peers (Coplan & Arbeau, 2009)
- Addition of Mildred Parten's (1932) classification of children's free play

Chapter 7: Physical and Cognitive Development in Middle and Late Childhood

- New discussion of Mark Johnson and his colleagues' (2009) view on how the prefrontal cortex likely orchestrates the functioning of other neural regions during development

- Discussion of a study on parents' roles in limiting children's sedentary activity, encouraging their exercise, and modeling exercise activities (Edwardson & Gorely, 2010)

- Coverage of a study on the effectiveness of a school-based program for increasing children's physical activity (Kriemler & others, 2010)

- Coverage of a study on the effect of fitness level on 9-year-old girls' performance on a cognitive control task (Hillman & others, 2009)

- Coverage of a large-scale U.S. study indicating a higher percentage of being overweight or obese for African American and Latino children than non-Latino White children (Benson, Baer, & Kaelber, 2009)

- Updated statistics on the percentage of children who receive special education services in the United States (National Center for Education Statistics, 2008a)

- New discussion of dysgraphia and dyscalculia

- New discussions of the brain's role in learning disabilities and ADHD, including new Figures 7.4 and 7.5

- Description of a meta-analysis indicating that behavior management treatments are effective in reducing the effects of ADHD (Fabiano & others, 2009)

- New coverage of autism spectrum disorders, including recent research and the recent increase in their occurrence or in their detection and labeling

- Expanded coverage of strategies for improving children's memory skills, including Patricia Bauer's (2009b) emphasis on improving consolidation and reconsolidation

- New material on the view that it is important for instructors to embed memory-relevant language in their teaching (Ornstein, Coffman, & Grammer, 2009; Ornstein & others, 2010)

- Expanded discussion of children's creative thinking, including research indicating a decline in creative thinking by U.S. schoolchildren and increased interest in teaching creative thinking in Chinese schools (Kim, 2010; Plucker, 2010)

- New material on the latest revision of the Stanford-Binet test, the Stanford-Binet 5

- Added new conclusion to the section on heredity/environment and intelligence and tied the conclusion to the nature/nurture issue first discussed in Chapter 1

- New discussions of the roles of nature/nurture and domain-specific aspects of giftedness

- Inclusion of commentary by Bill Gates about domain-specific giftedness

- New material on the complexity of second-language learning (Thomas & Johnson, 2008)

- Coverage of a research review indicating that bilingual children have lower formal language proficiency than monolingual children (Bialystok & Craik, 2010)

Chapter 8: Socioemotional Development in Middle and Late Childhood

- Inclusion of a study of self-regulation in children from low-income families (Buckner, Mezzacappa, & Beardslee, 2009)

- Coverage of a study on the increase in self-control in middle and late childhood and its link to lower levels of deviant behavior (Vazsonyi & Huang, 2010)

- Updated coverage of children's outcomes following a disaster (Kar, 2009)
- Updated conclusions about whether gender differences in moral orientation are as strong as Gilligan suggests (Blakemore, Berenbaum, & Liben, 2009)
- Expanded discussion of developmental changes in gender stereotypes (Blakemore, Berenbaum, & Liben, 2009)
- New summary of sex differences in the brain emphasizing caution in interpreting differences (Blakemore, Berenbaum, & Liben, 2009)
- Added commentary that any sex differences in the brain could be due to biological origins of the differences, behavioral experiences, or a combination of these factors

- Coverage of a recent large-scale assessment of a gender difference in writing (National Assessment of Educational Progress, 2007) and lack of a difference in math (Hyde & others, 2008)
- Discussion of a recent study indicating that relational aggression increases in middle and late childhood (Dishion & Piehler, 2009)
- Inclusion of information from a recent research review that girls engage in more relational aggression than boys in adolescence but not in childhood (Smith, Rose, & Schwartz-Mette, 2010)
- Description of a recent study linking parents' psychological control to a higher incidence of relational aggression in their children
- Updated description of gender differences in emotion (Blakemore, Berenbaum, & Liben, 2009)
- Description of a longitudinal study of children from ages 6 to 13 linking lack of reciprocal friendship to loneliness and depressed feelings in early adolescence (Pedersen & others, 2007)
- Description of three recent suicides in middle and late childhood and early adolescence that likely were influenced by bullying (Meyers, 2010)
- New emphasis on the importance of contexts in the study of bullying (Salmivalli & Peets, 2009; Schwartz & others, 2010)
- Coverage of two recent studies of bullies' popularity in the peer group (Veenstra & others, 2010; Witvliet & others, 2010)
- Description of a recent study on peer victimization and the extent of its link to lower academic achievement (Nakamoto & Schwartz, 2010)
- Coverage of a recent study on neighborhood disadvantage and child outcomes such as behavior problems and low verbal ability (Kohen & others, 2008)
- Description of a recent study linking chronic poverty to adverse cognitive development outcomes in children (Najman & others, 2009)
- New discussion of the recent results from the large-scale international assessment of fourth-grade students' math and science scores with a focus on how U.S. students compare to students in other countries (TIMMS, 2008)
- New coverage of Carol Dweck's recent research and ideas on improving students' growth mindset by teaching them about the brain's plasticity and how the brain changes when you put considerable effort into learning (Blackwell & others, 2007; Dweck & Master, 2009)
- New discussion of Carol Dweck's recent development of computer modules, called "Brainology," that explain how the brain works and how through work and effort students can make their brain work better (Blackwell & Dweck, 2008; Dweck & Master, 2009)

Chapter 9: Physical and Cognitive Development in Adolescence

- New discussion of precocious puberty (Blakemore, Berenbaum, & Liben, 2009)
- Inclusion of recent information that early-maturing girls are less likely to graduate from high school and more likely to cohabit and marry earlier (Cavanagh, 2009)

- New discussion of the pruning of synapses and what this means by the end of adolescence (Kuhn, 2009)
- New description of how the information about changes in the adolescent brain reflect the rapidly emerging field of developmental social neuroscience
- Updated information about causes of adolescent deaths in the United States (National Vital Statistics Reports, 2008)
- Description of a recent national study on the percentage of U.S. high school students who were currently sexually active (Eaton & others, 2008)
- Coverage of a recent study of adolescents' sexual experience and having multiple sexual partners from 1991 to 2007 (Santelli & others, 2009)
- Coverage of a recent study that revealed a link between maternal communication about sex and a reduction in risky sexual behavior by Latino adolescents (Trejos-Castillo & Vazsonyi, 2009)
- Discussion of a recent study that linked alcohol use, early menarche, and poor parent-child communication to early sexually intimate behavior in girls (Hipwell & others, 2010)
- Coverage of a recent study of early initiation of sexual intercourse in five countries (Madkour & others, 2010)
- Description of recent research on early sexual intercourse and subsequent grades (Wheeler, 2010)
- Description of recent research linking deviant peer relations in early adolescence with an increase in multiple sexual partners at age 16 (Lansford & others, 2010)
- Coverage of a recent study of middle school students indicating that better academic achievement was a protective factor in keeping boys and girls from engaging in early initiation of sexual intercourse (Laflin & others, 2008)
- Coverage of recent studies that revealed higher condom use by European adolescents than U.S. adolescents (Currie & others, 2008; Santelli, Sandfort, & Orr, 2009)
- Coverage of the reversal in increase of births to adolescents with a decline in 2007 and 2008, and a new Figure 9.3 (Hamilton, Martin, & Ventura, 2010)
- Discussion of the high fertility rate of Latina adolescents and comparison of their recent adolescent pregnancy and birth rates with other ethnic groups (Santelli, Abraido-Lanza, & Melnikas, 2009)
- New coverage of information comparing ethnic groups on the likelihood of having a second child in adolescence (Rosengard, 2009)
- Description of a national study documenting the high percentage of daughters of teenage mothers who become pregnant themselves as teenagers, and other risk factors in the daughters' lives for becoming pregnant (Meade, Kershaw, & Ickovics, 2008)
- Updated coverage of the increasing evidence that abstinence-only programs do not reduce adolescent pregnancy (Hentz & Fields, 2009)
- Updating of the trends in the percentage of U.S. adolescents who ate fruits and vegetables on a regular basis (Eaton & others, 2008)
- Coverage of a recent study of the role of peers in adolescent smoking (Holliday, Rothwell, & Moore, 2010)
- Discussion of a recent study on eating regular family meals and healthy eating patterns five years later (Burgess-Champoux & others, 2009)
- Discussion of a recent study linking low levels of exercise to depressive symptoms in young adolescents (Sund, Larsson, & Wichstrom, 2010)

- Description of a recent study that found vigorous physical activity was related to lower drug use in adolescents (Delisle & others, 2010)

- Coverage of a recent national study of adolescent sleep patterns, including developmental changes from the 9th through the 12th grade (Eaton & others, 2008)

- Updated coverage of the Monitoring the Future study's assessment of drug use by secondary school students (Johnston & others, 2010)

- Coverage of recent research that found parental monitoring was linked to lower substance abuse in adolescence (Tobler & Komro, 2010)

- Description of a recent research review that indicated adolescents who more frequently ate dinner with their family were less likely to have various problems (Sen, 2010)

- Expanded coverage of the pruning of synapses and what this means by the end of adolescence (Kuhn, 2009)

- Revised coverage of the personal fable based on recent research that indicates many adolescents perceive that they will experience an early death (Fischhoff & others, 2010; Reyna & Rivers, 2008)

- Expanded introduction to information processing and thinking in adolescence based on Deanna Kuhn's (2009) recent view on differences in childhood and adolescent cognitive development

- Updated statistics on school dropouts, including the substantial decrease in Latino dropouts since 2000 (National Center for Education Statistics, 2008b)

Chapter 10: Socioemotional Development in Adolescence

- Expanded and updated description of why college often stimulates a greater integration of identity at a higher level (Phinney, 2008)

- Coverage of a recent meta-analysis of 127 studies focused on developmental changes in Marcia's identity statuses (Kroger, Martinussen, & Marcia, 2010)

- Discussion of a recent study of Latino youth indicating a link between growth in identity exploration and an increase in self-esteem (Umana-Taylor, Gonzales-Backen, & Guimond, 2009)

- New information about Latino parents monitoring their daughters more closely than do non-Latino parents (Allen & others, 2008)

- Discussion of Joseph Allen and his colleagues' (2009) recent research linking secure attachment at age 14 with positive outcomes at age 21

- Description of a recent analysis that concluded that the most consistent outcomes of secure attachment in adolescence involve positive peer relations and the development of emotion regulation capacities (Allen & Miga, 2010)

- New material on which adolescents are most likely to conform to their peers (Prinstein & others, 2009)

- New coverage of three stages in the development of romantic relationships in adolescence (Connolly & McIsaac, 2009)

- New description of the percentage of adolescents who are early and late bloomers in developing romantic relationships (Connolly & McIsaac, 2009)

- Coverage of a recent study of adolescents' romantic experience and links to various aspects of adjustment (Furman, Lo, & Ho, 2009)

- Description of a recent study indicating that romantic involvement predicted an increase in depressive symptoms in adolescence (Starr & Davila, 2009)

- New section, The Media, that focuses on the dramatic increases in adolescents' media multitasking and Internet use (Roberts, Henrikson, & Foehr, 2009)
- New information about youths' communication with strangers on the Internet and cyberbullying (Subrahmanyam & Greenfield, 2008)
- Description of recent research indicating that many Internet sex crimes against minors involve social networking sites in some way (Mitchell & others, 2010)
- Coverage of a recent study linking parents' lack of knowledge of their young adolescents' whereabouts and the adolescents' engagement in delinquency later in adolescence (Lahey & others, 2008)
- Discussion of a recent study implicating harsh discipline at 8 to 10 years of age as a predictor of which adolescent delinquents would persist in criminal activity after age 21
- Coverage of a recent study of engaged parenting in low-income, urban families and its link to a lower level of delinquency (Ghazarian & Roche, 2010)
- Inclusion of new material on the roles of peers and schools in juvenile delinquency (Brown & Larson, 2009; Crosnoe & others, 2008)
- Description of a recent study on the positive influence of school connectedness in lowering conduct problems in early adolescence (Loukas, Roalson, & Herrera 2010)
- Coverage of recent estimates of the incidence of depression in adolescence (Graber & Sontag, 2009)
- Description of a recent study of mother-adolescent co-rumination and its link to adolescents' depression (Waller & Rose, 2010)
- Discussion of a recent study of young adolescents' friendships and depression (Brengden & others, 2010)
- Description of a recent study using data from the National Longitudinal Study of Adolescent Health that found a number of risks for suicidal behavior (Thompson, Kuruwita, & Foster, 2009)
- Description of a recent study on alcohol, depression, and suicide attempts in adolescence (Schilling & others, 2009)
- Inclusion of recent research on suicide attempts by young Latinas (Zayas & others, 2010)

Chapter 11: Physical and Cognitive Development in Early Adulthood

- Discussion of a recent study of more than 17,000 young adults in 21 countries that focused on links between health behavior and life satisfaction (Grant, Wardle, & Steptoe, 2009)
- Updated coverage of overweight and obesity, including projections of the percentage of Americans who will be overweight in 2030 (Beydoun & Wang, 2009)
- Coverage of a recent meta-analysis linking obesity with depression in women but not men (de Wit & others, 2010)
- Updated discussion of dieting including a recent research review of diet-plus-exercise in weight loss (Wu & others, 2009)
- Coverage of a recent study of the percentage of college students who abstain from drinking alcohol (Huang & others, 2009)
- New coverage of pregaming and gaming as becoming increasingly common rituals on college campuses, including recent research (DeJong, DeRicco, & Schneider, 2010; Ham & others, 2010; Read, Merrill, & Bytschkow, 2010)
- Updated material on trends in binge drinking by emerging adult women (Johnston & others, 2008)

- Inclusion of a recent meta-analysis of studies on gender differences in sexuality (Petersen & Hyde, 2010)
- New discussion of the positive role of sexuality in well-being, including recent research (Brody & Costa, 2009)
- Expanded coverage of causes of homosexual behavior, including a recent large-scale study in Sweden (King, 2011; Langstrom & others, 2010)
- Updated description of HIV and AIDS in the United States (National Center for Health Statistics, 2010b)
- Updated discussion of HIV and AIDS around the world, especially in sub-Saharan Africa (Campbell, 2009; UNAIDS, 2009)
- Discussion of recent research on a link between men's sexual narcissism and their sexual aggression (Widman & McNulty, 2010)
- New description of the red zone on college and university campuses and the time in their college years when women are most likely to have unwanted sexual experiences (Kimble & others, 2008)
- New discussion of Phyllis Moen's (2009a) view of the career mystique and how it has changed in recent years
- New coverage of the application of William Damon's (2008) ideas in *The Path to Purpose* to career development
- Updated coverage of the percentage of full-time U.S. college students who are employed (National Center for Education Statistics, 2008c)
- New section on unemployment, including information about the recent financial meltdown and recession
- Expanded discussion of issues involved in dual-earner couples based on Phyllis Moen's (2009a, b) recent views
- Updated gender and ethnicity data on the U.S. labor force projected through 2016 (Occupational Outlook Handbook, 2010–2011)

Chapter 12: Socioemotional Development in Early Adulthood

- Revised and updated discussion of adult attachment styles
- Updated and expanded material on the stability of adult attachment styles
- Discussion of recent research on links between anxious and avoidant attachment styles and various health problems (McWilliams & Bailey, 2010)
- Coverage of a recent analysis that revealed a link between insecure attachment in adults and depression (Bakersman-Kranenburg & van IJzendoorn, 2009)
- Description of a recent study linking recent secure attachment to parents with ease in forming friendships in college (Parade, Leerkes, & Blankson, 2010)
- Expanded description of adult friendships including the percentage of men and women who have a best friend and opportunities for making new friendships in adulthood (Blieszner, 2009)
- Coverage of a longitudinal study that linked emotional intimacy in early adulthood with marital adjustment in middle adulthood (Boden, Fischer, & Niehuis, 2010)
- Discussion of recent research documenting that in their twenties women display greater emotional intimacy with a closest other than do men (Boden, Fischer, & Niehuis, 2010)
- Updated coverage of the dramatic increase in the number of people who cohabit in the United States, including an updated Figure 12.2 (Popenoe, 2009)

- Description of a recent study on the percentage of women who cohabited before age 24

- Coverage of a recent study indicating that cohabiting women experience an elevated risk of partner violence (Brownridge, 2008)

- Description of a recent meta-analysis of links between cohabitation and marital quality/stability (Jose, O'Leary, & Moyer, 2010)

- Discussion of recent research that found a link between cohabitation prior to becoming engaged and negative marital outcomes for first marriages but not second marriages (Stanley & others, 2010)

- Updated coverage of the continuing decline in the rate of marriage in the U.S. from 2007 to 2009 (National Vital Statistics Reports, 2010)

- Updated statistics on the age of first marriage in the United States (U.S. Census Bureau, 2008b)

- Updated information on the percentage of married persons age 18 and older with "very happy" marriages, including an updated Figure 12.3 (Popenoe, 2009)

- Updated coverage of the age of first marriage in countries around the world (Waite, 2009)

- Expanded and updated discussion on the benefits of a good marriage, including a recent study on a lower proportion of time spent in marriage being linked to a likelihood of earlier death (Henretta, 2010)

- Updated coverage on the resumption of a decline in the rate of divorce in the U.S. from 2007 to 2009 following an increase from 2005 to 2007 (National Vital Statistics Reports, 2010)

- Updated percentage of divorced U.S. men and women: 1950 to 2007, including an updated Figure 12.4 (Popenoe, 2009)

- New description of partner characteristics that are linked to divorce (Hoelter, 2009)

- New material on the characteristics and timing of adults who get remarried (Sweeney, 2009, 2010)

- Updated and expanded discussion of the benefits and problems that characterize remarriage (Waite, 2009)

- Coverage of recent research on gender similarities and differences in relationships, including overall talk and relationship talk (Newman & others, 2008)

Chapter 13: Physical and Cognitive Development in Middle Adulthood

- Expanded commentary about time perspective in middle adulthood (Setterson, 2009)

- New material on the concept of *age identity* and the consistent finding that as adults get older their age identity is younger than their chronological age (Westerhof, 2009)

- New discussion of metabolic syndrome, including a recent meta-analysis of its link to all-cause mortality (Hui, Liu, & Ho, 2010)

- Updated information about the cause of death in middle adulthood with cancer recently replacing cardiovascular disease as the leading cause of death in middle adulthood (National Center for Health Statistics, 2008a)

- New description of later menopause being linked to increased risk of breast cancer (Mishra & others, 2009)

- Description of recent analyses confirming a link between combined estrogen/progestin hormone therapy and increased risk of cardiovascular disease (Toh & others, 2010)

- Coverage of recent research studies in a number of countries indicating that coinciding with the decrease in HRT in recent years has been a related decline in breast cancer (Dobson, 2009; Parkin, 2009)

- New material on possible alternatives to HRT

- New material on a recent large-scale study of the main sexual problems reported by U.S. men and women age 40 to 80 (Laumann & others, 2009)

- Description of the increasing evidence that religion has a positive link to health (McCullough & Willoughby, 2009)

- Coverage of a recent study indicating that certain aspects of religion are related to lower levels of worry, anxiety, and depressive symptoms (Rosmarin, Krumrei, & Andersson, 2009)

- New material on the factors that shape an individual's exploration of meaning in life and whether developing a sense of meaning in life is linked to positive developmental outcomes (Krause, 2008, 2009)

Chapter 14: Socioemotional Development in Middle Adulthood

- New discussion of a recent studying linking generativity with positive social engagement in such contexts as family life and community involvement (Cox & others, 2010)

- New material on the change in personality traits being more positive in middle age (Roberts & Mroczek, 2008)

- New coverage of a recent study on changes in marital satisfaction in middle age and aspects of the empty nest syndrome (Gorchoff, John, & Helson, 2008)

- Description of research on marital satisfaction in octogenarians and its ability to protect their happiness from daily fluctuations in perceived health (Waldinger & Schulz, 2010)

- Updated statistics on the percent of older adult women and men who are divorced or separated (U.S. Census Bureau, 2010)

- Expanded discussion of divorce in late adulthood, including cohort effects and gender differences (Peek, 2009)

- Added commentary about the percentage of older adults who cohabit likely to increase as baby boomers enter late adulthood

Chapter 15: Physical and Cognitive Development in Late Adulthood

- New discussion of the evolutionary theory of aging in the section on biological theories of aging (Austad, 2009; Kittas, 2010)

- New material on the role that telomerase might play in extending life (Effros, 2009)

- New material on the current consensus that under normal conditions it is unlikely that adults lose brain cells per se (Nelson, 2008)

- Coverage of recent information that new brain cells survive longer when rats are cognitively challenged to learn something (Shors, 2009)

- Description of recent research indicating links between aerobic fitness, greater volume in the hippocampus, and better memory (Erickson & others, 2009)

- Inclusion of a recent study on a link between exercise and frailty (Peterson & others, 2009)

- Description of a recent study in which exercise capacity and walking were the best predictors of mortality in older adults with cardiac dysfunction (Reibis & others, 2010)
- Coverage of recent research on obesity and mobility restrictions in older adults (Houston & others, 2009)
- Discussion of a recent large-scale study of 57- to 85-year-olds on links between sexual activity and health, including gender differences (Lindau & Gavrilova, 2010)
- Inclusion of recent research linking visual decline in older adults with a lower level of cognitive functioning (Clay & others, 2009)
- Discussion of recent research indicating that less frequent social activity in older adults was linked to more rapid loss of motor function (Buchman & others, 2009)
- Inclusion of recent research on a link between the frailty of older adults and their SES status (Szanton & others, 2010)
- Description of the percentage of individuals age 80 and older who experience a significant reduction in the sense of smell (Lafreiere & Mann, 2009)
- Inclusion of information about a recent study of sexual activity in older adults (Lindau & others, 2007)
- Discussion of cancer replacing cardiovascular disease as the leading cause of death in 65- to 74-year-olds (National Center for Health Statistics, 2008a)
- Description of a recent study linking exercise with a lower risk of falling and fewer falling incidents in older adults (Yokoya, Demura, & Sato, 2009)
- Coverage of a recent high-intensity strength training program for arthritis patients (Flint-Wagner & others, 2009)
- Inclusion of a recent study on a link between systolic blood pressure during exercise and increased long-term survival (Hedberg & others, 2009)
- Discussion of a recent study of more than 11,000 women that found low cardiorespiratory fitness was a significant predictor of all-cause mortality (Farrell & others, 2010)
- Coverage of a recent analysis of the effectiveness of strength training with older adults (Peterson & others, 2010)
- Coverage of a recent study of caloric restriction and verbal memory in older adults (Witte & others, 2009)
- Expanded discusion of working memory and aging, including explanation of deficits in working memory in older adults because of their less efficient inhibition in preventing irrelevant information from entering working memory and their increased distractibility (Lustig & Hasher, 2010; Rowe, Hasher, & Turcotte, 2010)
- Description of recent research indicating that when older adults engage in cognitively stimulating activities, the onset of rapid memory decline is delayed (Hall & others, 2009)
- Coverage of a recent study that found older adults engaged in superior reasoning about social conflicts than young and middle-aged adults (Grossman & others, 2010)
- Coverage of a recent research review on cognitive coordination of skills in older adults (Hertzog & others, 2009)
- Coverage of a recent study linking education to cognitive abilities in older adults, and how, for older adults with less education, engaging in cognitive activities improves episodic memory (Lachman & others, 2010)
- Discussion of a recent study on differences in connectivity between brain regions in younger and older adults (Leshikar & others, 2010)
- Expansion and updating of a number of aspects of depression in older adults based on a recent review (Fiske, Wetherell, & Gatz, 2009)
- Updated coverage of the estimated risk for developing dementia in women and men age 85 and older (Alzheimer's Association, 2010)

- Updated description of the percentage of individuals estimated to develop Alzheimer disease in the next 10 years at age 65, 75, and 85 for women and men, including a new Figure 15.7 (Alzheimer's Association, 2010)

- New coverage of why it is important to focus on biological and environmental risk factors, preventive strategies, and maintenance of cognitive reserves in middle adulthood in research on Alzheimer disease

- New discussion of the role that oxidative stress might play in Alzheimer disease (Bonda & others, 2010; Di Bona & others, 2010)

- New coverage of why it is important to focus on biological and environmental risk factors, preventive strategies, and maintenance of cognitive reserves in middle adulthood in research on Alzheimer disease

- New coverage of a research review indicating that fMRI measurement of neuron loss in the medial temporal lobe predicts memory loss and eventually dementia (Vellas & Aisen, 2010)

- Expanded discussion of drug treatment for Alzheimer disease, including recent indications of how effective the drugs are

- Inclusion of estimates of the percentage of individuals age 65 and older who have mild cognitive impairment (MCI) (Alzheimer's Association, 2010)

- Expanded coverage of MCI, including the use of fMRI scans with individuals who have MCI to predict which of these individuals are likely to develop Alzheimer disease

- Inclusion of information that the Federal Drug Administration has yet to approve any drugs for the treatment of MCI

- Updated coverage of new treatments for Parkinson disease, including stem cell research (Fricker-Gates & Gates, 2010)

- New discussion of research indicating that certain types of dance, such as the tango, can improve the motor skills of individuals with Parkinson disease (Hackney & Earhart, 2010a, b)

Chapter 16: Socioemotional Development in Late Adulthood

- Inclusion of recent research on institutionalized older adults that revealed that reminiscence therapy increased life satisfaction and reduced depression (Chiang & others, 2010)

- Discussion of a recent study that found a life-review course, "Looking for Meaning," reduced middle-aged and older adults' depressive symptoms (Pot & others, 2010)

- New discussion and recent research on life regrets as part of a life review (Choi & Jun, 2009)

- Coverage of a recent study of the components of conscientiousness that increased in the transition to late adulthood (Jackson & others, 2009)

- New material linking several "big five" personality factors to greater longevity (Iwasa & others, 2008)

- Added commentary about the burden and stress placed on many older adults because of the recent economic crisis (Keister & Destro, 2009)

- Updated data on the percentage of older adults living in poverty (U.S. Census Bureau, 2010)

- Coverage of a recent study indicating that low SES increases the risk of death in older adults (Krueger & Chang, 2008)

- Discussion of recent research on frequency of computer use in older adults and cognitive functioning (Tun & Lachman, 2010)
- Description of research on marital satisfaction in octogenarians and its ability to protect their happiness from daily fluctuations in perceived health (Waldinger & Schulz, 2010)
- Updated statistics on the percentage of older adult women and men who are divorced or separated (U.S. Census Bureau, 2010)
- Expanded discussion of divorce in late adulthood, including cohort effects and gender differences (Peek, 2009)
- Added commentary about the percentage of older adults who cohabit likely to increase as baby boomers enter late adulthood
- Expanded material on friendship in older adults, including comparison of the friendships of young adults and older adults (Zettel-Watson & Rook, 2009)
- Expanded description of loneliness and comparison of loneliness in younger and older adults (Schnittker, 2007; Koropeckyj-Cox, 2009)
- Coverage of a recent study in which loneliness predicted increased blood pressure four years later in middle-aged and older adults (Hawkley & others, 2010)
- Inclusion of information about a 12-year longitudinal study linking persistently low or declining feelings of usefulness to others and a higher risk of dying at a younger age (Gruenewald & others, 2009)
- Description of a recent analysis indicating that volunteering doesn't decline significantly until the mid-seventies (Morrow-Howell, 2010)
- Discussion of recent research on whether it is better for an older adult's well-being to give or to receive social support (Thomas, 2010)
- Description of a recent study in which volunteering was linked to less frailty in older adults (Jung & others, 2010)
- Expanded and updated discussion of volunteering, including recent information about developmental changes in volunteering (Burr, 2009)

Chapter 17: Death, Dying, and Grieving

- New information that discusses how most of what we know about death, dying, and grieving is based on older adults because older adults account for approximately two-thirds of the 2 million deaths each year in the United States
- Discussion of a recent study of contradictions in individuals' end-of-life decisions about themselves and relatives (Sviri & others, 2009)
- Coverage of a recent study of the percentage of patients who had a living will and had discussed health-care wishes with their family
- Inclusion of a recent Dutch study of euthanasia, including the percentage of dying persons who requested it and the percentage whose request was granted (Onwuteaka-Philipsen & others, 2010)
- Added commentary in the coverage of what constitutes a good death (Carr, 2009)
- Update on the countries and states in the United States that allow euthanasia (Smets & others, 2010; Watson, 2009)
- Coverage of a recent study indicating that as individuals move closer to death, they become more spiritual
- Added commentary about how difficult the coping process is for parents following the death of a child (Edwards & others, 2009)
- New discussion of prolonged grief and disenfranchised grief
- Description of recent research on aspects of death most likely to be linked to prolonged grief (Fujisawa & others, 2010)

- Inclusion of a recent study of a decrease in the life satisfaction over time in individuals age 80 and older whose spouse has died (Berg & others, 2009)
- Description of a recent study on meaning in life and anger in bereaved spouses (Kim, 2009)
- New information about the percentage of women and men ages 65 and older who are widowed in the United States (Administration on Aging, 2009)
- Updated information about the significant increase in the percentage of Americans who are cremated (Cremation Association of North America, 2008)
- Discussion of trends in death, mourning, and funerals (Callahan, 2009)

Acknowlegments

The development and writing of the first and second editions of *Essentials of Life-Span Development* was strongly influenced by a remarkable group of consultants, reviewers, and adopters.

Expert Consultants

I owe a special appreciation to leading experts who provided detailed feedback in their areas of expertise on *Life-Span Development. Essentials of Life-Span Development* has also benefited from the following experts' contributions:

K. Warner Schaie, *Pennsylvania State University*

Diane Hughes, *New York University*

Andrew Meltzoff, *University of Washington*

Ross Thompson, *University of California-Davis*

Maria Hernandez-Reif, *University of Alabama*

Roberta Gollinkoff, *University of Delaware*

William Hoyer, *Syracuse University*

Ellen Grigorenko, *Yale University*

L. Monique Ward, *University of Michigan*

Joseph Campos, *University of California-Berkeley*

Linda Mayes, *Yale University*

Margie Lachman, *Brandeis University*

John Schulenberg, *University of Michigan*

Art Kramer, *University of Illinois*

Phyllis Moen, *University of Minnesota*

Karen Fingerman, *Purdue University*

Deborah Carr, *Rutgers University*

Wolfgang Stroebe, *Utrecht University*

Applications Contributors

I am especially grateful to the contributors who helped develop the *How Would You . . . ?* questions for students in various majors who are taking the life-span development course:

Michael E. Barber, *Santa Fe Community College*

Maida Berenblatt, *Suffolk Community College*

Susan A. Greimel, *Santa Fe Community College*

Russell Isabella, *University of Utah*

Jean Mandernach, *University of Nebraska at Kearney*

General Reviewers

I gratefully acknowledge the comments and feedback from instructors around the nation who have reviewed *Essentials of Life-Span Development*. Recommendations from the following individuals helped shape *Essentials*:

Eileen Achorn, *University of Texas-San Antonio*

Michael E. Barber, *Santa Fe Community College*

Gabriel Batarseh, *Francis Marion University*

Troy E. Beckert, *Utah State University*

Stefanie Bell, *Pikes Peak Community College*

Maida Berenblatt, *Suffolk Community College*

Kathi Bivens, *Asheville Buncombe Technical Community College*

Alda Blakeney, *Kennesaw State University*

Candice L. Branson, *Kapiolani Community College*

Ken Brewer, *Northeast State Technical Community College*

Margaret M. Bushong, *Liberty University*

Krista Carter, *Colby Community College*

Stewart Cohen, *University of Rhode Island*

Rock Doddridge, *Asheville Buncombe Technical Community College*

Laura Duvall, *Heartland Community College*

Jenni Fauchier, *Metro Community College-Ft. Omaha*

Richard Ferraro, *University of North Dakota*

Terri Flowerday, *University of New Mexico-Albuquerque*

Laura Garofoli, *Fitchburg State College*

Sharon Ghazarian, *University of North Carolina-Greensboro*

Dan Grangaard, *Austin Community College*

Rodney J. Grisham, *Indian River Community College*

Rea Gubler, *Southern Utah University*

Myra M. Harville, *Holmes Community College*

Brett Heintz, *Delgado Community College*

Sandra Hellyer, *Butler University*

Randy Holley, *Liberty University*

Debra L. Hollister, *Valencia Community College*

Rosemary T. Hornack, *Meredith College*

Alycia Hund, *Illinois State University*

Rebecca Inkrott, *Sinclair Community College-Dayton*

Russell Isabella, *University of Utah*

Alisha Janowsky, *Florida Atlantic University*

Lisa Judd, *Western Technical College*

Tim Killian, *University of Arkansas-Fayetteville*

Shenan Kroupa, *Indiana University-Purdue University Indianapolis*

Pat Lefler, *Bluegrass Community and Technical College*

Jean Mandernach, *University of Nebraska-Kearney*

Carrie Margolin, *Evergreen State College*

Michael Jason McCoy, *Cape Fear Community College*

Carol Miller, *Anne Arundel Community College*

Gwynn Morris, *Meredith College*

Ron Mossler, *Los Angeles Community College*

Bob Pasnak, *George Mason University*

Curtis D. Proctor-Artz, *Wichita State University*

Janet Reis, *University of Illinois-Urbana*

Kimberly Renk, *University of Central Florida*

Vicki Ritts, *St. Louis Community College-Meramec*

Jeffrey Sargent, *Lee University*

James Schork, *Elizabethtown Community and Technical College*

Jason Scofield, *University of Alabama*

Christin E. Seifert, *Montana State University*

Elizabeth Sheehan, *Georgia State University*

Peggy Skinner, *South Plains College*

Christopher Stanley, *Winston-Salem State University*

Wayne Stein, *Brevard Community College-Melbourne*

Rose Suggett, *Southeast Community College*

Kevin Sumrall, *Montgomery College*

Joan Test, *Missouri State University*

Barbara VanHorn, *Indian River Community College*

John Wakefield, *University of North Alabama*

Laura Wasielewski, *St. Anselm College*

Lois Willoughby, *Miama Dade College-Kendall*

Paul Wills, *Kilgore College*

A. Claire Zaborowski, *San Jacinto College*

Pauline Davey Zeece, *University of Nebraska-Lincoln*

Design Reviewers

Cheryl Almeida, *Johnson and Wales University*

Candice L. Branson, *Kapiolani Community College*

Debra Hollister, *Valencia Community College*

Alycia Hund, *Illinois State University*

Jean Mandernach, *University of Nebraska-Kearney*

Michael Jason Scofield, *University of Alabama*

Christin Seifert, *Montana State University*

Life-Span Symposium

In the spring of 2010, McGraw-Hill held a symposium on life-span development for instructors from across the country. This event provided a forum for instructors to exchange ideas and experiences with colleagues they might not have met otherwise. It was also an opportunity for editors from McGraw-Hill to gather information about the needs and challenges of instructors of life-span development. The feedback we received has been invaluable and has contributed to the development of this edition of *Essentials of Life-Span Development*. We would like to thank the participants for their insights.

Mitchell Baker, *Moraine Valley Community College*

Chuck Calahan, *Purdue University*

Stephanie Ding, *Del Mar College*

Alycia Hund, *Illinois State University*

Gabriela Martorell, *Virginia Wesleyan College*

Daniel McConnell, *University of Southern Florida*

Jorge Milanes, *St. Johns River Community College*

Michael Miranda, *Kingsborough Community College*

Kaelin Olsen, *Utah State University*

Victoria Peeples, *University of Alabama*

Angi Semegon, *Santa Fe College*

The McGraw-Hill Team

A large number of outstanding professionals at McGraw-Hill helped me to produce this edition of *Essentials of Life-Span Development*. I especially want to thank Mike Sugarman, Publisher; Krista Bettino, Executive Editor; Dawn Groundwater, Director of Development; Judith Kromm, Senior Developmental Editor; Julia Flohr Larkin, Executive Marketing Manager; Holly Irish, Senior Production Editor; and Alex Ambrose, Lead Photo Research Manager.

Instructor and Student Resources

The resources listed here may accompany *Essentials of Life-Span Development*, Second Edition. Please contact your McGraw-Hill representative for details concerning policies, prices, and availability.

Instructor Resources

The instructor side of the **Online Learning Center** at http://www.mhhe.com/santrockessls2e contains the following instructor resources. Ask your local McGraw-Hill representative for your password.

- **Instructor's Manual**
- **Test Bank and Computerized Test Bank**
- **PowerPoint Slides**
- **McGraw-Hill's Visual Asset Database for Lifespan Development (VAD 2.0)** www.mhhe.com/vad

Create Craft your teaching resources to match the way you teach! With McGraw-Hill Create, www.mcgrawhillcreate.com, you can easily rearrange chapters, combine material from other content sources, and quickly upload content you have written, like your course syllabus or teaching notes. Find the content you need in Create by searching through thousands of leading McGraw-Hill textbooks. Arrange your book to fit your teaching style. Create even allows you to personalize your book's appearance by selecting the cover and adding your name, school, and course information. Order a Create book and you'll receive a complimentary print review copy in 3–5 business days or a complimentary electronic review copy (eComp) via email in about one hour. Go to www.mcgrawhillcreate.com today and register. Experience how McGraw-Hill Create empowers you to teach your students your way.

Blackboard McGraw-Hill Higher Education and Blackboard have teamed up. What does this mean for you?

Do More

1. **Your life, simplified.** Now you and your students can access McGraw-Hill's Connect™ and Create™ right from within your Blackboard course—all with a single sign-on. Say goodbye to the days of logging in to multiple applications.

2. **Deep integration of content and tools.** Not only do you get a single sign-on with Connect™ and Create™, you also get deep integration of McGraw-Hill content and content engines right in Blackboard. Whether you're choosing a book for your course or building Connect™ assignments, all the tools you need are right where you want them—inside Blackboard.

3. **Seamless Gradebooks.** Are you tired of keeping multiple gradebooks and manually synchronizing grades into Blackboard? We thought so. When a student completes an integrated Connect™ assignment, the grade for that assignment automatically (and instantly) feeds your Blackboard grade center.

4. **A solution for everyone.** Whether your institution is already using Blackboard or you just want to try Blackboard on your own, we have a solution for you. McGraw-Hill and Blackboard can now offer you easy access to industry leading technology and content, whether your campus hosts it, or we do. Be sure to ask your local McGraw-Hill representative for details.

Tegrity Tegrity Campus is a service that makes class time available all the time by automatically capturing every lecture in a searchable format for students to review when they study and complete assignments. With a simple one-click start and stop process, you capture all computer screens and corresponding audio. Students replay any part of any class with easy-to-use browser-based viewing on a PC or Mac. Educators know that the more students can see, hear, and experience class resources, the better they learn. With Tegrity Campus, students quickly recall key moments by using Tegrity Campus's unique search feature. This search helps students efficiently find what they need when they need it across an entire semester of class recordings. Help turn all your students' study time into learning moments immediately supported by your lecture.

Student Resources

Adaptive Diagnostic Tool This diagnostic tool is an unparalleled, intelligent learning system based on cognitive mapping that *diagnoses* your students' knowledge of a particular subject and then creates an individualized learning path geared toward student success in your course. It offers individualized assessment by delivering appropriate learning material in the form of questions at the right time, helping students attain mastery of the content. Whether the system is assigned by you or used independently by students as a study tool, the results can be recorded in an easy-to-use grade report that allows you to measure student progress at all times and coach your students to success.

As an added benefit, all content covered in this adaptive diagnostic is tied to learning objectives for your course so that you can use the results as evidence of subject mastery. This tool also provides a personal study plan that allows the student to estimate the time it will take and number of questions required to learn the subject matter. Your students will learn faster, study more efficiently, and retain more knowledge when using *Essentials of Life-Span Development*.

The *Milestones* Program Our new assessable video-based program tracks human development through each major life stage. Starting from infancy, students will watch each baby grow and achieve the major developmental milestones such as balance, development of fine motor control, and social interactions. The program continues through adulthood, capturing attitudes toward issues such as family, sexuality, and death and dying.

1

Introduction

Stories of Life-Span Development: How Did Ted Kaczynski Become Ted Kaczynski and Alice Walker Become Alice Walker?

Ted Kaczynski sprinted through high school, not bothering with his junior year and making only passing efforts at social contact. Off to Harvard at age 16, Kaczynski was a loner during his college years. One of his roommates at Harvard said that he avoided people by quickly shuffling by them and slamming the door behind him. After obtaining his Ph.D. in mathematics at the University of Michigan, Kaczynski became a professor at the University of California at Berkeley. His colleagues there remember him as hiding from social circum-

stances—no friends, no allies, no networking.

After several years at Berkeley, Kaczynski resigned and moved to a rural area of Montana, where he lived as a hermit in a crude shack for 25 years. Town residents described him as a bearded eccentric. Kaczynski traced his own difficulties to growing up as a genius in a kid's body and sticking out like a sore thumb in his surroundings as a child. In 1996, he was arrested and charged as the notorious Unabomber, America's most wanted killer. Over the

course of 17 years, Kaczynski had sent 16 mail bombs that left 23 people wounded or maimed, and 3 people dead. In 1998, he pleaded guilty to the offenses and was sentenced to life in prison.

A decade before Kaczynski mailed his first bomb, Alice Walker spent her days battling racism in Mississippi. She had recently won her first writing fellowship, but rather than use the money to follow her dream of moving to Senegal, Africa, she put herself into the heart and heat of the civil rights movement. Walker had

1

grown up knowing the brutal effects of poverty and racism. Born in 1944, she was the eighth child of Georgia sharecroppers who earned $300 a year. When Walker was 8, her brother accidentally shot her in the left eye with a BB gun. Since her parents had no car, it took them a week to get her to a hospital. By the time she received medical care, she was blind in that eye, and it had developed a disfiguring layer of scar tissue. Despite the counts against her, Walker overcame pain and anger and went on to win a Pulitzer Prize for her book *The Color Purple*. She became not only a novelist but also an essayist, a poet, a short-story writer, and a social activist.

Ted Kaczynski, the convicted unabomber, traced his difficulties to growing up as a genius in a kid's body and not fitting in when he was a child.

Alice Walker won the Pulitzer Prize for her book *The Color Purple*. Like the characters in her book, Walker overcame pain and anger to triumph and celebrate the human spirit.

What leads one individual, so full of promise, to commit brutal acts of violence and another to turn poverty and trauma into a rich literary harvest? If you have ever wondered why people turn out the way they do, you have asked yourself the central question we will explore in this book.

This book is a window into the journey of human development—your own and that of every other member of the human species. Every life is distinct, a new biography in the world. Examining the shape of life-span development helps us to understand it better. In this first chapter, we explore what it means to take a life-span perspective on development, examine the nature of development, and outline how science helps us to understand it. ∎

The Life-Span Perspective

Each of us develops partly like all other individuals, partly like some other individuals, and partly like no other individuals. Most of the time we see the qualities in an individual that make that person unique. But as humans, we have all traveled some common paths. Each of us—Leonardo da Vinci, Joan of Arc, George Washington, Martin Luther King, Jr., and you—walked at about 1 year, engaged in fantasy play as a young child, and became more independent as a youth. Each of us, if we live long enough, will experience hearing problems and the death of family members and friends. This is the general course of our **development**, the pattern of movement or change that begins at conception and continues through the human life span.

In this section we explore what is meant by the concept of development and why the study of life-span development is important. We outline the main characteristics of the life-span perspective and discuss various influences on development. In addition, we examine some contemporary concerns related to life-span development.

The Importance of Studying Life-Span Development

How might you benefit from studying life-span development? Perhaps you are, or will be, a parent or teacher. If so, responsibility for children is, or will be, a part of your everyday life. The more you learn about them, the better you can raise them or teach them. Perhaps you hope to gain some insight about your own history—as an infant, a child, an adolescent, or a young adult. Perhaps you want to know more about what your life will be like as you grow through the adult years—as a middle-aged adult, or as an adult in old age, for example. Or perhaps you just stumbled across this course, thinking that it sounded intriguing. Whatever your reasons, you will discover that the study of life-span development addresses some provocative questions about who we are, how we came to be this way, and where our future will take us.

In our exploration of development, we will examine the life span from the point of conception until the time when life (at least, life as we know it) ends. You will see yourself as an infant, as a child, and as an adolescent, and you will learn about how those years influenced the kind of individual you are today. And you will see yourself as a young adult, as a middle-aged adult, and as an adult in old age, and you will hopefully be motivated to consider how your experiences will affect your development through the remainder of your adult years.

development The pattern of movement or change that starts at conception and continues through the human life span.

life-span perspective The perspective that development is lifelong, multidimensional, multidirectional, plastic, multidisciplinary, and contextual; involves growth, maintenance, and regulation; and is constructed through biological, sociocultural, and individual factors working together.

Characteristics of the Life-Span Perspective

Growth and development are dramatic during the first two decades of life, but development is not something that happens only to children and adolescents. The *traditional approach* to the study of development emphasizes extensive change from birth to adolescence (especially during infancy), little or no change in adulthood, and decline in old age. Yet a great deal of change does occur in the decades after adolescence. The *life-span approach* emphasizes developmental change throughout adulthood as well as childhood (Schaie, 2009, 2010, 2011).

Recent increases in human life expectancy have contributed to greater interest in the life-span approach to development. The upper boundary of the *human life span* (based on the oldest age documented) is 122 years. The maximum life span of humans has not changed since the beginning of recorded history. What has changed is *life expectancy,* the average number of years that a person born in a particular year can expect to live. In the 20th century alone, life expectancy increased by 30 years, thanks to improvements in sanitation, nutrition, and medicine (see Figure 1.1). In 2009, the U.S. life expectancy was 78 years of age (U.S. Census Bureau, 2009). Today, for most individuals in developed countries, childhood and adolescence represent only about one-fourth of their lives.

The belief that development occurs throughout life is central to the life-span perspective or human development, but this perspective has other characteristics as well. According to life-span development expert Paul Baltes (1939–2006), the **life-span perspective** views development as lifelong, multidimensional, multidirectional, plastic, multidisciplinary and contextual, and as a process that involves growth, maintenance, and regulation of loss (Baltes, 1987, 2003; Baltes, Lindenberger, & Staudinger, 2006). In this view, it is important to understand that development is constructed through biological, sociocultural, and individual factors working together (Baltes, Reuter-Lorenz, & Rösler, 2006). Let's look at each of these characteristics.

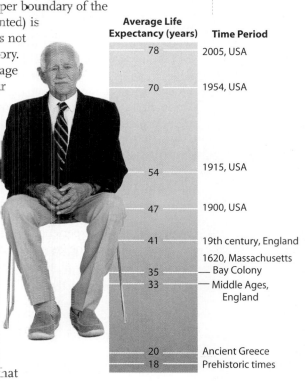

Average Life Expectancy (years)	Time Period
78	2005, USA
70	1954, USA
54	1915, USA
47	1900, USA
41	19th century, England
35	1620, Massachusetts Bay Colony
33	Middle Ages, England
20	Ancient Greece
18	Prehistoric times

Figure 1.1 Human Life Expectancy at Birth from Prehistoric to Contemporary Times
It took 5,000 years to extend human life expectancy from 18 to 41 years of age.

Development Is Lifelong

In the life-span perspective, early adulthood is not the endpoint of development; rather, no age period dominates development. Researchers increasingly study the experiences and psychological orientations of adults at different points in their lives. Later in this chapter we describe the age periods of development and their characteristics.

Development Is Multidimensional

Development consists of biological, cognitive, and socioemotional dimensions. Even within each of those dimensions, there are many components. The cognitive dimension, for example, includes attention, memory, abstract thinking, speed of processing information, and social intelligence. At every age, changes occur in every dimension. Changes in one dimension also affect development in the other dimensions.

To get an idea of how interactions occur, consider the development of Ted Kaczynski, the so-called Unabomber discussed at the opening of the chapter. When he was six months old, he was hospitalized with a severe allergic reaction, and his parents were rarely allowed to visit him. According to his mother, the previously happy baby was never the same. He became withdrawn and unresponsive. As Ted grew up, he had periodic "shutdowns" accompanied by rage. In his mother's view, a biological event in infancy warped the development of her son's mind and emotions.

Development consists of biological, cognitive, and socioemotional dimensions. Even within a dimension, there are many components—for example, attention, memory, abstract thinking, speed of processing information, and social intelligence are just a few of the components of the cognitive dimension.

Development Is Multidirectional

Throughout life, some dimensions or components of a dimension expand and others shrink. For example, when one language (such as English) is acquired early in development, the capacity for acquiring second and third languages (such as Spanish and Chinese) decreases later in development, especially after early childhood (Levelt, 1989). During adolescence, as individuals establish romantic relationships, their relationships with friends might decrease. During late adulthood, older adults might become wiser by being able to call on experience to guide their intellectual decision making (Karelitz, Jarvin, & Sternberg, 2011; Staudinger & Gluck, 2011), but they perform more poorly on tasks that require speed in processing information (Salthouse, 2010).

Development Is Plastic

Even at 10 years old, Ted Kaczynski was extraordinarily shy. Was he destined to remain forever uncomfortable with people? Developmentalists debate how much plasticity people have in various dimensions at different points in their development. *Plasticity* means the capacity for change. For example, can you still improve your intellectual skills when you are in your seventies or eighties? Or might these intellectual skills be fixed by the time you are in your thirties so that further improvement is impossible? In one research study, the reasoning abilities of older adults were improved through retraining (Willis & Schaie, 1994). However, possibly we possess less capacity for change when we become old. The search for plasticity and its constraints is a key element on the contemporary agenda for developmental research (Park & Goh, 2010).

Developmental Science Is Multidisciplinary

Psychologists, sociologists, anthropologists, neuroscientists, and medical researchers all share an interest in unlocking the mysteries of development through the life span. How do your heredity and health limit your intelligence? Do intelligence and social relationships change with age in the same way around the world? How do families and schools influence intellectual development? These are examples of research questions that cut across disciplines.

Development Is Contextual

All development occurs within a **context**, or setting. Contexts include families, schools, peer groups, churches, cities, neighborhoods, university laboratories, countries, and so on. Each of these settings is influenced by historical, economic, social, and cultural factors (Goodnow, 2010).

Contexts, like individuals, change (Schaie, 2011). Thus, individuals are changing beings in a changing world. As a result of these changes, contexts exert three types of influences (Baltes, 2003): (1) normative age-graded influences, (2) normative history-graded influences, and (3) nonnormative or highly individualized life events. Each of these types can have a biological or environmental impact on development. **Normative age-graded influences** are similar for individuals in a particular age group. These influences include biological processes such as puberty and menopause. They also include sociocultural, environmental processes such as beginning formal education (usually at about age 6 in most cultures) and retirement (which takes place in the fifties and sixties in most cultures).

Normative history-graded influences are common to people of a particular generation because of historical circumstances. For example, in their youth American baby boomers shared the experience of the Cuban missile crisis, the assassination of John F. Kennedy, and the Beatles invasion. Other examples of normative history-graded influences include economic, political, and social upheavals such as the Great Depression in the 1930s, World War II in the 1940s, the civil rights and women's rights movements of the 1960s and 1970s, the terrorist attacks of 9/11/2001, as well as the integration of computers and cell phones into everyday life during the 1990s. Long-term changes in the genetic and cultural makeup of a population (due to immigration or changes in fertility rates) are also part of normative historical change.

Nonnormative life events are unusual occurrences that have a major impact on the individual's life. These events do not happen to all people, and when they do occur they can influence people in different ways. Examples include the death of a parent when a child is young, pregnancy in early adolescence, a fire that destroys a home, winning the lottery, or getting an unexpected career opportunity.

Nonnormative life events, such as Hurricane Katrina in August 2005, are unusual circumstances that have a major impact on a person's life.

How Would You...?

As a social worker, how would you explain the importance of considering nonnormative life events when working with a new client?

context Setting in which development occurs, that is influenced by historical, economic, social, and cultural factors.

normative age-graded influences Biological and environmental influences that are similar for individuals in a particular age group.

normative history-graded influences Biological and environmental influences that are associated with history. These influences are common to people of a particular generation.

nonnormative life events Unusual occurrences that have a major impact on a person's life. The occurrence, pattern, and sequence of these events are not applicable to many individuals.

Development Involves Growth, Maintenance, and Regulation of Loss

Baltes and his colleagues (2006) assert that the mastery of life often involves conflicts and competition among three goals of human development: growth, maintenance, and regulation of loss. As individuals age into middle and late adulthood, the maintenance and regulation of loss in their capacities takes center stage away from growth. Thus, a 75-year-old man might aim not to improve his memory or his golf swing but to maintain his independence and to play golf at all. In Chapters 15 and 16, we will discuss these ideas about maintenance and regulation of loss in greater depth.

Development Is a Co-Construction of Biology, Culture, and the Individual

Development is a co-construction of biological, cultural, and individual factors working together (Baltes, Reuter-Lorenz, & Rösler, 2006). For example, the brain shapes culture, but it is also shaped by culture and the experiences that individuals have or pursue. In terms of individual factors, we can go beyond what our genetic inheritance and environment give us. We can create a unique developmental path by actively choosing from the environment the things that optimize our lives (Rathunde & Csikszentmihalyi, 2006).

Contemporary Concerns in Life-Span Development

Pick up a newspaper or magazine and you might see headlines like these: "Political Leanings May Be Written in the Genes," "Mother Accused of Tossing Children into Bay," "Gender Gap Widens," "FDA Warns About ADHD Drug," "Heart Attack Deaths Higher in African American Patients," "Test May Predict Alzheimer Disease." Researchers using the life-span perspective are examining these and many other topics of contemporary concern. The roles that health and well-being, parenting, education, and sociocultural contexts play in life-span development, as well as how social policy is related to these issues, are a particular focus of this textbook.

Health and Well-Being

Health professionals today recognize the power of lifestyles and psychological states in health and well-being (Hahn, Payne, & Lucas, 2011; Worthman, 2010). Clinical psychologists are among the health professionals who help people improve their well-being. Read about one clinical psychologist who helps adolescents who have become juvenile delinquents or substance abusers in the "Careers in Life-Span Development" profile.

CAREERS IN LIFE-SPAN DEVELOPMENT

Luis Vargas, Child Clinical Psychologist

Luis Vargas is Director of the Clinical Child Psychology Internship Program and a professor in the Department of Psychiatry at the University of New Mexico Health Sciences Center. He also is Director of Psychology at the University of New Mexico Children's Psychiatric Hospital.

Luis obtained an undergraduate degree in psychology from St. Edwards University in Texas, a master's degree in psychology from Trinity University in Texas, and a Ph.D. in clinical psychology from the University of Nebraska–Lincoln.

Luis' main interests are cultural issues and the assessment and treatment of children, adolescents, and families. He is motivated to find better ways to provide culturally responsive mental health services. One of his special interests is the treatment of Latino youth for delinquency and substance abuse.

Clinical psychologists like Luis Vargas seek to help people with psychological problems. They work in a variety of settings, including colleges and universities, clinics, medical schools, and private practice. Some clinical psychologists only conduct psychotherapy; others do psychological assessment and psychotherapy; some also do research. Clinical psychologists may specialize in a particular age group, such as children (child clinical psychologist) or older adults (often referred to as a geropsychologist).

Luis Vargas (*left*) conducting a child therapy session.

Clinical psychologists like Dr. Vargas have either a Ph.D. (which involves clinical and research training) or a Psy.D. degree (which only involves clinical training). This graduate training usually takes five to seven years and includes courses in clinical psychology and a one-year supervised internship in an accredited setting toward the end of the training. Most states require clinical psychologists to pass a test to become state licensed and to call themselves clinical psychologists.

Parenting and Education

Can two gay men raise a healthy family? Do children suffer if both parents work outside the home? Are U.S. schools failing to teach children how to read and write and calculate adequately? We hear many questions like these related to pressures on the contemporary family and the problems of U.S. schools (Johnson & others, 2011; McCombs, 2010; Patterson, 2009). In later chapters, we analyze child care, the effects of divorce, parenting styles, intergenerational relationships, early childhood education, relationships between childhood poverty and education, bilingual education, new educational efforts to improve lifelong learning, and many other issues related to parenting and education (Nieto, 2010).

Sociocultural Contexts and Diversity

Health, parenting, and education—like development itself—are all shaped by their sociocultural context (Cole & Cagigas, 2010). To analyze this context, four concepts are especially useful: culture, ethnicity, socioeconomic status, and gender.

Culture encompasses the behavior patterns, beliefs, and all other products of a particular group of people that are passed on from generation to generation. Culture results from the interaction of people over many years (Shiraev, 2011). A cultural group can be as large as the United States or as small as an isolated Appalachian town. Whatever its size, the group's culture influences the behavior of its members (Hall, 2010). **Cross-cultural studies** compare aspects of two or more cultures. The comparison provides information about the degree to which development is similar, or universal, across cultures, or is instead culture-specific (Kitayama, 2011; Shiraev & Levy, 2010).

Ethnicity (the word *ethnic* comes from the Greek word for "nation") is rooted in cultural heritage, nationality, race, religion, and language. African Americans, Latinos, Asian Americans, Native Americans, European Americans, and Arab Americans are a few examples of broad ethnic groups in the United States. Diversity exists within each ethnic group (Banks, 2010; Rowley, Kurtz-Costas, & Cooper, 2011).

Socioeconomic status (SES) refers to a person's position within society based on occupational, educational, and economic characteristics. Socioeconomic status implies certain inequalities. Differences in the ability to control resources and to participate in society's rewards produce unequal opportunities (Huston & Bentley, 2010).

Gender, the psychological and sociocultural dimensions of being female or male, is another important aspect of sociocultural contexts. Few aspects of our development are more central to our identity and social relationships than gender (Best, 2010; Eagly & Wood, 2011). We discuss sociocultural contexts and diversity in each chapter.

The conditions in which many of the world's women live are a serious concern (UNICEF, 2010). Inadequate educational opportunities, violence, and lack of political access are just some of the problems faced by many women. One analysis found that a higher percentage of girls than boys around the world have never had any education (UNICEF, 2004) (see Figure 1.2). The countries with the most uneducated females are in Africa. In contrast, Canada, the United States, and Russia have the highest percentages of educated women. In developing countries, 67 percent of women over the age

culture ... liefs, and behavior patterns, beliefs, and behavior patterns, group that ... products of a generation to ... sed on from **cross-cultural** ... ion. of one culture wit... other cultures. The ...mparisons mation about the deg...ore children's development ...for... universal, across cultures, the degree to which it is cu... specific.

ethnicity A range of characterist... rooted in cultural heritage, including nationality, race, religion, and language.

socioeconomic status (SES) Refers to the conceptual grouping of people with similar occupational, educational, and economic characteristics.

gender The psychological and sociocultural dimensions of being female or male.

Two Korean-born children on the day they became United States citizens. Asian American and Latino children are the fastest-growing immigrant groups in the United States. *How diverse are the students in your class on life-span development that you now are taking? How are their experiences in growing up likely similar to or different from yours?*

of 25 (compared with 50 percent of men) have never been to school. At the beginning of the 21st century, 80 million more boys than girls were in primary and secondary educational settings around the world (United Nations, 2002).

Social Policy

Social policy is a government's course of action designed to promote the welfare of its citizens. Values, economics, and politics all shape a nation's social policy. Out of concern that policy makers are doing too little to protect the well-being of children and older adults, life-span researchers are increasingly undertaking studies that they hope will lead to effective social policy (Balsano, Theokas, & Bobek, 2009).

How Would You...?
As a psychologist, how would you explain the importance of examining sociocultural factors in developmental research?

Children who grow up in poverty represent a special concern of researchers who see social policy as a way of improving children's lives (Tamis-LeMonda & McFadden, 2010). In 2007, 18 percent of U.S. children were living in families below the poverty line (Childstats.gov, 2009). As indicated in Figure 1.3, one study found that a higher percentage of children in poor families than in middle-income families were exposed to family turmoil, separation from a parent, violence, crowding, excessive noise, and poor housing (Evans & English, 2002).

Developmental psychologists are seeking ways to help families living in poverty improve their well-being, and they have offered many suggestions for improving government policies (Huston & Bentley, 2010). For example, the Minnesota Family Investment Program (MFIP) was designed in the 1990s primarily to influence the behavior of adults—specifically, to move adults off welfare rolls and into paid employment. A key element of the program was that it guaranteed that adults participating in the program would receive more income if they worked than if they did not. How did the increase in income affect their children? A study of the effects of MFIP found that higher incomes of working poor parents were linked with benefits for their children (Gennetian & Miller, 2002). The children's achievement in school improved, and their behavior problems decreased. A current MFIP study is examining the influence of specific services on low-income families at risk for child maltreatment and other negative outcomes for children (Minnesota Family Investment Program, 2009).

At the other end of the life span, older adults have health issues that social policy can address (Moody, 2009). Key concerns are escalating health-care costs and the access of older adults to adequate health care (Kim, Gordes, & Alon, 2010). One study found that the health-care system fails older adults in many areas (Wenger & others, 2003). For example, older adults received the recommended care for general medical conditions such as heart disease only 52 percent of the time; they received appropriate care for undernutrition and Alzheimer disease only 31 percent of the time.

Doly Akter, age 17, lives in a slum in Bangladesh, a country where nearly two-thirds of young women are married before they turn 18. With the support of UNICEF, Doly organized a club that has worked to improve hygiene and health in her neighborhood. Also, her group has managed to stop several child marriages by convincing parents that marriage isn't in their daughter's best interest and emphasizing the future benefits of staying in school. Doly says that the girls in her club are far more aware of their rights than their mothers ever were (UNICEF, 2007).

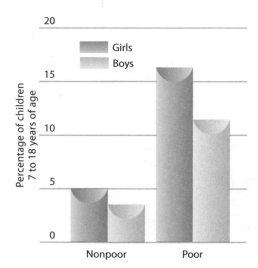

Figure 1.2 Percentage of Children 7 to 18 Years of Age Around the World Who Have Never Been to School of Any Kind
When UNICEF (2004) surveyed the education that children around the world are receiving, it found that far more girls than boys receive no formal schooling at all.

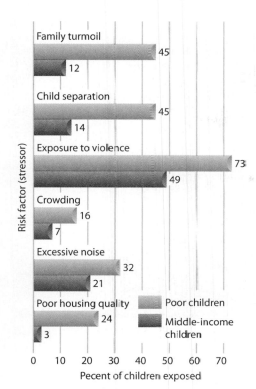

Figure 1.3 Exposure to Six Stressors Among Poor and Middle-Income Children

One study analyzed the exposure to six stressors among poor children and middle-income children (Evans & English, 2002). Poor children were much more likely to face each of these stressors.

biological processes Changes in an individual's physical nature.

cognitive processes Changes in an individual's thought, intelligence, and language.

Concerns about the well-being of older adults are heightened by two facts. First, the number of older adults in the United States is growing rapidly. Second, many of these older Americans are likely to need society's help. Compared with earlier decades, U.S. adults today are less likely to be married, more likely to be childless, and more likely to be living alone. As the older population continues to expand in the 21st century, an increasing number of older adults will be without either a spouse or children—traditionally the main sources of support for older adults (Cheng, Lee, & Chow, 2010). These individuals will need social relationships, networks, and supports (Antonucci & others, 2011).

The Nature of Development

In this section we explore what is meant by developmental processes and periods, as well as variations in the way age is conceptualized. We examine key developmental issues, how they describe development, and strategies we can use to evaluate them.

If you wanted to describe how and why Alice Walker or Ted Kaczynski developed during their lifetimes, how would you go about it? A chronicle of the events in any person's life can quickly become a confusing and tedious array of details. Two concepts help provide a framework for describing and understanding an individual's development: developmental processes and periods.

Biological, Cognitive, and Socioemotional Processes

At the beginning of this chapter, we defined development as the pattern of change that begins at conception and continues through the life span. The pattern is complex because it is the product of biological, cognitive, and socioemotional processes.

Biological Processes

Biological processes produce changes in an individual's physical nature. Genes inherited from parents, the development of the brain, height and weight gains, changes in motor skills, nutrition, exercise, the hormonal changes of puberty, and cardiovascular decline are all examples of biological processes that affect development.

Cognitive Processes

Cognitive processes refer to changes in an individual's thought, intelligence, and language. Watching a colorful mobile swinging above the crib, putting together a two-word sentence, memorizing a poem, imagining what it would be like to be a movie star, and solving a crossword puzzle all involve cognitive processes.

socioemotional processes Changes
in an individual's relationships with
other people, emotions, and
personality.

Socioemotional Processes

Socioemotional processes involve changes in the individual's relationships with other people, changes in emotions, and changes in personality. An infant's smile in response to a parent's touch, a toddler's aggressive attack on a playmate, a school-age child's development of assertiveness, an adolescent's joy at the senior prom, and the affection of an elderly couple all reflect the role of socioemotional processes in development.

PEANUTS © United Features Syndicate, Inc.

Connecting Biological, Cognitive, and Socioemotional Processes

Biological, cognitive, and socioemotional processes are inextricably intertwined (Diamond, 2009; Diamond, Casey, & Munakata, 2011). Consider a baby smiling in response to a parent's touch. This response depends on biological processes (the physical nature of touch and responsiveness to it), cognitive processes (the ability to understand intentional acts), and socioemotional processes (the act of smiling often reflects a positive emotional feeling, and smiling helps to connect us in positive ways with other human beings). Nowhere is the connection across biological, cognitive, and socioemotional processes more obvious than in two rapidly emerging fields:

- *developmental cognitive neuroscience,* which explores links between development, cognitive processes, and the brain (Diamond, Casey, & Munakata, 2011)

- *developmental social neuroscience,* which examines connections between socioemotional processes, development, and the brain (Bell, Greene, & Wolfe, 2010; de Haan & Gunnar, 2009).

In many instances, biological, cognitive, and socioemotional processes are bidirectional. For example, biological processes can influence cognitive processes and vice versa. For the most part, we will study the different processes of development (biological, cognitive, and socioemotional) in separate chapters, but the human being is an integrated individual with a mind and body that are interdependent. Thus, in many places throughout the book we will call attention to the connections between these processes.

Periods of Development

The interplay of biological, cognitive, and socioemotional processes (see Figure 1.4) over time gives rise to the developmental periods of the human life span. A *developmental period* is a time frame in a person's life that is characterized by certain features. The most widely used classification of developmental periods involves an eight-period sequence. For the purposes of organization and understanding, this book is structured according to these developmental periods.

The *prenatal period* is the time from conception to birth. It involves tremendous growth—from a single cell to a complete organism with a brain and behavioral capabilities—and takes place in approximately a nine-month period.

Infancy is the developmental period from birth to 18 or 24 months when humans are extremely dependent on adults. During this period, many psychological activities—language, symbolic thought, sensorimotor coordination, and social learning, for example—are just beginning.

Early childhood is the developmental period from the end of infancy to age 5 or 6. This period is sometimes called the "preschool years." During this time, young children learn to become more self-sufficient and to care for themselves. They also develop school readiness skills, such as the ability to follow instructions and identify letters, and they spend many hours playing with peers. First grade typically marks the end of early childhood.

Middle and late childhood is the developmental period from about 6 to 11 years of age, approximately corresponding to the elementary school years. During this period, the fundamental skills of reading, writing, and arithmetic are mastered. The child is formally exposed to the world outside the family and to the prevailing culture. Achievement becomes a more central theme of the child's world, and self-control increases.

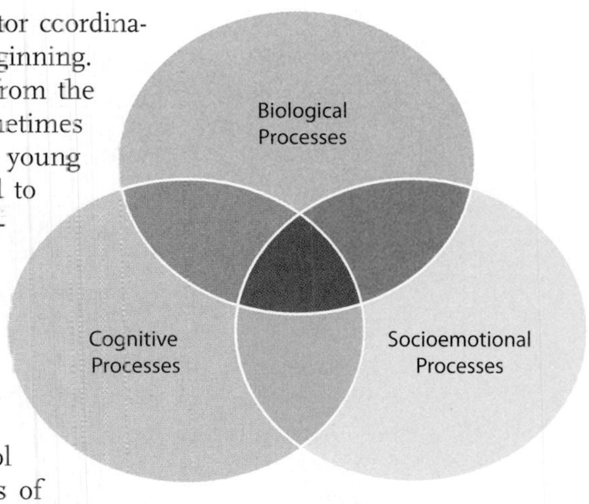

Adolescence encompasses the transition from childhood to early adulthood, entered at approximately 10 to 12 years of age and ending at 18 to 22 years of age. Adolescence begins with rapid physical changes—dramatic gains in height and weight, changes in body contour, and the development of sexual characteristics such as enlargement of the breasts, growth of pubic and facial hair, and deepening of the voice. At this point in development, the pursuit of independence and an identity are prominent. Thought is more logical, abstract, and idealistic. More time is spent outside the family.

Early adulthood is the developmental period that begins in the late teens or early twenties and lasts through the thirties. For young adults, this is a time for establishing personal and economic independence, career development, and for many, selecting a mate, learning to live with someone in an intimate way, starting a family, and rearing children.

Middle adulthood is the developmental period from approximately 40 years of age to about 60. It is a time of expanding personal and social involvement and responsibility; of assisting the next generation in becoming competent, mature individuals; and of reaching and maintaining satisfaction in a career.

Late adulthood is the developmental period that begins in the sixties or seventies and lasts until death. It is a time of life review, retirement, and adjustment to new social roles involving decreasing strength and health.

Late adulthood lasts longer than any other period of development. Because the number of people in this age group has been increasing dramatically, life-span developmentalists have been paying more attention to differences within late adulthood. According to Paul Baltes and Jacqui Smith (2003), a major change takes place in older adults' lives as they become the "oldest-old," at about 85 years of age. The "young-old" (classified as 65 through 84 in this analysis) have substantial potential for physical and cognitive fitness, retain much of their cognitive capacity, and can develop strategies to cope with the gains and losses of aging. In contrast, the oldest-old (85 and older) show considerable loss in cognitive skills, experience an increase in chronic stress, and are more frail (Baltes & Smith, 2003). Nonetheless, considerable variation exists in how much of their capabilities the oldest-old retain.

Life-span developmentalists who focus on adult development and aging increasingly describe life-span development in terms of four "ages" (Baltes, 2006):

First age: Childhood and adolescence

Second age: Prime adulthood, twenties through fifties

Third age: Approximately 60 to 79 years of age

Fourth age: Approximately 80 years and older

Figure 1.4
Processes Involved in Developmental Changes
Biological, cognitive, and socioemotional processes interact as individuals develop.

Biological Processes

Cognitive Processes

Socioemotional Processes

The major emphasis in this conceptualization is on the third and fourth ages, especially the increasing evidence that individuals in the third age are healthier and can lead more active, productive lives than their predecessors in earlier generations. However, when older adults reach their eighties, especially 85 and over (fourth age), health and well-being decline for many individuals.

Conceptions of Age

In our description of developmental periods, we linked an approximate age range with each period. But we also have noted that there are variations in the capabilities of individuals of the same age, and we have seen how age-related changes can be exaggerated. How important is age when we try to understand an individual?

According to some life-span experts, chronological age is not very relevant to understanding a person's psychological development (Hoyer & Roodin, 2009). Chronological age is the number of years that have elapsed since birth. But time is a crude index of experience, and it does not cause development. Chronological age, moreover, is not the only way of measuring age. Just as there are different domains of development, there are different ways of thinking about age.

Age has been conceptualized not just as chronological age but also as biological age, psychological age, and social age (Hoyer & Roodin, 2009). *Biological age* is a person's age in terms of biological health. Determining biological age involves knowing the functional capacities of a person's vital organs. One person's vital capacities may be better or worse than those of others of comparable chronological age. The younger the person's biological age, the longer the person is expected to live, regardless of chronological age.

Psychological age is an individual's adaptive capacities compared with those of other individuals of the same chronological age. Thus, older adults who continue to learn, are flexible, are motivated, and think clearly are engaging in more adaptive behaviors than their chronological age-mates who do not do these things (Park & Goh, 2010).

From a life-span perspective, an overall age profile of an individual involves not just chronological age but also biological age and psychological age. For example, a 70-year-old man (chronological age) might be in good physical health (biological age), but might be experiencing memory problems and having trouble coping with the demands placed on him by his wife's recent hospitalization (psychological age).

(a)

(b)

(a) Pam McSwain, age 60, competing in the Senior Olympics in Memphis, Tennessee in 2009.
(b) A sedentary, overweight middle-aged man. *Even if Pam McSwain's chronological age is older, might her biological age be younger than the middle-aged man's?*

Developmental Issues

Was Ted Kaczynski born a killer, or did his life turn him into one? Kaczynski himself thought that his childhood was the root of his troubles. He grew up as a genius in a boy's body and never fit in with other children. Did his early experiences determine his later life? Is your own journey through life marked out ahead of time, or can your experiences change your path? Are the experiences you have early in your journey more important than later ones? Is your journey more like taking an elevator up a skyscraper with distinct stops along the way or more like a cruise down a river with smoother ebbs and flows? These questions point to three issues about the nature of development: the roles played by nature and nurture, stability and change, and continuity and discontinuity.

Nature and Nurture

The **nature-nurture issue** concerns the extent to which development is influenced by nature and by nurture. *Nature* refers to an organism's biological inheritance, *nurture* to its environmental experiences.

According to those who emphasize the role of nature, just as a sunflower grows in an orderly way—unless flattened by an unfriendly environment—so too the human grows in an orderly way. An evolutionary and genetic foundation produces commonalities in growth and development (Cosmides, 2011; Goldsmith, 2011). We walk before we talk, speak one word before two words, grow rapidly in infancy and less so in early childhood, experience a rush of sex hormones in puberty, reach the peak of our physical strength in late adolescence and early adulthood, and then physically decline. Proponents of the importance of nature acknowledge that extreme environments—those that are psychologically barren or hostile—can depress development. However, they believe that basic growth tendencies are genetically programmed into humans (Mader, 2011).

By contrast, other psychologists emphasize the importance of nurture, or environmental experiences, in development (Gauvain & Parke, 2010; Grusec, 2011). Experiences run the gamut from the individual's biological environment (nutrition, medical care, drugs, and physical accidents) to the social environment (family, peers, schools, community, media, and culture).

Stability and Change

Is the shy child who hides behind the sofa when visitors arrive destined to become a wallflower at college dances, or might the child become a sociable, talkative individual? Is the fun-loving, carefree adolescent bound to have difficulty holding down a 9-to-5 job as an adult? These questions reflect the **stability-change issue**, involving the degree to which early traits and characteristics persist through life or change.

Many developmentalists who emphasize stability in development argue that stability is the result of heredity and possibly early experiences in life. For example, many argue that if an individual is shy throughout life (as Ted Kaczynski was), this stability is due to heredity and possibly early experiences in which the infant or young child encountered considerable stress when interacting with people. Some argue that unless infants experience warm, nurturant caregiving in the first year or so of life, their development will never be optimal (Finger & others, 2009).

Developmentalists who emphasize change take the more optimistic view that later experiences can produce change. Recall that in the life-span perspective, plasticity, the potential for change, exists throughout the life span (Park & Goh, 2010; Schaie, 2011). Experts such as Paul Baltes (2003) argue that with increasing age and on average older adults often show less capacity for change in the sense of learning new things than younger adults. However, many older adults continue to be good at practicing what they have learned in earlier times.

Continuity and Discontinuity

When developmental change occurs, is it gradual or abrupt? Think about your own development for a moment. Did you become the person you are gradually? Or did you experience sudden, distinct changes in your growth? For the most part, developmentalists who emphasize nurture describe development as a gradual, continuous process. Those who emphasize nature often describe development as a series of distinct stages.

The **continuity-discontinuity issue** focuses on the degree to which development involves either gradual, cumulative change (continuity) or distinct stages (discontinuity). In terms of continuity, as the oak grows from seedling to giant oak, its development is continuous. Similarly, a child's first word, though seemingly an abrupt, discontinuous event, is actually the result of weeks and months of growth and practice. Puberty might seem abrupt, but it is a gradual process that occurs over several years.

In terms of discontinuity, as an insect grows from a caterpillar to a chrysalis to a butterfly, it passes through a sequence of stages in which change is qualitatively rather than quantitatively different. Similarly, at some point a child moves from not being able to think abstractly about the world to being able to do so. This is a qualitative, discontinuous change in development rather than a quantitative, continuous change.

Evaluating the Developmental Issues

Developmentalists generally acknowledge that development is not all nature or all nurture, not all stability or all change, and not all continuity or all discontinuity. Nature *and* nurture, stability *and* change, continuity *and* discontinuity characterize development throughout the human life span.

Although most developmentalists do not take extreme positions on these three important issues, there is spirited debate regarding how strongly development is influenced by each of these factors (Gauvain & Parke, 2010; Kagan, 2010; Phillips & Lowenstein, 2011).

Theories of Development

How can we answer questions about the roles of nature and nurture, stability and change, and continuity and discontinuity in development? How can we determine, for example, whether memory declines in older adults can be prevented or whether special care can repair the harm inflicted by child neglect? The scientific method is the best tool we have to answer such questions (Smith & Davis, 2010).

The *scientific method* is essentially a four-step process: (1) conceptualize a process or problem to be studied, (2) collect research information (data), (3) analyze data, and (4) draw conclusions.

In step 1, when researchers are formulating a problem to study, they often draw on theories and develop hypotheses. A **theory** is an interrelated, coherent set of ideas that helps to explain phenomena and make predictions. It may suggest **hypotheses,** which are specific assertions and predictions that can be tested. For example, a theory on mentoring might state that sustained support and guidance from an adult makes a difference in the lives of children from impoverished backgrounds because the mentor gives the children opportunities to observe and imitate the behavior and strategies of the mentor.

This section outlines five theoretical orientations to development: psychoanalytic, cognitive, behavioral and social cognitive, ethological, and ecological. These theories look at development from different perspectives, and they disagree about certain aspects of development. But many of their ideas are complementary, and each contributes an important piece to the life-span development puzzle. Although the theories disagree about certain aspects of development, many of their ideas are complementary rather than contradictory. Together they let us see the total landscape of life-span development in all its richness.

Psychoanalytic Theories

psychoanalytic theories Theories that hold that development depends primarily on the unconscious mind and is heavily couched in emotion, that behavior is merely a surface characteristic, that it is important to analyze the symbolic meanings of behavior, and that early experiences are important in development.

Psychoanalytic theories describe development primarily in terms of unconscious (beyond awareness) processes that are heavily colored by emotion. Psychoanalytic theorists emphasize that behavior is merely a surface characteristic and that a true understanding of development requires analyzing the symbolic meanings of behavior and the deep inner workings of the mind. Psychoanalytic theorists also stress that early experiences with parents extensively shape development. These characteristics are highlighted in the main psychoanalytic theory, that of Sigmund Freud (1856–1939).

Freud's Theory

Freud was a pioneer in the treatment of psychological problems. Certain that by talking about their problems, his patients could be restored to psychological health, Freud developed a technique called *psychoanalysis*. As he listened to, probed, and analyzed his patients, he became convinced that their problems were the result of experiences early in life. He thought that as children grow up, their focus of pleasure and sexual impulses shifts from the mouth to the anus and eventually to the genitals. Consequently, he determined, we pass through five stages of psychosexual development: oral, anal, phallic, latency, and genital (see Figure 1.5). Our adult personality, Freud (1917) claimed, is determined by the way we resolve conflicts between sources of pleasure at each stage and the demands of reality.

Freud's followers significantly revised his psychoanalytic theory. Many of today's psychoanalytic theorists believe that Freud overemphasized sexual instincts; they place more emphasis on cultural experiences as determinants of an individual's development. Unconscious thought remains a central theme, but thought plays a greater role than Freud envisioned. Next, we will outline the ideas of an important revisionist of Freud's ideas—Erik Erikson.

Erikson's Psychosocial Theory

Erik Erikson recognized Freud's contributions but believed that Freud misjudged some important dimensions of human development. For one thing, Erikson (1950, 1968) said we develop in *psychosocial* stages, rather than in *psychosexual* stages, as Freud maintained. According to Freud, the primary motivation for human behavior is sexual in nature; according to Erikson, motivation is social and reflects a desire to affiliate with other people. According to Freud, our basic personality is shaped in the first five years of life; according to Erikson, developmental change occurs throughout the life span. Thus, Freud viewed early experiences as far more important than later experiences, whereas Erikson emphasized the importance of both early and later experiences.

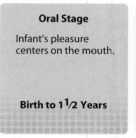

Oral Stage

Infant's pleasure centers on the mouth.

Birth to 1½ Years

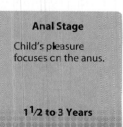

Anal Stage

Child's pleasure focuses on the anus.

1½ to 3 Years

Phallic Stage

Child's pleasure focuses on the genitals.

3 to 6 Years

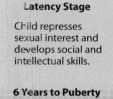

Latency Stage

Child represses sexual interest and develops social and intellectual skills.

6 Years to Puberty

Genital Stage

A time of sexual reawakening; source of sexual pleasure becomes someone outside the family.

Puberty Onward

Figure 1.5 Freudian Stages

Because Freud emphasized sexual motivation, his stages of development are known as *psychosexual stages*. In his view, if the need for pleasure at any stage is either undergratified or overgratified, an individual may become *fixated*, or locked in at that stage of development.

Erikson's theory A psychoanalytic theory in which eight stages of psychosocial development unfold throughout the human life span. Each stage consists of a unique developmental task that confronts individuals with a crisis that must be faced.

In **Erikson's theory,** eight stages of development unfold as we go through life (see Figure 1.6). At each stage, a unique developmental task confronts individuals with a crisis that must be resolved. According to Erikson, this crisis is not a catastrophe but a turning point marked by both increased vulnerability and enhanced potential. The more successfully an individual resolves the crises, the healthier development will be.

Trust versus mistrust is Erikson's first psychosocial stage, which is experienced in the first year of life. Trust in infancy sets the stage for a life-long expectation that the world will be a good and pleasant place to live.

Autonomy versus shame and doubt is Erikson's second stage. This stage occurs in late infancy and toddlerhood (1 to 3 years). After gaining trust in their caregivers, infants begin to discover that their behavior is their own. They start to assert their sense of independence or autonomy. They realize their *will.* If infants and toddlers are restrained too much or punished too harshly, they are likely to develop a sense of shame and doubt.

Initiative versus guilt, Erikson's third stage of development, occurs during the preschool years. As preschool children encounter a widening social world, they face new challenges that require active, purposeful, responsible behavior. Feelings of guilt may arise, though, if the child is irresponsible and is made to feel too anxious.

Industry versus inferiority is Erikson's fourth developmental stage, occurring approximately in the elementary school years. Children now need to direct their energy toward mastering knowledge and intellectual skills. The negative outcome is that the child may develop a sense of inferiority—feeling incompetent and unproductive.

During the adolescent years individuals face finding out who they are, what they are all about, and where they are going in life. This is Erikson's fifth developmental stage, *identity versus identity confusion.* If adolescents explore roles in a healthy manner and arrive at a positive path to follow in life, then they achieve a positive identity; if not, then identity confusion reigns.

Intimacy versus isolation is Erikson's sixth developmental stage, which individuals experience during the early adulthood years. At this time, individuals face the developmental task of forming intimate relationships. If young adults form healthy friendships and an intimate relationship with another, intimacy will be achieved; if not, isolation will result.

Generativity versus stagnation, Erikson's seventh developmental stage, occurs during middle adulthood. By *generativity,* Erikson means primarily a concern for helping the younger generation to develop and lead useful lives. The feeling of having done nothing to help the next generation is stagnation.

Integrity versus despair is Erikson's eighth and final stage of development, which individuals experience in late adulthood. During this stage, a person reflects on the past. If the person's life review reveals a life well spent, integrity will be achieved; if not, the retrospective glances likely will yield doubt or gloom—the despair Erikson described.

Erikson's Stages	Developmental Period
Integrity versus despair	Late adulthood (60s onward)
Generativity versus stagnation	Middle adulthood (40s, 50s)
Intimacy versus isolation	Early adulthood (20s, 30s)
Identity versus identity confusion	Adolescence (10 to 20 years)
Industry versus inferiority	Middle and late childhood (elementary school years, 6 years to puberty)
Initiative versus guilt	Early childhood (preschool years, 3 to 5 years)
Autonomy versus shame and doubt	Infancy (1 to 3 years)
Trust versus mistrust	Infancy (first year)

Figure 1.6 Erikson's Eight Life-Span Stages

Like Freud, Erikson proposed that individuals go through distinct, universal stages of development. In terms of the continuity-discontinuity issue, both favor the discontinuity side of the debate. Notice that the timing of Erikson's first four stages is similar to that of Freud's stages. *What are the implications of saying that people go through stages of development?*

Erik Erikson with his wife, Joan, an artist. Erikson generated one of the most important developmental theories of the twentieth century. *Which stage of Erikson's theory are you in? Does Erikson's description of this stage characterize you?*

Evaluating Psychoanalytic Theories

Contributions of psychoanalytic theories like Freud's and Erikson's to life-span development include an emphasis on a developmental framework, family relationships, and unconscious aspects of the mind. Criticisms include a lack of scientific support, too much emphasis on sexual underpinnings, and an image of people that is too negative.

Cognitive Theories

Whereas psychoanalytic theories stress the unconscious, cognitive theories emphasize conscious thoughts. Three important cognitive theories are Piaget's cognitive developmental theory, Vygotsky's sociocultural cognitive theory, and information-processing theory. All three focus on the development of complex thinking skills.

Piaget's Cognitive Developmental Theory

Piaget's theory states that children go through four stages of cognitive development as they actively construct their understanding of the world. Two processes underlie this cognitive construction of the world: organization and adaptation. To make sense of our world, we *organize* our experiences. For example, we separate important ideas from less important ideas, and we connect one idea to another. In addition to organizing our observations and experiences, we *adapt*, adjusting to new environmental demands.

Piaget (1954) also argued that we go through four stages in understanding the world (see Figure 1.7). Each stage is age-related and consists of a distinct way of thinking, a *different* way of understanding the world. Thus, according to Piaget, the

Sensorimotor Stage	**Preoperational Stage**	**Concrete Operational Stage**	**Formal Operational Stage**
The infant constructs an understanding of the world by coordinating sensory experiences with physical actions. An infant progresses from reflexive, instinctual action at birth to the beginning of symbolic thought toward the end of the stage.	The child begins to represent the world with words and images. These words and images reflect increased symbolic thinking and go beyond the connection of sensory information and physical action.	The child can now reason logically about concrete events and classify objects into different sets.	The adolescent reasons in more abstract, idealistic, and logical ways.
Birth to 2 Years of Age	**2 to 7 Years of Age**	**7 to 11 Years of Age**	**11 Years of Age Through Adulthood**

Figure 1.7 Piaget's Four Stages of Cognitive Development
According to Piaget, how a child thinks—not how much the child knows—determines the child's stage of cognitive development.

child's cognition is *qualitatively* different in one stage compared with another. What are Piaget's four stages of cognitive development?

The *sensorimotor stage,* which lasts from birth to about 2 years of age, is the first Piagetian stage. In this stage, infants construct an understanding of the world by coordinating sensory experiences (such as seeing and hearing) with physical, motor actions—hence the term *sensorimotor.*

The *preoperational stage,* which lasts from approximately 2 to 7 years of age, is Piaget's second stage. In this stage, children begin to go beyond simply connecting sensory information with physical action and represent the world with words, images, and drawings. However, according to Piaget, preschool children still lack the ability to perform what he calls *operations,* which are internalized mental actions that allow children to do mentally what they previously could only do physically. For example, if you imagine putting two sticks together to see whether they would be as long as another stick, without actually moving the sticks, you are performing a concrete operation.

The *concrete operational stage,* which lasts from approximately 7 to 11 years of age, is the third Piagetian stage. In this stage, children can perform operations that involve objects, and they can reason logically about specific or concrete examples. Concrete operational thinkers, however, cannot imagine the steps necessary to complete an algebraic equation, for they require a level of thinking that is too abstract for this stage of development.

The *formal operational stage,* which appears between the ages of 11 and 15 and continues through adulthood, is Piaget's fourth and final stage. In this stage, individuals move beyond concrete experiences and think in abstract and more logical terms. As part of thinking more abstractly, adolescents develop images of ideal circumstances. They might think about what an ideal parent is like and compare their parents to this ideal standard. They begin to entertain possibilities for the future and are fascinated with what they can be. In solving problems, they become more systematic, developing hypotheses about why something is happening the way it is and then testing these hypotheses. We will examine Piaget's cognitive developmental theory further in Chapters 3, 5, 7, and 9.

Jean Piaget, the famous Swiss developmental psychologist, changed the way we think about the development of children's minds. *What are some key ideas in Piaget's theory?*

Vygotsky's Sociocultural Cognitive Theory

Like Piaget, the Russian developmentalist Lev Vygotsky (1896–1934) reasoned that children actively construct their knowledge. However, Vygotsky (1962) gave social interaction and culture far more important roles in cognitive development than Piaget did. **Vygotsky's theory** is a sociocultural cognitive theory that emphasizes how culture and social interaction guide cognitive development.

Vygotsky portrayed the child's development as inseparable from social and cultural activities (Holzman, 2009). He stressed that cognitive development involves learning to use the inventions of society, such as language, mathematical systems, and memory strategies. Thus, in one culture children might learn to count with the help of a computer; in another they might learn by using beads. According to Vygotsky, children's social interaction with more-skilled adults and peers is indispensable to their cognitive development (Gauvain & Parke, 2010). Through this interaction, they learn to use the tools that will help them adapt and be successful in their culture. In Chapter 5 we examine ideas about learning and teaching that are based on Vygotsky's theory.

Lev Vygotsky was born the same year as Piaget, but he died much earlier, at the age of 37. There is considerable interest today in Vygotsky's sociocultural cognitive theory of child development. *What are some key characteristics of Vygotsky's theory?*

Information-Processing Theory

Information-processing theory emphasizes that individuals manipulate information, monitor it, and strategize about it. Unlike Piaget's theory but like Vygotsky's theory, information-processing theory does not describe development as stage-like.

Instead, according to this theory individuals develop a gradually increasing capacity for processing information, which allows them to acquire increasingly complex knowledge and skills (Martinez, 2010).

Robert Siegler (2006), a leading expert on children's information processing, states that thinking is information processing. In other words, when individuals perceive, encode, represent, store, and retrieve information, they are thinking. Siegler emphasizes that an important aspect of development is learning good strategies for processing information. For example, becoming a better reader might involve learning to monitor the key themes of the material being read.

Evaluating Cognitive Theories

Contributions of cognitive theories include a positive view of development and an emphasis on the active construction of understanding. Criticisms include skepticism about the pureness of Piaget's stages and too little attention to individual variations.

Behavioral and Social Cognitive Theories

Behavioral and social cognitive theories hold that development can be described in terms of behaviors learned through interactions with our surroundings. *Behaviorism* essentially holds that we can study scientifically only what can be directly observed and measured. Out of the behavioral tradition grew the belief that development is observable behavior that can be learned through experience with the environment. In terms of the continuity-discontinuity issue discussed earlier in this chapter, the behavioral and social cognitive theories emphasize continuity in development and argue that development does not occur in stage-like fashion. Let's explore two versions of behaviorism: Skinner's operant conditioning and Bandura's social cognitive theory.

Skinner's Operant Conditioning

According to B. F. Skinner (1904–1990), through *operant conditioning* the consequences of a behavior produce changes in the probability of the behavior's recurrence. A behavior followed by a rewarding stimulus is more likely to recur, whereas a behavior followed by a punishing stimulus is less likely to recur. For example, when an adult smiles at a child after the child has done something, the child is more likely to engage in that behavior again than if the adult gives the child a disapproving look.

In Skinner's (1938) view, such rewards and punishments shape development. For Skinner the key aspect of development is behavior, not thoughts and feelings. He emphasized that development consists of the pattern of behavioral changes that are brought about by rewards and punishments. For example, Skinner would say that shy people learned to be shy as a result of experiences they had while growing up. It follows that modifications in an environment can help a shy person become more socially oriented.

Albert Bandura has been one of the leading architects of social cognitive theory. *How does Bandura's theory differ from Skinner's?*

Bandura's Social Cognitive Theory

Some psychologists agree with the behaviorists' notion that development is learned and is influenced strongly by environmental interactions. However, unlike Skinner, they also see cognition as important in understanding development. **Social cognitive theory** holds that behavior, environment, and person/cognitive factors are the key factors in development.

ethology An approach that stresses that behavior is strongly influenced by biology, tied to evolution, and characterized by critical or sensitive periods.

American psychologist Albert Bandura (1925–) is the leading architect of social cognitive theory. Bandura (1986, 2004, 2009, 2010a,b) emphasizes that cognitive processes have important links with the environment and behavior. His early research program focused heavily on *observational learning* (also called *imitation* or *modeling*), which is learning that occurs through observing what others do. For example, a young boy might observe his father yelling in anger and treating other people with hostility; with his peers, the young boy later acts very aggressively, showing the same characteristics as his father's behavior. Social cognitive theorists stress that people acquire a wide range of behaviors, thoughts, and feelings through observing others' behavior and that these observations form an important part of life-span development.

What is *cognitive* about observational learning in Bandura's view? He proposes that people cognitively represent the behavior of others and then sometimes adopt this behavior themselves.

Bandura's (2004, 2009, 2010a,b) most recent model of learning and development includes three elements: behavior, the person/cognition, and the environment. An individual's confidence that he or she can control his or her success is an example of a person factor; strategies for achieving success are an example of a cognitive factor. As shown in Figure 1.8, behavior, person/cognitive, and environmental factors operate interactively.

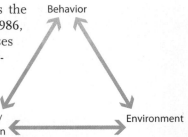

Figure 1.8 Bandura's Social Cognitive Model
The arrows illustrate how relations between behavior, person/cognition, and environment are reciprocal rather than one way. *Person/cognition* refers to cognitive processes (for example, thinking and planning) and personal characteristics (for example, believing that you can control your experiences).

Evaluating Behavioral and Social Cognitive Theories

Contributions of the behavioral and social cognitive theories include an emphasis on scientific research and environmental determinants of behavior. Criticisms include too little emphasis on cognition in Skinner's view and giving inadequate attention to developmental changes.

Ethological Theory

Ethology is the study of the behavior of animals in their natural habitat. Ethological theory stresses that behavior is strongly influenced by biology, is tied to evolution, and is characterized by critical or sensitive periods. These are specific time frames during which, according to ethologists, the presence or absence of certain experiences has a long-lasting influence on individuals.

European zoologist Konrad Lorenz (1903–1989) helped bring ethology to prominence. In his best-known research, Lorenz (1965) studied the behavior of greylag geese, which will follow their mothers as soon as they hatch. Lorenz separated the eggs laid by one goose into two groups. One group he returned to the goose to be hatched by her. The other group was hatched in an incubator. The goslings in the first group performed as predicted. They followed their mother as soon as they hatched. However, those in the second group, which saw Lorenz when they first hatched, followed him everywhere, as though he were their mother. Lorenz marked the goslings and then placed both groups under a box. Mother goose and "mother" Lorenz stood aside as the box lifted. Each group of goslings went directly to its "mother." Lorenz called this process *imprinting,* the rapid, innate learning that involves attachment to the first moving object seen.

John Bowlby (1969, 1989) illustrated an important application of ethological theory to human development. Bowlby stressed that attachment to a caregiver over the first year of life has important consequences throughout the life span. In his view, if this attachment is positive and secure, the individual will likely develop positively in childhood and adulthood. If the attachment is negative and insecure, development will likely not be optimal. In Chapter 4, we explore the concept of infant attachment in much greater detail.

Konrad Lorenz, a pioneering student of animal behavior, is followed through the water by three imprinted greylag geese. Describe Lorenz's experiment with the geese. *Do you think his experiment would have the same results with human babies? Explain.*

In Lorenz's view, imprinting needs to take place at a certain, very early time in the life of the animal, or else it will not take place. This point in time is called a *critical period*. A related concept is that of a *sensitive period*, and an example is the time during infancy when, according to Bowlby, attachment should occur in order to promote optimal development of social relationships.

Another theory that emphasizes biological foundations of development—evolutionary psychology—is presented in Chapter 2, along with views on the role of heredity in development. In addition, we examine a number of biological theories of aging in Chapter 15.

Evaluating Ethological Theory

Contributions of ethological theory include a focus on the biological and evolutionary basis of development, and the use of careful observations in naturalistic settings. Criticisms include too much emphasis on biological foundations and a belief that the critical and sensitive period concepts might be too rigid.

Ecological Theory

While ethological theory stresses biological factors, ecological theory emphasizes environmental factors. One ecological theory that has important implications for understanding life-span development was created by Urie Bronfenbrenner (1917–2005).

Bronfenbrenner's ecological theory (1986, 2004; Bronfenbrenner & Morris, 2006) holds that development reflects the influence of several environmental systems. The theory identifies five environmental systems: microsystem, mesosystem, exosystem, macrosystem, and chronosystem (see Figure 1.9).

The *microsystem* is the setting in which the individual lives. These contexts include the person's family, peers, school, and neighborhood. It is in the microsystem that the most direct interactions with social agents take place—with parents, peers, and teachers, for example. The individual is not a passive recipient of experiences in these settings, but someone who helps to construct the settings.

The *mesosystem* involves relations between microsystems or connections between contexts. Examples are the relation of family experiences to school experiences, school experiences to church

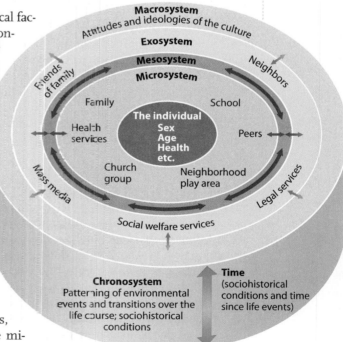

Figure 1.9 Bronfenbrenner's Ecological Theory of Development Bronfenbrenner's ecological theory consists of five environmental systems: microsystem, mesosystem, exosystem, macrosystem, and chronosystem.

eclectic theoretical orientation An
approach that selects and uses
whatever is considered the best in
many theories.

experiences, and family experiences to peer experiences. For example, children whose parents have rejected them may have difficulty developing positive relations with teachers.

The *exosystem* consists of links between a social setting in which the individual does not have an active role and the individual's immediate context. For example, a husband's or child's experience at home may be influenced by a mother's experiences at work. The mother might receive a promotion that requires more travel, which might increase conflict with the husband and change patterns of interaction with the child.

The *macrosystem* involves the culture in which individuals live. Remember from earlier in the chapter that culture refers to the behavior patterns, beliefs, and all other products of a group of people that are passed on from generation to generation. Remember also that cross-cultural studies—the comparison of one culture with one or more other cultures—provide information about the generality of development.

The *chronosystem* consists of the patterning of environmental events and transitions over the life course, as well as sociohistorical circumstances. For example, divorce is one transition. Researchers have found that the negative effects of divorce on children often peak in the first year after the divorce (Hetherington, 2006). By two years after the divorce, family interaction is more stable. As an example of sociohistorical circumstances, consider how the opportunities for women to pursue a career have increased since the 1960s.

Responding to growing interest in biological contributions to development, Bronfenbrenner (2004) added biological influences to his theory and relabeled it a *bioecological* theory. Nonetheless, it is still dominated by ecological, environmental contexts (Gauvain & Parke, 2010).

Urie Bronfenbrenner developed ecological theory, a perspective that is receiving increased attention today. His theory emphasizes the importance of both micro and macro dimensions of the environment in which the individual lives.

Evaluating Ecological Theory

Contributions of the theory include a systematic examination of macro and micro dimensions of environmental systems, and attention to connections between environmental systems. A further contribution of Bronfenbrenner's theory is an emphasis on a range of social contexts beyond the family, such as neighborhood, religious, school, and workplace, as influential in children's development (Gauvain & Parke, 2010). Criticisms include giving inadequate attention to biological factors, as well as too little emphasis on cognitive factors.

An Eclectic Theoretical Orientation

No single theory described in this chapter can explain entirely the rich complexity of life-span development, but each has contributed to our understanding of development. Psychoanalytic theory highlights the importance of the unconscious mind. Erikson's theory best describes the changes that occur in adult development. Piaget's, Vygotsky's, and the information-processing views provide the most complete description of cognitive development. The behavioral and social cognitive and ecological theories have been the most adept at examining the environmental determinants of development. The ethological theories have drawn attention to biology's role and the importance of sensitive periods in development.

In short, although theories are helpful guides, relying on a single theory to explain development is probably a mistake. This book instead takes an **eclectic theoretical orientation,** which does not follow any one theoretical approach but rather presents what are considered the best features of each theory. In this way, it represents the study of development as it actually exists—with different theorists making different assumptions, stressing different problems, and using

	Continuity/discontinuity, early versus later experiences	Biological and environmental factors
Psychoanalytic	Discontinuity between stages—continuity between early experiences and later development; early experiences very important; later changes in development emphasized in Erikson's theory	Freud's biological determination interacting with early family experiences; Erikson's more balanced biological-cultural interaction perspective
Cognitive	Discontinuity between stages in Piaget's theory; continuity between early experiences and later development in Piaget's and Vygotsky's theories; no stages in Vygotsky's theory or information-processing theory	Piaget's emphasis on interaction and adaptation; environment provides the setting for cognitive structures to develop; information-processing view has not addressed this issue extensively but mainly emphasizes biological-environmental interaction
Behavioral and social cognitive	Continuity (no stages); experience at all points of development important	Environment viewed as the cause of behavior in both views
Ethological	Discontinuity but no stages; critical or sensitive periods emphasized; early experiences very important	Strong biological view
Ecological	Little attention to continuity/discontinuity; change emphasized more than stability	Strong environmental view

Figure 1.10 Summary of Theories and Issues in Life-Span Development

different strategies to discover information. Figure 1.10 compares the main theoretical perspectives in terms of how they view important issues in life-span development.

Research in Life-Span Development

How do scholars and researchers with an eclectic orientation determine that one theory is somehow better than a different theory? The scientific method discussed earlier in this chapter provides a guide. Through scientific research, theories are tested and refined.

Generally, research in life-span development is designed to test hypotheses, which may be derived from the theories just described. Through research, theories are modified to reflect new data, and occasionally new theories arise. How are data about life-span development collected? What types of research designs are used to study life-span development? And what are some ethical considerations in conducting research on life-span development?

Methods for Collecting Data

Whether we are interested in studying attachment in infants, the cognitive skills of children, or social relationships in older adults, we can choose from several ways of collecting data. Here we outline the measures most often used, beginning with observation.

Observation

Scientific observation requires an important set of skills. For observations to be effective, they have to be systematic. We have to have some idea of what we are looking for. We have to know whom we are observing, when and where we will observe, how the observations will be made, and how they will be recorded.

Where should we make our observations? We have two choices: the laboratory and the everyday world.

When we observe scientifically, we often need to control certain factors that determine behavior but are not the focus of our inquiry (Langston, 2011). For

laboratory A controlled setting.

naturalistic observation Observation that occurs in a real-world setting without an attempt to manipulate the situation.

standardized test A test that is given with uniform procedures for administration and scoring.

this reason, some research in life-span development is conducted in a **laboratory**, a controlled setting where many of the complex factors of the "real world" are absent. For example, suppose you want to observe how children react when they see other people act aggressively. If you observe children in their homes or schools, you have no control over how much aggression the children observe, what kind of aggression they see, which people they see acting aggressively, or how other people treat the children. In contrast, if you observe the children in a laboratory, you can control these and other factors and therefore have more confidence about how to interpret your observations.

Laboratory research does have some drawbacks, however, including the following: (1) It is almost impossible to conduct research without the participants' knowing they are being studied. (2) The laboratory setting is unnatural and therefore can cause the participants to behave unnaturally. (3) People who are willing to come to a university laboratory may not fairly represent groups from diverse cultural backgrounds. (4) People who are unfamiliar with university settings, and with the idea of "helping science," may be intimidated by the laboratory setting.

Naturalistic observation provides insights that we sometimes cannot achieve in the laboratory. **Naturalistic observation** means observing behavior in real-world settings and making no effort to manipulate or control the situation. Life-span researchers conduct naturalistic observations at sporting events, child-care centers, work settings, malls, and other places people live in and frequent.

Naturalistic observation was used in one study that focused on conversations in a children's science museum (Crowley & others, 2001). When visiting exhibits at the museum with their children, parents were more than three times as likely to engage boys than girls in explanatory talk. The gender difference occurred regardless of whether the father, the mother, or both parents were with the child, although the gender difference was greatest for fathers' science explanations to sons and daughters. This finding suggests a gender bias that encourages boys more than girls to be interested in science.

Survey and Interview

Sometimes the best and quickest way to get information about people is to ask them for it. One technique is to *interview* them directly. A related method is the *survey* (sometimes referred to as a questionnaire) consisting of a standard set of questions designed to obtain peoples' self-reported attitudes or beliefs about a particular topic. Surveys are especially useful when information from many people is needed. In a good survey, the questions are clear and unbiased, allowing respondents to answer unambiguously.

Surveys and interviews can be used to study a wide range of topics from religious beliefs to sexual habits to attitudes about gun control to beliefs about how to improve schools. Surveys and interviews may be conducted in person, over the telephone, by mail, and over the Internet.

One problem with surveys and interviews is the tendency of participants to answer questions in a way that they think is socially acceptable or desirable rather than to say what they truly think or feel (McMillan & Wergin, 2010). For example, on a survey or in an interview some individuals might say that they do not take drugs even though they do.

Standardized Test

A **standardized test** has uniform procedures for administration and scoring. Many standardized tests allow performance comparisons; they provide information about individual differences among people (Drummond & Jones, 2010). One example is the Stanford-Binet intelligence test, which is described in Chapter 7. Your score on the Stanford-Binet test tells you how your performance compares with that of thousands of other people who have taken the test.

One criticism of standardized tests is that they assume a person's behavior is consistent and stable, yet personality and intelligence—two primary targets of standardized testing—can vary with the situation. For example, a person may perform poorly on a standardized intelligence test in an office setting but score much higher at home, where he or she is less anxious.

Case Study

A **case study** is an in-depth look at a single individual. Case studies are performed mainly by mental health professionals when, for either practical or ethical reasons, the unique aspects of an individual's life cannot be duplicated and tested in other individuals. A case study provides information about one person's experiences; it may focus on nearly any aspect of the subject's life that helps the researcher understand the person's mind, behavior, or other attributes. A researcher may gather information for a case study from interviews and medical records. In later chapters we discuss vivid case studies, such as that of Michael Rehbein, who had much of the left side of his brain removed at 7 years of age to end severe epileptic seizures.

A case study can provide a dramatic, in-depth portrayal of an individual's life, but we must be cautious when generalizing from this information. The subject of a case study is unique, with a genetic makeup and personal history that no one else shares. In addition, case studies involve judgments of unknown reliability. Researchers who conduct case studies rarely check to see if other professionals agree with their observations or findings (Stake, 2010).

Physiological Measures

Researchers are increasingly using physiological measures to study development at different points in the life span. For example, as puberty unfolds, the blood levels of certain hormones increase. To determine the nature of these hormonal changes, researchers analyze blood samples from adolescent volunteers (Susman & Dorn, 2009).

Another physiological measure that is increasingly being used is neuroimaging, especially *functional magnetic resonance imaging (fMRI)*, in which electromagnetic waves are used to construct images of a person's brain tissue and biochemical activity (Dennis & Cabeza, 2010). We have much more to say about neuroimaging and other physiological measures in later chapters.

Research Designs

In addition to a method for collecting data, you also need a research design to study life-span development. There are three main types of research design: descriptive, correlational, and experimental.

Descriptive Research

All of the data-collection methods that we have discussed can be used in **descriptive research**, which aims to observe and record behavior. For example, a researcher might observe the extent to which people are altruistic or aggressive toward each other. By itself, descriptive research cannot prove what causes some phenomenon, but it can reveal important information about people's behavior and provide a basis for more scientific studies (Babbie, 2011).

Correlational Research

In contrast to descriptive research, correlational research goes beyond describing phenomena; it provides information that helps to predict how people will behave. In **correlational research**, the goal is to describe the strength of the relation between two or more events or characteristics. The more strongly the two events are correlated (or related or associated), the more effectively we can predict one event from the other (Leedy & Ormrod, 2010).

For example, to study if children of permissive parents have less self-control than other children, you would need to carefully record observations of parents' permissiveness and their children's self-control. You might observe that the higher a parent was in permissiveness, the lower the child was in self-control. You would then analyze these data statistically to yield a **correlation coefficient**, a number based on a statistical analysis that is used to describe the degree of association between two variables. Correlation coefficients range from −1.00 to +1.00. A negative number means an inverse relation. In the above example, you might find an inverse correlation between permissive parenting and children's self-control with a coefficient of, say, −.30, meaning that parents who are permissive with their children are likely to have children who have low self-control. By contrast, you might find a positive correlation of +.30 between parental monitoring of children and children's self-control, meaning that parents who monitor their children effectively have children who have good self-control.

The higher the correlation coefficient (whether positive or negative), the stronger the association between the two variables. A correlation of 0 means that there is no association between the variables. A correlation of −.40 is stronger than a correlation of +.20 because we disregard whether the correlation is positive or negative in determining the strength of the correlation.

A word of caution is in order, however. Correlation does not equal causation (Howell, 2010; Levin & Fox, 2011). The correlational finding just mentioned does not mean that permissive parenting necessarily causes low self-control in children. It could mean that, but it also could mean that a child's lack of self-control caused the parents to throw up their arms in despair and give up trying to control the child. It also could mean that other factors, such as heredity or poverty, caused the correlation between permissive parenting and low self-control in children. Figure 1.11 illustrates these possible interpretations of correlational data.

Experimental Research

To study causality, researchers turn to *experimental research*. An **experiment** is a carefully regulated procedure in which one or more factors believed to influence the behavior being studied are manipulated while all other factors are held constant. If the behavior under study changes when a factor is manipulated, we say that the manipulated factor has caused the behavior to change. In other words, the experiment has demonstrated cause and effect. The cause is the factor that

Observed Correlation: As permissive parenting increases, children's self-control decreases.

Possible explanations for this observed correlation

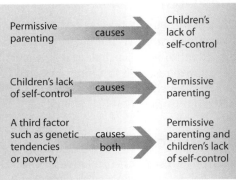

Figure 1.11 Possible Explanations for Correlational Data

was manipulated. The effect is the behavior that changed because of the manipulation. Nonexperimental research methods (descriptive and correlational research) cannot establish cause and effect because they do not involve manipulating factors in a controlled way (Jackson, 2011; Mitchell & Jolley, 2010).

Independent and Dependent Variables

Experiments include two types of changeable factors: independent and dependent variables. An *independent variable* is a manipulated, influential experimental factor. It is a potential cause. The label "independent" is used because this variable can be manipulated independently of other factors to determine its effect. An experiment may include one independent variable or several of them.

A *dependent variable* is a factor that can change in an experiment, in response to changes in the independent variable. As researchers manipulate the independent variable, they measure the dependent variable for any resulting effect.

For example, suppose that you wanted to study whether pregnant women could change the breathing and sleeping patterns of their newborn babies by meditating during pregnancy. You might require one group of pregnant women to engage in a certain amount and type of meditation each day, while another group would not meditate; the meditation is thus the independent variable. When the infants are born, you would observe and measure their breathing and sleeping patterns. These patterns are the dependent variable, the factor that changes as the result of your manipulation.

Experimental and Control Groups

Experiments can involve one or more experimental groups and one or more control groups. An experimental group is a group whose experience is manipulated. A control group is a comparison group that is as much like the experimental group as possible and that is treated in every way like the experimental group except for the manipulated factor (independent variable) The control group serves as a baseline against which the effects of the manipulated condition can be compared.

Random assignment is an important principle for deciding whether each participant will be placed in the experimental group or in the control group. Random assignment means that researchers assign participants to experimental and control groups by chance. It reduces the likelihood that the experiment's results will be due to any preexisting differences between groups (Graziano & Raulin, 2010; Stangor, 2011). In the example of the effects of meditation by pregnant women on the breathing and sleeping patterns of their newborns, you would randomly assign half of the pregnant women to engage in meditation over a period of weeks (the experimental group) and the other half to not meditate over the same number of weeks (the control group). Figure 1.12 illustrates the nature of experimental research.

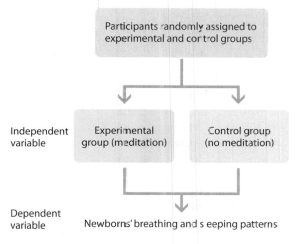

Figure 1.12 Principles of Experimental Research

Imagine that you decide to conduct an experimental study of the effects of meditation by pregnant women on their newborns' breathing and sleeping patterns. You would randomly assign pregnant women to experimental and control groups. Women in the experimental group would engage in meditation for a specified number of sessions and weeks. The control group would not. Then, when the infants are born, you would assess their breathing and sleeping patterns. If the breathing and sleeping patterns of newborns whose mothers were in the experimental group were more regular than those of the control group, you would conclude that meditation caused the positive effects.

Time Span of Research

Researchers in life-span development have a special concern with the relation between age and some other variable. To explore these relations, researchers can study different individuals of different ages and compare them, or they can study the same individuals as they age over time.

Cross-Sectional Approach

The **cross-sectional approach** is a research strategy that simultaneously compares individuals of different ages. A typical cross-sectional study might include three groups of children: 5-year-olds, 8-year-olds, and 11-year-olds. Another study might include a group of 15-year-olds, 25-year-olds, and 45-year-olds. The groups can be compared with respect to a variety of dependent variables: IQ, memory, peer relations, attachment to parents, hormonal changes, and so on. All of this can be accomplished in a short time. In some studies data are collected in a single day. Even in large-scale cross-sectional studies with hundreds of subjects, data collection does not usually take longer than several months to complete.

The main advantage of the cross-sectional study is that the researcher does not have to wait for the individuals to grow up or become older. Despite its efficiency, though, the cross-sectional approach has its drawbacks. It gives no information about how individuals change or about the stability of their characteristics. It can obscure the hills and valleys of growth and development. For example, a cross-sectional study of life satisfaction might reveal average increases and decreases, but it would not show how the life satisfaction of individual adults waxed and waned over the years. It also would not tell us whether the same adults who had positive or negative perceptions of life satisfaction in early adulthood maintained their relative degree of life satisfaction as they became middle-aged or older adults.

Longitudinal Approach

The **longitudinal approach** is a research strategy in which the same individuals are studied over a period of time, usually several years or more. For example, in a longitudinal study of life satisfaction, the same adults might be assessed periodically over a 70-year time span—at the ages of 20, 35, 45, 65, and 90, for example.

Longitudinal studies provide a wealth of information about vital issues such as stability and change in development and the importance of early experience for later development, but they do have drawbacks (Gibbons, Hedeker, & DuToit, 2010). They are expensive and time consuming. The longer the study lasts, the more participants drop out—they move, get sick, lose interest, and so forth. The participants who remain may be dissimilar to those who drop out, biasing the outcome of the study. Those individuals who remain in a longitudinal study over a number of years may be more responsible and conformity-oriented, for example, or they might have more stable lives.

Cohort Effects

A *cohort* is a group of people who are born at a similar point in history and share similar experiences as a result, such as living through the Vietnam war or growing up in the same city around the same time. These shared experiences may produce a range of differences among cohorts. For example, people who were teenagers during the Great Depression are likely to differ from people who were teenagers during the booming 1990s in their educational opportunities and economic status, in how they were raised, and in their attitudes toward sex and religion. In life-span development research, **cohort effects** are due to a person's time of birth, era, or generation but not to actual age.

(a)   (b)

Cohort effects are due to a person's time of birth or generation but not to age. Think for a moment about (a) the Great Depression and (b) today. How might your development be different depending on which of these time frames dominated your life? Your parents' lives? Your grandparents' lives?

Cohort effects are important because they can powerfully affect the dependent measures in a study ostensibly concerned with age. Researchers have shown it is especially important to be aware of cohort effects when assessing adult intelligence (Schaie, 2010, 2011). Individuals born at different points in time—such as 1920, 1940, and 1960—have had varying opportunities for education. Individuals born in earlier years had less access to education, and this fact may have a significant effect on how this cohort performs on intelligence tests.

Cross-sectional studies can show how different cohorts respond, but they can confuse age changes and cohort effects. Longitudinal studies are effective in studying age changes but only within one cohort.

Conducting Ethical Research

Researchers who study human development and behavior confront many ethical issues. For example, a developmentalist who wanted to study aggression in children would have to design the study in such a way that no child would be harmed physically or psychologically and would need to get permission from the university to carry out the study. Then the researcher would have to explain the study to the children's parents and obtain consent for the children to participate. Ethics in research may affect you personally if you ever serve as a participant in a study. In that event, you need to know your rights as a participant and the responsibilities of researchers to ensure that these rights are safeguarded.

Today, proposed research at colleges and universities must pass the scrutiny of a research ethics committee before the research can begin. In addition, the American Psychological Association (APA) has developed ethics guidelines for its members. This code of ethics instructs psychologists to protect their participants from mental and physical harm. The participants' best interests need to be kept foremost in the researcher's mind (Fisher, 2009).

APA's guidelines address four important issues:

1. *Informed consent*—all participants must know what their research participation will involve and what risks might develop. Even after informed consent is given, participants must retain the right to withdraw from the study at any time and for any reason.

2. *Confidentiality*—researchers are responsible for keeping all of the data they gather on individuals completely confidential and, when possible, completely anonymous.

3. *Debriefing*—after the study has been completed, participants should be informed of its purpose and the methods that were used. In most cases, the experimenter also can inform participants in a general manner beforehand about the purpose of the research without leading participants to behave in a way they think that the experimenter is expecting.

4. *Deception*—in some circumstances, telling the participants beforehand what the research study is about substantially alters the participants' behavior and invalidates the researcher's data. In all cases of deception, however, the psychologist must ensure that the deception will not harm the participants and that the participants will be *debriefed* (told the complete nature of the study) as soon as possible after the study is completed.

Summary

The Life-Span Perspective

- Development is the pattern of change that begins at conception and continues through the human life span. It includes both growth and decline.

- The life-span perspective includes these basic ideas: Development is lifelong, multidimensional, multidirectional, and plastic; its study is multidisciplinary; it is embedded in contexts; it involves growth, maintenance, and regulation; and it is a co-construction of biological, sociocultural, and individual factors.

- Health and well-being, parenting, education, sociocultural contexts and diversity, and social policy are all areas of contemporary concern for those who study life-span development.

The Nature of Development

- Three key developmental processes are biological, cognitive, and socioemotional. Development is influenced by an interplay of these processes.

- The life span is commonly divided into the prenatal period, infancy, early childhood, middle and late childhood, adolescence, early adulthood, middle adulthood, and late adulthood.

- We often think of age only in chronological terms, but a full evaluation of age requires the consideration of biological age and psychological age as well.

- Three important developmental issues are the nature-nurture issue, the continuity-discontinuity issue, and the stability-change issue.

Theories of Development

- According to psychoanalytic theories, including those of Freud and Erikson, development primarily depends on the unconscious mind and is heavily couched in emotion.

- Cognitive theories emphasize thinking, reasoning, language, and other cognitive processes. Three main cognitive theories are Piaget's, Vygotsky's, and information processing.

- Behavioral and social cognitive theories emphasize the environment's role in development. Two key behavioral and social cognitive theories are Skinner's operant conditioning and Bandura's social cognitive theory.

- Lorenz's ethological theory stresses the biological and evolutionary bases of development.

- According to Bronfenbrenner's ecological theory, development predominantly reflects the influence of five environmental systems—the microsystem, mesosystem, exosystem, and chronosystem.

- An eclectic orientation incorporates the best features of different theoretical approaches.

Research in Life-Span Development

- The main methods for collecting data about life-span development are observation, survey (questionnaire) or interview, standardized test, case study, and physiological measures.

- Three basic research designs are descriptive, correlational, and experimental.

- To examine the effects of time and age, researchers can conduct cross-sectional or longitudinal studies. Life-span researchers are especially concerned about cohort effects.

- Researchers have an ethical responsibility to safeguard the well-being of research participants.

Key Terms

2 Biological Beginnings

Stories of Life-Span Development: The Jim and Jim Twins

Jim Springer and Jim Lewis are identical twins. They were separated at 4 weeks of age and did not see each other again until they were 39 years old. Both worked as part-time deputy sheriffs, vacationed in Florida, drive Chevrolets, had dogs named Toy, and married and divorced women named Betty. One twin named his son James Allan, and the other named his son James Alan. Both liked math but not spelling, enjoyed carpentry and mechanical drawing, chewed their fingernails down to the nubs, had almost identical drinking and smoking habits, had hemorrhoids, put on 10 pounds at

about the same point in development, first suffered headaches at the age of 18, and had similar sleep patterns.

Jim and Jim do have some differences. One wears his hair over his forehead, the other slicks it back and has sideburns. One expresses himself best orally; the other is more proficient in writing. But, for the most part, their profiles are remarkably similar.

Another pair of identical twins, Daphne and Barbara, are called the "giggle sisters" because after being reunited they were always making each other laugh. A thorough search of their adoptive families'

histories revealed no gigglers. The giggle sisters ignored stress, avoided conflict and controversy whenever possible, and showed no interest in politics.

Jim and Jim and the giggle sisters were part of the Minnesota Study of Twins Reared Apart, directed by Thomas Bouchard and his colleagues. The study brings identical twins (who are identical genetically because they come from the same fertilized egg) and fraternal twins (who come from different fertilized eggs) from all over the world to Minneapolis to investigate their lives. There the twins complete personality and intelligence tests, and provide detailed medical histories, including information about diet and smoking, exercise habits, chest X-rays, heart stress tests, and EEGs. The twins are asked more than 15,000 questions about their family and childhood, personal interests, vocational orientation, values, and aesthetic judgments (Bouchard & others, 1990).

When genetically identical twins who were separated as infants show such striking similarities in their tastes and habits and choices, can we conclude that their genes must have caused these similarities? Although genes play a role, we also need to consider other possible causes. The twins shared not only the same genes but also some similar experiences. Some of the separated twins lived together for several months prior to their adoption; some had been reunited prior to testing (in some cases, many years earlier); adoption agencies often place twins in similar homes; and even strangers who spend several hours together and start comparing their lives are likely to come up with some coincidental similarities (Joseph, 2006).

The Minnesota study of identical twins points to both the importance of the genetic basis of human development and the need for further research on genetic and environmental factors.

The examples of Jim and Jim and the giggle sisters stimulate us to think about our genetic heritage and the biological foundations of our existence. Organisms are not like billiard balls, moved by simple, external forces to predictable positions on life's pool table. Environmental experiences and biological foundations work together to make us who we are. Our coverage of life's biological beginnings and experiences will emphasize the evolutionary perspective; genetic foundations; the interaction of heredity and environment; and charting growth from conception through the prenatal period, the birth process itself, and the postpartum period that follows birth. ∎

Jim Lewis (*left*)
Jim Springer (*right*).

The Evolutionary Perspective

From the perspective of evolutionary time, humans are relative newcomers to Earth. As our earliest ancestors left the forest to feed on the savannahs, and then to form hunting societies on the open plains, their minds and behaviors changed, and humans eventually became the dominant species on Earth. How did this evolution come about?

Natural Selection and Adaptive Behavior

Charles Darwin (1859) described *natural selection* as the evolutionary process by which those individuals of a species that are best *adapted* to their environment are the ones that are most likely to survive and reproduce. He reasoned that an intense, constant struggle for food, water, and resources must occur among the young of each generation, because many of them do not survive. Those that do survive and reproduce pass on their characteristics to the next generation. Darwin concluded that these survivors are better adapted to their world than are the nonsurvivors (Brooker, 2011; Johnson & Losos, 2010). The best-adapted individuals survive and leave the most offspring. Over the course of many generations, organisms with the characteristics needed for survival make up an increased percentage of the population (Mader, 2011).

Evolutionary Psychology

Although Darwin introduced the theory of evolution by natural selection in 1859, his ideas have only recently become a popular framework for explaining behavior.

How Would You...?
As a health-care professional, how would you explain technology and medicine working against natural selection?

Psychology's newest approach, **evolutionary psychology**, emphasizes the importance of adaptation, reproduction, and "survival of the fittest" in shaping behavior. ("Fit" in this sense refers to the ability to bear offspring that survive long enough to bear offspring of their own.) In this view, natural selection favors behaviors that increase reproductive success—that is, the ability to pass your genes to the next generation (Cosmides, 2011).

David Buss (2008, 2011) argues that just as evolution shapes our physical features, such as body shape and height, it also pervasively influences how we make decisions, how aggressive we are, our fears, and our mating patterns. For example, assume that our ancestors were hunters and gatherers on the plains and that men did most of the hunting and women stayed close to home, gathering seeds and plants for food. If you had to walk some distance from your home in an effort to track and slay a fleeing animal, you would need not only certain physical traits but also the ability to perform certain types of spatial thinking. Men born with these traits would be more likely than men without them to survive, to bring home lots of food, and to be considered attractive mates—and thus to reproduce and pass on these characteristics to their children. In other words, these traits would provide a reproductive advantage for males, and over many generations, men with good spatial thinking skills might become more numerous in the population. Critics point out that this scenario might or might not have actually happened.

Evolutionary Developmental Psychology

There is growing interest in using the concepts of evolutionary psychology to understand human development (Greve & Bjorklund, 2009). Following are some ideas proposed by evolutionary developmental psychologists (Bjorklund & Pellegrini, 2002).

One important concept is that an extended childhood period evolved because humans require time to develop a large brain and learn the complexity of human societies. Humans take longer to become reproductively mature than any other mammal (see Figure 2.1). During this extended childhood period, they develop a

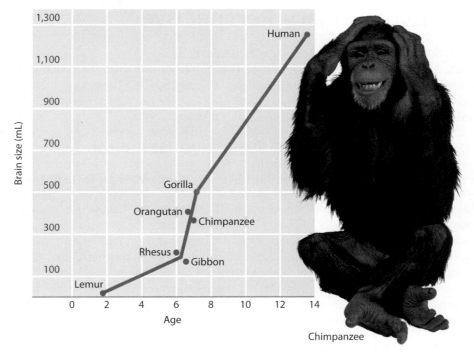

Figure 2.1 The Brain Sizes of Various Primates and Humans in Relation to the Length of the Juvenile Period

Compared with other primates, humans have both a larger brain and a longer juvenile period. *What conclusions can you draw from the relationship indicated by this graph?*

How Would You...?

As an educator, how would you apply the idea that psychological mechanisms are domain-specific to explain how a student with a learning disability in reading may perform exceptionally well in math?

large brain and the experiences needed to become competent adults in a complex society.

Another key idea is that many evolved psychological mechanisms are *domain-specific*. That is, the mechanisms apply only to a specific aspect of a person's makeup. According to evolutionary psychology, information processing is one example. In this view, the mind is not a general-purpose device that can be applied equally to a vast array of problems. Instead, as our ancestors dealt with certain recurring problems such as hunting and finding shelter, specialized modules evolved that process information related to those problems: for example, a module for physical knowledge for tracking animals, a module for mathematical knowledge for trading, and a module for language.

Evolved mechanisms are not always adaptive in contemporary society. Some behaviors that were adaptive for our prehistoric ancestors may not serve us well today. For example, the food-scarce environment of our ancestors likely led to humans' propensity to gorge when food is available and to crave high-caloric foods, a trait that might lead to an epidemic of obesity when food is plentiful.

Children in all cultures are interested in the tools that adults in their cultures use. For example, this 11-month-old boy from the Efe culture in the Democratic Republic of the Congo in Africa is trying to cut a papaya with an apopau (a smaller version of a machete). *Might the infant's behavior be evolutionary-based or be due to both biological and environmental conditions?*

Evaluating Evolutionary Psychology

Although the popular press gives a lot of attention to the ideas of evolutionary psychology, it remains just one theoretical approach. Like the theories described in Chapter 1, it has limitations, weaknesses, and critics. One criticism comes from Albert Bandura (1998), whose social cognitive theory was described in Chapter 1. Bandura acknowledges the important influence of evolution on human adaptation. However, he rejects what he calls "one-sided evolutionism," which sees social behavior as the product of evolved biological characteristics. An alternative is a *bidirectional view,* in which environmental and biological conditions influence each other. In this view, evolutionary pressures created changes in biological structures that allowed the use of tools, which enabled our ancestors to manipulate the environment, constructing new environmental conditions. In turn, environmental innovations produced new selection pressures that led to the evolution of specialized biological systems for consciousness, thought, and language.

In other words, evolution gave us bodily structures and biological potentialities; it does not dictate behavior. People have used their biological capacities to produce diverse cultures—aggressive and pacific, egalitarian and autocratic. As American scientist Stephen Jay Gould (1981) concluded, in most domains of human functioning, biology allows a broad range of cultural possibilities.

The "big picture" idea of natural selection leading to the development of human traits and behaviors is difficult to refute or test because it is on a time scale that does not lend itself to empirical study. Thus, studying specific genes in humans and other species—and their links to traits and behaviors—may be the best approach for testing ideas coming out of the evolutionary psychology perspective.

Genetic Foundations of Development

Genetic influences on behavior evolved over time and across many species. Our many traits and characteristics that are genetically influenced have a long evolutionary history that is retained in our DNA. In other words, our DNA is not just inherited from our parents; it's also what we've inherited as a species from the species that came before us. Let's take a closer look at DNA and its role in human development.

How are characteristics that suit a species for survival transmitted from one generation to the next? Darwin did not know because genes and the principles of genetics had not yet been discovered. Each of us carries a human "genetic code" that we inherited from our parents. Because a fertilized egg carries this human code, a fertilized human egg cannot grow into an egret, eagle, or elephant.

Each of us began life as a single cell weighing about one twenty-millionth of an ounce. This tiny piece of matter housed our entire genetic code—instructions that orchestrated growth from that single cell to a person made of trillions of cells, each containing a replica of the original code. That code is carried by our genes. What are genes and what do they do? For the answer, we need to look into our cells.

The nucleus of each human cell contains **chromosomes**, which are threadlike structures made up of deoxyribonucleic acid, or DNA. **DNA** is a complex molecule that has a double helix shape, like a spiral staircase, and contains genetic information. **Genes**, the units of hereditary information, are short segments of DNA, as you can see in Figure 2.2. They direct cells to reproduce themselves and to assemble proteins. Proteins, in turn, are the building blocks of cells as well as the regulators that direct the body's processes (Raven, 2011).

Each gene has its own designated place on a particular chromosome. Today, there is a great deal of enthusiasm about efforts to discover the specific locations of genes that are linked to certain functions (Starr, 2011). An important step in this direction was accomplished when the Human Genome Project and the Celera Corporation completed a preliminary map of the human *genome*—the complete set of developmental instructions for creating proteins that initiate the making of a human organism.

One of the big surprises of the Human Genome Project was a report indicating that humans have only about 30,000 genes (U.S. Department of Energy, 2001). More recently, the number of human genes has been revised further downward, to approximately 20,500 (Science Daily, 2008). Scientists had thought that humans had as many as 100,000 or more genes. They had also believed that each gene programmed just one protein. In fact, humans appear to have far more proteins than they have genes, so there cannot be a one-to-one correspondence between genes and proteins (Commoner, 2002). Each gene is not translated, in automaton-like fashion, into one and only one protein. A gene does not act independently, as developmental psychologist David Moore (2001) emphasized by titling his book *The Dependent Gene*. Rather than being a group of independent genes, the human genome consists of many genes that collaborate both with each other and with nongenetic factors inside and outside the body. The collaboration operates at many points. For example, the cellular "machinery" mixes, matches, and links small pieces of DNA to reproduce the genes, and that machinery is influenced by what is going on around it.

Whether a gene is turned "on"—that is, working to assemble proteins—is also a matter of collaboration. The activity of genes (*genetic expression*) is affected by their environment (Gottlieb, 2007). For example, hormones that circulate in the blood make their way into the cell, where they can turn genes "on" and "off." And the flow

Cell

Nucleus

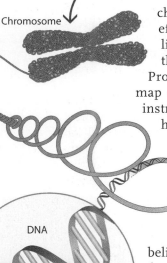

Chromosome

DNA

Figure 2.2 Cells, Chromosomes, DNA, and Genes

(*Top*) The body contains trillions of cells. Each cell contains a central structure, the nucleus. (*Middle*) Chromosomes are threadlike structures located in the nucleus of the cell. Chromosomes are composed of DNA. (*Bottom*) DNA has the structure of a spiraled double chain. A gene is a segment of DNA.

of hormones can be affected by environmental conditions such as light, day length, nutrition, and behavior. Numerous studies have shown that events outside of the cell and the person, as well as events inside the cell, can excite or inhibit gene expression (Gottlieb, 2007).

Genes and Chromosomes

Genes are not only collaborative; they are enduring How do they get passed from generation to generation and end up in all of the trillion cells in the body? Three processes explain the heart of the story: mitosis, meiosis, and fertilization.

Mitosis, Meiosis, and Fertilization

All cells in your body, except the sperm and egg, have 46 chromosomes arranged in 23 pairs. These cells reproduce by a process called **mitosis.**

During mitosis, the cell's nucleus—including the chromosomes—duplicates itself and the cell divides. Two new cells are formed, each containing the same DNA as the original cell, arranged in the same 23 pairs of chromosomes.

However, a different type of cell division—**meiosis**—forms eggs and sperm (or *gametes*). During meiosis, a cell of the testes (in men) or ovaries (in women) duplicates its chromosomes but then divides *twice*, thus forming four cells, each of which has only half of the genetic material of the parent cell. By the end of meiosis, each egg or sperm has 23 *unpaired* chromosomes.

During *fertilization*, an egg and a sperm fuse to create a single cell, called a zygote. In the zygote, the 23 unpaired chromosomes from the egg and the 23 unpaired chromosomes from the sperm combine to form one set of 23 paired chromosomes—one chromosome of each pair from the mother's egg and the other from the father's sperm. In this manner, each parent contributes half of the offspring's genetic material.

Figure 2.3 shows 23 paired chromosomes of a male and a female. The members of each pair of chromosomes are both similar and different: Each chromosome in the pair contains varying forms of the same genes, at the same location on the chromosome. A gene for hair color, for example, is located on both members of one pair of chromosomes, at the same location on each. However, one of those chromosomes might carry the gene for blond hair; the other might carry the gene for brown hair.

Do you notice any obvious differences between the chromosomes of the male and those of the female in Figure 2.3? The difference lies in the 23rd pair. Ordinarily, in females this pair consists of two chromosomes called *X chromosomes*; in males the 23rd pair consists of an X chromosome and a *Y chromosome*. The presence of a Y chromosome is what makes an individual a male.

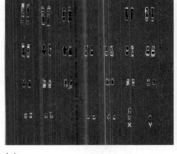

(a) (b)

Figure 2.3 The Genetic Difference Between Males and Females Set (*a*) shows the chromosome structure of a male, and set (*b*) shows the chromosome structure of a female. The last pair of 23 pairs of chromosomes is in the bottom right box of each set. Notice that the Y chromosome of the male is smaller than the X chromosome of the female.

Sources of Variability

Combining the genes of two parents in their offspring increases genetic variability in the population, which is valuable for a species because it provides more characteristics on which natural selection can operate (Raven, 2011). In fact, the human genetic process creates several important sources of variability.

First, the chromosomes in the zygote are not exact copies of those in the mother's ovaries and the father's testes. During the formation

mitosis Cellular reproduction in which the cell's nucleus duplicates itself with two new cells being formed, each containing the same DNA as the parent cell, arranged in the same 23 pairs of chromosomes.

meiosis A specialized form of cell division that occurs to form eggs and sperm (or gametes).

GENETIC FOUNDATIONS OF DEVELOPMENT

37

of the sperm and egg in meiosis, the members of each pair of chromosomes are separated, but which chromosome in the pair goes to the gamete is a matter of chance. In addition, before the pairs separate, pieces of the two chromosomes in each pair are exchanged, creating a new combination of genes on each chromosome (Klug & others, 2010). Thus, when chromosomes from the mother's egg and the father's sperm are brought together in the zygote, the result is a truly unique combination of genes.

Another source of variability comes from DNA (Lewis, 2010). Chance, a mistake by the cellular machinery, or damage caused by an environmental agent such as radiation may produce a *mutated gene*, a permanently altered segment of DNA.

Calvin and Hobbes — by Bill Watterson

CALVIN & HOBBES, Copyright © 1991 Watterson. Reprinted with permission of Universal Uclick. All Rights Reserved.

Even when their genes are identical, however, as for the identical twins described at the beginning of the chapter, people vary. The difference between *genotypes* and *phenotypes* helps us understand this source of variability. All of a person's genetic material makes up his or her **genotype**. There is increasing interest in studying *susceptibility genes* (Paquette & others, 2010), those that make an individual more vulnerable to specific diseases or acceleration of aging, and *longevity genes,* those that make an individual less vulnerable to certain diseases and be more likely to live to an older age (Bauer & others, 2010; Khabour & Barnawi, 2010); these are aspects of the individual's genotype. However, not all of the genetic material is apparent in an individual's observed and measurable characteristics. A **phenotype** consists of observable characteristics, including physical characteristics (such as height, weight, and hair color) and psychological characteristics (such as personality and intelligence).

For each genotype, a range of phenotypes can be expressed, providing another source of variability (Gottlieb, 2007). An individual can inherit the genetic potential to grow very large, for example, but good nutrition, among other things, will be essential to achieving that potential.

Genetic Principles

What determines how a genotype is expressed to create a particular phenotype? This question has not yet been fully answered. However, a number of genetic principles have been discovered, among them those of dominant and recessive genes, sex-linked genes, and polygenically determined characteristics.

Dominant and Recessive Genes

In some cases, one gene of a pair always exerts its effects; in other words, it is *dominant,* overriding the potential influence of the other gene, which is called the *recessive* gene. This is the *dominant-and-recessive genes principle.* A recessive gene exerts its influence only if the two genes of a pair are both recessive. If you inherit a recessive gene for a trait from each of your parents, you will show the trait. If you inherit a recessive gene from only one parent, you may never know that you carry the gene. Brown hair, farsightedness, and dimples override blond hair, nearsightedness, and freckles in the world of dominant and recessive genes. Can two brown-haired parents have a blond-haired child? Yes, they can. Suppose that each parent has a dominant gene for brown hair and a recessive gene for blond hair. Since dominant genes override recessive genes, the parents have brown hair, but both are *carriers* of blondness and pass on their recessive genes for blond hair. With no dominant gene to override them, the recessive genes can make the child's hair blond.

Sex-Linked Genes

Most mutated genes are recessive. When a mutated gene is carried on the X chromosome, the result is called *X-linked inheritance*. It may have very different implications for males than for females. Remember that males have only one X chromosome. Thus, if there is an altered, disease-creating gene on the X chromosome, males have no "backup" copy to counter the harmful gene and therefore may carry an X-linked disease. However, females have a second X chromosome, which is likely to be unchanged. As a result, they are not likely to have the X-linked disease. Thus, most individuals who have X-linked diseases are males. Females who have one changed copy of the X gene are known as carriers, and they usually do not show any signs of the X-linked disease. Fragile X syndrome, which we will discuss later in the chapter, is an example of X-linked inheritance.

Polygenic Inheritance

Genetic transmission is usually more complex than the simple examples we have examined thus far (Fry, 2009). Few characteristics reflect the influence of only a single gene or pair of genes. Most are determined by the interaction of many different genes; they are said to be *polygenically* determined. Even a simple characteristic, such as height, reflects the interaction of many genes, as well as the influence of the environment. Most diseases such as cancer and diabetes, develop as a consequence of complex gene interactions and environmental factors (Crosslin & others, 2009).

The term *gene-gene interaction* is increasingly used to describe studies that focus on the interdependence of two or more genes in influencing characteristics, behavior, diseases, and development (Li & others, 2008). For example, recent studies have documented gene-gene interaction in cancer (Bapat & others, 2010), cardiovascular disease (Jylhava & others, 2009), and arthritis (Chen & others, 2010).

Chromosome- and Gene-Linked Abnormalities

In some (relatively rare) cases, genetic inheritance involves an abnormality. Some of these abnormalities come from whole chromosomes that do not separate properly during meiosis. Others are produced by defective genes.

Chromosome Abnormalities

Sometimes, when a gamete is formed, the combined sperm and ovum do not have their normal set of 23 chromosomes. The most notable examples involve Down syndrome and abnormalities of the sex chromosomes. Figure 2.4 describes some chromosome abnormalities, including their treatment and incidence.

Down Syndrome Down syndrome is one of the most common genetically linked causes of mental retardation; it is also characterized by certain physical features. An individual with Down syndrome has a round face, a flattened skull, an extra fold of skin over the eyelids, a thickened tongue, short limbs, and retardation of motor and mental abilities. The syndrome is caused by the presence of an extra copy of chromosome 21. It is not known why the extra chromosome is present, but the health of the male sperm or female ovum may be involved.

Name	Description	Treatment	Incidence
Down syndrome	An extra chromosome causes mild to severe retardation and physical abnormalities.	Surgery, early intervention, infant stimulation, and special learning programs	1 in 1,900 births at age 20 1 in 300 births at age 35 1 in 30 births at age 45
Klinefelter syndrome (XXY)	An extra X chromosome causes physical abnormalities.	Hormone therapy can be effective	1 in 600 male births
Fragile X syndrome	An abnormality in the X chromosome can cause mental retardation, learning disabilities, or short attention span.	Special education, speech and language therapy	More common in males than in females
Turner syndrome (XO)	A missing X chromosome in females can cause mental retardation and sexual underdevelopment.	Hormone therapy in childhood and puberty	1 in 2,500 female births
XYY syndrome	An extra Y chromosome can cause above-average height.	No special treatment required	1 in 1,000 male births

Figure 2.4 Some Chromosome Abnormalities

Treatment of these abnormalities does not necessarily erase the problem but may improve the individual's adaptive behavior and quality of life.

These athletes, some of whom have Down syndrome, are participating in a Special Olympics competition. Notice the distinctive facial features of the individuals with Down syndrome, such as a round face and a flattened skull. *What causes Down syndrome?*

Down syndrome appears approximately once in every 700 live births. Women between the ages of 16 and 34 are less likely to give birth to a child with Down syndrome than are younger or older women. African American children are rarely born with Down syndrome.

Sex-Linked Chromosome Abnormalities

Recall that a newborn normally has either an X and a Y chromosome, or two X chromosomes. Human embryos must possess at least one X chromosome to be viable. The most common sex-linked chromosome abnormalities involve the presence of an extra chromosome (either an X or a Y) or the absence of one X chromosome in females.

Klinefelter syndrome is a genetic disorder in which males have an extra X chromosome, making them XXY instead of XY. Males with this disorder have undeveloped testes, and they usually have enlarged breasts and become tall. Klinefelter syndrome occurs approximately once in every 800 live male births.

Fragile X syndrome is a genetic disorder that results from an abnormality in the X chromosome, which becomes constricted and often breaks. A lower level of intelligence often is an outcome, and it may take the form of mental retardation, a learning disability, or a short attention span (Lewis, 2010). This disorder occurs more frequently in males than in females, possibly because the second X chromosome in females negates the effects of the other, abnormal X chromosome.

Turner syndrome is a chromosome disorder in females in which either an X chromosome is missing, making the person XO instead of XX, or part of one X chromosome is deleted. Females with Turner syndrome are short in stature and have a webbed neck. In some cases, they are infertile. They have difficulty in mathematics, but their verbal ability is often quite good. Turner syndrome occurs in approximately 1 of every 2,500 live female births.

How Would You...?
As a social worker, how would you respond to a 30-year-old pregnant woman who is concerned about the risk of giving birth to a baby with Down syndrome?

The *XYY syndrome* is a chromosomal disorder in which the male has an extra Y chromosome. Early interest in this syndrome focused on the belief that the extra Y chromosome found in some males contributed to aggression and violence. However, researchers subsequently found that XYY males are no more likely to commit crimes than are XY males (Witkin & others, 1976).

Gene-Linked Abnormalities

Abnormalities can be produced not only by an uneven number of chromosomes, but also by defective genes. Figure 2.5 describes some gene-linked abnormalities, including their treatment and incidence.

Phenylketonuria (PKU) is a genetic disorder in which the individual cannot properly metabolize phenylalanine, an amino acid that naturally occurs in many food sources. It results from a recessive gene and occurs about once in every 10,000 to 20,000 live births. Today, phenylketonuria is easily detected in newborns, and it is treated by a diet that prevents an excess accumulation of phenylalanine (van Spronsen & Enns, 2010). If phenylketonuria is left untreated, however, excess phenylalanine builds up in the child, producing mental retardation and hyperactivity. Phenylketonuria accounts for approximately 1 percent of institutionalized individuals who are mentally retarded, and it occurs primarily in Whites.

Sickle-cell anemia, which occurs most often in African Americans, is a genetic disorder that impairs the body's red blood cells. Red blood cells, which carry oxygen throughout the body, are usually shaped like a disk. In sickle-cell anemia, a recessive gene causes the red blood cell to become a hook-shaped "sickle" that cannot carry oxygen properly and dies quickly. As a result, the body's cells do not receive adequate oxygen, causing anemia and early death. About 1 in 400 African American babies is affected by sickle-cell anemia. One in 10 African Americans is a carrier, as is 1 in 20 Latin Americans.

A boy with fragile X syndrome.

How Would You...?
As a health-care professional, how would you explain the heredity-environment interaction to new parents who are upset when they discover that their child has a treatable genetic defect?

Name	Description	Treatment	Incidence
Cystic fibrosis	Glandular dysfunction that interferes with mucus production; breathing and digestion are hampered, resulting in a shortened life span.	Physical and oxygen therapy, synthetic enzymes and antibiotics; most individuals live to middle age.	1 in 2,000 births
Diabetes	Body does not produce enough insulin, which causes abnormal metabolism of sugar.	Early onset can be fatal unless treated with insulin.	1 in 2,500 births
Hemophilia	Delayed blood clotting causes internal and external bleeding.	Blood transfusions/injections can reduce or prevent damage due to internal bleeding.	1 in 10,000 males
Huntington disease	Central nervous system deteriorates, producing problems in muscle coordination and mental deterioration.	Does not usually appear until age 35 or older; death likely 10 to 20 years after symptoms appear.	1 in 20,000 births
Phenylketonuria (PKU)	Metabolic disorder that, left untreated, causes mental retardation.	Special diet can result in average intelligence and normal life span.	1 in 10,000 to 1 in 20,000 births
Sickle-cell anemia	Blood disorder that limits the body's oxygen supply; it can cause joint swelling, as well as heart and kidney failure.	Penicillin, medication for pain, antibiotics, and blood transfusions.	1 in 400 African American children (lower among other groups)
Spina bifida	Neural tube disorder that causes brain and spine abnormalities.	Corrective surgery at birth, orthopedic devices, and physical/medical therapy.	2 in 1,000 births
Tay-Sachs disease	Deceleration of mental and physical development caused by an accumulation of lipids in the nervous system.	Medication and special diet are used, but death is likely by 5 years of age.	1 in 30 American Jews is a carrier.

Figure 2.5 Some Gene-Linked Abnormalities
The treatments for these abnormalities do not necessarily erase the problem but may improve the individual's adaptive behavior and quality of life.

behavior genetics The field that seeks to discover the influence of heredity and environment on individual differences in human traits and development.

Other diseases that result from genetic abnormalities include cystic fibrosis, diabetes, hemophilia, Huntington disease, spina bifida, and Tay-Sachs disease. Someday, scientists may identify why these and other genetic abnormalities occur and discover how to cure them.

Genetic counselors, usually physicians or biologists who are well-versed in the field of medical genetics, understand the kinds of diseases just described, the odds of encountering them, and helpful strategies for offsetting some of their effects (Wider, Foroud, & Wszolek, 2010). To read about the career and work of a genetic counselor, see "Careers in Life-Span Development."

CAREERS IN LIFE-SPAN DEVELOPMENT

Holly Ishmael, Genetic Counselor

Holly Ishmael is a genetic counselor at Children's Mercy Hospital in Kansas City. She obtained an undergraduate degree in psychology and then a master's degree in genetic counseling from Sarah Lawrence College.

Genetic counselors work as members of a health-care team, providing information and support to families with birth defects or genetic disorders. They identify families at risk by analyzing inheritance patterns and explore options with the family. Some genetic counselors, like Holly, become specialists in prenatal and pediatric genetics; others might specialize in cancer genetics or psychiatric genetic disorders.

Holly says, "Genetic counseling is a perfect combination for people who want to do something science-oriented, but need human contact and don't want to spend all of their time in a lab or have their nose in a book" (Rizzo, 1999, p. 3).

Genetic counselors have specialized graduate degrees in the areas of medical genetics and counseling. They enter graduate

Holly Ishmael (*left*) in a genetic counseling session.

school with undergraduate backgrounds from a variety of disciplines, including biology, genetics, psychology, public health, and social work. There are approximately thirty graduate genetic counseling programs in the United States. If you are interested in this profession, you can obtain further information from the National Society of Genetic Counselors at www.nsgc.org.

The Interaction of Heredity and Environment: The Nature-Nurture Debate

Is it possible to untangle the influence of heredity from that of environment and discover the role of each in producing individual differences in development? When heredity and environment interact, how does heredity influence the environment, and vice versa?

Behavior Genetics

Behavior genetics is the field that seeks to discover the influence of heredity and environment on individual differences in human traits and development. Behavior geneticists often study either twins or adoption situations (Silberg, Maes, & Eaves, 2010).

In a **twin study**, the behavioral similarities between identical twins (who are genetically identical) is compared with the behavioral similarities between fraternal twins. Recall that although fraternal twins share the same womb, they are no more genetically alike than are brothers or sisters born years apart. By comparing groups of identical and fraternal twins, behavior geneticists capitalize on this basic knowledge that identical twins are more similar genetically than are fraternal twins: If they observe that a behavioral trait is more often shared by identical twins than by fraternal twins, they can infer that the trait has a genetic basis (Mustelin & others, 2009). For example, one study revealed a higher incidence of conduct problems shared by identical twins than by fraternal twins; the researchers discerned an important role for heredity in conduct problems (Scourfield & others, 2004).

However, several issues complicate the interpretation of twin studies. For example, perhaps the environments of identical twins are more similar than those of fraternal twins. Parents and caregivers might stress the similarities of identical twins more than those of fraternal twins, and identical twins might perceive themselves as a "set" and play together more than fraternal twins do. If so, the observed similarities between identical twins might have a significant environmental basis.

In an **adoption study**, investigators seek to discover whether the behavior and psychological characteristics of adopted children are more like those of their adoptive parents, who have provided a home environment, or more like those of their biological parents, who have contributed their heredity (Loehlin, Horn, & Ernst, 2007). Another form of the adoption study compares adoptees with their adoptive siblings and their biological siblings.

Heredity-Environment Correlations

The difficulties that researchers encounter in interpreting the results of twin and adoption studies reflect the complexities of heredity-environment interactions. Some of these interactions are *heredity-environment correlations*, which means that individuals' genes may influence the types of environments to which they are exposed. In a sense individuals "inherit" environments that may be related or linked to genetic "propensities" (Loehlin, 2010; Plomin & others, 2009). Behavior geneticist Sandra Scarr (1993) described three ways in which heredity and environment are correlated:

- *Passive genotype-environment correlations* occur because biological parents, who are genetically related to the child, provide a rearing environment for the child. For example, the parents might have a genetic predisposition to be intelligent and read skillfully. Because they read well and enjoy reading, they provide their children with books to read. The likely outcome is that their children, given their own inherited predispositions from their parents and their book-filled environment, will become skilled readers.

- *Evocative genotype-environment correlations* occur because a child's characteristics elicit certain types of environments. For example, active, smiling children receive more social stimulation than passive, quiet children do. Cooperative, attentive children evoke more pleasant and instructional responses from the adults around them than uncooperative, distractible children do.

- *Active (niche-picking) genotype-environment correlations* occur when children seek out environments that they find compatible and stimulating. *Niche-picking* refers to finding a setting that is suited to

twin study A study in which the behavioral similarity of identical twins is compared with the behavioral similarity of fraternal twins.

adoption study A study in which investigators seek to discover whether, in behavior and psychological characteristics, adopted children are more like their adoptive parents, who provided a home environment, or more like their biological parents, who contributed their heredity. Another form of the adoption study is to compare adoptive and biological siblings.

How might heredity-environment correlations be at work in a child learning to play the piano?

epigenetic view Emphasizes that development is the result of an ongoing, bidirectional interchange between heredity and environment.

gene x environment (g x e) interaction The interaction of a specified measured variation in DNA and a specific measured aspect of the environment.

one's abilities. Children select from their surrounding environment some aspect that they respond to, learn about, or ignore. Their active selections of environments are related to their particular genotype. For example, outgoing children tend to seek out social contexts in which to interact with people, whereas shy children don't. Children who are musically inclined are likely to select musical environments in which they can successfully perform their skills.

The Epigenetic View and Gene X Environment (G X E) Interaction

Notice that Scarr's view gives the preeminent role in development to heredity: her analysis describes how heredity may influence the types of environments that children experience. Critics argue that the concept of heredity-environment correlation gives heredity too great an influence in determining development because it does not consider the role of prior environmental influences in shaping the correlation itself (Gottlieb, 2007). In this section we look at some approaches that place greater emphasis on the role of the environment.

How Would You...?
As a human development and family studies professional, how would you apply the epigenetic view to explain why one identical twin can develop alcoholism, while the other twin does not?

The Epigenetic View

In line with the concept of a collaborative gene, Gilbert Gottlieb (2007) proposed an **epigenetic view**, which states that development is the result of an ongoing, bidirectional interchange between heredity and the environment. Figure 2.6 compares the heredity-environment correlation and epigenetic views of development.

Let's look at an example that reflects the epigenetic view. A baby inherits genes from both parents at conception. During prenatal development, toxins, nutrition, and stress can influence some genes to stop functioning while others become stronger or weaker. During infancy, additional environmental experiences, such as toxins, nutrition, stress, learning, and encouragement, continue to modify genetic activity and the activity of the nervous system that directly underlies behavior. Heredity and environment thus operate together—or collaborate—to produce a person's intelligence, temperament, health, ability to pitch a baseball, ability to read, and so on (Gottlieb, 2007; Wright & Christiani, 2010).

Gene X Environment (G X E) Interaction

An increasing number of studies are exploring how the interaction between heredity and environment influences development, including interactions that involve specific DNA sequences (Goldman & others, 2010; Keers & others, 2010). One study found that individuals who have a short version of a genotype labeled 5-HTTLPR (a gene involving the neurotransmitter serotonin) have an elevated risk of developing depression only if they *also* have stressful lives (Caspi & others, 2003). Thus, the specific gene did not link directly to the development of depression, but rather interacted with environmental exposure to stress to predict whether individuals would develop depression; however, some studies have not replicated this finding (Risch & others, 2009). In a recent study, adults who experienced parental loss as young children were more likely to have unresolved attachment as adults only when they had the short version of the 5-HTTLPR gene (Caspers & others, 2009). The long version of the serotonin transporter gene apparently provided some protection and ability to cope better with parental loss. The type of research just described is referred to as **gene x environment (g x e) interaction**—the interaction of a specific measured variation in DNA and a specific measured aspect of the environment (Diamond, 2009).

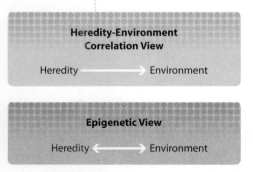

Figure 2.6 Comparison of the Heredity-Environment Correlation and Epigenetic Views

Conclusions About Heredity-Environment Interaction

If an attractive, popular, intelligent girl is elected president of her high school senior class, is her success due to heredity or to environment? Of course, the answer is "both."

The relative contributions of heredity and environment are not additive. That is, we can't say that such-and-such a percentage of nature and such-and-such a percentage of experience make us who we are. Nor is it accurate to say that full genetic expression happens once, at the time of conception or birth, after which we carry our genetic legacy into the world to see how far it takes us. Genes produce proteins throughout the life span, in many different environments. Or they don't produce these proteins, depending in part on how harsh or nourishing those environments are.

The emerging view is that complex behaviors have some *genetic loading* that gives each individual a propensity for a particular developmental trajectory (Goldsmith, 2011; Guo & Tillman, 2009). However, the individual's actual development requires more: a particular environment. And that environment is complex, just like the mixture of genes we inherit (Gauvain & Parke, 2010; Grusec, 2011). Environmental influences range from the things we lump together under "nurture" (such as parenting, family dynamics, schooling, and neighborhood quality) to biological encounters (such as viruses, birth complications, and even biological events in cells).

Imagine for a moment that there is a cluster of genes that are somehow associated with youth violence. (This example is hypothetical because we don't know of any such combination.) The adolescent who carries this genetic mixture might experience a world of loving parents, regular nutritious meals, lots of books, and a series of competent teachers. Or the adolescent's world might include parental neglect, a neighborhood in which gunshots and crime are everyday occurrences, and inadequate schooling. In which of these environments are the adolescent's genes likely to manufacture the biological underpinnings of criminality?

Fertilization of an ovum by a sperm marks the moment of conception.

If heredity and environment interact to determine the course of development, is that all there is to answering the question of what causes development? Are humans completely at the mercy of their genes and their environment as they develop through the life span? Genetic heritage and environmental experiences are pervasive influences on development. But in thinking about what causes development, recall from Chapter 1 our discussion of development as the co-construction of biology, culture, *and* the individual. Not only are we the outcomes of our heredity and the environment we experience, but we also can author a unique developmental path by changing our environment. As one psychologist recently concluded:

> In reality, we are both the creatures and creators of our worlds. We are . . . the products of our genes and environments. Nevertheless . . . the stream of causation that shapes the future runs through our present choices . . . Mind matters . . . Our hopes, goals, and expectations influence our future. (Myers, 2010, p. 168)

Prenatal Development

We turn now to a description of how the process of development unfolds from its earliest moment—the moment of *conception*—when two parental cells, with their unique genetic contributions, meet to create a new individual.

Conception occurs when a single sperm cell from a male unites with an ovum (egg) in a female's fallopian tube in a process called fertilization. Over the next few months the genetic code discussed earlier directs a series of changes in the fertilized egg, but many events and hazards will influence how that egg develops and becomes a person.

The Course of Prenatal Development

Prenatal development lasts approximately 266 days, beginning with fertilization and ending with birth. It can be divided into three periods: germinal, embryonic, and fetal.

The Germinal Period

The **germinal period** is the period of prenatal development that takes place in the first two weeks after conception. It includes the creation of the fertilized egg (the *zygote*), cell division, and the attachment of the multicellular organism to the uterine wall.

Rapid cell division by the zygote begins the germinal period. (Recall from earlier in the chapter that this cell division occurs through a process called *mitosis*.) Within one week after conception, the differentiation of these cells—their specialization for different tasks—has already begun. At this stage the organism, now called the *blastocyst*, consists of a hollow ball of cells that will eventually develop into the embryo, and the *trophoblast*, an outer layer of cells that later provides nutrition and support for the embryo. *Implantation*, the embedding of the blastocyst in the uterine wall, takes place in the second week after conception. Figure 2.7 summarizes these significant developments in the germinal period.

The Embryonic Period

The **embryonic period** is the period of prenatal development that occurs from two to eight weeks after conception. During the embryonic period, the rate of cell differentiation intensifies, support systems for cells form, and organs appear.

The mass of cells is now called an *embryo*, and three layers of cells form. The embryo's *endoderm* is the inner layer of cells, which will develop into the digestive and respiratory systems. The *ectoderm* is the outermost layer, which will become the nervous system, sensory receptors (ears, nose, and eyes, for example), and skin parts (hair and nails, for example). The *mesoderm* is the middle layer, which will become the circulatory system, bones, muscles, excretory

How Would You...?
As a social worker, how would you counsel a woman who continues to drink alcohol in the early weeks of pregnancy because she believes she can't harm the baby until it has developed further?

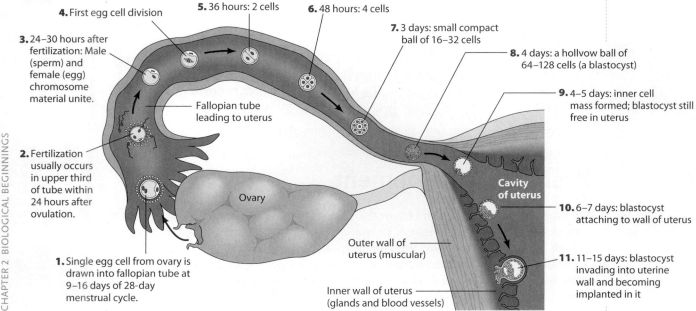

4. First egg cell division

5. 36 hours: 2 cells

6. 48 hours: 4 cells

7. 3 days: small compact ball of 16–32 cells

3. 24–30 hours after fertilization: Male (sperm) and female (egg) chromosome material unite.

8. 4 days: a hollvow ball of 64–128 cells (a blastocyst)

9. 4–5 days: inner cell mass formed; blastocyst still free in uterus

Fallopian tube leading to uterus

2. Fertilization usually occurs in upper third of tube within 24 hours after ovulation.

Ovary

Cavity of uterus

10. 6–7 days: blastocyst attaching to wall of uterus

1. Single egg cell from ovary is drawn into fallopian tube at 9–16 days of 28-day menstrual cycle.

Outer wall of uterus (muscular)

Inner wall of uterus (glands and blood vessels)

11. 11–15 days: blastocyst invading into uterine wall and becoming implanted in it

Figure 2.7 Major Developments in the Germinal Period

How Would You...?
As a human development and family studies professional, how would you characterize the greatest risks at each period of prenatal development?

system, and reproductive system. Every body part eventually develops from these three layers. The endoderm primarily produces internal body parts, the mesoderm primarily produces parts that surround the internal areas, and the ectoderm primarily produces surface parts. **Organogenesis** is the name given to the process of organ formation during the first two months of prenatal development. While they are being formed, the organs are especially vulnerable to environmental influences.

As the embryo's three layers form, life-support systems for the embryo develop rapidly. These systems include the amnion, the umbilical cord (both of which develop from the fertilized egg, not the mother's body), and the placenta. The amnion is like a bag or an envelope; it contains a clear fluid in which the developing embryo floats. The amniotic fluid provides an environment that is temperature- and humidity-controlled, as well as shockproof. The *umbilical cord*, which contains two arteries and one vein, connects the baby to the placenta. The *placenta* consists of a disk-shaped group of tissues in which small blood vessels from the mother and the offspring intertwine but do not join.

Very small molecules—oxygen, water, salt, and nutrients from the mother's blood, as well as carbon dioxide and digestive wastes from the baby's blood—pass back and forth between the mother and the embryo or fetus. Large molecules cannot pass through the placental wall; these include red blood cells and harmful substances, such as most bacteria, maternal wastes, and hormones. The mechanisms that govern the transfer of substances across the placental barrier are complex and still not entirely understood (Barta & Drugan, 2010; Wick & others, 2010).

The Fetal Period

The **fetal period**, which lasts about seven months, is the prenatal period that extends from two months after conception until birth in typical pregnancies. Growth and development continue their dramatic course during this time.

Three months after conception, the fetus is about 3 inches long and weighs about 1 ounce. It has become active, moving its arms and legs, opening and closing its mouth, and moving its head. The face, forehead, eyelids, nose, and chin are distinguishable, as are the upper arms, lower arms, hands, and lower limbs. In most cases, the genitals can be identified as male or female. By the end of the fourth month of pregnancy, the fetus has grown to 6 inches in length and weighs 4 to 7 ounces. At this time, a growth spurt occurs in the body's lower parts. For the first time, the mother can feel arm and leg movements.

By the end of the fifth month, the fetus is about 12 inches long and weighs close to a pound. Structures of the skin have formed—including toenails and fingernails. The fetus is more active, showing a preference for a particular position in the womb. By the end of the sixth month, the fetus is about 14 inches long and has gained another 6 to 12 ounces. The eyes and eyelids are completely formed, and a fine layer of hair covers the head. A grasping reflex is present and irregular breathing movements occur.

As early as six months of pregnancy (about 24 to 25 weeks after conception), the fetus for the first time has a chance of surviving outside the womb—that is, it is *viable*. Infants that are born early, or between 24 and 37 weeks of pregnancy, usually need help breathing because their lungs are not yet fully mature. By the end of the seventh month, the fetus is about 16 inches long and now weighs about 3 pounds.

During the last two months of prenatal development, fatty tissues develop and the functioning of various organ systems—heart and kidneys, for example—steps up. During the eighth and ninth months, the fetus grows longer and gains substantial weight—about 4 more pounds. At birth, the average American baby weighs 7½ pounds and is about 20 inches long. In addition to describing prenatal development in terms of germinal, embryonic, and fetal periods, prenatal development also can be divided into equal three-month periods, called *trimesters*.

organogenesis Organ formation that takes place during the first two months of prenatal development.

fetal period The prenatal period of development that begins two months after conception and lasts for seven months, on the average.

Figure 2.8 gives an overview of the main events during each trimester. Remember that the three trimesters are not the same as the three prenatal periods we have discussed. The germinal and embryonic periods occur in the first trimester. The fetal period begins toward the end of the first trimester and continues through the second and third trimesters.

The Brain

One of the most remarkable aspects of the prenatal period is the development of the brain (Nelson, 2011). By the time babies are born, they have approximately 100 billion **neurons**, or nerve cells, which handle information processing at the cellular level in the brain. During prenatal development, neurons move to specific locations and start to become connected. The basic architecture of the human brain is assembled during the first two trimesters of prenatal development. In typical development, the third trimester of prenatal development and the first two

First trimester (first 3 months)

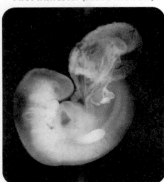

Conception to 4 weeks
- Is less than $1/10$ inch long
- Beginning development of spinal cord, nervous system, gastrointestinal system, heart, and lungs
- Amniotic sac envelops the preliminary tissues of entire body
- Is called a "zygote," then a "blastocyst"

8 weeks
- Is just over 1 inch long
- Face is forming with rudimentary eyes, ears, mouth, and tooth buds
- Arms and legs are moving
- Brain is forming
- Fetal heartbeat is detectable with ultrasound
- Is called an "embryo"

12 weeks
- Is about 3 inches long and weighs about 1 ounce
- Can move arms, legs, fingers, and toes
- Fingerprints are present
- Can smile, frown, suck, and swallow
- Sex is distinguishable
- Can urinate
- Is called a "fetus"

Second trimester (middle 3 months)

16 weeks
- Is about 6 inches long and weighs about 4 to 7 ounces
- Heartbeat is strong
- Skin is thin, transparent
- Downy hair (lanugo) covers body
- Fingernails and toenails are forming
- Has coordinated movements; is able to roll over in amniotic fluid

20 weeks
- Is about 12 inches long and weighs close to 1 pound
- Heartbeat is audible with ordinary stethoscope
- Sucks thumb
- Hiccups
- Hair, eyelashes, eyebrows are present

24 weeks
- Is about 14 inches long and weighs about 1 to $1^1/2$ pounds
- Skin is wrinkled and covered with protective coating (vernix caseosa)
- Eyes are open
- Waste matter is collected in bowel
- Has strong grip

Third trimester (last 3 months)

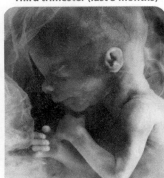

28 weeks
- Is about 16 inches long and weighs about 3 pounds
- Is adding body fat
- Is very active
- Rudimentary breathing movements are present

32 weeks
- Is $16^1/2$ to 18 inches long and weighs 4 to 5 pounds
- Has periods of sleep and wakefulness
- Responds to sounds
- May assume the birth position
- Bones of head are soft and flexible
- Iron is being stored in liver

36 to 38 weeks
- Is 19 to 20 inches long and weighs 6 to $7^1/2$ pounds
- Skin is less wrinkled
- Vernix caseosa is thick
- Lanugo is mostly gone
- Is less active
- Is gaining immunities from mother

Figure 2.8 Growth and Development in the Three Trimesters of Prenatal Development

years of postnatal life are characterized by connectivity and functioning of neurons (Nelson, 2011).

As the human embryo develops inside its mother's womb, the nervous system begins forming as a long, hollow tube located on the embryo's back. This pear-shaped *neural tube*, which forms at about 18 to 24 days after conception, develops out of the ectoderm. The tube closes at the top and bottom ends at about 24 days after conception. Figure 2.9 shows that the nervous system still has a tubular appearance 6 weeks after conception.

Two birth defects related to a failure of the neural tube to close are anencephaly and spina bifida. When fetuses have anencephaly (that is, when the head end of the neural tube fails to close), the highest regions of the brain fail to develop and they die in the womb, during childbirth, or shortly after birth (Levene & Chervenak, 2009). Spina bifida, an incomplete development of the spinal cord, results in varying degrees of paralysis of the lower limbs. Individuals with spina bifida usually need assistive devices such as crutches, braces, or wheelchairs. A strategy that can help to prevent neural tube defects is for women to take adequate amounts of the B vitamin folic acid, a topic we will discuss later in the chapter (Rasmussen & Clemmensen, 2010). Both maternal diabetes and obesity also place the fetus at risk for developing neural tube defects (Yazdy & others, 2010).

In a normal pregnancy, once the neural tube has closed, a massive proliferation of new immature neurons begins to take place about the 5th prenatal week and continues throughout the remainder of the prenatal period. The generation of new neurons is called *neurogenesis*. At the peak of neurogenesis, it is estimated that as many as 200,000 neurons are being generated every minute.

At approximately 6 to 24 weeks after conception, *neuronal migration* occurs (Nelson, 2011). Cells begin moving outward from their point of origin to their appropriate locations and creating the different levels, structures, and regions of the brain (Cozzi & others, 2010). Once a cell has migrated to its target destination, it must mature and develop a more complex structure.

At about the 23rd prenatal week, connections between neurons begin to form, a process that continues postnatally (Nelson, 2011). We will have much more to say about the structure of neurons, their connectivity, and the development of the infant brain in Chapter 3.

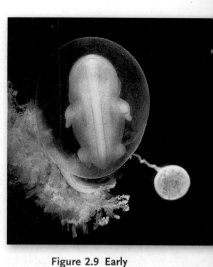

Figure 2.9 Early Formation of the Nervous System The photograph shows the primitive, tubular appearance of the nervous system at six weeks in the human embryo.

Prenatal Tests

Together with her doctor, a pregnant woman will decide the extent to which she should undergo prenatal testing. A number of tests can indicate whether a fetus is developing normally; these include ultrasound sonography, fetal MRI, chorionic villus sampling, amniocentesis, and maternal blood screening. The decision to have a given test depends on several criteria, such as the mother's age, medical history, and genetic risk factors.

An ultrasound test is generally performed 7 weeks into a pregnancy and at various times later in pregnancy. *Ultrasound sonography* is a noninvasive prenatal medical procedure in which high-frequency sound waves are directed into the pregnant woman's abdomen (Cignini & others, 2010). The echo from the sounds is transformed into a visual representation of the fetus's inner structures. This technique can detect many structural abnormalities in the fetus, including microencephaly, a form of mental retardation involving an abnormally small brain; it can also give clues to the baby's sex and indicate whether there is more than one fetus. Ultrasound results are available as soon as the images are read by a radiologist.

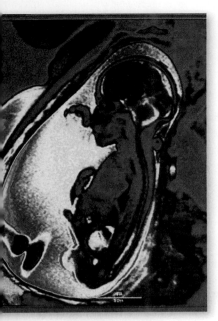

Figure 2.10 A Fetal MRI

Increasingly, MRI is being used to diagnose fetal malformations.

The development of brain-imaging techniques has led to increasing use of *fetal MRI* to diagnose fetal malformations (Weston, 2010) (see Figure 2.10). MRI stands for magnetic resonance imaging and uses a powerful magnet and radio images to generate detailed images of the body's organs and structures. Currently, ultrasound is still the first choice in fetal screening, but fetal MRI can provide more detailed images than ultrasound. In many instances, ultrasound will indicate a possible abnormality and fetal MRI will then be used to obtain a clearer, more detailed image (Obenauer & Maestre, 2008). Among the fetal malformations that fetal MRI may be able to detect better than ultrasound sonography are certain central nervous system, chest, gastrointestinal, genital/urinary, and placental abnormalities (Baysinger, 2010; Daltro & others, 2010; Panigrahy, Borzaga, & Blumi, 2010).

At some point between the 10th and 12th weeks of pregnancy, chorionic villus sampling may be used to screen for genetic defects and chromosome abnormalities. *Chorionic villus sampling* (*CVS*) is a prenatal medical procedure in which a tiny tissue sample from the placenta is removed and analyzed. The results are available in about 10 days.

Between the 15th and 18th weeks of pregnancy, *amniocentesis* may be performed. In this procedure, a sample of amniotic fluid is withdrawn by syringe and tested for chromosome or metabolic disorders. The later in the pregnancy amniocentesis is performed, the better its diagnostic potential. However, the earlier it is performed, the more useful it is in deciding how to handle a pregnancy when the fetus is found to have a disorder. It may take two weeks for enough cells to grow so that amniocentesis test results can be obtained.

Amniocentesis brings a small risk of miscarriage: about 1 woman in every 200 to 300 miscarries after amniocentesis. Although earlier reports indicated that chorionic villus sampling brings a slightly higher risk of pregnancy loss than amniocentesis, a U.S. study of more than 40,000 pregnancies found that loss rates for CVS decreased from 1998 to 2003 and that there is no longer a difference in pregnancy loss risk between CVS and amniocentesis (Caughey, Hopkins, & Norton, 2006).

During the 16th to 18th weeks of pregnancy, maternal blood screening may be performed. *Maternal blood screening* identifies pregnancies that have an elevated risk for birth defects such as spina bifida and Down syndrome. The current blood test is called the *triple screen* because it measures three substances in the mother's blood. After an abnormal triple screen result, the next step is usually an ultrasound examination. If an ultrasound does not explain the abnormal triple screen results, amniocentesis typically is used.

Infertility and Reproductive Technology

How Would You...?
As a psychologist, how would you advise a 25-year-old mother who is concerned about the possibility of birth defects but has no genetic history of these types of problems?

Recent advances in biological knowledge have also opened up many choices for infertile people. Approximately 10 to 15 percent of couples in the United States experience infertility, which is defined as the inability to conceive a child after 12 months of regular intercourse without contraception. The cause of infertility can rest with either the woman or the man, or both. The woman may not be ovulating (releasing eggs to be fertilized); she may be producing abnormal ova; her fallopian tubes (by which ova normally reach the womb) may be blocked; or she may have a condition that prevents implantation of the embryo into the uterus. The man may produce too few sperm; the sperm may lack motility (the ability to move adequately); or he may have a blocked passageway (Kini & others, 2010; Walsh, Pera, & Turek, 2009).

Surgery can correct some causes of infertility; for others, hormone-based drugs may be effective. Of the 2 million U.S. couples who seek help for infertility

every year, about 40,000 try assisted reproduction technologies. *In vitro fertilization (IVF)*, the technique that produced the world's first "test tube baby" in 1978, involves eggs and sperm being combined in a laboratory dish. If any eggs are successfully fertilized, one or more of the resulting fertilized eggs is transferred into the woman's uterus.

teratogen Any agent that can potentially cause a birth defect or negatively alter cognitive and behavioral outcomes.

The creation of families by means of assisted reproduction techniques raises important questions about the physical and psychological consequences for children. For example, one result of fertility treatments is an increase in multiple births (Steel & Sutcliffe, 2010). Twenty-five to 30 percent of pregnancies achieved by fertility treatments—including in vitro fertilization—result in multiple births. Any multiple birth increases the likelihood that the babies will have life-threatening and costly problems, such as extremely low birth weight (McDonald & others, 2010).

Hazards to Prenatal Development

For most babies, the course of prenatal development goes smoothly. Their mother's womb protects them as they develop. Despite this protection, however, the environment can affect the embryo or fetus in many well-documented ways.

General Principles

A **teratogen** is any agent that can potentially cause a birth defect or negatively alter cognitive and behavioral outcomes. The field of study that investigates the causes of birth defects is called *teratology*. Teratogens include drugs, incompatible blood types, environmental pollutants, infectious diseases, nutritional deficiencies, maternal stress, advanced maternal and paternal age, and environmental pollutants.

The dose, genetic susceptibility, and time of exposure to a particular teratogen influence both the severity of the damage to an embryo or fetus and the type of defect: (1) *Dose*—the dose effect is rather obvious—the greater the dose of an agent, such as a drug, the greater the effect. (2) *Genetic susceptibility*—the type or severity of abnormalities caused by a teratogen is linked to the genotype of the pregnant woman and the genotype of the embryo or fetus. (3) *Time of exposure*—For example, teratogens do more damage when they occur at some points in development than at others. The probability of a structural defect is greatest early in the embryonic period, when organs are being formed. After organogenesis is complete, teratogens are less likely to cause anatomical defects. Instead, exposure during the fetal period is more likely to stunt growth or create problems in the way organs function. To examine some key teratogens and their effects, let's begin with drugs.

Prescription and Nonprescription Drugs

Prescription drugs that can function as teratogens include antibiotics, such as streptomycin and tetracycline; some antidepressants; certain hormones, such as progestin and synthetic estrogen; and Accutane (often prescribed for acne) (Bayraktar & others, 2010; Teichert & others, 2010). Nonprescription drugs that can be harmful include diet pills and aspirin. Recent research revealed that low doses of aspirin pose no harm to the fetus but that high doses can contribute to maternal and fetal bleeding (James, Brancazio, & Price, 2008).

Psychoactive Drugs

Psychoactive drugs are drugs that act on the nervous system to alter states of consciousness, modify perceptions, and change moods. Examples include caffeine, alcohol, and nicotine, as well as illegal drugs such as cocaine, methamphetamine, marijuana, and heroin.

Caffeine People often consume caffeine by drinking coffee, tea, or colas, or by eating chocolate. A recent study revealed that pregnant women who consumed 200 or more milligrams of caffeine a day had an increased risk of miscarriage (Weng, Odouli, & Li, 2008). Taking into account such results, the Food and Drug Administration recommends that pregnant women either not consume caffeine or consume it only sparingly.

Alcohol Heavy drinking by pregnant women can be devastating to offspring. **Fetal alcohol spectrum disorders (FASD)** are a cluster of abnormalities and problems that appear in the offspring of mothers who drink alcohol heavily during pregnancy. The abnormalities include facial deformities and defective limbs, face, and heart (Klingenberg & others, 2010). Most children with FASD have learning problems, and many are below average in intelligence; some are mentally retarded (Dalen & others, 2009). Although mothers of FASD infants are heavy drinkers, many mothers who are heavy drinkers may not have children with FASD or may have one child with FASD and other children who do not have it.

What are some guidelines for alcohol use during pregnancy? Even drinking just one or two servings of beer or wine or one serving of hard liquor a few days a week can have negative effects on the fetus, although it is generally agreed that this level of alcohol use will not cause fetal alcohol spectrum disorders. The U.S. Surgeon General recommends that *no* alcohol be consumed during pregnancy. And research suggests that it may not be wise to consume alcohol at the time of conception. One study revealed that intakes of alcohol by both men and women during the weeks of conception increased the risk of early pregnancy loss (Henriksen & others, 2004).

Fetal alcohol spectrum disorders (FASD) are characterized by a number of physical abnormalities and learning problems. Notice the wide-set eyes, flat cheekbones, and thin upper lip in this child with FASD.

Nicotine Cigarette smoking by pregnant women can also adversely influence prenatal development, birth, and postnatal development (Blood-Siegfried & Rende, 2010). Preterm births and low birth weights, fetal and neonatal deaths, respiratory problems, sudden infant death syndrome (SIDS, also known as crib death), and cardiovascular problems are all more common among the offspring of mothers who smoked during pregnancy (Feng & others, 2010; Lazic & others, 2010). Maternal smoking during pregnancy has also been identified as a risk factor for the development of attention deficit hyperactivity disorder in offspring (Knopik, 2009). A recent research review indicates that environmental tobacco smoke, or secondhand smoke, is linked to increased risk of low birth weight in offspring (Leonardi-Bee & others, 2008).

Cocaine Does cocaine use during pregnancy harm the developing embryo and fetus? The most consistent finding is that cocaine exposure during prenatal development is associated with reduced birth weight, length, and head circumference (Smith & others, 2001). In other studies, prenatal cocaine exposure has been linked to lower arousal, less effective self-regulation, higher excitability, and lower quality of reflexes at 1 month of age (Ackerman, Riggins, & Black, 2010; Lester & others, 2002); impaired motor development at 2 years of age and a slower rate of growth through 10 years of age (Richardson, Goldschmidt, & Willford, 2008); impaired language development and information processing, including attention deficits (especially in sustained attention) in preschool and elementary school children (Accornero & others, 2006; Ackerman, Riggins, & Black, 2010); and increased likelihood of being in a special education program that involves support services (Levine & others, 2008).

Some researchers argue that these findings should be interpreted cautiously (Accornero & others, 2006). Why? Because other factors in the lives of pregnant women who use cocaine (such as poverty, malnutrition, and other substance abuse) often cannot be ruled out as possible contributors to the problems found in their children (Hurt & others, 2005). For example, cocaine users are more likely than nonusers to smoke cigarettes, use marijuana, drink alcohol, and take amphetamines.

Despite these cautions, the weight of research evidence indicates that children born to mothers who use cocaine are likely to have neurological, medical, and cognitive deficits (Field, 2007; Mayer & Zhang, 2009). Cocaine use by pregnant women is never recommended.

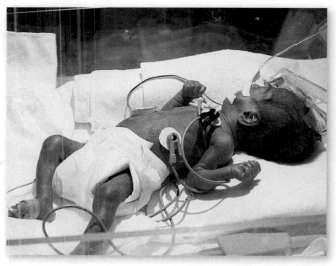

This baby was exposed to cocaine prenatally. *What are some of the possible effects on development of being exposed to cocaine prenatally?*

Methamphetamine Methamphetamine, like cocaine, is a stimulant, speeding up an individual's nervous system. Babies born to mothers who use methamphetamine, or "meth," during pregnancy are at risk for a number of problems, including high infant mortality, low birth weight, memory deficits, and developmental and behavioral problems (Forester & Merz, 2007; Lu & others, 2009).

Marijuana An increasing number of studies find that marijuana use by pregnant women also has negative outcomes for offspring. For example, a recent study found that prenatal marijuana exposure was related to lower intelligence in children (Goldschmidt & others, 2008). Another study indicated that prenatal exposure to marijuana was linked to marijuana use at 14 years of age (Day, Goldschmidt, & Thomas, 2005). In sum, marijuana use is not recommended for pregnant women.

Heroin It is well documented that infants whose mothers are addicted to heroin show several behavioral difficulties at birth (Steinhausen, Blattmann, & Pfund, 2007). The difficulties include withdrawal symptoms, such as tremors, irritability, abnormal crying, disturbed sleep, and impaired motor control. Many still show behavioral problems at their first birthday and attention deficits may appear later in development. The most common treatment for heroin addiction, methadone, is associated with very severe withdrawal symptoms in newborns.

Incompatible Blood Types

Incompatibility between the mother's and the father's blood types poses another risk to prenatal development. Blood types are created by differences in the surface structure of red blood cells. One such difference creates the familiar blood groups—A, B, O, and AB. A second difference creates what is called Rh-positive and Rh-negative blood. If a surface marker, called the *Rh factor*, is present in an individual's red blood cells, the person is said to be Rh-positive; if the Rh marker is not present the person is said to be Rh-negative. If a pregnant woman is Rh-negative and her partner is Rh-positive, the fetus may be Rh-positive. If the fetus's blood is Rh-positive and the mother's is Rh-negative, the mother's immune system may produce antibodies that will attack the fetus. This can result in any number of problems, including miscarriage or stillbirth, anemia, jaundice, heart defects, brain damage, or death soon after birth (Moise, 2005).

Generally, the first Rh-positive baby of an Rh-negative mother is not at risk, but with each subsequent pregnancy the risk increases. A serum (RhoGAM) may be given to the mother within three days of the child's birth to prevent her body from making antibodies that will attack future Rh-positive fetuses. Also, babies affected by Rh incompatibility can be given blood transfusions before or right after birth.

How Would You...?
As a social worker, how would you advise women in their childbearing years who frequently abuse drugs and other psychoactive substances?

How Would You...?
As a human development and family studies professional, how would you justify the need for educational programming for couples planning to become pregnant?

Environmental Hazards

Many aspects of our modern industrial world can endanger the embryo or fetus. Some specific hazards to the embryo or fetus include radiation, toxic wastes, and other environmental pollutants (O'Connor & Roy, 2008).

X-ray radiation can affect the developing embryo or fetus, especially in the first several weeks after conception, when women do not yet know they are pregnant (Urbano & Tait, 2004). Women and their physicians should weigh the risk of an X-ray when the woman is or might be pregnant. However, a routine diagnostic X-ray of a body area other than the abdomen, with the woman's abdomen protected by a lead apron, is generally considered safe (Brent, 2009).

Maternal Diseases

Maternal diseases and infections can produce defects in offspring by crossing the placental barrier, or they can cause damage during birth. Rubella (German measles) is one disease that can cause prenatal defects. Women who plan to have children should have a blood test before they become pregnant to determine if they are immune to the disease (Coonrod & others, 2008).

Syphilis (a sexually transmitted infection) is more damaging later in prenatal development—four months or more after conception. Damage includes eye lesions, which can cause blindness, and skin lesions.

Another infection that has received widespread attention is genital herpes. Newborns contract this virus when they are delivered through the birth canal of a mother with genital herpes (Hollier & Wendel, 2008). About one-third of babies delivered through an infected birth canal die; another one-fourth suffer brain damage. If an active case of genital herpes is detected in a pregnant woman close to her delivery date, a cesarean section can be performed (in which the infant is delivered through an incision in the mother's abdomen) to keep the virus from infecting the newborn (Sellner & others, 2009).

AIDS is a sexually transmitted infection that is caused by the human immunodeficiency virus (HIV), which destroys the body's immune system. A mother can infect her offspring with HIV/AIDS in three ways: (1) across the placenta during gestation, (2) through contact with maternal blood or fluids during delivery, and (3) through breast feeding. The transmission of AIDS through breast feeding is a particular problem in many developing countries (UNICEF, 2011). Babies born to HIV-infected mothers can be (1) infected and symptomatic (show HIV symptoms), (2) infected but asymptomatic (not show HIV symptoms), or (3) not infected at all. An infant who is infected and asymptomatic may still develop HIV symptoms up to 15 months of age.

The more widespread disease of diabetes, characterized by high levels of sugar in the blood, also affects offspring (Huda & others, 2010). A research review indicated that newborns with physical defects are more likely to have diabetic mothers than newborns without such defects (Eriksson, 2009). Moreover, women who have gestational diabetes (a condition in which women without previously diagnosed diabetes develop high blood glucose levels during pregnancy) may deliver very large infants (weighing 10 pounds or more), and the infants themselves are at risk for diabetes (Gluck & others, 2009).

Other Parental Factors

So far we have discussed a number of drugs, environmental hazards, maternal diseases, and incompatible blood types that can harm the embryo or fetus. Here we will explore other characteristics of the mother and father that can affect prenatal and child development, including nutrition, age, and emotional states and stress.

Maternal Diet and Nutrition A developing embryo or fetus depends completely on its mother for nutrition, which comes from the mother's blood. The nutritional status of the embryo or fetus is determined by the mother's total caloric intake, as well as her intake of proteins, vitamins, and minerals. Children born to malnourished mothers are more likely than other children to be malformed.

Being overweight before and during pregnancy can also put the embryo or fetus at risk, and an increasing number of pregnant women in the United States are overweight (Griffiths & others, 2010; Sullivan & others, 2010). A recent research review concluded that obesity during pregnancy is linked to increased maternal risks of infertility, hypertensive disorders, diabetes, and delivery by cesarean section (Arendas, Qui, & Gruslin, 2008). In this review, obesity during pregnancy put the fetus at increased risk for macrosomia (excessive birth weight), intrauterine fetal death, stillbirth, and admission to the neonatal intensive care unit (NICU).

One aspect of maternal nutrition that is important for normal prenatal development is folic acid, a B-complex vitamin (Rasmussen & Clemmensen, 2010). A recent study of more than 34,000 women taking folic acid either alone or as part of a multivitamin for at least one year prior to conceiving was linked with a 70 percent lower risk of delivering at 20 to 28 weeks and a 50 percent lower risk of delivering at 28 to 32 weeks (Bukowski & others, 2008). Another recent study revealed that toddlers of mothers who did not use folic acid supplements in the first trimester of pregnancy had more behavioral problems (Roza & others, 2010). Also, as we indicated earlier in the chapter, lack of folic acid is related to neural tube defects in offspring (Levene & Chervenak, 2009). The U.S. Department of Health and Human Services (2009) recommends that pregnant women consume a minimum of 400 micrograms of folic acid per day (about twice the amount the average woman gets in one day). Orange juice and spinach are examples of foods that are rich in folic acid.

Because the fetus depends entirely on its mother for nutrition, it is important for the pregnant woman to have good nutritional habits. In Kenya, this government clinic provides pregnant women with information about how their diet can influence the health of their fetus and offspring. What might the information about diet be like?

Eating fish is often recommended as part of a healthy diet, but pollution has made many fish a risky choice for pregnant women. Some fish contain high levels of mercury, which is released into the air both naturally and by industrial processes (Genuis, 2009). When mercury falls into the water it can accumulate in large fish, such as shark, swordfish, king mackerel, and some species of large tuna (Mayo Clinic, 2009). Mercury is easily transferred across the placenta, and the embryo's developing brain and nervous system are highly sensitive to the metal. Researchers have found that prenatal mercury exposure is linked to adverse outcomes, including miscarriage, preterm birth, and lower intelligence (Xue & others, 2007).

Maternal Age When possible harmful effects on the fetus and infant are considered, two maternal ages are of special interest: adolescence and 35 years and older (Malizia, Hacker, & Penzias, 2009). The mortality rate of infants born to adolescent mothers is double that of infants born to mothers in their twenties. Adequate prenatal care decreases the probability that a child born to an adolescent girl will have physical problems. However, adolescents are the least likely of women in all age groups to obtain prenatal assistance from clinics and health services.

Maternal age is also linked to the risk that a child will have Down syndrome (Ghosh & others, 2010). A baby with Down syndrome rarely is born to a mother 16 to 34 years of age. However, when the mother reaches 40 years of age, the probability is slightly over 1 in 100 that a baby born to her will have Down syndrome, and by age 50 it is almost 1 in 10. When mothers are 35 years and older, risks also increase for low birth weight, preterm delivery, and fetal death (Mibugua Gitau & others, 2009).

We still have much to learn about the role of the mother's age in pregnancy and childbirth. As women remain active, exercise regularly, and are careful about their nutrition, their reproductive systems may remain healthier at older ages than was thought possible in the past.

How Would You...?
As a health-care professional, how would you advise an expectant mother who is experiencing extreme psychological stress?

Emotional States and Stress When a pregnant woman experiences intense fears, anxieties, and other emotions or negative mood states, physiological changes occur that may affect her fetus (Leung & others, 2010). A mother's stress may also influence the fetus indirectly by increasing the likelihood that the mother will engage in unhealthy behaviors, such as taking drugs and receiving poor prenatal care.

High maternal anxiety and stress during pregnancy can have long-term consequences for the offspring (Dunkel Schetter, 2011). A research review indicated that pregnant women with high levels of stress are at increased risk for having a child with emotional or cognitive problems, attention deficit hyperactivity disorder (ADHD), and language delay (Taige & others, 2007).

Might maternal depression also have an adverse effect on prenatal development and birth? A recent study revealed that maternal depression is linked to preterm birth and slower prenatal growth rates (Diego & others, 2009). In this study, mothers who were depressed had elevated cortisol levels, which likely contributed to the negative outcomes for the fetus and newborn.

In one study, in China, the longer fathers smoked, the higher the risk that their children would develop cancer (Ji & others, 1997). *What are some other paternal factors that can influence the development of the fetus and the child?*

Paternal Factors So far, we have discussed how characteristics of the mother—such as drug use, disease, diet and nutrition, age, and emotional states—can influence prenatal development and the development of the child. Might there also be some paternal risk factors? Indeed, there are several. Men's exposure to lead, radiation, certain pesticides, and petrochemicals may cause abnormalities in sperm that lead to miscarriage or diseases such as childhood cancer (Cordier, 2008). The father's smoking during the mother's pregnancy also can cause problems for the offspring. In one study, heavy paternal smoking was associated with the risk of early miscarriage (Venners & others, 2004). This negative outcome may be related to secondhand smoke.

Much of our discussion on prenatal development has focused on what can go wrong. Prospective parents should take steps to avoid the vulnerabilities to fetal development that we have described. But it is important to keep in mind that most of the time, prenatal development does not go awry, and development occurs along a positive path.

Prenatal Care

Although prenatal care varies enormously from one woman to another, it usually involves a defined schedule of visits for medical care, which typically includes screening for manageable conditions and treatable diseases that can affect the baby or the mother. In addition to medical care, prenatal programs often include comprehensive educational, social, and nutritional services.

Information about pregnancy, labor, delivery, and caring for the newborn can be especially valuable for first-time mothers (Lowdermilk, Perry, & Cashion, 2011; Murray & McKinney, 2010). Prenatal care is also very important for women in poverty because it links them with other social services (Mattson & Smith, 2011).

An innovative program that is rapidly expanding in the United States is CenteringPregnancy (Steming, 2008). This program is relationship-centered and provides complete prenatal care in a group setting. It replaces traditional 15-minute physician visits with 90-minute peer group support sessions and self-examination led by a physician or certified nurse-midwife. Groups of up to 10 women (and often their partners) meet regularly beginning at 12 to 16 weeks of pregnancy. The sessions emphasize empowering women to play an active role in experiencing a positive pregnancy. A recent study revealed that CenteringPregnancy groups made more prenatal visits, had higher breast feeding rates, and were more satisfied with their prenatal care than were women in individual care (Klima & others, 2009).

Some prenatal programs for parents focus on home visitation (Eckenrode & others, 2010). Research evaluations indicate that the Nurse-Family Partnership created by David Olds and his colleagues (2004, 2007) is successful. The Nurse-Family Partnership involves home visits by trained nurses beginning in the second or third trimester of prenatal development. The extensive program consists of approximately 50 home visits beginning during the prenatal period and extending through the child's first two years. The home visits focus on the mother's health, access to health care, parenting, and improvement of the mother's life by providing her guidance in education, work, and relationships. Research revealed that the Nurse-Family Partnership has numerous positive outcomes, including fewer pregnancies, better work circumstances, and stability in relationship partners for the mother, and improved academic success and social development for the child (Olds & others, 2004, 2007).

A CenteringPregnancy program. This rapidly increasing program alters routine prenatal care by bringing women out of exam rooms and into relationship-oriented groups.

Birth and the Postpartum Period

The long wait for the moment of birth is over, and the infant is about to appear. What happens during childbirth, and what can be done to make the experience a positive one?

Nature writes the basic script for how birth occurs, but parents make important choices about the conditions surrounding birth. We look first at the sequence of physical steps through which a child is born.

The Birth Process

The birth process occurs in three stages. It may take place in different contexts and in most cases involves one or more attendants.

Stages of Birth

The first stage of the birth process is the longest. Uterine contractions are 15 to 20 minutes apart at the beginning and last up to a minute. These contractions cause the woman's cervix to stretch and open. As the first stage progresses, the contractions come closer together, occurring every two to five minutes. Their intensity increases. By the end of the first stage, contractions dilate the cervix to an opening of about 10 centimeters (4 inches), so that the baby can move from the uterus to the birth canal. For a woman having her first child, the first stage lasts an average of 6 to 12 hours; for subsequent children, this stage typically is much shorter.

The second birth stage begins when the baby's head starts to move through the cervix and the birth canal. It terminates when the baby completely emerges from the mother's body. With each contraction, the mother bears down hard to push the baby out of her body. By the time the baby's head is out of the mother's body, the contractions come almost every minute and last for about a minute. This stage typically lasts approximately 45 minutes to an hour.

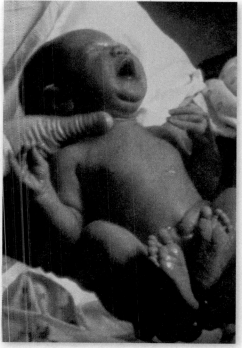

After the long journey of prenatal development, birth takes place. During birth the baby is on a threshold between two worlds. *What are the characteristics of the three stages of birth?*

Afterbirth is the third stage, during which the placenta, umbilical cord, and other membranes are detached and expelled. This final stage is the shortest of the three birth stages, lasting only minutes.

Childbirth Setting and Attendants

In the United States, 99 percent of births take place in hospitals, a figure that has remained constant for several decades (Martin & others, 2005). Who helps a mother during birth varies across cultures. In U.S. hospitals, it has become the norm for fathers or birth coaches to be with the mother throughout labor and delivery. In the East African Nigoni culture, men are completely excluded from the childbirth process. When a woman is ready to give birth, female relatives move into the woman's hut and the husband leaves, taking his belongings (clothes, tools, weapons, and so on) with him. He is not permitted to return until after the baby is born. In some cultures, childbirth is an open, community affair. For example, in the Pukapukan culture in the Pacific Islands, women give birth in a shelter that is open to villagers, who may observe the birth.

Midwives *Midwifery* is practiced in most countries throughout the world (Wickham, 2009). In Holland, more than 40 percent of babies are delivered by *midwives* rather than by doctors. However, in 2003, 91 percent of U.S. births were attended by physicians, and only 8 percent of women who delivered a baby were attended by a midwife (Martin & others, 2005). Nevertheless, the 8 percent figure for 2003 represents a substantial increase from less than 1 percent in 1975 (Martin & others, 2005). Ninety-five percent of the midwives who delivered babies in the United States in 2003 were certified nurse-midwives.

Doulas In some countries, a doula attends a childbearing woman. *Doula* is a Greek word that means "a woman who helps." A *doula* is a caregiver who provides continuous physical, emotional, and educational support for the mother before, during, and after childbirth. Doulas remain with the parents throughout labor, assessing and responding to their needs. Researchers have found positive effects when a doula is present at the birth of a child (Berghella, Baxter, & Chauhan, 2008).

In the United States, most doulas work as independent providers hired by the expectant parents. Doulas typically function as part of a "birthing team," serving as an adjunct to the midwife or the hospital's obstetric staff.

Methods of Childbirth

U.S. hospitals often allow the mother and her obstetrician a range of options regarding their method of delivery. Key choices involve the use of medication, whether to use any of a number of nonmedicated techniques to reduce pain, and when to have a cesarean delivery.

Medication Three basic kinds of drugs that are used for labor are analgesia, anesthesia, and oxytocin/pitocin.

Analgesia is used to relieve pain. Analgesics include tranquilizers, barbiturates, and narcotics such as Demerol.

Anesthesia is used in late first-stage labor and during delivery to block sensation in an area of the body or to block consciousness. There is a trend toward not using general anesthesia, which blocks consciousness, in normal births because general anesthesia can be transmitted through the placenta to the fetus (Lieberman & others, 2005). An *epidural block* is regional anesthesia that numbs the woman's body from the waist down. Researchers are continuing to explore safer drug mixtures for use at lower doses to improve the effectiveness and safety of epidural anesthesia (Balaji, Dhillon, & Russell, 2009).

Oxytocin is a synthetic hormone that is used to stimulate contractions; pitocin is the most widely used oxytocin. The benefits and risks of oxytocin as a part of childbirth continue to be debated (Vasdev, 2008).

Predicting how a drug will affect an individual woman and her fetus is difficult (Lowdermilk, Perry, & Cashion, 2011). A particular drug might have only a minimal effect on one fetus yet have a much stronger effect on another. The drug's dosage is also a factor (Weiner & Buhimschi, 2009). Stronger doses of tranquilizers and narcotics given to decrease the mother's pain potentially have a more negative effect on the fetus than do mild doses. It is important for the mother to assess her level of pain and have a voice in the decision as to whether or not she should receive medication.

Natural and Prepared Childbirth For a brief time not long ago, the idea of avoiding all medication during childbirth gained favor in the United States. Instead, many women chose to reduce the pain of childbirth through techniques known as natural childbirth and prepared childbirth. Today, at least some medication is used in the typical childbirth, but elements of natural childbirth and prepared childbirth remain popular (Oates & Abraham, 2010).

Natural childbirth is a childbirth method in which no drugs are given to relieve pain or assist in the birth process. The mother and her partner are taught to use breathing methods and relaxation techniques during delivery. French obstetrician Ferdinand Lamaze developed a method similar to natural childbirth that is known as **prepared childbirth**, or the Lamaze method. It includes a special breathing technique to control pushing in the final stages of labor, as well as more detailed education about anatomy and physiology. The Lamaze method has become very popular in the United States. The pregnant woman's partner usually serves as a coach; the partner attends childbirth classes with her and helps her with her breathing and relaxation during delivery. In sum, proponents of current prepared childbirth methods conclude that when information and support are provided, women *know* how to give birth.

Other Nonmedicated Techniques to Reduce Pain The effort to reduce stress and control pain during labor has recently led to an increase in the use of some older and some newer nonmedicated techniques (Kalder & others, 2010; Simkin & Bolding, 2004). These include waterbirth, massage, and acupuncture.

Waterbirth involves giving birth in a tub of warm water. Some women go through labor in the water and get out for delivery; others remain in the water for delivery. The rationale for waterbirth is that the baby has been in an amniotic sac for many months and that delivery in a similar environment is likely to be less stressful for the baby and the mother (Meyer, Weible, & Woeber, 2010). Mothers get into the warm water when contractions become closer together and more intense. Getting into the water too soon can cause labor to slow or stop. Reviews

What is the rationale for the waterbirth technique?

natural childbirth A childbirth method in which no drugs are given to relieve pain or assist in the birth process. The mother and her partner are taught to use breathing methods and relaxation techniques during delivery.

prepared childbirth Developed by French obstetrician Ferdinand Lamaze, this childbirth strategy is similar to natural childbirth but includes a special breathing technique to control pushing in the final stages of labor and a more detailed anatomy and physiology course.

of research have indicated mixed results for waterbirths (Cluett & Burns, 2009; Pinette, Wax, & Wilson, 2004). Waterbirth has been practiced more often in European countries such as Switzerland and Sweden than in the United States in recent decades, but is increasingly being included in U.S. birth plans.

Massage is increasingly used as a procedure prior to and during delivery (Stager, 2009–2010). Researchers have found that massage can reduce pain and anxiety during labor (Chang, Chen, & Huang, 2006). A recent study revealed that massage therapy reduced pain in pregnant women and alleviated prenatal depression in both parents and improved their relationships (Field & others, 2008).

Acupuncture, the insertion of very fine needles into specific locations in the body, is used as a standard procedure to reduce the pain of childbirth in China, although it only recently has begun to be used for this purpose in the United States (Moleti, 2009). One study revealed that acupuncture resulted in less time spent in labor and a reduction in the need for oxytocin to augment labor (Gaudernack, Forbord, & Hole, 2006).

How Would You...?
As a health-care professional, how would you advise a woman in her first trimester about the options available for her baby's birth and for her own comfort during the delivery process?

Cesarean Delivery Normally, the baby's head comes through the vagina first. But if the baby is in a *breech position,* its buttocks are the first part to emerge from the vagina. In 1 of every 25 deliveries, the baby's head is still in the uterus when the rest of the body is out. Because breech births can cause respiratory problems, if the baby is in a breech position a surgical procedure known as a cesarean delivery is usually performed. In a *cesarean delivery* (or cesarean section), the baby is removed from the uterus through an incision made in the mother's abdomen (Lee, El-Sayed, & Gould, 2008). The benefits and risks of cesarean sections continue to be debated (Bangdiwala & others, 2010).

The Transition from Fetus to Newborn

Much of our discussion of birth so far has focused on the mother. However, birth also involves considerable stress for the baby. If the delivery takes too long, the baby can develop *anoxia,* a condition in which the fetus or newborn has an insufficient supply of oxygen. Anoxia can cause brain damage (Aylott, 2006).

The baby has considerable capacity to withstand the stress of birth. Large quantities of adrenaline and noradrenaline, hormones that protect the fetus in the event of oxygen deficiency, are secreted in the newborn's body during the birth process (Van Beveren, 2010).

Immediately after birth, the umbilical cord is cut and the baby is on its own. Before birth, oxygen came from the mother via the umbilical cord, but now the baby is self-sufficient and can breathe independently.

Almost immediately after birth, a newborn is taken to be weighed, cleaned up, and tested for signs of developmental problems that might require urgent attention (Therrell & others, 2010). The **Apgar Scale** is widely used to assess the health of newborns at one and five minutes after birth. The Apgar Scale evaluates infants' heart rate, respiratory effort, muscle tone, body color, and reflex irritability. An obstetrician or nurse does the evaluation and gives the newborn a score, or reading, of 0, 1, or 2 on each of these five health signs. A total score of 7 to 10 indicates that the newborn's condition is good. A score of 5 indicates that there may be developmental difficulties. A score of 3 or below signals an emergency and warns that the baby might not survive. The Apgar Scale is especially good at assessing the newborn's ability to respond to the stress of delivery and its new environment (Reynolds, 2010). It also identifies high-risk infants who need resuscitation.

Nurses often play important roles in the birth of a baby. To read about the work of a nurse who specializes in the care of women during labor and delivery, see "Careers in Life-Span Development."

Linda Pugh, Perinatal Nurse

Perinatal nurses work with childbearing women to support health and growth during the childbearing experience. Linda Pugh, Ph.D., R.N.C., is a perinatal nurse on the faculty at The Johns Hopkins University School of Nursing. She is certified as an inpatient obstetric nurse and specializes in the care of women during labor and delivery. She teaches undergraduate and graduate students, educates professional nurses, and conducts research. In addition, Pugh consults with hospitals and organizations about women's health issues and many of the topics we discuss in this chapter.

Her research interests include nursing interventions with low-income breast feeding women, discovering ways to prevent and ameliorate fatigue during childbearing, and using breathing exercises during labor.

Linda Pugh (*right*) with a mother and her newborn.

Low Birth Weight and Preterm Infants

Three related conditions pose threats to many newborns: low birth weight, preterm birth, and being small for date. *Low birth weight* infants weigh less than 5½ pounds at birth. *Very low birth weight* newborns weigh under 3 pounds, and *extremely low birth weight* newborns weigh under 2 pounds. Preterm infants are born three weeks or more before the pregnancy has reached its full term—in other words, 35 or fewer weeks after conception. Small for date infants (also called *small for gestational age infants*) have a birth weight that is below normal when the length of the pregnancy is considered. They weigh less than 90 percent of all babies of the same gestational age. Small for date infants may be preterm or full term. One study found that small for date infants have a 400 percent greater risk of death (Regev & others, 2003).

In 2006, 12.8 percent of U.S. infants were born preterm—a 36 percent increase since the 1980s (National Center for Health Statistics, 2009). The increase in preterm birth is likely due to such factors as the increasing number of births to women 35 years of age or older, increasing rates of multiple births, increased management of maternal and fetal conditions (for example, inducing labor preterm if medical technology indicates that it will increase the likelihood of survival), increased substance abuse (tobacco, alcohol), and increased stress (Goldenberg & Culhane, 2007). Ethnic variations characterize preterm birth (Balchin & Steer, 2007). For example, in 2006 the likelihood of being born preterm was 12.8 percent for all U.S. infants, but the rate was 18.5 percent for African American infants (National Center for Health Statistics, 2009).

Incidence and Causes of Low Birth Weight

Most, but not all, preterm babies are also low birth weight babies. The incidence of low birth weight varies considerably from one country to another. In some developing countries, such as Bangladesh, where poverty is rampant and the health and nutrition of mothers are poor, the percentage of low birth weight babies reaches as high as 50 percent. In the United States, there has been an increase in low birth weight infants in the last two decades, and the U.S. low birth weight rate of 8.1 percent in 2004 is considerably higher than that of many other developed countries (Cuevas & others, 2005). For example, only 4 percent of the infants born in Sweden, Finland, the Netherlands, and Norway are low birth weight, and only 5 percent of those born in New Zealand, Australia, France, and Japan are low birth weight.

Recently, there has been considerable interest in the role that progestin might play in reducing preterm births (O'Brien & Lewis, 2009). Recent research indicates that progestin is most effective when it is given to women with a history of previous spontaneous birth at less than 37 months (da Fonseca & others, 2009), to women who have a short cervical length of 15 mm or less (da Fonseca & others, 2009), and to women with a singleton rather than twins (Norman & others, 2010).

Consequences of Low Birth Weight

Although most preterm and low birth weight infants are healthy, as a group they have more health and developmental problems than do normal birth weight infants (Minde & Zelkowitz, 2008). The number and severity of these problems increase when infants are born very early and as their birth weight decreases. Survival rates for infants who are born very early and very small have risen, but with this improved survival rate have come increases in rates of severe brain damage (Casey, 2008).

For preterm birth, the terms *extremely preterm* and *very preterm* are increasingly used (Lowdermilk, Perry, & Cashion, 2011). *Extremely preterm infants* are those born less than 28 weeks preterm, and *very preterm infants* are those born at less than 33 weeks of gestational age.

Low birth weight children are more likely than their normal birth weight counterparts to develop a learning disability, attention deficit hyperactivity disorder, or breathing problems such as asthma (Santo, Portuguez, & Nunes, 2009). Approximately 50 percent of all low birth weight children are enrolled in special education programs.

A new mother learning how to practice kangaroo care. *What is kangaroo care?*

Nurturing Low Birth Weight and Preterm Infants

Two increasingly used interventions in the neonatal intensive care unit (NICU) are kangaroo care and massage therapy. *Kangaroo care* involves skin-to-skin contact in which the baby, wearing only a diaper, is held upright against the parent's bare chest, much as a baby kangaroo is carried by its mother. Kangaroo care is typically practiced for two to three hours per day over an extended time in early infancy.

Why use kangaroo care with preterm infants? Preterm infants often have difficulty coordinating their breathing and heart rate, and the close physical contact with the parent provided by kangaroo care can help stabilize the preterm infant's heartbeat, temperature, and breathing (Nyqvist & others, 2010). Preterm infants who experience kangaroo care also gain more weight than their counterparts who are not given this care (Gathwala, Singh, & Balhara, 2008). A recent study also revealed that kangaroo care decreased pain responses in preterm infants (Johnston & others, 2009).

Many preterm infants experience less touch than full-term infants do because they are isolated in temperature-controlled incubators. Research by Tiffany Field and her colleagues (2001, 2007; Diego, Field, & Hernandez-Reif, 2008; Field, Diego, & Hernandez-Reif, 2008, 2010) has led to a surge of interest in the role that massage might play in improving developmental outcomes for preterm infants. In Field's first study in this area, massage therapy consisting of firm stroking with the palms of the hands was given three times per day for 15-minute periods to preterm infants (Field & others, 1986). The massage therapy led to 47 percent greater weight gain than did standard medical treatment. The massaged infants also were more active and alert than preterm infants who were not massaged, and they performed better on developmental tests.

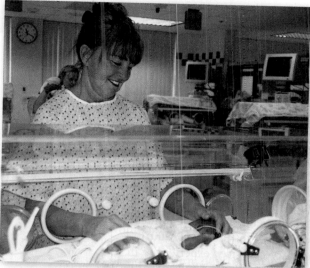

Tiffany Field is shown here massaging a newborn infant. *What types of infants have massage therapy been shown to help?*

In later studies, Field demonstrated the benefits of massage therapy for infants who faced a variety of problems. For example, preterm infants exposed to cocaine in utero who received massage therapy gained weight and improved their scores on developmental tests (Field, 2001). In another investigation, newborns born to HIV-positive mothers were randomly assigned to a massage therapy group or to a control group that did not receive the therapy (Scafidi & Field, 1996). The massaged infants showed superior performance on a wide range of assessments, including daily weight gain. Another study investigated 1- to 3-month-old infants born to depressed adolescent mothers (Field & others, 1996). The infants of depressed mothers who received massage therapy had lower stress—as well as improved emotionality, sociability, and soothability—compared with the non-massaged infants of depressed mothers. In a review of the use of massage therapy with preterm infants, Field and her colleagues (2004) concluded that the most consistent findings involve two positive results: (1) increased weight gain and (2) discharge from the hospital from three to six days earlier.

Bonding

A special component of the parent-infant relationship is *bonding,* the formation of a connection, especially a physical bond between parents and the newborn in the period shortly after birth. In the mid-20th century, U.S. hospitals seemed almost determined to deter bonding. Anesthesia given to the mother during delivery would make the mother drowsy, interfering with her ability to respond to and stimulate the newborn. Mothers and newborns were often separated shortly after delivery, and preterm infants were isolated from their mothers even more than from full-term mothers. In recent decades these practices have changed, but to some extent they are still followed in many hospitals.

Do these practices do any harm? Some physicians believe that during the "critical period" shortly after birth the parents and newborn need to form an emotional attachment as a foundation for optimal development in years to come (Kennell, 2006; Kennell & McGrath, 1999). Although some research supports this bonding hypothesis (Klaus & Kennell, 1976), a body of research challenges the significance of the first few days of life as a critical period (Bakeman & Brown, 1980; Rode & others, 1981). Indeed, the extreme form of the bonding hypothesis—that the newborn *must* have close contact with the mother in the first few days of life to develop optimally—simply is not true.

Nevertheless, the weakness of the bonding hypothesis should not be used as an excuse to keep motivated mothers from interacting with their newborns. Such contact brings pleasure to many mothers and may dispel maternal anxiety about the baby's health and safety. In some cases—including preterm infants, adolescent mothers, and mothers from disadvantaged circumstances—early close contact is key to establishing a climate for improved interaction after the mother and infant leave the hospital.

How Would You...?
As a health-care professional, how would you advise hospital administrators about implementing kangaroo care or massage therapy in the newborn intensive care unit?

behavior that promotes the organism's survival in a natural habitat.

- Evolutionary psychology holds that adaptation, reproduction, and "survival of the fittest" are important in shaping behavior. Evolutionary developmental psychology emphasizes that an extended "juvenile" period is needed to develop a large brain and learn the complexity of human social communities.

stitute genes, the units of hereditary information that direct cells to reproduce and manufacture proteins. Genes act collaboratively, not independently.

- Genes are passed on to new cells when chromosomes are duplicated during the processes of mitosis and meiosis.

postpartum period The period after childbirth when the mother adjusts, both physically and psychologically, to the process of childbirth. This period lasts for about six weeks or until her body has completed its adjustment and returned to a near prepregnant state.

Many hospitals now offer a *rooming-in* arrangement, in which the baby remains in the mother's room most of the time during its hospital stay. However, if parents choose not to use this rooming-in arrangement, the weight of the research suggests that this decision will not harm the infant emotionally (Lamb, 1994).

The Postpartum Period

(*Left*) An HIV-infected mother breast feeding her baby in Nairobi, Africa; (*Right*) A Rhwandan mother bottle feeding her baby. *What are some concerns about breast versus bottle feeding in impoverished African countries?*

Fabella Memorial Hospital in the Philippines reported saving 8 percent of its annual budget. Still, there are many places in the world where the baby-friendly initiatives have not been implemented (UNICEF, 2004).

The advantages of breast feeding in impoverished countries are substantial (UNICEF, 2011). However, these advantages must be balanced against the risk of passing HIV to the baby through breast milk if the mother has the virus; the majority of mothers with HIV don't know that they are infected (Gumbo & others, 2010; Oladokun, Brown, & Osinusi, 2010). In some areas of Africa more than 30 percent of mothers have the virus.

In the first two years of life, an infant's body and brain undergo remarkable growth and development. In this chapter we explore how this takes place: through physical growth, motor development, sensory and perceptual development, cognitive development, and language development. ▌

Physical Growth and Development in Infancy

At birth, an infant has few of the physical abilities we associate with being human. Its head, which is huge relative to the rest of the body, flops around uncontrollably. Apart from some basic reflexes and the ability to cry, the newborn is unable to perform many actions. Over the next 12 months, however, the infant becomes capable of sitting, standing, stooping, climbing, and usually walking. During the

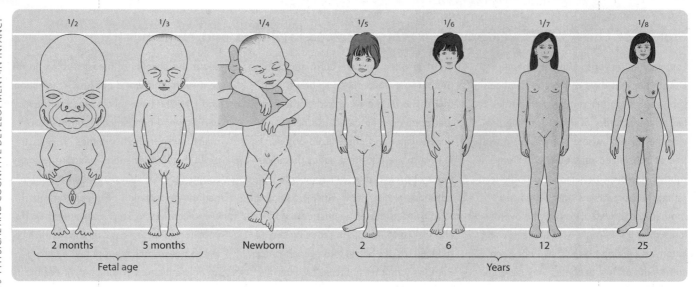

Figure 3.1 Changes in Proportions of the Human Body During Growth
As individuals develop from infancy through adulthood, one of the most noticeable physical changes is that the head becomes smaller in relation to the rest of the body. The fractions listed refer to head size as a proportion of total body length at different ages.

second year, while growth slows, rapid increases in such activities as running and climbing take place. Let's now examine in greater detail the sequence of physical development in infancy.

Patterns of Growth

cephalocaudal pattern The sequence in which the earliest growth always occurs at the top— the head—with physical growth in size, weight, and feature differentiation gradually working from top to bottom.

proximodistal pattern The sequence in which growth starts at the center of the body and moves toward the extremities.

During prenatal development and early infancy, the head occupies an extraordinary proportion of the total body (see Figure 3.1). The **cephalocaudal pattern** is the sequence in which the earliest growth always occurs at the top—the head—with physical growth and differentiation of features gradually working their way down from top to bottom (shoulders, middle trunk, and so on). This same pattern occurs in the head area, as the top parts of the head—the eyes and brain—grow faster than the lower parts, such as the jaw.

Sensory and motor development generally proceed according to the cephalocaudal pattern. For example, infants see objects before they can control their torso, and they can use their hands long before they can crawl or walk. However, development does not follow a rigid blueprint. One study found that infants reached for toys with their feet four weeks earlier, on average, than they reached for them with their hands (Galloway & Thelen, 2004).

Growth also follows the **proximodistal pattern**, a sequence in which growth starts at the center of the body and moves toward the extremities. For example, infants control the muscles of their trunk and arms before they control their hands, and they use their whole hands before they can control several fingers.

Height and Weight

The average North American newborn is 20 inches long and weighs 7½ pounds. Ninety-five percent of full-term newborns are 18 to 22 inches long and weigh between 5½ and 10 pounds.

In the first several days of life, most newborns lose 5 to 7 percent of their body weight before they adjust to feeding by sucking, swallowing, and digesting. They then grow rapidly, gaining an average of 5 to 6 ounces per week during the first month. They double their birth weight by the age of 4 months and nearly triple it by their first birthday. Infants grow about 1 inch per month during the first year, reaching approximately 1½ times their birth length by their first birthday.

Growth slows considerably in the second year of life. By 2 years of age, children weigh approximately 26 to 32 pounds, having gained a quarter to half a pound per month during the second year; now they have reached about one-fifth of their adult weight. At 2 years of age, the average child is 32 to 35 inches tall, nearly half of his or her eventual adult height.

The Brain

At birth, the infant that began as a single cell has a brain that contains tens of billions of nerve cells, or neurons. Extensive brain development continues after birth, through infancy, and later (Diamond, Casey, & Munakata, 2011; Nelson, 2011). Because the brain is still developing so rapidly in infancy, the infant's head should be protected from falls or other injuries and the baby should never be shaken. *Shaken baby syndrome*, which includes brain swelling and hemorrhaging, affects hundreds of babies in the United States each year (Croucher, 2010; Fanconi & Lips, 2010).

The Brain's Development

At birth, the brain weighs about 25 percent of its adult weight. By the second birthday, it is about 75 percent of its adult weight. However, the brain's areas do not mature uniformly.

Mapping the Brain Scientists analyze and categorize areas of the brain in numerous ways (Nelson, 2011). Of greatest interest is the portion farthest from the spinal cord, known as the *fore-brain,* which includes the cerebral cortex and several structures beneath it. The *cerebral cortex* covers the forebrain like a wrinkled cap. It has two halves, or hemispheres. Based on ridges and valleys in the cortex, scientists distinguish four main areas, called lobes, in each hemisphere: the *frontal lobes,* the *occipital lobes,* the *temporal lobes,* and the *parietal lobes* (see Figure 3.2).

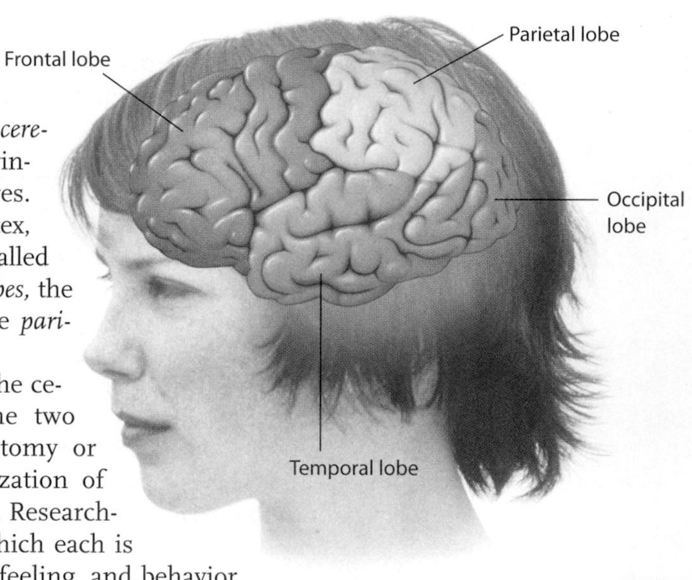

Although these areas are found in the cerebral cortex of each hemisphere, the two hemispheres are not identical in anatomy or function. **Lateralization** is the specialization of function in one hemisphere or the other. Researchers continue to explore the degree to which each is involved in various aspects of thinking, feeling, and behavior (Diamond, Casey, & Munakata, 2011). At birth, the hemispheres of the cerebral cortex have already started to specialize: Newborns show greater electrical brain activity in the left hemisphere than in the right hemisphere when listening to speech sounds (Hahn, 1987).

The most extensive research on brain lateralization has focused on language (Bortfield, Fava, & Boas, 2009). Speech and grammar are localized in the left hemisphere in most people, but some aspects of language, such as appropriate language use in different contexts and the use of metaphor and humor, involve the right hemisphere (Hornickel, Skoe, & Kraus, 2008). Thus, language is not controlled exclusively by the brain's left hemisphere. Further, most neuroscientists agree that complex functions—such as reading, performing music, and creating art—are the outcome of communication between both sides of the brain (Stroofbant, Buijs, & Vingerhoets, 2009).

How are the areas of the brain different in the newborn and the infant than in an adult, and why do the differences matter? Important differences have been documented at both the cellular and the structural levels.

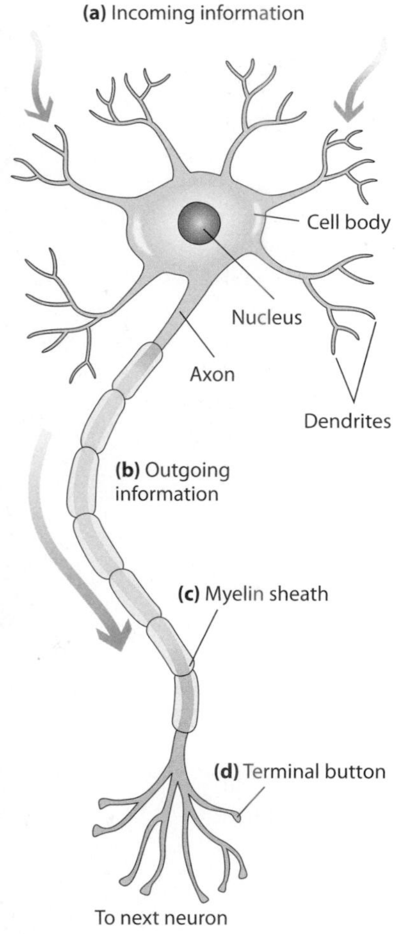

Changes in Neurons Within the brain, neurons send electrical and chemical signals, communicating with each other. As we indicated in Chapter 2, a *neuron* is a nerve cell that handles information processing (see Figure 3.3). Extending from the neuron's cell body are two types of fibers, known as *axons* and *dendrites.* Generally, the axon carries signals away from the cell body and dendrites carry signals toward it. A *myelin sheath,* which is a layer of fat cells, encases many axons (see Figure 3.3). The myelin sheath provides insulation and helps electrical signals travel faster down the axon. At the end of the axon are terminal buttons, which release chemicals called *neurotransmitters* into *synapses,* tiny gaps between neurons. Chemical interactions in synapses connect axons and dendrites, allowing information to pass from one neuron to another.

Neurons change in two very significant ways during the first years of life. First, *myelination,* the process of encasing axons with fat cells, begins prenatally and continues throughout childhood, even into adolescence (Paus, 2009). Second, connectivity among neurons increases, creating new neural pathways, as Figure 3.4 illustrates. New dendrites

Figure 3.2 The Brain's Four Lobes
Shown here are the locations of the brain's four lobes: frontal, occipital, temporal, and parietal.

(a) Incoming information

Cell body

Nucleus

Axon

Dendrites

(b) Outgoing information

(c) Myelin sheath

(d) Terminal button

To next neuron

Figure 3.3 The Neuron

(a) The dendrites of the cell body receive information from other neurons, muscles, or glands. (b) Axons transmit information away from the cell body. (c) A myelin sheath covers most axons and speeds information transmission. (d) As the axon ends, it branches out into terminal buttons.

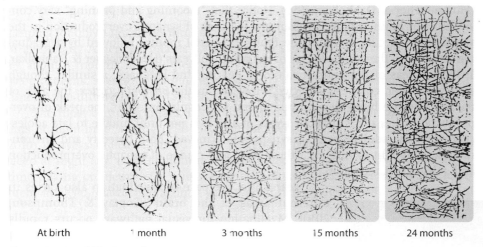

| At birth | 1 month | 3 months | 15 months | 24 months |

Figure 3.4 Dendritic Spreading

Note the increase in connectedness between neurons over the course of the first two years of life.

Reprinted by permission of the publisher from *The Postnatal Development of the Human Cerebral Cortex, Volumes I-VIII*, by J. LeRoy Conel, Cambridge, Mass.: Harvard University Press. Copyright © 1939, 1941, 1947, 1951, 1955, 1959, 1963, 1967 by the President and Fellows of Harvard.

grow, connections among dendrites increase, and synaptic connections between axons and dendrites proliferate. Whereas myelination speeds up neural transmissions, the expansion of dendritic connections facilitates the spreading of neural pathways in infant development.

Researchers have discovered an intriguing aspect of synaptic connections: Nearly twice as many of these connections are made as will ever be used (Huttenlocher & Dabholkar, 1997). The connections that are used become strengthened and survive, while the unused ones are replaced by other pathways or disappear. In the language of neuroscience, these connections will be "pruned" (Nelson, 2011).

Changes in Regions of the Brain Figure 3.5 vividly illustrates the dramatic growth and later pruning of synapses in the visual, auditory, and prefrontal cortex

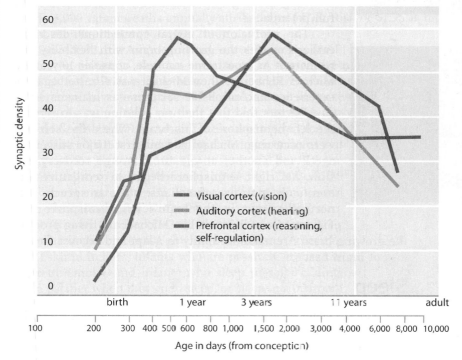

Figure 3.5 Synaptic Density in the Human Brain from Infancy to Adulthood

The graph shows the dramatic increase and then pruning in synaptic density for three regions of the brain: visual cortex, auditory cortex, and prefrontal cortex. Synaptic density is believed to be an important indication of the extent of connectivity between neurons.

Breast Feeding Versus Bottle-Feeding

For the first four to six months of life, human milk or an alternative formula is the baby's source of nutrients and energy. For years, debate has focused on whether breast feeding is better for the infant than bottle-feeding. The growing consensus is that breast feeding is better for the baby's health (Walker, 2010; Wilson, 2010). Since the 1970s, breast feeding by U.S. mothers has become widespread.

Human milk or an alternative formula is a baby's source of nutrients for the first four to six months. The growing consensus is that breast feeding is better for the baby's health, although in some cases there are reasons for new mothers to use formula. *Why is breast feeding strongly recommended by pediatricians?*

What are some of the benefits of breast feeding? During the first two years of life and beyond, these benefits include appropriate weight gain and lowered risk of childhood obesity (Lamb & others, 2010); lower risk of SIDS (Stuebe & Schwartz, 2010); fewer gastrointestinal infections (Garofalo, 2010); and fewer lower respiratory tract infections (Ip & others, 2009). However, in a large-scale review, no evidence for the benefits of breast feeding was found for children's cognitive development and cardiovascular functioning (Agency for Healthcare Quality and Research, 2007). Benefits of breast feeding for the mother include a lower incidence of breast cancer (Akbari & others, 2010) and a reduction in ovarian cancer (Stuebe & Schwartz, 2010).

Many health professionals have argued that breast feeding facilitates the development of an attachment bond between mother and infant (Britton, Britton, & Gronwaldt, 2006; Wittig & Spatz, 2008). However, a recent research review found that the positive effect of breast feeding on the mother-infant relationship is not supported by research (Jansen, de Weerth, & Riksen-Walraven, 2008). The review concluded that recommending breast feeding should not be based on its role in improving the mother-infant relationship but rather on its positive effects on infant and maternal health.

Are there circumstances when mothers should not breast feed? Yes: A mother should not breast feed if she (1) is infected with AIDS or any other infectious disease that can be transmitted through her milk, (2) has active tuberculosis, or (3) is taking any drug that may not be safe for the infant (Berlin, Paul, & Vesell, 2009; Gumbo & others, 2010).

Some women cannot breast feed their infants because of physical difficulties; others feel guilty if they terminate breast feeding early. Mothers also may worry that they are depriving their infants of important emotional and psychological benefits if they bottle-feed rather than breast feed. Some researchers have found, however, that there are no psychological differences between breast fed and bottle-fed infants (Ferguson, Harwood, & Shannon, 1987; Young, 1990).

A further issue in interpreting the benefits of breast feeding was underscored in a recent large-scale research review (Agency for Healthcare Quality and Research, 2007). While highlighting a number of benefits of breast feeding for children and mothers, the report issued a caution about research on breast feeding: None of the findings imply causality. Breast feeding versus bottle-feeding studies are correlational, not experimental, and women who breast feed tend to be wealthier, older, better educated, and likely more health-conscious than those who bottle-feed, which could explain why breast fed children are healthier.

Nutritional Needs

Individual differences among infants in terms of their nutrient reserves, body composition, growth rates, and activity patterns make it difficult to define actual nutrient needs (Schiff, 2009). However, because parents need guidelines,

nutritionists recommend that infants consume approximately 50 calories per day for each pound they weigh—more than twice an adult's requirement per pound.

A national study of more than 3,000 randomly selected 4- to 24-month-olds documented that many U.S. parents are feeding their babies too few fruits and vegetables and too much junk food (Fox & others, 2004). Up to one-third of the babies ate no vegetables and fruit; almost half of the 7- to 8-month-old babies were fed desserts, sweets, or sweetened drinks. By 15 months, French fries were the most common vegetables the babies ate.

In sum, adequate early nutrition is an important aspect of healthy development. To be healthy, children need a nurturant, supportive environment (Black & others, 2009). One individual who has stood out as an advocate of caring for children is T. Berry Brazelton, who is featured in "Careers in Life-Span Development."

dynamic systems theory The perspective on motor development that seeks to explain how motor behaviors are assembled for perceiving and acting.

CAREERS IN LIFE-SPAN DEVELOPMENT

T. Berry Brazelton, Pediatrician

T. Berry Brazelton is America's best-known pediatrician as a result of his numerous books, television appearances, and newspaper and magazine articles about parenting and children's health. He takes a family-centered approach to child development issues and communicates with parents in easy-to-understand ways.

Dr. Brazelton founded the Child Development Unit at Boston Children's Hospital and created the Brazelton Neonatal Behavioral Assessment Scale, a widely used measure of the newborn's health and well-being. He also has conducted a number of research studies on infants and children and has been president of the Society for Research in Child Development, a leading research organization.

T Berry Brazelton with a young child.

Motor Development

Meeting infants' nutritional needs help them to develop the strength and coordination required for motor development. How do infants develop their motor skills, and which skills do they develop when?

The Dynamic Systems View

According to **dynamic systems theory**, infants assemble motor skills for perceiving and acting; perception and action are coupled together (Adolph, Karasik, & Tamis-LeMonda, 2010; Thelen & Smith, 2006). In order to develop motor skills, infants must perceive something in the environment that motivates them to act, then use their perceptions to fine-tune their movements. Motor skills thus represent solutions to the infant's goals.

How is a motor skill developed, according to this theory? When infants are motivated to do something, they might create a new motor behavior. The new behavior is the result of many converging factors: the development of the nervous system, the body's physical properties and its possibilities for movement, the goal the child is motivated to reach, and environmental support for the skill. For example, babies will learn to walk only when their nervous system has matured sufficiently to allow them to control certain leg muscles, their legs have grown enough to support their weight, and they have decided they want to walk.

Mastering a motor skill requires the infant's active efforts to coordinate several components of the skill (Adolph & Joh, 2009). Infants explore and select possible solutions to the demands of a new task; they assemble adaptive patterns by modifying their current movement patterns. The first step, for example, occurs when the infant is motivated by a new challenge—such as the desire to cross a room—and initiates this task by taking a few stumbling steps. The infant then "tunes" these movements to make them smoother and more effective. The tuning is achieved through repeated cycles of action and perception of the consequences of that action. According to the dynamic systems view, even universal milestones, such as crawling, reaching, and walking, are learned through this process of adaptation: Infants modulate their movement patterns to fit a new task by exploring and selecting possible configurations (Thelen & Smith, 2006).

Thus, according to dynamic systems theory, motor development is not a passive process in which genes dictate the unfolding of a sequence of skills. Rather, the infant actively puts together a skill in order to achieve a goal within the constraints set by the infant's body and environment. Nature and nurture, the infant and the environment, are all working together as part of an ever-changing system (Adolph & Joh, 2009).

As we examine the course of motor development, we will describe how dynamic systems theory applies to some specific skills. First, though, let's examine how the story of motor development begins with reflexes.

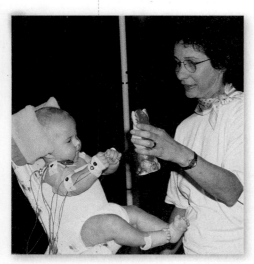

Esther Thelen is shown conducting an experiment to discover how infants learn to control their arms to reach and grasp for objects. A computer device is used to monitor the infant's arm movements and to track muscle patterns. Thelen's research is conducted from a dynamic systems perspective. *What is the nature of this perspective?*

Reflexes

The newborn is not completely helpless. Among other things, the newborn has some basic reflexes. *Reflexes* are built-in reactions to stimuli, and they govern the newborn's movements. Reflexes are genetically carried survival mechanisms that are automatic and involuntary. They allow infants to respond adaptively to their environment before they have had the opportunity to learn. For example, if immersed in water, the newborn automatically holds its breath and contracts its throat to keep water out.

Other important examples are the rooting and sucking reflexes. Both have survival value for newborn mammals, who must find a mother's breast to obtain nourishment. The *rooting reflex* occurs when the infant's cheek is stroked or the side of the mouth is touched. In response, the infant turns its head toward the side that was touched in an apparent effort to find something to suck. The *sucking reflex* occurs when newborns automatically suck an object placed in their mouth. This reflex enables newborns to get nourishment before they have associated a nipple with food.

Another example is the *Moro reflex,* which occurs in response to a sudden, intense noise or movement. When startled, the newborn arches its back, throws back its head, and flings out its arms and legs. Then the newborn rapidly closes its arms and legs. The Moro reflex is believed to be a way of grabbing for support while falling; it would have had survival value for our primate ancestors. An overview of the reflexes we have discussed, along with others, is presented in Figure 3.7.

gross motor skills Motor skills that involve large-muscle activities, such as walking.

Some reflexes—coughing, sneezing, blinking, shivering, and yawning, for example—persist throughout life. They are as important for the adult as they are for the infant. Other reflexes, though, disappear several months after birth, as the infant's brain matures and voluntary control over many behaviors develops. The rooting, sucking, and Moro reflexes, for example, all tend to disappear when the infant is 3 to 4 months old.

The movements of some reflexes eventually become incorporated into more complex, voluntary actions. One important example is the *grasping reflex,* which occurs when something touches the infant's palm. The infant responds by grasping tightly. By the end of the third month, the grasping reflex diminishes, and the infant shows a more voluntary grasp. For example, when an infant sees a mobile turning slowly above a crib, it may reach out and try to grasp it. As its motor development becomes smoother, the infant will grasp objects, carefully manipulate them, and explore their qualities.

Gross Motor Skills

Gross motor skills are skills that involve large-muscle activities, such as moving one's arms and walking. Newborn infants cannot voluntarily control their posture. Within a few weeks, though, they can hold their heads erect, and soon they can lift their heads while prone. By 2 months of age, babies can sit while supported on a lap or an infant seat, but they cannot sit independently until they are 6 or 7 months of age. Standing also develops gradually during the first year of life. By about 8 months of age, infants usually learn to pull themselves up and hold on to a chair, and by about 10 to 12 months of age they can often stand alone.

Locomotion and postural control are closely linked, especially in walking upright (Adolph & Joh, 2009). To walk upright, the baby must be able both to balance

Reflex	Stimulation	Infant's Response	Developmental Pattern
Blinking	Flash of light, puff of air	Closes both eyes	Permanent
Babinski	Sole of foot stroked	Fans out toes, twists foot in	Disappears after 9 months to 1 year
Grasping	Palms touched	Grasps tightly	Weakens after 3 months, disappears after 1 year
Moro (startle)	Sudden stimulation, such as hearing loud noise or being dropped	Startles, arches back, throws head back, flings out arms and legs and then rapidly closes them to center of body	Disappears after 3 to 4 months
Rooting	Cheek stroked or side of mouth touched	Turns head, opens mouth, begins sucking	Disappears after 3 to 4 months
Stepping	Infant held above surface and feet lowered to touch surface	Moves feet as if to walk	Disappears after 3 to 4 months
Sucking	Object touching mouth	Sucks automatically	Disappears after 3 to 4 months
Swimming	Infant put face down in water	Makes coordinated swimming movements	Disappears after 6 to 7 months
Tonic neck	Infant placed on back	Forms fists with both hands and usually turns head to the right (sometimes called the "fencer's pose" because the infant looks like it is assuming a fencer's position)	Disappears after 2 months

Figure 3.7 Infant Reflexes

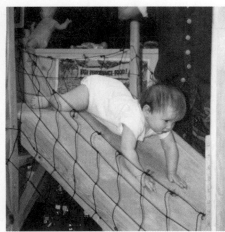

Newly crawling infant

Experienced walker

Figure 3.8 The Role of Experience in Crawling and Walking Infants' Judgments of Whether to Go Down a Slope

Karen Adolph (1997) found that locomotor experience rather than age was the primary predictor of adaptive responding on slopes of varying steepness. Newly crawling and walking infants could not judge the safety of the various slopes. With experience, they learned to avoid slopes where they would fall. When expert crawlers began to walk, they again made mistakes and fell, even though they had judged the same slope accurately when crawling. Adolph referred to this as the *specificity of learning* because it does not transfer across crawling and walking.

on one leg as the other is swung forward and to shift its weight from one leg to the other (Thelen & Smith, 2006).

Infants must also learn what kinds of places and surfaces are safe for crawling or walking (Adolph & Joh, 2009). Karen Adolph (1997) investigated how experienced and inexperienced crawling and walking infants go down steep slopes (see Figure 3.8). Newly crawling infants, who averaged about 8½ months in age, rather indiscriminately went down the steep slopes, often falling in the process (with their mothers next to the slope to catch them). After weeks of practice, the crawling babies became more adept at judging which slopes were too steep to crawl down and which ones they could navigate safely.

You might expect that babies who learned that a slope was too steep for crawling would know when they began walking whether a slope was safe. But Adolph's research indicated that newly walking infants could not judge the safety of the slopes. Only when infants became experienced walkers were they able to accurately match their skills with the steepness of the slopes. They rarely fell downhill, either refusing to go down the steep slopes or going down backward in a cautious manner. Experienced walkers assessed the situation perceptually—looking, swaying, touching, and thinking before they moved down the slope. With experience, both crawlers and walkers learned to avoid the risky slopes where they would fall, integrating perceptual information with the development of a new motor behavior. In this research, we again see the importance of perceptual-motor coupling in the development of motor skills.

The First Year: Milestones and Variations

Figure 3.9 summarizes important accomplishments in gross motor skills during the first year, culminating in the ability to walk easily. The timing of these milestones, especially the later ones, may vary by as much as two to four months, and experiences can modify the onset of these accomplishments. For example, since 1992, when pediatricians began recommending that parents put their infants to sleep on their backs, there has been an increase in the number of babies who skip the stage of crawling (Davis & others, 1998). Moreover, some infants do not follow the standard sequence of motor accomplishments. For example, many American infants never crawl on their belly or on their hands and knees. They may discover an idiosyncratic form of locomotion before walking, such as rolling, or not engage in any form of locomotion until they get upright. In the African Mali tribe, most infants do not crawl (Bril, 1999).

According to Karen Adolph and Sarah Berger (2005), "The old-fashioned view that growth and motor development reflect merely the age-related output of maturation is, at best, incomplete. Rather, infants acquire new skills with the help of their caregivers in a real-world environment of objects, surfaces, and planes" (p. 273).

Development in the Second Year

The motor accomplishments of the first year bring increasing independence, allowing infants to explore their environment more extensively and to initiate interaction with others more readily. In the second year of life, toddlers become more mobile as their motor skills are honed. Child development experts believe that motor activity during the second year is vital to the child's competent development

How Would You...?
As a human development and family studies professional, how would you advise parents who are concerned that their infant is one or two months behind the average gross motor milestones?

and that few restrictions, except those having to do with safety, should be placed on their adventures (Fraiberg, 1959).

By 13 to 18 months, toddlers can pull a toy attached to a string and use their hands and legs to climb up steps. By 18 to 24 months, toddlers can walk quickly or run stiffly for a short distance, balance on their feet in a squatting position while playing with objects on the floor, walk backward without losing their balance, stand and kick a ball without falling, stand and throw a ball, and jump in place.

Practice is especially important in learning to walk (Adolph & Joh, 2009). Infants and toddlers accumulate an immense number of experiences with balance and locomotion. For example, the average toddler traverses almost 40 football fields a day and has 15 falls an hour (Adolph, 2010).

fine motor skills Motor skills that involve more finely tuned movements, such as finger dexterity.

Fine Motor Skills

Whereas gross motor skills involve large-muscle activity, **fine motor skills** involve finely tuned movements. Grasping a toy, using a spoon, buttoning a shirt, or anything that requires finger dexterity demonstrates fine motor skills. At birth, infants have very little control over fine motor skills, but they do have many components of what will become finely coordinated arm, hand, and finger movements.

The onset of reaching and grasping marks a significant achievement in infants' ability to interact with their surroundings (van Hof, van der Kamp, & Savelsbergh, 2008). During the first two years of life, infants refine how they reach and grasp. Initially, they reach by moving the shoulder and elbow crudely, swinging toward an object. Later, when they reach for an object they move the wrist, rotate the hand, and coordinate the thumb and forefinger. An infant does not have to see his or her own hand in order to reach for an object (Clifton & others, 1993); rather, reaching is guided by cues from muscles, tendons, and joints.

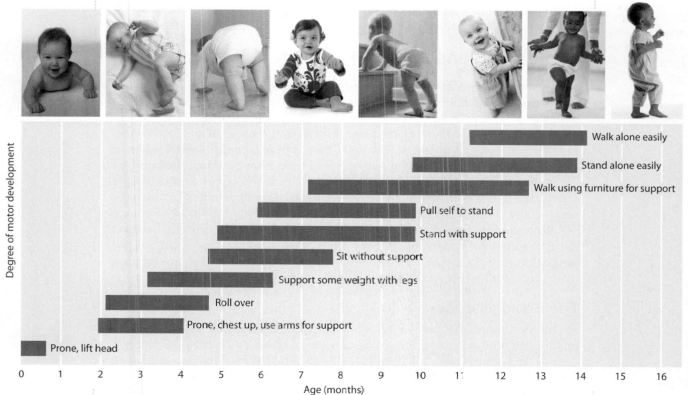

Figure 3.9 Milestones in Gross Motor Development
The horizontal red bars indicate the range in which most infants reach various milestones in gross motor development.

sensation The product of the interaction between information and the sensory receptors—the eyes, ears, tongue, nostrils, and skin.

perception The interpretation of what is sensed.

ecological view The view that perception functions to bring organisms in contact with the environment and to increase adaptation.

Experience plays a role in reaching and grasping (Needham, 2009). In one study, 3-month-old infants participated in play sessions wearing "sticky mittens"—"mittens with palms that stuck to the edges of toys and allowed the infants to pick up the toys" (Needham, Barrett, & Peterman, 2002, p. 279) (see Figure 3.10). Infants who participated in sessions with the mittens grasped and manipulated objects earlier in their development than a control group of infants who did not receive the "mitten" experience. The experienced infants looked at the objects longer, swatted at them more during visual contact, and were more likely to mouth the objects.

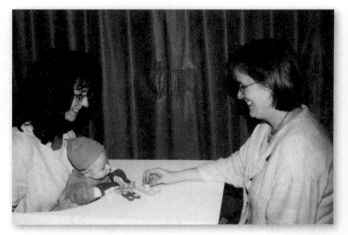

Figure 3.10 Infants' Use of "Sticky Mittens" to Explore Objects Amy Needham and her colleagues (2002) found that "sticky mittens" enhanced young infants' object exploration skills.

Just as infants need to exercise their gross motor skills, they also need to exercise their fine motor skills (Needham, 2009). Especially when they can manage a pincer grip, infants delight in picking up small objects. Many develop the pincer grip and begin to crawl at about the same time, and infants at this time pick up virtually everything in sight, especially on the floor, and put the objects in their mouth. Thus, parents need to be vigilant in monitoring objects within the infant's reach.

Sensory and Perceptual Development

Can a newborn see? If so, what can it perceive? How do sensations and perceptions develop? Can an infant put together information from two modalities, such as sight and sound? These are among the intriguing questions that we explore in this section.

Exploring Sensory and Perceptual Development

How does a newborn know that her mother's skin is soft rather than rough? How does a 5-year-old know what color his hair is? Infants and children "know" these things as a result of information that comes through the senses.

Sensation occurs when information interacts with sensory *receptors*—the eyes, ears, tongue, nostrils, and skin. The sensation of hearing occurs when waves of pulsating air are collected by the outer ear and transmitted through the bones of the inner ear to the auditory nerve. The sensation of vision occurs as rays of light contact the eyes, become focused on the retina, and are transmitted by the optic nerve to the visual centers of the brain.

Perception is the interpretation of what is sensed. The air waves that contact the ears might be interpreted as noise or as musical sounds, for example. The physical energy transmitted to the retina of the eye might be interpreted as a particular color, pattern, or shape, depending on how it is perceived.

The Ecological View

For the past several decades, much of the research on perceptual development in infancy has been guided by the ecological view proposed by Eleanor and James J. Gibson (E. Gibson, 1969, 1989, 2001; J. Gibson, 1966, 1979). They argue that we do not have to take bits and pieces of data from sensations and build up representations of the world in our minds. Instead, our perceptual system can select from the rich information that the environment itself provides.

According to the Gibsons' **ecological view**, we directly perceive information that exists in the world around us. Perception brings us into contact with the environment in order to interact with and adapt to it. Perception is designed for action. It gives people such information as when to duck, when to turn their bodies through a narrow passageway, and when to put their hands up to catch something.

visual preference method A method used to determine whether infants can distinguish one stimulus from another by measuring the length of time they attend to different stimuli.

Studying the Infant's Perception

Studying the infant's perception is not an easy task. Unlike most research participants, infants cannot write, type on a computer keyboard, or speak well enough to explain to an experimenter what their responses are to a given stimulus or condition. Yet scientists have developed several ingenious research methods to examine infants' sensory and perceptual development (Bendersky & Sullivan, 2007).

The Visual Preference Method Robert Fantz (1963), a pioneer in this effort, made an important discovery: Infants look at different things for different lengths of time. Fantz placed infants in a "looking chamber," which had two visual displays on the ceiling above the infant's head. An experimenter viewed the infant's eyes by looking through a peephole. If the infant was gazing at one of the displays, the experimenter could see the display's reflection in the infant's eyes. This allowed the experimenter to determine how long the infant looked at each display. Fantz (1963) found that infants only 2 days old would gaze longer at patterned stimuli (such as faces or concentric circles) than at red, white, or yellow discs. Similar results were found with infants 2 to 3 weeks old (see Figure 3.11). Fantz's research method—studying whether infants can distinguish one stimulus from another by measuring the length of time they attend to different stimuli—is referred to as the **visual preference method.**

Habituation and Dishabituation Another way in which researchers study infant perception is to present a stimulus (such as a sight or a sound) a number of times. If the infant decreases its response to the stimulus after several presentations, this indicates that the infant is no longer interested in the stimulus. If the researcher now presents a new stimulus, the infant's response will recover—indicating the infant could discriminate between the old and new stimuli.

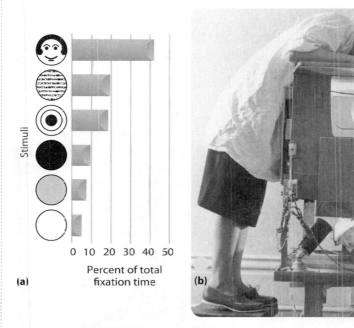

(a)

(b)

Figure 3.11 Fantz's Experiment on Infants' Visual Perception
(a) Infants 2 to 3 weeks old preferred to look at some stimuli more than others. In Fantz's experiment, infants preferred to look at patterns rather than at color or brightness. For example, they looked longer at a face, a piece of printed matter, or a bull's-eye than at red, yellow, or white discs. (b) Fantz used a "looking chamber" to study infants' perception of stimuli.

habituation Decreased responsiveness to a stimulus after repeated presentations of the stimulus.

dishabituation Recovery of a habituated response after a change in stimulation.

Habituation is the name given to decreased responsiveness to a stimulus after repeated presentations of the stimulus. **Dishabituation** is the recovery of a habituated response after a change in stimulation. Newborn infants can habituate to repeated sights, sounds, smells, or touches (Bendersky & Sullivan, 2007). Among the measures researchers use in habituation studies are sucking behavior (sucking behavior stops when the infant attends to a novel object), heart and respiration rates, and the length of time the infant looks at an object.

Equipment Technology can facilitate the use of most methods for investigating the infant's perceptual abilities. Videotape equipment allows researchers to investigate elusive behaviors. High-speed computers make it possible to perform complex data analysis in minutes. Other equipment records respiration, heart rate, body movement, visual fixation, and sucking behavior, which provide clues to what the infant is perceiving. Recently, researchers also are beginning to use tracking of an infant's eye movements as the infant follows a moving object to evaluate early visual ability (Franchak & others, 2010) (see Figure 3.12).

Figure 3.12 An Infant Wearing Eye-Tracking Headgear
Photo from Karen Adolph's laboratory at New York University.

Visual Perception

Psychologist William James (1890/1950) called the newborn's perceptual world a "blooming, buzzing confusion." A century later, we can safely say that he was wrong (Johnson, 2010a). Even the newborn perceives a world with some order.

Visual Acuity and Color

Just how well can infants see? The newborn's vision is estimated to be 20/600 on the well-known Snellen eye examination chart (Banks & Salapatek, 1983). This means that an object 20 feet away is only as clear to the newborn's eyes as it would be if it were viewed from a distance of 600 feet by an adult with normal vision (20/20). By 6 months of age, though, an *average* infant's vision is 20/40 (Aslin & Lathrop, 2008). Figure 3.13 shows a computer estimation of what a picture of a face looks like to an infant at different ages from a distance of about 6 inches.

Figure 3.13 Visual Acuity During the First Months of Life
The first three photographs represent a computer estimation of what a picture of a face looks like to a 1-month-old, a 3-month-old, and 1-year-old (which approximates that of an adult, shown in the fourth photograph).

The infant's color vision also improves. By 8 weeks, and possibly even by 4 weeks, infants can discriminate among some colors (Kelly, Borchert, & Teller, 1997).

Perceiving Patterns

Do infants recognize patterns? As we discussed earlier, Fantz (1963) found that even 2- to 3-week-old infants prefer to look at patterned displays rather than at nonpatterned displays. For example, they prefer to look at a normal human face rather than at one with scrambled features, and prefer to look at a bull's-eye target or black and white stripes rather than at a plain circle.

Perceiving Occluded Objects

Look around the context in which you are right now. You likely see that some objects are partly occluded by other objects that are in front of them—possibly a desk behind a chair, some books behind a computer, or a car parked behind a tree. Do infants perceive an object as complete when it is occluded by an object in front of it?

In the first two months of postnatal development, infants do not perceive occluded objects as complete, instead only perceiving what is visible (Johnson, 2010b). Beginning at about 2 months of age, infants develop the ability to perceive that occluded objects are whole (Slater, Field & Hernandez-Reif, 2007). How does perceptual completion develop? In Scott Johnson's (2004, 2010a, b, c) research, learning, experience, and self-directed exploration via eye movements play key roles in the development of perceptual completion in young infants.

Many objects that are occluded appear and disappear behind closer objects, as when you are walking down the street and see cars appear and disappear behind buildings. Infants develop the ability to track briefly occluded moving objects at about 3 to 5 months (Bertenthal, 2008). A recent study explored the ability of 5- to 9-month-old infants to track moving objects that disappeared gradually behind an occluded partition, disappeared abruptly, or imploded (shrank quickly) (Bertenthal, Longo, & Kenny, 2007) (see Figure 3.14). In this study, the infants were more likely to accurately track the moving object when it disappeared gradually rather than abruptly or imploding.

Depth Perception

To investigate whether infants have depth perception, Eleanor Gibson and Richard Walk (1960) constructed a miniature cliff with a drop-off covered by glass. They placed 6- to 12-month-old infants on the edge of this visual cliff and had their mothers coax them to crawl onto the glass (see Figure 3.15). Most infants would not crawl out on the glass, choosing instead to remain on the shallow side, an indication that they could perceive depth, according to Gibson and Walk. Although researchers do not know exactly how early in life infants can perceive depth, they have found that infants develop the ability to use binocular (two-eyed) cues to depth by about 3 to 4 months of age.

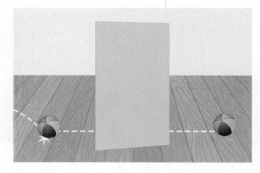

(a) Gradual occlusion

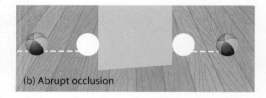

(b) Abrupt occlusion

(c) Implosion

Figure 3.14 Infants' Predictive Tracking of a Briefly Occluded Moving Ball

The top drawing shows the visual scene that infants experienced. At the beginning of each event, a multicolored ball bounded up and down with an accompanying bouncing sound, and then rolled across the floor until it disappeared behind the partition. Drawings (a), (b), and (c) show the three stimulus events the 5- to 9-month-old infants experienced: (a) *Gradual Occlusion*. The ball gradually disappears behind the right side of the occluding partition located in the center of the display. (b) *Abrupt Occlusion*. The ball abruptly disappears when it reaches the location of the white circle and then abruptly reappears 2 seconds later at the location of the second white circle on the other side of the occluding partition. (c) *Implosion*. The rolling ball quickly decreases in size as it approaches the occluding partition and rapidly increases in size as it reappears on the other side of the occluding partition.

Figure 3.15 Examining Infants' Depth Perception on the Visual Cliff

Eleanor Gibson and Richard Walk (1960) found that most infants would not crawl out on the glass, indicating that they had depth perception, according to Gibson and Walk. Critics have suggested that other factors, such as fear of heights, might account for the infants' reluctance to crawl across the visual cliff.

Other Senses

Other sensory systems besides vision also develop during infancy. In this section, we explore development in hearing, touch and pain, smell, and taste.

Hearing

During the last two months of pregnancy, as the fetus nestles in its mother's womb, it can hear sounds such as the mother's voice (Kisilevsky & others, 2009). In one study, researchers had sixteen women read *The Cat in the Hat* aloud to their fetuses during the last months of pregnancy (DeCasper & Spence, 1986). Then, shortly after their babies were born, the mothers read aloud either *The Cat in the Hat* or a story with a different rhyme and pace, *The King, the Mice and the Cheese* (which had not been read during prenatal development). The infants sucked on a nipple in a different way when the mothers read the two stories, suggesting that the infants recognized the pattern and tone of *The Cat in the Hat.*

Newborns are especially sensitive to human speech sounds (Saffran, Werker, & Warner, 2006). Just a few days after birth, newborns will turn to the sound of a familiar caregiver's voice.

What changes in hearing take place during infancy? They involve perception of a sound's loudness, pitch, and localization. Immediately after birth, infants cannot hear soft sounds quite as well as adults can; a stimulus must be louder for the newborn to hear it (Trehub & others, 1991). Infants are also less sensitive to the pitch of a sound than adults are. *Pitch* is the frequency of a sound; a soprano voice sounds high pitched, a bass voice low pitched. Infants are less sensitive to low-pitched sounds and are more likely to hear high-pitched sounds (Aslin, Jusczyk, & Pisoni, 1998). By 2 years of age, infants have considerably improved their ability to distinguish sounds with different pitches.

Even newborns can determine the general location from where a sound is coming, but by 6 months they are more proficient at *localizing* sounds, detecting their origins. The ability to localize sounds continues to improve in the second year (Saffran, Werker, & Warner, 2006).

Touch and Pain

Newborns respond to touch. A touch to the cheek produces a turning of the head; a touch to the lips produces sucking movements. Newborns can also feel pain (Gunnar & Quevado, 2007). The issue of an infant's pain perception often becomes important to parents who give birth to a son and need to consider whether he should be circumcised (Gunnar & Quevedo, 2007). An investigation by Megan Gunnar and her colleagues (1987) found that although newborn infant males cry intensely during circumcision, they also display amazing resiliency. Within several minutes after the surgery (which is performed without anesthesia), they can nurse and interact in a normal manner with their mothers.

Smell

Newborns can differentiate among odors (Doty & Shah, 2008). For example, the expressions on their faces indicate that they like the scents of vanilla and strawberry but do not like the scent of rotten eggs or fish (Steiner, 1979).

It may take time to develop other odor preferences, however. By the time they were 6 days old, breast-fed infants in one study showed a clear preference for smelling their mother's breast pad than a clean breast pad (MacFarlane, 1975).

When they were 2 days old they did not show this preference, indicating that they require several days of experience to recognize this scent.

Taste

Sensitivity to taste might be present even before birth (Doty & Shah, 2008). In one very early experiment, when saccharin was added to the amniotic fluid of a near-term fetus, swallowing increased (Windle, 1940). In another study, even at only 2 hours of age, babies made different facial expressions when they tasted sweet, sour, and bitter solutions (Rosenstein & Oster, 1988) (see Figure 3.16). At about 4 months, infants begin to prefer salty tastes, which as newborns they had found to be aversive (Harris, Thomas, & Booth, 1990).

Intermodal Perception

How do infants put all these stimuli together? Imagine yourself playing basketball or tennis. You are experiencing many visual inputs: the ball coming and going, other players moving around, and so on. However, you are experiencing many auditory inputs as well: the sound of the ball bouncing or being hit, the grunts and groans, and so on. There is good correspondence between much of the visual and auditory information: When you see the ball bounce, you hear a bouncing sound; when a player stretches to hit a ball, you hear a groan. When you look at and listen to what is going on, you do not experience just the sounds or just the sights; you put all these things together. You experience a unitary episode. This is **intermodal perception**, which involves integrating information from two or more sensory modalities, such as vision and hearing (Brenner & others, 2010; Walker & others, 2010).

Early, exploratory forms of intermodal perception exist even in newborns (Bahrick & Hollich, 2008). For example, newborns turn their eyes and their head toward the sound of a voice or rattle when the sound is maintained for several seconds (Clifton & others, 1981). Intermodal perception becomes sharper with experience in the first year of life (Bahrick & Hollich, 2008). In the first six months, infants have difficulty connecting sensory input from different modes (such as vision and sound), but in the second half of the first year they show an increased ability to make this connection mentally.

Nature, Nurture, and Perceptual Development

Now that we have discussed many aspects of perceptual development, let's explore one of developmental psychology's key issues as it relates to perceptual development: the nature-nurture issue. There has been a longstanding interest in how strongly infants' perception is influenced by nature or nurture (Aslin, 2009; Johnson, 2010a, b, c; Slater & others, 2010). In the field of perceptual development, those who emphasize nature are referred to as *nativists* and those who emphasize learning and experience are called *empiricists*.

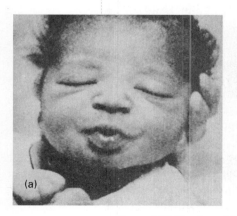
(a)

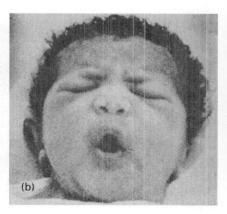
(b)

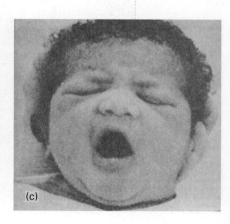
(c)

Figure 3.16 Newborns' Facial Responses to Basic Tastes
Facial expressions elicited by (a) a sweet solution (b) a sour solution and (c) a bitter solution.

In the nativist view, the ability to perceive the world in a competent, organized way is inborn or innate. At the beginning of our discussion of perceptual development, we examined the Gibsons' ecological view because it has played such a pivotal role in guiding research in perceptual development. This approach leans toward a nativist explanation of perceptual development because it holds that perception is direct and evolved over time to allow the detection of size and shape constancy, a three-dimensional world, intermodal perception, and so on early in infancy. However, the Gibsons' view is not entirely nativist because they emphasized that perceptual development involves distinctive features that are detected at different ages (Slater & others, 2010).

The Gibsons' ecological view is quite different from Piaget's constructivist view, which reflects an empiricist approach to explaining perceptual development. According to Piaget, much of perceptual development in infancy must await the development of a sequence of cognitive stages in which infants become able to construct more complex perceptual tasks. Thus, in Piaget's view the ability to perceive size and shape constancy, a three-dimensional world, intermodal perception, and so on develops later in infancy than the Gibsons envision.

Today it is clear that an extreme empiricist position on perceptual development is unwarranted. Much of early perception develops from innate (nature) capabilities, and the basic foundation of many perceptual abilities can be detected in newborns, whereas others unfold through maturation (Arterberry, 2008). However, as infants develop, environmental experiences (nurture) refine or calibrate many perceptual functions, and they may be the driving force behind some functions (Amos & Johnson, 2011). The accumulation of experience with and knowledge about their perceptual world contributes to infants' ability to perceive coherent perceptions of people and things (Slater & others, 2010). Thus, a full portrait of perceptual development includes the influence of nature, nurture, and a developing sensitivity to information (Arterberry, 2008).

Perceptual Motor Coupling

A central theme of the ecological approach is the interplay between perception and action. Action can guide perception, and perception can guide action. Only by moving one's eyes, head, hands, and arms and by moving from one location to another can an individual fully experience his or her environment and learn how to adapt to it. Thus, perception and action are coupled (Kim & Johnson, 2011).

Babies, for example, continually coordinate their movements with perceptual information to learn how to maintain balance, reach for objects in space, and move across various surfaces and terrains (Adolph & others, 2010; Thelen & Smith, 2006). They are motivated to move by what they perceive. Consider the sight of an attractive toy across the room. In this situation, infants must perceive the current state of their bodies and learn how to use their limbs to reach the toy. Although their movements at first are awkward and uncoordinated, babies soon learn to select patterns that are appropriate for reaching their goals.

Equally important is the other part of the perception-action coupling. That is, action educates perception (Adolph & others, 2010; Soska, Adolph, & Johnson, 2010). For example, watching an object while exploring it manually helps infants discover its texture, size, and hardness. Moving around in their environment teaches babies about how objects and people look

What characterizes perceptual motor coupling in infant development?

from different perspectives, or whether surfaces will support their weight. In short, infants perceive in order to move and move in order to perceive. Perceptual and motor development do not occur in isolation from each other but instead are coupled.

Cognitive Development

The competent infant not only develops motor and perceptual skills, but also develops cognitive skills. Our coverage of cognitive development in infancy focuses on Piaget's theory and sensorimotor stages as well as on how infants learn, remember, and conceptualize.

schemes In Piaget's theory, actions or mental representations that organize knowledge.

assimilation Piagetian concept of using existing schemes to deal with new information or experiences.

accommodation Piagetian concept of adjusting schemes to fit new information and experiences.

organization Piaget's concept of grouping isolated behaviors and thoughts into a higher-order, more smoothly functioning cognitive system.

Piaget's Theory

Piaget's theory is a general, unifying story of how biology and experience sculpt cognitive development. The Swiss child psychologist Jean Piaget thought that, just as our physical bodies have structures that enable us to adapt to the world, we build mental structures that help us to adapt to the world. *Adaptation* involves adjusting to new environmental demands. Piaget stressed that children actively construct their own cognitive worlds; information is not just poured into their minds from the environment. He sought to discover how children at different points in their development think about the world and how systematic changes in their thinking occur.

Processes of Development

What processes do children use as they construct their knowledge of the world? Piaget developed several concepts to answer this question.

Schemes According to Piaget (1954), as the infant or child seeks to construct an understanding of the world, the developing brain creates **schemes.** These are actions or mental representations that organize knowledge. In Piaget's theory, infants create behavioral schemes (physical activities), whereas toddlers and older children create mental schemes (cognitive activities) (Lamb, Bornstein, & Teti, 2002). A baby's schemes are structured by simple actions that can be performed on objects such as sucking, looking, and grasping. Older children's schemes include strategies and plans for solving problems.

Assimilation and Accommodation To explain how children use and adapt their schemes, Piaget offered two concepts: assimilation and accommodation. **Assimilation** occurs when children use their existing schemes to deal with new information or experiences. **Accommodation** occurs when children adjust their schemes to take new information and experiences into account.

Think about a toddler who has learned the word *car* to identify the family's car. The toddler might call all moving vehicles on roads "cars," including motorcycles and trucks; the child has assimilated these objects to his or her existing scheme. But the child soon learns that motorcycles and trucks are not cars and fine-tunes the category to exclude those vehicles. The child has accommodated the scheme.

Organization To make sense out of their world, said Piaget, children cognitively organize their experiences. **Organization**, in Piaget's theory, is the grouping of isolated behaviors and thoughts into a higher-order system. Continual refinement of this organization is an inherent part of development. A child who has only a vague idea about how to use a hammer may also have a vague idea about how to use other tools. After learning how to use each one, she relates these uses to one another, thereby organizing her knowledge.

equilibration A mechanism that Piaget proposed to explain how children shift from one stage of thought to the next.

sensorimotor stage The first of Piaget's stages, which lasts from birth to about 2 years of age; infants construct an understanding of the world by coordinating sensory experiences with motoric actions.

object permanence The Piagetian term for understanding that objects and events continue to exist, even when they cannot directly be seen, heard, or touched.

Equilibration and Stages of Development Assimilation and accommodation always take the child to a higher level, according to Piaget. In trying to understand the world, the child inevitably experiences cognitive conflict, or *disequilibrium*. That is, the child is constantly faced with inconsistencies and counterexamples to his or her existing schemes. For example, if a child believes that pouring water from a short, wide container into a tall, narrow container changes the amount of water in the container, the child might wonder where the "extra" water came from and whether there is actually more water to drink. This puzzle creates disequilibrium; and in Piaget's view the resulting search for equilibrium creates motivation for change. The child assimilates and accommodates, adjusting old schemes, developing new schemes, and organizing and reorganizing the old and new schemes. Eventually, the organization is fundamentally different from the old organization; it becomes a new way of thinking.

Equilibration is the name Piaget gave to this mechanism by which children shift from one stage of thought to the next. Equilibration does not, however, happen all at once. There is considerable movement between states of cognitive equilibrium and disequilibrium as assimilation and accommodation work in concert to produce cognitive change.

A result of these processes, according to Piaget, is that individuals go through four stages of development. A different way of understanding the world makes one stage more advanced than another. Cognition is *qualitatively* different in one stage compared with another. In other words, the way children reason at one stage is different from the way they reason at another stage. Here our focus is on Piaget's stage of infant cognitive development. In Chapters 5, 7, and 9, we explore the last three Piagetian stages.

The Sensorimotor Stage

The **sensorimotor stage** lasts from birth to about age 2. In this stage, infants construct an understanding of the world by coordinating sensory experiences (such as seeing and hearing) with physical, motor actions—hence the term "sensorimotor." At the beginning of this stage, newborns have little more than reflexes to work with. At the end of the sensorimotor stage, 2-year-olds can produce complex sensorimotor patterns and use primitive symbols. We first summarize Piaget's descriptions of how infants develop. Later we consider criticisms of his view.

Object permanence is the understanding that objects continue to exist even when they cannot be seen, heard, or touched. Acquiring the sense of object permanence is one of the infant's most important accomplishments, according to Piaget.

How could anyone know whether or not an infant had a sense of object permanence? The principal way in which object permanence is studied is by watching an infant's reaction when an interesting object disappears (see Figure 3.17). If infants search for the object, it is inferred that they know it continues to exist.

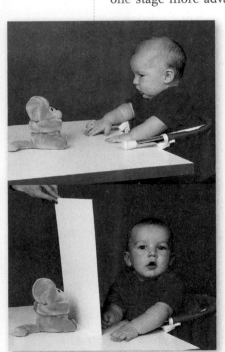

Figure 3.17 Object Permanence Piaget argued that object permanence is one of infancy's landmark cognitive accomplishments. For this 5-month-old boy, "out of sight" is literally out of mind. The infant looks at the toy monkey (*top*), but, when his view of the toy is blocked (*bottom*), he does not search for it. Several months later, he will search for the hidden toy monkey, reflecting the presence of object permanence.

Evaluating Piaget's Sensorimotor Stage Piaget opened up a new way of looking at infants with his view that their main task is to coordinate their sensory impressions with their motor activity. However, the infant's cognitive world is not as neatly packaged as Piaget portrayed it, and some of Piaget's explanations for the cause of change are debated. In the past several decades, there have been many research studies on infant development using sophisticated experimental techniques. Much of the new research suggests that Piaget's view of sensorimotor development needs to be modified (Aslin, 2010; Johnson, 2010a, b, c; Oakes & others. 2010).

A-not-B error (also called AB̄ error) is the term used to describe the tendency of infants to reach where an object was located earlier rather than where the object was last hidden. Older infants are less likely to make the A-not-B error because their concept of object permanence is more complete.

Researchers have found, however, that the A-not-B error does not show up consistently (Sophian, 1985). The evidence indicates that A-not-B errors are sensitive to the delay between hiding the object at B and the infant's attempt to find it (Diamond, 1985). Thus, the A-not-B error might be due to a failure in memory. Another explanation is that infants tend to repeat a previous motor behavior (Clearfield & others, 2006).

A number of theorists, such as Eleanor Gibson (1989) and Elizabeth Spelke (2004), have concluded that infants' perceptual abilities are highly developed very early in life. For example, intermodal perception—the ability to coordinate information from two or more sensory modalities, such as vision and hearing—develops much earlier than Piaget would have predicted (Spelke & Owsley, 1979).

Object permanence also develops earlier than Piaget thought. In his view, object permanence does not develop until approximately 8 to 9 months. However, research by Renée Baillargeon and her colleagues (2004; Baillargeon & others, 2009) documents that infants as young as 3 to 4 months expect objects to be *substantial* (in the sense that other objects cannot move through them) and *permanent* (in the sense that they continue to exist when they are hidden).

Today researchers believe that infants see objects as bounded, unitary, solid, and separate from their background, possibly at birth or shortly thereafter, but definitely by 3 to 4 months, much earlier than Piaget envisioned. Young infants still have much to learn about objects, but the world appears both stable and orderly to them.

In considering the big issue of whether nature or nature plays a more important role in infant development, Elizabeth Spelke (de Hevia & Spelke, 2010; Izard & Spelke, 2010; Spelke, 2004; Spelke & Kinzler, 2009) comes down clearly on the side of nature. Spelke endorses a **core knowledge approach**, which states that infants are born with domain-specific innate knowledge systems. Among these knowledge systems are those involving space, number sense, object permanence, and language (which we will discuss later in this chapter). Strongly influenced by evolution, the core knowledge domains are theorized to be "prewired" to allow infants to make sense of their world. After all, Spelke concludes, how could infants possibly grasp the complex world in which they live if they did not come into the world equipped with core sets of knowledge? In this approach, the innate core knowledge domains form a foundation around which more mature cognitive functioning and learning develop. The core knowledge approach argues that Piaget greatly underestimated the cognitive abilities of infants, especially young infants.

In criticizing the core knowledge approach, British developmental psychologist Mark Johnson (2008) says that the infants Spelke assesses in her research have already accumulated hundreds, and in some cases even thousands, of hours of experience in grasping what the world is about, which gives considerable room for the environment's role in the development of infant cognition (Highfield, 2008). According to Johnson (2008), infants likely come into the world with "soft biases to perceive and attend to different aspects of the environment, and to learn about the world in particular ways."

Many researchers conclude that Piaget was not specific enough about how infants learn about their world and that, like Spelke, infants are more competent than Piaget

Today researchers believe that infants see objects as bounded, unitary, solid, and separate from their background, possibly at birth or shortly thereafter, but definitely by 3 to 4 months, much earlier than Piaget envisioned. Young infants still have much to learn about objects, but the world appears both stable and orderly to them.

A-not-B error Also called AB̄ error, the term used to describe the tendency of infants to reach where an object was located earlier rather than where the object was last hidden.

core knowledge approach States that infants are born with domain-specific innate knowledge systems.

attention The focusing of mental resources on select information.

joint attention Process that occurs when individuals focus on the same object and an ability to track another's behavior is present, one individual directs another's attention, and reciprocal interaction is present.

thought they were (Amos & Johnson, 2011; Brenner & others, 2010; Schultz, 2010). As they have examined the specific ways in which infants learn, the field of infant cognition has become very specialized. If there is a unifying theme, it is that investigators in the field of infant development seek to understand more precisely how developmental changes in cognition take place, as well as the larger issue of nature and nurture (Aslin, 2009; Diamond, Casey, & Munakata, 2011). As they seek to identify more precisely the contributions of nature and nurture to infant development, researchers face the difficult task of determining whether the course of acquiring information, which is very rapid in some domains, is best accounted for by an innate set of biases (that is, core knowledge) or by the extensive input of environmental experiences to which the infant is exposed (Aslin, 2009).

Learning, Remembering, and Conceptualizing

In Chapter 1, we described the behavioral and social cognitive theories, as well as information-processing theory. These theories emphasize that cognitive development does not unfold in a stage-like process as Piaget proposed, but rather advances more gradually. In this section we explore what researchers using these approaches can tell us about how infants learn, remember, and conceptualize.

Conditioning

In Chapter 1, we discussed Skinner's theory of operant conditioning, in which the consequences of a behavior produce changes in the probability of the behavior's occurrence. Infants can learn through operant conditioning: If an infant's behavior is followed by a rewarding stimulus, the behavior is likely to recur.

Operant conditioning has been especially helpful to researchers in their efforts to determine what infants perceive. For example, infants will suck faster on a nipple when the sucking behavior is followed by a visual display, music, or a human voice (Rovee-Collier, 2007).

Carolyn Rovee-Collier (1987) has demonstrated that infants can retain information from the experience of being conditioned. In a characteristic experiment, Rovee-Collier places a 2½-month-old baby in a crib under an elaborate mobile (see Figure 3.18). She then ties one end of a ribbon to the baby's ankle and the other end to the mobile. Subsequently, she observes that the baby kicks and makes the mobile move. The movement of the mobile is the reinforcing stimulus (which increases the baby's kicking behavior) in this experiment. Weeks later, the baby is returned to the crib, but its foot is not tied to the mobile. The baby kicks, suggesting that it has retained the information that if it kicks a leg, the mobile will move.

Figure 3.18 The Technique Used in Rovee-Collier's Investigation of Infant Memory
In Rovee-Collier's experiment, operant conditioning was used to demonstrate that infants as young as 2½ months of age can retain information from the experience of being conditioned. *What did infants recall in Rovee-Collier's experiment?*

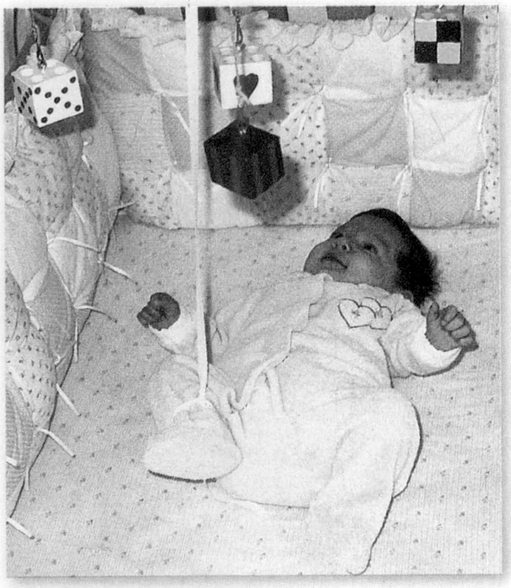

Attention

Attention, the focusing of mental resources on select information, improves cognitive processing on many tasks. Even newborns can detect a contour and fix their attention on it. Older infants scan patterns more thoroughly (Colombo, 2007). By 4 months, infants can selectively attend to an object.

Closely linked with attention are the processes of habituation and dishabituation, which we discussed earlier in this chapter. Infants' attention is strongly governed by novelty and habituation. When an object becomes familiar, attention becomes shorter, making infants more vulnerable to distraction (Kavsek, 2009; Richards, 2010).

Another aspect of attention that is an important aspect of infant development is **joint attention**, in which individuals focus on the same object or event. Joint attention requires (1) the ability to track

A father and his
infant engaging
in joint attention.
*What about this
photograph tells
you that joint
attention is occur-
ring? Why is joint
attention an
important aspect
of infant
development?*

How Would You...?
As a human
development and
family studies
professional, what
strategies would
likely help parents
improve an infant's
development of
attention?

another's behavior, such as following someone's gaze; (2) one person directing another's attention; and (3) reciprocal interaction. Early in infancy, joint attention usually involves a caregiver pointing or using words to direct an infant's attention. Emerging forms of joint attention occur at about 7 to 8 months, but it is not until 10 to 11 months that joint attention skills are frequently observed (Meltzoff & Brooks, 2009). By their first birthday, infants have begun to direct adults' attention to objects that capture their interest (Heimann & others, 2006).

Joint attention plays important roles in many aspects of infant development and considerably increases infants' ability to learn from other people (Colombo, Kapa, & Curtendale, 2010; Meltzoff & Brooks, 2009). Nowhere is this more apparent than in observations of interchanges between caregivers and infants as infants are learning language. When caregivers and infants frequently engage in joint attention, infants say their first word earlier and develop a larger vocabulary (Flom & Pick, 2003).

Imitation

Infant development researcher Andrew Meltzoff (2004, 2007) has conducted numerous studies of infants' imitative abilities. He sees infants' imitative abilities as biologically based, because infants can imitate a facial expression within the first few days after birth. He also emphasizes that the infant's imitative abilities do not resemble a hardwired response but rather involve flexibility and adaptability. In Meltzoff's observations of infants during the first 72 hours of life, the infants gradually displayed more complete imitation of an adult's facial expression, such as protruding the tongue or opening the mouth wide (see Figure 3.19).

Meltzoff (2007) concludes that infants don't blindly imitate everything they see and often make creative errors. He also argues that beginning at birth there is an interplay between learning by observing and learning by doing (Piaget emphasized learning by doing).

Not all experts on infant development accept Meltzoff's conclusion that newborns are capable of imitation. Some say that these babies were engaging in little more than automatic responses to a stimulus.

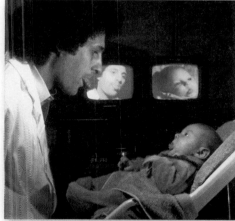

Figure 3.19 Infant Imitation
Infant development researcher Andrew Meltzoff protrudes his tongue in an attempt to get the infant to imitate his behavior. *How do Meltzoff's findings about imitation compare with Piaget's descriptions of infants' abilities?*

deferred imitation Imitation that occurs after a delay of hours or days.

memory A central feature of cognitive development, pertaining to all situations in which an individual retains information over time.

implicit memory Memory without conscious recollection; involves skills and routine procedures that are automatically performed.

explicit memory Memory of facts and experiences that individuals consciously know and can state.

Meltzoff (2005) has also studied **deferred imitation**, which occurs after a time delay of hours or days. Piaget held that deferred imitation does not occur until about 18 months. Meltzoff's research suggested that it occurs much earlier. In one study, Meltzoff (1988) demonstrated that 9-month-old infants could imitate actions—such as pushing a recessed button in a box, which produced a beeping sound—that they had seen performed 24 hours earlier.

Memory

Meltzoff's studies of deferred imitation suggest that infants have another important cognitive ability: **memory,** which involves the retention of information over time. Sometimes information is retained only for a few seconds, and at other times it is retained for a lifetime. What can infants remember, and when?

Some researchers, such as Rovee-Collier (2007), have concluded that infants as young as 2 to 6 months can remember some experiences through 1½ to 2 years of age. However, critics such as Jean Mandler (2000), a leading expert on infant cognition, argue that the infants in Rovee-Collier's experiments are displaying only implicit memory. **Implicit memory** refers to memory without conscious recollection—memories of skills and routine procedures that are performed automatically. In contrast, **explicit memory** refers to conscious memory of facts and experiences.

When people think about memory, they are usually referring to explicit memory. Most researchers find that babies do not show explicit memory until the second half of the first year (Bauer, 2009). Explicit memory improves substantially during the second year of life (Bauer, 2009). In one longitudinal study, infants were assessed several times during their second year (Bauer & others, 2000). The older infants showed more accurate memory and required fewer prompts to demonstrate their memory than did younger infants. Figure 3.20 summarizes how long infants of different ages can remember information (Bauer, 2009). As indicated in Figure 3.20, researchers have documented that 6-month-olds can remember information for 24 hours but by 20 months infants can remember information they encountered 12 months earlier.

Let's examine another aspect of memory. Do you remember your third birthday party? Probably not. Most adults can remember little, if anything, from the first 3 years of their life. This is called *infantile* or *childhood amnesia*. The few memories that adults are able to report of their life at age 2 or 3 are at best very sketchy (Fivush, 2011; Sabbagh, 2009). Moreover, even by elementary-school age, children have lost most memories of their early childhood years (Newcombe, 2008).

What is the cause of infantile amnesia? One reason older children and adults have difficulty recalling events from their infant and early childhood years is that during these years the prefrontal lobes of the brain are immature, and this area of the brain is believed to play an important role in storing memories of events (Diamond, Casey, & Munakata, 2011).

In sum, most of young infants' conscious memories appear to be rather fragile and short-lived, although their implicit memory of perceptual-motor actions can be substantial (Bauer, 2009).

Concept Formation and Categorization

Along with attention, imitation, and memory, concepts are a key aspect of infants' cognitive development (Madole, Oakes, & Rakison, 2010; Quinn & others, 2010). To understand what concepts are, we first have to define *categories:* they are groups of objects, events, and characteristics based on common properties. *Concepts* are ideas about what categories represent, or, said another way, the sort of

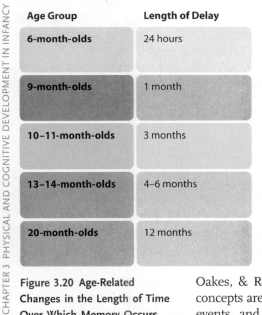

Age Group	Length of Delay
6-month-olds	24 hours
9-month-olds	1 month
10–11-month-olds	3 months
13–14-month-olds	4–6 months
20-month-olds	12 months

Figure 3.20 Age-Related Changes in the Length of Time Over Which Memory Occurs

thing we think category members are. Concepts and categories help us to simplify and summarize information. Without concepts, you would see each object and event as unique; you would not be able to make any generalizations.

Do infants have concepts? Yes, they do, although we do not know just how early concept formation begins (Quinn & others, 2010). Using habituation experiments like those described earlier in the chapter, some researchers have found that infants as young as 3 months of age can group together objects with similar appearances (Quinn & others, 2009). This research capitalizes on the knowledge that infants are more likely to look at a novel object than at a familiar one. For example, in a characteristic study, young infants are shown a series of photographs of different types of cats in pairs (Quinn & Eimas, 1996). As they are shown more pictures of cats, they habituate to the animals, looking at them less and less. Then, after seeing a series of cats paired in photographs, when they are shown a photograph of a cat paired with a photograph of a dog, they take a longer look at the dog, indicating an ability to group together objects characterized by similar properties.

Figure 3.21 Categorization in 9- to 11-Month-Olds
These are the stimuli used in the study that indicated 9- to 11-month-old infants categorized birds as animals and airplanes as vehicles even though the objects were perceptually similar (Mandler & McDonough, 1993).

Jean Mandler (2009) argues that these early categorizations are best described as *perceptual categorization*. That is, the categorizations are based on similar perceptual features of objects, such as size, color, and movement, as well as parts of objects, such as legs for animals. Mandler (2004) concludes that it is not until about 7 to 9 months that infants form *conceptual* categories rather than just making perceptual discriminations between different categories. In one study of 9- to 11-month-olds, infants classified birds as animals and airplanes as vehicles even though the objects were perceptually similar—airplanes and birds with their wings spread (Mandler & McDonough, 1993) (see Figure 3.21).

Further advances in categorization occur in the second year of life (Booth, 2006). Many infants' "first concepts are broad and global in nature, such as 'animal' or 'indoor thing.' Gradually, over the first two years these broad concepts become more differentiated into concepts such as 'land animal,' then 'dog,' or to 'furniture,' then 'chair'" (Mandler, 2006, p. 1).

In sum, the infant's advances in processing information—through attention, memory, imitation, and concept formation—is much richer, more gradual and less stage-like, and occurs earlier than was envisioned by earlier theorists (Diamond, Casey, & Munakata, 2011; Oakes & others, 2010). As leading infant researcher Jean Mandler (2004) concluded, "The human infant shows a remarkable degree of learning power and complexity in what is being learned and in the way it is represented" (p. 304).

How Would You...?
As an educator, how would you talk with parents about the importance of concept development in their infants?

Language Development

In 1799, villagers in the French town of Aveyron observed a nude boy running through the woods and captured him. Known as the Wild Boy of Aveyron, he was judged to be about 11 years old and believed to have lived in the woods alone for six years (Lane, 1976). When found, he made no effort to communicate, and he never did learn to communicate effectively.

Sadly, a modern-day wild child was discovered in Los Angeles in 1970. Despite intensive intervention, the child, named Genie by researchers, has never acquired more than a primitive form of language. Both of these cases—the Wild Boy of Aveyron and Genie—raise questions about the biological and environmental

language A form of communication, whether spoken, written, or signed, that is based on a system of symbols. Language consists of the words used by a community and the rules for varying and combining them.

infinite generativity The ability to produce an endless number of meaningful sentences using a finite set of words and rules.

determinants of language, topics that we also examine later in the chapter. First, though, we need to define language.

Defining Language

Language is a form of communication—whether spoken, written, or signed—that is, based on a system of symbols. Language consists of the words used by a community and the rules for varying and combining them. All human languages have some common characteristics, such as organizational rules and infinite generativity (Berko Gleason, 2009). Rules describe the way the language works; **infinite generativity** is the ability to produce an endless number of meaningful sentences using a finite set of words and rules.

How Language Develops

Whatever language they learn, infants all over the world follow a similar path in language development. What are some key milestones in this development?

Figure 3.22 From Universal Linguist to Language-Specific Listener

In Patricia Kuhl's research laboratory, babies listen to tape-recorded voices that repeat syllables. When the sounds of the syllables change, the babies quickly learn to look at the bear. Using this technique, Kuhl has demonstrated that babies are universal linguists until about 6 months of age, but in the next six months become language-specific listeners. *Does Kuhl's research give support to the view that either "nature" or "nurture" is the source of language acquisition?*

Babbling and Gestures

Babies actively produce sounds from birth onward. The effect of these early communications is to attract attention. Babies' sounds and gestures go through the following sequence during the first year:

- *Crying.* Babies cry even at birth. Crying can signal distress, but as we will discuss in Chapter 6, there are different types of cries that signal different things.

- *Cooing.* Babies first coo at about 2 to 4 months. Coos are gurgling sounds that are made in the back of the throat and usually express pleasure during interaction with the caregiver.

- *Babbling.* In the middle of the first year, babies babble—that is, they produce strings of consonant-vowel combinations such as "ba, ba, ba, ba."

- *Gestures.* Infants start using gestures, such as showing and pointing, at about 8 to 12 months (Goldin-Meadow, 2010). They may wave bye-bye, nod to mean "yes," and show an empty cup to want more milk. A recent study found that parents in high socio-economic status (SES) families were more likely to use gestures when communicating with their 14-month-old infants (Rowe & Goldin-Meadow, 2009). Further, the infants' use of gestures at 14 months in high-SES families was linked to a larger vocabulary at 54 months.

Recognizing Language Sounds

Long before they begin to learn words, infants can make fine distinctions among the sounds of a language (Stoel-Gammon & Sosa, 2010). In Patricia Kuhl's (2000, 2009) research, *phonemes* (the basic sound units of a language) from languages all over the world are piped through a speaker for infants to hear (see Figure 3.22). A box with a toy bear in it is placed where the infant can see it. A string of identical syllables is played; then the syllables are changed (for example, *ba ba ba ba,* and then *pa pa pa pa*). If the infant turns its head when the syllables change, the box lights up and the bear dances and drums, rewarding the infant for noticing the change.

Kuhl's research has demonstrated that from birth up to about 6 months, infants are "citizens of the world": They can tell when sounds change most of the time no matter what language the syllables come from. But over the next six months, infants get even better at perceiving changes in sounds from their "own" language, the one their parents speak, and gradually lose the ability to recognize differences that are not important in their own language (Kuhl, 2009).

First Words

Infants understand words before they can produce or speak them (Pan & Uccelli, 2009). For example, as early as 5 months many infants recognize their name. However, the infant's first spoken word, a milestone eagerly anticipated by every parent, usually doesn't occur until 10 to 15 months of age and at an average of about 13 months. Yet long before babies say their first words, they have been communicating with their parents, often by gesturing and using their own special sounds. The appearance of first words is a continuation of this communication process (Berko Gleason, 2009).

A child's first words include those that name important people (*dada*), familiar animals (*kitty*), vehicles (*car*), toys (*ball*), food (*milk*), body parts (*eye*), clothes (*hat*), household items (*clock*), and greeting terms (*bye*). Children often express various intentions with their single words, so that "cookie" might mean, "That's a cookie" or "I want a cookie."

As indicated earlier, children understand their first words earlier than they speak them. On the average, infants understand about 50 words at about 13 months, but they can't say this many words until about 18 months. Thus, in infancy *receptive vocabulary* (words the child understands) considerably exceeds *spoken vocabulary* (words the child uses).

The infant's spoken vocabulary rapidly increases once the first word is spoken (Waxman, 2009). Whereas the average 13-month-old can speak about 50 words, a 2-year-old can speak about 200 words. This rapid increase in vocabulary that begins at approximately 18 months is called the *vocabulary spurt* (Bloom, Lifter, & Broughton, 1985).

Like the timing of a child's first word, the timing of the vocabulary spurt varies (Dale & Goodman, 2004). Figure 3.23 shows the range for these two language milestones in 14 children. On average, these children said their first word at 13 months and had a vocabulary spurt at 19 months. However, the ages for the first word of individual children varied from 10 to 17 months and, for their vocabulary spurt, from 13 to 25 months.

Children sometimes overextend or underextend the meanings of the words they use (Woodward & Markman, 1998). *Overextension* is the tendency to apply a word to objects that are inappropriate for the word's meaning. For example, children at first may say "*dada*" not only for "father" but also for other men, strangers, or boys. With time, overextensions decrease and eventually disappear. *Underextension* is the tendency to apply a word too narrowly; it occurs when children fail to use a word to name a relevant event or object. For example, a child might use the word *boy* to describe a 5-year-old neighbor but not apply the word to a male infant or to a 9-year-old male.

Two-Word Utterances

By the time children are 18 to 24 months of age, they usually produce two-word utterances. To convey meaning with just two words, the child relies heavily on gesture, tone, and context. The wealth of meaning

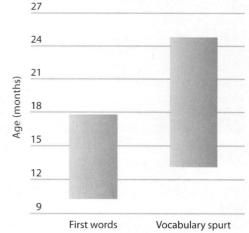

Figure 3.23 Variation in Language Milestones

What are some possible explanations for variations in the timing of these milestones?

telegraphic speech The use of short and precise words without grammatical markers such as articles, auxiliary verbs, and other connectives.

children can communicate with a two-word utterance includes the following (Slobin, 1972): identification—"See doggie"; location—"Book there"; repetition—"More milk"; negation—"Not wolf"; possession—"My candy"; attribution—"Big car"; and question—"Where ball?" These examples are from children whose first language is English, German, Russian, Finnish, Turkish, or Samoan.

Notice that two-word utterances omit many parts of speech and are remarkably succinct. In fact, in every language a child's first combinations of words have this economical quality; they are telegraphic. **Telegraphic speech** is the use of short, precise words without grammatical markers such as articles, auxiliary verbs, and other connectives. Telegraphic speech is not limited to two words; "Mommy give ice cream" and "Mommy give Tommy ice cream" are also examples of telegraphic speech.

Around the world, young children learn to speak in two-word utterances, in most cases, at about 18 to 24 months of age. *What are some examples of these two-word utterances?*

Typical Age	Language Milestones
Birth	Crying
2 to 4 months	Cooing begins
5 months	Understands first word
6 months	Babbling begins
7 to 11 months	Change from universal linguist to language-specific listener
8 to 12 months	Uses gestures, such as showing and pointing Comprehension of words appears
13 months	First word spoken
18 months	Vocabulary spurt starts
18 to 24 months	Uses two-word utterances Rapid expansion of understanding of words

Figure 3.24 Some Language Milestones in Infancy

Despite great variations in the language input received by infants, around the world they follow a similar path in learning to speak.

Biological and Environmental Influences

We have discussed a number of language milestones in infancy; Figure 3.24 summarizes the time at which infants typically reach these milestones. But what makes this amazing development possible? Everyone who uses language in some way "knows" its rules and has the ability to create an infinite number of words and sentences. Where does this knowledge come from? Is it the product of biology, or is language learned and influenced by experiences?

Biological Influences

The ability to speak and understand language requires a certain vocal apparatus as well as a nervous system with certain capabilities. The nervous system and vocal apparatus of humans' predecessors changed over hundreds of thousands, or millions, of years. With advances in the nervous system and vocal structures, *Homo sapiens* went beyond the grunting and shrieking of other animals to develop speech. Although estimates vary, many experts believe that humans acquired language about 100,000 years ago, which in evolutionary time represents a very recent acquisition. It gave humans an enormous edge over other animals and increased the chances of human survival.

Some language scholars view the remarkable similarities in how children acquire language all over the world as strong evidence that language has a biological basis. There is evidence that particular regions of the brain are predisposed to be used for language (Shafer & Garrido-Nag, 2010). Two regions involved in language were first discovered in studies of brain-damaged individuals: *Broca's area,* an area in the left frontal lobe of the brain that is involved in producing words; and

Wernicke's area, a region of the brain's left hemisphere that is involved in language comprehension (see Figure 3.25). Damage to either of these areas produces types of *aphasia*, a loss or impairment of language processing. Individuals with damage to Broca's area have difficulty producing speech but can comprehend what others say; those with damage to Wernicke's area have poor comprehension and often produce fluent but nonsensical speech.

Linguist Noam Chomsky (1957) proposed that humans are biologically "prewired" to learn language at a certain time and in a certain way. He said that children are born into the world with a **language acquisition device (LAD)**, a biological endowment that enables the child to detect the various features and rules of language. Children are prepared by nature with the ability to detect the sounds of language, for example, and follow linguistic rules such as those governing how to form plurals and ask questions.

Chomsky's LAD is a theoretical construct, not a physical part of the brain. Is there evidence for the existence of a LAD? Supporters of the LAD concept cite the uniformity of language milestones across languages and cultures, evidence that children create language even in the absence of well-formed input, and the importance of language's biological underpinnings. But as we will see, critics argue that even if infants have something like a LAD, it cannot explain the whole story of language acquisition.

Environmental Influences

Decades ago, behaviorists opposed Chomsky's hypothesis and argued that language represents nothing more than chains of responses acquired through reinforcement (Skinner, 1957). A baby happens to babble "Ma-ma"; Mama rewards the baby with hugs and smiles; the baby says "Mama" more and more frequently. Bit by bit, said the behaviorists, the baby's language is built up in this way. According to behaviorists, language is a complex learned skill, much like playing the piano or dancing.

The behavioral view of language learning has several problems. First, it does not explain how people create novel sentences—sentences they have never heard or spoken before. Second, children learn the syntax of their native language even if they are not reinforced for doing so. Social psychologist Roger Brown (1973) spent long hours observing parents and their young children. He found that parents did not directly or explicitly reward or correct the syntax of most children's utterances. That is, parents did not say "good," "correct," "right," "wrong," and so on. Parents also did not offer direct corrections such as, "You should say 'two shoes,' not 'two shoe.'" However, as we will see shortly, many parents do expand on their young children's grammatically incorrect utterances and recast many of those that contain grammatical errors (Clark, 2009).

The behavioral view is no longer considered a viable explanation of how children acquire language. But a great deal of research describes ways in which children's environmental experiences influence their language skills (Berko Gleason & Ratner, 2009). Many language experts argue that a child's experiences, the particular language to be learned, and the context in which learning takes place can strongly influence language acquisition (Goldfield & Snow, 2009).

Language is not learned in a social vacuum. Most children are bathed in language from a very early age (Sacks, 2009). The support

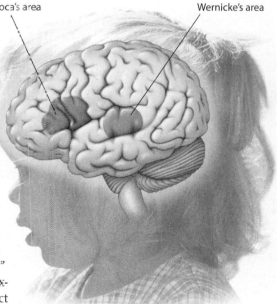

language acquisition device (LAD) Chomsky's term that describes a biological endowment enabling the child to detect the features and rules of language, including phonology, syntax, and semantics.

How Would You...?

As a social worker, how would you intervene in a family in which a child like Genie (described on page 93) has lived in social isolation for years?

Broca's area

Wernicke's area

Figure 3.25 Broca's Area and Wernicke's Area

Broca's area is located in the frontal lobe of the brain's left hemisphere, and it is involved in the control of speech. Wernicke's area is a portion of the left hemisphere's temporal lobe that is involved in understanding language.

child-directed speech Language spoken in a higher pitch than normal with simple words and sentences.

and involvement of caregivers and teachers greatly facilitate a child's language learning (Otto, 2010; Wagner, 2010). For example, one study found that when mothers immediately smiled and touched their 8-month-old infants after they babbled, the infants subsequently made more complex speech-like sounds than when mothers responded to their infants in a random manner (Goldstein, King, & West, 2003) (see Figure 3.26).

In particular, researchers have found that a child's vocabulary development is linked to the family's socioeconomic status and the type of talk that parents direct to the child. Betty Hart and Todd Risley (1995) observed the language environments of children whose parents were professionals and children whose parents were on welfare. Compared with the professional parents, the parents on welfare talked much less to their young children, talked less about past events, and provided less elaboration. The children of the professional parents had a much larger vocabulary at 36 months than the children of the welfare parents did. Keep in mind, though, that individual variations characterize language development and that some welfare parents do spend considerable time talking to their children.

One intriguing component of the young child's linguistic environment is **child-directed speech**, language spoken in a higher pitch than normal, using simple words and sentences (Clark, 2009). It is hard for most adults to use child-directed speech when not in the presence of a baby. As soon as adults start talking to a baby, though, they often shift into child-directed speech. Much of this is automatic and something most parents are not aware they are doing. Even 4-year-olds speak in simpler ways to 2-year-olds than to their 4-year-old friends. Child-directed speech serves the important function of capturing the infant's attention and maintaining communication.

Adults often use strategies other than child-directed speech to enhance the child's acquisition of language, including recasting, expanding, and labeling. *Recasting* is rephrasing something the child has said, perhaps turning it into a question or restating the child's immature utterance in the form of a fully grammatical sentence. For example, if the child says, "The dog was barking," the adult can respond by asking, "When was the dog barking?" Effective recasting lets the child indicate an interest and then elaborates on that interest. *Expanding* is restating, in a linguistically sophisticated form, what a child has said. For example, a child says, "Doggie eat," and the parent replies, "Yes, the doggie is eating." *Labeling* is identifying the names of objects. Young children are forever being asked to identify the names of objects. Roger Brown (1958) called this "the original word game" and claimed that much of a child's early vocabulary is motivated by this adult pressure to identify the words associated with objects.

Figure 3.26 Social Interaction and Babbling

One study focused on two groups of mothers and their 8-month-old infants (Goldstein, King, & West, 2003). One group of mothers was instructed to smile and touch their infants immediately after the babies cooed and babbled; the other group was also told to smile and touch their infants but in a random manner, unconnected to sounds the infants made. The infants whose mothers immediately responded in positive ways to their babbling subsequently made more complex, speechlike sounds, such as "da" and "gu."

Parents use these strategies naturally and in meaningful conversations. Parents do not (and should not) use any deliberate method to teach their children to talk, even with children who are slow in learning language. Children usually benefit when parents guide their discovery of language rather than overloading them; "following in order to lead"

How Would You...?
As a human development and family studies professional, how would you encourage parents to talk with their infants and toddlers?

helps a child learn language. If children are not ready to take in some information, they are likely to indicate this, perhaps by turning away. Thus, giving the child more information is not always better.

Infants toddlers, and young children benefit when adults read books to and with them, a process called *shared reading* (DeLoache & Ganea, 2009). In one study, reading daily to children at 14 to 24 months was positively related to the children's language and cognitive development at 36 months (Raikes & others, 2006).

Researchers find that the encouragement of language development, not drill and practice, is the key. Language development is not a simple matter of imitation and reinforcement. What are some effective ways in which parents can facilitate children's language development?

What characterizes shared reading in lives of infants, toddlers, and young children?

An Interactionist View

If language acquisition depended only on biology, Genie and the Wild Boy of Aveyron (discussed earlier in the chapter) should have talked without difficulty. A child's experiences do influence language acquisition (Goldfield & Snow, 2009). But we have seen that language also has strong biological foundations (Shafer & Garrido-Nag, 2010); no matter how much you converse with a dog, it won't learn to talk. Unlike dogs, children are biologically prepared to learn language. Children all over the world acquire language milestones at about the same time and in about the same order. An interactionist view emphasizes that both biology and experience contribute to language development (Gathercole & Hoff, 2010).

This interaction of biology and experience can be seen in variations in the acquisition of language. Children vary in their ability to acquire language, and this variation cannot be readily explained by differences in environmental input alone. For children who are slow in developing language skills, however, opportunities to talk and be talked with are important. Children whose parents provide them with a rich verbal environment show many positive benefits. Parents who pay attention to what their children are trying to say, expand their children's utterances, read to them, and label things in the environment, are providing valuable, if unintentional, benefits (Berko Gleason, 2009).

Summary

Physical Growth and Development in Infancy

- Most development follows cephalocaudal and proximodistal patterns.

- Physical growth is rapid in the first year but rate of growth slows in the second year.

- Dramatic changes characterize the brain's development in the first two years.

- Newborns usually sleep 16 to 17 hours a day, but by 4 months many American infants approach adult-like sleeping patterns. Sudden infant death syndrome (SIDS) is a condition that occurs when a sleeping infant suddenly stops breathing and dies without an apparent cause.

- Infants need to consume about 50 calories per day for each pound they weigh. The growing consensus is that breast feeding is more beneficial than bottle-feeding.

Motor Development

- Dynamic systems theory seeks to explain how motor behaviors are assembled for perceiving and acting. This theory emphasizes that experience plays an important role in motor development, and that perception and action are coupled.

- Reflexes—automatic movements—govern the newborn's behavior.

- Key gross motor skills, which involve large-muscle activities, developed during infancy include control of posture and walking.

- Fine motor skills involve finely tuned movements. The onset of reaching and grasping marks a significant accomplishment, and this becomes more refined during the first two years of life.

Sensory and Perceptual Development

- Sensation occurs when information interacts with sensory receptors. Perception is the interpretation of sensation.

- Created by the Gibsons, the ecological view states that perception brings people into contact with the environment to interact with and adapt to it.

- The infant's visual acuity increases dramatically in the first year of life. By 3 months of age, infants show size and shape constancy. In Gibson and Walk's classic study, infants had depth perception as young as 6 months of age.

- The fetus can hear several weeks prior to birth. Just after being born, infants can hear but their sensory threshold is higher than that of adults. Newborns can respond to touch, feel pain, differentiate among odors, and may be sensitive to taste at birth.

- A basic form of intermodal perception is present in newborns and sharpens over the first year of life.

- In perception, nature advocates are referred to as nativists and nurture proponents are called empiricists. A strong empiricist approach is unwarranted. A full account of perceptual development includes the roles of nature, nurture, and the infant's developing sensitivity to information.

Cognitive Development

- In Piaget's theory, children construct their own cognitive worlds, building mental structures to adapt to their world. Schemes, assimilation and accommodation, organization, and equilibration are key processes in Piaget's theory. According to Piaget, there are four qualitatively different stages of thought. In sensorimotor thought, the first of Piaget's four stages, the infant organizes and coordinates sensations with physical movements. The stage lasts from birth to about 2 years of age. One key accomplishment of this stage is object permanence. In the past decades, revisions of Piaget's view have been proposed based on research.

- A different approach than Piaget's focuses on infants' operant conditioning, attention, imitation, memory, and concept formation.

Language Development

- Rules describe the way language works. Language is characterized by infinite generativity.

- Infants reach a number of milestones in development, including first words and two-word utterances.

- Chomsky argues that children are born with the ability to detect basic features and rules of language. The behavioral view has not been supported by research. How much of language is biologically determined, and how much depends on interaction with others, is a subject of debate among linguists and psychologists. However, all agree that both biological capacity and relevant experience are necessary. Parents should talk extensively with an infant, especially about what the baby is attending to.

Key Terms

Socioemotional Development in Infancy

4

Stories of Life-Span Development: Darius and His Father

An increasing number of fathers are staying home to care for their children (Lamb, 2010; O'Brien & Moss, 2010), Consider 17-month-old Darius. On weekdays, Darius' father, a writer, cares for him during the day while his mother works full-time as a landscape architect. Darius' father is doing a great job of caring for him. He keeps Darius nearby while he is writing and spends lots of time talking to him and playing with him. From their interactions, it is clear that they genuinely enjoy each other's company.

Last month, Darius began spending one day a week at a child-care center.

His parents selected the center after observing a number of centers and interviewing teachers and center directors. His parents placed him in the center because they wanted him to get some experience with peers and his father to have some time out from caregiving.

Darius' father looks to the future and imagines the Little League games Darius will play in and the many other activities he can enjoy with his son. Remembering how little time his own father spent with him, he is dedicated to making sure that Darius has an involved, nurturing relationship with his father.

When Darius' mother comes home in the evening, she spends considerable time with him. Darius is securely attached to both his mother and his father.

In Chapter 3, you read about how infants perceive, learn, and remember. Infants also are socioemotional beings, capable of displaying emotions and initiating social interaction with people close to them. The main topics that we explore in this chapter are emotional and personality development, attachment, and the social contexts of the family and child care.

Emotional and Personality Development

Anyone who has been around infants for even a brief time can tell that they are emotional beings. Not only do infants express emotions, but they also vary in temperament. Some are shy and others are outgoing. Some are active and others much less so. Let's explore these and other aspects of emotional and personality development in infants.

Emotional Development

Imagine what your life would be like without emotion. Emotion is the color and music of life, as well as the tie that binds people together. How do psychologists define and classify emotions, and why are they important to development? How do emotions develop during the first two years of life?

What Are Emotions?

We will define **emotion** as feeling, or *affect*, that occurs when a person is in a state or an interaction that is important to him or her, especially to his or her well-being. In many instances, emotions involve an individual's communication with the world. Although emotion consists of more than communication, in infancy it is the communication aspect that is at the forefront of emotion (Campos, 2009).

Psychologists classify the broad range of emotions in many ways, but almost all classifications designate an emotion as either positive (pleasant) or negative (unpleasant). Positive emotions include pleasant states such as happiness, joy, love, and enthusiasm. Negative emotions include anxiety, anger, guilt, and sadness.

Biological and Environmental Influences

Emotions are influenced both by biological foundations and by a person's experiences (Kagan, 2010; Kopp, 2011). For example, children who are blind from birth and have never observed the smile or frown on another person's face smile and frown in the same way that children with normal vision do. Moreover, facial expressions of basic emotions such as happiness, surprise, anger, and fear are the same across cultures.

How do East Asian mothers handle their infants' and children's emotional development differently than non-Latina White mothers?

These biological factors, however, are only part of the story of emotion. Display rules—rules governing when, where, and how emotions should be expressed—are not universal (Shiraev & Levy, 2010). For example, researchers have found that East Asian infants display less frequent and less intense positive and negative emotions than do non-Latino White infants (Cole & Tan, 2007). Throughout childhood, East Asian parents encourage their children to show emotional reserve rather than to be emotionally expressive (Chen & others, 1998).

Emotions serve important functions in our relationships (Stern, 2010; Thompson, 2010). As we discuss later in this section, emotions are the first language with which parents and infants communicate. Emotion-linked interchanges provide the foundation for the infant's developing attachment to the parent.

Early Emotions

Emotions that infants express in the first six months of life include surprise, interest, joy, anger, sadness, fear, and disgust (see Figure 4.1). Other emotions that appear in infancy include jealousy, empathy, embarrassment, pride, shame, and guilt; most of these occur for the first time at some point in the second half of the first year or during the second year. These later-developing emotions have been called *self-conscious or other-conscious emotions* because they involve the emotional reactions of others (Lewis, 2007; Saarni & others, 2006).

Some experts on infant socioemotional development, such as Jerome Kagan (2010), conclude that the structural immaturity of the infant brain makes it unlikely that emotions that require thought—such as guilt, pride, despair, shame, empathy, and jealousy—can be experienced in the first year. Thus, both Kagan (2010) and Campos (2009) argue that so-called "self-conscious" emotions don't occur until after the first year, a view that increasingly reflects that of most developmental psychologists.

Emotional Expressions and Relationships

Emotional expressions are involved in infants' first relationships. The ability of infants to communicate emotions permits coordinated interactions with their caregivers and the beginning of an emotional bond between them (Thompson, 2010). Not only do parents change their emotional expressions in response to those of their infants (and each other's), but infants also modify their emotional expressions in response to those of their parents. In other words, these interactions are mutually regulated. Because of this coordination, the interactions between parents and infants are described as *reciprocal,* or *synchronous,* when all is going well. Sensitive, responsive parents help their infants grow emotionally, whether the infants respond in distressed or happy ways (Stern, 2010).

Crying Cries and smiles are two emotional expressions that infants display when interacting with parents. These are babies' first forms of emotional communication. Crying is the most important mechanism newborns have for communicating with their world. Cries may also provide information about the health of the newborn's central nervous system.

Babies have at least three types of cries:

- **Basic cry:** A rhythmic pattern that usually consists of a cry, followed by a briefer silence, then a shorter whistle that is somewhat higher in pitch than the main cry, then another brief rest before the next cry. Some experts believe that hunger is one of the conditions that incite the basic cry.

- **Anger cry:** A variation of the basic cry, with more excess air forced through the vocal cords.

basic cry A rhythmic pattern usually consisting of a cry, a briefer silence, a shorter inspiratory whistle that is higher pitched than the main cry, and then a brief rest before the next cry.

anger cry A cry similar to the basic cry, with more excess air forced through the vocal cords.

How Would You...?
As a human development and family studies professional, how would you respond to the parents of a 13-month-old baby who are concerned because their son has suddenly started crying every morning when they drop him off at child care despite the fact that he has been going to the same child care for over six months?

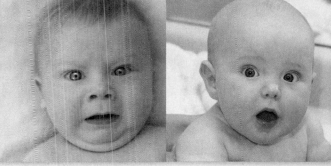

Joy   Sadness   Fear   Surprise

Figure 4.1 Expression of Different Emotions in Infants

pain cry A sudden appearance of loud crying without preliminary moaning, followed by breath holding.

reflexive smile A smile that does not occur in response to external stimuli. It appears during the first month after birth, usually during sleep.

social smile A smile in response to an external stimulus, which, early in development, typically is a face.

stranger anxiety An infant's fear and wariness of strangers; it tends to appear in the second half of the first year of life.

• **Pain cry:** A sudden long, initial loud cry followed by the holding of the breath; no preliminary moaning is present. The pain cry may be stimulated by physical pain or by any high-intensity stimulus.

Most adults can determine whether an infant's cries signify anger or pain (Zeskind, Klein, & Marshall, 1992). Parents can distinguish among the cries of their own baby better than among those of another baby.

Should parents respond to an infant's cries? Many developmental psychologists recommend that parents soothe a crying infant, especially in the first year. This reaction should help infants develop a sense of trust and secure attachment to the caregiver. One study examined how mothers responded when their 2- to 6-month-old infants were inoculated (Jahromi, Putnam, & Stifter, 2004). A combination of holding and gently rocking the baby resulted in reduced intensity and duration of infant crying.

How Would You...?
As a health-care professional, how would you explain to a worried parent that a sudden loud cry does not necessarily signify physical pain?

Smiling Smiling is critical as a means of developing a new social skill and is a key social signal (Campos, 2009). Two types of smiling can be distinguished in infants:

• **Reflexive smile:** A smile that does not occur in response to external stimuli and appears during the first month after birth, usually during sleep.

• **Social smile:** A smile that occurs in response to an external stimulus, typically a face in the case of the young infant. Social smiling occurs as early as 4 weeks in response to a caregiver's voice (Campos, 2005).

Daniel Messinger (2008) recently described the developmental course of infant smiling. From 2 to 6 months after birth, infants' social smiling increases considerably, in both self-initiated smiles and smiles in response to others' smiles. At 6 to 12 months, smiles that couple what is called the Duchenne marker (eye constriction) and mouth-opening occur in the midst of highly enjoyable interactions and play with parents (see Figure 4.2). In the second year, smiling continues to occur in such positive circumstances with parents, and in many cases an increase in smiling occurs when interacting with peers. Also in the second year, toddlers become increasingly aware of the social meaning of smiles, especially in their relationship with parents.

Fear

One of a baby's earliest emotions is fear, which typically first appears at about 6 months and peaks at about 18 months. However, abused and neglected infants can show fear as early as 3 months (Campos, 2005). The most frequent expression of an infant's fear involves **stranger anxiety**, in which an infant shows fear and wariness of strangers.

Stranger anxiety usually emerges gradually. It first appears at about 6 months in the form of wary reactions. By 9 months, fear of strangers is often more intense, and it continues to escalate through the infant's first birthday (Emde, Gaensbauer, & Harmon, 1976).

Not all infants show distress when they encounter a stranger. Besides individual variations, whether an infant shows stranger anxiety also depends on the social context and the characteristics of the stranger.

Infants show less stranger anxiety when they are in familiar settings. For example, in one study, 10-month-olds showed little stranger anxiety when they met a stranger in their own home but much greater fear when they encountered a stranger in a research laboratory (Sroufe, Waters, & Matas, 1974). Also, infants show less stranger anxiety when they are sitting on their mothers' laps than when placed in an infant seat several feet away from their mothers (Bohlin &

Figure 4.2 A 6-Month-Old's Strong Smile

This strong smile reflects the Duchenne marker (eye constriction) and mouth opening.

Hagekull, 1993). Thus, it appears that when infants feel secure they are less likely to show stranger anxiety.

separation protest An infant's distressed crying when the caregiver leaves.

social referencing "Reading" emotional cues in others to help determine how to act in a particular situation.

Who the stranger is and how the stranger behaves also influence stranger anxiety in infants. Infants are less fearful of child strangers than of adult strangers. They also are less fearful of friendly, outgoing, smiling strangers than of passive, unsmiling strangers (Bretherton, Stolberg, & Kreye, 1981).

In addition to stranger anxiety, infants experience fear of being separated from their caregivers. The result is **separation protest**—crying when the caregiver leaves. Separation protest tends to peak at about 15 months among U.S. infants. A study of four different cultures found, similarly, that separation protest peaked at about 13 to 15 months (Kagan, Kearsley, & Zelazo, 1978). As indicated in Figure 4.3, the percentage of infants who engaged in separation protest varied across cultures, but the infants reached a peak of protest at about the same age—just before the middle of the second year.

Social Referencing

Infants not only express emotions like fear but "read" the emotions of other people (Kim, Walden, & Knieps, 2010). **Social referencing** involves "reading" emotional cues in others to help determine how to act in a particular situation. The development of social referencing helps infants interpret ambiguous situations more accurately, as when they encounter a stranger (Thompson, 2009a, b). By the end of the first year, a parent's facial expression—either smiling or fearful—influences whether an infant will explore an unfamiliar environment.

Infants become better at social referencing in the second year of life. At this age, they tend to "check" with their mother before they act; they look at her to see if she is happy, angry, or fearful.

Emotional Regulation and Coping

During the first year, the infant gradually develops an ability to inhibit, or minimize, the intensity and duration of emotional reactions (Kopp, 2011). From early in infancy, babies put their thumbs in their mouths to soothe themselves. In their second year, they may say things to help soothe themselves. When placed in his bed for the night, after a little crying and whimpering, a 20-month-old was overheard saying, "Go sleep, Alex. Okay." But at first, infants depend mainly on caregivers to help them soothe their emotions, as when a caregiver rocks an infant to sleep, sings lullabies, gently strokes the infant, and so on.

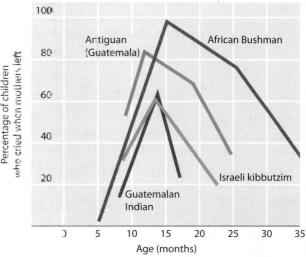

Figure 4.3 Separation Protest in Four Cultures

Note that separation protest peaked at about the same time in all four cultures in this study (13 to 15 months of age) (Kagan, Kearsley, & Zelazo, 1978). However, a higher percentage (100 percent) of infants in an African Bushman culture engaged in separation protest compared to only about 60 percent of infants in Guatemalan Indian and Israeli Kibbutzim cultures. *What might explain the fact that separation protest peaks at about the same time in these cultures?*

Caregivers' actions influence the infant's neurobiological regulation of emotions (Laible & Thompson, 2007). By soothing the infant, caregivers help infants modulate their emotions and reduce the level of stress hormones (de Haan & Gunnar, 2009). Many developmental psychologists believe it is a good strategy for a caregiver to soothe an infant before the infant gets into an intense, agitated, uncontrolled state (Thompson, 2006).

Later in infancy, when they become aroused, infants sometimes redirect their attention or distract themselves in order to reduce their arousal (Grolnick, Bridges, & Connell, 1996). By age 2, children can use language to define their feeling states and the context that is upsetting them (Kopp, 2011). A 2-year-old might say, "Feel bad. Dog scare." This type of communication may cue caregivers to help the child regulate emotion.

temperament An individual's
behavioral style and characteristic
way of emotionally responding.

easy child A child who is generally in
a positive mood, who quickly establishes regular routines in infancy, and
who adapts easily to new experiences.

difficult child A child who tends to
react negatively and cry frequently,
who engages in irregular daily routines, and who is slow to accept
new experiences.

slow-to-warm-up child A child who
has a low activity level, is somewhat
negative, and displays a low intensity of mood.

Contexts can influence emotional regulation (Thompson, 2010). Infants are often affected by fatigue, hunger, time of day, which people are around them, and where they are. Infants must learn to adapt to different contexts that require emotional regulation. Further, new demands appear as the infant becomes older and parents modify their expectations. For example, a parent may take it in stride if a 6-month-old infant screams in a restaurant but may react very differently if a 1½-year-old starts screaming.

Temperament

Do you get upset easily? Does it take much to get you angry, or to make you laugh? Even at birth, babies seem to have different emotional styles. One infant is cheerful and happy much of the time; another seems to cry constantly. These tendencies reflect **temperament**, or individual differences in behavioral styles, emotions, and characteristic ways of responding. With regard to its link to emotion, temperament refers to individual differences in how quickly the emotion is shown, how strong it is, how long it lasts, and how quickly it fades away (Campos, 2009).

Describing and Classifying Temperament

How would you describe your temperament or the temperament of a friend? Researchers have described and classified the temperament of individuals in different ways. Here we examine three of those ways.

Chess and Thomas' Classification Psychiatrists Alexander Chess and Stella Thomas (Chess & Thomas, 1977; Thomas & Chess, 1991) identified three basic types, or clusters, of temperament:

- **Easy child:** This child is generally in a positive mood, quickly establishes regular routines in infancy, and adapts easily to new experiences.
- **Difficult child:** This child reacts negatively and cries frequently, engages in irregular daily routines, and is slow to accept change.
- **Slow-to-warm-up child:** This child has a low activity level, is somewhat negative, and displays a low intensity of mood.

In their longitudinal investigation, Chess and Thomas found that 40 percent of the children they studied could be classified as easy, 10 percent as difficult, and 15 percent as slow to warm up. Notice that 35 percent did not fit any of the three patterns. Researchers have found that these three basic clusters of temperament are moderately stable across the childhood years.

A recent study revealed that young children with a difficult temperament showed more problems when they experienced low-quality child care and fewer problems when they experienced high-quality child care than did young children with an easy temperament (Pluess & Belsky, 2009).

Kagan's Concept of Behavioral Inhibition Another way of classifying temperament focuses on the differences between a shy, subdued, timid child and a sociable, extraverted, bold child. Jerome Kagan (2002, 2010) regards shyness with strangers (peers or adults) as one feature of a broad temperament category called *inhibition to the unfamiliar*. Inhibited children react to many aspects of unfamiliarity with initial avoidance, distress, or subdued affect, beginning around 7 to 9 months.

"Oh, he's cute, all right, but he's got the temperament of a car alarm."

© Barbara Smaller/The New Yorker Collection/www.cartoonbank.com

Effortful Control (Self-Regulation) Mary Rothbart and John Bates (2006) stress that effortful control (self-regulation) is an important dimension of temperament. Infants who are high in effortful control show an ability to keep their arousal from getting too high and have strategies for soothing themselves. By contrast, children who are low in effortful control are often unable to control their arousal; they are easily agitated and become intensely emotional.

An important point about temperament classifications such as Chess and Thomas' and Rothbart and Bates' is that children should not be pigeonholed as having only one temperament dimension, such as "difficult" or "negative affectivity." A good strategy when attempting to classify a child's temperament is to think of temperament as consisting of multiple dimensions (Bates, 2008; Bates, Schermerhorn, & Goodnight, 2011). For example, a child might be extraverted, show little emotional negativity, and have good self-regulation. Another child might be introverted, show little emotional negativity, and have a low level of self-regulation.

Biological Foundations and Experience

How does a child acquire a certain temperament? Kagan (2010) argues that children inherit a physiology that predisposes them to have a particular type of temperament. However, through experience they may learn to modify their temperament to some degree. For example, children may inherit a physiology that predisposes them to be fearful and inhibited but then learn to reduce their fear and inhibition to some degree.

How might caregivers help a child become less fearful and inhibited? An important first step is to find out what frightens the child. Comforting and reassuring the child, and addressing their specific fears, are also good strategies.

Biological Influences Physiological characteristics have been linked with different temperaments (Kagan, 2010). In particular, an inhibited temperament is associated with a unique physiological pattern that includes a high and stable heart rate, high levels of the hormone cortisol, and high activity in the right frontal lobe of the brain (Kagan, 2010). This pattern may be tied to the excitability of the amygdala, a structure in the brain that plays an important role in fear and inhibition. Twin and adoption studies also suggest that heredity has a moderate influence on differences in temperament within a group of people (Goldsmith, 2011; Plomin & others, 2009).

Gender, Culture, and Temperament Gender may be an important factor shaping the context that influences temperament. Parents might react differently to an infant's temperament based on whether the baby is a boy or a girl (Blakemore, Berenbaum, & Liben, 2009). For example, in one study, mothers were more responsive to the crying of irritable girls than to that of irritable boys (Crockenberg, 1986).

Similarly, the reaction to an infant's temperament may depend in part on culture (Kagan, 2010). For example, an active temperament might be valued in some cultures (such as the United States) but not in others (such as China) (Gartstein & others, 2009). Indeed, children's temperament can vary across cultures. For example, behavioral inhibition is valued more highly in China than in North America (Cole & Tan, 2007).

In short, many aspects of a child's environment can encourage or discourage the persistence of temperament characteristics (Bates, Schermerhorn, & Goodnight, 2011). One useful way of thinking about these relationships applies the concept of goodness of fit, which we examine next.

Goodness of Fit and Parenting

Goodness of fit refers to the match between a child's temperament and the environmental demands the child must cope with. Suppose Jason is an active toddler who is made to sit still for long periods and Jack is a slow-to-warm-up toddler

goodness of fit Refers to the match between a child's temperament and the environmental demands with which the child must cope.

who is abruptly pushed into new situations on a regular basis. Both Jason and Jack face a lack of fit between their temperament and environmental demands. Lack of fit can produce adjustment problems (Bates, Schermerhorn, & Goodnight, 2011; Rothbart & Bates, 2006).

Many parents don't come to believe in the importance of temperament until the birth of their second child. They viewed their first child's behavior as stemming from how they treated the child. But then they find that some strategies that worked with their first child are not as effective with the second child. Some problems experienced with the first child (such as those associated with feeding, sleeping, and coping with strangers) may not arise with the second child, but new problems arise. Such experiences strongly suggest that children differ from each other very early in life, and that these differences have important implications for parent-child interaction (Putnam, Sanson, & Rothbart, 2002).

What are the implications of temperamental variations for parenting? Although research does not yet allow for many highly specific conclusions, temperament experts Ann Sanson and Mary Rothbart (1995) recommend the following strategies for temperament-sensitive parenting:

How Would You...?
As a social worker, how would you apply information about an infant's temperament to maximize the goodness of fit in a clinical setting?

- *Attention to and respect for individuality.* One implication is that it is difficult to generate general prescriptions for "good parenting." A goal might be accomplished in one way with one child and in another way with another child, depending on the child's temperament. Parents need to be flexible and sensitive to the infant's signals and needs.

- *Structuring the child's environment.* Crowded, noisy environments can pose greater problems for some children (such as a "difficult child") than for others (such as an "easy child"). We might also expect that a fearful, withdrawing child would benefit from slower entry into new contexts.

- *Avoid applying negative labels to the child.* Acknowledging that some children are harder to parent than others is often helpful, and advice on how to handle particular kinds of difficult circumstances can be helpful. However, labeling a child "difficult" runs the risk of becoming a self-fulfilling prophecy. That is, if a child is identified as "difficult," people may treat him or her in a way that elicits "difficult" behavior.

Personality Development

Emotions and temperament are key aspects of *personality*, the enduring personal characteristics of individuals. Let's now examine characteristics that are often thought of as central to personality development during infancy: trust and the development of self and independence.

Trust

According to Erik Erikson (1968), the first year of life is characterized by the trust-versus-mistrust stage of development. Upon emerging from a life of regularity, warmth, and protection in the mother's womb, the infant faces a world that is less secure. Erikson proposed that infants learn trust when they are cared for in a consistently nurturant manner. If the infant is not well fed and kept warm on a consistent basis, a sense of mistrust is likely to develop.

In Erikson's view, the issue of trust versus mistrust is not resolved once and for all in the first year of life. It arises again at each successive stage of development, and the outcomes can be positive or negative. For example, children who leave infancy with a sense of trust can still have their sense of mistrust activated at a later stage, perhaps if their parents are separated or divorced.

The Developing Sense of Self

According to leading expert Ross Thompson (2007), it is difficult to study the self in infancy mainly because infants cannot tell us how they experience themselves.

Infants cannot verbally express their views of the self. They also cannot understand complex instructions from researchers.

A rudimentary form of self-recognition—being attentive and positive toward one's image in a mirror—appears as early as 3 months (Mascolo & Fischer, 2007; Pipp, Fischer, & Jennings, 1987). However, a central, more complete index of self-recognition—the ability to recognize one's physical features—does not emerge until the second year (Thompson, 2006)

One ingenious strategy to test infants' visual self-recognition is the use of a mirror technique in which an infant's mother first puts a dot of rouge on the infant's nose. Then, an observer watches to see how often the infant touches its nose. Next, the infant is placed in front of a mirror and observers detect whether nose touching increases. Why does this matter? The idea is that increased nose touching indicates that the infant recognizes itself in the mirror and is trying to touch or rub off the rouge because the rouge violates the infant's view of itself; that is, the infant thinks something is not right, since it believes its real self does not have a dot of rouge on it.

Figure 4.4 displays the results of two investigations that used the mirror technique. The researchers found that before they were 1 year old, infants did not recognize themselves in the mirror (Amsterdam, 1968; Lewis & Brooks-Gunn, 1979). Signs of self-recognition began to appear among some infants when they were 15 to 18 months old. By the time they were 2 years old, most children recognized themselves in the mirror. In sum, infants begin to develop a self-understanding, called self-recognition, at approximately 18 months of age (Hart & Karmel, 1996; Lewis, 2005).

In one study, biweekly assessments of infants from 15 to 23 months of age were conducted (Courage, Edison, & Howe, 2004). Self-recognition emerged gradually over this period, first appearing in the form of mirror recognition, followed by use of the personal pronoun and then by recognizing a photo of themselves. These aspects of self-recognition are often referred to as the first indications of toddlers' understanding of the mental state of "me," "that they are objects in their own mental representation of the world" (Lewis, 2005, p. 363).

Mirrors are not familiar to infants in all cultures. Thus, physical self-recognition may be a more important marker of self-recognition in Western cultures than in non-Western cultures (Thompson & Virmani, 2010).

Late in the second year and early in the third year, toddlers show other emerging forms of self-awareness that reflect a sense of "me" (Thompson & Virmani, 2010). For example, they refer to themselves by saying "Me big"; they label internal experiences such as emotions; they monitor themselves, as when a toddler says, "Do it myself"; and they say that things are theirs (Bullock & Lutkenhaus, 1990; Fasig, 2000). A recent study revealed that it is not until the second year that infants develop a conscious awareness of their own bodies. This developmental change in body awareness marks the beginning of children's representation of their own three-dimensional body shape and appearance, providing an early step in the development of their self-image and identity (Brownell & others, 2010).

Independence

Not only does the infant develop a sense of self in the second year of life, but independence also becomes a more central theme in the infant's life. Erikson (1968) stressed that independence is an important issue in the second year of life. Erikson's second stage of development is identified as autonomy versus

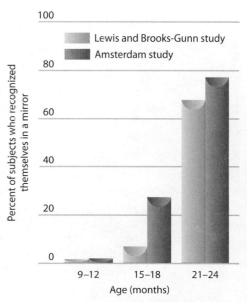

Figure 4.4 The Development of Self-Recognition in Infancy
The graph shows the findings of two studies in which infants less than 1 year of age did not recognize themselves in the mirror. A slight increase in the percentage of infant self-recognition occurred around 15 to 18 months of age. By 2 years of age, a majority of children recognized themselves. *Why do researchers study whether infants recognize themselves in a mirror?*

How Would You...?
As a human development and family studies professional, how would you work with a parent who shows signs of being overly protective or critical to the point of impairing their toddler's autonomy?

EMOTIONAL AND PERSONALITY DEVELOPMENT

109

Erikson believed that autonomy versus shame and doubt is the key developmental theme of the toddler years. *What are some good strategies for parents to use with their toddlers?*

shame and doubt. Autonomy builds as the infant's mental and motor abilities develop. At this point, not only can infants walk, but they can also climb, open and close, drop, push and pull, and hold and let go. Infants feel pride in these new accomplishments and want to do everything themselves, whether the activity is flushing a toilet, pulling the wrapping off a package, or deciding what to eat. It is important to recognize toddlers' motivation to do what they are capable of doing at their own pace. Then they can learn to control their muscles and their impulses themselves. Conversely, when caregivers are impatient and do for toddlers what they are capable of doing themselves, shame and doubt develop. To be sure, every parent has rushed a child from time to time, and one instance of rushing is unlikely to result in impaired development. It is only when parents consistently overprotect toddlers or criticize accidents (wetting, soiling, spilling, or breaking, for example) that children are likely to develop an excessive sense of shame and doubt about their ability to control themselves and their world.

Erikson also argued that the stage of autonomy versus shame and doubt has important implications for the development of independence and identity during adolescence. The development of autonomy during the toddler years gives adolescents the courage to be independent individuals who can choose and guide their own future.

Social Orientation and Attachment

So far, we have discussed how emotions and emotional competence change as children develop. We have also examined the role of emotional style; in effect, we have seen how emotions set the tone of our experiences in life. But emotions also write the lyrics because they are at the core of our interest in the social world and our relationships with others.

Social Orientation and Understanding

As socioemotional beings, infants show a strong interest in their social world and are motivated to orient themselves toward it and to understand it. In earlier chapters we described many of the biological and cognitive foundations that contribute to the infant's development of social orientation and understanding. We will call attention to relevant biological and cognitive factors as we explore social orientation; locomotion; intention, goal-directed behavior, and cooperation; and social referencing. Discussing biological, cognitive, and social processes together reminds us of an important aspect of development that was pointed out in Chapter 1—that these processes are intricately intertwined (Diamond, 2009).

Social Orientation

From early in their development, infants are captivated by the social world. Young infants stare intently at faces and are attuned to the sounds of human voices, especially their caregiver's face (Conradt & Ablow, 2010; Johnson, 2010). Later, they become adept at interpreting the meaning of facial expressions. *Face-to-face play* often begins to characterize caregiver-infant interactions when the infant is about 2 to 3 months of age. Such play is part of many mothers' motivation to create a positive emotional state in their infants (Thompson, 2010).

Infants also learn about the social world through contexts other than face-to-face play with a caregiver (Stern 2010; Tronick, 2010). Even though infants as young as 6 months show an interest in each other, their interaction with peers increases considerably in the latter half of the second year. Between 18 and 24 months, children markedly increase their imitative and reciprocal play—for example, imitating nonverbal actions like jumping and running (Eckerman & Whitehead, 1999). One recent study involved presenting 1- and 2-year-olds with a simple cooperative task that consisted of pulling a lever to get an attractive toy (Brownell, Ramani, & Zerwas, 2006) (see Figure 4.5). Any coordinated actions of the 1-year-olds appeared to be coincidental rather than cooperative, whereas the 2-year-olds' behavior was characterized as active cooperation to reach a goal.

Figure 4.5 The Cooperation Task
The cooperation task consisted of two handles on a box, atop which was an animated musical toy, surreptitiously activated by remote control when both handles were pulled. The handles were placed far enough apart that one child could not pull both handles. The experimenter demonstrated the task, saying, "Watch! If you pull the handles, the doggie will sing" (Brownell, Ramani, & Zerwas, 2006).

Locomotion

Recall from earlier in the chapter how important independence is for infants, especially in the second year of life. As infants develop the ability to crawl, walk, and run, they are able to explore and expand their social world. These newly developed self-produced locomotor skills allow the infant to independently initiate social interchanges on a more frequent basis (Thompson, 2009a).

Locomotion is also important for its motivational implications (Thompson, 2008). Once infants have the ability to move in goal-directed pursuits, the rewards gained from these pursuits leads to further efforts to explore and develop skills.

Intention, Goal-Directed Behavior, and Cooperation

The ability to perceive people as engaging in intentional and goal-directed behavior is an important social-cognitive accomplishment, and this initially occurs toward the end of the first year (Thompson, 2009a). Joint attention and gaze-following help the infant understand that other people have intentions (Meltzoff & Brooks, 2009). By their first birthday, infants have begun to direct their caregiver's attention to objects that capture their interest (Heimann & others, 2006).

Infants' Social Sophistication and Insight

In sum, researchers are discovering that infants are more socially sophisticated and insightful at younger ages than was previously envisioned (Thompson, 2010; Tronick, 2010). This sophistication and insight is reflected in infants' perceptions of others' actions as intentionally motivated and goal-directed (Brune & Woodward, 2007) and their motivation to share and participate in that intentionality by their first birthday (Tomasello, 2009). The more advanced social-cognitive skills of infants could be expected to influence their understanding and awareness of attachment to a caregiver.

body

attachment A close emotional bond between two people.

Attachment

Attachment is a close emotional bond between two people. There is no shortage of theories about infant attachment. Three theorists discussed in Chapter 1—Freud, Erikson, and Bowlby—proposed influential views of attachment.

Freud theorized that infants become attached to the person or object that provides them with oral satisfaction. For most infants, this is the mother, since she is most likely to feed the infant. Is feeding as important as Freud thought? A classic study by Harry Harlow (1958) indicates that the answer is no (see Figure 4.6).

Harlow removed infant monkeys from their mothers at birth; for six months they were reared by two surrogate (substitute) "mothers." One surrogate mother was made of wire, the other of cloth. Half of the infant monkeys were fed by the wire mother, half by the cloth mother. Periodically, the amount of time the infant monkeys spent with either the wire or the cloth mother was computed. Regardless of which mother fed them, the infant monkeys spent far more time with the cloth mother. Even if the wire mother, but not the cloth mother, provided nourishment, the infant monkeys spent more time with the cloth mother. And when Harlow frightened the monkeys, those who were "raised" by the cloth mother ran to that mother and clung to it; those who were raised by the wire mother did not. Whether the mother provided comfort seemed to determine whether the monkeys associated that mother with security. This study clearly demonstrated that feeding is not the crucial element in the attachment process, and that contact comfort is important.

Physical comfort also plays a role in Erik Erikson's (1968) view of the infant's development. Recall Erikson's proposal that during the first year of life infants are in the stage of trust versus mistrust. Physical comfort and sensitive care, according to Erikson (1968), are key to establishing a basic trust in infants. The infant's sense of trust, in turn, is the foundation for attachment and sets the stage for a lifelong expectation that the world will be a good and pleasant place.

The ethological perspective of British psychiatrist John Bowlby (1969, 1989) also stresses the importance of attachment in the first year of life and the responsiveness of the caregiver. Bowlby believes that both the infant and its primary caregivers are biologically predisposed to form attachments. He argues that the newborn is biologically equipped to elicit attachment behavior. The baby cries, clings, coos, and smiles. Later, the infant crawls, walks, and follows the mother. The immediate result is to keep the primary caregiver nearby; the long-term effect is to increase the infant's chances of survival (Thompson, 2006).

Attachment does not emerge suddenly but rather develops in a series of phases, moving from a baby's general preference for human figures to a partnership with primary caregivers. Following are four such phases based on Bowlby's conceptualization of attachment (Schaffer, 1996):

- *Phase 1: From birth to 2 months.* Infants instinctively direct their attachment to human figures. Strangers, siblings, and parents are equally likely to elicit smiling or crying from the infant.

- *Phase 2: From 2 to 7 months.* Attachment becomes focused on one figure, usually the primary caregiver, as the baby gradually learns to distinguish familiar from unfamiliar people.

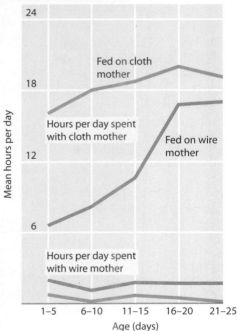

Figure 4.6 Contact Time With Wire and Cloth Surrogate Mothers

Regardless of whether the infant monkeys were fed by a wire or a cloth mother, they overwhelmingly preferred to spend contact time with the cloth mother. *How do these results compare with what Freud's theory and Erikson's theory would predict about human infants?*

CHAPTER 4 SOCIOEMOTIONAL DEVELOPMENT IN INFANCY

112

- *Phase 3: From 7 to 24 months.* Specific attachments develop. With increased locomotor skills, babies actively seek contact with regular caregivers, such as the mother or father.

- *Phase 4: From 24 months on.* Children become aware of other people's feelings, goals, and plans and begin to take these into account in forming their own actions.

Bowlby argued that infants develop an *internal working model* of attachment, a simple mental model of the caregiver, their relationship to him or her, and the self as deserving of nurturant care. The infant's internal working model of attachment with the caregiver influences the infant's, and later the child's, subsequent responses to other people (Goldsmith 2007). The internal model of attachment also has played a pivotal role in the discovery of links between attachment and subsequent emotion, understanding, conscious development, and self-concept (Thompson, 2006).

Attachment, then, emerges from the social-cognitive advances that allow infants to develop expectations for the caregiver's behavior and to determine the affective quality of their relationship (Laible & Thompson, 2007). These advances include recognizing the caregiver's face, voice, and other features, as well as expecting that the caregiver will provide pleasure in social interaction and relief from distress

Individual Differences in Attachment

Although attachment to a caregiver intensifies midway through the first year, isn't it likely that the quality of a baby's attachment experiences varies? Mary Ainsworth (1979) thought so. Ainsworth created the **Strange Situation**, an observational measure of infant attachment in which the infant experiences a series of introductions, separations, and reunions with the caregiver and an adult stranger in a prescribed order. In using the Strange Situation, researchers hope that their observations will provide information about the infant's motivation to be near the caregiver and the degree to which the caregiver's presence provides the infant with security and confidence.

Based on how babies respond in the Strange Situation, they are described as being securely attached or insecurely attached (in one of three ways) to the caregiver:

- **Securely attached babies** use the caregiver as a secure base from which to explore the environment. When in the presence of their caregiver, securely attached infants explore the room and examine toys that have been placed in it. When the caregiver departs, securely attached infants might protest mildly; when the caregiver returns, these infants reestablish positive interaction with her, perhaps by smiling or climbing on her lap. Subsequently, they often resume playing with the toys in the room.

- **Insecure avoidant babies** show insecurity by avoiding the caregiver. In the Strange Situation, these babies engage in little interaction with the caregiver, are not distressed when she leaves the room, usually do not reestablish contact with her upon her return, and may even turn their back on her. If contact is established, the infant usually leans away or looks away.

- **Insecure resistant babies** often cling to the caregiver and then resist her by fighting against the closeness, perhaps by kicking or pushing away. In the Strange

Strange Situation An observational measure of infant attachment that requires the infant to move through a series of introductions, separations, and reunions with the caregiver and an adult stranger in a prescribed order.

securely attached babies Babies that use the caregiver as a secure base from which to explore the environment.

insecure avoidant babies Babies that show insecurity by avoiding the mother.

insecure resistant babies Babies that often cling to the caregiver, then resist her by fighting against the closeness, perhaps by kicking or pushing away.

What is the nature of secure and insecure attachment?

SOCIAL ORIENTATION AND ATTACHMENT

insecure disorganized babies
Babies that show insecurity by
being disorganized and disoriented.

Situation, these babies often cling anxiously to the caregiver and don't explore the playroom. When the caregiver leaves, they often cry loudly and push away if she tries to comfort them upon her return.

- **Insecure disorganized babies** are disorganized and disoriented. In the Strange Situation, these babies might appear dazed, confused, and fearful. To be classified as disorganized, babies must show strong patterns of avoidance and resistance or display certain specified behaviors, such as extreme fearfulness around the caregiver.

How Would You...?
As a psychologist, how would you identify an insecurely attached toddler? How would you encourage a parent to strengthen the attachment bond?

Do individual differences in attachment matter? Ainsworth proposed that secure attachment in the first year of life provides an important foundation for psychological development later in life. The securely attached infant moves freely away from the caregiver but keeps track of where she is through periodic glances. The securely attached infant responds positively to being picked up by others and, when put back down, freely moves away to play. An insecurely attached infant, by contrast, avoids the caregiver or is ambivalent toward her, fears strangers, and is upset by minor, everyday separations.

If early attachment to a caregiver is important, it should relate to a child's social behavior later in development. For some children, early attachments seem to foreshadow later functioning (Raikes & Thompson, 2009). In an extensive longitudinal study conducted by Alan Sroufe and his colleagues (2005a, b), early secure attachment (assessed by the Strange Situation at 12 and 18 months) was linked with positive emotional health, high self-esteem, self-confidence, and socially competent interaction with peers, teachers, camp counselors, and romantic partners through adolescence. And a recent meta-analysis found that disorganized attachment was more strongly linked to externalizing problems (aggression and hostility, for example) than were avoidant attachment and resistant attachment (Fearon & others, 2010).

For some children, though, there is little continuity (Thompson & Goodvin, 2005). Not all research reveals the power of infant attachment to predict subsequent development. In one longitudinal study, attachment classification (secure and insecure attachment) in infancy did not predict attachment classification at 18 years of age (Lewis, Feiring, & Rosenthal, 2000). In this study, the infants whose attachment was insecure did not necessarily have an insecure attachment classification at age 18. Instead, the best predictor of an insecure attachment classification at 18 was the occurrence of parental divorce in the intervening years. Other research suggests that consistently positive caregiving over a number of years is an important factor in connecting early attachment and the child's functioning later in development.

Some developmental psychologists believe that too much emphasis has been placed on the attachment bond in infancy. Jerome Kagan (1987, 2002), for example, sees infants as highly resilient and adaptive; he and others stress that genetic characteristics and temperament play more important roles in a child's social competence than the attachment theorists, such as Bowlby and Ainsworth, are willing to acknowledge (Chaudhuri & Williams, 1999). For example, if some infants inherit a low tolerance for stress, this, rather than an insecure attachment bond, may be responsible for an inability to get along with peers.

Another criticism of attachment theory is that it ignores the diversity of socializing agents and contexts that exists in an infant's world. A culture's value system can influence the nature of attachment (Shiraev & Levy, 2010). In northern Germany, for example, expectations for an infant's independence may be responsible for infants showing little distress upon a brief separation from the mother, whereas the Japanese mother's motivation for extreme close proximity to her infant may explain why Japanese infants

In the Hausa culture, siblings and grandmothers provide a significant amount of care for infants. *How might these variations in care affect attachment?*

become upset when they are separated from the mother. Also, in some cultures infants show attachments to many people. Among the Hausa (who live in Nigeria), both grandmothers and siblings provide a significant amount of care for infants (Harkness & Super, 1995). Infants in agricultural societies tend to form attachments to older siblings, who have major responsibility for their younger siblings' care. Researchers recognize the importance of competent, nurturant caregivers in an infant's development (Bornstein & Lansford, 2010). At issue, though, is whether or not secure attachment, especially to a single caregiver, is essential (Lamb, 2005).

Despite such criticisms, there is ample evidence that security of attachment is important to development (Bigelow & others, 2010; Sroufe, Coffino, & Carlson, 2010; Thompson & Newton, 2009). Secure attachment in infancy is important because it reflects a positive parent-infant relationship and provides the foundation that supports healthy socioemotional development in the years that follow.

Caregiving Styles and Attachment

How Would You...?
As a health-care professional, how would you use an infant's attachment style and/or a parent's caregiving style to determine if an infant may be at risk for neglect or abuse?

Is the style of caregiving linked with the quality of the infant's attachment? Securely attached babies have caregivers who are sensitive to their signals and are consistently available to respond to the infant's needs (Cassidy, 2008). These caregivers often let their babies take an active part in determining the onset and pacing of interactions in the first year of life. A recent study revealed that sensitive maternal responding was linked to infant attachment security (Finger & others, 2009). Another study found that maternal sensitivity in parenting was related to secure attachment in infants in two different cultures: the United States and Colombia (Carbonell & others, 2002). Although maternal sensitivity is positively linked to the development of secure attachment in infancy, it is important to note that the link is not especially strong (Campos, 2009).

How do the caregivers of insecurely attached babies interact with them? Caregivers of avoidant babies tend to be unavailable or rejecting (Cassidy, 2008). They often don't respond to their babies' signals and have little physical contact with them. When they do interact with their babies, they may behave in an angry and irritable way. Caregivers of resistant babies tend to be inconsistent; sometimes they respond to their babies' needs, and sometimes they don't. In general, they tend not to be very affectionate with their babies and show little synchrony when interacting with them. Caregivers of disorganized babies often neglect or physically abuse them (Cicchetti, 2011; Cicchetti & others, 2010).

A recent study found links between disorganized attachment in infancy, a specific gene, and level of maternal responsiveness. In this study, a disorganized attachment style developed in infancy only when infants had the short version of the serotonin transporter gene—5-HTTLPR (Spangler & others, 2009). Infants were not characterized by this attachment style when they had the long version of the gene (Spangler & others, 2009). Further, this gene-environment interaction occurred only when mothers showed a low level of responsiveness toward their infants.

Social Contexts

Now that we have explored the infant's emotional and personality development and attachment, let's examine the social contexts in which these occur. We begin by studying a number of aspects of the family and then turn to a social context in which infants increasingly spend time: child care.

The Family

The family can be thought of as a constellation of subsystems—a complex whole made up of interrelated, interacting parts—defined in terms of generation, gender, and role. Each family member participates in several subsystems. The father and child represent one subsystem, the mother and father another; the mother, father, and child represent yet another; and so on.

These subsystems have reciprocal influences on each other, as Figure 4.7 highlights. For example, Jay Belsky (1981) stresses that marital relations, parenting, and infant behavior and development can have both direct and indirect effects on each other. An example of a direct effect is the influence of the parents' behavior on the child. An indirect effect is how the relationship between the spouses mediates the way a parent acts toward the child. For example, marital conflict might reduce the efficiency of parenting, in which case marital conflict would indirectly affect the child's behavior. The simple fact that two people are becoming parents may have profound effects on their relationship.

The Transition to Parenthood

Whether people become parents through pregnancy, adoption, or stepparenting, they face disequilibrium and must adapt to it. Parents want to develop a strong attachment with their infant, but they still want to maintain strong attachments to their spouse and friends, and possibly to continue their careers. Parents ask themselves how this new being will change their lives. A baby places new restrictions on partners; no longer will they be able to rush out to a movie at a moment's notice, and money may not be readily available for vacations and other luxuries. Dual-career parents ask, "Will it harm the baby to place her in child care? Will we be able to find responsible baby-sitters?"

In a longitudinal investigation of couples from late pregnancy until 3½ years after the baby was born, couples enjoyed more positive marital relations before the baby was born than afterward (Cowan & Cowan, 2000, 2009; Cowan & others, 2005). Still, almost one-third reported an increase in marital satisfaction. Some couples said that the baby had both brought them closer together and moved them farther apart; being parents enhanced their sense of themselves and gave them a new, more stable identity as a couple. Babies opened men up to greater concern with intimate relationships, and the demands of juggling work and family roles stimulated women to manage family tasks more efficiently and pay attention to their own personal growth.

The Bringing Home Baby project is a workshop for new parents that emphasizes strengthening the couple's relationship, understanding and becoming acquainted with the baby, resolving conflict, and developing parenting skills. Evaluations of the project revealed that parents who participated improved in their ability to work together as parents; fathers were more involved with their baby and sensitive to the baby's behavior; mothers had fewer symptoms of postpartum depression; and their baby showed better overall development than was the case among parents and babies in a control group (Gottman, 2009; Gottman, Gottman, & Shapiro, 2009).

Reciprocal Socialization

For many years, socialization was viewed as a one-way process: Children were considered to be the products of their parents' socialization techniques. According to more recent research, however, parent-child interaction is reciprocal (Gauvain & Parke, 2010; Stern, 2010). **Reciprocal socialization** is socialization that is bidirectional. That is, children socialize their parents just as parents socialize their children (Grusec, 2011). The parent responds to the child's behavior with **scaffolding**, in which the parent times interactions so that the infant experiences turn-taking with the parent. Scaffolding can be used to support children's efforts at any age.

Figure 4.7 Interaction Between Children and Their Parents: Direct and Indirect Effects
Children socialize parents just as parents socialize children.

Marital relationship

Child behavior and development

Parenting

How Would You...?

As an educator, how would you explain the value of games and the role of scaffolding in the development of infants and toddlers?

A recent study of Hmong families living in the United States revealed that maternal scaffolding, especially in the form of cognitive support, of young children's problem solving during the summer before kindergarten predicted the children's reasoning skills in kindergarten (Stright, Herr, & Neitzel, 2009).

The game peek-a-boo, in which parents initially cover their babies, then remove the covering, and finally register "surprise" at the babies' reappearance, reflects the concept of scaffolding. As infants become more skilled at this game, they gradually do some of the covering and uncovering themselves. Parents try to time their actions in such a way that the infant takes turns with the parent.

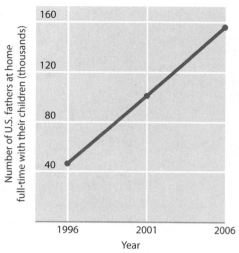

Figure 4.8 Increase in the Number of U.S. Fathers Staying at Home Full-Time With Their Children

Maternal and Paternal Caregiving

Much of our discussion of attachment has focused on mothers as caregivers. Do mothers and fathers differ in their caregiving roles? In general, mothers on average still spend considerably more time in caregiving with infants and children than do fathers (Blakemore, Berenbaum, & Liben, 2009). Mothers especially are more likely to engage in the managerial role with their children, coordinating their activities, making sure their health-care needs are fulfilled, and so on (Gauvain & Parke, 2010).

However, an increasing number of U.S. fathers stay home full-time with their children (Lamb, 2010). As indicated in Figure 4.8, there was a 300-plus percent increase in stay-at-home fathers in the United States from 1996 to 2006. A large portion of the full-time fathers have career-focused wives who provide the main family income (O'Brien & Moss, 2010). One study revealed that the stay-at-home fathers were as satisfied with their marriage as traditional parents, although they indicated that they missed their daily life in the workplace (Rochlen & others, 2008). In this study, the stay-at-home fathers reported that they tended to be ostracized when they took their children to playgrounds and often were excluded from parent groups.

Observations of fathers and their infants suggest that fathers have the ability to act as sensitively and responsively with their infants as mothers do (Parke & others, 2008). Consider the Aka pygmy culture in Africa, in which fathers spend as much time interacting with their infants as mothers do (Hewlett, 1991, 2000; Hewlett & MacFarlan, 2010). Remember, however, that although fathers can be active, nurturant, involved caregivers, as in the case of Aka pygmies, in many cultures men have not chosen to follow this pattern (Lamb, 2005).

Do fathers behave differently toward infants than mothers do? Maternal interactions usually center on child-care activities—feeding, changing diapers, and bathing. Paternal interactions are more likely to include play (Parke & Buriel, 2006). Fathers engage in more rough-and-tumble play. They bounce infants, throw them up in the air, tickle them, and so on (Lamb, 1986, 2000). Mothers do play with their infants, but their play is less physical and arousing than that of fathers.

Do children benefit when fathers are positively involved in their caregiving? A study of more than 7,000 children who were assessed from infancy to adulthood revealed that those who were extensively involved in their children's lives (such as engaging in various activities with them and showing a strong interest in their education) were more successful in school (Flouri & Buchanan, 2004).

An Aka pygmy father with his infant son. In the Aka culture, fathers were observed to be holding or nearby their infants 47 percent of the time (Hewlett, 1991).

Child Care

Many U.S. children today experience multiple caregivers. Most do not have a parent staying home to care for them; instead, the children receive "child care"—that is, some type of care provided by others. Many parents worry that child care will have adverse effects, such as reducing their infants' emotional attachment to them, retarding the infants' cognitive development, failing to teach them how to control anger, or allowing them to be unduly influenced by their peers. Are these concerns justified?

In the United States, approximately 15 percent of children age 5 and younger experience more than one child-care arrangement. A recent study of 2- and 3-year-old children revealed that an increase in the number of child-care arrangements the children experienced was linked to an increase in behavioral problems and a decrease in prosocial behavior (Morrissey, 2009).

Parental Leave

Today far more young children are in child care than at any other time in U.S. history. About 2 million children in the United States currently receive formal, licensed child care, and uncounted millions of children are cared for by unlicensed baby-sitters. In part, these numbers reflect the fact that U.S. adults cannot receive paid leave from their jobs to care for their young children.

Child-care policies around the world vary (Tolani & Brooks-Gunn, 2008). Europe has led the way in creating new standards of parental leave: In 1992, the European Union (EU) mandated a paid 14-week maternity leave. In most European countries today, working parents on leave receive from 70 percent of the worker's prior wage up to the full wage, and paid leave averages about 16 weeks (Tolani & Brooks-Gunn, 2008). The United States currently allows up to 12 weeks of unpaid leave for parents who are caring for a newborn.

How are child-care policies in many European countries, such as Sweden, different than those in the United States?

Most countries restrict eligible benefits to women who have been employed for a minimum length of time prior to childbirth. In Denmark, even unemployed mothers are eligible for extended parental leave related to childbirth. In Germany, child-rearing leave is available to almost all parents. The Nordic countries (Denmark, Norway, and Sweden) have extensive gender-equity family leave policies for childbirth that emphasize the contributions of both women and men (Tolani & Brooks-Gunn, 2008). For example, in Sweden parents can take an 18-month, job-protected parental leave with benefits to be shared by parents and applied to full-time or part-time work.

Variations in Child Care

Because the United States does not have a policy of paid leave for child care, child care in the United States has become a major national concern (Phillips & Lowenstein, 2011; Thompson, 2009c). Many factors influence the effects of child care, including the age of the child, the type of child care, and the quality of the program.

The type of child care varies extensively. Child care is provided in large centers with elaborate facilities and in private homes. Some child-care centers are commercial operations; others are nonprofit centers run by churches, civic groups, and employers.

Some child-care providers are professionals; others are untrained adults who want to earn extra money. Figure 4.9 presents the primary care arrangement for U.S. children under age 5 with employed mothers (Clarke-Stewart & Miner, 2008).

Child-care quality makes a difference. What constitutes a high-quality child-care program for infants? In high-quality child care (Clarke-Stewart & Miner, 2008, p. 273):

> caregivers encourage the children to be actively engaged in a variety of activities, have frequent, positive interactions that include smiling, touching, holding, and speaking at the child's eye level, respond properly to the child's questions or requests, and encourage children to talk about their experiences, feelings, and ideas.

High-quality child care also involves providing children with a safe environment, access to age-appropriate toys and participation in age-appropriate activities, and a low caregiver-child ratio that allows caregivers to spend considerable time with children on an individual basis.

Children are more likely to experience poor-quality child care if they come from families with few resources (psychological, social and economic) (Cabrera, Hutchens, & Peters, 2006). Many researchers have examined the role of poverty in quality of child care (Lucas & others, 2008). One study found that extensive child care was harmful to low-income children only when the care was of low quality (Votrub-Drzal & others, 2004). Even if the child was in child care more than 45 hours a week, high-quality care was associated with fewer internalizing problems (anxiety, for example) and externalizing problems (aggressive and destructive behaviors, for example). A recent study revealed that children from low-income families benefited in terms of school readiness and language development when their parents selected higher-quality child care (McCartney & others, 2007).

To read about one individual who provides quality child care to individuals from impoverished backgrounds, see "Careers in Life-Span Development."

How Would You...?
As an educator, how would you design the ideal child-care program to promote optimal infant development?

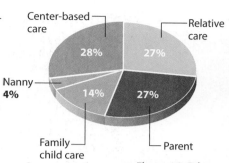

Figure 4.9 Primary Care Arrangements in the United States for Children Under 5 Years of Age With Employed Mothers

Center-based care 28%
Relative care 27%
Nanny 4%
Family child care 14%
Parent 27%

CAREERS IN LIFE-SPAN DEVELOPMENT

Wanda Mitchell, Child-Care Director

Wanda Mitchell is the Center Director at the Hattie Daniels Day Care Center in Wilson, North Carolina. Her responsibilities include directing the operation of the center, which involves creating and maintaining an environment in which young children can learn effectively, and for ensuring that the center meets state licensing requirements. Wanda obtained her undergraduate degree from North Carolina A & T University, majoring in Child Development. Prior to her current position, she had been an education coordinator for Head Start and an instructor at Wilson Technical Community College. Describing her work, Wanda says, "I really enjoy working in my field. This is my passion. After graduating from college, my goal was to advance in my field."

Wanda Mitchell, child-care director, working with some of the children at her center.

The National Longitudinal Study of Child Care

In 1991, the National Institute of Child Health and Human Development (NICHD) began a comprehensive longitudinal study of child-care experiences. Data were collected from a diverse sample of almost 1,400 children and their families at 10 locations across the United States over a period of seven years. Researchers used multiple methods (trained observers, interviews, questionnaires, and testing) and measured many facets of children's development, including physical health, cognitive development, and socioemotional development. Following are some of the results of what is now referred to as the NICHD Study of Early Child Care and Youth Development or NICHD SECCYD (NICHD Early Child Care Network, 2001, 2002, 2003, 2004, 2005, 2006).

- *Quality of care.* Evaluations of quality of care were based on such characteristics as group size, child–adult ratio, physical environment, caregiver characteristics (such as formal education, specialized training, and child-care experience), and caregiver behavior (such as sensitivity to children). An alarming conclusion is that a majority of the child care in the first three years of life was of unacceptable low quality. Positive caregiving by nonparents in child-care settings was infrequent—only 12 percent of the children in the study experienced positive nonparental child care (such as positive talk and language stimulation). Further, infants from low-income families experienced lower-quality child care than did infants from higher-income families. When quality of caregivers' care was high, children performed better on cognitive and language tasks, were more cooperative with their mothers during play, showed more positive and skilled interaction with peers, and had fewer behavior problems. Caregiver training and good child–staff ratios were linked with higher cognitive and social competence when children were 54 months of age. In recent research involving the NICHD sample, links were found between nonrelative child care from birth to 4½ years of age and adolescent development at 15 years of age (Vandell & others, 2010). In this analysis, better quality of early care was related to a higher level of academic achievement and a lower level of externalizing problems at 15.

- *Amount of child care.* The quantity of child care predicted some outcomes (Vandell & others, 2010). When children spent extensive amounts of time in child care beginning in infancy, they experienced fewer sensitive interactions with their mother, showed more behavior problems, and had higher rates of illness. In general, when children spent 30 hours or more per week in child care, their development was less than optimal.

- *Family and parenting influences.* The influence of families and parenting was not weakened by extensive child care. Parents played a significant role in helping children regulate their emotions. Especially important parenting influences were being sensitive to children's needs, being involved with children, and providing cognitive stimulation. Indeed, parental sensitivity has been the most consistent predictor of secure attachment (Friedman, Melhuish, & Hill, 2009). An important final point about the extensive NICHD SECCYD research is that findings have consistently shown that family factors are considerably stronger and more consistent predictors of a wide variety of child outcomes than are child-care experiences (quality, quantity, type).

What are some strategies parents can follow in regard to child care? Child-care expert Kathleen McCartney (2003, p. 4) offers this advice:

- *Recognize that the quality of your parenting is a key factor in your child's development.*
- *Make decisions that will improve the likelihood that you will be good parents.* "For some this will mean working full-time"—for personal fulfillment, income, or both. "For others, this will mean working part-time or not working outside the home."
- *Monitor your child's development.* "Parents should observe for themselves whether their children seem to be having behavior problems." They should

How Would You...?
As a psychologist, based on the findings from the NICHD study, how would you advise parents about their role in their child's development versus the role of nonparental child care?

- also talk with child-care providers and their pediatrician about their child's behavior.
- *Take some time to find the best child care.* Observe different child-care facilities and be certain that you like what you see. "Quality child care costs money, and not all parents can afford the child care they want."

Summary

Emotional and Personality Development

- Emotion is feeling, or affect, that occurs when a person is in a state or an interaction that is important to them. Infants display a number of emotions early in their development, such as crying, smiling, and fear. Two fears that infants develop are stranger anxiety and separation from a caregiver. As infants develop, it is important for them to increase their emotion regulation.

- Temperament is an individual's behavioral style and characteristic way of emotional responding. Chess and Thomas classified infants as (1) easy, (2) difficult, or (3) slow to warm up. Kagan proposed that inhibition to the unfamiliar is an important temperament category. Rothbart and Bates emphasized that effortful control (self-regulation) is an important temperament dimension. Goodness of fit can be an important aspect of a child's adjustment.

- Erikson argued that an infant's first year is characterized by the stage of trust versus mistrust. Independence becomes a central theme in the second year of life, which is characterized by the stage of autonomy versus shame and doubt.

Social Orientation and Attachment

- Infants show a strong interest in the social world and are motivated to understand it. Infants are more socially sophisticated and insightful at an earlier age than previously envisioned.

- Attachment is a close emotional bond between two people. In infancy, contact comfort and trust are important in the development of attachment. Securely attached babies use the caregiver, usually the mother, as a secure base from which to explore the environment. Three types of insecure attachment are avoidant, resistant, and disorganized. Caregivers of secure babies are more sensitive to the babies' signals and are consistently available to meet their needs.

Social Contexts

- The transition to parenthood requires considerable adaptation and adjustment on the part of parents. In general, mothers spend more time in caregiving than fathers; fathers tend to engage in more physical, playful interaction with infants than mothers.

- The quality of child care is uneven, and child care remains a controversial topic. Quality child care can be achieved and seems to have few adverse effects on children.

Key Terms

emotion 102
basic cry 103
anger cry 103
pain cry 104
reflexive smile 104
social smile 104
stranger anxiety 104

separation protest 105
social referencing 105
temperament 106
easy child 106
difficult child 105
slow-to-warm-up
   child 106

goodness of fit 107
attachment 112
Strange Situation 113
securely attached
   babies 113
insecure avoidant
   babies 113

insecure resistant
   babies 113
insecure disorganized
   babies 114
reciprocal
   socialization 116
scaffolding 116

5 Physical and Cognitive Development in Early Childhood

Stories of Life-Span Development: Reggio Emilia's Children

The Reggio Emilia approach is an educational program for young children that was developed in the northern Italian city of Reggio Emilia. Children of single parents and children with disabilities have priority in admission; other children are admitted according to a scale of needs. Parents pay on a sliding scale based on income.

The children are encouraged to learn by investigating and exploring topics that interest them. A wide range of stimulating media and materials are available for children to use as they learn music, movement, drawing, paint-ing, sculpting, collage, puppetry, and photography, among other things.

In this program, children often explore topics in a group, which fosters a sense of community, respect for diversity, and a collaborative approach to problem solving (Hyson, Copple, & Jones, 2006). In this group setting, two co-teachers guide the children in their exploration. The Reggio Emilia teachers consider each project as an adventure. It can start from an adult's suggestion, from a child's idea, or from an unexpected event such as a snowfall. Every project is based on what the children say and do. The teachers allow children enough time to think of and craft a project.

At the core of the Reggio Emilia approach is an image of children who are competent and have rights, especially the right to outstanding care and education. Parent participation is considered essential, and cooperation is a major theme in the schools. Many experts on early childhood education believe that the Reggio Emilia approach provides a supportive, stimulating context in which children are motivated to explore their world in a competent and confident manner (New, 2007).

Parents and educators who clearly understand how young children develop can play an active role in creating programs that foster their natural interest in learning, rather than stifling it. In this chapter, the first of two chapters on early childhood (ages 3 to 5), we explore the physical, cognitive, and language changes that typically occur as the toddler develops into the preschooler, and then look at early childhood education.

A Reggio Emilia classroom in which young children explore topics that interest them.

Physical Changes

Remember from Chapter 3 that a child's growth in infancy is rapid and follows cephalocaudal and proximodistal patterns. Fortunately, the growth rate slows in early childhood; otherwise, we would be a species of giants.

Body Growth and Change

Despite the slowing of growth in height and weight that characterizes early childhood, this growth is still the most obvious physical change during this period of development. Yet unseen changes in the brain and nervous system are no less significant in preparing children for advances in cognition and language.

Height and Weight

The average child grows 2½ inches in height and gains between 5 and 7 pounds a year during early childhood. As the preschool child grows older, the percentage of increase in height and weight decreases with each additional year. Girls are only slightly smaller and lighter than boys during these years, a difference that continues until puberty. In addition, girls have more fatty tissue than boys, and boys have more muscle tissue than girls.

During the preschool years, both boys and girls slim down as the trunk of the body lengthens (Hockenberry, 2010). Although the head is still somewhat large for the body, by the end of the preschool years most children have lost the top-heavy look they had as toddlers. Body fat also shows a slow, steady decline during the preschool years. The chubby baby often looks much leaner by the end of early childhood.

Growth patterns vary from one individual to another. Think back to your preschool years. That was probably the first time you noticed that some children were taller than you, some shorter; some were fatter, some thinner; some were stronger, some weaker. Much of the variation was due to heredity, but environmental experiences were also involved. A review of the height and weight of children around the world concluded that the two most important contributors to height differences are ethnic origin and nutrition (Meredith, 1978). Urban, middle-socioeconomic status, and firstborn children were taller than rural, lower-socioeconomic status, and later-born children. In the United States, African American children are also taller than White children.

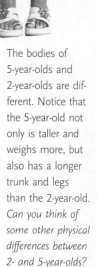

The bodies of 5-year-olds and 2-year-olds are different. Notice that the 5-year-old not only is taller and weighs more, but also has a longer trunk and legs than the 2-year-old. *Can you think of some other physical differences between 2- and 5-year-olds?*

The Brain

One of the most important physical developments during early childhood is the continuing development of the brain and other parts of the nervous system (Nelson, 2011). The increasing maturation of the brain, combined with opportunities to experience a widening world, contribute to children's emerging cognitive abilities. In particular, changes in the brain during early childhood enable children to plan their actions, attend to stimuli more effectively, and make considerable strides in language development.

Although the brain does not grow as rapidly during early childhood as in infancy, it does undergo remarkable changes. By repeatedly obtaining brain scans of the same children for up to four years, researchers have found that children's brains experience rapid, distinct spurts of growth (Gogtay & Thompson, 2010). The overall size of the brain does not increase dramatically from ages 3 to 15; what does change dramatically are local patterns within the brain. The amount of brain material in some areas can nearly double in as little as a year, followed by a dramatic loss of tissue as unneeded cells are pruned and the brain continues to reorganize itself. From 3 to 6 years of age the most rapid growth in the brain takes place in the part of the frontal lobes known as the *prefrontal cortex* (see Figure 5.1), which plays a key role in planning and organizing new actions and maintaining attention to tasks (Gogtay & Thompson, 2010; Diamond, Casey, & Munakata, 2011).

The continuation of two changes that began before birth contributes to the brain's growth during early childhood. First, the number and size of dendrites increase, and second, myelination continues. Recall from Chapter 3 that **myelination** is the process through which axons (nerve fibers that carry signals away from the cell body) are covered with a layer of fat cells, which increases the speed and efficiency of information traveling through the nervous system. Myelination is important in the development of a number of abilities (Nelson, 2011). For example, myelination in the areas of the brain related to hand-eye coordination is not complete until about age 4. Myelination in the areas of the brain related to focusing attention is not complete until the end of middle or late childhood.

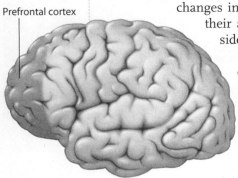

Prefrontal cortex

Figure 5.1 The Prefrontal Cortex The brain pathways and circuitry involving the prefrontal cortex (shaded in purple) show significant advances in development during middle and late childhood. *What cognitive processes are linked with these changes in the prefrontal cortex?*

Motor Development

Running as fast as you can, falling down, getting right back up and running just as fast as you can . . . building towers with blocks . . . scribbling, scribbling, and scribbling some more . . . cutting paper with scissors . . . During your preschool years, you probably developed the ability to perform all these activities. What physical changes made this possible?

Gross Motor Skills

The preschool child no longer has to make an effort simply to stay upright and move around. As children move their legs with more confidence and carry themselves more purposefully, moving around in the environment becomes more automatic.

Around age 3, children enjoy simple movements such as hopping, jumping, and running back and forth, just for the sheer delight of performing them. They delight in showing how they can run across a room and jump all of 6 inches. The run-and-jump will win no Olympic medals, but for the 3-year-old it is a source of considerable pride and accomplishment.

At age 4, children are still enjoying the same kinds of activities, but they have become more adventurous. They scramble over low jungle gyms as they display their athletic prowess. Although they have been able to climb stairs with one foot on each step for some time, they are just beginning to be able to come down the same way.

How Would You...? As a health-care professional, how would you advise parents who want to get their talented 4-year-old child into a soccer league for preschool children?

By age 5, children are even more adventuresome than when they were 4. It is not unusual for self-assured 5-year-olds to perform hair-raising stunts on practically any climbing object. Five-year-olds also run hard and enjoy races with each other and their parents.

Fine Motor Skills

By the time they turn 3, children have had the ability to pick up the tiniest objects between their thumb and forefinger for some time, but they are still somewhat clumsy at it. Three-year-olds can build surprisingly high block towers, each block placed with intense concentration but often not in a completely straight line. When 3-year-olds play with a simple jigsaw puzzle, they are rather rough in placing the pieces. Even when they recognize the hole a piece fits into, they are not very precise in positioning the piece. They often try to force the piece into the hole or pat it vigorously.

By age 4, children's fine motor coordination has improved substantially and becomes much more precise. Sometimes 4-year-olds have trouble building high towers with blocks because, in their desire to place each of the blocks perfectly, they may upset those already in the stack. Fine motor coordination continues to improve so that by age 5, hand, arm, and body all move together under better command of the eye. Mere towers no longer interest the 5-year-old, who now wants to build a house or a church, complete with steeple, though adults might still need to be told what each finished project is meant to be.

Nutrition and Exercise

Eating habits are important aspects of development during early childhood (Schiff, 2011; Wardlaw & Smith, 2011). What children eat affects their skeletal growth, body shape, and susceptibility to disease. Exercise and physical activity are also very important aspects of young children's lives (Lumpkin, 2011).

Overweight Young Children

Being overweight has become a serious health problem in early childhood (Marcdante, Kleigman, & Behrman, 2011). A recent national study revealed that 45 percent of children's meals exceed recommendations for saturated and trans fat, which can raise cholesterol levels and increase the risk of heart disease (Center for Science in the Public Interest, 2008). This study also found that one-third of children's daily caloric intake comes from restaurants, twice the percentage consumed away from home in the 1980s. Further, 93 percent of almost 1,500 possible choices at 13 major fast-food chains exceeded 430 calories—one-third of what the National Institute of Medicine recommends that 4- to 8-year-old children consume in a day. Nearly every combination of children's meals at KFC, Taco Bell, Sonic, Jack in the Box, and Chick-fil-A were too high in calories.

How Would You...?
As a health-care professional, how would you work with parents to increase the nutritional value of meals and snacks they provide to their young children?

Young children's eating behavior is strongly influenced by their caregivers' behavior (Black & Hurley, 2007; Ventura, Gromis, & Lohse, 2010). Children's eating behavior improves when caregivers eat with children on a predictable schedule, model eating healthy food, make mealtimes pleasant occasions, and engage in certain feeding styles. Distractions created by television, family arguments, and competing activities should be minimized so that children can focus on eating. Experts recommend a sensitive, responsive caregiver feeding style, in which the caregiver is nurturant, provides clear information about what is expected, and responds appropriately to children's cues (Black & Lozoff, 2008). Forceful and restrictive caregiver behaviors are not recommended, as they can lead to excessive weight gain.

The Centers for Disease Control and Prevention (2011) has established categories for obesity, overweight and at risk for being overweight. These categories are determined by body mass index (BMI), which is computed by a formula that takes

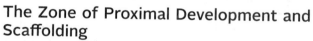

Rochel Gelman (1969) showed that when children's attention to relevant aspects of the conservation task is improved, they are more likely to conserve. Gelman has also demonstrated that attentional training on one dimension, such as number, improves preschool children's performance on another dimension, such as mass. Thus, Gelman believes that conservation appears earlier than Piaget thought and that attention is especially important in explaining conservation.

Vygotsky's Theory

Like Piaget, Vygotsky was a constructivist, but Vygotsky's theory is a **social constructivist approach**, and it emphasizes the social contexts of learning and the construction of knowledge through social interaction (Gauvain & Parke, 2010). In Chapter 1, we described some basic elements of Vygotsky's theory. Here we expand on his theory, exploring his ideas about the zone of proximal development, scaffolding, and the young child's use of language.

The Zone of Proximal Development and Scaffolding

Vygotsky's belief in the importance of social influences, especially instruction, on children's cognitive development is reflected in his concept of the zone of proximal development (Holzman, 2009). **Zone of proximal development (ZPD)** is Vygotsky's term for the range of tasks that are too difficult for the child to master alone but can be learned with the guidance and assistance of adults or more-skilled children. Thus, the lower limit of the ZPD is the level of skill reached by the child working independently. The upper limit is the level of additional responsibility the child can accept with the assistance of an able instructor (see Figure 5.6). The ZPD captures the child's cognitive skills that are in the process of maturing and can be accomplished only with the assistance of a more-skilled person (Alvarez & del Rio, 2007). Vygotsky (1962) called these the "buds" or "flowers" of development, to distinguish them from the "fruits" of development, which the child can already accomplish independently.

Closely linked to the idea of the ZPD is the concept of scaffolding, which was introduced in Chapter 4 in the context of parent-infant interaction. *Scaffolding* means changing the level of support. Over the course of a teaching session, a more-skilled person (a teacher or advanced peer) adjusts the amount of guidance to fit the child's current performance. When the student is learning a new task, the skilled person may use direct instruction. As the student's competence increases, less guidance is given.

Language and Thought

According to Vygotsky, children use speech not only for social communication but also to help them solve tasks. Vygotsky (1962) further believed that young children use language to plan, guide, and monitor their behavior. This use of language for self-regulation is called *private speech*. For Piaget, private speech is egocentric and immature, but for Vygotsky it is an important tool of thought during the early-childhood years (Wertsch, 2007).

Vygotsky said that language and thought initially develop independently of each other and then merge. He emphasized that all

Upper limit

Level of additional responsibility child can accept with assistance of an able instructor

Zone of proximal development (ZPD)

Lower limit

Level of problem solving reached on these tasks by child working alone

Figure 5.6 Vygotsky's Zone of Proximal Development

Vygotsky's zone of proximal development has a lower limit and an upper limit. Tasks in the ZPD are too difficult for the child to perform alone. They require assistance from an adult or a more-skilled child. As children experience the verbal instruction or demonstration, they organize the information in their existing mental structures, so they can eventually perform the skill or task alone.

How Would You...?

As an educator, how would you apply Vygotsky's ZPD theory and the concept of scaffolding to help a young child complete a puzzle?

mental functions have external, or social, origins. Children must use language to communicate with others before they can focus inward on their own thoughts. Children also must communicate externally and use language for a long time before they can make the transition from external to internal speech. This transition period occurs between ages 3 and 7 and involves talking to oneself. After a while, self-talk becomes second nature to children, and they can act without verbalizing. When this occurs, children have internalized their egocentric speech in the form of *inner speech*, which becomes their thoughts.

Vygotsky saw children who use a lot of private speech as more socially competent than those who don't. He argued that private speech represents an early transition toward becoming more socially communicative. For Vygotsky, when young children talk to themselves they are using language to govern their behavior and guide themselves. For example, a child working on a puzzle might say to herself, "Which pieces should I put together first? I'll try those green ones first. Now I need some blue ones. No, that blue one doesn't fit there. I'll try it over here." Researchers have found support for Vygotsky's view that private speech plays a positive role in children's development (Winsler, Carlton, & Barry, 2000). Children use private speech more when tasks are difficult, when they have made errors, and when they are not sure how to proceed (Berk, 1994). Researchers have also found that children who use private speech are more attentive and improve their performance more than do children who do not use private speech (Berk & Spuhl, 1995).

Teaching Strategies Based on Vygotsky's Theory

Vygotsky's theory has been embraced by many teachers and has been successfully applied to education (Holzman, 2009). Here are some ways in which educators can apply Vygotsky's theory:

1. *Assess the child's ZPD.* Like Piaget, Vygotsky did not believe that formal, standardized tests are the best way to assess children's learning. Rather, Vygotsky argued that assessment should focus on determining the child's zone of proximal development. The skilled helper presents the child with tasks of varying difficulty to determine the best level at which to begin instruction.

2. *Use the child's zone of proximal development in teaching.* Teaching should begin toward the zone's upper limit, so that the child can reach the goal with help and move to a higher level of skill and knowledge. Offer just enough assistance. You might ask, "What can I do to help you?" Or simply observe the child's intentions and attempts, providing support only when it is needed.

3. *Use more-skilled peers as teachers.* Remember that it is not just adults that are important in helping children learn. Children also benefit from the support and guidance of more-skilled children.

4. *Monitor and encourage children's use of private speech.* Be aware of the developmental change from talking to oneself externally when solving a problem during the preschool years to talking to oneself privately in the early elementary school years. In the elementary school years, encourage children to internalize and self-regulate their talk to themselves.

5. *Place instruction in a meaningful context.* Educators today are moving away from abstract presentations of material, instead providing students with opportunities to experience learning in real-world settings. For example, instead of just memorizing math formulas, students work on math problems with real-world implications.

Tools of the Mind is an early-childhood education curriculum that emphasizes children's development of self-regulation and the cognitive foundations of literacy. The curriculum was created by Elena Bodrova and Deborah Leong (2007) and has been implemented in more than 200 classrooms. Most of the children in the Tools of the Mind programs are at-risk because of their living circumstances, which in many instances are characterized by poverty and other difficult conditions, such as being homeless and having parents with drug problems.

With these applications of Vygotsky's theory in mind, let's examine an early childhood program that reflects these applications. Tools of the Mind is grounded in Vygotsky's (1962) theory, with special attention to cultural tools and the development of self-regulation, the zone of proximal development, scaffolding, private speech, shared activity, and play as important activity. In a Tools of the Mind classroom, dramatic play has a central role. Teachers guide children in creating themes that are based on the children's interests, such as treasure hunt, store, hospital, and restaurant. Teachers also incorporate field trips, visitor presentations, videos, and books in the development of children's play. They also help children develop a play plan, which increases the maturity of their play. Play plans describe what the children expect to do in the play period, including the imaginary context, roles, and props to be used. The play plans increase the quality of their play and self-regulation.

Scaffolding children's writing is another important theme in the Tools of the Mind classroom. Teachers guide children in planning their own message by drawing a line to stand for each word the child says. Children then repeat the message, pointing to each line as they say the word. Then the child writes on the lines, trying to represent each word with some letters or symbols.

Research assessments of children's writing in Tools of the Mind classrooms revealed that they have more advanced writing skills than do children in other early childhood programs (Bodrova & Leong, 2007). For example, they write more complex messages, use more words, spell more accurately, show better letter recognition, and have a better understanding of the concept of a sentence. Also, one study assessed the effects of the Tools of the Mind curriculum on at-risk preschool children (Diamond & others, 2007). The results indicated that the Tools of the Mind curriculum improved the self-regulatory and cognitive control skills (such as resisting distractions and temptations) of such children. Other research on the Tools of the Mind curriculum has found that it improves young children's cognitive skills (Barnett & others, 2006; Saifer, 2007).

Evaluating Vygotsky's Theory

How does Vygotsky's theory compare with Piaget's? We already have mentioned several comparisons, such as Vygotsky's emphasis on the importance of inner speech in development and Piaget's view that such speech is immature. Figure 5.7

	Vygotsky	Piaget
Sociocultural Context	Strong emphasis	Little emphasis
Constructivism	Social constructivist	Cognitive constructivist
Stages	No general stages of development proposed	Strong emphasis on stages (sensorimotor, preoperational, concrete operational, and formal operational)
Key Processes	Zone of proximal development, language, dialogue, tools of the culture	Schema, assimilation, accommodation, operations, conservation, classification
Role of Language	A major role; language plays a powerful role in shaping thought	Language has a minimal role; cognition primarily directs language
View on Education	Education plays a central role, helping children learn the tools of the culture	Education merely refines the child's cognitive skills that have already emerged
Teaching Implications	Teacher is a facilitator and guide, not a director; establish many opportunities for children to learn with the teacher and more-skilled peers	Also views teacher as a facilitator and guide, not a director; provide support for children to explore their world and discover knowledge

Figure 5.7 Comparison of Vygotsky's and Piaget's Theories

compares the two theories. The implication of Piaget's theory for teaching is that children need support to explore their world and discover knowledge. The main implication of Vygotsky's theory is that students need many opportunities to learn with a teacher and more-skilled peers. In both theories, teachers serve as facilitators and guides rather than as directors and molders.

Even though their theories were proposed at about the same time, most of the world learned about Vygotsky's theory later than they did about Piaget's, so Vygotsky's theory has not yet been evaluated as thoroughly. Vygotsky's view of the importance of sociocultural influences on children's development fits with the current belief that it is important to evaluate contextual factors in learning (Gauvain & Parke, 2010).

Some critics say that Vygotsky overemphasized the role of language in thinking. His emphasis on collaboration and guidance also has potential pitfalls. Might facilitators be too helpful in some cases, as when a parent becomes too overbearing and controlling? Further, some children might become lazy and expect help when they might have done something on their own.

Information Processing

Piaget's and Vygotsky's theories provided important ideas about how young children think and how their thinking changes. More recently, the information-processing approach has generated research that illuminates how children process information during the preschool years (Galotti, 2010). What are the limitations and advances in the young child's ability to pay attention to the environment, to remember, to develop strategies and solve problems, and to understand their own mental processes and those of others?

Attention

Recall that in Chapter 3 we defined *attention* as the focusing of mental resources on select information. The child's ability to pay attention improves significantly during the preschool years (Posner & Rothbart, 2007). Toddlers wander around, shift attention from one activity to another, and seem to spend little time focused on any one object or event. By comparison the preschool child might be observed watching television for half an hour.

Young children especially make advances in two aspects of attention: executive attention and sustained attention (Rothbart & Gartstein, 2008). **Executive attention** involves planning actions, allocating attention to goals, detecting and compensating for errors, monitoring progress on tasks, and dealing with novel or difficult circumstances. **Sustained attention** is focused and extended engagement with an object, task, event, or other aspect of the environment.

In at least two ways, however, the preschool child's control of attention is still deficient:

1. *Salient versus relevant dimensions.* Preschool children are likely to pay attention to stimuli that stand out, or are *salient*, even when those stimuli are not relevant to solving a problem or performing a task. For example, if a flashy, attractive clown presents the directions for solving a problem, preschool children are likely to pay more attention to the clown than to the directions. After age 6 or 7, children attend more efficiently to the dimensions of the task that are relevant, such as the directions for solving a problem. This change reflects a shift to cognitive control of attention, so that children act less impulsively and reflect more.

2. *Planfulness.* When experimenters ask children to judge whether two complex pictures are the same, preschool children tend to use a haphazard comparison strategy, not examining all the details before making a judgment. By comparison, elementary school age children are more likely to systematically compare the details across the pictures, one detail at a time (Vurpillot, 1968).

executive attention Involves action planning, allocating attention to goals, error detection and compensation, monitoring progress on tasks, and dealing with novel or difficult circumstances.

sustained attention Focused and extended engagement with an object, task, event, or other aspect of the environment.

In Central European countries such as Hungary, kindergarten children participate in exercises designed to improve their attention (Posner & Rothbart, 2007). For example, in one eye-contact exercise, the teacher sits in the center of a circle of children and each child is required to catch the teacher's eye before being permitted to leave the group. In other exercises created to improve attention, teachers have children participate in stop-go activities during which they have to listen for a specific signal, such as a drumbeat or an exact number of rhythmic beats, before stopping the activity. Recently, computer exercises have been developed to improve children's attention (Jaeggi, Berman, & Jonides, 2009; Tang & Posner, 2009).

The ability of preschool children to control and sustain their attention is related to school readiness (Posner & Rothbart, 2007). For example, a study of more than 1,000 children revealed that their ability to sustain their attention at 54 months of age was linked to their school readiness (which included achievement and language skills) (NICHD Early Child Care Research Network, 2005). A later study showed that children whose parents and teachers rated them higher on a scale of having attention problems at 54 months of age had a lower level of social skills in peer relations in the first and third grades than their counterparts who were rated lower on the attention problems scale (NICHD Early Child Care Research Network, 2009).

What are some advances in children's attention in early childhood?

Memory

Memory—the retention of information over time—is a central process in children's cognitive development. In Chapter 3, we saw that most of an infant's memories are fragile and, for the most part, short-lived—except for the memory of perceptual-motor actions, which can be substantial (Mandler, 2004). Thus, we saw that to understand the infant's capacity to remember we need to distinguish *implicit memory* from *explicit memory*. Explicit memory itself, however, comes in many forms. One distinction is between relatively permanent or *long-term memory* and short-term memory.

Short-Term Memory In **short-term memory**, individuals retain information for up to 30 seconds if there is no rehearsal of the information. Using *rehearsal* (repeating information after it has been presented), we can keep information in short-term memory for a much longer period. One method of assessing short-term memory is the memory-span task. You hear a short list of stimuli—usually digits—presented at a rapid pace (one per second, for example). Then you are asked to repeat the digits.

Research with the memory-span task suggests that short-term memory increases during early childhood. For example, in one investigation memory span increased from about 2 digits in 2- to 3-year-old children to about 5 digits in 7-year-old children, yet between ages 7 and 13 memory span increased by only 1½ digits (Dempster, 1981) (see Figure 5.8). Keep in mind, though, that memory span varies from one individual to another.

Why does memory span change with age? Rehearsal of information is important; older children rehearse the digits more than younger children do. Also important are efficiency of processing and speed, especially the speed with which memory items can be identified (Schneider, 2004).

The speed-of-processing explanation highlights a key point in the information-processing perspective: The speed with which a child processes information is an important aspect of the child's cognitive abilities, and there is abundant evidence that the speed with which many cognitive tasks are completed improves dramatically during the childhood years (Kail, 2007).

How Accurate Are Young Children's Long-Term Memories? While toddlers' short-term memory span increases during the early childhood years, their memory also becomes more accurate. Young children can remember a great deal of information if they are given appropriate cues and prompts. Increasingly, young children are even being allowed to testify in court, especially if they are the only witnesses to abuse or a crime. Several factors can influence the accuracy of a young child's memory, however (Bruck & Ceci, 1999):

- *There are age differences in children's susceptibility to suggestion.* Preschoolers are the most suggestible age group (Lehman & others, 2010). For example, preschool children are more susceptible to believing misleading or incorrect information given after an event (Ghetti & Alexander, 2004). Despite these age differences, there is still concern about the reaction of older children when they are subjected to suggestive interviews (Ceci & others, 2007).

- *There are individual differences in susceptibility.* Some preschoolers are highly resistant to interviewers' suggestions, whereas others immediately succumb to the slightest suggestion. A recent study revealed that preschool children's ability to produce a high-quality narrative was linked to their resistance to suggestion (Kulkofsky & Klemfuss, 2008).

- *Interviewing techniques can produce substantial distortions in children's reports about highly salient events.* Children are suggestible not just about peripheral details but also about the central aspects of an event (Bruck, Ceci, & Hembrooke, 1998). In some cases, children's false reports can be tinged with sexual connotations. In laboratory studies, young children have made false claims about "silly events" that involved body contact (such as "Did the nurse lick your knee?" or "Did she blow in your ear?"). A significant number of preschool children have falsely reported that someone touched their private parts, kissed them, or hugged them, when these events clearly did not happen. Nevertheless, young children are capable of recalling much that is relevant about an event (Fivush, 1993). When young children do recall information accurately, the interviewer often has a neutral tone, misleading questions are avoided, and there is no reason for the child to make a false report (Bruck & Ceci, 1999).

In sum, whether a young child's eyewitness testimony is accurate or not may depend on a number of factors, such as

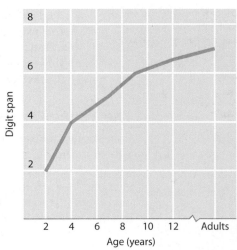

Figure 5.8
Developmental Changes in Memory Span
In one study, from 2 years of age to 7 years of age, children's memory span increased about 3 digits to 5 digits (Dempster, 1981). Between 7 and 13 years of age, memory span had increased on average only another 1½ digits, to 7 digits. *What factors might contribute to the increase in memory span during childhood?*

Four-year-old Jennifer Royal was the only eyewitness to one of her playmates' being shot to death. She was allowed to testify in open court and the clarity of her statements helped to convict the gunman. *What are some issues involved in whether young children should be allowed to testify in court?*

theory of mind Refers to the awareness of one's own mental processes and the mental processes
of others.

the type, number, and intensity of the suggestive techniques the child
has experienced. It appears that the reliability of young children's
reports has as much to do with the skills and motivation of the interviewer as with any natural limitations on young children's memory
(Ceci & others, 2007).

The Young Child's Theory of Mind

Even young children are curious about the nature of the human mind. They have
a **theory of mind,** a term that refers to awareness of one's own mental processes
and those of others. Studies of theory of mind view the child as "a thinker who
is trying to explain, predict, and understand people's thoughts, feelings, and
utterances" (Harris, 2006). Children's theory of mind changes as they develop
through childhood (Gelman, 2009; Wellman, 2011). The main changes occur at
ages 2 to 3, 4 to 5, and beyond age 5.

Ages 2 to 3 In this time frame, children begin to understand the following three
mental states: (1) *Perceptions*—the child realizes that other people see what is in front
of their eyes and not necessarily what is in front of the child's eyes. (2) *Emotions*—
the child can distinguish between positive and negative emotions. A child might
say, "Vic feels bad." (3) *Desires*—the child understands that if someone wants something, he or she will try to get it. A child might say, "I want my mommy."

Children refer to desires earlier and more frequently than they refer to cognitive states such as thinking and knowing (Harris, 2006). Two- to 3-year-olds understand the way desires are related to actions and to simple emotions (Harris,
2006). For example, they understand that people will
search for what they want and that if they obtain it,
they are likely to feel happy, but if they don't, they will
keep searching for it and are likely to feel sad or angry
(Hadwin & Perner, 1991).

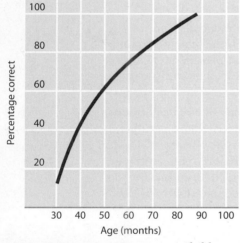

Ages 4 to 5 Children come to understand that the mind
can represent objects and events accurately or inaccu-
rately. The realization that people can have *false beliefs*—
beliefs that are not true—develops in a majority of children by the time they are 5 years old (Wellman, Cross, &
Watson, 2001) (see Figure 5.9).

In a classic false-belief task, children are told a story
about Sally and Anne. In the story, Sally places a toy in
a basket and then leaves the room. In her absence, Anne
takes the toy from the basket and places it in a box.
Children are asked where Sally will look for the toy when she returns.
The major finding is that 3-year-olds tend to fail false-belief tasks,
saying that Sally will look in the box (even though Sally could not
know that the toy has been moved to this new location). Four-year-
olds and older children tend to pass the task, correctly saying that
Sally will have a "false belief"—she will think the object is in the
basket, even though that belief is now false. The conclusion from
these studies is that children younger than age 4 do not understand
that it is possible to have a false belief.

Young children's understanding of thinking has some limitations (Wellman, 2011). They often underestimate when mental activity is likely occurring. For example, they fail to attribute mental
activity to someone who is sitting quietly, reading, or talking (Flavell,
Green, & Flavell, 1995). Their understanding of their own thinking
is also limited.

Beyond Age 5 It is only beyond the preschool years that children
have a deepening appreciation of the mind itself rather than just an

**Figure 5.9 Development Changes
in False-Belief Performance**
False-belief performance—the
child's understanding that a
person has a false belief that
contradicts reality—dramatically
increases from 2½ years of age
through the middle of the elementary school years. In a
summary of the results of many
studies, 2½-year-olds gave correct
responses about 20 percent of
the time (Wellman, Cross, &
Watson, 2001). At 3 years 8
months, they were correct about
50 percent of the time, and after
that, gave increasingly correct
responses.

understanding of mental states (Wellman, 2011). Not until middle and late childhood do children see the mind as an active constructor of knowledge or a processing center (Flavell, Green, & Flavell, 2000). It is only then that they move from understanding that beliefs can be false to realizing that the same event can be open to multiple interpretations (Carpendale & Chandler, 1996).

Individual Differences As in other developmental research, there are individual differences in when children reach certain milestones in their theory of mind (Pellicano, 2010; Wellman, 2011). For example, children who talk with their parents about feelings frequently as 2-year-olds show better performance on theory of mind tasks (Ruffman, Slade, & Crowe, 2002), as do children who frequently engage in pretend play (Harris, 2000).

Executive function, which describes several functions (such as inhibition and planning) that are important for flexible, future-oriented behavior, also may be connected to the development of a theory of mind (Doherty, 2008). For example, in one executive function task, children are asked to say the word "night" when they see a picture of a sun and the word "day" when they see a picture of a moon and stars. Children who perform better at executive function tasks seem also to have a better understanding of theory of mind (Sabbagh & others, 2006).

Another individual difference in understanding the mind involves autism (Doherty, 2008). Children with autism show a number of behaviors that differ from those of most children their age, including deficits in social interaction and communication as well as repetitive behaviors or interests. Researchers have found that autistic children have difficulty developing a theory of mind, especially when it comes to understanding other people's beliefs and emotions (Peterson & others, 2009; Williams & Happe, 2010).

Language Development

Toddlers move rather quickly from producing two-word utterances to creating three-, four-, and five-word combinations. Between ages 2 and 3, they begin the transition from saying simple sentences that express a single proposition to saying complex sentences.

As young children learn the special features of their own language, there are extensive regularities in how they acquire that particular language (Berko Gleason, 2009). For example, all children learn the prepositions *on* and *in* before other prepositions. Children learning other languages, such as Russian or Chinese, also acquire the particular features of those languages in a consistent order.

Understanding Phonology and Morphology

Phonology refers to the sound system of a language, including the sounds used and how they may be combined. During the preschool years, most children gradually become more sensitive to the sounds of spoken words and increasingly capable of producing all the sounds of their language. By their third birthday they can produce all the vowel sounds and most of the consonant sounds (Menn & Stoel-Gammon, 2009).

By the time children move beyond two-word utterances, they demonstrate a knowledge of morphology rules (Tager-Flusberg & Zukowski, 2009). **Morphology** refers to the units of meaning involved in word formation. Children begin using the plural and possessive forms of nouns (such as *dogs* and *dog's*). They put appropriate endings on verbs (such as -*s* when the subject is third-person singular and -*ed* for the past tense). They use prepositions (such as *in* and *on*), articles (such as *a* and *the*), and various forms of the verb *to be* (such as "I *was* going to the store"). Some of the best evidence for changes in children's use of morphological rules

syntax The ways words are combined to form acceptable phrases and sentences.

semantics The meaning of words and sentences.

pragmatics The appropriate use of language in different contexts.

occurs in their overgeneralization of the rules, as when a preschool child says "foots" instead of "feet," or "goed" instead of "went."

In a classic experiment that was designed to study children's knowledge of morphological rules, such as how to make a plural, Jean Berko (1958) presented preschool and first-grade children with cards such as the one shown in Figure 5.10. The children were asked to look at the card while the experimenter read aloud the words on the card. Then the children were asked to supply the missing word. This might sound easy, but Berko was interested in the children's ability to apply the appropriate morphological rule, in this case to say "wugs" with the *z* sound that indicates the plural.

Although the children's answers were not perfect, they were much better than chance. What makes Berko's study impressive is that most of the words were made up for the experiment. Thus, the children could not base their responses on remembering past instances of hearing the words. That they could make the plurals or past tenses of words they had never heard before was proof that they knew the morphological rules.

This is a wug.

Now there is another one. There are two of them. There are two _____.

Figure 5.10 Stimuli in Berko's Study of Young Children's Understanding of Morphological Rules In Jean Berko's (1958) study, young children were presented cards, such as this one with a "wug" on it. Then the children were asked to supply the missing word; in supplying the missing word, they had to say it correctly too. "Wugs" is the correct response here.

Changes in Syntax and Semantics

Preschool children also learn and apply rules of **syntax,** which involves the way words are combined to form acceptable phrases and sentences (Tager-Flusberg & Zukowski, 2009). They show a growing mastery of complex rules for how words should be ordered. Consider *wh-* questions, such as "Where is Daddy going?" or "What is that boy doing?" To ask these questions properly, the child must know two important differences between *wh-* questions and affirmative statements (for instance, "Daddy is going to work" and "That boy is waiting for the school bus"). First, a *wh-* word must be added at the beginning of the sentence. Second, the auxiliary verb must be inverted—that is, exchanged with the subject of the sentence. Young children learn quite early where to put the *wh-* word, but they take much longer to learn the auxiliary-inversion rule. Thus, preschool children might ask, "Where Daddy is going?" and "What that boy is doing?"

Gains in **semantics,** the aspect of language that refers to the meaning of words and sentences, also characterize early childhood. Vocabulary development is dramatic (Pan & Uccelli, 2009). Some experts have concluded that between 18 months and 6 years, young children learn about one new word every waking hour (Gelman & Kalish, 2006)! By the time they enter first grade, it is estimated that children know about 14,000 words (Clark, 1993).

Advances in Pragmatics

Changes in **pragmatics,** the appropriate use of language in different contexts, also characterize young children's language development (Bryant, 2009). A 6-year-old is simply a much better conversationalist than a 2-year-old. What are some of the improvements in pragmatics during the preschool years?

Young children begin to engage in extended discourse (Akhtar & Herold, 2008). For example, they learn culturally specific rules of conversation and politeness, and become sensitive to the need to adapt their speech to different settings. Their developing linguistic skills and increasing ability to take the perspective of others contribute to their generation of more competent narratives.

As children grow older, they become increasingly able to talk about things that are not here (grandma's house, for example) and not now (what happened to them yesterday or might happen tomorrow, for example). A preschool child can tell you what she wants for lunch tomorrow, something that would not have been possible at the two-word stage of language development.

Around age 4 or 5, children learn to change their speech style to suit the situation. For example, even 4-year-old children speak differently to a 2-year-old than to a same-aged peer; they use shorter sentences with the 2-year-old. They also speak differently to an adult than to a same-aged peer, using more polite and formal language with the adult (Shatz & Gelman, 1973).

Young Children's Literacy

Concern about U.S. children's ability to read and write has led to a careful examination of preschool and kindergarten children's experiences, with the hope that a positive orientation toward reading and writing can be developed early in life (Jalongo, 2011; Wagner, 2010). Parents and teachers need to provide young children with a supportive environment for the development of literacy skills (Christie, Enz, & Vukelich, 2011; Reese, Sparks, & Leyva, 2010). Children should be active participants and be immersed in a wide range of interesting listening, talking, writing, and reading experiences (Beatty & Pratt, 2011). A recent study revealed that children whose mothers had more education had more advanced emergent literacy levels than did children whose mothers had less education (Korat, 2009). Another study found that literacy experiences (such as how often the child was read to), the quality of the mother's engagement with her child (such as attempts to cognitively stimulate the child), and provision of learning materials (such as age-appropriate learning materials and books) were important home literacy experiences in low-income families that were linked to the children's language development in positive ways (Rodriquez & others, 2009).

Instruction should be built on what children already know about oral language, reading, and writing. Further, early precursors of literacy and academic success include language skills, phonological and syntactic knowledge, letter identification, and conceptual knowledge about print and its conventions and functions (Morrow, 2009).

The devl and the babe goste

A DEVL NAPD IN THE BRITE SUNLITE he SED IT IS HOLOWENE I HAV to GET UP AND GET. reDE to SCer The littL CHILJRIN WEN ThAEGO to CHRICOR CHRETE FRST He MADE A JACAL ETRN He PUT 2 CEDLS IN it to RELE SCer THem THN He MADE A COL JRIN to CAST SPELS ON The CHIL JRIN.

Anna Mudd began writing stories when she was 4 years old. Above is her story, "The devl and the babe goste," which she wrote as a 6-year-old. The story includes poetic images, sophisticated syntax, and vocabulary that reflects advances in language development. *What are some guidelines parents and teachers can follow in helping young children develop literacy skills?*

The advances in language that take place in early childhood lay the foundation for later development in the elementary school years, which we will discuss in Chapter 7.

Early Childhood Education

How do other early education programs treat children, and how do the children fare? Our exploration of early childhood education focuses on variations in programs, education for children who are disadvantaged, and some controversies in early childhood education.

child-centered kindergarten Education that involves the whole child by considering both the child's physical, cognitive, and socioemotional development and the child's needs, interests, and learning styles.

Montessori approach An educational philosophy in which children are given considerable freedom and spontaneity in choosing activities and are allowed to move from one activity to another as they desire.

Variations in Early Childhood Education

There are many variations in the way young children are educated (Folari, 2011; Morrison, 2011; Shonkoff, 2010). The foundation of early childhood education is the child-centered kindergarten.

The Child-Centered Kindergarten

Nurturing is a key aspect of the **child-centered kindergarten**, which emphasizes the education of the whole child and concern for his or her physical, cognitive, and socioemotional development (Marion, 2010). Instruction is organized around the child's needs, interests, and learning styles. Emphasis is on the process of learning, rather than what is learned (Hendrick & Weissman, 2010). The child-centered kindergarten honors three principles: (1) Each child follows a unique developmental pattern; (2) young children learn best through firsthand experiences with people and materials; and (3) play is extremely important in the child's total development. *Experimenting, exploring, discovering, trying out, restructuring, speaking,* and *listening* are frequent activities in excellent kindergarten programs. Such programs are closely attuned to the developmental status of 4- and 5-year-old children.

The Montessori Approach

Montessori schools are patterned on the educational philosophy of Maria Montessori (1870–1952), an Italian physician-turned-educator who at the beginning of the twentieth century crafted a revolutionary approach to young children's education. The **Montessori approach** is a philosophy of education in which children are given considerable freedom and spontaneity in choosing activities. They are allowed to move from one activity to another as they desire. The teacher acts as a facilitator rather than a director. The teacher shows the child how to perform intellectual

Larry Page and Sergey Brin, founders of the highly successful Internet search engine, Google, have said that their early years at Montessori schools were a major factor in their success (International Montessori Council, 2006). During an interview with Barbara Walters, they said they learned how to be self-directed and self-starters at Montessori (ABC News, 2005). They commented that Montessori experiences encouraged them to think for themselves and allowed them the freedom to develop their own interests.

activities, demonstrates interesting ways to explore curriculum materials, and offers help when the child requests it (Drake, 2008; Lillard, 2008). "By encouraging children to make decisions from an early age, Montessori programs seek to develop self-regulated problem solvers who can make choices and manage their time effectively" (Hyson, Copple, & Jones, 2006, p. 14). The number of Montessori schools in the United States has expanded dramatically in recent years, from one school in 1959 to 355 schools in 1970 to more than 4,000 today.

Some developmental psychologists favor the Montessori approach, but others believe that it neglects children's socioemotional development. For example, although the Montessori approach fosters independence and the development of cognitive skills, it deemphasizes verbal interaction between the teacher and child and between peers. Montessori's critics also argue that it restricts imaginative play and that its heavy reliance on self-corrective materials may not adequately allow for creativity and for a variety of learning styles.

Developmentally Appropriate Education

Many educators and psychologists conclude that preschool and young elementary school children learn best through active, hands-on teaching methods such as games and dramatic play. They know that children develop at varying rates and that schools need to allow for these individual differences. They also argue that schools should focus on improving children's socioemotional development as well as their cognitive development. Educators refer to this type of schooling as **developmentally appropriate practice (DAP)**, which is based on knowledge of the typical development of children within a particular age span (age-appropriateness), as well as on the uniqueness of the individual child (individual-appropriateness). DAP emphasizes the importance of creating settings that encourage children to be active learners and reflect children's interests and capabilities (Bredekamp, 2011; Kostelnik, Soderman, & Whiren, 2011). Desired outcomes for DAP include thinking critically, working cooperatively, solving problems, developing self-regulatory skills, and enjoying learning. The emphasis in DAP is on the process of learning rather than on its content (Barbarin & Miller, 2009; Ritchie, Maxwell, & Bredekamp, 2009).

Do developmentally appropriate educational practices improve young children's development? Some researchers have found that young children in developmentally appropriate classrooms are likely to feel less stress, be more motivated, be more socially skilled, have better work habits, be more creative, have better language skills, and demonstrate better math skills than children in developmentally inappropriate classrooms (Hart & others, 2003). However, not all studies find DAP to have significant positive effects (Hyson, Copple, & Jones, 2006). Among the reasons that it is difficult to generalize about research on developmentally appropriate education is that individual programs often vary, and developmentally appropriate education is an evolving concept. Recent changes in the concept have given more attention to sociocultural factors and the teacher's active involvement and implementation of systematic intentions, as well as how strongly academic skills should be emphasized and how they should be taught.

How Would You...?
As an educator, how would you design a developmentally appropriate lesson to teach kindergartners the concept of gravity?

Education for Young Children Who Are Disadvantaged

For many years, U.S. children from low-income families did not receive any education before they entered the first grade. Often when they began first grade they were already several steps behind their classmates in readiness to learn. In the summer of 1965, the federal government began an effort to break the cycle of poverty and poor education for young children through **Project Head Start.** Head Start is a compensatory program designed to give children from low-income

How Would You...?

As a health-care professional, how would you explain the importance of health services being a component of an effective Head Start program?

families the opportunity to acquire skills and experiences that are important for success in school (Zigler & Styfco, 2010). After almost half a century, Head Start continues to be the largest federally funded program for U.S. children, with almost 1 million children enrolled in it annually (Hagen & Lamb-Parker, 2008). In 2007, 3 percent of Head Start children were 5 years old, 51 percent were 4 years old, 36 percent were 3 years old, and 10 percent were under age 3 (Administration for Children & Families, 2008).

Early Head Start was established in 1995 to serve children from birth to age 3. In 2007, half of all new funds appropriated for Head Start programs were used for the expansion of Early Head Start. Researchers have found these programs to have positive effects (Hoffman & Ewen, 2007).

Head Start programs are not all created equal. One estimate is that 40 percent of the 1,400 Head Start programs are of questionable quality (Zigler & Styfco, 1994). More attention needs to be given to developing consistently high-quality Head Start programs (Chambers, Cheung, & Slavin, 2006). One person who is strongly motivated to make Head Start a valuable learning experience for young children from disadvantaged backgrounds is Yolanda Garcia. To read about her work, see "Careers in Life-Span Development."

CAREERS IN LIFE-SPAN DEVELOPMENT

Yolanda Garcia, Director of Children's Services, Head Start

Yolanda Garcia has been the director of the Children's Services Department of the Santa Clara, California, County Office of Education since 1980. As director, she is responsible for managing child development programs for 2,500 3- to 5-year-old children in 127 classrooms. Her training includes two master's degrees, one in public policy and child welfare from the University of Chicago and another in education administration from San Jose State University.

Yolanda Garcia, Director of Children's Services/Head Start, working with a Head Start child in Santa Clara, California.

Garcia has served on many national advisory committees that have resulted in improvements in the staffing of Head Start programs. Most notably, she served on the Head Start Quality Committee that recommended the development of Early Head Start and revised performance standards for Head Start programs. Garcia currently is a member of the American Academy of Science Committee on the Integration of Science and Early Childhood Education.

Evaluations support the positive influence of quality early childhood programs on both the cognitive and social worlds of disadvantaged young children (Ryan, Fauth, & Brooks-Gunn, 2006). A recent national evaluation of Head Start revealed that the program had a positive influence on the language and cognitive development of the 3- and 4-year-olds (Puma & others, 2010). However, by the end of the first grade, there were few lasting outcomes. One exception was a larger vocabulary for those who went to Head Start as 4-year-olds and better oral comprehension for those who went to Head Start as 3-year-olds. Another recent study found that when young children initially began Head Start, they were well below their more academically advantaged peers in literacy and math (Hindman & others, 2010). However, by the end of the first grade, the Head Start children were on par with national averages in literacy and math.

One high-quality early childhood education program (although not a Head Start program) is the Perry Preschool program in Ypsilanti, Michigan, a two-year preschool program that includes weekly home visits from program personnel. In analyses of the long-term effects of the program, adults who had been in the Perry Preschool program were compared with a control group of adults from the same background who did not receive the enriched early childhood education (Schweinhart & others, 2005; Weikert, 1993). Those who had been in the Perry Preschool program had fewer teen pregnancies and higher high school graduation rates, and at age 40 more were in the workforce, owned their own homes, had a savings account, and had fewer arrests.

Controversies in Early Childhood Education

Two current controversies in early childhood education involve what the curriculum for early childhood education should be and whether preschool education should be universal in the United States.

How Would You...?
As a psychologist, how would you advise preschool teachers to balance the development of young children's skills for academic achievement with opportunities for healthy social interaction?

Controversy Over Curriculum

A current controversy in early childhood education involves what the curriculum for early childhood education should be (Barbarin & Miller, 2009; Bredekamp, 2011; Marion, 2010). On one side are those who advocate a child-centered, constructivist approach much like that emphasized by the National Association for the Education of Young Children (NAEYC), along the lines of developmentally appropriate practice. On the other side are those who advocate an academic, direct-instruction approach.

In reality, many high-quality early-childhood education programs include both academic and constructivist approaches. Many education experts, such as Lilian Katz (1999), though, worry about academic approaches that place too much pressure on young children to achieve and don't provide opportunities to actively construct knowledge. Competent early childhood programs also should focus on both cognitive development *and* socioemotional development, not exclusively on cognitive development (Bredekamp, 2011; NAEYC, 2009).

Universal Preschool Education

Another controversy in early childhood education focuses on whether preschool education should be instituted for all U.S. 4-year-old children. Edward Zigler and his colleagues (2006) argue that the United States should have universal preschool education. They emphasize that quality preschools prepare children for later academic success. Zigler and his colleagues (2006) cite research showing that quality preschool programs increase the likelihood that once children go to elementary and secondary school they will be less likely to be retained in a grade or drop out of school. They also point to analyses indicating that universal preschool would bring cost savings on the order of billions of dollars because of a diminished need for remedial and justice services (Karoly & Bigelow, 2005).

Critics of universal preschool education argue that the gains attributed to preschool and kindergarten education are often overstated. They especially stress that research has not proven that nondisadvantaged children improve as a result of attending a preschool. Thus, the critics say it is more important to improve preschool education for young children who are disadvantaged rather than funding preschool education for all 4-year-old children. Some critics, especially home-schooling advocates, emphasize that young children should be educated by their parents, not by schools. Thus, universal preschool education remains a subject of controversy.

Summary

Physical Changes

- The average child grows 2½ inches in height and gains between 5 and 7 pounds a year during early childhood. Growth patterns vary from one child to another, though. Some of the brain's increase in size in early childhood is due to increases in the number and size of dendrites, some to myelination. From ages 3 to 6, the most rapid growth in the brain occurs in the frontal lobes.

- Gross and fine motor skills increase dramatically during early childhood.

- Too many young children in the United States are being raised on diets that are too high in fat. The child's life should be centered on activities, not meals. Other nutritional concerns include malnutrition in early childhood and the inadequate diets of many children living in poverty.

- Accidents are the leading cause of death in young children. A special concern is the poor health status of many young children in low-income families. There has been a dramatic increase in HIV/AIDS in young children in developing countries in recent decades.

Cognitive Changes

- According to Piaget, in the preoperational stage children cannot yet perform operations, but they begin to present the world with symbols, to form stable concepts, and to reason. Preoperational thought is characterized by two substages: symbolic function (2 to 4 years) and intuitive thought (4 to 7 years). Centration and a lack of conservation also characterize the preoperational stage.

- Vygotsky's theory represents a social constructivist approach to development. Vygotsky argues that it is important to discover the child's zone of proximal development to improve the child's learning.

- Young children make substantial strides in executive and sustained attention. Significant improvement in short-term memory occurs during early childhood. Theory of mind is the awareness of one's own mental processes and the mental processes of others. Children begin to understand mental states involving perceptions, emotions, and desires at 2 to 3 years of age and at 4 to 5 years of age realize that people can have false beliefs.

Language Development

- Young children increase their grasp of language's rule systems. In terms of phonology, children become more sensitive to the sounds of spoken language. Berko's classic study demonstrated that young children understand morphological rules.

- Preschool children learn and apply rules of syntax and how words should be ordered. In terms of semantics, vocabulary development increases dramatically in early childhood.

- Young children's conversational skills improve in early childhood.

- Early precursors of literacy and academic success develop in early childhood.

Early Childhood Education

- The child-centered kindergarten emphasizes the education of the whole child. The Montessori approach has become increasingly popular. Developmentally appropriate practice focuses on the typical patterns of children (age appropriateness) and the uniqueness of each child (individual appropriateness).

- The U.S. government has tried to break the poverty cycle with programs such as Head Start. Model programs have had positive effects on young children's education.

- Controversy over early childhood education involves what the curriculum should be and whether universal preschool education should be implemented.

Key Terms

6 Socioemotional Development in Early Childhood

Stories of Life-Span Development: Craig Lesley's Complicated Early Emotional and Social Life

In his memoir *Burning Fence: A Western Memoir of Fatherhood*, award-winning novelist Craig Lesley describes one memory from his early childhood:

Lifting me high above his head, my father placed me in the crotch of the Bing cherry tree growing beside my mother's parents' house in The Dalles. A little frightened at the dizzying height, I pressed my palms into the tree's rough, peeling bark. My father stood close, reassuring. I could see his olive skin, dazzling smile, and sharp-creased army uniform.

"Rudell, don't let him fall." My mother watched, her arms held out halfway, as if to catch me. . . .

The cherries were ripe and robins flittered through the green leaves, pecking at the Bings. Tipping my head back I could see blue sky beyond the extended branches.

"That's enough. Bring him down now." My mother's arms reached out farther.

Laughing, my father grabbed me under the arms, twirled me around, and plunked me into the grass. I wobbled a little. Imprinted on my palms was the pattern of the tree bark, and I brushed off the little bark pieces on my dungarees.

In a moment, my grandmother gave me a small glass of lemonade. . . .

This first childhood memory of my father remains etched in my mind. . . .

When I grew older, I realized that my father had never lifted me into the cherry tree. After Rudell left, I never saw him until I was fifteen. My grandfather had put me in the tree. Still, the memory of my father lifting me into the tree persists. Even today, I remain half-convinced by the details, the press of bark against my palms, the taste of lemonade, the texture of my father's serge uniform. Apparently, my mind has cross-wired the photographs of my handsome father in his army uniform with the logical reality that my grandfather set me in the crotch of the tree.

Why can I remember the event so vividly? I guess because I wanted so much for my father to be there. I have no easy answers. (Lesley, 2005, pp. 8–10)

Like millions of children, Lesley experienced a family torn by divorce; he would also experience abuse by a stepfather. When his father left, Lesley was an infant, but even as a preschooler he felt his father's absence. Once he planned to win a gift for his father so that his grandmother "could take it to him and then he'd come to see me" (Lesley, 2005, p. 16). In just a few years, the infant had become a child with a complicated emotional and social life.

In early childhood, young children's emotional lives and personalities develop in significant ways, and their small worlds widen. In addition to the continuing influence of family relationships, peers assume a more significant role in children's development, play fills the days of many young children's lives—and, for many, more time is spent watching television.

Emotional and Personality Development

Many changes characterize young children's socioemotional development in early childhood. Children's developing minds and social experiences produce remarkable advances in the development of the self, emotional maturity, moral understanding, and gender awareness.

The Self

We learned in Chapter 4 that during the second year of life children make considerable progress in self-recognition. In the early childhood years, young children develop in many ways that enable them to enhance their self-understanding.

Initiative Versus Guilt

In Chapter 1, you read about Erik Erikson's (1968) eight developmental stages, which are encountered during certain time periods in the human life span. As you learned in Chapter 4, Erikson's first stage, trust versus mistrust, describes what he considers to be the main developmental task of infancy. According to Erikson, the psychosocial stage associated with early childhood is *initiative versus guilt*. By now, children have become convinced that they are persons of their own; during early childhood, they begin to discover what kind of person they will become. They identify intensely with their parents, who most of the time appear to them to be powerful and beautiful, though often unreasonable, disagreeable, and sometimes even dangerous. During early childhood, children use their perceptual, motor, cognitive, and language skills to make things happen. They have a surplus of energy that permits them to forget failures quickly and to approach new areas that seem desirable—even if dangerous—with undiminished zest and some increased sense of direction. On their own initiative, then, children at this stage exuberantly move out into a wider social world.

The great governor of initiative is *conscience*. Children's initiative and enthusiasm may bring them not only rewards but also guilt, which lowers self-esteem.

Self-Understanding and Understanding Others

Recent research studies have revealed that young children are more psychologically aware—of themselves and others—than was formerly thought (Carpendale & Lewis, 2011; Thompson & Virmani, 2010). This increased awareness reflects young children's expanding psychological sophistication.

In Erikson's portrait of early childhood, the young child clearly has begun to develop **self-understanding**, which is the representation of self, the substance and content of self-conceptions (Harter, 2006). Though not the whole of personal identity, self-understanding provides its rational underpinnings. Mainly through interviews,

What character-
izes young
children's self-
understanding?

researchers have probed children's conceptions of many aspects of self-understanding (Harter, 2006).

As we saw in Chapter 4, early self-understanding involves
self-recognition. In early childhood, young children think the
self can be described by material characteristics such as size,
shape, and color. They distinguish themselves from others
through physical and material attributes. Says 4-year-old Sandra,
"I'm different from Jennifer because I have brown hair and she
has blond hair." Says 4-year-old Ralph, "I am different from
Hank because I am taller and I am different from my sister
because I have a bicycle." Physical activities are also a central
component of the self in early childhood (Keller, Ford, &
Meacham, 1978). For example, preschool children often describe
themselves in terms of activities such as play. In sum, in early
childhood, children often provide self-descriptions that involve
body attributes, material possessions, and physical activities.

Although young children mainly describe themselves in
terms of concrete, observable features and activities, at age 4
to 5, as they hear others use psychological trait and emotion
terms, they begin to include these in their self-descriptions
(Marsh, Ellis, & Craven, 2002). Thus, in a self-description a
4-year-old might say, "I'm not scared. I'm always happy."

Young children's self-descriptions are typically unrealistically positive, as reflected
in the comment of the 4-year-old who says he is always happy, which he is not (Harter,
2006). They express this optimism because they don't yet distinguish between their
desired competence and their actual competence, tend to confuse ability and effort
(thinking that differences in ability can be changed as easily as can differences in
effort), don't engage in spontaneous social comparison of their abilities with those
of others, and tend to compare their present abilities with what they could do at an
earlier age (which usually makes them look quite good) (Thompson, 2008).

Understanding Others Children also make advances in their understanding of
others (Carpendale & Lewis, 2011). Young children's theory of mind includes understanding that other people have emo-
tions and desires. And at age 4 to 5 children
not only start describing themselves in
terms of psychological traits but also begin to
perceive others in terms of psychological
traits. Thus, a 4-year-old might say, "My
teacher is nice."

It is important for children to develop
an understanding that people don't always
give accurate reports of their beliefs (Gee &
Heyman, 2007). Researchers have found
that even 4-year-olds understand that people
may make statements that aren't true in
order to obtain what they want or to avoid

Young children are more psychologically aware of themselves and
others than used to be thought.
Some children are better than
others at understanding people's
feelings and desires—and, to
some degree, these individual
differences are influenced by
conversations caregivers have
with young children about
feelings and desires.

trouble (Lee & others, 2002). For example, one recent study revealed
that 4- and 5-year-olds were increasingly skeptical of another child's
claim to be sick when the children were informed that the child was
motivated to avoid having to go to camp (Gee & Heyman, 2007).
Another recent study found that at age 3 children mistrusted people
who made a single error, but it wasn't until age 4 that, when deciding
whom to trust, children took into account the relative frequency of
errors informants made (Pasquini & others, 2007). This and other
research on young children's social understanding provides clear
evidence that young children are not as egocentric as Piaget believed
them to be.

Children also begin to develop an understanding for joint commitments. A recent study revealed that 3-year-olds, but not 2-year-olds, recognize when an adult is committed and when they themselves are committed to an activity that involves obligation to a partner (Grafenhain & others, 2009).

Both the extensive theory of mind research and the recent research on young children's social understanding underscore that young children are not as egocentric as Piaget envisioned (Sokol & others, 2010). Ross Thompson (2009e), a leading expert on children's socioemotional development, recently questioned why Piaget's concept of egocentrism has become ingrained in people's thinking about young children given the fact that the current research on social awareness in infancy and early childhood is dissonant with Piaget's egocentrism concept.

Emotional Development

The young child's growing awareness of self is linked to the ability to feel an expanding range of emotions. Young children, like adults, experience many emotions during the course of a day. Their emotional development allows them to try to make sense of other people's emotional reactions and to begin to control their own emotions.

Expressing Emotions

Recall from Chapter 4 that even young infants experience emotions such as joy and fear, but to experience *self-conscious emotions* children must be able to refer to themselves and be aware of themselves as distinct from others (Lewis, 2007). Pride, shame, embarrassment, and guilt are examples of self-conscious emotions. These emotions do not appear to develop until self-awareness appears around 18 months of age.

During the early childhood years, emotions such as pride and guilt become more common. They are especially influenced by parents' responses to children's behavior. For example, a young child may experience shame when a parent says, "You should feel bad about biting your sister."

Understanding Emotions

Among the most important changes in emotional development in early childhood is an increased understanding of emotions. Young children increasingly understand that certain situations are likely to evoke particular emotions, facial expressions indicate specific emotions, and emotions affect behavior and can be used to influence others (Cole & others, 2009). A recent meta-analysis revealed that emotion knowledge (such as understanding emotional cues—for example, when a young child understands that a peer feels sad about being left out of a game) was positively related to 3- to 5-year-olds' social competence (such as offering an empathic response to the child who is left out) and negatively related to their internalizing (high level of anxiety, for example) and externalizing problems (high level of aggressive behavior, for example) (Trentacosta & Fine, 2009). A recent study also found that young children's emotion understanding was linked to an increase in prosocial behavior (Ensor, Spencer, & Hughes, 2010).

Between ages 2 and 4, children considerably increase the number of terms they use to describe emotions. During this time, they are also learning about the causes and consequences of feelings (Denham, Bassett, & Wyatt, 2007).

When they are 4 to 5 years old, children show an increased ability to reflect on emotions. They also begin to understand that the same event can elicit different feelings in different people. Moreover, they show growing awareness that they need to manage their emotions to meet social standards. And by age 5 most children can accurately determine emotions that are produced by challenging circumstances and describe strategies they might call on to cope with everyday stress (Cole & others, 2009).

Regulating Emotions

As we saw in Chapter 4, emotion regulation is an important aspect of development (Kopp, 2011). In particular, it plays a key role in children's ability to manage the demands and conflicts they face in interacting with others (Lewis, Todd, & Xu, 2011).

Emotion-Coaching and Emotion-Dismissing Parents Parents can play an important role in helping young children regulate their emotions (Engle & McElwain, 2010; Sallquist & others, 2010). Depending on how they talk with their children about emotion, parents can be described as taking an *emotion-coaching* or an *emotion-dismissing* approach (Gottman, 2009). The distinction between these approaches is most evident in the way the parent deals with the child's negative emotions (anger, frustration, sadness, and so on). *Emotion-coaching parents* monitor their children's emotions, view their children's negative emotions as opportunities for teaching, assist them in labeling emotions, and coach them in how to deal effectively with emotions. In contrast, *emotion-dismissing parents* view their role as to deny, ignore, or change negative emotions. Emotion-coaching parents interact with their children in a less rejecting manner, use more scaffolding and praise, and are more nurturant than are emotion-dismissing parents (Gottman & DeClaire, 1997). Moreover, children of emotion-coaching parents are better at soothing themselves when they get upset, are more effective in regulating their negative affect, focus their attention better, and have fewer behavior problems than do children of emotion-dismissing parents.

Regulation of Emotion and Peer Relations Emotions play a strong role in determining the success of a child's peer relationships (Howes, 2009). Specifically, the ability to modulate one's emotions is an important skill that benefits children in their relationships with peers. Moody and emotionally negative children are more likely to experience rejection by peers, whereas emotionally positive children are more popular (Stocker & Dunn, 1990). A recent study revealed that 4-year-olds recognized and generated strategies for controlling their anger more than did 3-year-olds (Cole & others, 2009).

An emotion-coaching parent. *What are some differences in emotion-coaching and emotion-dismissing parents?*

Moral Development

Unlike a crying infant, a screaming 5-year-old is likely to be considered responsible for making a fuss. The parents may worry about whether the 5-year-old is a "bad" child. Although there are some who view children as innately good, many developmental psychologists believe that just as parents help their children become good readers, musicians, or athletes, parents must nurture goodness and help their children develop morally. **Moral development** involves the development of thoughts, feelings, and behaviors regarding rules and conventions about what people should do in their interactions with other people. Major developmental theories have focused on different aspects of moral development.

Moral Feelings

Feelings of anxiety and guilt are central to the account of moral development provided by Freud's psychoanalytic theory (introduced in Chapter 1). According to Freud, to reduce anxiety, avoid punishment, and maintain parental affection, children identify with their parents, internalizing their standards of right and wrong, and in this way develop the *superego*, the moral element of the personality.

Freud's ideas are not backed by research, but guilt certainly can motivate moral behavior. Other emotions, however, also contribute to moral development, including positive feelings. One important example is *empathy,* or responding to another person's feelings with an emotion that echoes those feelings (Eisenberg & others, 2009).

Infants have the capacity for some purely empathic responses, but empathy often requires the ability to discern another person's emotional states, or what is called *perspective taking*. Learning how to identify a wide range of emotional states in others, and to anticipate what kinds of action will improve another person's emotional state, help to advance children's moral development.

Moral Reasoning

Interest in how children think about moral issues was stimulated by Piaget (1932), who extensively observed and interviewed children from ages 4 through 12. Piaget watched children play marbles to learn how they used and thought about the game's rules. He also asked children about ethical issues—theft, lies, punishment, and justice, for example. He concluded that children go through two distinct stages in how they think about morality:

* From ages 4 to 7, children display **heteronomous morality**, the first stage of moral development in Piaget's theory. Children think of justice and rules as unchangeable properties, removed from the control of people.

* From ages 7 to 10, children are in a period of transition, showing some features of the first stage of moral reasoning and some of the second stage, autonomous morality.

* From about age 10 and older, children show **autonomous morality**.

They become aware that rules and laws are created by people, and in judging an action they consider the actor's intentions as well as its consequences.

Because young children are heteronomous moralists, they judge the rightness or goodness of behavior by considering its consequences, not the intentions of the actor. For example, to the heteronomous moralist, breaking twelve cups accidentally is worse than breaking one cup intentionally. As children develop into moral autonomists, intentions become more important than consequences.

The heteronomous thinker also believes that rules are unchangeable and are handed down by all-powerful authorities. When Piaget suggested to young children that they use new rules in a game of marbles, they resisted. By contrast, older children—moral autonomists—accept change and recognize that rules are merely conventions, subject to change.

The heteronomous thinker also believes in **immanent justice**, the concept that if a rule is broken, punishment will be meted out immediately. The young child believes that a violation is connected automatically to its punishment. Thus, young children often look around worriedly after doing something wrong, expecting the inevitable punishment. Immanent justice also implies that if something unfortunate happens to someone, that person must have transgressed earlier. Older children, who are moral autonomists, recognize that punishment occurs only if someone witnesses the wrongdoing and that, even then, punishment is not inevitable.

How do these changes in moral reasoning occur? Piaget argued that, as children develop, they become more sophisticated in their thinking about social matters, especially about the possibilities and conditions of cooperation. Piaget stressed that this social understanding comes about through the mutual give-and-take of peer relations. In the peer group, where others have power and status similar to the child's, plans are negotiated and coordinated, and disagreements are reasoned about and eventually settled. Parent-child relations, in which parents have the power and children do not, are less likely to advance moral reasoning, because rules are often handed down in an authoritarian manner.

heteronomous morality The first stage of moral development in Piaget's theory, occurring from approximately 4 to 7 years of age. Justice and rules are conceived of as unchangeable properties of the world, removed from the control of people.

autonomous morality The second stage of moral development in Piaget's theory, displayed by older children (about 10 years of age and older). The child becomes aware that rules and laws are created by people and, in judging an action, one should consider the actor's intentions as well as the consequences.

immanent justice The concept that, if a rule is broken, punishment will be meted out immediately.

Piaget extensively observed and interviewed 4- to 12-year-old children as they played games to learn how they used and thought about the games' rules.

gender identity The sense of being male or female, which most children acquire by the time they are 3 years old.

gender roles Sets of expectations that prescribe how females or males should think, act, and feel.

social role theory A theory that gender differences result from the contrasting roles of men and women.

Moral Behavior

The behavioral and social cognitive approach, initially described in Chapter 1, focuses on moral behavior rather than moral reasoning. It holds that the processes of reinforcement, punishment, and imitation explain the development of moral behavior. When children are rewarded for behavior that is consistent with laws and social conventions, they are likely to repeat that behavior. When models who behave morally are provided, children are likely to adopt their actions. And when children are punished for immoral behavior, those behaviors are likely to be reduced or eliminated. However, because punishment may have adverse side effects, as discussed later in this chapter, it needs to be used judiciously and cautiously.

If a mother has rewarded a 4-year-old boy for telling the truth when he broke a glass at home, does this mean that he is likely to tell the truth to his preschool teacher when he knocks over a vase and breaks it? Not necessarily; the situation influences behavior. More than half a century ago, a comprehensive study of thousands of children in many situations—at home, at school, and at church, for example—found that a totally honest child is virtually nonexistent; so is a child who cheats in all situations (Hartshorne & May, 1928–1930). Behavioral and social cognitive researchers emphasize that what children do in one situation is often only weakly related to what they do in other situations. A child might cheat in class but not in a game; a child might steal a piece of candy when alone but not when others are present.

Social cognitive theorists also emphasize that the ability to resist temptation is closely tied to the development of self-control (Mischel, 2004), which involves learning to delay gratification. According to social cognitive theorists, cognitive factors are important in the child's development of self-control (Bandura, 2010a).

Gender

How Would You...?
As a health-care professional, how would you expect a child in the heteronomous stage of moral development to judge the behaviors of a doctor who unintentionally caused pain to a child during a medical procedure?

Recall from Chapter 1 that *gender* refers to the social and psychological dimensions of being male or female, and even preschool children display many of these dimensions. **Gender identity** is the sense of being male or female, which most children acquire by the time they are 3 years old. **Gender roles** are sets of expectations that prescribe how females or males should think, act, and feel. During the preschool years, most children increasingly act in ways that match their culture's gender roles.

How do these and other gender differences come about? Biology clearly plays a role, as we saw in Chapter 2. Among the possible biological influences are chromosomes, hormones, and evolution. However, our focus in this chapter is on the social aspects of gender.

Social Influences

Many social scientists do not locate the cause of psychological gender differences in biological dispositions. Rather, they argue that these differences are due to social experiences (Best, 2010). Their explanations include both social and cognitive theories.

First imagine that this is a photograph of a baby girl. *What expectations would you have for her?* Then imagine that this is a photograph of a baby boy. *What expectations would you have for him?*

Social Theories of Gender Three main social theories of gender have been proposed: social role theory, psychoanalytic theory, and social cognitive theory. Alice Eagly (2001, 2009; Eagly & Wood, 2011) proposed **social role theory**, which states that gender differences result from the contrasting roles of women and men. In most cultures around the world, women have less power and status than men do, and they control fewer resources (UNICEF, 2010). Compared with men, women perform more domestic work, spend fewer hours in paid employment, receive lower pay, and are more thinly represented in the highest levels of organizations. In Eagly's (2009; Eagly & Wood, 2011) view, as women adapted to roles with less

154

power and less status in society, they showed more cooperative, less dominant profiles than men did. Thus, the social hierarchy and division of labor are important causes of gender differences in power, assertiveness, and nurture (Carli & Eagly, 2011).

The **psychoanalytic theory of gender** stems from Freud's view that the preschool child develops a sexual attraction to the opposite-sex parent. This is the process known as the Oedipus (for boys) or Electra (for girls) complex. At age 5 or 6, the child renounces this attraction because of anxious feelings. Subsequently, the child identifies with the same-sex parent, unconsciously adopting that parent's characteristics. However, developmental psychologists have observed that gender development does not proceed in the manner that Freud proposed (Callan, 2001). Children become gender-typed much earlier than age 5 or 6, and they become masculine or feminine even when the same-sex parent is not present in the family.

The social cognitive approach discussed in Chapter 2 provides an alternative explanation. According to the **social cognitive theory of gender**, children's gender development occurs through observation and imitation of what other people say and do, and through being rewarded and punished for gender-appropriate and gender-inappropriate behavior (Bussey & Bandura, 1999). From birth onward, males and females are treated differently. When infants and toddlers show gender differences, adults tend to reward them. Parents often use rewards and punishments to teach their daughters to be feminine ("Karen, you are being a good girl when you play gently with your doll") and their sons to be masculine ("Keith, a boy as big as you are is not supposed to cry"). Parents, however, are only one of many sources from which children learn gender roles (Martin & Ruble, 2010). Culture, schools, peers, the media, and other family members also provide gender role models (Best, 2010). For example, children learn about gender by observing other adults in the neighborhood and on television. As children grow older, peers become increasingly important. Let's look more closely at the influence of parents and peers.

Parental Influences Parents influence their children's gender development by action and by example (Gore, 2009). Both mothers and fathers are psychologically important to their children's gender development (Grusec & Davidov, 2007). Cultures around the world, however, tend to give mothers and fathers different roles (Shiraev, 2011). A research review provided these conclusions (Bronstein, 2006):

- *Mothers' socialization strategies.* In many cultures, mothers socialize their daughters to be more obedient and responsible than their sons. They also place more restrictions on their daughters' autonomy.

- *Fathers' socialization strategies.* Fathers show more attention to their sons than to their daughters, engage in more activities with their sons, and put forth more effort to promote their sons' intellectual development.

Thus, according to Bronstein (2006, pp. 269–270), "Despite an increased awareness in the United States and other Western cultures of the detrimental effects of gender stereotyping, many parents continue to foster behaviors and perceptions that are consonant with traditional gender role norms."

Peer Influences Parents provide the earliest discrimination of gender roles, but before long, peers join the process of responding to and modeling masculine and feminine behavior (Blakemore, Berenbaum, & Liben, 2009). In fact, peers become so important to gender development that the playground has been described as "gender school" (Luria & Herzog, 1985).

Peers extensively reward and punish gender behavior (Leaper & Friedman, 2007). For example, when children play in ways that the culture considers sex-appropriate, their peers tend to reward them. But peers often reject children who act in a manner that is considered more characteristic of the other gender (Matlin, 2008). A little girl

psychoanalytic theory of gender
A theory deriving from Freud's view that the preschool child develops a sexual attraction to the opposite-sex parent, by approximately 5 or 6 years of age renounces this attraction because of anxious feelings, and subsequently identifies with the same-sex parent, unconsciously adopting the same-sex parent's characteristics.

social cognitive theory of gender
A theory that emphasizes that children's gender development occurs through the observation and imitation of gender behavior and through the rewards and punishments children experience for gender-appropriate and gender-inappropriate behavior.

How Would You...?
As a human development and family studies professional, how would you describe the ways in which parents influence their children's notions of gender roles?

EMOTIONAL AND PERSONALITY DEVELOPMENT

155

gender schema theory The theory
that gender typing emerges as children gradually develop gender schemas of what is gender-appropriate
and gender-inappropriate in their
culture.

who brings a doll to the park may find herself
surrounded by new friends; a little boy might
be jeered. However, there is greater pressure
for boys to conform to a traditional male role
than for girls to conform to a traditional
female role (Fagot, Rogers, & Leinbach, 2000).
For example, a preschool girl who wants to
wear boys' clothing receives considerably more approval
than a boy who wants to wear a dress. The very term
"tomboy" implies broad social acceptance of girls' adopting traditional male behaviors.

Gender molds important aspects of peer relations. It
influences the composition of children's groups, the size
of groups, and interactions within a group (Maccoby,
1998, 2002).

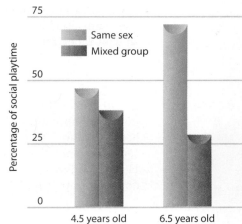

- *Gender composition of children's groups.* Around age 3, children already show a
  preference to spend time with same-sex playmates. This preference increases
  until around age 12, and during the elementary school years children spend a
  large majority of their free time with children of their own sex (see Figure 6.1).

- *Group size.* From about age 5, boys are more likely to associate together in larger
  clusters than girls are. Boys are also more likely to participate in organized group
  games than girls are. In one study, same-sex groups of six children were permitted to use play materials in any way they wished (Benenson, Apostolaris, & Parnass, 1997). Girls were more likely than boys to play in dyads or triads, while boys
  were more likely to interact in larger groups and seek to attain a group goal.

- *Interaction in same-sex groups.* Boys are more likely than girls to engage in
  rough-and-tumble play, competition, conflict, ego displays, risk taking, and
  seeking dominance. By contrast, girls are more likely to engage in "collaborative discourse," in which they talk and act in a more reciprocal manner.

**Figure 6.1 Devel-
opmental Changes
in Percentage of
Time Spent in
Same-Sex and
Mixed-Group
Settings**
Observations of
children show that
they are more
likely to play in
same-sex than
mixed-sex groups.
This tendency
increases between
4 and 6 years
of age.

Cognitive Influences

Observation, imitation, rewards and punishment—these are the mechanisms by
which gender develops, according to social cognitive theory. Interactions between
the child and the social environment are the main keys to gender development.
Some critics argue that this explanation pays too little attention to the child's own
mind and understanding, and portrays the child as passively acquiring gender
roles (Martin & Ruble, 2010).

One influential cognitive theory is **gender schema theory**, which states that
gender typing emerges as children gradually develop gender schemas of what is
gender-appropriate and gender-inappropriate in their culture (Martin & Ruble,
2010). A *schema* is a cognitive structure, a network of associations that guide an
individual's perceptions. A *gender schema* organizes the world in terms of female
and male. Children are internally motivated to perceive the world and to act in
accordance with their developing schemas. Bit by bit, children pick up what is
gender-appropriate and gender-inappropriate in their culture, and develop gender
schemas that shape how they perceive the world and what they remember. Children are motivated to act in ways that conform with these gender schemas. Thus,
gender schemas fuel gender typing.

How Would You...?
As an educator,
how would you
create a classroom
climate that pro-
motes healthy
gender develop-
ment for both
boys and girls?

Families

Attachment to a caregiver is a key social relationship during infancy, but we saw
in Chapter 4 that some experts maintain that secure attachment and the infant's
early experiences have been overdramatized as determinants of life-span development. Social and emotional development is also shaped by other relationships and

by temperament, contexts, and social experiences in the early child-hood years and later (Parke & Clarke-Stewart, 2011). In this section, we discuss social relationships in early childhood beyond attachment.

Parenting

How Would You...?
As a human development and family studies professional, how would you characterize the parenting style that prevails within your own family?

To understand variations in parenting, let's consider the styles parents use when they interact with their children, how they discipline their children, and the cooperative practice of coparenting.

Baumrind's Parenting Styles

Baumrind (1971) stresses that parents should be neither punitive nor aloof. Rather, they should develop rules for their children and be affectionate with them. She has described four parenting styles:

- **Authoritarian parenting** is a restrictive, punitive style in which parents exhort the child to follow their directions and respect their work and effort. The authoritarian parent places firm limits and controls on the child and allows little verbal exchange. For example, an authoritarian parent might say, "You do it my way or else." Authoritarian parents also might spank the child frequently, enforce rules rigidly but not explain them, and show anger toward the child. Children of authoritarian parents are often unhappy, fearful, and anxious about comparing themselves with others; they also fail to initiate activity, and have weak communication skills.

- **Authoritative parenting** encourages children to be independent but still places limits and controls on their actions. Extensive verbal give-and-take is allowed, and parents are warm and nurturant toward the child. An authoritative parent might put his arm around the child in a comforting way and say, "You know you shouldn't have done that. Let's talk about how you could handle the situation better next time." Authoritative parents show pleasure and support in response to their children's constructive behavior. They also expect independent, age-appropriate behavior. Children whose parents are authoritative are often cheerful, self-controlled and self-reliant, and achievement-oriented; they tend to maintain friendly relations with peers, cooperate with adults, and cope well with stress.

- **Neglectful parenting** is a style in which the parent is uninvolved in the child's life. Children whose parents are neglectful develop the sense that other aspects of the parents' lives are more important than they are. These children tend to be socially incompetent. Many have poor self-control and don't handle independence well. They frequently have low self-esteem, are immature, and may be alienated from the family. In adolescence, they may show patterns of truancy and delinquency.

- **Indulgent parenting** is a style in which parents are highly involved with their children but place few demands or controls on them. Such parents let their children do what they want. Some parents deliberately rear their children in this way because they believe the combination of warm involvement and few restraints will produce a creative, confident child. However, children whose parents are indulgent rarely learn respect for others and have difficulty controlling their behavior. They might be domineering, egocentric, and noncompliant, and have unsatisfactory peer relations.

These four classifications of parenting involve combinations of acceptance and responsiveness on the one hand and demand and control on the other (Maccoby & Martin, 1983). How these dimensions combine to produce authoritarian, authoritative, neglectful, and indulgent parenting is shown in Figure 6.2.

authoritarian parenting A restrictive punitive style in which parents exhort the child to follow their directions and to respect work and effort. The authoritarian parent places firm limits and controls on the child and allows little verbal exchange. Authoritarian parenting is associated with children's social incompetence.

authoritative parenting A parenting style in which parents encourage their children to be independent but still place limits and controls on their actions. Extensive verbal give-and-take is allowed, and parents are warm and nurturant toward the child. Authoritative parenting is associated with children's social competence.

neglectful parenting A style of parenting in which the parent is very uninvolved in the child's life; it is associated with children's social incompetence, especially a lack of self-control.

indulgent parenting A style of parenting in which parents are highly involved with their children but place few demands or controls on them. Indulgent parenting is associated with children's social incompetence, especially a lack of self-control.

Keep in mind that research on parenting styles and children's development is *correlational*, not causal, in nature. Thus, if a study reveals that authoritarian parenting is linked to higher levels of aggression by children, it may be that aggressive children elicited authoritarian parenting just as much as authoritarian parenting produced aggressive children. Also recall from Chapter 1 that a third factor may influence the correlation between two factors. Thus, in the example of the correlation between authoritarian parenting and aggressive children, possibly authoritarian parents (first factor) and aggressive children (second factor) share genes (third factor) that predispose them to behave in ways that produced the correlation.

Parenting Styles in Context

Among Baumrind's four parenting styles, authoritative parenting clearly conveys the most benefits to the child and to the family as a whole. Do the benefits of authoritative parenting transcend the boundaries of ethnicity, socioeconomic status, and household composition? Although some exceptions have been found, evidence linking authoritative parenting with competence on the part of the child occurs in research across a wide range of ethnic groups, social strata, cultures, and family structures (Steinberg & Silk, 2002).

Nevertheless, researchers have found that in some ethnic groups, aspects of the authoritarian style may be associated with more positive outcomes than Baumrind predicts. In the Arab world, many families are very authoritarian, dominated by the father's rule, and children are taught strict codes of conduct and family loyalty (Booth, 2002). As another example, Asian American parents often continue aspects of traditional Asian child-rearing practices that have sometimes been described as authoritarian. The parents exert considerable control over their children's lives. However, Ruth Chao (2001, 2005, 2007; Chao & Tseng, 2002) argues that the style of parenting used by many Asian American parents is distinct from the domineering control that is characteristic of the authoritarian style. Instead, Chao argues that it reflects concern and involvement in children's lives and is best conceptualized as a type of training. The high academic achievement of Asian American children may be a consequence of their parents' "training" (Stevenson & Zusho, 2002).

	Accepting, responsive	Rejecting, unresponsive
Demanding, controlling	Authoritative	Authoritarian
Undemanding, uncontrolling	Indulgent	Neglectful

Figure 6.2 Classification of Parenting Styles
The four types of parenting styles (authoritative, authoritarian, indulgent, and neglectful) involve the dimensions of acceptance and responsiveness, on the one hand, and demand and control on the other. For example, authoritative parenting involves being both accepting/responsive and demanding/controlling.

How Would You...?
As a psychologist, how would you use the research on parenting styles to design a parent education class that teaches effective skills for interacting with young children?

Punishment

Use of corporal punishment is legal in every state in the United States. A national survey of U.S. parents with 3- and 4-year-old children found that 26 percent of parents reported spanking their children frequently, and 67 percent reported yelling at their children frequently (Regalado & others, 2004). A cross-cultural comparison found that individuals in the United States and Canada were among those with the most favorable attitudes toward corporal punishment and were most likely to remember it being used by their parents (see Figure 6.3) (Curran & others, 2001).

A research review concluded that corporal punishment by parents is associated with higher levels of immediate compliance and aggression by the children (Gershoff, 2002). The review also found that corporal punishment is linked to lower levels of moral internalization and mental health (Gershoff, 2002). A recent study also discovered that a history of harsh physical discipline was related to adolescent depression and externalized problems, such as juvenile delinquency (Bender & others, 2007).

What are some reasons for avoiding spanking or similar punishments? They include the following:

- When adults punish a child by yelling, screaming, or spanking, they are presenting children with out-of-control models for handling stressful situations. Children may imitate this behavior.

- Punishment can instill fear, rage, or avoidance. For example, spanking the child may cause the child to avoid being near the parent and to fear the parent.

- Punishment tells children what not to do rather than what to do. Children should be given feedback, such as "Why don't you try this?"

- Parents might unintentionally become so aroused when they are punishing the child that they become abusive (Durrant, 2008).

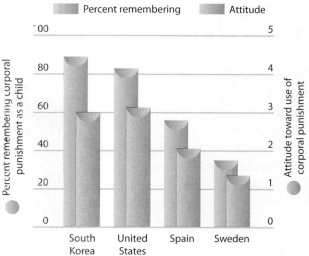

FIGURE 6.3 Corporal Punishment in Different Countries

A 5-point scale was used to assess attitudes toward corporal punishment with scores closer to 1 indicating an attitude against its use and scores closer to 5 suggesting an attitude favoring its use. *Why are studies of corporal punishment correlational studies, and how does that method affect their interpretations?*

Most child psychologists recommend handling misbehavior by reasoning with the child, especially explaining the consequences of the child's actions for others. *Time out*, in which the child is removed from a setting that offers positive reinforcement, can also be effective. For example, when the child has misbehaved, a parent might forbid TV viewing for a specified time.

Debate about the effects of punishment on children's development continues (Grusec, 2011; Knox, 2010; Thompson, 2009e). A research review of 26 studies concluded that only severe or predominant use of spanking, not mild spanking, compared unfavorably with alternative discipline practices (Larzelere & Kuhn, 2005). There are few longitudinal studies of punishment and few studies that distinguish adequately between moderate and heavy use of punishment. Thus, in the view of some experts, it is still difficult to determine whether the effects of physical punishment are harmful to children's development, although such a view might be distasteful to some individuals (Grusec, 2009). It is nonetheless clear that when physical punishment involves abuse, it can be very harmful to children's development, as discussed later in this chapter (Cicchetti & Toth, 2011).

Coparenting

The relationship between marital conflict and the use of punishment highlights the importance of *coparenting*, the support that parents give each other in raising a child. Poor coordination between parents, undermining by one parent of the other, lack of cooperation and warmth, and aloofness by one parent are conditions that place children at risk (McHale & Sullivan, 2008). In addition, one study revealed that coparenting is more beneficial than either maternal or paternal parenting in terms of children's development of self-control (Karreman & others, 2008).

Parents who do not spend enough time with their children or have problems in child rearing can benefit from counseling and therapy. To read about the work of marriage and family counselor Darla Botkin, see "Careers in Life-Span Development."

Darla Botkin, Marriage and Family Therapist

Darla Botkin is a marriage and family therapist who teaches, conducts research, and engages in marriage and family therapy. She is on the faculty of the University of Kentucky. Botkin obtained a bachelor's degree in elementary education with a concentration in special education, and went on to receive a master's degree in early childhood education. She spent the next six years working with children and their families in a variety of settings, including child care, elementary school, and Head Start. These experiences led her to recognize the interdependence of

Darla Botkin (*left*), conducting a family therapy session.

the developmental settings that children and their parents experience (such as home, school, and work). She returned to graduate school and obtained a Ph.D. in family studies from the University of Tennessee. She then became a faculty member in the Family Studies program at the University of Kentucky. Completing further coursework and clinical training in marriage and family therapy, she became certified as a marriage and family therapist.

Botkin's current interests include working with young children in family therapy, gender and ethnic issues in family therapy, and the role of spirituality in family wellness.

Child Maltreatment

Unfortunately, punishment sometimes leads to the abuse of infants and children (Cicchetti, 2011). In 2006, approximately 905,000 U.S. children were victims of child abuse (U.S. Department of Health and Human Services, 2008). Eighty-four percent of these children were abused by a parent or parents.

Types of Child Maltreatment

The four main types of child maltreatment are physical abuse, child neglect, sexual abuse, and emotional abuse (National Clearinghouse on Child Abuse and Neglect, 2004):

- *Physical abuse* is characterized by the infliction of physical injury as a result of punching, beating, kicking, biting, burning, shaking, or otherwise harming a child. The parent or other person may not intend to hurt the child; the injury may result from excessive physical punishment (Milot & others, 2010).

- *Child neglect* is characterized by failure to provide for the child's basic needs. Neglect can be physical (abandonment, for example), educational (allowing chronic truancy, for example), or emotional (marked inattention to the child's needs, for example) (Newton & Vandeven, 2010). Child neglect is by far the most common form of child maltreatment. In every country where relevant data have been collected, neglect occurs up to three times as often as abuse (Benoit, Coolbear, & Crawford, 2008).

- *Sexual abuse* includes fondling of genitals, intercourse, incest, rape, sodomy, exhibitionism, and commercial exploitation through prostitution or production of pornographic materials (Bahali & others, 2010; Leventhal, Murphy, & Asnes, 2011).

- *Emotional abuse (psychological/verbal abuse/mental injury)* includes acts or omissions by parents or other caregivers that have caused, or could cause, serious behavioral, cognitive, or emotional problems (van Harmelen & others, 2010).

Although any of these forms of child maltreatment may be found separately, they often occur in combination. Emotional abuse is almost always present when other forms are identified.

The Context of Abuse

No single factor causes child maltreatment (Cicchetti & Toth, 2011). A combination of factors, including the culture, characteristics of the family, and developmental characteristics of the child, likely contribute to child maltreatment (Appleton & Stanley, 2009; Prinz & others, 2009).

The extensive violence that characterizes American culture, including TV violence, is reflected in the occurrence of violence in the family (Durrant, 2008). The family itself is obviously a key part of the context of abuse (Kennedy, 2009). The interactions among all family members need to be considered, regardless of who performs violent acts against the child. For example, even though the father may be the one who physically abuses the child, the behavior of the mother, the child, and siblings should also be evaluated.

About one-third of parents who were abused themselves when they were young go on to abuse their own children (Cicchetti, Toth, & Rogusch, 2006). Thus, some, but not a majority, of parents are involved in an intergenerational transmission of abuse.

Developmental Consequences of Abuse

Among the consequences of maltreatment in childhood and adolescence are poor emotion regulation, attachment problems, problems in peer relations, difficulty in adapting to school, and other psychological problems, such as depression and delinquency (Cicchetti & Toth, 2011). Compared to their peers, adolescents who experienced abuse or neglect as children are more likely to engage in violent romantic relationships, delinquency, sexual risk taking, and substance abuse (Shin, Hong, & Hazen, 2010; Wekerle & others, 2009). Later, during the adult years, individuals who were maltreated as children often have difficulty establishing and maintaining healthy intimate relationships (Dozier, Stovall-McClough, & Albus, 2009). A recent study also revealed that adults who had experienced maltreatment as children were at increased risk for financial and employment-related difficulties (Zielinski, 2009).

What can be done to prevent or reduce the incidence of child maltreatment? In one study of maltreating mothers and their 1-year-olds, two approaches were effective: (1) home visits that emphasized improved parenting and coping with stress, and (2) psychotherapy that focused on improving maternal-infant attachment (Cicchetti, Toth, & Rogusch, 2005).

Sibling Relationships and Birth Order

How do developmental psychologists characterize sibling relationships? And how does birth order influence behavior, if at all?

Sibling Relationships

Approximately 80 percent of American children have one or more siblings—that is, sisters and brothers (Dunn, 2007). Any of you who have grown up with siblings probably have rich memories of your relationships with them. Two- to 4-year-old siblings in each other's presence have a conflict once every 10 minutes, on average; the rate of conflict declines somewhat from ages 5 to 7 (Kramer, 2006). What do parents do when they encounter siblings having a verbal or physical confrontation? One study revealed that they do one of three things: (1) intervene and try to help them resolve the conflict, (2) admonish or threaten them, or (3) do nothing at all (Kramer & Perozynski, 1999). Of interest is that in families with two siblings ages 2 to 5 the most frequent parental reaction is to do nothing at all.

Laurie Kramer (2006), who has conducted a number of research studies on siblings, says that not intervening and letting sibling conflict escalate are not good strategies. She developed a program titled "More Fun With Sisters and Brothers" that teaches 4- to 8-year-old siblings social skills for developing positive interactions (Kramer

How Would You...?
As a health-care professional, how would you work with parents during infant and toddler checkups to prevent child maltreatment?

How Would You...?
As an educator, how would you explain the potential impact of maltreatment at home on a child's performance in school?

& Radey, 1997). Among the skills taught in the program are how to appropriately initiate play, how to accept and refuse invitations to play, perspective taking, how to deal with angry feelings, and how to manage conflict.

However, conflict is only one of the many dimensions of sibling relations (Steelman & Koch, 2009). Sibling relations include helping, sharing, teaching, fighting, compromising, and playing, and siblings can act as emotional supports, rivals, and communication partners. A recent review concluded that sibling relationships in adolescence are not as close, are less intense, and are more egalitarian than in childhood (East, 2009).

Judy Dunn (2007), a leading expert on sibling relationships, described three important characteristics of sibling relationships:

1. *The emotional quality of the relationship.* Siblings often express both intensive positive and negative emotions toward each other. Many children and adolescents have mixed feelings toward their siblings.

2. *The familiarity and intimacy of the relationship.* Siblings typically know each other very well, and this intimacy suggests that they can either provide support or tease and undermine each other, depending on the situation.

3. *The variation in sibling relationships.* Some siblings describe their relationships more positively than others do. Thus, there is considerable variation in sibling relationships. We just noted that many siblings have mixed feelings about each other, but some children and adolescents describe their siblings mainly in warm, affectionate ways, whereas others primarily talk about how irritating and mean a sibling is.

Birth Order

Whether a child has older or younger siblings has been linked to the development of certain personality characteristics. For example, a recent review concluded that "firstborns are the most intelligent, achieving, and conscientious, while later-borns are the most rebellious, liberal, and agreeable" (Paulhus, 2008, p. 210). Compared with later-born children, firstborn children have also been described as more adult-oriented, helpful, conforming, and self-controlled. However, when such birth-order differences are reported, they often are small.

What accounts for such differences related to birth order? Proposed explanations usually point to variations in interactions associated with a particular position in the family. In one study, mothers became more negative, coercive, and restraining and played less with the firstborn following the birth of a second child (Dunn & Kendrick, 1982).

What about children who don't have siblings? The popular conception is that an only child is a "spoiled brat" with undesirable characteristics such as dependency, lack of self-control, and self-centered behavior. But researchers present a more positive portrayal. Only children are often achievement-oriented and display desirable personality characteristics, especially in comparison with later-borns and children from large families (Falbo & Poston, 1993; Jiao, Ji, & Jing, 1996).

So far, our discussion suggests that birth order might be a strong predictor of behavior. However, an increasing number of family researchers stress that, when all the factors that influence behavior are considered, birth order itself has limited ability to predict behavior. Think about some of the other important factors in children's lives that influence their behavior. They include heredity, models of competency or incompetency that parents present to children on a daily basis, peer and school influences, socioeconomic and sociohistorical factors, and cultural variations. When someone says that firstborns are always like this but last-borns are always like that, he or she is making overly simplistic statements that do not adequately take into account the complexity of influences on a child's development.

The one-child family is becoming much more common in China because of the strong motivation to limit the population growth in the People's Republic of China. The policy is still relatively new, and its effects on children have not been fully examined. *In general, though, what have researchers found the only child to be like?*

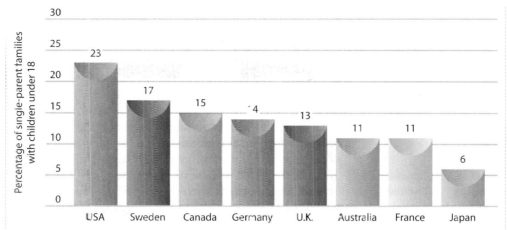

Figure 6.4 Single-Parent Families in Different Countries

The Changing Family in a Changing Society

Beyond variations in number of siblings, the families that children experience differ in many important ways. As shown in Figure 6.4, the United States has one of the highest percentages of single-parent families in the world. Among two-parent families, there are those in which both parents work, or have divorced parents who have remarried, or gay or lesbian parents. Differences in culture and socioeconomic status (SES) also influence families. How do these variations in families affect children?

Working Parents

More than one of every two U.S. mothers with a child under age 5 is in the labor force; more than two of every three with a child ages 6 to 17 is. Maternal employment is a part of modern life, but its effects are still being debated.

Parental employment can have positive and negative effects on parenting (Han, 2009). Recent research indicates that what matters for children's development is the nature of the parents' work rather than whether one or both parents works outside the home (Goldberg & Lucas-Thompson, 2008). Ann Crouter (2006) described how parents bring their experiences at work into their homes. She concluded that parents who experience poor working conditions, such as long hours, overtime work, stressful working conditions, and lack of autonomy at work, are likely to be more irritable at home and engage in less effective parenting than their counterparts who experience better working conditions. A consistent finding is that the children (especially girls) of working mothers engage in less gender stereotyping and have more egalitarian views of gender than do children of non-working mothers (Goldberg & Lucas-Thompson, 2008).

Children in Divorced Families

Divorce rates changed rather dramatically in the United States and many countries around the world in the late 20th century (Amato & Dorius, 2011). The U.S. divorce rate increased dramatically in the 1960s and 1970s but has declined since the 1980s. However, the divorce rate in the United States is still much higher than in most other countries.

It is estimated that 40 percent of children born to married parents in the United States will experience their parents' divorce (Hetherington & Stanley-Hagan, 2002) Let's examine some important questions about children in divorced families:

- *Are children better adjusted in intact, never-divorced families than in divorced families?* Most researchers agree that children from divorced families show poorer adjustment than their counterparts in never-divorced families (Amato &

and connections that include the prefrontal cortex. In this view, the prefrontal cortex coordinates which neural connections are the most effective for solving a problem at hand.

Motor Development

During middle and late childhood, children's motor skills become much smoother and more coordinated than they were in early childhood. For example, only one child in a thousand can hit a tennis ball over the net at the age of 3, yet by the age of 10 or 11 most children can learn to play the sport. Running, climbing, skipping rope, swimming, bicycle riding, and skating are just a few of the many physical skills elementary school children can master. In gross motor skills that involve large muscle activity, boys usually outperform girls.

Increased myelination of the central nervous system is reflected in the improvement of fine motor skills during middle and late childhood. Children can more adroitly use their hands as tools. Six-year-olds can hammer, paste, tie shoes, and fasten clothes. By 7 years of age, children's hands have become steadier. At this age, children prefer a pencil to a crayon for printing, and they reverse letters less often. Printing becomes smaller. At 8 to 10 years of age, they can use their hands independently with more ease and precision. Fine motor coordination develops to the point at which children can write rather than print words. Cursive letter size becomes smaller and more even. At 10 to 12 years of age, children begin to show manipulative skills similar to the abilities of adults. They can master the complex, intricate, and rapid movements needed to produce fine-quality crafts or to play a difficult piece on a musical instrument. Girls usually outperform boys in their use of fine motor skills.

Exercise

Elementary school children are far from physical maturity, so they need to be active (Graham, Holt/Hale, & Parker, 2010; Rink, 2009). They become more fatigued by long periods of sitting than by running, jumping, or bicycling. Physical action, such as batting a ball, skipping rope, or balancing on a beam, is essential for children this age to refine their developing skills. It is becoming increasingly clear that exercise plays an important role in children's growth and development (Crawford & others, 2010; Fahey, Insel, & Roth, 2011).

Are U.S. children getting enough exercise? In one historical comparison, the percentage of children involved in daily P.E. programs in schools decreased from 80 percent in 1969 to 20 percent in 1999 (Health Management Resources, 2001) (see Figure 7.1). Educators and policy makers in many other countries around the world, including China, Finland, and Great Britain, have become very concerned about the sedentary lifestyles of many children in their countries (Fogelholm, 2008).

Television watching is linked with low activity and obesity in children (Wells & others, 2008). A related concern is the dramatic increase in computer use by children. Researchers have found that the total time that children and adolescents spend in front of a television or computer places them at risk for reduced activity and being overweight (Rey-Lopez & others, 2008).

Parents and schools can increase children's exercise. A recent study revealed that the extent to which parents limited their children's sedentary behavior, encouraged them to exercise, and engaged in

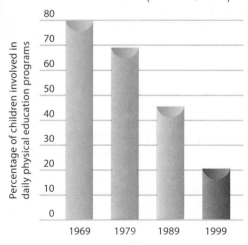

Figure 7.1 Percentage of Children Involved in Daily Physical Education Programs in the United States from 1969 to 1999

There has been a dramatic drop in the percentage of children participating in daily physical education programs in the United States, from 80 percent in 1969 to only 20 percent in 1999.

How Would You...?
As an educator, how would you structure the curriculum to ensure that elementary school students are getting adequate physical activity throughout the day?

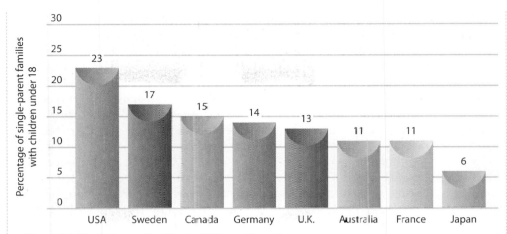

Figure 6.4 **Single-Parent Families in Different Countries**

The Changing Family in a Changing Society

Beyond variations in number of siblings, the families that children experience differ in many important ways. As shown in Figure 6.4, the United States has one of the highest percentages of single-parent families in the world. Among two-parent families, there are those in which both parents work, or have divorced parents who have remarried, or gay or lesbian parents. Differences in culture and socioeconomic status (SES) also influence families. How do these variations in families affect children?

Working Parents

More than one of every two U.S. mothers with a child under age 5 is in the labor force; more than two of every three with a child ages 6 to 17 is. Maternal employment is a part of modern life, but its effects are still being debated.

Parental employment can have positive and negative effects on parenting (Han, 2009). Recent research indicates that what matters for children's development is the nature of the parents' work rather than whether one or both parents works outside the home (Goldberg & Lucas-Thompson, 2008). Ann Crouter (2006) described how parents bring their experiences at work into their homes. She concluded that parents who experience poor working conditions, such as long hours, overtime work, stressful working conditions, and lack of autonomy at work, are likely to be more irritable at home and engage in less effective parenting than their counterparts who experience better working conditions. A consistent finding is that the children (especially girls) of working mothers engage in less gender stereotyping and have more egalitarian views of gender than do children of non-working mothers (Goldberg & Lucas-Thompson, 2008).

Children in Divorced Families

Divorce rates changed rather dramatically in the United States and many countries around the world in the late 20th century (Amato & Dorius, 2011). The U.S. divorce rate increased dramatically in the 1960s and 1970s but has declined since the 1980s. However, the divorce rate in the United States is still much higher than in most other countries.

It is estimated that 40 percent of children born to married parents in the United States will experience their parents' divorce (Hetherington & Stanley-Hagan, 2002). Let's examine some important questions about children in divorced families:

- *Are children better adjusted in intact, never-divorced families than in divorced families?* Most researchers agree that children from divorced families show poorer adjustment than their counterparts in never-divorced families (Amato &

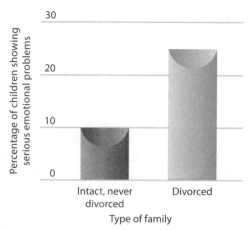

Figure 6.5 Divorce and Children's Emotional Problems

In Hetherington's research, 25 percent of children from divorced families showed serious emotional problems compared with only 10 percent of children from intact, never-divorced families. However, keep in mind that a substantial majority (75 percent) of the children from divorced families did not show serious emotional problems.

Dorius, 2011; Hetherington, 2006; Lansford, 2009; see Figure 6.5). Those who have experienced multiple divorces are at greater risk. Children in divorced families are more likely than those in never-divorced families to have academic problems, to exhibit externalized problems (such as acting out and delinquency) and experience internalized problems (such as anxiety and depression), to be less socially responsible, to have less competent intimate relationships, to drop out of school, to become sexually active at an early age, to take drugs, to associate with antisocial peers, to have low self-esteem, and to be less securely attached as young adults (Lansford, 2009). A recent study revealed that adolescent girls with divorced parents were especially vulnerable to developing depressive symptoms (Oldehinkel & others, 2008). Another study found that experiencing parental divorce in childhood was associated with insecure attachment in early adulthood (Brockmeyer, Treboux, & Crowell, 2005). Yet another study revealed that when individuals experienced the divorce of their parents in childhood and adolescence, they were more likely to have unstable romantic and marital relationships and low levels of education in adulthood (Amato, 2006). Keep in mind, however, that a majority of children (75 percent) in divorced families do not have significant adjustment problems.

- *Should parents stay together for the sake of the children?* Whether parents should stay in an unhappy or conflicted marriage for the sake of their children is one of the most commonly asked questions about divorce (Hetherington, 2006). If the stresses and disruptions in family relationships associated with an unhappy marriage that erode the well-being of children are reduced by the move to a divorced, single-parent family, divorce can be advantageous. However, if the diminished resources and increased risks associated with divorce are accompanied by inept parenting and sustained or increased conflict, not only between the divorced couple but also among the parents, children, and siblings, the best choice for the children would be for an unhappy marriage to be continued (Hetherington & Stanley-Hagan, 2002). It is difficult to determine how these "ifs" will play out when parents either remain together in an acrimonious marriage or become divorced.

Note that marital conflict may have negative consequences for children in the context of marriage or divorce (Cummings & Merrilees, 2009). A longitudinal study revealed that conflict in never-divorced families was associated with emotional problems in children (Amato, 2006). Indeed, many of the problems experienced by children from divorced homes begin during the predivorce period, a time when parents often are in active conflict. Thus, when children from divorced homes show problems, the problems may be due not only to the divorce itself but also to the marital conflict that led to it (Thompson, 2008).

E. Mark Cummings and his colleagues (Cummings & Davies, 2010; Cummings & Merrilees, 2009) have proposed *emotion security theory*, which has its roots in attachment theory and states that children appraise marital conflict in terms of their sense of security and safety in the family. They make a distinction between marital conflict that is negative for children (such as hostile emotional displays and destructive conflict tactics) and marital conflict that can be positive for children (such as marital disagreement that involves

What concerns are involved in whether parents should stay together for the sake of the children or become divorced?

164

a calm discussion of each person's perspective and working together to reach a solution).

How Would You...?
As a human development and family studies professional, how would you apply the guidelines on communicating about divorce to help parents discuss the death of a family member with their children?

- *How much do family processes matter after a divorce?* They matter a great deal (Lansford, 2009; Parke & Clarke-Stewart, 2011). When divorced parents' relationship with each other is harmonious, and when they use authoritative parenting, children's adjustment improves (Hetherington, 2006). A number of researchers have shown that a disequilibrium, which includes diminished parenting skills, occurs in the year following the divorce—but by two years after the divorce, restabilization has occurred and parenting skills have improved (Hetherington, 1989).

- *What factors influence an individual child's vulnerability to suffering negative consequences as a result of divorce?* Among the factors involved are the child's adjustment prior to the divorce, as well as the child's personality and temperament, gender, and custody situation (Hetherington, 2006). Children whose parents later divorce show poorer adjustment before the breakup (Lansford, 2009). Children who are socially mature and responsible, who show few behavioral problems, and who have an easy temperament are better able to cope with their parents' divorce. Children with a difficult temperament often have problems in coping with their parents' divorce (Hetherington, 2006).

- *What role does socioeconomic status play in the lives of children whose parents have divorced?* Mothers who have custody of their children experience the loss of about one-fourth to one-half of their predivorce income, compared with a loss of only one-tenth by fathers who have custody. This income loss for divorced mothers is accompanied by increased workloads, high rates of job instability, and residential moves to less desirable neighborhoods with inferior schools (Lansford, 2009).

Gay Male and Lesbian Parents

Increasingly, gay male and lesbian couples are creating families that include children. Approximately 20 percent of lesbians and 10 percent of gay men are parents (Patterson & Farr, 2010). There may be more than 1 million gay and lesbian parents in the United States today.

Like heterosexual couples, gay male and lesbian parents vary greatly. They may be single, or they may have same-gender partners. Many lesbian mothers and gay fathers are noncustodial parents because they lost custody of their children to heterosexual spouses after a divorce.

Most children of gay and lesbian parents were born in a heterosexual relationship that ended in a divorce: in most cases, it was probably a relationship in which one or both parents only later identified themselves as gay male or lesbian. In other cases, lesbians and gay men became parents as a result of donor insemination and surrogates, or through adoption. Parenthood among lesbians and gay men is controversial. Opponents claim that being raised by male or lesbian parents harms the child's development. But researchers have found few differences between children growing up with lesbian mothers or gay fathers on the one hand, and children growing up with heterosexual parents on the other (Patterson & Wainright, 2010). For example, children growing up in gay or lesbian families are just as popular with

What are the research findings regarding the development and psychological well-being of children raised by gay and lesbian couples?

their peers, and no differences are found in the adjustment and mental health of children living in these families when they are compared with children in heterosexual families (Hyde, 2007). Contrary to the once-popular expectation that being raised by a gay or lesbian parent would result in the child's growing up to be gay or lesbian, in fact the overwhelming majority of children from gay or lesbian families have a heterosexual orientation (Golombok & Tasker, 2010).

Cultural, Ethnic, and Socioeconomic Variations

Parenting can be influenced by culture, ethnicity, and socioeconomic status (Tamis-LeMonda & McFadden, 2010). Recall from Bronfenbrenner's ecological theory (see Chapter 1) that a number of social contexts influence the child's development. In Bronfenbrenner's theory, culture, ethnicity, and socioeconomic status are classified as part of the macrosystem because they represent broader, societal contexts.

Cross-Cultural Studies Different cultures often give different answers to such basic questions as what the father's role in the family should be, what support systems are available to families, and how children should be disciplined (Fiese & Winter, 2008; Hewlett & MacFarlan, 2010). There are important cross-cultural variations in parenting (Bornstein & Lansford, 2010; Gauvain & Parke, 2010). In some cultures, such as rural areas of many countries, authoritarian parenting is widespread.

Cultural change, brought about by such factors as increasingly frequent international travel, the Internet and electronic communications, and economic globalization, is affecting families in many countries around the world. There are trends toward greater family mobility, migration to urban areas, and separation as some family members work in cities or countries far from their homes. Other trends include smaller families, fewer extended-family households, and increases in maternal employment (Brown & Larson, 2002). These trends can change the nature of the resources available to children. For example, when several generations no longer live close by, children may lose the support and guidance of grandparents, aunts, and uncles. On the positive side, smaller families may produce more openness and communication between parents and children.

Ethnicity Families within various ethnic groups in the United States differ in their typical size, structure, composition, reliance on kinship networks, and levels of income and education (Liu & others, 2009). Large and extended families are more common among minority groups than among the White majority. For example, 19 percent of Latino families have three or more children, compared with 14 percent of African American and 10 percent of White families. African American and Latino children interact more with grandparents, aunts, uncles, cousins, and more distant relatives than do White children.

Single-parent families are more common among African Americans and Latinos than among White Americans (Brown & Lesane-Brown, 2009). In comparison with two-parent households, single parents often have more limited resources in terms of time, money, and energy (Wilson, M. N., 2008). Ethnic minority parents also are less educated and more likely to live in low-income circumstances than their White counterparts. Still, many impoverished ethnic minority families manage to find ways to raise competent children (Hattery & Smith, 2007).

Of course, individual families vary, and how ethnic minority families deal with stress depends on many factors (Galindo & Durham, 2009; Gauvain & Parke, 2010: Parke & Clarke-Stewart, 2011). Whether the parents are native-born or immigrants, how long the family has been in this country, its socioeconomic status, and its national origin all make a difference (Parke & others, 2008). The characteristics of the family's social context also influence its adaptation. What are the attitudes toward the family's ethnic group within its neighborhood or city? Can the family's children attend good schools? Are there community groups that welcome people from the family's ethnic group? Do members of the family's ethnic group form community groups of their own?

*What are some
characteristics
of families within
different ethnic
groups?*

Ethnic minority children and their parents are expected to move beyond their own cultural background and to identify with aspects of the dominant culture. They undergo varying degrees of *acculturation*, which refers to cultural changes that occur when one culture comes into contact with another (Kitayama, 2011). Asian American parents, for example, may feel pressure to modify the traditional training style of parental control discussed earlier as they encounter the more permissive parenting that is typical of the dominant culture.

Status Low-income families have less access to resources than do higher-income families (Bennett, 2011; Koppelman & Goodhart, 2011). The resources in question include nutrition, health care, protection from danger, and enriching educational and socialization opportunities, such as tutoring and lessons in various activities. These differences are compounded in low-income families characterized by long-term poverty (Brandon, 2009).

In America and most Western cultures, researchers have identified differences in child-rearing practices among different socioeconomic-status (SES) groups (Hoff, Laursen, & Tardif, 2002, p. 246):

- "Lower-SES parents (1) are more concerned that their children conform to society's expectations, (2) create a home atmosphere in which it is clear that parents have authority over children," (3) are more likely to use physical punishment in disciplining their children, and (4) are more directive and less conversational with their children.

- "Higher-SES parents (1) are more concerned with developing children's initiative" and delay of gratification, (2) "create a home atmosphere in which children are more nearly equal participants and in which rules are discussed as opposed to being laid down" in an authoritarian manner, (3) are less likely to use physical punishment, and (4) "are less directive and more conversational" with their children.

Peer Relations, Play, and Television

The family is an important social context for children's development. However, children's development also is strongly influenced by what goes on in other social contexts, such as in peer groups and when children are playing or watching television (Chung-Hall & Chen, 2010; Gentile, Mathieson, & Crick, 2010).

Peer Relations

As children grow older, they spend an increasing amount of time with their *peers*—children of about the same age or maturity level.

What are the functions of a child's peer group? One of its most important functions is to provide a source of information and comparison about the world outside the family. Children receive feedback about their abilities from their peer group. They evaluate what they do in terms of whether it is better than, as good as, or worse than what other children do. It is hard to make these judgments at home because siblings are usually older or younger.

Good peer relations can be necessary for normal socioemotional development (Hartup, 2009; Prinstein & others, 2009). Special concerns in peer relations focus on children who are withdrawn and aggressive (Rubin & Coplan, 2010; Smith, Rose, & Schwartz-Mette, 2010). Withdrawn children who are rejected by peers or are victimized and feel lonely are at risk for depression. Children who are aggressive with their peers are at risk for developing a number of problems, including delinquency and dropping out of school (Dodge, 2010).

Recall from our discussion of gender that by about age 3, children already prefer to spend time with same-sex rather than opposite-sex playmates, and this preference increases in early childhood. During these same years, the frequency of peer interactions, both positive and negative, picks up considerably. Although aggressive interactions and rough-and-tumble play increase, the proportion of aggressive exchanges, compared to friendly exchanges, decreases. Many preschool children spend considerable time in peer interaction just conversing with playmates about such matters as "negotiating roles and rules in play, arguing, and agreeing" (Rubin, Bukowski, & Parker, 2006). We discuss peer relations further in Chapter 8.

Play

An extensive amount of peer interaction during childhood involves play, but social play is only one type of play. *Play* is a pleasurable activity that is engaged in for its own sake, and its functions and forms vary.

Functions of Play

Play makes important contributions to young children's cognitive and socioemotional development (Coplan & Arbeau, 2009). Theorists have focused on different aspects of play and have highlighted a long list of functions of play.

According to Freud and Erikson, play helps the child master anxieties and conflicts. Because tensions are relieved through play, the child can cope better with life's problems. Play permits the child to work off excess physical energy and release pent-up tensions. Therapists use *play therapy* both to allow the child to work off frustrations and to analyze the child's conflicts and ways of coping with them (Sanders, 2008). Children may feel less threatened and be more likely to express their true feelings in the context of play.

Play is also an important context for cognitive development (Coplan & Arbeau, 2009). Both Piaget and Vygotsky concluded that play is the child's work. Piaget (1962) maintained that play advances children's cognitive development. At the same time, he said that children's cognitive development *constrains* the way they play. Play permits children to practice their competencies and acquired skills in a relaxed, pleasurable way. Piaget thought that cognitive structures need to be exercised, and play provides the perfect setting for this exercise.

Vygotsky (1962) also considered play to be an excellent setting for cognitive development. He was especially interested in the symbolic and make-believe aspects of play, as when a child substitutes a stick for a horse and rides the stick as if it were a horse. For young children, the imaginary situation is real. Parents should encourage such imaginary play, because it advances the child's cognitive development, especially creative thought.

Daniel Berlyne (1960) described play as exciting and pleasurable in itself because it satisfies our exploratory drive. This drive involves curiosity and a desire for information about something new or unusual. Play encourages exploratory behavior by offering children the possibilities of novelty, complexity, uncertainty, surprise, and incongruity.

More recently, play has been described as an important context for the development of language and communication skills (Coplan & Arbeau, 2009). Language and communication skills may be enhanced through discussions and negotiations regarding roles and rules in play as young children practice various words and phrases. These types of social interactions during play can benefit young children's literacy skills (Coplan & Arbeau, 2009). And, as we saw in Chapter 5, play is a central focus of the child-centered kindergarten and is thought to be an essential aspect of early childhood education (Feeney & others, 2010).

Parten's Classic Study of Play

Many years ago, Mildred Parten (1932) developed an elaborate classification of children's play. Based on observations of children in free play at nursery school, Parten proposed the following types of play:

- *Unoccupied play* is not play as it is commonly understood. The child may stand in one spot or perform random movements that do not seem to have a goal. In most nursery schools, unoccupied play is less frequent than other forms of play.

- *Solitary play* happens when the child plays alone and independently of others. The child seems engrossed in the activity and does not care much about anything else that is happening. Two- and 3-year-olds engage more frequently in solitary play than older preschoolers do.

- *Onlooker play* takes place when the child watches other children play. The child may talk with the other children and ask questions but does not enter into their play behavior. The child's active interest in other children's play distinguishes onlooker play from unoccupied play.

- *Parallel play* occurs when the child plays separately from others but with toys like those the others are using or in a manner that mimics their play. The older children are, the less frequently they engage in this type of play. However, even older preschool children engage in parallel play quite often.

- *Associative play* involves social interaction with little or no organization. In this type of play, children seem to be more interested in each other than in the tasks they are performing. Borrowing or lending toys and following or leading one another in line are examples of associative play.

- *Cooperative play* consists of social interaction in a group with a sense of group identity and organized activity. Children's formal games, competition aimed at winning, and groups formed by a teacher for doing things together aimed at winning, and groups formed by a teacher for doing things together are examples of cooperative play. Cooperative play is the prototype for the games of middle childhood. Little cooperative play is seen in the preschool years.

Types of Play

Whereas Parten's classification system focuses primarily on the social aspects of play, the contemporary perspective on play emphasizes both the cognitive and the social aspects of it (Sumaroka & Bornstein, 2008). Among the most widely studied types of children's play are sensorimotor and practice play, pretense/symbolic play, social play, constructive play, and games (Bergen, 1988).

sensorimotor play Behavior engaged in by infants to derive pleasure from exercising their existing sensorimotor schemes.

practice play Play that involves repetition of behavior when new skills are being learned or when physical or mental mastery and coordination of skills are required for games or sports.

pretense/symbolic play Play in which the child transforms the physical environment into a symbol.

social play Play that involves social interactions with peers.

Sensorimotor and Practice Play **Sensorimotor play** is behavior by infants intended to derive pleasure from exercising their sensorimotor schemes. The development of sensorimotor play follows Piaget's description of sensorimotor thought, which we discussed in Chapter 4. Infants initially engage in exploratory and playful visual and motor transactions in the second quarter of the first year of life. For example, at 9 months, infants begin to select novel objects for exploration and play, especially responsive objects such as toys that make noise or bounce.

Practice play involves the repetition of behavior when new skills are being learned or when physical or mental mastery and coordination of skills are required for games or sports. Sensorimotor play, which often involves practice play, is primarily confined to infancy, whereas practice play can occur throughout life. During the preschool years, children often engage in practice play.

Pretense/Symbolic Play **Pretense/symbolic play** occurs when the child transforms the physical environment into a symbol. Between 9 and 30 months, children increase their use of objects in symbolic play. They learn to transform objects—substituting them for other objects and acting toward them as if they were these other objects. For example, a preschool child treats a table as if it were a car and says, "I'm fixing the car," as he grabs a leg of the table.

Many experts on play consider the preschool years the "golden age" of symbolic/pretense play that is dramatic or sociodramatic in nature. This type of make-believe play often appears at about 18 months and reaches a peak at ages 4 to 5, then gradually declines.

Some child psychologists believe that pretend play is an important aspect of young children's development and often reflects advances in their cognitive development, especially as an indication of symbolic understanding. For example, Catherine Garvey (2000) and Angeline Lillard (2006) emphasize that hidden in young children's pretend-play narratives are remarkable capacities for role-taking, balancing of social roles, metacognition (thinking about thinking), testing of the distinction between reality and pretense, and numerous nonegocentric capacities that reveal young children's remarkable cognitive skills. In one recent analysis, a major accomplishment in early childhood is the development of children's ability to share their pretend play with peers (Coplan & Arbeau, 2009). And in recent research, pretend play has been found to contribute to young children's self-regulation, mainly because of the self-monitoring and social sensitivity required in creating and enacting a sociodramatic narrative in cooperation with other children (Diamond & others, 2007).

Social Play **Social play** is play that involves interaction with peers. It increases dramatically during the preschool years. For many children, social play is the main

What role does gender play in children's peer relations?

context for their social interactions with peers (Coplan & Arbeau, 2009). Social play includes varied interchanges such as turn taking, conversations about numerous topics, social games and routines, and physical play (Sumaroka & Bornstein, 2008). It often involves a high degree of pleasure on the part of the participants.

How Would You...?
As an educator, how would you integrate play into the learning process?

Constructive Play

Constructive play combines sensorimotor/practice play with symbolic representation. It occurs when children engage in the self-regulated creation of a product or solution. Constructive play increases in the preschool years as symbolic play increases and sensorimotor play decreases. Constructive play is also a frequent form of play in the elementary school years, both in and out of the classroom.

Games Games are activities that are engaged in for pleasure and have rules. Often they involve competition. Preschool children may begin to participate in social games that involve simple rules of reciprocity and turn taking. However, games take on a much stronger role in the lives of elementary school children. In one study, the highest incidence of game playing occurred between ages 10 and 12 (Eiferman, 1971). After age 12, games decline in popularity (Bergen, 1988).

constructive play Play that combines sensorimotor and repetitive activity with symbolic representation of ideas. Constructive play occurs when children engage in self-regulated creation or construction of a product or a problem solution.

games Activities engaged in for pleasure that include rules and often competition with one or more individuals.

Television

Few developments in society in the second half of the 20th century had a greater impact on children than television (Bickham 2009). Although it is only one of the many types of mass media that affect children's behavior, television is the most influential. The persuasive capabilities of television are staggering (Scharrer & Demers, 2009).

Many children spend more time in front of the television set than they do with their parents. Just how much television do young children watch? Survey results vary, with the figures ranging from an average of two to four hours a day (Roberts & Foehr, 2008). Compared with their counterparts in other developed countries, children in the United States watch television for considerably longer periods. Television can have a negative influence on children by making them passive learners, distracting them from doing homework, teaching them stereotypes, providing them with violent models of aggression, and presenting them with unrealistic views of the world (Murray & Murray, 2008). However, television can have a positive influence on children's development by presenting motivating educational programs, portraying information about the world beyond their immediate environment, and providing models of prosocial behavior (Wilson, 2008).

How Would You...?
As a human development and family studies professional, how would you talk with parents about strategies for improving television viewing by their children?

Effects of Television on Children's Aggression

The extent to which children are exposed to violence and aggression on television raises special concerns (Gentile, Mathieson, & Crick, 2010; Scharrer & Demers, 2009). For example, Saturday morning cartoon shows average more than 25 violent acts per hour. In one experiment, preschool children were randomly assigned to one of two groups: One group watched television shows taken directly from violent Saturday morning cartoons on 11 days; the second group watched television cartoon shows with all the violence removed (Steuer, Applefield, & Smith, 1971). The children were then observed during play at their preschool. The preschool children who had seen the TV cartoon shows with violence kicked, choked, and pushed their playmates more than did the preschool children who

"Mrs. Horton, could you stop by school today?"
Copyright © Martha Campbell.

had watched nonviolent TV cartoon shows. Because the children were randomly assigned to the two conditions (TV cartoons with violence versus nonviolent TV cartoons), we can conclude that exposure to TV violence *caused* the increased aggression in the children in this investigation.

Other research has found links between watching television violence as a child and acting aggressively years later. For example, in one study, exposure to media violence at ages 6 to 10 was linked with aggressive behavior in young adulthood (Huesmann & others, 2003).

In addition to television violence, there is increased concern about children who play violent video games, especially those that are highly realistic (Escobar-Chaves & Anderson, 2008). A recent research review concluded that playing violent video games is linked to aggression in both males and females (Anderson, Gentile, & Buckley, 2007).

Effects of Television on Children's Prosocial Behavior

Television can also teach children that it is better to behave in positive, prosocial ways than in negative, antisocial ways (Bryant, 2007). Researchers have found that when children watch positive social interchanges in which children are taught how to use social skills on the TV show *Sesame Street,* they subsequently are likely to imitate these positive social behaviors (Bryant, 2007).

How is television violence linked to children's aggression?

Summary

Emotional and Personality Development

- In Erikson's theory, early childhood is a period when development involves resolving the conflict of initiative versus guilt. Young children improve their self-understanding and understanding of others.

- Young children's range of emotions expands during early childhood as they increasingly experience self-conscious emotions such as pride, shame, and guilt. Children benefit from having emotion-coaching parents.

- Moral development involves thoughts, feelings, and actions regarding rules and regulations about what people should do in their interactions with others. Piaget proposed cognitive changes in children's moral reasoning. Behavioral and social cognitive theorists argue that there is considerable situational variability in moral behavior.

- Gender refers to the social and psychological dimensions of being male or female. Both psychoanalytic theory and social cognitive theory emphasize the adoption of parents' gender characteristics.

Peers are especially adept at rewarding gender-appropriate behavior. Gender schema theory emphasizes the role of cognition in gender development.

Families

- Authoritarian, authoritative, neglectful, and indulgent are four main parenting styles. Authoritative parenting is the style most often associated with children's social competence. Ethnic variations characterize parenting styles. Physical punishment is widely used by U.S. parents, but there are a number of reasons why it is not a good choice. Coparenting has positive effects on children's development.

- Child maltreatment may take the form of physical abuse, child neglect, sexual abuse, and emotional abuse.

- Siblings interact with each other in positive and negative ways. Birth order is related in certain ways to child characteristics, but by itself it is not a good predictor of behavior.

- In general, having both parents employed full-time outside the home has not been shown to have negative effects on children. If divorced parents develop a harmonious relationship and practice authoritative parenting, children's adjustment improves. Researchers have found few differences between children growing up in gay or lesbian families and children growing up in heterosexual families. Culture, ethnicity, and socioeconomic status are linked to a number of aspects of families and children's development.

Peer Relations, Play, and Television

- Peers are powerful socialization agents. Peers provide a source of information and comparison about the world outside the family.

- Play's functions include affiliation with peers, tension release, advances in cognitive development, exploration, and provision of a safe haven. The contemporary perspective on play emphasizes both the cognitive and the social aspects of play. Among the most widely studied types of children's play are sensorimotor play, practice play, pretense/symbolic play, social play, constructive play, and games.

- Television can have both negative and positive influences on children's development.

Key Terms

self-understanding 149
moral development 152
heteronomous morality 153
autonomous morality 153
immanent justice 153
gender identity 154

gender roles 154
social role theory 154
psychoanalytic theory of gender 155
social cognitive theory of gender 155

gender schema theory 156
authoritarian parenting 157
authoritative parenting 157
neglectful parenting 157
indulgent parenting 157
sensorimotor play 170

practice play 170
pretense/symbolic play 170
social play 170
constructive play 171
games 171

7 Physical and Cognitive Development in Middle and Late Childhood

Stories of Life-Span Development: Angie and Her Weight

The following comments are by Angie, an elementary-school-age girl:

> When I was eight years old, I weighed 125 pounds. My clothes were the size that large teenage girls wear. I hated my body, and my classmates teased me all the time. I was so overweight and out of shape that when I took a P.E. class my face would get red and I had trouble breathing. I was jealous of the kids who played sports and weren't overweight like I was.
>
> I'm nine years old now and I've lost 30 pounds. I'm much happier and proud of myself. How did I lose the weight? My mom said she had finally decided enough was enough. She took me to a pediatrician who specializes in helping children lose weight and keep it off. The pediatrician counseled my mom about my eating and exercise habits, then had us join a group that he had created for overweight children and their parents. My mom and I go to the group once a week, and we've now been participating in the program for six months. I no longer eat fast-food meals, and my mom is cooking more healthy meals. Now that I've lost weight, exercise is not as hard for me, and I don't get teased by the kids at school. My mom's pretty happy, too, because she's lost 15 pounds herself since we've been in the counseling program.

Not all overweight children are as successful as Angie at reducing their weight. Indeed, being overweight in childhood has become a major national concern in the United States. Later in the chapter, we further explore being overweight in childhood.

During the middle and late childhood years, which last from approximately 6 years of age to 10 or 11 years of age, children grow taller, heavier, and stronger, and become more adept at using their physical skills. During these years, disabilities may emerge that call for special attention and intervention. It is also in this age period that children's cognitive abilities increase dramatically. Their command of grammar becomes proficient, they learn to read, and they may acquire a second language.

Physical Changes and Health

Continued growth and change in proportions characterize children's bodies during middle and late childhood. During this time period, some important changes in the brain also take place and motor skills improve. Developing a healthy lifestyle that involves regular exercise and good nutrition is a key aspect of making these years a time of healthy growth and development.

Body Growth and Change

The period of middle and late childhood involves slow, consistent growth. This is a period of calm before the rapid growth spurt of adolescence. During the elementary school years, children grow an average of 2 to 3 inches a year until, at the age of 11, the average girl is 4 feet, 10¼ inches tall, and the average boy is 4 feet, 9 inches tall. During the middle and late childhood years, children gain about 5 to 7 pounds a year. The weight increase is due mainly to increases in the size of the skeletal and muscular systems, as well as the size of some body organs.

Proportional changes are among the most pronounced physical changes in middle and late childhood (Hockenberry & Wilson, 2009). Head and waist circumference decrease in relation to body height. A less noticeable physical change is that bones continue to ossify during middle and late childhood, though they still yield to pressure and pull more than do mature bones.

Muscle mass and strength gradually increase during these years as "baby fat" decreases. The loose movements and knock-knees of early childhood give way to improved muscle tone. Thanks both to heredity and to exercise, children double their strength capabilities during these years. Because of their greater number of muscle cells, boys are usually stronger than girls.

The Brain

Total brain volume stabilizes by the end of middle and late childhood, but significant changes in various structures and regions of the brain continue to occur (Gogtay & Thompson, 2010). As children develop, activation in some brain areas increases while it decreases in other areas (Diamond, Casey, & Munakata, 2011; Nelson, 2011). One shift in activation that occurs is from diffuse, larger areas to more focal, smaller areas (Turkeltaub & others, 2003). This shift is characterized by synaptic pruning, in which areas of the brain not being used lose synaptic connections and those areas being used show an increase in connections. In one study, researchers found less diffusion and more focal activation in the prefrontal cortex from 7 to 30 years of age (Durston & others, 2006). This shift in activation was accompanied by increased efficiency in cognitive performance, especially *cognitive control*, which involves effective control and flexibility in a number of areas. These areas include controlling attention, reducing interfering thoughts, inhibiting motor actions, and flexibility in switching between competing choices (Diamond, Casey, & Munakata, 2011).

Leading researchers in developmental cognitive neuroscience have recently proposed that the prefrontal cortex likely orchestrates the functions of many other brain regions during development (Johnson & others, 2009). As part of this organizational role, the prefrontal cortex may provide an advantage to neural networks and connections that include the prefrontal cortex. In this view, the prefrontal cortex coordinates which neural connections are the most effective for solving a problem at hand.

Motor Development

During middle and late childhood, children's motor skills become much smoother and more coordinated than they were in early childhood. For example, only one child in a thousand can hit a tennis ball over the net at the age of 3, yet by the age of 10 or 11 most children can learn to play the sport. Running, climbing, skipping rope, swimming, bicycle riding, and skating are just a few of the many physical skills elementary school children can master. In gross motor skills that involve large muscle activity, boys usually outperform girls.

Increased myelination of the central nervous system is reflected in the improvement of fine motor skills during middle and late childhood. Children can more adroitly use their hands as tools. Six-year-olds can hammer, paste, tie shoes, and fasten clothes. By 7 years of age, children's hands have become steadier. At this age, children prefer a pencil to a crayon for printing, and they reverse letters less often. Printing becomes smaller. At 8 to 10 years of age, they can use their hands independently with more ease and precision. Fine motor coordination develops to the point at which children can write rather than print words. Cursive letter size becomes smaller and more even. At 10 to 12 years of age, children begin to show manipulative skills similar to the abilities of adults. They can master the complex, intricate, and rapid movements needed to produce fine-quality crafts or to play a difficult piece on a musical instrument. Girls usually outperform boys in their use of fine motor skills.

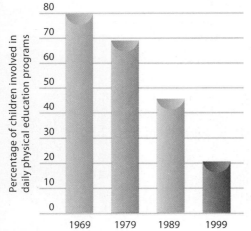

Exercise

Elementary school children are far from physical maturity, so they need to be active (Graham, Holt/Hale, & Parker, 2010; Rink, 2009). They become more fatigued by long periods of sitting than by running, jumping, or bicycling. Physical action, such as batting a ball, skipping rope, or balancing on a beam, is essential for children this age to refine their developing skills. It is becoming increasingly clear that exercise plays an important role in children's growth and development (Crawford & others, 2010; Fahey, Insel, & Roth, 2011).

Are U.S. children getting enough exercise? In one historical comparison, the percentage of children involved in daily P.E. programs in schools decreased from 80 percent in 1969 to 20 percent in 1999 (Health Management Resources, 2001) (see Figure 7.1). Educators and policy makers in many other countries around the world, including China, Finland, and Great Britain, have become very concerned about the sedentary lifestyles of many children in their countries (Fogelholm, 2008).

Television watching is linked with low activity and obesity in children (Wells & others, 2008). A related concern is the dramatic increase in computer use by children. Researchers have found that the total time that children and adolescents spend in front of a television or computer places them at risk for reduced activity and being overweight (Rey-Lopez & others, 2008).

Parents and schools can increase children's exercise. A recent study revealed that the extent to which parents limited their children's sedentary behavior, encouraged them to exercise, and engaged in

How Would You...?
As an educator, how would you structure the curriculum to ensure that elementary school students are getting adequate physical activity throughout the day?

Figure 7.1 Percentage of Children Involved in Daily Physical Education Programs in the United States from 1969 to 1999

There has been a dramatic drop in the percentage of children participating in daily physical education programs in the United States, from 80 percent in 1969 to only 20 percent in 1999.

y-axis: Percentage of children involved in daily physical education programs (0–80)
x-axis: 1969, 1979, 1989, 1999

exercise themselves were linked to children's exercise practices (Edwardson & Gorely, 2010). In another recent study, elementary school children who participated in a school-based exercise intervention (five physical education classes a week plus physical activity exercises to do out of school) increased their exercise activity and lowered their adiposity level more than their counterparts who did not participate in the intervention (Kriemler & others, 2010).

Increasing children's exercise levels has positive outcomes (Rink, 2009). For example, one study found that 45 minutes of moderate physical activity and 15 minutes of vigorous physical activity daily were related to decreased odds of children being overweight (Wittmeier, Mollard, & Kriellaars, 2008).

Researchers also have found that exercise is linked to children's cognitive development. For example, one study revealed that aerobic exercise was linked to increases in an important cognitive activity—planning—in overweight 9-year-old children (Davis & others, 2007). In another study, a group of 9-year-old girls who were more physically fit showed better performance on a cognitive control task than a group of 9-year-old girls who were less physically fit. The control task involved inhibiting unnecessary information to obtain correct solutions (Hillman & others, 2009).

Here are some ways to get children to exercise more:

- Offer more physical activity programs run by volunteers at school facilities.
- Improve physical fitness activities in schools.
- Have children plan community and school activities that really interest them.
- Encourage families to focus more on physical activity, and encourage parents to exercise more.

Health, Illness, and Disease

For the most part, middle and late childhood is a time of excellent health. Disease and death are less prevalent at this time than during other periods in childhood and in adolescence. However, many children in middle and late childhood face health problems that harm their development (Nyaronga & Wickrama, 2009).

Overweight Children

Being overweight is an increasing child health problem (Blake, 2011; Schiff, 2011). Recall from Chapter 5 that being overweight is defined in terms of body mass index (BMI), which is computed by a formula that takes into account height and weight. Children at or above the 97th percentile are included in the obesity category, and those at or above the 95th percentile in the overweight category, and children at or above the 85th percentile are at risk for being overweight (Centers for Disease Control and Prevention, 2011). Over the last three decades, the percentage of U.S. children who are at risk for being overweight has doubled from 15 percent in the 1970s to almost 30 percent today, and the percentage of children who are overweight has tripled (Paxson & others, 2006). Recently, however, the increase in child obesity began to level off. A large-scale U.S. study revealed that child obesity increased from 7 percent to 11 percent from 1980 to 1994 but was essentially the same from 2002 to 2006 (Ogden, Carroll, & Flegal,

2008). Still, the levels of child obesity, overweight, and risk for being overweight are still far too high (Donatelle, 2011; Thompson, Manore, & Vaughan, 2011).

Note that girls are more likely than boys to be overweight, and this gender difference occurs in many countries (Sweeting, 2008). Additionally, another large-scale U.S.

What are some trends in the eating habits and weight of young children?

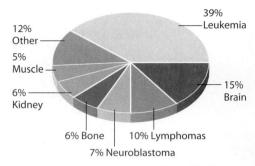

12% Other		39% Leukemia
5% Muscle		
6% Kidney		15% Brain
	6% Bone	10% Lymphomas
	7% Neuroblastoma	

Figure 7.2 Types of Cancer in Children Cancers in children have a different profile from adult cancers, which attack mainly the lungs, colon, breast, prostate, and pancreas.

study showed that African American and Latino children were more likely to be overweight or obese than non-Latino White children (Benson, Baer, & Kaelber, 2009).

Being overweight causes a large amount of concern because it raises the risk for many medical and psychological problems (Oliver & others, 2010; Raghuveer, 2010). Overweight children are at risk for developing pulmonary problems, such as sleep apnea (which involves upper-airway obstruction), and hip problems (Goodwin & others, 2010). Diabetes, hypertension (high blood pressure), and elevated blood cholesterol levels also are common in children who are overweight (Amed & others, 2010; Genovesi & others, 2010). Once considered rare in children, hypertension has become increasingly common in overweight children (Jago & others 2010). And many obese children have low self-esteem (Griffiths & others, 2010).

How Would You...?
As a social worker, how would you use your knowledge of overweight risk factors to design a workshop for parents and children about healthy lifestyle choices?

Cancer

Cancer is the second leading cause of death in U.S. children 5 to 14 years of age. One in every 330 children in the United States develops cancer before the age of 19. The incidence of cancer in children has slightly increased in recent years (National Cancer Institute, 2008a).

Child cancers mainly attack the white blood cells (leukemia), brain, bone, lymph system, muscles, kidneys, and nervous system. All are characterized by an uncontrolled proliferation of abnormal cells. As indicated in Figure 7.2, the most common cancer in children is leukemia, a cancer in which bone marrow manufactures an abundance of abnormal white blood cells, which crowd out normal cells, making the child susceptible to bruising and infection (Eden, 2010; Kaatsch, 2010).

Because of advancements in cancer treatment, children with cancer are surviving longer (National Cancer Institute, 2008b). For example, in the 1960s, less than 5 percent of children with an acute form of leukemia survived for more than five years; today, approximately 25 percent of these children survive for five years or more.

Child life specialists are among the health professionals who work to make the lives of children with diseases less stressful. To read about the work of child life specialist Sharon McLeod, see "Careers in Life-Span Development."

CAREERS IN LIFE-SPAN DEVELOPMENT

Sharon McLeod, Child Life Specialist

Sharon McLeod is a child life specialist who is clinical director of the Child Life and Recreational Therapy Department at the Children's Hospital Medical Center in Cincinnati. Under McLeod's direction, the goals of the Child Life Department are to promote children's optimal growth and development, reduce the stress of health-care experiences, and provide support to child patients and their families. These goals are accomplished through therapeutic play and developmentally appropriate activities, educating and psychologically preparing children for medical procedures, and serving as a resource for parents and other professionals regarding children's development and health-care issues.

McLeod says that human growth and development provides the foundation for her profession of child life specialist. She also describes her best times as a student when she con-

Sharon McLeod, child life specialist, working with a child at Children's Hospital Medical Center in Cincinnati.

ducted fieldwork, had an internship, and experienced hands-on theories and concepts she learned in her courses.

Children With Disabilities

The elementary school years are a time when some disabilities become prominent for some children. What are some of the disabilities that children have? What characterizes the educational issues involving children with disabilities?

The Scope of Disabilities

Disability	Percentage of All Children in Public Schools
Learning disabilities	5.4
Speech and language impairments	3.0
Mental retardation	1.1
Emotional disturbance	0.9

Figure 7.3 U.S. Children With a Disability Who Receive Special Education Services
Figures are for the 2006–2007 school year. Learning disabilities and attention deficit hyperactivity disorder are combined in the learning disabilities category (National Center for Education Statistics, 2008a).

Approximately 14 percent of all children from ages 3 to 21 years in the United States receive special education or related services (National Center for Education Statistics 2008a). Figure 7.3 shows the four largest groups of students with a disability who were served by federal programs in the 2006–2007 school year (National Center for Education Statistics, 2008a). Notice that students with a learning disability were by far the largest group, followed by children with speech or language impairments, mental retardation, and emotional disturbance.

Learning Disabilities

The U.S. government defines whether a child should be classified as having a learning disability as the following: A child with a **learning disability** has difficulty in learning that involves understanding or using spoken or written language, and the difficulty can appear in listening, thinking, reading, writing, and spelling. A learning disability also may involve difficulty in doing mathematics. To be classified as a learning disability, the learning problem is not primarily the result of visual, hearing, or motor disabilities; mental retardation; emotional disorders; or due to environmental, cultural, or economic disadvantage.

About three times as many boys as girls are classified as having a learning disability. Among the explanations for this gender difference are a greater biological vulnerability among boys and *referral bias*. That is, boys are more likely to be referred by teachers for treatment because of troublesome behavior.

Approximately 80 percent of children with a learning disability have a reading problem (Shaywitz, Gruen, & Shaywitz, 2007). Three types of learning disabilities are dyslexia, dysgraphia, and discalculia:

- *Dyslexia* is a category reserved for individuals who have a severe impairment in their ability to read and spell (Ise & Schulte-Korne, 2010).

- *Dysgraphia* is a learning disability that involves difficulty in handwriting (Rosenblum, Abri, & Josman, 2010). Children with dysgraphia may write very slowly, their writing products may be virtually illegible, and they may make numerous spelling errors because of their inability to match up sounds and letters.

- *Dyscalculia*, also known as developmental arithmetic disorder, is a learning disability that involves difficulty in math computation (Rykhlevskaia & others, 2010).

The precise causes of learning disabilities have not yet been determined (Hallahan, Kauffman, & Pullen, 2009; Rosenberg, Westling, & McLeskey, 2011). To reveal any regions of the brain that might be involved in learning disabilities, researchers use brain-imaging techniques, such as magnetic resonance imaging (Shaywitz, Lyon, & Shaywitz, 2006) (see Figure 7.4). This research indicates that it is unlikely learning disabilities reside in a single, specific brain location. More likely, learning disabilities are due to

learning disability Describes a child who has difficulty in learning that involves understanding or using spoken or written language, and the difficulty can appear in listening, thinking, reading, writing, and spelling. A learning disability also may involve difficulty in doing mathematics. To be classified as a learning disability, the learning problem is not primarily the result of visual, hearing, or motor disabilities; mental retardation; emotional disorders; or due to environmental, cultural, or economic disadvantage.

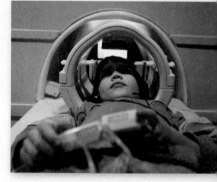

Figure 7.4 Brain Scans and Learning Disabilities
An increasing number of studies are using MRI brain scans to examine the brain pathways involved in learning disabilities. Shown here is 9-year-old Patrick Price, who has dyslexia. Patrick is going through an MRI scanner disguised by drapes to look like a child-friendly castle. Inside the scanner, children must lie virtually motionless as words and symbols flash on a screen, and they are asked to identify them by clicking different buttons.

attention deficit hyperactivity disorder (ADHD) A disability in which children consistently show one or more of the following characteristics: (1) inattention, (2) hyperactivity, and (3) impulsivity.

problems in integrating information from multiple brain regions or subtle difficulties in brain structures and functions.

Interventions with children who have a learning disability often focus on improving reading ability (Bursuck & Damer, 2011). Intensive instruction over a period of time by a competent teacher can help many children (Berninger, 2006; Waber, 2010).

Attention Deficit Hyperactivity Disorder (ADHD)

Attention deficit hyperactivity disorder (ADHD) is a disability in which children consistently show one or more of these characteristics over a period of time: (1) inattention, (2) hyperactivity, and (3) impulsivity. Children who are inattentive have such difficulty focusing on any one thing that they may get bored with a task after only a few minutes—or even seconds. Children who are hyperactive show high levels of physical activity, seeming to be almost constantly in motion. Children who are impulsive have difficulty curbing their reactions; they do not do a good job of thinking before they act. Depending on the characteristics that children with ADHD display, they can be diagnosed as (1) ADHD with predominantly inattention, (2) ADHD with predominantly hyperactivity/impulsivity, or (3) ADHD with both inattention and hyperactivity/impulsivity.

The number of children diagnosed and treated for ADHD has increased substantially in recent decades. The disorder is diagnosed as much as four to nine times more in boys than in girls. There is controversy, however, about the increased diagnosis of ADHD (Stolzer, 2009). Some experts attribute the increase mainly to heightened awareness of the disorder; others are concerned that many children are being incorrectly diagnosed (Parens & Johnston, 2009).

Definitive causes of ADHD have not been found. However, a number of causes have been proposed (Farone & Mick, 2010; Stolzer, 2009). Some children likely inherit a tendency to develop ADHD from their parents (Durston, 2010; Pennington & others, 2009). Other children likely develop ADHD because of damage to their brain during prenatal or postnatal development (Linblad & Hjern, 2010). Among early possible contributors to ADHD are cigarette and alcohol exposure during prenatal development and low birth weight (Knopik, 2009).

As with learning disabilities, the development of brain-imaging techniques is leading to a better understanding of ADHD (Hoeksema & others, 2010). A recent study revealed that peak thickness of the cerebral cortex occurred three years later (10.5 years) in children with ADHD than in children without ADHD (peak at 7.5 years) (Shaw & others, 2007). The delay was more prominent in the prefrontal regions of the brain that are especially important in attention and planning (see Figure 7.5). Researchers also are exploring the roles that various neurotransmitters, such as serotonin and dopamine, might play in ADHD (Levy, 2009; Rondou, Haegeman, & Van Craenenbroeck, 2010; Zhou & others, 2010).

Stimulant medication such as Ritalin or Adderall (which has fewer side effects than Ritalin) is effective in improving the attention of many children with ADHD, but it usually does not improve their attention to the same level as children who do not have ADHD (Brams, Mao, & Doyle, 2009; Stray, Ellertson, & Stray, 2010). A recent meta-analysis (statistical analysis that combines the results of many different studies) concluded that behavior management treatments are effective in reducing the effects of ADHD (Fabiano & others,

Many children with ADHD show impulsive behavior, such as this child who is throwing a paper airplane at other children. *How would you handle this situation if you were a teacher and this were to happen in your classroom?*

How Would You...? As a health-care professional, how would you respond to these statements by a parent? "I do not believe that ADHD is a real disorder. Children are supposed to be active."

How Would You...? As an educator, how would you explain the nature of learning disabilities to a parent whose child has recently been diagnosed with a learning disability?

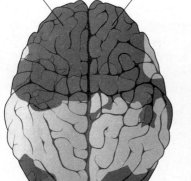

Prefrontal cortex — Prefrontal cortex

■ Greater than 2 years delay
■ 0 to 2 years delay

Figure 7.5 Regions of the Brain in Which Children With ADHD Had a Delayed Peak in the Thickness of the Cerebral Cortex *Note:* The greatest delays occurred in the prefrontal cortex.

How Would You...?
As a human development and family studies professional, how would you advise parents who are hesitant about medicating their child who was recently diagnosed with a mild form of ADHD?

2009). Researchers have often found that a combination of medication (such as Ritalin) and behavior management improves the behavior of children with ADHD better than medication alone or behavior management alone, although not in all cases (Parens & Johnston, 2009).

Autism Spectrum Disorders

Autism spectrum disorders (ASD), also called pervasive developmental disorders, range from the more severe disorder called *autistic disorder* to the milder disorder called *Asperger syndrome*. Autism spectrum disorders are characterized by problems in social interaction, problems in verbal and nonverbal communication, and repetitive behaviors (Boutot & Myles, 2011; Hall, 2009). Children with these disorders may also show atypical responses to sensory experiences (National Institute of Mental Health, 2008). Autism spectrum disorders can often be detected in children as early as 1 to 3 years of age.

Recent estimates of autism spectrum disorders indicate that they are increasing in occurrence or are increasingly being detected and labeled (Neal, 2009). Once thought to affect only 1 in 2,500 individuals, today's estimates suggest that they occur in about 1 in 150 individuals (Centers for Disease Control and Prevention, 2007).

Autistic disorder is a severe developmental autism spectrum disorder that has its onset in the first three years of life and includes deficiencies in social relationships; abnormalities in communication; and restricted, repetitive, and stereotyped patterns of behavior.

Asperger syndrome is a relatively mild autism spectrum disorder in which the child has relatively good verbal language, milder nonverbal language problems, and a restricted range of interests and relationships (Bennett & others, 2008). Children with Asperger syndrome often engage in obsessive repetitive routines and preoccupations with a particular subject. For example, a child may be obsessed with baseball scores or railroad timetables.

What causes the autism spectrum disorders? The current consensus is that autism is a brain dysfunction with abnormalities in brain structure and neurotransmitters (Anderson & others, 2009). Genetic factors likely play a role in the development of autism spectrum disorders (El-Fishawy & State, 2010; Shen & others, 2010). A recent study revealed that mutations—missing or duplicated pieces of DNA on chromosome 16—can raise a child's risk of developing autism a hundredfold (Weiss & others, 2008). There is no evidence that family socialization causes autism. Mental retardation is present in some children with autism; others show average or above-average intelligence (Hoekstra & others, 2010). Boys are four times as likely as girls to have autism spectrum disorders (Gong & others, 2009).

Children with autism benefit from a well-structured classroom, individualized instruction, and small-group instruction. Behavior modification techniques are sometimes effective in helping autistic children learn (Boutot & Myles, 2011; Kasari & Lawton, 2010). A recent research review concluded that when behavior modifications are intensely provided and used early in the autistic child's life, they are more effective than when used intermittently and later in life (Howlin, Magiati, & Charman, 2009).

Educational Issues

Until the 1970s most U.S. public schools either refused enrollment to children with disabilities or inadequately served them. This changed in 1975, when *Public Law 94-142*, the Education for All Handicapped Children Act, required that all students with disabilities be given a free, appropriate public education. In 1990, Public Law 94-142 was recast as the *Individuals with Disabilities Education Act* (IDEA). IDEA was amended in 1997 and then reauthorized in 2004 and renamed the Individuals with Disabilities Education Improvement Act.

autism spectrum disorders (ASD) Also called pervasive developmental disorders, they range from the severe disorder labeled autistic disorder to the milder disorder called Asperger syndrome. These disorders are characterized by problems in social interaction, verbal and nonverbal communication, and repetitive behaviors.

What characterizes autism spectrum disorders?

individualized education plan (IEP) A written statement that spells out a program tailored to a child with a disability.

least restrictive environment (LRE) The concept that a child with a disability must be educated in a setting that is as similar as possible to the one in which children who do not have a disability are educated.

inclusion Educating a child with special education needs full-time in the regular classroom.

IDEA mandates free, appropriate education for all children. *What services does IDEA mandate for children with disabilities?*

IDEA spells out broad mandates for services to children with disabilities of all kinds (Friend, 2011). These services include evaluation and eligibility determination, appropriate education and an individualized education plan (IEP), and education in the least restrictive environment (LRE).

An **individualized education plan (IEP)** is a written statement that spells out a program that is specifically tailored for a student with a disability. The **least restrictive environment (LRE)** is a setting that is as similar as possible to the one in which children who do not have a disability are educated. This provision of the IDEA has given a legal basis to efforts to educate children with a disability in the regular classroom. The term **inclusion** describes educating a child with special education needs full-time in the regular classroom (Hick & Thomas, 2009; Valle & Connor, 2011).

Many legal changes regarding children with disabilities have been extremely positive (Carter, Prater, & Dyches, 2009; Rosenberg, Westling, & McLeskey, 2011). Compared with several decades ago, far more children today are receiving competent, specialized services. For many children, inclusion in the regular classroom, with modifications or supplemental services, is appropriate. However, some leading experts on special education argue that some children with disabilities may not benefit from inclusion in the regular classroom. James Kauffman and his colleagues, for example, advocate a more individualized approach that does not necessarily involve full inclusion but allows options such as special education outside the regular classroom with trained professionals and adapted curricula (Kauffman, McGee, & Brigham, 2004). They go on to say, "We sell students with disabilities short when we pretend that they are not different from typical students. We make the same error when we pretend that they must *not* be expected to put forth extra effort if they are to learn to do some things—or learn to do something in a different way" (p. 620). Like general education, special education should challenge students with disabilities "to become all they can be."

Cognitive Changes

Do children enter a new stage of cognitive development in middle and late childhood? How do children process information in this age period? What is the nature of children's intelligence? Let's explore these questions.

Piaget's Cognitive Developmental Theory

According to Piaget (1952), the preschool child's thought is preoperational. Preschool children can form stable concepts, and they have begun to reason, but their thinking is flawed by egocentrism and magical belief systems. As we discussed in Chapter 5, however, Piaget may have underestimated the cognitive skills of preschool children. Some researchers argue that under the right conditions, young children may display abilities that are characteristic of Piaget's next stage of cognitive development, the stage of concrete operational thought (Gelman, 1969). Here we will cover the characteristics of concrete operational thought and evaluate Piaget's portrait of this stage.

The Concrete Operational Stage

Piaget proposed that the *concrete operational stage* lasts from approximately 7 to 11 years of age. In this stage, children can perform concrete operations, and they can reason logically as long as reasoning can be applied to specific or concrete examples. Remember that *operations* are mental actions that are reversible, and *concrete operations* are operations that are applied to real, concrete objects.

The conservation tasks described in Chapter 5 indicate whether children are capable of concrete operations. For example, recall that in one task involving conservation of matter, the child is presented with two identical balls of clay. The experimenter rolls one ball into a long, thin shape; the other remains in its original ball shape. The child is then asked if there is more clay in the ball or in the long, thin piece of clay. By the time children reach the age of 7 or 8, most answer that the amount of clay is the same. To answer this problem correctly, children have to imagine the clay rolling back into a ball. This type of imagination involves a reversible mental action applied to a real, concrete object. Concrete operations allow the child to consider several characteristics rather than focus on a single property of an object. In the clay example, the preoperational child is likely to focus on height *or* width. The concrete operational child coordinates information about both dimensions.

What other abilities are characteristic of children who have reached the concrete operational stage? One important skill is the ability to classify or divide things into different sets or subsets and to consider their interrelationships. Consider the family tree of four generations that is shown in Figure 7.6 (Furth & Wachs, 1975). This family tree suggests that the grandfather (A) has three children (B, C, and D), each of whom has two children (E through J), and that one of these children (J) has three children (K, L, and M). A child who comprehends the classification system can move up and down a level, across a level, and up and down and across within the system. The concrete operational child understands that person J can at the same time be father, brother, and grandson, for example.

Children who have reached the concrete operational stage are also capable of **seriation**, which is the ability to order stimuli along a quantitative dimension (such as length). To see if students can serialize, a teacher might haphazardly place eight sticks of different lengths on a table. The teacher then asks the students to order the sticks by length. Many young children end up with two or three small groups of "big" sticks or "little" sticks, rather than a correct ordering of all eight sticks. Another mistaken strategy they use is to line up the tops of the sticks evenly but ignore the bottoms. The concrete operational thinker simultaneously understands that each stick must be longer than the one that precedes it and shorter than the one that follows it.

Another aspect of reasoning about the relations between classifications is **transitivity**, which is the ability to logically combine relations to understand certain conclusions. In this case, consider three sticks (A, B, and C) of differing lengths. A is the longest, B is intermediate in length, and C is the shortest. Does the child understand that if A is longer than B and B is longer than C, then A is longer than C? In Piaget's theory, concrete operational thinkers do; preoperational thinkers do not.

seriation The concrete operation that involves ordering stimuli along a quantitative dimension (such as length).

transitivity The ability to logically combine relations to understand certain conclusions.

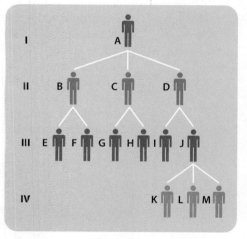

Figure 7.6 Classification: An Important Ability in Concrete Operational Thought

A family tree of four generations (*I to IV*): The preoperational child has trouble classifying the members of the four generations; the concrete operational child can classify the members vertically, horizontally, and obliquely (up and down and across). For example, the concrete operational child understands that a family member can be a son, a brother, and a father, all at the same time.

Evaluating Piaget's Concrete Operational Stage

How Would You...? As a psychologist, how would you characterize the contribution Piaget made to our current understanding of cognitive development in childhood?

Has Piaget's portrait of the concrete operational child stood the test of research? According to Piaget various aspects of a stage should emerge at the same time. In fact, however, some concrete operational abilities do not appear in synchrony. For example, children do not learn to conserve at the same time they learn to cross-classify.

Furthermore, education and culture exert stronger influences on children's development than Piaget reasoned (Holzman, 2009; Irvine & Berry, 2010). Some preoperational children can be trained to reason at a concrete operational stage. And the age at which children acquire conservation skills is related to how much practice their culture provides in these skills.

Thus, although Piaget was a giant in the field of developmental psychology, his conclusions about the concrete operational stage have been challenged. In Chapter 9, after examining the final stage in his theory of cognitive development, we will further evaluate Piaget's contributions and the criticisms of his theory.

Neo-Piagetians argue that Piaget got some things right but that his theory needs considerable revision. They give more emphasis to how children use attention, memory, and strategies to process information (Case & Mueller, 2001). They especially believe that a more accurate portrayal of children's thinking requires attention to children's strategies, the speed at which children process information, the particular task involved, and the division of problems into smaller, more precise steps (Morra & others, 2008). These are issues addressed by the information-processing approach, and we discuss some of them later in this chapter.

Information Processing

If we examine how children handle information during middle and late childhood instead of analyzing the type of thinking they display, what do we find? During these years, most children dramatically improve their ability to sustain and control attention. Other changes in information processing during middle and late childhood involve memory, thinking, and metacognition.

Memory

In Chapter 5, we concluded that short-term memory increases considerably during early childhood but after the age of 7 does not show as much increase. **Long-term memory**, a relatively permanent and unlimited type of memory, increases with age during middle and late childhood. In part, improvements in memory reflect children's increased knowledge and their increased use of strategies. Keep in mind that it is important not to view memory in terms of how children add something to it but rather to underscore how children actively construct their memory (Ornstein & Light, 2011; Ornstein & others, 2010).

Knowledge and Expertise Much of the research on the role of knowledge in memory has compared experts and novices. *Experts* have acquired extensive knowledge about

An outstanding teacher, and education in the logic of science and mathematics, are important cultural experiences that promote the development of operational thought. *Might Piaget have underestimated the roles of culture and schooling in children's cognitive development?*

a particular content area; this knowledge influences what they notice and how they organize, represent, and interpret information. This in turn affects their ability to remember, reason, and solve problems. When individuals have expertise about a particular subject, their memory also tends to be good regarding material related to that subject (Martinez, 2010).

For example, one study found that 10- and 11-year-olds who were experienced chess players ("experts") were able to remember more information about chess pieces than college students who were not chess players ("novices") (Chi, 1978). In contrast, when the college students were presented with other stimuli, they were able to remember them better than the children were. Thus, the children's expertise in chess gave them superior memories, but only in chess.

There are developmental changes in expertise (Blair & Somerville, 2009). Older children usually have more expertise about a subject than younger children, which can contribute to their better memory for the subject.

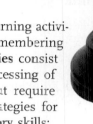

Strategies Long-term memory depends on the learning activities individuals engage in when learning and remembering information (Ashcraft & Radvansky, 2010). **Strategies** consist of deliberate mental activities to improve the processing of information. They do not occur automatically but require effort and work. Following are some effective strategies for adults to use to help children improve their memory skills:

strategies Consist of deliberate mental activities to improve the processing of information.

elaboration An important strategy that involves engaging in more extensive processing of information.

- *Guide children to elaborate about the information they are to remember.* **Elaboration** involves more extensive processing of the information, such as thinking of examples or relating the information to one's own life. Elaboration makes the information more meaningful (Schneider, 2011).

- *Encourage children to engage in mental imagery.* Mental imagery can help even young school children to remember visuals. However, for remembering verbal information, mental imagery works better for older children than for younger children (Schneider, 2004).

- *Motivate children to remember material by understanding it rather than by memorizing it.* Children will remember information better over the long term if they understand the information rather than just rehearse and memorize it. Rehearsal works well for encoding information into short-term memory, but when children need to retrieve the information from long-term memory, it is much less efficient. For most information, encourage children to understand it, give it meaning, elaborate on it, and personalize it.

- *Repeat and vary instructional information, and link it to other information early and often.* These recommendations improve children's consolidation and reconsolidation of the information they are learning (Bauer, 2009b). Varying the themes of a lesson increases the number of associations in memory storage, and linking the information expands the network of associations in memory storage; both strategies expand the routes for retrieving information from storage in the brain.

- *Embed memory-relevant language when instructing children.* Teachers who use mnemonic devices and metacognitive questions that encourage children to think about their thinking can improve student performance (Ornstein & Light, 2011). In recent research that involved extensive observations of a number of first-grade teachers in the classroom, Peter Ornstein & his colleagues (2007, 2010) found that for the time segments observed, the teachers' rarely used strategy suggestions or metacognitive (thinking about thinking) questions. However, lower-achieving students increased their performance when they were placed in classrooms with teachers who frequently embedded memory-relevant information in their teaching (Ornstein & others, 2007).

Fuzzy Trace Theory Might something other than knowledge and strategies be responsible for the improvement in memory during the elementary school years? Charles Brainerd and Valerie Reyna (2004) argue that fuzzy traces account for much of this improvement. Their **fuzzy trace theory** states that memory is best understood by considering two types of memory representations: (1) verbatim memory trace and (2) gist. The *verbatim memory trace* consists of the precise details of the information, whereas *gist* refers to the central idea of the information. When gist is used, fuzzy traces are built up. Although individuals of all ages extract gist, young children tend to store and retrieve verbatim traces. At some point during the early elementary school years, children begin to use gist more and, according to the theory, this contributes to the improved memory and reasoning of older children because fuzzy traces are more enduring and less likely to be forgotten than verbatim traces.

Thinking

Thinking involves manipulating and transforming information in memory. Two important aspects of thinking are being able to think critically and creatively.

Critical Thinking Currently, there is considerable interest among psychologists and educators in critical thinking (Bonney & Sternberg, 2011; Fairweather & Cramond, 2011). **Critical thinking** involves thinking reflectively and productively, and evaluating evidence. In this book, the "How Would You . . . ?" questions in the margins of each chapter challenge you to think critically about a topic or an issue related to the discussion.

Jacqueline and Martin Brooks (2001) lament that few schools really teach students to think critically and develop a deep understanding of concepts. Deep understanding occurs when students are stimulated to rethink previously held ideas. In Brooks and Brooks' view, schools spend too much time getting students to give a single correct answer in an imitative way, rather than encouraging them to expand their thinking by coming up with new ideas and rethinking earlier conclusions. They observe that too often teachers ask students to recite, define, describe, state, and list, rather than to analyze, infer, connect, synthesize, criticize, create, evaluate, think, and rethink. Many successful students complete their assignments, do well on tests and get good grades, yet they don't ever learn to think critically and deeply. They think superficially, staying on the surface of problems rather than stretching their minds and becoming deeply engaged in meaningful thinking.

Creative Thinking Cognitively competent children not only think critically, but also creatively (Hennesey, 2011; Sternberg, 2010a). **Creative thinking** is the ability to think in novel and unusual ways and to come up with unique solutions to problems. Thus, intelligence and creativity are not the same thing. This difference was recognized by J. P. Guilford (1967), who distinguished between **convergent thinking**, which produces one correct answer and characterizes the kind of thinking that is required on conventional tests of intelligence, and **divergent thinking**, which produces many different answers to the same question and characterizes creativity. For example, a typical item on a conventional intelligence test is "How many quarters will you get in return for 60 dimes?" In contrast, the following question has many possible answers: "What images come to mind when you hear the phrase 'sitting alone in a dark room' or 'some unique uses for a paper clip'?"

It is important to recognize that children will show more creativity in some domains than others (Runco & Spritzker, 2010). A child who shows creative thinking skills in mathematics may not exhibit these skills in art, for example. An important goal is to help children learn to think creatively.

MINDS AT WORK

A special concern today is that the creative thinking of children in the United States appears to be declining. A study of approximately 300,000 U.S. children and adults found that creativity scores rose until 1990, but since then have been steadily declining (Kim, 2010). Among the likely causes of this decline are the number of hours U.S. children watch TV and play videogames instead of engaging in creative activities, as well as the lack of emphasis on creative thinking skills in schools (Beghetto & Kaufman, 2011; Runco, 2011; Sternberg, 2011d). In some countries, though, there has been increasing emphasis on creative thinking in schools. For example, historically, creative thinking has typically been discouraged in Chinese schools. However, Chinese educators are now encouraging teachers to spend more classroom time on creative activities (Plucker, 2010).

Metacognition

Metacognition is cognition about cognition, or knowing about knowing (Flavell, 2004). Many studies classified as "metacognitive" have focused on *metamemory,* or knowledge about memory. This includes general knowledge about memory, such as knowing that recognition tests are easier than recall tests. It also encompasses knowledge about one's own memory, such as a student's ability to monitor whether she has studied enough for a test that is coming up next week.

Young children do have some general knowledge about memory (Schneider, 2011). By 5 or 6 years of age, children usually already know that familiar items are easier to learn than unfamiliar ones, that short lists are easier than long ones, that recognition is easier than recall, and that forgetting is more likely to occur over time (Lyon & Flavell, 1993). However, in other ways young children's metamemory is limited. They don't understand that related items are easier to remember than unrelated ones and that remembering the gist of a story is easier than remembering information verbatim (Kreutzer, Leonard, & Flavell, 1975). By the fifth grade, children do understand that gist recall is easier than verbatim recall.

Young children also have only limited knowledge about their own memory. They have an inflated opinion of their memory abilities. For example, in one study a majority of young children predicted that they would be able to recall all 10 items on a list of 10 items. When tested for this, however, none of the young children managed this feat (Flavell, Friedrichs, & Hoyt, 1970). As they move through the elementary school years, children can give more realistic evaluations of their memory skills.

In addition to metamemory, metacognition includes knowledge about memory strategies (White, Fredrikson, & Collins, 2010). In the view of Michael Pressley (2007), the key to education is helping students learn a rich repertoire of strategies that result in solutions to problems. Good thinkers routinely use strategies and effective planning to solve problems. Good thinkers also know when and where to use strategies. Understanding when and where to use strategies often results from monitoring the learning situation (Serra & others, 2010).

Intelligence

How can intelligence be defined? **Intelligence** is the ability to solve problems and to adapt and learn from experiences. Interest in intelligence has often focused on individual differences and assessment. *Individual differences* are the stable, consistent ways in which people are different from each other. We can talk about individual differences in personality or any other domain, but it is in the domain of intelligence that the most attention has been directed at individual differences. For example, an intelligence test purports to inform us about whether a student can reason better than others who have taken the test. Let's go back in history and see what the first intelligence test was like.

Cognitive developmentalist John Flavell (*left*) is a pioneer in providing insights about children's thinking. Among his many contributions are establishing the field of metacognition and conducting numerous studies in this area, including metamemory and theory of mind studies.

mental age (MA) Binet's measure of an individual's level of mental development, compared with that of others.

intelligence quotient (IQ) A person's mental age divided by chronological age, multiplied by 100.

normal distribution A symmetrical distribution with most scores falling in the middle of the possible range of scores and few scores appearing toward the extremes of the range.

The Binet Tests

In 1904, the French Ministry of Education asked psychologist Alfred Binet to devise a method of identifying children who were unable to learn in school. School officials wanted to reduce crowding by placing students who did not benefit from regular classroom teaching in special schools. Binet and his student Theophile Simon developed an intelligence test to meet this request. The test is called the *1905 Scale*. It consists of 30 questions on topics ranging from the ability to touch one's ear to the ability to draw designs from memory and define abstract concepts.

Binet developed the concept of **mental age (MA)**, an individual's level of mental development relative to others. Not much later, in 1912, William Stern created the concept of **intelligence quotient (IQ)**, a person's mental age divided by chronological age (CA), multiplied by 100. That is: IQ = MA/CA × 100. If mental age is the same as chronological age, then the person's IQ is 100. If mental age is above chronological age, then IQ is more than 100. If mental age is below chronological age, then IQ is less than 100.

The Binet test has been revised many times to incorporate advances in the understanding of intelligence and intelligence tests. These revisions are called the *Stanford-Binet tests* (Stanford University is where the revisions have been done). In 2004, the test—now called the *Stanford-Binet 5*—was revised to analyze an individual's response in five content areas: fluid reasoning, knowledge, quantitative reasoning, visual-spatial reasoning, and working memory. A general composite score also is still obtained.

By administering the test to large numbers of people of different ages (from preschool through late adulthood) from different backgrounds, researchers have found that scores on the Stanford-Binet approximate a normal distribution (see Figure 7.7). A **normal distribution** is symmetrical, with a majority of the scores falling in the middle of the possible range of scores and few scores appearing toward the extremes of the range.

The Wechsler Scales

Another set of tests widely used to assess students' intelligence is called the *Wechsler scales,* developed by psychologist David Wechsler. They include the *Wechsler Preschool and Primary Scale of Intelligence—Third Edition (WPPSI-III)* to test children from the ages of 2 years 6 months to 7 years 3 months of age; the *Wechsler Intelligence Scale for Children—Fourth Edition (WISC-IV)* for children and

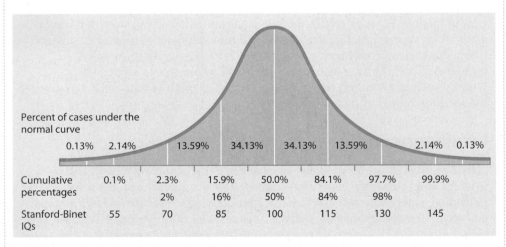

Figure 7.7 The Normal Curve and Stanford-Binet IQ Scores
The distribution of IQ scores approximates a normal curve. Most of the population falls in the middle range of scores. Notice that extremely high and extremely low scores are very rare. Slightly more than two-thirds of the scores fall between 85 and 115. Only about 1 in 50 individuals has an IQ of more than 130, and only about 1 in 50 individuals has an IQ of less than 70.

adolescents 6 to 16 years of age; and the *Wechsler Adult Intelligence Scale—Fourth Edition (WAIS-IV)*.

The Wechsler subscales not only provide an overall IQ score, but they also yield several composite indexes, such as the Verbal Comprehension Index, the Working Memory Index, and the Processing Speed Index. These types of indexes allow the examiner to quickly determine the areas in which the child is strong or weak. Three of the Wechsler subscales are shown in Figure 7.8.

Types of Intelligence

Is it more appropriate to think of a child's intelligence as a general ability or as a number of specific abilities? Robert Sternberg and Howard Gardner have proposed influential theories oriented to this second viewpoint.

Sternberg's Triarchic Theory Robert J. Sternberg (1986, 2004, 2008, 2009, 2010a, b, 2011a, b, e) developed the **triarchic theory of intelligence**, which states that intelligence comes in three forms: (1) *analytical intelligence*, which refers to the ability to analyze, judge, evaluate, compare, and contrast; (2) *creative intelligence*, which consists of the ability to create, design, invent, originate, and imagine; and (3) *practical intelligence*, which involves the ability to use, apply, implement, and put ideas into practice.

Sternberg (2011a, b) says that children with different triarchic patterns "look different" in school. Students with high analytic ability tend to be favored in conventional schooling. They often do well under direct instruction, in which the teacher lectures and gives students objective tests. They often are considered to be "smart" students who get good grades, show up in high-level tracks, do well on traditional tests of intelligence and the SAT, and later get admitted to competitive colleges.

In contrast, children who are high in creative intelligence often are not on the top rung of their class. Many teachers have specific expectations about how assignments should be done, and creatively intelligent students may not conform to those expectations. Instead of giving conformist answers, they give unique answers, for which they might get reprimanded or marked down. No teacher wants to discourage creativity, but Sternberg stresses that too often a teacher's desire to improve students' knowledge suppresses creative thinking.

Like children high in creative intelligence, children who are practically intelligent often do not relate well to the demands of school. However, many of these children do well outside of the classroom's walls. They may have excellent social skills and good common sense. As adults, some become successful managers, entrepreneurs, or politicians in spite of having undistinguished school records.

Gardner's Eight Frames of Mind Howard Gardner (1983, 1993, 2002) suggests there are eight types of intelligence, or "frames of

Verbal Subscales

Similarities

A child must think logically and abstractly to answer a number of questions about how things might be similar.

Example: "In what way are a lion and a tiger alike?"

Comprehension

This subscale is designed to measure an individual's judgment and common sense.

Example: "What is the advantage of keeping money in a bank?"

Nonverbal Subscales

Block Design

A child must assemble a set of multicolored blocks to match designs that the examiner shows.
Visual-motor coordination, perceptual organization, and the ability to visualize spatially are assessed.

Example: "Use the four blocks on the left to make the pattern on the right."

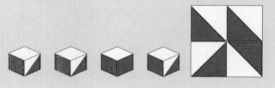

Figure 7.8 Sample Subscales of the Wechsler Intelligence Scale for Children—Fourth Edition (WISC-IV)

The Wechsler includes 11 subscales, 6 verbal and 5 nonverbal. Three of the subscales are shown here. Simulated items are similar to those found in the *Wechsler Intelligence Scale for Children—Fourth Edition.*

COGNITIVE CHANGES

189

mind." These are described here, with examples of the types of vocations in which they are reflected as strengths (Campbell, Campbell, & Dickinson, 2004):

Verbal: The ability to think in words and use language to express meaning. Occupations: Authors, journalists, speakers.

Mathematical: The ability to carry out mathematical operations. Occupations: Scientists, engineers, accountants.

Spatial: The ability to think three-dimensionally. Occupations: Architects, artists, sailors.

Bodily-kinesthetic: The ability to manipulate objects and be physically adept. Occupations: Surgeons, craftspeople, dancers, athletes.

Musical: A sensitivity to pitch, melody, rhythm, and tone. Occupations: Composers, musicians, and sensitive listeners.

Interpersonal: The ability to understand and interact effectively with others. Occupations: Successful teachers, mental health professionals.

Intrapersonal: The ability to understand oneself. Occupations: Theologians, psychologists.

Naturalist: The ability to observe patterns in nature and understand natural and human-made systems. Occupations: Farmers, botanists, ecologists, landscapers.

According to Gardner, everyone has all of these intelligences to varying degrees. As a result, we prefer to learn and process information in different ways. People learn best when they can do so in a way that uses their stronger intelligences.

Evaluating the Multiple-Intelligences Approaches Sternberg's and Gardner's approaches have much to offer. They have stimulated teachers to think more broadly about what makes up children's competencies. And they have motivated educators to develop programs that instruct students in multiple domains. These approaches have also contributed to interest in assessing intelligence and classroom learning in innovative ways, such as by evaluating student portfolios (Moran & Gardner, 2007).

How Would You...?
As a psychologist, how would you use Gardner's theory of multiple intelligences to respond to children who are distressed by their below-average score on a traditional intelligence test?

When Gardner's multiple intelligences approach is applied to education, children can pursue activities of special interest to them. Every day, each child can choose from activities that draw on Gardner's eight frames of mind. In the elementary school shown here, children can choose from activities that range from gardening to architecture to gliding to dancing.

Still, doubts about multiple-intelligences approaches persist. A number of psychologists think that the multiple-intelligences views have taken the concept of specific intelligences too far (Reeve & Charles, 2008). Some argue that a research base to support the three intelligences of Sternberg or the eight intelligences of Gardner has not yet emerged. One expert on intelligence, Nathan Brody (2007), observes that people who excel at one type of intellectual task are likely to excel in others. Thus, individuals who do well at memorizing lists of digits are also likely to be good at solving verbal problems and spatial layout problems. If musical skill reflects a distinct type of intelligence, ask other critics, why not label the skills of outstanding chess players, prizefighters, painters, and poets as types of intelligence?

The argument between those who support the concept of general intelligence and those who advocate the multiple-intelligences view is ongoing (Brody, 2007; Sternberg, 2009, 2010a, 2011e). Sternberg (2011a, b) actually accepts that there is a general intelligence for the kinds of analytical tasks that traditional IQ tests assess but thinks that the range of tasks those tests measure is far too narrow.

Culture and Intelligence

Differences in conceptions of intelligence occur not only among psychologists but also among cultures (Sternberg, 2011c; Zhang & Sternberg, 2011). What is viewed as intelligent in one culture may not be thought of as intelligent in another. For example, people in Western cultures tend to view intelligence in terms of reasoning and thinking skills, whereas people in Eastern cultures see intelligence as a way for members of a community to engage successfully in social roles (Nisbett, 2003).

Interpreting Differences in IQ Scores

The IQ scores that result from tests such as the Stanford-Binet and Wechsler scales provide information about children's mental abilities. However, interpreting what performance on an intelligence test means is debated.

The Influence of Genetics How strong is the effect of genetics on intelligence? This question is difficult to answer because, as we discussed in Chapter 2, teasing apart heredity and environment is virtually impossible. Also, most research on heredity and environment does not include environments that differ radically. Thus, it is not surprising that many genetic studies show environment to be a fairly weak influence on intelligence.

One strategy for examining the role of heredity in intelligence is to compare the IQs of identical and fraternal twins, which we initially discussed in Chapter 2. Recall that identical twins have exactly the same genetic makeup but fraternal twins do not. If intelligence is genetically determined, say some investigators, identical twins' IQs should be more similar than the intelligence of fraternal twins. A research review of many studies found that the difference in the average correlation of intelligence between identical and fraternal twins was 0.15, a relatively low correlation (Grigorenko, 2000) (see Figure 7.9).

Today, most researchers agree that genetics and environment interact to influence intelligence. For most people, this means that modifications in environment can change their IQ scores considerably. Although genetic endowment may always influence a person's intellectual ability, the environmental influences and opportunities we provide children and adults do make a difference.

Environmental Influences One environmental influence on intelligence is schooling (Gustafsson, 2007). The biggest effects have been

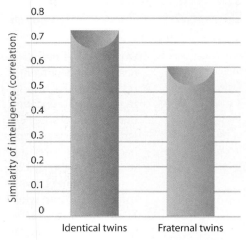

Figure 7.9 Correlation Between Intelligence Test Scores and Twin Status

The graph represents a summary of research findings that have compared the intelligence test scores of identical and fraternal twins. An approximate .15 difference has been found with a higher correlation for identical twins (.75) and a lower correlation for fraternal twins (.60).

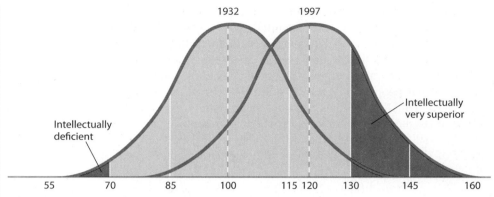

1932   1997

Intellectually
very superior

Intellectually
deficient

55   70   85   100   115 120   130   145   160

Figure 7.10 The Increase in IQ Scores from 1932 to 1997
As measured by the Stanford-Binet intelligence test, American children seem to be getting smarter. Scores of a group tested in 1932 fell along a bell-shaped curve with half below 100 and half above. Studies show that if children took that same test today, half would score above 120 on the 1932 scale. Very few of them would score in the "intellectually deficient" end, on the left side, and about one-fourth would rank in the "very superior" range.

Students in an elementary school in South Africa. *How might schooling influence the development of children's intelligence?*

found when large groups of children have been deprived of formal education for an extended period, resulting in lower intelligence (Ceci & Gilstrap, 2000). Another possible effect of education can be seen in rapidly increasing IQ test scores around the world (Flynn, 1999, 2007). IQ scores have been increasing so fast that a high percentage of people regarded as having average intelligence at the turn of the century would be considered below average in intelligence today (see Figure 7.10). If a representative sample of people today took the Stanford-Binet test version used in 1932, about 25 percent would be defined as having very superior intelligence, a label usually accorded to fewer than 3 percent of the population. Because the increase has taken place in a relatively short time, it can't be due to heredity, but rather may be due to increasing levels of education attained by a much greater percentage of the world's population, or to other environmental factors such as the explosion of information to which people are exposed. The worldwide increase in intelligence test scores that has occurred over a short time frame has been called the *Flynn effect* after the researcher who discovered it, James Flynn.

Researchers are increasingly concerned about improving the early environment of children who are at risk for impoverished intelligence (Barajas, Philipsen, & Brooks-Gunn, 2008). For various reasons, many low-income parents have difficulty providing an intellectually stimulating environment for their children. Programs that educate parents to be more sensitive caregivers and better teachers, as well as support services such as quality child-care programs, can make a difference in a child's intellectual development (Coltrane & others, 2008). Thus the efforts to counteract a deprived early environment's effect on intelligence emphasize prevention rather than remediation.

A review of the research on early interventions concluded that (1) high-quality child-care center–based interventions are associated with increases in children's intelligence and school achievement; (2) the interventions are most successful with poor children and children whose parents have little education; (3) the positive benefits continue through adolescence, but are not as strong as in early childhood or the beginning of elementary school; and (4) the programs that continue into middle and late childhood have the best long-term results (Brooks-Gunn, 2003).

In sum, there is a consensus among psychologists that both heredity and environment influence intelligence (Grigorenko & Takanishi, 2010; Sternberg, 2011a, b). This consensus reflects the nature-nurture issue that was highlighted in Chapter 1. Recall that this issue focuses on the extent to which development is influenced by nature (heredity) and nurture (environment). Although psychologists agree that intelligence is the product of both nature and nurture, there is still disagreement about how strongly each influences intelligence.

Group Differences On the average, African American schoolchildren in the United States score 10 to 15 points lower on standardized intelligence tests than non-Latino White American schoolchildren do (Brody, 2000). Children from Latino families also score lower than non-Latino White children. These are *average scores*, however; there is significant overlap in the distribution of scores. About 15 to 25 percent of African American schoolchildren score higher than half of White schoolchildren do, and many White schoolchildren score lower than most African American schoolchildren. As African Americans have gained social, economic, and educational opportunities, the gap between African Americans and Whites on standardized intelligence tests has begun to narrow. This gap especially narrows in college, where African American and White students often experience more similar environments than in the elementary and high school years (Myerson & others, 1998).

Creating Culture-Fair Tests **Culture-fair tests** are tests of intelligence that are intended to be free of cultural bias. Two types of culture-fair tests have been devised. The first includes items that are familiar to children from all socioeconomic and ethnic backgrounds, or items that at least are familiar to the children taking the test. For example, a child might be asked how a bird and a dog are different, on the assumption that all children have been exposed to birds and dogs. The second type of culture-fair test has no verbal questions.

Why is it so hard to create culture-fair tests? Most tests tend to reflect what the dominant culture thinks is important (Shiraev & Levy, 2010). If tests have time limits, that will bias the test against groups not concerned with time. If languages differ, the same words might have different meanings for different language groups. Even pictures can produce bias because some cultures have less experience with drawings and photographs. Because of such difficulties in creating culture-fair tests, Robert Sternberg (2009, 2011c) concludes that there are no culture-fair tests, only *culture-reduced tests*.

Extremes of Intelligence

Intelligence tests have been used to discover indications of mental retardation or intellectual giftedness, the extremes of intelligence. At times, they have been misused for this purpose. Keeping in mind the theme that an intelligence test should not be used as the sole indicator of mental retardation or giftedness, we will explore the nature of these intellectual extremes.

Mental Retardation **Mental retardation** is a condition of limited mental ability in which an individual has a low IQ, usually below 70 on a traditional intelligence test, and has difficulty adapting to everyday life. About 5 million Americans fit this definition of mental retardation.

There are several classifications of mental retardation (Hallahan, Kaufmann, & Pullen, 2009). About 89 percent of the mentally retarded fall into the mild category, with IQs of 55 to 70; most of them are able to live independently as adults and work at a variety of jobs. About 6 percent are classified as moderately retarded, with IQs of 40 to 54; these people can attain a second-grade level of skills and may be able to support themselves as adults through some types of labor. About 3.5 percent of the mentally retarded are in the severe category, with IQs of 25 to 39; these individuals learn to talk and accomplish very simple tasks but require extensive supervision. Less than 1 percent have IQs below 25; they fall into the profoundly mentally retarded classification and need constant supervision.

How Would You...?
As a social worker, how would you explain the role and purpose of intelligence test scores to a parent whose child is preparing to take a standardized intelligence test?

A child with Down syndrome. *What causes Down syndrome? In which major classification of mental retardation does the condition fall?*

organic retardation Mental retardation that involves some physical damage and is caused by a genetic disorder or brain damage.

cultural-familial retardation Retardation characterized by no evidence of organic brain damage, but the individual's IQ generally is between 50 and 70.

gifted Having above-average intelligence (an IQ of 130 or higher) and/or superior talent for something.

At 2 years of age, art prodigy Alexandra Nechita colored in coloring books for hours and also took up pen and ink. She had no interest in dolls or friends. By age 5 she was using watercolors. Once she started school, she would start painting as soon as she got home. At the age of 8, in 1994, she saw the first public exhibit of her work. In succeeding years, working quickly and impulsively on canvases as large as 5 feet by 9 feet, she has completed hundreds of paintings, some of which sell for close to $100,000 apiece. As a teenager, she continued to paint—relentlessly and passionately. It is, she said, what she loves to do. *What are some characteristics of children who are gifted?*

Mental retardation can have an organic cause, or it can be social and cultural in origin:

- **Organic retardation** is mental retardation that is caused by a genetic disorder or by brain damage; the word *organic* refers to the tissues or organs of the body, indicating physical damage. Most people who suffer from organic retardation have IQs that range between 0 and 50. However, children with Down syndrome have an average IQ of approximately 50. As discussed in Chapter 2, Down syndrome is caused by an extra copy of chromosome 21.

- **Cultural-familial retardation** is a mental deficit in which no evidence of organic brain damage can be found; individuals' IQs generally range from 50 to 70. Psychologists suspect that such mental deficits result from the normal variation that distributes people along the range of intelligence scores combined with growing up in a below-average intellectual environment.

Giftedness There have always been people whose abilities and accomplishments outshine others'—the whiz kid in class, the star athlete, the natural musician. People who are **gifted** have above-average intelligence (an IQ of 130 or higher) or superior talent for something or both. When it comes to programs for the gifted, most school systems select children who have intellectual superiority and academic aptitude, whereas children who are talented in the visual and performing arts (arts, drama, dance, music), athletics, or other special aptitudes tend to be overlooked (Sternberg, Jarvin, & Grigorenko, 2011; Winner, 2009).

What are the characteristics of children who are gifted? Despite speculation that giftedness is linked with having a mental disorder, no relation between giftedness and mental disorder has been found. Similarly, the idea that gifted children are maladjusted is a myth, as Lewis Terman (1925) found when he conducted an extensive study of 1,500 children whose Stanford-Binet IQs averaged 150. The children in Terman's study were socially well adjusted, and many went on to become successful doctors, lawyers, professors, and scientists. Studies support the conclusion that gifted people tend to be more mature than others, have fewer emotional problems than others, and grow up in a positive family climate (Feldman, 2001).

Ellen Winner (1996) described three criteria that characterize gifted children, whether in art, music, or academic domains:

1. *Precocity.* Gifted children are precocious. They begin to master an area earlier than their peers. Learning in their domain is more effortless for them than for ordinary children. In most instances, these gifted children are precocious because they have an inborn high ability in a particular domain or domains.

2. *Marching to a different drummer.* Gifted children learn in a qualitatively different way than ordinary children. One way that they march to a different drummer is that they need minimal help, or scaffolding, from adults to learn. In many instances, they resist any kind of explicit instruction. They often make discoveries on their own and solve problems in unique ways.

3. *A passion to master.* Gifted children are driven to understand the domain in which they have high ability. They display an intense, obsessive interest and an ability to focus. They motivate themselves, says Winner, and do not need to be "pushed" by their parents.

Is giftedness a product of heredity or environment? The answer is, likely both (Sternberg, 2009). Individuals who are gifted recall that they had signs of high ability in a particular area at a very young age, prior to or at the beginning of formal training

A young Bill Gates, founder of Microsoft and now one of the world's richest people. Like many highly gifted students, Gates was not especially fond of school. He hacked a computer security system when he was 13 and as a high school student, he was allowed to take some college math classes. He dropped out of Harvard University and began developing a plan for what was to become Microsoft Corporation. *What are some ways that schools can enrich the education of such highly talented students as Gates to make it a more challenging, interesting, and meaningful experience?*

(Howe & others, 1995). This suggests the importance of innate ability in giftedness. However, researchers have also found that individuals with world-class status in the arts, mathematics, science, and sports all report strong family support and years of training and practice (Bloom, 1985). Deliberate practice is an important characteristic of individuals who become experts in a particular domain. For example, in one study, the best musicians engaged in twice as much deliberate practice over their lives as did the least successful ones (Ericsson, Krampe, & Tesch-Romer, 1993).

Individuals who are highly gifted are typically not gifted in many domains, and research on giftedness is increasingly focused on domain-specific developmental paths (Matthews, 2009). During the childhood years, the domain(s) in which individuals are gifted usually emerges. Thus, at some point in the childhood years, the child who is to become a gifted artist or the child who is to become a gifted mathematician begins to show expertise in that domain. Regarding domain-specific giftedness, software genius Bill Gates (1998), the founder of Microsoft and one of the world's richest people, commented that when you are good at something, you may have to resist the urge to think that you will be good at everything. Because he has been so successful at software development, he has found that people also expect him to be brilliant in other domains in which he is far from gifted.

An increasing number of experts argue that the education of children who are gifted in the United States requires a significant overhaul (Clark, 2008). Ellen Winner (1996, 2006) argues that too often children who are gifted are socially isolated and underchallenged in the classroom. It is not unusual for other students to label them "nerds" or "geeks." Many eminent adults report that school was a negative experience for them, that they were bored and sometimes knew more than their teachers (Bloom, 1985). Winner argues that American students will benefit more from their education when standards are raised for all children. She recommends that some underchallenged students be allowed to attend advanced classes in their domain of exceptional ability, such as allowing some precocious middle school students to take college classes in their area of expertise. For example, at age 13, Bill Gates took college math classes and hacked a computer security system; Yo-Yo Ma, famous cellist, graduated from high school at 15 and attended Juilliard School of Music in New York City.

How Would You...?
As an educator, how would you structure educational programs for children who are gifted that would challenge and expand their unique cognitive abilities?

Language Development

Children gain new skills as they enter school that make it possible to learn to read and write: These include increased use of language to talk about things that are not physically present, learning what a word is, and learning how to recognize and talk about sounds (Berko Gleason, 2003). They also learn the *alphabetic principle*, that the letters of the alphabet represent sounds of the language.

Vocabulary, Grammar, and Metalinguistic Awareness

During middle and late childhood, changes occur in the way children's mental vocabulary is organized. When asked to say the first word that comes to mind when they hear a word, preschool children typically provide a word that often follows the word in a sentence. For example, when asked to respond to "dog" the young child

metalinguistic awareness Refers to knowledge about language, such as knowing what a preposition is or the ability to discuss the sounds of a language.

whole-language approach An approach to reading instruction based on the idea that instruction should parallel children's natural language learning. Reading materials should be whole and meaningful.

phonics approach The idea that reading instruction should teach the basic rules for translating written symbols into sounds.

may say "barks," or to the word "eat" respond with "lunch." At about 7 years of age, children begin to respond with a word that is the same part of speech as the stimulus word. For example, a child may now respond to the word "dog" with "cat" or "horse." To "eat," they now might say "drink." This is evidence that children now have begun to categorize their vocabulary by parts of speech (Berko Gleason, 2003).

The process of categorizing becomes easier as children increase their vocabulary. Children's vocabulary increases from an average of about 14,000 words at age 6 to an average of about 40,000 words by age 11.

Children make similar advances in grammar (Lidz, 2010). During the elementary school years, children's improvement in logical reasoning and analytical skills helps them understand such constructions as the appropriate use of comparatives (*shorter, deeper*) and subjectives ("If you were president . . . "). During the elementary school years, children become increasingly able to understand and use complex grammar, such as the following sentence: *The boy who kissed his mother wore a hat.* They also learn to use language in a more connected way, producing connected discourse. They become able to relate sentences to one another to produce descriptions, definitions, and narratives that make sense. Children must be able to do these things orally before they can be expected to deal with them in written assignments.

These advances in vocabulary and grammar during the elementary school years are accompanied by the development of **metalinguistic awareness**, which is knowledge about language, such as knowing what a preposition is or the ability to discuss the sounds of a language. Metalinguistic awareness allows children "to think about their language, understand what words are, and even define them" (Berko Gleason, 2009, p. 4). It improves considerably during the elementary school years (Pan & Uccelli, 2009). Defining words becomes a regular part of classroom discourse, and children increase their knowledge of syntax as they study and talk about the components of sentences such as subjects and verbs (Meltzi & Ely, 2009).

Children also make progress in understanding how to use language in culturally appropriate ways—a process called pragmatics (Siegal & Surian, 2010). By the time they enter adolescence, most children know the rules for the use of language in everyday contexts—that is, what is appropriate and inappropriate to say.

Reading

Before learning to read, children learn to use language to talk about things that are not present; they learn what a word is; and they learn how to recognize sounds and talk about them. Children who begin elementary school with a robust vocabulary have an advantage when it comes to learning to read (Paris & Paris, 2006). A fluent vocabulary helps readers access word meaning effortlessly (Beaty, 2009).

How should children be taught to read? Currently, debate focuses on the whole-language approach versus the phonics approach (Combs, 2010; Tompkins, 2011a, b).

The **whole-language approach** stresses that reading instruction should parallel children's natural language learning. In some whole-language classes, beginning readers are taught to recognize whole words or even entire sentences, and to use the context of what they are reading to guess at the meaning of words. Reading materials that support the whole-language approach are whole and meaningful—that is, children are given material in its complete form, such as stories and poems, so that they learn to understand language's communicative function. Reading is connected with listening and writing skills. Although there are variations in whole-language programs, most share the premise that reading should be integrated with other skills and subjects, such as science and social studies, and that it should focus on real-world material. Thus, a class might read newspapers, magazines, or books, and then write about and discuss them.

In contrast, the **phonics approach** emphasizes that reading instruction should teach basic rules for translating written symbols into sounds. Early phonics-centered reading instruction should involve simplified materials. Only after children have learned correspondence rules that relate spoken phonemes to the alphabet letters that are used to represent them should they be given complex reading materials, such as books and poems (Cunningham & Allington, 2009).

What are some good strategies for guiding children to read effectively?

Which approach is better? Research suggests that children can benefit from both approaches, but instruction in phonics needs to be emphasized (Snowling & Goble, 2011; Tompkins, 2011a, b). An increasing number of experts in the field of reading now conclude that direct instruction in phonics is a key aspect of learning to read (Fox & Alexander, 2011; Mayer, 2008).

Bilingualism and Second-Language Learning

Are there sensitive periods in learning a second language? That is, if individuals want to learn a second language, how important is the age at which they begin to learn it? What is the best way in the United States to teach children who come from homes in which English is not the primary language?

Second-Language Learning

For many years, it was claimed that if individuals did not learn a second language prior to puberty they would never reach native-language learners' proficiency in the second language (Johnson & Newport, 1991). However, recent research indicates a more complex conclusion: There are sensitive periods for learning a second language. Additionally, these sensitive periods likely vary across different areas of language systems (Paradis, 2010; Thomas & Johnson, 2008). For example, late language learners, such as adolescents and adults, may learn new vocabulary more easily than new sounds or new grammar (Neville, 2006). Also, children's ability to pronounce words with a native-like accent in a second language typically decreases with age, with an especially sharp drop occurring after the age of about 10 to 12. Adults tend to learn a second language faster than children, but their level of second-language mastery is not as high as children's. And the way children and adults learn a second language differs somewhat. Compared with adults, children are less sensitive to feedback, less likely to use explicit strategies, and more likely to learn a second language from large amounts of input (Thomas & Johnson, 2008).

Students in the United States are far behind their counterparts in many developed countries in learning a second language. For example, in Russia, schools have 10 grades, called *forms,* which roughly correspond to the 12 grades in American schools. Russian children begin school at age 7 and begin learning English in the third form. Because of this emphasis on teaching English, most Russian citizens under the age of 40 today are able to speak at least some English. The United States is the only technologically advanced Western nation that does not have a national foreign language requirement at the high school level, even for students in rigorous academic programs.

U.S. students who do not learn a second language may be missing more than the chance to acquire a skill. *Bilingualism*—the ability to speak two languages—has a positive effect on children's cognitive development. Children who are fluent in two languages perform better than their single-language counterparts on tests of

8 Socioemotional Development in Middle and Late Childhood

Stories of Life-Span Development: Learning in Troubled Schools

In *The Shame of the Nation,* Jonathan Kozol (2005) described his visits to 60 U.S. schools in urban low-income areas in 11 states. He saw many schools in which the minority population was 80 to 90 percent. Kozol observed numerous inequities—unkempt classrooms, hallways, and restrooms; inadequate textbooks and supplies; and lack of resources. He also saw teachers mainly instructing students to memorize material by rote, especially as preparation for mandated tests, rather than stimulating them to engage in higher-level thinking. Kozol also frequently observed teachers using threatening disciplinary tactics to control the classroom.

However, some teachers Kozol observed were effective in educating children in these undesirable conditions. At P.S. 30 in the South Bronx, Mr. Bedrock teaches fifth grade. One student in his class, Serafina, recently lost her mother to AIDS. When Kozol visited the class, he was told that two other children had taken the role of "allies in the child's struggle for emotional survival" (Kozol, 2005, p. 291). Textbooks are in short supply for the class, and the social studies text is so out of date it claims that Ronald Reagan is the country's president. But Mr. Bedrock told Kozol that it's a "wonderful" class this year. About their teacher, 56-year-old Mr. Bedrock, one student said, "He's getting old . . . but we love him anyway" (p. 292). Kozol found the students orderly, interested, and engaged.

The years of middle and late childhood bring many changes to children's social and emotional lives. The development of their self-conceptions, moral reasoning, and gendered behavior is significant. Transformations in their relationships with parents and peers occur, and schooling takes on a more academic flavor.

Emotional and Personality Development

self-esteem The global evaluative dimension of the self. Self-esteem is also referred to as self-worth or self-image.

self-concept Domain-specific evaluations of the self.

In this section, we explore how the self continues to develop during middle and late childhood and the emotional changes that take place during these years. We also discuss children's moral development and many aspects of the role that gender plays in their development in middle and late childhood.

The Self

What is the nature of the child's self-understanding and self-esteem during the elementary school years? What role do self-efficacy and self-regulation play in children's achievement?

The Development of Self-Understanding

In middle and late childhood, especially from 8 to 11 years of age, children increasingly describe themselves with psychological characteristics and traits in contrast to the more concrete self-descriptions of younger children. Older children are more likely to describe themselves as *"popular, nice, helpful, mean, smart,* and *dumb"* (Harter, 2006, p. 526).

In addition, during the elementary school years, children become more likely to recognize social aspects of the self (Harter, 2006). They include references to social groups in their self-descriptions, such as referring to themselves as Girl Scouts, as Catholics, or as someone who has two close friends (Livesly & Bromley, 1973).

Children's self-understanding in the elementary school years also includes increasing reference to social comparison (Davis-Kean, Jager, & Collins, 2010). At this point in development, children are more likely to distinguish themselves from others in comparative rather than in absolute terms. That is, elementary-school-age children are no longer as likely to think about what they do or do not do, but are more likely to think about what they can do in comparison with others.

Consider a series of studies in which Diane Ruble (1983) investigated children's use of social comparison in their self-evaluations. Children were given a difficult task and then offered feedback on their performance, as well as information about the performances of other children their age. The children were then asked for self-evaluations. Children younger than 7 made virtually no reference to the information about other children's performances. However, many children older than 7 included socially comparative information in their self-descriptions.

In sum, in middle and late childhood, self-description increasingly involves psychological and social characteristics, including social comparison.

Self-Esteem and Self-Concept

High self-esteem and a positive self-concept are important characteristics of children's well-being (Kaplan, 2009). Investigators sometimes use the terms *self-esteem* and *self-concept* interchangeably or do not precisely define them, but there is a meaningful difference between them.

Self-esteem refers to global evaluations of the self; it is also called *self-worth* or *self-image*. For example, a child may perceive that she is not merely a person but a *good* person. **Self-concept** refers to domain-specific evaluations of the self.

How Would You...?
As a psychologist, how would you explain the role of social comparison for the development of a child's sense of self?

What characterizes self-understanding in middle and late childhood?

How Would You...?

As an educator, how would you work with a child to develop a healthy self-concept concerning their academic ability?

Children can make self-evaluations in many domains of their lives—academic, athletic, appearance, and so on. In sum, *self-esteem* refers to global self-evaluations, *self-concept* to domain-specific evaluations.

Self-esteem reflects perceptions that do not always match reality (Baumeister & others, 2003). A child's self-esteem might reflect a belief about whether he or she is intelligent and attractive, for example, but that belief is not necessarily accurate. Thus, high self-esteem may refer to accurate, justified perceptions of one's worth as a person and one's successes and accomplishments but it can also refer to an arrogant, grandiose, unwarranted sense of superiority over others (Krueger, Vohs, & Baumeister, 2008). In the same manner, low self-esteem may reflect either an accurate perception of one's shortcomings or a distorted, even pathological insecurity and inferiority.

Variations in self-esteem have been linked with many aspects of children's development. However, much of the research is *correlational* rather than *experimental*. Recall from Chapter 1 that correlation does not equal causation. Thus, if a correlational study finds an association between children's low self-esteem and low academic achievement, low academic achievement could cause the low self-esteem as much as low self-esteem causes low academic achievement.

In fact, there are only moderate correlations between school performance and self-esteem, and these correlations do not suggest that high self-esteem produces better school performance (Baumeister & others, 2003). In fact, efforts to increase students' self-esteem have not always led to improved school performance (Davies & Brember, 1999).

Children with high self-esteem have greater initiative, but this can produce positive or negative outcomes (Baumeister & others, 2003). High-self-esteem children are prone to both prosocial and antisocial actions (Krueger, Vohs, & Baumeister, 2008). A recent study revealed that over time aggressive children with high self-esteem increasingly valued the rewards that aggression can bring and belittled their victims (Menon & others, 2007).

In addition, a current concern is that too many of today's children grow up receiving praise for mediocre or even poor performance and as a consequence have inflated self-esteem (Stipek, 2005). They may have difficulty handling competition and criticism. This theme is vividly captured by the title of a book, *Dumbing Down Our Kids: Why American Children Feel Good About Themselves But Can't Read, Write, or Add* (Sykes, 1995).

Increasing Children's Self-Esteem

Teachers, social workers, health-care professionals and others are often concerned about low self-esteem in the children they serve. Researchers have suggested several strategies to improve self-esteem in at-risk children (Bednar, Wells, & Peterson, 1995; Harter, 2006).

- *Identify the causes of low self-esteem.* Intervention should target the causes of low self-esteem. Children have the highest self-esteem when they perform competently in domains that are important to them. Therefore, it is helpful to encourage children to identify and value their areas of competence. These may include areas such as academic skills, athletic skills, physical attractiveness, and social acceptance.

- *Provide emotional support and social approval.* Some children with low self-esteem come from conflicted families or conditions of abuse or neglect—situations in which emotional support is unavailable. In some cases, alternative sources of support can be arranged either informally through the encouragement of a teacher, a coach, or another significant adult, or more formally, through programs such as Big Brothers and Big Sisters.

- *Help children achieve.* Achievement also can improve children's self-esteem. For example, the straightforward teaching of real skills to children often results in increased achievement and, thus, in enhanced self-esteem. Children develop higher self-esteem when they know which tasks will achieve their goals and when they have successfully performed them or similar tasks.

self-efficacy The belief that one can master a situation and produce favorable outcomes.

• *Help children cope.* Self-esteem can be built when a child faces a problem and tries to cope with it, rather than avoiding it. If coping rather than avoidance prevails, children often face problems realistically, honestly, and nondefensively. This produces favorable self-evaluative thoughts, which lead to the self-generated approval that raises self-esteem.

Self-Efficacy

Self-efficacy is the belief that one can master a situation and produce favorable outcomes. Albert Bandura (2001, 2006, 2009a, 2010a, 2010b), whose social cognitive theory we described in Chapter 1, states that self-efficacy is a critical factor in whether or not students achieve. Self-efficacy is the belief that "I can"; helplessness is the belief that "I cannot." Students with high self-efficacy endorse such statements as "I know that I will be able to learn the material in this class" and "I expect to be able to do well at this activity."

How Would You...?

As an educator, how would you encourage enhanced self-efficacy in a student who says, "I can't do this work!"?

Dale Schunk (2008, 2011) has applied the concept of self-efficacy to many aspects of students' achievement. In his view, self-efficacy influences a student's

How can parents help children develop higher self-esteem?

choice of activities. Students with low self-efficacy for learning may avoid many learning tasks, especially those that are challenging. By contrast, high-self-efficacy counterparts eagerly work at learning tasks (Schunk & Zimmerman, 2006). Students with high self-efficacy are more likely to expend effort and persist longer at a learning task than students with low self-efficacy.

Self-Regulation

One of the most important aspects of the self in middle and late childhood is the increased capacity for self-regulation (Veenman, (2011). This increased capacity is characterized by deliberate efforts to manage one's behavior, emotions, and thoughts that lead to increased social competence and achievement (Eisenberg, Spinrad, & Eggum, 2010; Winne & Nesbit, 2010). For example, a recent study revealed that children from low-income families who had a higher level of self-regulation made better grades in school than their counterparts who had a lower level of self-regulation (Buckner, Mezzacappa, & Beardslee, 2009). Another recent study found that self-control increased from 4 to 10 years of age and that high self-control was linked to lower levels of deviant behavior (Vazsonyi & Huang, 2010).

The increased capacity in self-regulation is linked to developmental advances in the brain's prefrontal cortex, which was discussed in Chapter 7 (Diamond, Casey, & Munakata, 2011). In that discussion, increased focal activation in the prefrontal cortex was linked to improved cognitive control. Such cognitive control includes self-regulation.

Industry Versus Inferiority

In Chapter 1, we described Erik Erikson's (1968) eight stages of human development. His fourth stage, industry versus inferiority, appears during middle and late childhood. The term *industry* expresses a dominant theme of this period: Children become interested in how things are made and how they work. When children are encouraged in their efforts to make, build, and work—whether building a model airplane, constructing a tree house, fixing a bicycle, solving an addition

velopment, which he believed are universal. Development, which he believed are universal. Development of the other, said Kohlberg, is fostered by opportunities to take the perspective of others and to experience conflict between one's current stage of moral thinking and the reasoning of someone at a higher stage.

The Kohlberg Stages

Kohlberg's stages fall into three levels of moral thinking, each of which is characterized by two stages (see Figure 8.1).

problem, or cooking—their sense of industry increases. Conversely, parents who see their children's efforts at making things as "mischief" or "making a mess" will tend to foster a sense of inferiority in their children.

Emotional Development

In Chapter 6, we saw that preschoolers become more adept at talking about their own and others' emotions. They also show a growing awareness of the need to

Gender Similarities and Differences

What is the reality behind gender stereotypes? Let's examine some of the similarities and differences between boys and girls, keeping in mind that (1) the differences are averages—not all boys versus all girls; (2) even when differences are reported, there is considerable gender overlap; and (3) the differences may be due primarily to biological factors, sociocultural factors, or both. First, we examine physical similarities and differences, and then we turn to cognitive and socioemotional similarities and differences.

Physical Development Women have about twice the body fat of men, most concentrated around breasts and hips. In males, fat is more likely to go to the abdomen. On the average, males grow to be 10 percent taller than females. Other physical differences are less obvious. From conception on, females have a longer life expectancy than males, and females are less likely than males to develop physical or mental disorders. Males have twice the risk of coronary disease as females.

Does gender matter when it comes to brain structure and function? Human brains are much alike, whether the brain belongs to a male or a female (Halpern & others, 2007). However, researchers have found some differences in the brains of males and females (Hofer & others, 2007). For example, female brains are smaller than male brains, but female brains have more folds; the larger number of folds (called convolutions) allows more surface brain tissue within the skulls of females than males (Luders & others, 2004). An area of the parietal lobe that functions in visuospatial skills is larger in males than females (Frederikse & others, 2000). And the areas of the brain involved in emotional expression show more metabolic activity in females than males (Gur & others, 1995).

Although some differences in brain structure and function have been found, either many of these differences are small or research is inconsistent regarding the differences. Also, when sex differences in the brain have been revealed, in many cases they have not been directly linked to psychological differences (Blakemore, Berenbaum, & Liben, 2009). Although research on sex differences in the brain is still in its infancy, it is likely that there are far more similarities than differences in the brains of females and males. A further point is worth noting: Anatomical sex differences in the brain may be due to the biological origins of these differences, behavioral experiences (which underscores the brain's continuing plasticity), or a combination of these factors.

How Would You...?
As a psychologist, how would you discuss gender similarities and differences with a parent or teacher who is concerned about a child's academic progress and social skills?

Cognitive Development No gender differences in general intelligence have been revealed, but some gender differences have been found in some cognitive areas (Blakemore, Berenbaum, & Liben, 2009). Research has shown that in general girls and women have slightly better verbal skills than boys and men, although in some verbal skills areas the differences are substantial (Blakemore, Berenbaum, & Liben, 2009). For example, in recent national assessments, girls were significantly better than boys in reading and writing (National Assessment of Educational Progress, 2005, 2007).

Are there gender differences in math? A very large-scale study of more than 7 million U.S. students in grades 2 through 11 revealed no differences in math scores for boys and girls (Hyde & others, 2008). One area of math that has been examined for possible gender differences is visuospatial skills, which include being able to rotate objects mentally and determine what they would look like when rotated. These types of skills are important in courses such as plane and solid geometry and geography. A research review revealed that boys have better visuospatial skills than girls (Halpern & others, 2007). For example, despite equal participation in the National Geography Bee, in most years all 10 finalists are boys (Liben, 1995). However, some experts argue that the gender difference in visuospatial skills is small (Hyde, 2007).

Socioemotional Development Three areas of socioemotional development in which gender similarities and differences have been studied extensively are aggression, emotion, and prosocial behavior.

One of the most consistent gender differences is that boys are more physically aggressive than girls are (Brengden, 2009). The difference occurs in all cultures and appears very early in children's development (White, 2001). The physical aggression difference is especially pronounced when children are provoked. Both biological and environmental factors have been proposed to account for gender differences in aggression. Biological factors include heredity and hormones. Environmental factors include cultural expectations, adult and peer models, and social agents that reward aggression in boys and punish aggression in girls.

Although boys are consistently more physically aggressive than girls, might girls show as much or more verbal aggression, such as yelling, than boys? When verbal aggression is examined, gender differences often disappear; sometimes, though, verbal aggression is more pronounced in girls (Eagly & Steffen, 1986).

Recently, increased interest has been shown in *relational aggression*, which involves harming someone by manipulating a relationship (Crick & others, 2009). Relational aggression includes such behaviors as trying to make others dislike a certain individual by spreading malicious rumors about the person. Relational aggression increases in middle and late childhood (Dishion & Piehler, 2009). Mixed findings have characterized research on whether girls show more relational aggression than boys, but one consistency in findings is that relational aggression comprises a greater percentage of girls' overall aggression than is the case for boys (Putallaz & others, 2007). One research review revealed that girls engage in more relational aggression than boys in adolescence but not in childhood (Smith, Rose, & Schwartz-Mette, 2010).

Are there gender differences in emotion? Girls are more likely to express their emotions openly and intensely than are boys, especially in displaying sadness and fear (Blakemore, Berenbaum, & Liben, 2009). Girls also are better at reading others' emotions and more likely to show empathy than are boys (Blakemore, Berenbaum, & Liben, 2009). Males usually show less self-regulation of emotion than females, and this low self-control can translate into behavioral problems (Eisenberg, Spinrad, & Smith, 2004).

Are there gender differences in prosocial behavior? Across childhood and adolescence, females engage in more prosocial behavior than do males. Females also view themselves as more prosocial and empathic than do males (Eisenberg & others, 2009). However, the greatest gender difference in prosocial behavior occurs with kind and considerate behavior, in which females engage more than males. There is only a small difference between boys and girls: in the extent to which they share, with girls sharing slightly more than boys.

Gender-Role Classification

Not long ago, it was accepted that boys should grow up to be masculine and girls to be feminine. In the 1970s, however, as both females and males became dissatisfied with the burdens imposed by their stereotypic roles, alternatives to femininity and masculinity were proposed. Instead of describing masculinity and femininity as a continuum in which more of one means less of the other, it was proposed that individuals could have both masculine and feminine traits.

This thinking led to the development of the concept of **androgyny**, the presence of positive masculine and feminine characteristics in the same person (Bem, 1977; Spence & Helmreich, 1978). The androgynous boy might be assertive (masculine) and nurturing (feminine). The androgynous girl might be powerful (masculine) and sensitive to others' feelings (feminine). Measures have been developed to assess androgyny (see Figure 8.3).

androgyny The presence of positive masculine and feminine characteristics in the same individual.

Examples of masculine items

Defends open beliefs
Forceful
Willing to take risks
Dominant
Aggressive

Examples of feminine items

Does not use harsh language
Affectionate
Loves children
Understanding
Gentle

Figure 8.3 The Bem Sex-Role Inventory
These items are from the Bem Sex-Role Inventory (BSRI). When taking the BSRI, an individual is asked to indicate on a 7-point scale how well each of 60 characteristics describes herself or himself. The scale ranges from 1 (never or almost never true) to 7 (always or almost always true). Individuals who score high on the masculine items and low on the feminine items are categorized as masculine; those who score high on the feminine items and low on the masculine items are categorized as feminine; and those who score high on both the masculine and feminine items are categorized as androgynous.

EMOTIONAL AND PERSONALITY DEVELOPMENT

Gender experts, such as Sandra Bem, argue that androgynous individuals are more flexible, competent, and mentally healthy than their masculine or feminine counterparts. To some degree, though, which gender-role classification is best depends on the context involved. For example, in close relationships, feminine and androgynous orientations might be more desirable. One study found that girls and individuals high in femininity showed a stronger interest in caring than did boys and individuals high in masculinity (Karniol, Groz, & Schorr, 2003). However, masculine and androgynous orientations might be more desirable in traditional academic and work settings because of the achievement demands in these contexts.

Despite talk about the "sensitive male," William Pollack (1999) argues that little has been done to change traditional ways of raising boys. He says that the "boy code" tells boys that they should show little if any emotion and should act tough. Boys learn the boy code in many contexts—sandboxes, playgrounds, schoolrooms, camps, hangouts. The result, according to Pollack, is a "national crisis of boyhood." Pollack and others suggest that boys would benefit from being socialized to express their anxieties and concerns and to better regulate their aggression.

Gender in Context

Both the concept of androgyny and gender stereotypes talk about people in terms of personality traits such as "aggressive" or "caring." However, which traits people display may vary with the situation (Leaper & Friedman, 2007). Thus, the nature and extent of gender differences may depend on the context (Blakemore, Berenbaum, & Liben, 2009).

In China, especially in rural areas, females and males are usually socialized to behave, feel, and think differently. The old patriarchal traditions of male supremacy have not been completely uprooted. Chinese women still make considerably less money than Chinese men do, and, in rural China (such as here in the village of Lixian Sichuan) male supremacy still governs many women's lives.

Consider helping behavior. The stereotype is that females are better than males at helping. But it depends on the situation. Females are more likely than males to volunteer their time to help children with personal problems and to engage in caregiving behavior. However, in situations in which males feel a sense of competence and that involve danger, males are more likely than females to help (Eagly & Crowley, 1986). For example, a male is more likely than a female to stop and help a person stranded by the roadside with a flat tire. Indeed, one study documented that males are more likely to help when the context is masculine in nature (MacGeorge, 2003).

The importance of considering gender in context is nowhere more apparent than when examining what is culturally prescribed behavior for females and males in different countries around the world (Best, 2010; Shiraev & Levy, 2010). Although there has been greater acceptance of androgyny and similarities in male and female behavior in the United States, in many countries gender roles have remained gender-specific. For example, in many Middle Eastern countries, the division of labor between males and females is dramatic. Males are socialized and schooled to work in the public sphere, females in the private world of home and child rearing. For example, in Iran, the dominant view is that the man's duty is to provide for his family and the woman's is to care for her family and household. China also has been a male-dominant culture. Although women have made some strides in China, especially in urban areas, the male role is still dominant. Most males in China do not accept androgynous behavior and gender equity.

Families

Our further discussion of parenting and families in this section focuses on how parent-child interactions typically change in middle and late childhood, parents as managers, and how children are affected by living with stepparents.

Developmental Changes in Parent-Child Relationships

As children move into the middle and late childhood years, parents spend considerably less time with them. In one study, parents spent less than half as much time with their children aged 5 to 12 in caregiving, instruction, reading, talking, and playing as when the children were younger (Hill & Stafford, 1980). Although parents spend less time with their children in middle and late childhood than in early childhood, parents continue to be extremely important in their children's lives. In an analysis of the contributions of parents in middle and late childhood, the following conclusion was reached: "Parents serve as gatekeepers and provide scaffolding as children assume more responsibility for themselves and . . . regulate their own lives" (Huston & Ripke, 2006, p. 422).

Parents especially play an important role in supporting and stimulating children's academic achievement in middle and late childhood (Huston & Ripke, 2006). The value parents place on education can mean the difference in whether children do well in school. Parents not only influence children's in-school achievement but they also make decisions about children's out-of-school activities. Whether children participate in such activities as sports, music, and other activities is heavily influenced by the extent to which parents sign up children for such activities and encourage their participation (Simpkins & others, 2006).

Elementary school children tend to receive less physical discipline than they did as preschoolers. Instead of spanking or coercive holding, their parents are more likely to use deprivation of privileges, appeals to the child's self-esteem, comments designed to increase the child's sense of guilt, and statements that the child is responsible for his or her actions.

During middle and late childhood, some control is transferred from parent to child. The process is gradual, and it produces *coregulation* rather than control by either the child or the parent alone (Maccoby, 1984). Parents continue to exercise general supervision and control, while children are allowed to engage in moment-to-moment self-regulation. The major shift to autonomy does not occur until about the age of 12 or later. A key developmental task as children move toward autonomy is learning to relate to adults outside the family on a regular basis—adults who interact with the child much differently than parents, such as teachers.

Parents as Managers

Parents can play important roles as managers of children's opportunities, as monitors of their behavior, and as social initiators and arrangers (Gauvain & Parke, 2010; Parke & Buriel, 2006; Parke & Clarke-Stewart, 2011). Mothers are more likely than fathers to engage in a managerial role in parenting.

Researchers have found that family management practices are positively related to students' grades and self-responsibility, and negatively to school-related problems (Eccles, 2007). Among the most important family management practices in this regard are maintaining a structured and organized family environment, such as establishing routines for homework, chores, bedtime, and so on, and effectively monitoring the child's behavior. A research review of family functioning in African American students' academic achievement found that when African American parents monitored their son's academic achievement by ensuring that homework was completed, restricted time spent on nonproductive distractions (such as video-games and TV), and participated in a consistent, positive dialogue with teachers and school officials, their son's academic achievement benefited (Mandara, 2006).

Stepfamilies

Not only has divorce become commonplace in the United States, so has getting remarried (Gosselin, 2010; Higginbotham, Skogrand, & Torres, 2010). It takes time for parents to marry, have children, get divorced, and then remarry. Consequently, there are far more elementary and secondary school children than infants or pre-school children living in stepfamilies.

The number of remarriages involving children has grown steadily in recent years. Also, divorces occur at a 10 percent higher rate in remarriages than in first marriages (Cherlin & Furstenberg, 1994). About half of all children whose parents divorce will have a stepparent within four years of the separation.

Remarried parents face some unique tasks. The couple must define and strengthen their marriage and at the same time renegotiate the biological parent-child relationships and establish stepparent-stepchild and stepsibling relationships (Ganong, Coleman, & Hans, 2006). The complex histories and multiple relationships make adjustment difficult in a stepfamily. Only one-third of stepfamily couples stay remarried.

In some cases, the stepfamily may have been preceded by the death of a spouse. However, by far the largest number of stepfamilies is preceded by divorce rather than death (Pasley & Moorefield, 2004). Three common types of stepfamily structure are (1) stepfather, (2) stepmother, and (3) blended or complex. In step-father families, the mother typically had custody of the children and remarried, introducing a stepfather into her children's lives. In stepmother families, the father usually had custody and remarried, introducing a stepmother into his children's lives. In a blended or complex stepfamily, both parents bring children from previous marriages to live in the newly formed stepfamily.

In Hetherington's (2006) most recent longitudinal analyses, children and adolescents who had been in a simple stepfamily (stepfather or stepmother) for a number of years were adjusting better than in the early years of the remarried family and were functioning well in comparison to children and adolescents in conflicted families that have not gone through a divorce, and children and adolescents in complex (blended) stepfamilies. More than 75 percent of the adolescents in long-established simple stepfamilies described their relationships with their stepparents as "close" or "very close." Hetherington (2006) concluded that in long-established simple stepfamilies adolescents seem to eventually benefit from the presence of a stepparent and the resources provided by the stepparent.

How does living in a stepfamily influence a child's development?

Children often have better relationships with their custodial parents (mothers in stepfather families, fathers in stepmother families) than with stepparents (Santrock, Sitterle, & Warshak, 1988). Also, children in simple families (stepmother, stepfather) often show better adjustment than their counterparts in complex (blended) families (Hetherington, 2006).

As in divorced families, children in stepfamilies show more adjustment problems than children in never-divorced families (Hetherington, 2006). The adjustment problems are similar to those found among children of divorced parents—academic problems and lower self-esteem, for example (Anderson & others, 1999). However, it is important to recognize that a majority of children in stepfamilies do not have problems. In one analysis, 25 percent of children from stepfamilies showed adjustment problems compared with 10 percent in intact, never-divorced families (Hetherington & Kelly, 2002).

popular children Children who are frequently nominated as a best friend and are rarely disliked by their peers.

average children Children who receive an average number of both positive and negative nominations from their peers.

Peers

Having positive relationships with peers is especially important in middle and late childhood (Rubin, Cheah, & Menzer, 2010). Engaging in positive interactions with peers, resolving conflicts with peers in nonaggressive ways, and having quality friendships in middle and late childhood not only have positive outcomes at this time in children's lives, but also are linked to more positive relationship outcomes in adolescence and adulthood (Huston & Ripke, 2006). For example, in one longitudinal study, being popular with peers and engaging in low levels of aggression at 8 years of age were related to higher levels of occupational status at 48 years of age (Huesmann & others, 2006). Another study found that peer competence (a composite measure that included social contact with peers, popularity with peers, friendship, and social skills) in middle and late childhood was linked to having better relationships with coworkers in early adulthood (Collins & van Dulmen, 2006).

Developmental Changes

As children enter the elementary school years, reciprocity becomes especially important in peer interchanges. Researchers estimate that the percentage of time spent in social interaction with peers increases from approximately 10 percent at 2 years of age to more than 30 percent in middle and late childhood (Rubin, Bukowski, & Parker, 2006). In an early classic study, a typical day in elementary school included approximately 300 episodes with peers (Barker & Wright, 1951). As children move through middle and late childhood, the size of their peer group increases, and peer interaction is less closely supervised by adults (Rubin, Bukowski, & Parker, 2006). Until about 12 years of age, children's preference for same-sex peer groups increases.

Peer Status

Which children are likely to be popular with their peers and which ones are disliked? Developmentalists address this and similar questions by examining *sociometric status,* a term that describes the extent to which children are liked or disliked by their peer group (Cillessen, 2009). Sociometric status is typically assessed by asking children to rate how much they like or dislike each of their classmates. Status may also be assessed by asking children to nominate the children they like the most and those they like the least.

Developmentalists have distinguished five peer statuses (Wentzel & Asher, 1995):

- **Popular children** are frequently nominated as a best friend and are rarely disliked by their peers.

- **Average children** receive an average number of both positive and negative nominations from their peers.

neglected children Children who are infrequently nominated as a best friend but are not disliked by their peers.

rejected children Children who are infrequently nominated as a best friend and are actively disliked by their peers.

controversial children Children who are frequently nominated both as someone's best friend and as being disliked.

- **Neglected children** are infrequently nominated as a best friend but are not disliked by their peers.

- **Rejected children** are infrequently nominated as someone's best friend and are actively disliked by their peers.

- **Controversial children** are frequently nominated both as someone's best friend and as being disliked.

Popular children have a number of social skills that contribute to their being well liked. They give out reinforcements, listen carefully, maintain open lines of communication with peers, are happy, control their negative emotions, act like themselves, show enthusiasm and concern for others, and are self-confident without being conceited (Hartup, 1983; Rubin, Bukowski, & Parker, 1998).

What characterizes the social skills of peer-rejected boys who are aggressive? John Coie (2004, pp. 252–253) provided three reasons why aggressive, peer-rejected boys have problems in social relationships:

- "First, the rejected, aggressive boys are more impulsive and have problems sustaining attention. As a result, they are more likely to be disruptive of ongoing activities in the classroom and in focused group play.

How Would You...?
As a social worker, how would you help a rejected child develop more positive relationships with peers?

- Second, rejected, aggressive boys are more emotionally reactive. They are aroused to anger more easily and probably have more difficulty calming down once aroused. Because of this they are more prone to become angry at peers and attack them verbally and physically. . . .

- Third, rejected children have fewer social skills in making friends and maintaining positive relationships with peers."

What are some examples of positive relationships with peers in middle and late childhood?

Social Cognition

How Would You...?
As a psychologist, how would you characterize differences in the social cognition of aggressive children compared to children who behave in less hostile ways?

Social cognition involves thoughts about social matters, such as an aggressive boy's interpretation of an encounter as hostile and his classmates' perception of his behavior as inappropriate (Dodge, 2010). Children's social cognition about their peers becomes increasingly important for understanding peer relationships in middle and late childhood. Of special interest are the ways in which children process information about peer relations and their social knowledge (Dodge, 2010).

Kenneth Dodge (1983) argues that children go through five steps in processing information about their social world. They decode social cues, interpret, search for a response, select an optimal response, and enact. Dodge has found that aggressive boys are more likely to perceive another child's actions as hostile when the child's intention is ambiguous. And, when aggressive boys search for cues to determine a peer's intention, they respond more rapidly, less efficiently, and less reflectively than do nonaggressive children. These are among the social cognitive factors believed to be involved in children's conflicts.

Social knowledge also is involved in children's ability to get along with peers. They need to know what goals to pursue in poorly defined or ambiguous situations, how to initiate and maintain a social bond, and what scripts to follow to get other children to be their friends. For example, as part of the script for getting friends, it helps to know that saying nice things, regardless of what the peer does or says, will make the peer like the child more.

Bullying

Significant numbers of students are victimized by bullies (Vernberg & Biggs, 2010). In a national survey of more than 15,000 students in grades 6 through 10, nearly one of every three students said that they had experienced occasional or frequent involvement as a victim or perpetrator in bullying (Nansel & others, 2001). In this study, bullying was defined as verbal or physical behavior intended to disturb someone less powerful (see Figure 8.4). Boys are more likely to be bullies than girls, but gender differences regarding victims of boys is less clear (Salmivalli & Peets, 2009).

Who is likely to be bullied? In the study just described, boys and younger middle school students were most likely to be affected (Nansel & others, 2001). Children who said they were bullied reported more loneliness and difficulty in making friends, while those who did the bullying were more likely to have low grades and to smoke and drink alcohol. Researchers have found that anxious, socially withdrawn, and aggressive children are often the victims of bullying (Hanish & Guerra, 2004). Anxious and socially withdrawn children may be victimized because they are nonthreatening and unlikely to retaliate if bullied, whereas aggressive children may be the targets of bullying because their behavior is irritating to bullies (Rubin, Bukowski, & Parker, 2006).

Social contexts also influence bullying (Schwartz & others, 2010). Recent research indicates that 70 to 80 percent of victims and their bullies are in the same school classroom (Salmivalli & Peets, 2009). Classmates are often aware of bullying incidents and in many cases witness bullying. The larger social context of the peer group plays an important role in bullying (Salmivalli & Peets, 2009). In many cases, bullies torment victims to gain higher status in the peer group and bullies need others to witness their power displays. Many bullies are not rejected by the peer group. In one study, bullies were only rejected by peers for whom they were a potential threat (Veenstra & others, 2010). In another study, bullies often affiliated with each other or in some cases maintained their position in the popular peer group (Wivliet & others, 2010).

What are the outcomes of bullying? One study indicated that bullies and their victims in adolescence were more likely to experience depression and engage in suicide ideation and attempt suicide than their counterparts who were not involved in bullying (Brunstein Klomek & others, 2007). A recent meta-analysis of 33 studies revealed a small but significant link between peer victimization and lower academic achievement (Nakamoto & Schwartz, 2010). Another study revealed that bullies, victims, or those who were both bullies and victims had more health problems (such as headaches, dizziness, sleep problems, and anxiety) than their counterparts who were not involved in bullying (Srabstein & others, 2006). Recently, bullying has been linked to these suicides: An 8-year-old jumped out of a two-story building in Houston; a 13-year-old girl hanged himself in Houston; and teenagers harassed a girl so mercilessly that she killed herself in Massachusetts (Meyers, 2010).

Extensive interest is developing in preventing and treating bullying and victimization (Biggs & Vernberg, 2010; Guerra & Williams, 2010; Singh, Orpinas, & Horne, 2010). A research review revealed mixed results for school-based intervention (Vreeman & Carroll, 2007). School-based interventions vary greatly, ranging from involving the whole school in an antibullying campaign to individualized social skills training. One of the most promising bullying intervention programs has been created by Dan Olweus. This program focuses on 6- to 15-year-olds with the goal of decreasing opportunities and rewards for bullying. School staff is instructed in ways to improve peer relations and make schools safer. When properly implemented, the program reduces bullying by 30 to 70 percent (Olweus, 2003).

How Would You...?
As a health-care professional, how would you characterize the health risks that bullying poses to the victims of bullying?

How Would You...?
As an educator, how would you design and implement a bullying reduction program at your school?

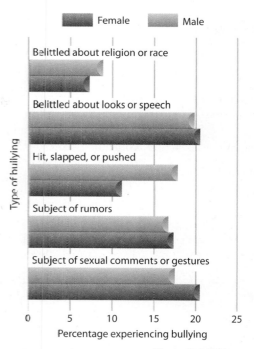

Figure 8.4 Bullying Behaviors Among U.S. Youth

The percentages reflect the extent to which bullied students said that they had experienced a particular type of bullying. In terms of gender, note that when they were bullied, boys were more likely to be hit, slapped, or pushed than girls were.

Friends

Like adult friendships, children's friendships are typically characterized by similarity Throughout childhood, friends are more similar than dissimilar in terms of age, sex, race, and many other factors. Friends often have similar attitudes toward school, similar educational aspirations, and closely aligned achievement orientations.

Why are children's friendships important? Willard Hartup (1983, 1996, 2009) has studied peer relations and friendship for more than three decades. He recently concluded that friends can be cognitive and emotional resources from childhood through old age. Friends can foster self-esteem and a sense of well-being. More specifically, children's friendships can serve six functions (Gottman & Parker, 1987):

- *Companionship*. Friendship provides children with a familiar partner and playmate, someone who is willing to spend time with them and join in collaborative activities.

- *Stimulation*. Friendship provides children with interesting information, excitement, and amusement.

- *Physical support*. Friendship provides time, resources, and assistance.

- *Ego support*. Friendship provides the expectation of support, encouragement, and feedback, which helps children maintain an impression of themselves as competent, attractive, and worthwhile individuals.

- *Social comparison*. Friendship provides information about where the child stands vis-à-vis others and whether the child is doing okay.

- *Affection and intimacy*. Friendship provides children with a warm, close, trusting relationship with another individual. *Intimacy in friendships* is characterized by self-disclosure and the sharing of private thoughts. Research reveals that intimate friendships may not appear until early adolescence (Berndt & Perry, 1990).

What are some characteristics of children's friendships?

Although having friends can be a developmental advantage, not all friendships are alike (Vitaro, Boivin, & Bukowski, 2009). People differ in the company they keep—that is, who their friends are. Developmental advantages occur when children have friends who are socially skilled and supportive. However, it is not developmentally advantageous to have coercive and conflict-ridden friendships (Laursen & Pursell, 2009).

The importance of friendship was underscored in a two-year longitudinal study (Wentzel, Barry, & Caldwell, 2004). Sixth-grade students who did not have a friend engaged in less prosocial behavior (cooperation, sharing, helping others), had lower grades, and were more emotionally distressed (depression, low well-being) than their counterparts who had one or more friends. Two years later, in the eighth grade, the students who did not have a friend in the sixth grade were still more emotionally distressed. In another longitudinal study of children from 6 to 13 years of age, the number of years without at least one reciprocal friendship predicted loneliness and depression in early adolescence (Pedersen & others, 2007).

Schools

For most children, entering the first grade signals new obligations. They develop new relationships and develop new standards by which to judge themselves. School provides children with a rich source of new ideas to shape their sense of self. They will spend many years in schools as members of small societies in which there are tasks to be accomplished, people to be socialized and socialized by, and rules that define and limit behavior, feelings, and attitudes. By the time students graduate from high school, they have spent 12,000 hours in the classroom.

Contemporary Approaches to Student Learning

Because there are so many approaches for teaching children, controversy swirls about the best way to teach children (Johnson & others, 2011; Parkay & Stanford, 2010). There also is considerable interest in education about the best way to hold schools and teachers accountable for whether children are learning (Popham, 2011).

Constructivist and Direct Instruction Approaches

The **constructivist approach** is learner centered and it emphasizes the importance of individuals actively constructing their knowledge and understanding with guidance from the teacher. In the constructivist view, teachers should not attempt to simply pour information into children's minds. Rather, children should be encouraged to explore their world, discover knowledge, reflect, and think critically with careful monitoring and meaningful guidance from the teacher (Abruscato & DeRosa, 2010; Eby, Herrell, & Jordan, 2011). The constructivist belief is that for too long in American education children have been required to sit still, be passive learners, and rotely memorize irrelevant as well as relevant information.

Today, constructivism may include an emphasis on collaboration—children working with each other in their efforts to know and understand (Holzman, 2009; Slavin, 2011). A teacher with a constructivist instructional philosophy would not have children memorize information rotely but would give them opportunities to meaningfully construct the knowledge and understand the material while guiding their learning (Maxim, 2010).

By contrast, the **direct instruction approach** is structured and teacher centered. It is characterized by teacher direction and control, high teacher expectations for students' progress, maximum time spent by students on academic tasks, and efforts by the teacher to keep negative affect to a minimum. An important goal in the direct instruction approach is maximizing student learning time (Borich, 2011).

Advocates of the constructivist approach argue that the direct instruction approach turns children into passive learners and does not adequately challenge them to think in critical and creative ways (Abruscato & DeRosa, 2010). The direct instruction enthusiasts say that the constructivist approaches do not give enough attention to the content of a discipline, such as history or science. They also believe that the constructivist approaches are too relativistic and vague.

Some experts in educational psychology believe that many effective teachers use both a constructivist *and* a direct instruction approach rather than either exclusively (Bransford & others, 2006). Further, some circumstances may call more for a constructivist approach, others for a direct instruction approach. For example, experts increasingly recommend an explicit, intellectually engaging direct instruction approach when teaching students with a reading or a writing disability (Berninger, 2006).

Accountability

Since the 1990s, the U.S. public and governments at every level have demanded increased accountability from schools. One result has been the spread of state-mandated tests to measure just what students had or had not learned (Popham, 2011). Many states identified objectives for students in their state and created tests to measure whether students were meeting those objectives. This approach became national policy in 2002 when the No Child Left Behind (NCLB) legislation was signed into law.

Advocates argue that statewide standardized testing will have a number of positive effects. These include improved student performance; more time teaching the subjects that are tested; high expectations for all students; identification of poorly performing schools, teachers, and administrators; and improved confidence in schools as test scores rise.

Critics argue that the NCLB legislation is doing more harm than good (Yell & Drasgow, 2009). One criticism stresses that using a single test as the sole indicator of students' progress and competence presents a very narrow view of students' skills (Lewis, 2007). This criticism is similar to the one leveled at IQ tests, which we described in Chapter 7. To assess student progress and achievement, many psychologists and educators emphasize that a number of measures should be used, including tests, quizzes, projects, portfolios, classroom observations, and so on. Also, the tests used as part of NCLB don't measure creativity, motivation, persistence, flexible thinking, and social skills (Stiggins, 2008). Critics point out that teachers end up spending far too much class time "teaching to the test" by drilling students and having them memorize isolated facts at the expense of teaching that focuses on thinking skills, which students need for success in life (Pressley, 2007). Also, some individuals are concerned that in the era of No Child Left Behind policy there is a neglect of students who are gifted in the effort to raise the achievement level of students who are not doing well (Clark, 2008).

Consider also the following: Each state is allowed to have different criteria for what constitutes passing or failing grades on tests designated for NCLB inclusion. An analysis of NCLB data indicated that almost every fourth-grade student in Mississippi knows how to read but only half of Massachusetts' students do (Birman & others, 2007). Clearly, Mississippi's standards for passing the reading test are far below those of Massachusetts. In the recent analysis of state-by-state comparisons, many states have taken the safe route and kept the standard for passing low. Thus, while one of NCLB's goals was to raise standards for achievement in U.S. schools, apparently allowing states to set their own standards likely has lowered achievement standards.

Despite such criticisms, the U.S. Department of Education is committed to implementing No Child Left Behind, and schools are making accommodations to meet the requirement of this law. Indeed, most educators support the importance of high expectations and high standards of excellence for students and teachers. At issue, however, is whether the tests and procedures mandated by NCLB are the best ones for achieving these high standards (Nitko & Brookhart, 2011).

Socioeconomic Status, Ethnicity, and Culture

Children from low-income, ethnic minority backgrounds have more difficulties in school than do their middle-socioeconomic-status, White counterparts. Why? Critics argue that schools have not done a good job of educating low-income, ethnic minority students to overcome the barriers to their achievement (Entwisle, Alexander, & Olson, 2010; Tamis-LeMonda & McFadden, 2010). And recent comparisons of student achievement indicate that U.S. students have lower achievement in math and science than a number of countries, especially those in eastern Asia (TIMMS, 2008). Let's further explore the roles of socioeconomic status, ethnicity, and culture in schools.

How Would You...?
As a health-care professional, how would you advise school administrators about health and nutrition challenges faced by low-income students that may impact their performance on achievement tests?

The Education of Students From Low-Income Backgrounds

Many children in poverty face problems that present barriers to their learning (Tamis-LeMonda & McFadden, 2010). They might have parents who don't set high educational standards for them, who are incapable of reading to them, or who don't have enough money to pay for educational materials and experiences, such as books and trips to zoos and museums. They might be malnourished or live in areas where crime and violence are a way of life. One study revealed that neighborhood disadvantage (involving such characteristics as low neighborhood income and high unemployment) was linked to less consistent, less stimulating, and more punitive parenting, and ultimately to negative child outcomes such as behavioral problems and low verbal ability (Kohen & others, 2008). Another study revealed that the longer children experienced poverty the more detrimental the poverty was to their cognitive development (Najman & others, 2009).

Compared with schools in higher-income areas, schools in low-income areas are more likely to have more students with low achievement test scores, low graduation rates, and small percentages of students going to college; they are more likely to have young teachers with less experience; and they are more likely to encourage rote learning (Koppelman & Goodhart, 2011; Spring, 2010). Many of the schools' buildings and classrooms are old and crumbling. These are the types of undesirable conditions Jonathan Kozol (2005) observed in many inner-city schools, including the South Bronx in New York City, as described at the beginning of the chapter.

In *The Shame of a Nation*, Jonathan Kozol (2005) criticized the inadequate quality and lack of resources in many U.S. schools, especially those in the poverty areas of inner cities, that have high concentrations of ethnic minority children. Kozol praises teachers like Angela Lively (*above*), who keeps a box of shoes in her Indianapolis classroom for students in need.

The schools that children from impoverished backgrounds attend often have fewer resources than schools in higher-income neighborhoods (Tamis-LeMonda & McFadden, 2010). In low-income areas, schools are more likely to be staffed by young teachers with less experience than schools in higher-income neighborhoods (Liu & Hernandez, 2008). Teachers in schools in low-income areas also are more likely to encourage rote learning, whereas teachers in schools in higher-income areas are more likely to work with children to improve their thinking skills (Spring, 2010). In sum, far too many schools in low-income neighborhoods provide students with environments that are not conducive to effective learning (Huston & Bentley, 2010; Rowley, Kurtz-Costas, & Cooper, 2010).

Ethnicity in Schools

More than one-third of all African American and almost one-third of all Latino students attend schools in the 47 largest city school districts in the United States, compared with only 5 percent of all White and 22 percent of all Asian American students. Many of these inner-city schools are still segregated, are grossly under-funded, and do not provide adequate opportunities for children to learn effectively. Thus, the effects of socioeconomic status (SES) and the effects of ethnicity are often intertwined (Banks, 2010; Bennett, 2011).

Even outside of inner-city schools, school segregation remains a factor in U.S. education (Koppelman & Goodhart, 2011). Almost one-third of all African American and Latino students attend schools in which 90 percent or more of the students are from minority groups (Banks, 2010).

The school experiences of students from different ethnic groups vary considerably (Banks, 2010). African American and Latino students are much less likely than non-Latino White or Asian American students to be enrolled in academic, college preparatory programs and are much more likely to be enrolled in remedial and special education programs. Asian American students are far more likely than other ethnic minority groups to take advanced math and science courses in high school. African American students are twice as likely as Latinos, Native Americans, or Whites to be suspended from school.

Following are some strategies for improving relationships among ethnically diverse students:

- *Turn the class into a jigsaw classroom.* When Elliot Aronson was a professor at the University of Texas at Austin, the school system contacted him for ideas on how to reduce the increasing racial tension in classrooms. Aronson (1986) developed the concept of "jigsaw classroom," in which students from different cultural backgrounds are placed in a cooperative group in which they have to construct different parts of a project to reach a common goal. Aronson used the term

Adolescence is a transitional period in the human life span, entered at approximately 10 to 12 years of age and exited at about 18 to 22 years of age. We begin this chapter by examining some general characteristics of adolescence followed by coverage of major physical changes and health issues of adolescence. Then we describe the significant cognitive changes that characterize adolescence. Last, we consider various aspects of schools for adolescents.

The Nature of Adolescence

There is a long history of worrying about how adolescents will "turn out." In 1904, G. Stanley Hall proposed the "storm-and-stress" view that adolescence is a turbulent time charged with conflict and mood swings. However, when Daniel Offer and his colleagues (1988) studied the self-images of adolescents in a number of countries, at least 73 percent of the adolescents displayed a healthy self-image rather than an image of storm-and-stress.

In matters of taste and manners, the young people of every generation have seemed unnervingly radical and different from adults—different in how they look, in how they behave, in the music they enjoy, in their hairstyles, and in the clothing they choose. It is an enormous error, though, to confuse adolescents' enthusiasm for trying on new identities and enjoying moderate amounts of outrageous behavior with hostility toward parental and societal standards. Acting out and boundary testing are time-honored ways in which adolescents move toward accepting, rather than rejecting, parental values.

Most adolescents negotiate the lengthy path to adult maturity successfully, but too large a group does not (Balsano, Theokas, & Bobek, 2009). Ethnic, cultural, gender, socioeconomic, age, and lifestyle differences influence the actual life trajectory

Growing up has never been easy. However, adolescence is not best viewed as a time of rebellion, crisis, pathology, and deviance. A far more accurate vision of adolescence describes it as a time of evaluation, of decision making, of commitment, and of carving out a place in the world. Most of the problems of today's youth are not with the youth themselves. What adolescents need is access to a range of legitimate opportunities and to long-term support from adults who deeply care about them. *What might be some examples of such support and caring?*

of every adolescent (Swanson, Edwards, & Spencer, 2010). Different portrayals of adolescence emerge, depending on the particular group of adolescents being described (Rowley, Kurtz-Costas, & Cooper, 2010). Today's adolescents are exposed to a complex menu of lifestyle options through the media, and many face the temptations of drug use and sexual activity at increasingly young ages. Too many adolescents are not provided with adequate opportunities and support to become competent adults (Entwisle, Alexander, & Olson, 2010; McLoyd & others, 2009).

puberty A period of rapid physical and sexual maturation that occurs mainly during early adolescence.

menarche A girl's first menstruation.

Physical Changes

One father remarked that the problem with his teenage son was not that he grew, but that he did not know when to stop growing. In addition to pubertal changes, other physical changes we will explore involve sexuality and the brain.

Puberty

Puberty is not the same as adolescence. For most of us, puberty ends long before adolescence does, although puberty is the most important marker of the beginning of adolescence. **Puberty** is a period of rapid physical maturation involving hormonal and bodily changes that occur primarily during early adolescence. Puberty is not a single, sudden event. We know whether a young boy or girl is going through puberty, but pinpointing puberty's beginning and end is difficult. Among the most noticeable changes are signs of sexual maturation and increases in height and weight.

Sexual Maturation, Height, and Weight

Think back to the onset of your puberty. Of the striking changes that were taking place in your body, what was the first to occur? Researchers have found that male pubertal characteristics typically develop in this order: increase in penis and testicle size, appearance of straight pubic hair, minor voice change, first ejaculation (which usually occurs through masturbation or a wet dream), appearance of kinky pubic hair, onset of maximum growth in height and weight, growth of hair in armpits, more detectable voice changes, and, finally, growth of facial hair.

What is the order of appearance of physical changes in females? First, either the breasts enlarge or pubic hair appears. Later, hair appears in the armpits. As these changes occur, the female grows in height and her hips become wider than her shoulders. **Menarche**—a girl's first menstruation—comes rather late in the pubertal cycle.

ZITS By Jerry Scott and Jim Borgman

© ZITS Partnership. Reprinted with permission of King Features Syndicate.

hormones Powerful chemical substances secreted by the endocrine glands and carried through the body by the bloodstream.

hypothalamus A structure in the higher portion of the brain that monitors eating and sex.

pituitary gland An important endocrine gland that controls growth and regulates other glands, including the gonads.

gonads The sex glands—the testes in males and the ovaries in females.

Marked weight gains coincide with the onset of puberty. During early adolescence, girls tend to outweigh boys, but by about age 14 boys begin to surpass girls. Similarly, at the beginning of the adolescent period, girls tend to be as tall as or taller than boys of their age, but by the end of the middle school years most boys have caught up, or, in many cases, surpassed girls in height.

As indicated in Figure 9.1, the growth spurt occurs approximately two years earlier for girls than for boys. The mean age at the beginning of the growth spurt in girls is 9; for boys, it is 11. The peak rate of pubertal change occurs at 11½ years for girls and 13½ years for boys. During their growth spurt, girls increase in height about 3½ inches per year, boys about 4 inches. Boys and girls who are shorter or taller than their peers before adolescence are likely to remain so during adolescence.

Precocious puberty is the term used for the very early onset and rapid progression of puberty. Judith Blakemore and her colleagues (2009) described the following characteristics of precocious puberty. It occurs about 10 times more often in girls than in boys. It is usually diagnosed when the onset of puberty happens before 8 years of age in girls and before 9 years of age in boys and is usually treated by medically suppressing gonadotropic secretions, which temporarily halts pubertal change. This treatment is usually given because children who experience precocious puberty may have short stature, early sexual capability, and the potential for engaging in age-inappropriate behavior (Blakemore, Berenbaum, & Liben, 2009).

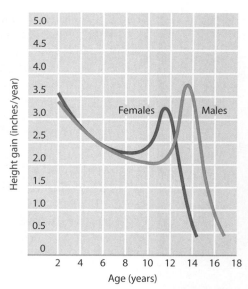

Figure 9.1 Pubertal Growth Spurt
On average, the peak of the growth spurt during puberty occurs two years earlier for girls (11½) than for boys (13½). *How are hormones related to the growth spurt and to the difference between the average height of adolescent boys and that of girls?* From J. M. Tanner et al., in *Archives of Diseases in Childhood 41*, 1966. Reproduced with permission from BMJ Publishing Group.

What are some of the differences in the ways girls and boys experience pubertal growth?

Hormonal Changes Behind the first whisker in boys and the widening of hips in girls is a flood of **hormones**, powerful chemical substances secreted by the endocrine glands and carried through the body by the bloodstream. The endocrine system's role in puberty involves the interaction of the hypothalamus, the pituitary gland, and the gonads. The **hypothalamus** is a structure in the brain that monitors eating and sex. The **pituitary gland** is an important endocrine gland that controls growth and regulates other glands; among these, the **gonads**—the testes in males, the ovaries in females—are particularly important in giving rise to pubertal changes in the body.

The concentrations of certain hormones increase dramatically during adolescence (Susman & Dorn, 2009; Wankowska & Polkowska, 2010). *Testosterone* is a hormone associated in boys with the development of genitals, an increase in height, and a change in voice. *Estradiol* is a type of estrogen; in girls it is associated with breast, uterine, and skeletal development. In one study, testosterone levels increased eighteenfold in boys but only twofold in girls during puberty; estradiol increased eightfold in girls but only twofold in boys (Nottelmann & others, 1987). Thus, both testosterone and estradiol are present in the hormonal makeup of both boys and girls, but testosterone dominates in male pubertal development, estradiol in female pubertal development.

The same influx of hormones that grows hair on a male's chest and increases the fatty tissue in a female's breasts may also contribute to psychological develop-

How Would You...?
As a psychologist, how would you explain the role of biological and physical changes on adolescent mood swings?

ment in adolescence (Susman & Dorn, 2009). However, hormonal effects by themselves do not account for adolescent development (Graber Brooks-Gunn, & Warren, 2006). For example, in one study, social factors accounted for two to four times as much variance as did hormonal factors in young adolescent girls' depression and anger (Brooks-Gunn & Warren, 1989). Behavior and moods also can affect hormones. Stress, eating patterns, exercise, sexual activity, tension, and depression can activate or suppress various aspects of the hormonal system. In sum, the hormone-behavior link is complex (Susman & Dorn, 2009).

Timing and Variations in Puberty

Imagine a toddler displaying all the features of puberty—a 3-year-old girl with fully developed breasts or a preschool boy with a deep voice. That is what we would see by the year 2250 if the age at which puberty arrives were to keep getting younger at its present pace. In Norway today, menarche occurs at just over 13 years of age, compared with 17 years of age in the 1840s. In the United States—where children mature up to a year earlier than children in European countries—the average age of menarche has declined significantly since the mid-19th century. Fortunately, however, we are unlikely to see pubescent toddlers, since what has happened in the past century is likely the result of improved nutrition and health (Hermann-Giddens, 2007).

Why do the changes of puberty occur when they do, and how can variations in their timing be explained? The basic genetic program for puberty is wired into the species, but nutrition, health, and other environmental factors also affect puberty's timing and makeup (Susman & Dorn, 2009).

For most boys, the pubertal sequence may begin as early as age 10 or as late as 13½ and may end as early as age 13 or as late as 17. Thus the normal range is wide enough that, given two boys of the same chronological age, one might complete the pubertal sequence before the other one has begun it. For girls, menarche is considered within the normal range if it appears between the ages of 9 and 15.

Body Image

One psychological aspect of physical change in puberty is certain: Adolescents are preoccupied with their bodies and develop images of what their bodies are like. Preoccupation with body image is strong throughout adolescence, but it is especially acute during puberty, a time when adolescents are more dissatisfied with their bodies than in late adolescence.

Gender differences characterize adolescents' perceptions of their bodies. In general, girls are less happy with their bodies and have more negative body images than boys throughout puberty (Bearman & others, 2006). As pubertal change proceeds, girls often become more dissatisfied with their bodies, probably because their body fat increases. In contrast, boys become more satisfied as they move through puberty, probably because their muscle mass increases (Bearman & others, 2006).

How Would You...?
As a human development and family studies professional, how would you counsel parents about communicating with their adolescent daughter about changes in her behavior that likely reflect a downward turn in her body image?

Early and Late Maturation

Some of you entered puberty early, others late, and still others right on time. Adolescents who mature earlier or later than their peers perceive themselves differently. In the Berkeley Longitudinal Study some years ago, early-maturing boys perceived themselves more positively and had more successful peer relations than did their late-maturing counterparts (Jones, 1965). When the late-maturing boys were in their thirties, however, they had developed a stronger sense of identity than the early-maturing boys had (Peskin, 1967). This may have occurred because the late-maturing boys had more time to explore life's options, or because the early-maturing boys continued to focus on their advantageous physical status instead of on career development and achievement. More recent research confirms, though, that at least during adolescence it is advantageous to be an early-maturing rather than a late-maturing boy (Graber, Brooks-Gunn, & Warren, 2006).

corpus callosum The location where fibers connect the brain's left and right hemispheres.

amygdala The region of the brain that is the seat of emotions.

How Would You...?

As a health-care professional, how would you use your knowledge of puberty to reassure adolescents who are concerned that they are maturing slower than their friends?

An increasing number of researchers have found that early maturation increases girls' vulnerability to a number of problems (Cavanagh, 2009; Ge & Natusaki, 2010). Early-maturing girls are more likely to smoke, drink, be depressed, have an eating disorder, struggle for earlier independence from their parents, and have older friends; and their bodies are likely to elicit responses from males that lead to earlier dating and earlier sexual experiences (Wiesner & Ittel, 2002). Early-maturing girls also are less likely to graduate from high school and they cohabit and marry earlier (Cavanagh, 2009).

The Brain

Along with the rest of the body, the brain is changing during adolescence, but the study of adolescent brain development is in its infancy. As advances in technology take place, significant strides will also likely be made in charting developmental changes in the adolescent brain (Paus, 2009). What do we know now?

Recall from Chapter 3 that researchers have discovered that nearly twice as many synaptic connections are made than we will ever use (Huttenlocher & Dabholkar, 1997). The connections that we do use are strengthened and survive, while the unused ones are replaced by other pathways or disappear. That is, in the language of neuroscience, these connections will be "pruned." What results from this pruning is that by the end of adolescence individuals have "fewer, more selective, more effective neuronal connections than they did as children" (Kuhn, 2009, p. 153). And this pruning indicates that the activities adolescents choose to engage in and not to engage in influence which neural connections will be strengthened and which will disappear.

Using fMRI brain scans, scientists have discovered that adolescents' brains undergo significant structural changes (Bava & others, 2010; Lenroot & others, 2009). The **corpus callosum**, where fibers connect the brain's left and right hemispheres, thickens in adolescence, and this improves adolescents' ability to process information (Giedd, 2008). We described advances in the development of the *prefrontal cortex*—the highest level of the frontal lobes involved in reasoning, decision making, and self-control—in Chapters 5 and 7. However, the prefrontal cortex doesn't finish maturing until the emerging adult years, approximately 18 to 25 years of age, or later, whereas the **amygdala**—the seat of emotions such as anger—matures earlier than the prefrontal cortex. Figure 9.2 shows the locations of the corpus callosum, prefrontal cortex, and amygdala.

Many of the changes in the adolescent brain that have been described involve the rapidly emerging field of *developmental social neuroscience*, which involves connections between development, the brain, and socioemotional processes (de Haan & Gunnar, 2009). For example, consider leading researcher Charles Nelson's (2003) view that, although adolescents are capable of very strong emotions, their prefrontal cortex hasn't adequately developed to the point at which they can control these passions. It is as if their brain doesn't have the brakes to slow down their emotions. Or consider this interpretation of the development of emotion and cognition in adolescents: "early activation of strong 'turbo-charged' feelings with a relatively un-skilled set of 'driving skills' or cognitive abilities to modulate strong emotions and motivations" (Dahl, 2004, p. 18).

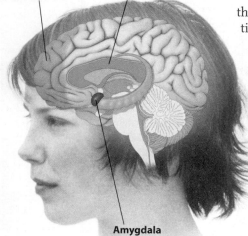

Prefrontal cortex
This "judgment" region reins in intense emotions but doesn't finish developing until at least emerging adulthood.

Corpus callosum
These nerve fibers connect the brain's two hemispheres; they thicken in adolescence to process information more effectively.

Amygdala
The seat of emotions such as anger; this area develops quickly before other regions that help to control it.

Figure 9.2

Changes in the Adolescent Brain

Of course, a major issue is which comes first, biological changes in the brain or experiences that stimulate these changes? (Lerner, Boyd, & Du, 2008). Consider a study in which the prefrontal cortex thickened and more brain connections formed when adolescents resisted peer pressure (Paus & others, 2007). Scientists have yet to determine whether the brain changes come first or whether the brain changes are the result of experiences with peers, parents, and others. Once again, we encounter the nature/nurture issue that is so prominent in an examination of development through the life span.

Adolescent Sexuality

Not only are adolescents characterized by substantial changes in physical growth and the development of the brain, but adolescence also is a bridge between the asexual child and the sexual adult. Adolescence is a time of sexual exploration and experimentation, of sexual fantasies and realities, of incorporating sexuality into one's identity.

Developing a Sexual Identity

Mastering emerging sexual feelings and forming a sense of sexual identity is a multifaceted and lengthy process. It involves learning to manage sexual feelings (such as sexual arousal and attraction), developing new forms of intimacy, and learning the skills to regulate sexual behavior to avoid undesirable consequences.

An adolescent's sexual identity involves activities, interests, styles of behavior, and an indication of sexual orientation (whether an individual has same-sex or other-sex attractions) (Buzwell & Rosenthal, 1996). For example, some adolescents have a high anxiety level about sex, others a low level. Some adolescents are strongly aroused sexually, others less so. Some adolescents are very active sexually, others not at all. Some adolescents are sexually inactive in response to their strong religious upbringing; others go to church regularly, yet their religious training does not inhibit their sexual activity (Thorton & Camburn, 1989).

It is commonly believed that most gay and lesbian individuals quietly struggle with same-sex attractions in childhood, do not engage in heterosexual dating, and gradually recognize that they are gay or lesbian in middle to late adolescence. Many youth do follow this developmental pathway, but others do not (Diamond & Savin-Williams, 2009). For example, many youth have no recollection of early same-sex attractions and experience a more abrupt sense of their same-sex attraction in late adolescence. Researchers also have found that the majority of adolescents with same-sex attractions also experience some degree of other-sex attractions. Even though some adolescents who are attracted to individuals of their same sex fall in love with these individuals, others claim that their same-sex attractions are purely physical (Diamond & Savin-Williams, 2009).

In sum, gay and lesbian youth have diverse patterns of initial attraction, often have bisexual attractions, and may have physical or emotional attraction to same-sex individuals but do not always fall in love with them (Diamond, Fagundes, & Butterworth, 2011). In Chapter 11, we further explore same-sex and heterosexual attraction.

The Timing of Adolescent Sexual Behaviors

The timing of sexual initiation varies by country as well as by gender and other socioeconomic characteristics. In one cross-cultural study, among females, the proportion having first intercourse by age 17 ranged from 72 percent in Mali to 47 percent in the United States and 45 percent in Tanzania (Singh & others, 2000). The percentage of males who had their first intercourse by age 17 ranged from 76 percent in Jamaica to 64 percent in the United States and 63 percent in Brazil. Within the United States, male, African American, and inner-city adolescents report being the most sexually active, whereas Asian American adolescents have the most restrictive sexual timetable (Feldman, Turner, & Araujo, 1999).

A national survey revealed that 63 percent of U.S. twelfth-graders (64 percent of males, 62 percent of females) reported that they had experienced sexual intercourse

How Would You...?
As a psychologist, how would you describe the cultural and ethnic differences in the timing of an adolescent's first sexual experience?

compared with 34 percent of ninth-graders (39 percent of males, 29 percent of females) (MMWR, 2006). By age 20, 77 percent of U.S. youth have engaged in sexual intercourse (Dworkin & Santelli, 2007). One national study indicated that 35 percent of U.S. high school students were currently sexually active (Eaton & others, 2008). Another national study of adolescent sexual behavior from 1991 to 2007 revealed that sexual experience and having multiple sexual partners in adolescence declined from the early 1990s through the early 2000s, and then increased recently (Santelli & others, 2009).

Many adolescents are not emotionally prepared to handle sexual experiences, especially in early adolescence. Early sexual activity is linked with risky behaviors such as drug use, delinquency, and school-related problems (Dryfoos & Barkin, 2006). A recent study of adolescents in five countries, including the United States, found that substance use was related to early sexual intercourse (Madkour & others, 2010). A recent study also revealed that alcohol use, early menarche, and poor parent-child communication were linked to early sexually intimate behavior in girls (Hipwell & others, 2010). A research review also found that earlier onset of sexual intercourse was linked to a lower level of parental monitoring (Zimmer-Gembeck & Helfand, 2008). In another study, maternal communication about sex (the extent mothers talked with their adolescents about having sexual intercourse and the negative implications of pregnancy for both young men and women, for example) was linked with less risky sexual behavior by Latino adolescents (Trejos-Castillo & Vazsonyi, 2009). Further, recent research indicated that associating with more deviant peers in early adolescence was related to having more sexual partners at age 16 (Lansford & others, 2010). And a recent study of middle school students revealed that better academic achievement was a protective factor in keeping boys and girls from engaging in early initiation of sexual intercourse (Laflin, Wang, & Barry, 2008).

What are some risks for early initiation of sexual intercourse?

Contraceptive Use

Sexual activity carries with it considerable risks if appropriate safeguards are not taken. Youth encounter two kinds of risks: unintended, unwanted pregnancy and sexually transmitted infections. Both of these risks can be reduced significantly if contraception is used.

The good news is that adolescents are increasing their use of contraceptives (Frost, Darroch, & Ramez, 2008). For example, a large-scale study revealed a substantial increase in the use of a contraceptive (61.5 percent in 2007 compared with 46.2 percent in 1991) by U.S. high school students during the last time they had sexual intercourse (Centers for Disease Control and Prevention, 2008).

Although adolescent contraceptive use is increasing, many sexually active adolescents still do not use contraceptives, or they use them inconsistently (Parkes & others, 2009; Tschann & others, 2010). Younger adolescents are less likely than older adolescents to take contraceptive precautions.

Researchers also have found that U.S. adolescents use condoms less than their counterparts in Europe. Recent studies of 15-year-olds revealed that in Europe 72 percent of the girls and 81 percent of the boys used condoms at last intercourse (Currie & others, 2008); by comparison, in the U.S., 62 percent of the girls and 75 percent of the boys used condoms at last intercourse (Santelli, Sandfort, & Orr, 2009). Pill use also continues to be higher in European countries (Santelli, Sandfort, & Orr, 2009). Such comparisons provide insight into why adolescent pregnancy rates are much higher in the United States than in European countries.

Sexually Transmitted Infections

Some forms of contraception, such as birth control pills or implants, do not protect against sexually transmitted infections, or STIs. **Sexually transmitted infections (STIs)** are contracted primarily through sexual contact, including oral-genital

How Would You...? As a social worker, how would you design an educational campaign to increase adolescents' effective use of contraception?

and anal-genital contact. Every year more than 3 million American adolescents (about one-fourth of those who are sexually experienced) acquire an STI (Centers for Disease Control and Prevention, 2008). In a single act of unprotected sex with an infected partner, a teenage girl has a 1 percent risk of getting HIV, a 30 percent risk of acquiring genital herpes, and a 50 percent chance of contracting gonorrhea (Glei, 1999). Other very widespread STIs are chlamydia and human papillomavirus (HPV) (Weiss & others, 2010). In Chapter 11, we will consider these and other sexually transmitted infections.

Adolescent Pregnancy

In cross-cultural comparisons, the United States continues to have one of the highest adolescent pregnancy and childbearing rates in the industrialized world, despite a considerable decline in the 1990s (Cooksey, 2009). The U.S. adolescent pregnancy rate is eight times as high as in the Netherlands. This dramatic difference exists in spite of the fact that U.S. adolescents are no more sexually active than their counterparts in the Netherlands.

Despite the negative comparisons of the United States with many other developed countries, there have been some encouraging trends in U.S. adolescent pregnancy rates. In 2004, births to adolescent girls fell to a record low (Child Trends, 2006). In fact, the rate of births to adolescent girls has dropped 30 percent since 1991. Reasons for these declines include increased contraceptive use and fear of sexually transmitted infections such as AIDS (Joyner, 2009). However, the U.S. adolescent birth rate increased by 5 percent in 2005 and 2006, but resumed its downward trend in 2007 and 2008 (Hamilton, Martin, & Ventura, 2010) (see Figure 9.3).

Latina adolescents have a higher teen birth rate than non-Latina White and African American adolescents (Santelli, Abraido-Lanza, & Melnikas, 2009). Latinas also have had the smallest recent declines in adolescent pregnancy and birth rates among ethnic groups in the United States (Ventura & others, 2008). Latina and African American adolescent girls who have a child are more likely than non-Latina Whites to have a second child during adolescence (Rosengard, 2009).

Daughters of teenage mothers are at risk for teenage childbearing, thus perpetuating an intergenerational cycle. A study using data from the National Longitudinal Survey of Youth revealed that daughters of teenage mothers were 66 percent more likely to become teenage mothers themselves (Meade, Kershaw, & Ickovics, 2008). In this study, risks that increased the likelihood the daughters of the teenage mothers would become pregnant included low parental monitoring and poverty.

Outcomes Adolescent pregnancy creates risks for both the mother and the baby. Adolescent mothers often drop out of school. Although many adolescent mothers resume their education later in life, they generally never catch up economically with women who postpone childbearing until their twenties. Infants born to adolescent mothers are more likely to have low birth weights—a prominent factor in infant mortality—as well as neurological problems and childhood illness (Chedraui, 2008).

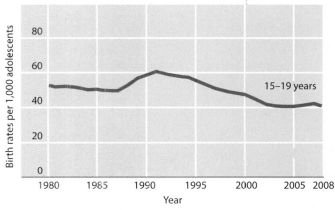

Though the consequences of America's high adolescent pregnancy rate are cause for great concern, it often is not pregnancy alone that leads to negative consequences for an adolescent mother and her offspring (Cavazos-Rehg & others, 2010a, b). Adolescent mothers are more likely to come from low-SES backgrounds (Joyner, 2009). Many adolescent mothers also were not good students before they

Figure 9.3 Birth Rates for U.S. Adolescents from 1980 to 2008 Source: Hamilton, Martin, & Ventura, (2010).

became pregnant (Malamitsi-Puchner & Boutsikou, 2006). However, not every adolescent female who bears a child lives a life of poverty and low achievement. Thus, although adolescent pregnancy is a high-risk circumstance and adolescents who do not become pregnant generally fare better than those who do, some adolescent mothers do well in school and have positive outcomes (Leadbeater & Way, 2000).

Serious, extensive efforts are needed to help pregnant adolescents and young mothers enhance their educational and occupational opportunities (Cavazos-Rehg & others, 2010a). Adolescent mothers also need help in obtaining competent child care and in planning for the future.

Adolescents can benefit from age-appropriate family life education. Family and consumer science educators teach life skills, such as effective decision making, to adolescents. "Careers in Life-Span Development" describes the work of one family and consumer science educator.

CAREERS IN LIFE-SPAN DEVELOPMENT

Lynn Blankenship, Family and Consumer Science Educator

Lynn Blankenship is a family and consumer science educator. She has an undergraduate degree in this area from the University of Arizona. She has taught for more than 20 years, the last 14 at Tucson High Magnet School.

Lynn was awarded the Tucson Federation of Teachers Educator of the Year Award for 1999–2000 and the Arizona Teacher of the Year in 1999.

Lynn especially enjoys teaching life skills to adolescents. One of her favorite activities is having students care for an automated baby that imitates the needs of real babies. She says that this program has a profound impact on students because the baby must be cared for around the clock for the duration of the assignment. Lynn also coordinates real-world work experiences and training for students in several child-care facilities in the Tucson area.

Family and consumer science educators like Lynn Blankenship may specialize in early childhood education or instruct middle and high school students about such matters as nutrition, inter-

Lynn Blankenship (*center*) teaching life skills to students.

personal relationships, human sexuality, parenting, and human development. Hundreds of colleges and universities throughout the United States offer two- and four-year degree programs in family and consumer science. These programs usually require an internship. Additional education courses may be needed to obtain a teaching certificate. Some family and consumer educators go on to graduate school for further training, which provides a background for possible jobs in college teaching or research.

Reducing Adolescent Pregnancy Girls Inc. has four programs that are intended to increase adolescent girls' motivation to avoid pregnancy until they are mature enough to make responsible decisions about motherhood (Roth & others, 1998). Growing Together, a series of five two-hour workshops for adolescent girls and their mothers, and Will Power/Won't Power, a series of six two-hour sessions that focus on assertiveness training, are designed for 12- to 14-year-old girls. For older adolescent girls, Taking Care of Business provides nine sessions that emphasize career planning as well as information about sexuality, reproduction, and contraception. The program Health Bridge coordinates health and education services—girls can participate in this program as one of their Girls Inc. club activities. Girls who participated in these programs were less likely to get pregnant than girls who did not participate (Girls Inc., 1991).

Currently, a major controversy in sex education is whether schools should have an abstinence-only program or a program that emphasizes contraceptive knowledge (Hentz & Fields, 2009). Two research reviews found that abstinence-only programs do not delay the initiation of sexual intercourse and do not reduce HIV risk behaviors (Kirby, Laris, & Rollier, 2007; Underhill, Montgomery, & Operario, 2007). Further, another study revealed that adolescents who experienced comprehensive sex education were less likely to report adolescent pregnancies than those who were given abstinence-only sex education or no education (Kohler, Manhart, & Lafferty, 2008). A number of leading experts on adolescent sexuality conclude that sex education programs that emphasize contraceptive knowledge do not increase the incidence of sexual intercourse and are more likely to reduce the risk of adolescent pregnancy and sexually transmitted infections than abstinence-only programs (Constantine, 2008; Hentz & Fields, 2009).

Issues in Adolescent Health

Adolescence is a critical juncture in the adoption of behaviors that are relevant to health (Coker & others, 2010; Ozer & Irwin, 2009). Many of the behaviors that are linked to poor health habits and early death in adults begin during adolescence. Conversely, the early formation of healthy behavior patterns, such as regular exercise and a preference for foods low in fat and cholesterol, not only has immediate health benefits but helps in adulthood to delay or prevent disability and mortality from heart disease, stroke, diabetes, and cancer (Schiff, 2011).

Nutrition and Exercise

Concerns are growing about adolescents' nutrition and exercise (Biro & others, 2010; Jessor, Turbin, & Costa, 2010; Seo & Sa, 2010). The percentage of overweight U.S. 12- to 19-year-olds increased from 11 to 17 percent from the early 1990s through 2004 (Eaton & others, 2006). One study found that 80 percent of the male and 92 percent of the female adolescents in the 95th percentile and higher for body mass index (BMI) became obese adults (Wang & others, 2008). A comparison of adolescents in 28 countries found that U.S. and British adolescents were more likely to eat fried food and less likely to eat fruits and vegetables than adolescents in most other countries that were studied (World Health Organization, 2000).

U.S. adolescents are decreasing their intake of fruits and vegetables. The National Youth Risk Survey found that U.S. high school students decreased their intake of fruits and vegetables from 1999 through 2007 (Eaton & others, 2008) (see Figure 9.4). A special concern in American culture is the amount of fat in our diet (Frisco, 2009). Many of today's adolescents virtually live on fast-food meals, which contribute to the high fat levels in their diet. A longitudinal study revealed that 24 percent of males and 21 percent of 15-year-old females reported intake of fast food three or more times per week (Larson & others, 2008). At 20 years of age, the percent increased to 33 percent for males but remained at 21 percent for the females. And a recent study found that eating regular family meals during early adolescence was linked to healthy eating habits five years later (Burgess-Champoux & others, 2009).

Researchers have found that individuals become less active as they reach and progress through adolescence (Butcher & others,

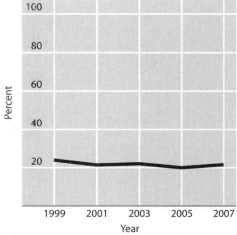

Figure 9.4 Percentage of U.S. High School Students Who Ate Fruits and Vegetables Five or More Times a Day, 1999 to 2007
Note: The graph shows the percentage of high school students over time who had eaten fruits and vegetables (100% fruit juice, fruit, green salad, potatoes—excluding french fries, fried potatoes, or potato chips—carrots, or other vegetables) five or more times per day during the preceding seven days (Eaton & others, 2008).

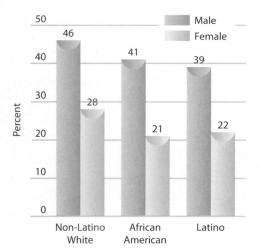

Figure 9.5 Exercise Rates of U.S. High School Students: Gender and Ethnicity

Note: Data are for high school students who were physically active doing any kind of physical activity that increased their heart rate and made them breathe hard some of the time for a total of at least 60 minutes per day on five or more of the seven days preceding the survey.

2008). A recent national study revealed that only 31 percent of U.S. 15-year-olds met the federal government's moderate to vigorous exercise recommendations per day (a minimum of 60 minutes a day) and only 17 percent met the recommendations on weekends (Nader & others, 2008). This study also found that adolescent boys were more likely to engage in moderate to vigorous exercise than were girls. Another national study of U.S. adolescents revealed that physical activity increased until 13 years of age in boys and girls but then declined through 18 years of age (Kahn & others, 2008).

Ethnic differences in exercise participation rates of U.S. adolescents also occur, and these rates vary by gender. As indicated in Figure 9.5, in the National Youth Risk Survey, non-Latino White boys exercised the most, African American girls the least (Eaton & others, 2008).

Exercise is linked to a number of positive physical outcomes in adolescence (van der Heijden & others, 2010). Regular exercise has a positive effect on adolescents' weight status. A study revealed that regular exercise from age 9 to 16 was associated with regular weight in girls (McMurray & others, 2008). Other positive outcomes of exercise in adolescence are reduced triglyceride levels, lower blood pressure, a lower incidence of type II diabetes (Butcher & others, 2008), and lower drug use (Delisle & others, 2010). Negative outcomes have been shown for low levels of exercise as well. One study revealed that low levels of exercise were related to young adolescents' depressive symptoms (Sund, Larsson, & Wichstraom, 2010). And another recent study found that vigorous physical activity was linked to lower drug use in adolescence (Delisle & others, 2010).

Watching television and using computers for long hours may be involved in lower levels of physical fitness in adolescence (Rey-Lopez & others, 2008). For example, one study revealed that the more frequently adolescents watched television and used computers, the less likely they were to engage in regular exercise (Chen, Liou, & Wu, 2008).

How Would You...?
As a health-care professional, how would you explain the benefits of physical fitness in adolescence to adolescents, parents, and teachers?

Sleep Patterns

Like nutrition and exercise, sleep is an important influence on well-being. Might changing sleep patterns in adolescence contribute to adolescents' health-compromising behaviors? Recently there has been a surge of interest in adolescent sleep patterns (Brand & others, 2010; Wolfson, 2010).

In a national survey of youth, only 31 percent of U.S. adolescents got eight or more hours of sleep on an average school night (Eaton & others, 2008). In this study, the percentage of adolescents getting this much sleep on an average school night decreased as they got older.

The National Sleep Foundation (2006) conducted a U.S. survey of 1,602 caregivers and their 11- to 17-year-olds. Forty-five percent of the adolescents got inadequate sleep on school nights (less than eight hours). Older adolescents (ninth- to twelfth-graders) got markedly less sleep on school nights than younger adolescents (sixth- to eighth-graders)—62 percent of the older adolescents got inadequate sleep compared to 21 percent of the younger adolescents. Adolescents who got inadequate sleep (eight hours or less) on school nights were more likely to feel more tired or sleepy, more cranky and irritable, fall asleep in school, be in a depressed mood, and drink caffeinated beverages than their counterparts who got optimal sleep (nine or more hours).

Mary Carskadon and her colleagues (2006; Jenni & Carskadon, 2007; Tarokh & Carskadon, 2008) have conducted a number of research studies on adolescent sleep patterns. They found that when given the opportunity adolescents will sleep an average of 9 hours and 25 minutes a night. Most get considerably less than nine hours of sleep, however, especially during the week. This shortfall creates a sleep deficit, which adolescents often attempt to make up on the weekend. The researchers also found that older adolescents tend to be sleepier during the day than younger adolescents. They theorized that this sleepiness was not due to academic work or social pressures. Rather, their research suggests that adolescents' biological clocks undergo a shift as they get older, delaying their period of wakefulness by about one hour. A delay in the nightly release of the sleep-inducing hormone melatonin, which is produced in the brain's pineal gland, seems to underlie this shift. Melatonin is secreted at about 9:30 p.m. in younger adolescents and approximately an hour later in older adolescents.

In Mary Carskadon's sleep laboratory at Brown University, an adolescent girl's brain activity is being monitored. Carskadon (2005) says that in the morning, sleep-deprived adolescents' "brains are telling them it's nightt me . . . and the rest of the world is saying it's time to go to school" (p. 19).

How Would You...?
As an educator, how would you use developmental research to convince your school board to change the starting time of high school?

Carskadon concludes that early school starting times may cause grogginess, inattention in class, and poor performance on tests. Based on her research, school officials in Edina, Minnesota, decided to start classes at 8:30 a.m. rather than the usual 7:25 a.m. Since then, there have been fewer referrals for discipline problems, and the number of students who report being ill or depressed has decreased. The school system reports that test scores have improved for high school students, but not for middle school students. This finding supports Carskadon's suspicion that early start times are likely to be more stressful for older than for younger adolescents.

Leading Causes of Death in Adolescence

The three leading causes of death in adolescence are accidents, homicide, and suicide (National Vital Statistics Reports, 2008). Almost half of all deaths from 15 to 24 years of age are due to unintentional injuries, approximately three-fourths of them involving motor vehicle accidents. Risky driving habits, such as speeding, tailgating, and driving under the influence of alcohol or other drugs, may be more important contributors to these accidents than lack of driving experience (Dunlop & Romer, 2010; Shope, 2010). In about 50 percent of motor vehicle fatalities involving adolescents, the driver has a blood alcohol level of 0.10 percent—twice the level needed to be designated as "under the influence" in some states. A high rate of intoxication is also found in adolescents who die as pedestrians, or while using recreational vehicles.

Homicide is the second leading cause of death in adolescence (National Vital Statistics Reports, 2008), especially among African American male adolescents. The rate of the third cause, adolescent suicide, has tripled since the 1950s. Suicide accounts for 6 percent of the deaths in the 10 to 14 age group and 12 percent of deaths in the 15 to 19 age group. We will discuss suicide further in Chapter 10.

Substance Use and Abuse

Each year since 1975, Lloyd Johnston and his colleagues at the Institute of Social Research at the University of Michigan have monitored the drug use of America's high school seniors in a wide range of public and private high schools. Since 1991, they also have surveyed drug use by eighth- and tenth-graders. In 2009, the study surveyed more than 45,000 secondary school students (Johnston & others, 2010).

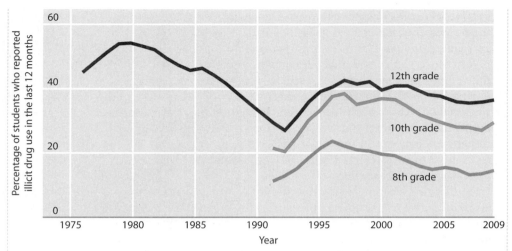

Figure 9.6 Trends in Drug Use by U.S. Eighth-, Tenth-, and Twelfth-Grade Students
This graph shows the percentage of U.S. eighth-, tenth-, and twelfth-grade students who reported having taken an illicit drug in the last 12 months from 1991 to 2009, for eighth- and tenth-graders, and from 1975 to 2008, for twelfth-graders (Johnston & others, 2010).

How Would You...?
As a health-care professional, how would you use research on the rates and risks of adolescents' substance abuse to advocate for government funding of drug and alcohol education programs?

According to this study, the proportions of 8th-, 10th-, and 12th-grade U.S. students who used any illicit drug declined in the late 1990s and first decade of the 21st century (Johnston & others, 2010) (see Figure 9.6). Nonetheless, even with the recent decline in use, the United States still has one of the highest rates of adolescent drug use of any industrialized nation.

A special concern involves adolescents who begin to use drugs early in adolescence or even in childhood (Patrick, Abar, & Maggs, 2009). A longitudinal study of individuals from 8 to 42 years of age also found that early onset of drinking was linked to increased risk of heavy drinking in middle age (Pitkänen, Lyrra, & Pulkkinen, 2005).

Parents play an important role in preventing adolescent drug abuse (Harakeh & others, 2010; Miller & Plant, 2010). Researchers have found that parental monitoring is linked with a lower incidence of problem behavior by adolescents, including substance abuse (Tobler & Komro, 2010). A recent research review found that when adolescents ate dinner more often with their family they were less likely to have problems, such as substance abuse (Sen, 2010).

Peers also influence whether adolescents become substance abusers. A recent study revealed that whether a best friend or boyfriend/girlfriend smoked was related to the adolescent's regular smoking pattern (Holliday, Rothwell, & Moore, 2010).

Educational success is also a strong buffer for the emergence of drug problems in adolescence. A recent analysis by Jerald Bachman and his colleagues (2008) revealed that early educational achievement considerably reduced the likelihood that adolescents would develop drug problems, including alcohol abuse, smoking, and abuse of various illicit drugs. Another recent study found that for adolescent girls, but not boys, being an "A" or "B" student was linked to a lower probability of engaging in illegal substance use, compared to "C" students (Wheeler, 2010).

How Would You...?
As a human development and family studies professional, how would you explain to parents the importance of parental monitoring in preventing adolescent substance abuse?

Eating Disorders

Earlier in the chapter under the topic of nutrition and exercise, we described the increase in being overweight in adolescence. Let's now examine two different eating problems—anorexia nervosa and bulimia nervosa—that are far more common in adolescent girls than boys.

Anorexia Nervosa

Although most U.S. girls have been on a diet at some point, slightly less than 1 percent ever develop anorexia nervosa. **Anorexia nervosa** is an eating disorder that involves the relentless pursuit of thinness through starvation. It is a serious disorder that can lead to death. Three main characteristics apply to people suffering from anorexia nervosa: (1) weight less than 85 percent of what is considered normal for their age and height; (2) an intense fear of gaining weight that does not decrease with weight loss; and (3) a distorted image of their body shape (Rigaud & others, 2007). Even when they are extremely thin, they see themselves as too fat. They never think they are thin enough, especially in the abdomen, buttocks, and thighs. They usually weigh themselves frequently, often take their body measurements, and gaze critically at themselves in mirrors.

Anorexia nervosa typically begins in the early to middle adolescent years, often following an episode of dieting and some type of life stress. It is about 10 times more likely to occur in females than males. When anorexia nervosa does occur in males, the symptoms and other characteristics (such as a distorted body image and family conflict) are usually similar to those reported by females who have the disorder (Ariceli & others, 2005).

Most individuals with anorexia are non-Latina White adolescent or young adult females from well-educated, middle- and upper-income families and are competitive and high achieving (Schmidt, 2003). They set high standards, become stressed about not being able to reach the standards, and are intensely concerned about how others perceive them (Liechty, 2010; Woelders & others, 2011). Unable to meet these high expectations, they turn to something they can control: their weight. Offspring of mothers with anorexia nervosa are at risk for becoming anorexic themselves (Striegel-Moore & Bulik, 2007). Problems in family functioning are increasingly being found to be linked to the appearance of anorexia nervosa in adolescent girls (Benninghoven & others, 2007), and a recent research review indicated that family therapy is often the most effective treatment of adolescent girls with anorexia nervosa (Bulik & others, 2007).

The fashion image in U.S. culture contributes to the incidence of anorexia nervosa (Striegel-Moore & Bulik, 2007). The media portray thin as beautiful in their choice of fashion models, whom many adolescent girls strive to emulate. And many adolescent girls who strive to be thin hang out together.

Bulimia Nervosa

Whereas people with anorexia control their eating by restricting it, most individuals with bulimia cannot. **Bulimia nervosa** is an eating disorder in which the individual consistently follows a binge-and-purge pattern. They go on an eating binge and then purge by self-inducing vomiting or using a laxative. Although many people binge and purge occasionally and some experiment with it, a person is considered to have a serious bulimic disorder only if the episodes occur at least twice a week for three months (Napierski-Pranel, 2009).

As with those who have anorexia, most people with bulimia are preoccupied with food, have a strong fear of becoming overweight, are depressed or anxious, and have a distorted body image. A study revealed that they overvalued their body weight and shape, and this overvaluation was linked to higher depression and lower self-esteem (Hrabosky & others, 2007). Unlike people who have anorexia, people who binge and purge typically fall within a normal weight range, which makes bulimia more difficult to detect.

Approximately 1 to 2 percent of U.S. women are estimated to develop bulimia nervosa, and about 90 percent are women. Bulimia nervosa typically begins in late adolescence or early adulthood. Many women who develop bulimia nervosa were somewhat overweight before the onset of the disorder, and the binge eating often began during an episode of dieting. As with anorexia nervosa, about 70 percent of individuals who develop bulimia nervosa eventually recover from the disorder (Agras & others, 2004).

anorexia nervosa An eating disorder that involves the relentless pursuit of thinness through starvation.

bulimia nervosa An eating disorder in which the individual consistently follows a binge-and-purge pattern.

Anorexia nervosa has become an increasing problem for adolescent girls and young adult women. *What are some possible causes of anorexia nervosa?*

How Would You...?
As a health-care professional, how would you educate parents to identify the signs and symptoms that may signal an eating disorder?

Adolescent Cognition

Adolescents' developing power of thought opens up new cognitive and social horizons. Let's examine what their developing power of thought is like, beginning with Piaget's theory (1952).

Piaget's Theory

As we discussed in Chapter 7, Piaget proposed that around 7 years of age children enter the *concrete operational stage* of cognitive development. They can reason logically about concrete events and objects, and they make gains in the ability to classify objects and to reason about the relationships between classes of objects. Around age 11, according to Piaget, the fourth and final stage of cognitive development, the *formal operational stage,* begins.

The Formal Operational Stage

What are the characteristics of the formal operational stage? Formal operational thought is more abstract than concrete operational thought. Adolescents are no longer limited to actual, concrete experiences as anchors for thought. They can conjure up make-believe situations, abstract propositions, and events that are purely hypothetical, and can try to reason logically about them.

The abstract quality of thinking during the formal operational stage is evident in the adolescent's verbal problem-solving ability. The concrete operational thinker needs to see the concrete elements A, B, and C to be able to make the logical inference that if A = B and B = C, then A = C, whereas the formal operational thinker can solve this problem merely through verbal presentation.

Another indication of the abstract quality of adolescents' thought is their increased tendency to think about thought itself. One adolescent commented, "I began thinking about why I was thinking what I was. Then I began thinking about why I was thinking about what I was thinking about what I was." If this sounds abstract, it is, and it characterizes the adolescent's enhanced focus on thought and its abstract qualities.

Accompanying the abstract nature of formal operational thought is thought full of idealism and possibilities, especially during the beginning of the formal operational stage, when assimilation dominates. Adolescents engage in extended speculation about ideal characteristics—qualities they desire in themselves and in

Might adolescents' ability to reason hypothetically and to evaluate what is ideal versus what is real lead them to engage in demonstrations, such as this protest related to better ethnic relations?

others. Such thoughts often lead adolescents to compare themselves with others in regard to such ideal standards. And their thoughts are often fantasy flights into future possibilities.

At the same time that adolescents think more abstractly and idealistically, they also think more logically. Children are likely to solve problems through trial and error; adolescents begin to think more as a scientist thinks, devising plans to solve problems and systematically testing solutions. This type of problem solving requires **hypothetical-deductive reasoning**, which involves creating a hypothesis and deducing its implications, which provides ways to test the hypothesis. Thus, formal operational thinkers develop hypotheses about ways to solve problems and then systematically deduce the best path to follow to solve the problem.

Evaluating Piaget's Theory

Researchers have challenged some of Piaget's ideas on the formal operational stage (Kuhn, 2009, 2011). Among their findings is that there is much more individual variation than Piaget envisioned: Only about one in three young adolescents is a formal operational thinker, and many American adults never become formal operational thinkers; neither do many adults in other cultures

Furthermore, education in the logic of science and mathematics promotes the development of formal operational thinking. This point recalls a criticism of Piaget's theory that we discussed in Chapter 7: Culture and education exert stronger influences on cognitive development than Piaget argued (Daniels, 2011).

Piaget's theory of cognitive development has been challenged on other points as well (Halford & Andrews, 2011; Quinn, 2011). As we noted in Chapter 7, Piaget conceived of stages as unitary structures of thought, with various aspects of a stage emerging at the same time. However, most contemporary developmentalists agree that cognitive development is not as stage-like as Piaget thought (Kuhn, 2009). Furthermore, children can be trained to reason at a higher cognitive stage, and some cognitive abilities emerge earlier than Piaget thought (Diamond, Casey, & Munakata, 2011). Some understanding of the conservation of number has been demonstrated as early as age 3, although Piaget did not think it emerged until 7. Other cognitive abilities can emerge later than Piaget thought (Kuhn, 2009, 2011). As we just noted, many adolescents still think in concrete operational ways or are just beginning to master formal operations, and even many adults are not formal operational thinkers.

Despite these challenges to Piaget's ideas, we owe him a tremendous debt (Miller, 2011). Piaget was the founder of the present field of cognitive development, and he developed a long list of masterful concepts of enduring power and fascination: assimilation, accommodation, object permanence, egocentrism, conservation, and others. Psychologists also owe him the current vision of children as active, constructive thinkers. And they have a debt to him for creating a theory that generated a huge volume of research on children's cognitive development.

Piaget also was a genius when it came to observing children. His careful observations demonstrated inventive ways to discover how children act on, and adapt to, their world. He also showed us how children need to make their experiences fit their schemes yet simultaneously adapt their schemes to experience. Piaget also revealed how cognitive change is likely to occur if the context is structured to allow gradual movement to the next higher level. Concepts do not emerge suddenly, full-blown, but instead develop through a series of partial accomplishments that lead to increasingly comprehensive understanding (Aslin, 2009).

Adolescent Egocentrism

Adolescent egocentrism is the heightened self-consciousness of adolescents. David Elkind (1976) maintains that adolescent egocentrism has two key components—the imaginary audience and personal fable. The **imaginary audience** is adolescents'

hypothetical-deductive reasoning Piaget's formal operational concept that adolescents have the cognitive ability to develop hypotheses, or best guesses, about ways to solve problems, such as an algebraic equation.

adolescent egocentrism The heightened self-consciousness of adolescents.

imaginary audience Involves adolescents' belief that others are as interested in them as they themselves are; attention-getting behavior motivated by a desire to be noticed, visible, and "on stage."

the seventh grade (Hirsch & Rapkin, 1987). Compared with their earlier feelings as sixth-graders, the seventh-graders were less satisfied with school, were less committed to school, and liked their teachers less. The drop in school satisfaction occurred regardless of how academically successful the students were.

The transition to middle or junior high school takes place at a time when many changes—in the individual, in the family, and in school—are occurring simultaneously. These changes include puberty and related concerns about body image; the emergence of at least some aspects of formal operational thought, including accompanying changes in social cognition; increased responsibility and decreased dependency on parents; change to a larger, more impersonal school structure; change from one teacher to many teachers and from a small, homogeneous set of peers to a larger, more heterogeneous set of peers; and an increased focus on achievement and performance. Moreover, when students make the transition to middle or junior high school, they experience the **top-dog phenomenon**, moving from being the oldest, biggest, and most powerful students in the elementary school to being the youngest, smallest, and least powerful students in the middle or junior high school.

The transition from elementary to middle or junior high school occurs at the same time as a number of other developmental changes. What are some of these other developmental changes?

There can also be positive aspects to the transition to middle or junior high school. Students are more likely to feel grown up, have more subjects from which to select, have more opportunities to spend time with peers and locate compatible friends, and enjoy increased independence from direct parental monitoring. They also may be more challenged intellectually by academic work.

Effective Schools for Young Adolescents

How Would You...?
As an educator, how would you design school programs to enhance students' smooth transition into middle school?

Educators and psychologists worry that junior high and middle schools have become watered-down versions of high schools, mimicking their curricular and extracurricular schedules. Critics argue that these schools should offer activities that reflect a wide range of individual differences in biological and psychological development among young adolescents. The Carnegie Foundation (1989) issued an extremely negative evaluation of our nation's middle schools. It concluded that most young adolescents attended massive, impersonal schools; were taught from irrelevant curricula; trusted few adults in school; and lacked access to health care and counseling. It recommended that the nation should develop smaller "communities" or "houses" to lessen the impersonal nature of large middle schools, have lower student-to-counselor ratios (10 to 1 instead of several hundred to 1), involve parents and community leaders in schools, develop new curricula, have teachers team teach in more flexibly designed curriculum blocks that integrate several disciplines, boost students' health and fitness with more in-school programs, and help students who need public health care to get it. Twenty-five years later, experts are still finding that middle schools throughout the nation need a major redesign if they are to be effective in educating adolescents (Eccles & Roeser, 2010).

High School

Just as there are concerns about U.S. middle school education, so are there concerns about U.S. high school education (Smith, 2009). Critics stress that in many high schools expectations for success and standards for learning are too low. Critics also argue that too often high schools foster passivity and that schools should create a variety of pathways for students to achieve an identity. Many students graduate from high school with inadequate reading, writing, and mathematical skills—including many who go on to college and have to enroll in remediation classes there. Other students drop out of high school and do not have skills that will allow them to obtain decent jobs, much less to be informed citizens.

In the last half of the 20th century and the first several years of the 21st century, U.S. high school dropout rates declined (National Center for Education Statistics, 2008b) (see Figure 9.7). In the 1940s, more than half of U.S. 16- to 24-year-olds had dropped out of school; by 2006, this figure had decreased to 9.3 percent. The dropout rate of Latino adolescents remains high, although it has been decreasing in the 21st century (from 28 percent in 2000 to 22 percent in 2006). The highest dropout rate in the United States, though, likely occurs for Native American youth—less than 50 percent finish their high school education.

Students drop out of schools for many reasons (Christenson & Thurlow, 2004). In one study, almost 50 percent of the dropouts cited school-related reasons for leaving school, such as not liking school or being expelled or suspended (Rumberger, 1995). Twenty percent of the dropouts (but 40 percent of the Latino students) cited economic reasons for leaving school. One-third of the female students dropped out for personal reasons, such as pregnancy or marriage.

According to one review, the most effective programs to discourage dropping out of high school provide early reading programs, tutoring, counseling, and mentoring (Lehr & others, 2003). They also emphasize the creation of caring environments and relationships, use block scheduling, and offer community service opportunities.

service learning A form of education that promotes social responsibility and service to the community.

Service Learning

Service learning is a form of education that promotes social responsibility and service to the community. In service learning, adolescents engage in activities such as tutoring, helping older adults, working in a hospital, assisting at a child-care center, or cleaning up a vacant lot to make a play area. An important goal of service learning is that adolescents become less self-centered and more strongly motivated to help others (Zaff & others, 2011). Service learning is often more effective when two conditions are met (Nucci, 2006): (1) giving students some degree of choice in the service activities in which they participate, and (2) providing students opportunities to reflect about their participation.

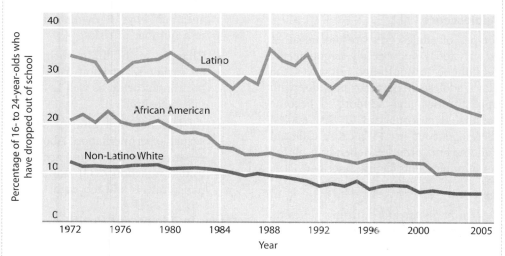

Figure 9.7 Trends in High School Dropout Rates
From 1972 through 2005, the school dropout rate for Latinos remained very high (22 percent of 16- to 24-year-olds in 2005). The African American dropout rate was still higher (10 percent) than the non-Latino White rate (6 percent) in 2005. (*Source:* National Center for Education Statistics, 2008b.)

10 Socioemotional Development in Adolescence

Stories of Life-Span Development: Jewel Cash, Teen Dynamo

The mayor of the city says she is "everywhere." She recently persuaded the city's school committee to consider ending the practice of locking tardy students out of their classrooms. She also swayed a neighborhood group to support her proposal for a winter jobs program. According to one city councilman, "People are just impressed with the power of her arguments and the sophistication of the argument" (Silva, 2005, pp. B1, B4). She is Jewel E. Cash, and she is only 16 years old.

A junior at Boston Latin Academy, Jewel was raised in one of Boston's housing projects by her mother, a single parent. Today she is a member of the Boston Student Advisory Council, mentors children, volunteers at a women's shelter, manages and dances in two troupes, and is a member of a neighborhood watch group—among other activities. Jewel is far from typical, but her activities illustrate that cognitive and socioemotional development allows even adolescents to be capable, effective individuals.

Significant changes characterize socio-emotional development in adolescence. These changes include searching for identity. Changes also occur in the social contexts of adolescents' lives, with transformations occurring in relationships with families and peers in cultural contexts. Adolescents also may develop sociemotional problems, such as delinquency and depression.

Jewel Cash, seated next to her mother, participating in a crime watch meeting at a community center.

Identity

Jewel Cash told an interviewer from the *Boston Globe*, "I see a problem and I say, 'How can I make a difference?'. . . I can't take on the world even though I can try. . . . I'm moving forward but I want to make sure I'm bringing people with me" (Silva, 2005, pp. B1, B4). Jewel's confidence and positive identity sound at least as impressive as her activities. This section examines how adolescents develop characteristics like these. How much did you understand yourself during adolescence, and how did you acquire the stamp of your identity? Is your identity still developing?

What Is Identity?

Questions about identity surface as common, virtually universal, concerns during adolescence. Some decisions made during adolescence might seem trivial: whom to date, whether or not to break up, which major to study, whether to study or play, whether or not to be politically active, and so on. Over the years of adolescence, however, such decisions begin to form the core of what the individual is all about as a human being—what is called his or her identity.

Identity is a self-portrait composed of many pieces, including these:

- The career and work path the person wants to follow (vocational/career identity)
- Whether the person is conservative, liberal, or middle-of-the-road (political identity)
- The person's spiritual beliefs (religious identity)
- Whether the person is single, married, divorced, and so on (relationship identity)
- The extent to which the person is motivated to achieve and is intellectual (achievement, intellectual identity)
- Whether the person is heterosexual, homosexual, or bisexual (sexual identity)
- Which part of the world or country a person is from and how intensely the person identifies with his or her cultural heritage (cultural/ethnic identity)
- The kind of things a person likes to do, which can include sports, music, hobbies, and so on (interest)
- The individual's personality characteristics, such as being introverted or extraverted, anxious or calm, friendly or hostile, and so on (personality)
- The individual's body image (physical identity)

What are some important dimensions of identity?

Synthesizing the identity components can be a long and drawn-out process, with many negations and affirmations of various roles and faces. Identity development gets done in bits and pieces. Decisions are not made once and for all, but have to be made again and again. Identity development does not happen neatly, and it does not happen cataclysmically (Coté, 2009; Kroger, Martinussen, & Marcia, 2010).

Erikson's View

It was Erik Erikson (1950, 1968) who first understood that questions about identity are central to understanding adolescent development. Today, as a result of Erikson's masterful thinking and analysis, identity is considered a key aspect of adolescent development.

Erikson's theory was introduced in Chapter 1. Recall that his fifth developmental stage, which individuals experience during adolescence, is *identity versus identity confusion*. During this time, said Erikson, adolescents are faced with deciding who they are, what they are all about, and where they are going in life.

The search for an identity during adolescence is aided by a *psychosocial moratorium,* which is Erikson's term for the gap between childhood security and adult autonomy. During this period, society leaves adolescents relatively free of responsibilities and free to try out different identities. Adolescents in effect search their culture's identity files, experimenting with different roles and personalities. They may want to pursue one career one month (lawyer, for example) and another career the next month (doctor, actor, teacher, social worker, or astronaut, for example). They may dress neatly one day, sloppily the next. This experimentation is a deliberate effort on the part of adolescents to find out where they fit in the world. Most adolescents eventually discard undesirable roles.

Developmental Changes

Although questions about identity may be especially important during adolescence, identity formation neither begins nor ends during these years (McAdams & Cox, 2011). It begins with the appearance of attachment, the development of the sense of self, and the emergence of independence in infancy; the process reaches its final phase with a life review and integration in old age. What is important about identity development in adolescence, especially late adolescence, is that for the first time, physical development, cognitive development, and socioemotional development advance to the point at which the individual can begin to sort through and synthesize childhood identities and identifications to construct a viable path toward adult maturity.

How do individual adolescents go about the process of forming an identity? Eriksonian researcher James Marcia (1980, 1994) believes that Erikson's theory of identity development contains four *statuses* of identity, or ways of resolving the identity crisis: identity diffusion, identity foreclosure, identity moratorium, and identity achievement. What determines an individual's identity status? Marcia classifies individuals based on the existence or extent of their crisis or commitment (see Figure 10.1). **Crisis** is defined as a period of identity development during which the individual is exploring alternatives. Most researchers use the term *exploration* rather than crisis. **Commitment** is personal investment in identity.

The four statuses of identity are described as follows:

- **Identity diffusion** is the status of individuals who have not yet experienced a crisis or made any commitments. Not only are they undecided about occupational and ideological choices, they are also likely to show little interest in such matters.

- **Identity foreclosure** is the status of individuals who have made a commitment but have not experienced a crisis. This occurs most often when parents hand down commitments to their adolescents, usually in an authoritarian way,

How Would You...?

As a psychologist, how would you apply Marcia's theory of identity formation to describe your current identity status or that of adolescents you know?

before adolescents have had a chance to explore different approaches, ideologies, and vocations on their own.

- **Identity moratorium** is the status of individuals who are in the midst of a crisis but whose commitments are either absent or are only vaguely defined.

- **Identity achievement** is the status of individuals who have undergone a crisis and have made a commitment.

Researchers are developing a consensus that the key changes in identity are more likely to take place in emerging adulthood, the period from about 18 to 25 years of age (Juang & Syed, 2010; Swanson, 2010). For example, Alan Waterman (1985, 1992) has found that from the years preceding high school through the last few years of college, the number of individuals who are identity achieved increases, whereas the number of individuals who are identity diffused decreases. Many young adolescents are identity diffused. College upperclassmen are more likely than high school students or college freshmen to be identity achieved.

Why might college produce some key changes in identity? Increased complexity in the reasoning skills of college students combined with a wide range of new experiences that highlight contrasts between home and college and between themselves and others stimulate them to reach a higher level of integrating various dimensions of their identity (Phinney, 2008).

A recent meta-analysis of 124 studies revealed that during adolescence and emerging adulthood, identity moratorium status rose steadily to age 19 and then declined; identity achievement rose across late adolescence and emerging adulthood; and foreclosure and diffusion statuses declined across the high school years but fluctuated in the late teens and emerging adulthood (Kroger, Martinussen, & Marcia, 2010). The studies also found that a large portion of individuals were not identity achieved by the time they reached their twenties.

Resolution of the identity issue during adolescence and emerging adulthood does not mean that identity will be stable through the remainder of life (McAdams & Cox, 2011). Many individuals who develop positive identities follow what are called "MAMA" cycles; that is, their identity status changes from *moratorium* to *achievement* to *moratorium* to *achievement* (Marcia, 1994). These cycles may be repeated throughout life (Francis, Fraser, & Marcia, 1989). Marcia (2002) points out that the first identity is just that—it is not, and should not be expected to be, the final product.

Ethnic Identity

Throughout the world, ethnic minority groups have struggled to maintain their ethnic identities while blending in with the dominant culture (Erikson, 1968). **Ethnic identity** is an enduring aspect of the self that includes a sense of membership

identity moratorium Marcia's term for adolescents who are in the midst of a crisis, but their commitments are either absent or vaguely defined.

identity achievement Marcia's term for adolescents who have undergone a crisis and have made a commitment.

ethnic identity An enduring, basic aspect of the self that includes a sense of membership in an ethnic group and the attitudes and feelings related to that membership.

Identity Status

Position on Occupation and Ideology	Identity Diffusion	Identity Foreclosure	Identity Moratorium	Identity Achievement
Crisis	Absent	Absent	Present	Present
Commitment	Absent	Present	Absent	Present

Figure 10.1 Marcia's Four Statuses of Identity

According to Marcia, an individual's status in developing an identity can be described as identity diffusion, identity foreclosure, identity moratorium, or identity achievement. The status depends on the presence or absence of (1) a crisis or exploration of alternatives and (2) a commitment to an identity. *What is the identity status of most young adolescents?*

in an ethnic group, along with the attitudes and feelings related to that membership. Thus, for adolescents from ethnic minority groups, the process of identity formation has an added dimension: the choice between two or more sources of identification—their own ethnic group and the mainstream, or dominant, culture (Phinney, 2008). Many adolescents resolve this choice by developing a *bicultural identity*. That is, they identify in some ways with their ethnic group and in other ways with the majority culture.

For ethnic minority individuals, adolescence and emerging adulthood are often a special juncture in their development (Juang & Syed, 2010; Swanson, 2010; Syed & Azmitia, 2010). Although children are aware of some ethnic and cultural differences, individuals consciously confront their ethnicity for the first time in adolescence. Unlike children, adolescents have the ability to interpret ethnic and cultural information, to reflect on the past, and to speculate about the future. Researchers are increasingly finding that a positive ethnic identity is related to positive outcomes for ethnic minority adolescents (Rivas-Drake, 2010; Umana-Taylor, Updegraff, & Gonzales-Backen, 2010). For example, a recent study of Latino youth indicated that growth in identity exploration was linked with a positive increase in self-esteem (Umana-Taylor, Gonzales-Backen, & Guimond, 2009).

The indicators of identity change often differ for each succeeding generation (Phinney & Ong, 2007). First-generation immigrants are likely to be secure in their identities and unlikely to change much; they may or may not develop a new identity. The degree to which they begin to feel "American" appears to be related to whether or not they learn English, develop social networks beyond their ethnic group, and become culturally competent in their new country. Second-generation immigrants are more likely to think of themselves as "American," possibly because citizenship is granted at birth. Their ethnic identity is likely to be linked to retention of their ethnic language and social networks. In the third and later generations, the issues become more complex. Historical, contextual, and political factors that are unrelated to acculturation may affect the extent to which members of this generation retain their ethnic identities. For non-European ethnic groups, racism and discrimination influence whether ethnic identity is retained.

Michelle Chin, age 16: "Parents do not understand that teenagers need to find out who they are, which means a lot of experimenting, a lot of mood swings, a lot of emotions and awkwardness. Like any teenager, I am facing an identity crisis. I am still trying to figure out whether I am a Chinese American or an American with Asian eyes."

How Would You...? As a human development and family studies professional, how would you design a community program that assists ethnic minority adolescents to develop a healthy bicultural identity?

Families

Adolescence typically alters the relationship between parents and their children (Bakken & Brown, 2010; Keijsers & Laird, 2010). Among the most important aspects of family relationships in adolescence are those that involve autonomy, attachment, and parent-adolescent conflict.

Autonomy and Attachment

With most adolescents, parents are likely to find themselves engaged in a delicate balancing act, weighing competing needs for autonomy and control, for independence and connection.

The Push for Autonomy

The typical adolescent's push for autonomy and responsibility puzzles and angers many parents. As parents see their teenager slipping from their grasp, they may have an urge to take stronger control. Heated emotional exchanges may ensue, with either side calling names, making threats, and doing whatever seems necessary to gain control. Parents may seem frustrated because they *expect* their teenager to heed their advice, to want to spend time with the family, and to grow up to do what is right. Most parents anticipate that their teenager will have some difficulty adjusting to the changes that adolescence brings, but few parents imagine and predict just how strong an adolescent's desires will be to spend time with peers or how intensely adolescents will want to show that it is they—not their parents—who are responsible for their successes and failures.

Adolescents' ability to attain autonomy and gain control over their behavior is acquired through appropriate adult reactions to their desire for control (Duncan & Sawyer, 2010; McElhaney & others, 2009; Sher-Censor, Parke, & Coltrane, 2010). At the onset of adolescence, the average individual does not have the knowledge to make appropriate or mature decisions in all areas of life. As the adolescent pushes for autonomy the wise adult relinquishes control in those areas where the adolescent can make reasonable decisions, but continues to guide the adolescent to make reasonable decisions in areas in which the adolescent's knowledge is more limited. Gradually adolescents acquire the ability to make mature decisions on their own.

Gender differences characterize autonomy-granting in adolescence. Boys are given more independence than girls. In one study, this was especially true in U.S. families with a traditional gender-role orientation (Bumpus, Crouter, & McHale, 2001). Also, Latino parents protect and monitor their daughters more closely than is the case for non-Latino parents (Allen & others, 2008; Updegraff & others, 2010).

The Role of Attachment

Recall from Chapter 4 that one of the most widely discussed aspects of socioemotional development in infancy is secure attachment to caregivers. In the past decade, researchers have explored whether secure attachment also might be an important concept in adolescents' relationships with their parents (Laursen & Collins, 2009; Rosenthal & Kobak, 2010). For example, Joseph Allen and his colleagues (2009) found that adolescents who were securely attached at age 14 were more likely to report that they were in an exclusive relationship, comfortable with intimacy in relationships, and increasing financial independence at age 21. In a recent analysis, it was concluded that the most consistent outcomes of secure attachment in adolescence involve positive peer relations and development of the adolescent's emotion regulation capacities (Allen & Miga, 2010).

Parent-Adolescent Conflict

Although parent-adolescent conflict increases in early adolescence, it does not reach the tumultuous proportions G. Stanley Hall envisioned at the beginning of the 20th century (Laursen & Collins, 2009). Rather, much of the conflict involves the everyday events of family life, such as keeping a bedroom clean, dressing neatly, getting home by a certain time, and not talking forever on the phone. The conflicts rarely involve major dilemmas such as drugs or delinquency.

Conflict with parents often escalates during early adolescence, remains somewhat stable during the high school years, and then lessens as the adolescent reaches 17 to 20 years of age. Parent-adolescent relationships become more positive if adolescents go away to college than if they attend college while living at home (Sullivan & Sullivan, 1980).

What are strategies parents can use to guide adolescents in effectively handling their increased motivation for autonomy?

Stacey Christensen, age 16: "I am lucky enough to have open communication with my parents. Whenever I am in need or just need to talk, my parents are there for me. My advice to parents is to let your teens grow at their own pace, be open with them so that you can be there for them. We need guidance, our parents need to help but not be too overwhelming."

FAMILIES

255

Figure 10.2 Old and New Models of Parent-Adolescent Relationships

The everyday conflicts that characterize parent-adolescent relationships may actually serve a positive developmental function. These minor disputes and negotiations facilitate the adolescent's transition from being dependent on parents to becoming an autonomous individual. Recognizing that conflict and negotiation can serve a positive developmental function can tone down parental hostility.

The old model of parent-adolescent relationships suggested that as adolescents mature they detach themselves from parents and move into a world of autonomy apart from parents. The old model also suggested that parent-adolescent conflict is intense and stressful throughout adolescence. The new model emphasizes that parents serve as important attachment figures and support systems while adolescents explore a wider, more complex social world. The new model also emphasizes that, in most families, parent-adolescent conflict is moderate rather than severe and that the everyday negotiations and minor disputes not only are normal but also can serve the positive developmental function of helping the adolescent make the transition from childhood dependency to adult independence (see Figure 10.2).

Still, a high degree of conflict characterizes some parent-adolescent relationships. And this prolonged, intense conflict is associated with various adolescent problems: movement out of the home, juvenile delinquency, school dropout, pregnancy and early marriage, membership in religious cults, and drug abuse (Brook & others, 1990).

How Would You...? As a social worker, how would you counsel a mother who is experiencing stress about anticipated family conflicts as her child enters adolescence?

Peers

Peers play powerful roles in the lives of adolescents (Dishion & Piehler, 2009). When you think back to your own adolescent years, you probably recall many of your most enjoyable moments as experiences shared with peers. Peer relations undergo important changes in adolescence, including changes in friendships, peer groups, and the beginning of romantic relationships.

Friendships

For most children, being popular with their peers is a strong motivator. Beginning in early adolescence, however, teenagers typically prefer to have a smaller number of friendships that are more intense and intimate than those of young children.

Harry Stack Sullivan (1953) was the most influential theorist to discuss the importance of adolescent friendships. In contrast to other psychoanalytic theorists who focused almost exclusively on parent-child relationships, Sullivan argued that friends are also important in shaping the development of children and adolescents. Everyone, said Sullivan, has basic social needs, such as the need for tenderness (secure attachment), playful companionship, social acceptance, intimacy, and sexual relations. Whether or not these needs are fulfilled largely determines our emotional well-being. For example, if the need for playful companionship goes unmet, then we become bored and depressed; if the need for social acceptance is not met, we suffer a lowered sense of self-worth.

During adolescence, said Sullivan, friends become increasingly important in meeting social needs. In particular, Sullivan argued that the need for intimacy intensifies during early adolescence, motivating teenagers to seek out close friends. If adolescents fail to forge such close friendships, they experience loneliness and a reduced sense of self-worth. The nature of relationships with friends during adolescence can foreshadow the quality of romantic relationships in emerging adulthood. For example, a longitudinal study revealed that having more secure relationships with close friends at age 16 was linked with more positive romantic relationships at age 20 to 23 (Simpson & others, 2007).

Many of Sullivan's ideas have withstood the test of time (Buhrmester & Chong, 2009). For example, adolescents report disclosing intimate and personal information to their friends more often than do younger children (Buhrmester, 1998) (see Figure 10.3). Adolescents also say they depend more on friends than on parents to satisfy their needs for companionship, reassurance of worth, and intimacy. The ups and downs of experiences with friends shape adolescents' well-being.

Although most adolescents develop friendships with individuals who are close to their own age, some adolescents become best friends with younger or older individuals. Adolescents who interact with older youth engage in deviant behavior more frequently, but it is not known whether the older youth guide younger adolescents toward deviant behavior or whether the younger adolescents were already prone to deviant behavior before they developed the friendship with the older youth.

What changes take place in friendship during the adolescent years?

Peer Groups

How extensive is peer pressure in adolescence? What roles do cliques and crowds play in adolescents' lives? As we see next, researchers have found that the standards of peer groups and the influence of crowds and cliques become increasingly important during adolescence.

Peer Pressure

Young adolescents conform more to peer standards than children do. Around the eighth and ninth grades, conformity to peers—especially to their antisocial standards—peaks (Brown & Larson, 2009). At this point, adolescents are most likely to go along with a peer to steal hubcaps off a car, draw graffiti on a wall, or steal cosmetics from a store counter. One study found that U.S. adolescents are more likely than Japanese adolescents to put pressure on their peers to resist parental influence (Rothbaum & others, 2000). Adolescents are more likely to conform to their peers when they are uncertain about their social identity and when they are in the presence of someone they perceive to have higher status than they do (Prinstein & Dodge, 2010; Prinstein & others, 2009).

Cliques and Crowds

Cliques and crowds assume more important roles in the lives of adolescents than children (Brown & Larson,

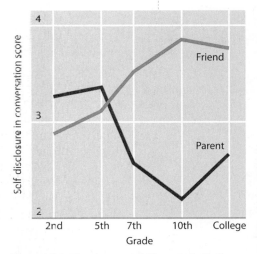

Figure 10.3 Developmental Changes in Self-Disclosing Conversations
Self-disclosing conversations with friends increased dramatically in adolescence while declining in an equally dramatic fashion with parents. However, self-disclosing conversations with parents began to pick up somewhat during the college years. The measure of self-disclosure involved a 5-point rating scale completed by the children and youth, with a higher score representing greater self-disclosure. The data shown represent the means for each age group.

2009). **Cliques** are small groups that range from 2 to about 12 individuals and average about 5 to 6 individuals. The clique members are usually of the same sex and about the same age.

Cliques can form because adolescents engage in similar activities, such as being in a club or on a sports team. Some cliques also form because of friendship. Several adolescents may form a clique because they have spent time with each other, share mutual interests, and enjoy each other's company. Not necessarily friends, they often develop a friendship if they stay in the clique. What do adolescents do in cliques? They share ideas and hang out together. Often they develop an in-group identity in which they believe that their clique is better than other cliques.

Crowds are larger than cliques and less personal. Adolescents are usually members of a crowd based on reputation, and they may or may not spend much time together. Many crowds are defined by the activities adolescents engage in (such as "jocks" who are good at sports or "druggies" who take drugs).

Dating and Romantic Relationships

Adolescents spend considerable time either dating or thinking about dating. Dating can be a form of recreation, a source of status, a setting for learning about close relationships, as well as a way of finding a mate.

Developmental Changes in Dating and Romantic Relationships

Three stages characterize the development of romantic relationships in adolescence (Connolly & McIssac, 2009):

1. *Entering into romantic attractions and affiliations at about age 11 to 13.* This initial stage is triggered by puberty. From age 11 to 13, adolescents become intensely interested in romance and it dominates many conversations with same-sex friends. Developing a crush on someone is common and the crush often is shared with a same-sex friend. Young adolescents may or may not interact with the individual who is the object of their infatuation. When dating occurs, it usually occurs in a group setting.

2. *Exploring romantic relationships at approximately age 14 to 16.* At this point in adolescence, two types of romantic involvement occur: (a) *Casual dating* emerges between individuals who are mutually attracted. These dating experiences are often short lived, last a few months at best, and usually endure only for a few weeks. (b) *Dating in groups* is common and reflects the importance of peers in adolescents' lives. Friends often act as a third-party facilitator of a potential dating relationship by communicating their friend's romantic interest and confirming whether the other person feels a similar attraction.

3. *Consolidating dyadic romantic bonds at about age 17 to 19.* At the end of the high school years, more serious romantic relationships develop. This is characterized by strong emotional bonds more closely resembling those in adult romantic relationships. These bonds often are more stable and enduring than earlier bonds, typically lasting one year or more.

How Would You...?
As a psychologist, how would you explain the risks of dating and romantic relationships during early adolescence?

Two variations on these stages in the development of romantic relationships in adolescence involve early and late bloomers (Connolly & McIssac, 2009). *Early bloomers* include 15 to 20 percent of 11- to 13-year-olds who say that they currently are in a romantic relationship and 35 percent who indicate that they have had some prior experience in romantic relationships. *Late bloomers* comprise approximately 10 percent of 17- to 19-year-olds who say that they have had no experience with romantic relationships and another 15 percent who report that they have not engaged in any romantic relationships that lasted more than 4 months.

What are some
developmental
changes in dating
and romantic
relationships in
adolescence?

How Would You...?
As a human development and family studies professional, how would you explain to parents the developmental challenges faced by a gay or lesbian adolescent?

Dating in Gay and Lesbian Youth

Recently, researchers have begun to study romantic relationships in gay and lesbian youth (Diamond, Fagundes, & Butterworth, 2011; Diamond & Savin-Williams, 2009). Many sexual minority youth date other-sex peers, which can help them to clarify their sexual orientation or disguise it from others (Diamond, Fagundes, & Butterworth, 2011). Most gay and lesbian youth have had some same-sex sexual experience, often with peers who are "experimenting," and then go on to a primarily heterosexual orientation (Diamond & Savin-Willliams, 2009).

Sociocultural Contexts and Dating

The sociocultural context exerts a powerful influence on adolescents' dating patterns (Crissey, 2009) This influence may be seen in differences in dating patterns among ethnic groups within the United States. Values, religious beliefs, and traditions often dictate the age at which dating begins, how much freedom in dating is allowed, whether dates must be chaperoned by adults or parents, and the roles of males and females in dating. For example, Latino and Asian American cultures have more conservative standards regarding adolescent dating than does the Anglo-American culture. Dating may become a source of conflict within a family if the parents have immigrated from cultures in which dating begins at a late age, little freedom in dating is allowed, dates are chaperoned, and dating is especially restricted for adolescent girls. When immigrant adolescents choose to adopt the ways of the dominant U.S. culture (such as unchaperoned dating), they often clash with parents and extended-family members who have more traditional values.

Dating and Adjustment

Researchers have linked dating and romantic relationships with various measures of how well adjusted adolescents are (Connolly & McIssac, 2009; Eklund, Kerr, & Stattin, 2010). For example, a recent study of 200 10th graders revealed that the more romantic experiences they had, the more they

What are some ethnic variations in dating during adolescence?

reported higher levels of social acceptance, friendship competence, and romantic competence; however, having more romantic experience also was linked to a higher level of substance use, delinquency, and sexual behavior (Furman, Low, & Ho, 2009). A recent study of adolescent girls found that those who engaged in *co-rumination* (excessive discussion of problems with friends) were more likely to be involved in a romantic relationship, and together co-rumination and romantic involvement predicted an increase in depressive symptoms (Starr & Davila, 2009).

Dating and romantic relationships at an early age can be especially problematic (Connolly & McIssac, 2009). Researchers have found that early dating and "going with" someone are linked with adolescent pregnancy and problems at home and school (Florsheim, Moore, & Edgington, 2003).

Culture and Adolescent Development

We live in an increasingly diverse world, one in which there is increasing contact between adolescents from different cultures and ethnic groups. In this section, we explore these differences as they relate to adolescents. We explore how adolescents in various cultures spend their time, and some of the rites of passage they undergo. We also examine how ethnicity and the media affect U.S. adolescents and their development.

Cross-Cultural Comparisons

How Would You...?
As a health-care professional, how would you explain to policy makers and insurance providers the importance of cultural context when creating guidelines for adolescent health coverage?

What traditions remain for adolescents around the globe? What circumstances are changing adolescents' lives?

Traditions and Changes in Adolescence Around the Globe

Depending on the culture being observed, adolescence may involve many different experiences (Larson, Wilson, & Rickman, 2009).

Health Adolescent health and well-being have improved in some respects but not in others. Overall, fewer adolescents around the world die from infectious diseases and malnutrition now than in the past (UNICEF, 2011). However, a number of adolescent health-compromising behaviors (especially illicit drug use and unprotected sex) are increasing in frequency. Extensive increases in the rates of HIV in adolescents have occurred in many sub-Saharan countries (UNICEF, 2011).

Gender Around the world, the experiences of male and female adolescents continue to be quite different (Kitayama, 2011; Larson, Wilson, & Rickman, 2009). Except in a few regions, such as Japan, the Philippines, and Western countries, males have far

Asian Indian adolescents in a marriage ceremony

Muslim school in Middle East with boys only

Street youth in Rio de Janeiro

greater access to educational opportunities than females (UNICEF, 2011). In many countries, adolescent females have less freedom than males to pursue a variety of careers and engage in various leisure activities. Gender differences in sexual expression are widespread, especially in India, Southeast Asia, Latin America, and Arab countries where there are far more restrictions on the sexual activity of adolescent females than on males. These gender differences do appear to be narrowing over time, however. In some countries, educational and career opportunities for women are expanding, and control over adolescent girls' romantic and sexual relationships is weakening.

Family In some countries, adolescents grow up in closely knit families with extensive extended-kin networks that retain a traditional way of life. For example, in Arab countries, "adolescents are taught strict codes of conduct and loyalty" (Brown & Larson, 2002, p. 6). However, in Western countries such as the United States, parenting is less authoritarian than in the past, and much larger numbers of adolescents are growing up in divorced families and stepfamilies.

In many countries around the world, current trends "include greater family mobility, migration to urban areas, family members working in distant cities or countries, smaller families, fewer extended-family households, and increases in mothers' employment" (Brown & Larson, 2002, p. 7). Unfortunately, many of these changes may reduce the ability of families to spend time with their adolescents.

Peers Some cultures give peers a stronger role in adolescence than others (Brown & Larson, 2002). In most Western nations, peers figure prominently in adolescents' lives, in some cases taking on roles that are otherwise assumed by parents. Among street youth in South America, the peer network serves as a surrogate family that supports survival in dangerous and stressful settings. In other regions of the world, such as in Arab countries, peer relations are restricted, especially for girls (Booth, 2002).

Adolescents' lives, then, are characterized by a combination of change and tradition. Researchers have found both similarities and differences in the experiences of adolescents in different countries (Larson, Wilson, & Rickman, 2009).

Rites of Passage

Another variation in the experiences of adolescents in different cultures is whether the adolescents go through a rite of passage. Some societies have elaborate ceremonies that signal the adolescent's move to maturity and achievement of adult status (Kottak, 2009). A **rite of passage** is a ceremony or ritual that marks an individual's transition from one status to another. Most rites of passage focus on the transition to adult status. In many primitive cultures, rites of passage are the avenue through which adolescents gain access to sacred adult practices, to knowledge, and to sexuality. These rites often involve dramatic practices intended to facilitate the adolescent's separation from the immediate family, especially the mother. The transformation is usually characterized by some form of ritual death and rebirth, or by means of contact with the spiritual world. Bonds are forged between the adolescent and the adult instructors through shared rituals, hazards, and secrets to allow the adolescent to enter the adult world. This kind of ritual provides a forceful and discontinuous entry into the adult world at a time when the adolescent is perceived to be ready for the change.

rite of passage A ceremony or ritual that marks an individual's transition from one status to another. Most rites of passage focus on the transition to adult status.

These Congolese Kota boys painted their faces as part of a rite of passage to adulthood. *What rites of passage do American adolescents have?*

An especially rich tradition of rites of passage for adolescents has prevailed in African cultures, especially sub-Saharan Africa. Under the influence of Western industrialized culture, many of these rites are disappearing today, although they are still prevalent in locations where formal education is not readily available.

Do we have such rites of passage for American adolescents? We certainly do not have universal formal ceremonies that mark the passage from adolescence to adulthood. Certain religious and social groups do, however, have initiation ceremonies that indicate that an advance in maturity has been reached: the Jewish bar and bat mitzvah, the Catholic confirmation, and social debuts, for example. School graduation ceremonies come the closest to being culture-wide rites of passage in the United States. The high school graduation ceremony has become nearly universal for middle-class adolescents and increasing numbers of adolescents from low-income backgrounds.

How Would You...?

As an educator, how would you modify high school graduation to be a more meaningful rite of passage for adolescents in the United States?

Ethnicity

Earlier in this chapter we explored the identity development of ethnic minority adolescents. Here, we further examine immigration and the relationship between ethnicity and socioeconomic status.

Immigration

Relatively high rates of immigration are contributing to the growth of ethnic minorities in the United States. Immigrants often experience stressors uncommon to or less prominent among longtime residents such as language barriers, dislocations and separations from support networks, changes in socioeconomic status (SES), and the dual struggle to preserve identity and to acculturate (Ho & Berman, 2010; Tamis-LeMonda & McFadden, 2010).

Many of the families that have immigrated in recent decades to the United States, such as Mexican Americans and Asian Americans, come from collectivist cultures in which family obligation is strong (Fuligni, Hughes, & Way, 2009). For adolescents this family obligation may take the form of assisting parents in their occupations and contributing to the family's welfare (Tamis-LeMonda & McFadden, 2010). This often means helping out in jobs in construction, gardening, cleaning, or restaurants. In some cases, the long hours immigrant youth work in such jobs can be detrimental to their academic achievement.

Jason Leonard age 15: "I want America to know that most of us Black teens are not troubled people from broken homes and headed to jail.... In my relationships with my parents, we show respect for each other and we have values in our house. We have traditions we celebrate together, including Christmas and Kwanzaa."

Ethnicity and Socioeconomic Status

Much of the research on ethnic minority adolescents has failed to tease apart the influences of ethnicity and socioeconomic status (SES). These can interact in ways that exaggerate the influence of ethnicity because ethnic minority individuals are overrepresented in the lower socioeconomic levels of American society. Consequently, researchers too often have given ethnic explanations for aspects of adolescent development that were largely due instead to SES.

Not all ethnic minority families are poor. However, poverty contributes to the stressful life experiences of many ethnic minority adolescents (Kao & Turney, 2010; McLoyd & others, 2009). Thus, many ethnic minority adolescents experience a double disadvantage: (1) prejudice, discrimination, and bias because of their ethnic minority status; and (2) the stressful effects of poverty (Seaton & others, 2010).

Although some ethnic minority youth come from middle-income backgrounds, economic advantage does not entirely enable them to escape the prejudice, discrimination, and bias associated with being a member of an ethnic minority group (Bennett, 2011; Koppelman & Goodhart, 2011). Even Japanese Americans, who are often characterized as a "model minority" because of their strong achievement orientation and family cohesiveness, still experience stress associated with ethnic minority status.

juvenile delinquent An adolescent who breaks the law or engages in behavior that is considered illegal.

The Media

The culture adolescents experience involves not only cultural values, SES, and ethnicity, but also media influences (Kistler & others, 2010). A major trend in the use of technology is the dramatic increase in media multitasking (Roberts, Henriksen, & Foehr, 2009). A recent estimate indicates that when media multitasking is taken into account, 8- to 18-year-olds use media an average of 8 hours per day (Roberts & Foehr, 2008). For example, it is not unusual for adolescents to simultaneously watch TV while text messaging their friends. In some cases, adolescents engage in media multitasking—such as text messaging, listening to an iPOD, and updating a YouTube site—at the same time as doing homework. It is hard to imagine how that can be a good thing for doing homework efficiently, although there is little research on media multitasking.

Television viewing and video-game playing often peak in early adolescence and then begin to decline at some point in late adolescence in response to competing media and the demands of school and social activities (Roberts, Henriksen, & Foehr, 2009). As their TV viewing and video-game playing decline, older adolescents spend more time listening to music and using the computer.

Youth throughout the world are increasingly using the Internet (Mikami & others, 2010; Pujazacn-Zazik & Park, 2010). Special concerns have emerged about children's and adolescents' access to information on the Internet, which has been largely unregulated. A national survey indicated that 42 percent of U.S. 10- to 17-year-olds had been exposed to Internet pornography in the last 12 months, with 66 percent of the exposure being unwanted (Wolak, Mitchell, & Finkelhor, 2007). Also, there has been a substantial increase in youth harassment and cyberbullying on the Internet (Subrahmanyam & Greenfield, 2008). Parents need to monitor and regulate their adolescents' use of the Internet. For example, a recent study revealed that many Internet sex crimes against minors involved social networking sites in some way (Mitchell & others, 2010). Criminals used the social networking sites to initiate sexual relationships, disseminate information or photos of the victim, and to contact the victim's friends.

The digitally mediated social environment of adolescents and emerging adults includes e-mail, chat rooms, instant messaging, blogs, social networking sites such as Facebook and MySpace, videosharing and photosharing, multiplayer online computer games, and virtual worlds (Uhls & Greenfield, 2009). Most of these digitally mediated social interactions began on computers but also have recently shifted to cell phones, especially smart phones (Roberts, Henrikson, & Foehr, 2009).

Is multitasking beneficial or distracting for adolescents?

Adolescent Problems

In Chapter 9, we described several adolescent problems: substance abuse, sexually transmitted infections, and eating disorders. In this chapter, we examine the problems of juvenile delinquency, depression, and suicide. We also explore interrelationships among adolescent problems and how such problems can be prevented or remedied.

Juvenile Delinquency

The label **juvenile delinquent** is applied to an adolescent who breaks the law or engages in behavior that is considered illegal. Like other categories of disorders, juvenile delinquency is a broad concept; legal infractions range from littering to murder. Because the adolescent technically becomes a juvenile delinquent only after being judged guilty of a crime by a court of law, official records do not accurately reflect the number of illegal acts juvenile delinquents commit.

Males are more likely to engage in delinquency than females. However, delinquency caseloads involving females increased from 19 percent in 1985 to 27 percent in 2005 (Puzzanchera & Sickmund, 2008).

Delinquency rates among minority groups and lower-socioeconomic-status youth are especially high in proportion to the overall population of these groups. However, such groups have less influence over the judicial decision-making process in the United States and, therefore, may be judged delinquent more readily than their White, middle-socioeconomic-status counterparts.

Causes of Delinquency

What causes delinquency? Many causes have been proposed, including heredity, identity problems, community influences, and family experiences. Erik Erikson (1968), for example, argues that adolescents whose development has restricted them from acceptable social roles, or made them feel that they cannot measure up to the demands placed on them, may choose a negative identity. Adolescents with a negative identity may find support for their delinquent image among peers, reinforcing the negative identity. For Erikson, delinquency is an attempt to establish an identity, although a negative one.

Although delinquency is less exclusively a phenomenon of lower socioeconomic status (SES) than it was in the past, some characteristics of lower-SES culture might promote delinquency (Ghazarian & Roche, 2010). The norms of many lower-SES peer groups and gangs are antisocial, or counterproductive, to the goals and norms of society at large. Getting into and staying out of trouble are prominent features of life for some adolescents in low-income neighborhoods (Thio, 2010). Being "tough" and "masculine" are high-status traits for lower-SES boys, and these traits are often measured by the adolescents' success in performing and getting away with delinquent acts. Furthermore, adolescents in communities with high crime rates observe many models who engage in criminal activities. These communities may be characterized by poverty, unemployment, and feelings of alienation toward the middle class. Quality schooling, educational funding, and organized neighborhood activities may be lacking in these communities.

Certain characteristics of family support systems are also associated with delinquency (Farrington, 2009). Parental monitoring of adolescents is especially important in determining whether an adolescent becomes a delinquent. For example, a study of families living in high-risk neighborhoods revealed that parents' lack of knowledge of their young adolescents' whereabouts was linked to whether the adolescents engaged in delinquency later in adolescence (Lahey & others, 2008). A recent study of low-income urban families found that engaged parenting was linked with less youth delinquency (Ghazarian & Roche, 2010). Researchers also have found that having an older sibling and friends who are delinquents can have a strong influence on whether an adolescent becomes a delinquent (Brown & Larson, 2009).

Peers and schools also can influence whether adolescents engage in juvenile delinquency (Glaser, Shelton, & van den Bree, 2010). One study found that associating with delinquent peers increased the risk of becoming delinquent (Brown & Larson, 2009), while another discovered that having academically oriented friends reduced the risk of becoming delinquent (Crosnoe & others, 2008). A recent study also revealed that young adolescents' school connectedness buffered the effects of negative family relations and poor self-control on the development of conduct problems (Loukas, Roalson, & Herrera, 2010).

Rodney Hammond is an individual whose goal is to help at-risk adolescents, such as juvenile delinquents, cope more effectively with their lives. Read about his work in "Careers in Life-Span Development."

How Would You...?
As a social worker, how would you apply your knowledge of juvenile delinquency and adolescent development to improve the juvenile justice system?

Rodney Hammond, Health Psychologist

Rodney Hammond described his college experiences:

> When I started as an undergraduate at the University of Illinois, Champaign-Urbana, I hadn't decided on my major. But to help finance my education, I took a part-time job in a child development research program sponsored by the psychology department. There, I observed inner-city children in settings designed to enhance their learning. I saw firsthand the contribution psychology can make, and I knew I wanted to be a psychologist. (American Psychological Association, 2003, p. 26)

Rodney Hammond went on to obtain a doctorate in school and community psychology with a focus on children's development. For a number of years, he trained clinical psychologists at Wright State University in Ohio and directed a program to reduce violence in ethnic minority youth. There, he and his associates taught at-risk youth how to use social skills to effectively manage conflict and to recognize situations that could lead to violence. Today, Rodney is Director of Violence Prevention at the Centers for Disease Control and Prevention in Atlanta Georgia. Rodney says that if you are interested in people and problem solving, psychology is a wonderful way to put these together.

School psychology was one of Rodney Hammond's doctoral concentrations. School psychologists focus on improving

Rodney Hammond

the psychological and intellectual well-being of elementary, middle/junior, and high school students. They give psychological tests, interview students and their parents, consult with teachers, and may provide counseling to students and their families. They may work in a centralized office in a school district or in one or more schools. School psychologists usually have a master's or doctoral degree in school psychology. In graduate school, they take courses in counseling, assessment, learning, and other areas of education and psychology.

Depression and Suicide

What is the nature of depression in adolescence? What causes an adolescent to commit suicide?

Depression

How extensive is depression in adolescence? Rates of ever experiencing major depressive disorder range from 15 to 20 percent for adolescents (Graber & Sontag, 2009). By about age 15, adolescent females have a rate of depression that is twice that of adolescent males. Among the reasons for this gender difference are that females tend to ruminate in their depressed mood and amplify it; females' self-images, especially their body images, are more negative than males'; females face more discrimination than males do; and puberty occurs earlier for girls than for boys (Nolen-Hoeksema, 2011). As a result, girls experience a piling up of changes and life experiences in the middle school years that can increase depression (Hammen, 2009).

Certain family factors place adolescents at risk for developing depression (Liem, Cavell, & Lustig, 2010; Waller & Rose, 2010). These include having a depressed parent, emotionally unavailable parents, parents who have high marital

conflict, and parents with financial problems. A recent study also revealed that mother-adolescent co-rumination, especially when focused on their mother's problems, were linked to adolescents' depression (Waller & Rose, 2010).

Poor peer relationships also are associated with adolescent depression (Kistner & others, 2006). Not having a close relationship with a best friend, having less contact with friends, having friends who are depressed, and experiencing peer rejection all increase depressive tendencies in adolescents (Brengden & others, 2010). As we saw earlier in the chapter, problems in adolescent romantic relationships can also trigger depressive symptoms, especially for girls (Starr & Davila, 2009).

What are some characteristics of adolescents who become depressed? What are some factors that are linked with suicide attempts by adolescents?

Suicide

Suicide behavior is rare in childhood but escalates in adolescence and then increases further in emerging adulthood (Park & others, 2006). Suicide is the third leading cause of death in 10- to 19-year-olds today in the United States (Piruccello, 2010). After increasing to high levels in the 1990s, suicide rates in adolescents have declined in recent years.

Although a suicide threat should always be taken seriously, far more adolescents contemplate or attempt it unsuccessfully than actually commit it. In a national study, in 2005, 17 percent of U.S. high school students said that they had seriously considered or attempted suicide in the last 12 months (Eaton & others, 2006). Females were more likely to attempt suicide than males, but males were more likely to succeed in committing suicide. Males use more lethal means, such as guns, in their suicide attempts, whereas adolescent females are more likely to cut their wrists or take an overdose of sleeping pills—methods less likely to result in death.

How Would You...?

As a psychologist, how would you talk with an adolescent who has just threatened suicide?

What is the psychological profile of the suicidal adolescent? Suicidal adolescents often have depressive symptoms (Nrugham, Holen, & Sund, 2010). Although not all depressed adolescents are suicidal, depression is the most frequently cited factor associated with adolescent suicide (Bethell & Rhoades, 2008). Further, a study indicated that adolescents who used alcohol while they were sad or depressed were at risk for attempting suicide (Schilling & others, 2009). And a national study found that these factors were linked with suicide risk: depressive symptoms, a sense of hopelessness, engaging in suicide ideation, having a family background of suicidal behavior, and having friends with a history of suicidal behavior (Thompson, Kuruwita, & Foster, 2009). And a recent study revealed that frequent, escalating stress, especially at home, was linked with suicide attempts in young Latinas (Zayas & others, 2010).

The Interrelation of Problems and Successful Prevention/Intervention Programs

We have described some of the major adolescent problems in this chapter and in Chapter 9, including substance abuse; juvenile delinquency; school-related problems, such as dropping out of school; adolescent pregnancy and sexually transmitted infections; eating disorders; depression; and suicide. The four problems that affect the most adolescents are (1) drug abuse, (2) juvenile delinquency, (3) sexual problems, and (4) school-related problems (Dryfoos, 1990; Dryfoos & Barkin, 2006). The adolescents most at risk have more than one of these problems.

Researchers are increasingly finding that problem behaviors in adolescence are interrelated (Hipwell & others, 2010; McMurran & others, 2010). For example, heavy substance abuse is related to early sexual activity, lower grades, dropping out of school, and delinquency (Mason, Hitchings, & Spoth, 2007). Early initiation of sexual activity is associated with the use of cigarettes and alcohol, the use of marijuana and other illicit drugs, lower grades, dropping out of school, and delinquency (Aalsma & others, 2010). Delinquency is related to early sexual activity, early pregnancy, substance abuse, and dropping out of school (Chew & others, 2010). As many as 10 percent of adolescents in the United States have been estimated to engage in all four of these problem behaviors (for example, adolescents who have dropped out of school are behind in their grade level, are users of heavy drugs, regularly use cigarettes and marijuana, and are sexually active but do not use contraception). In 1990, it was estimated that another 15 percent of high-risk youth engage in two or three of the four main problem behaviors (Dryfoos, 1990). Recently, this figure was increased to 20 percent of all U.S. adolescents (Dryfoos & Barkin, 2006).

A review of the programs that have been successful in preventing or reducing adolescent problems found these common components (Dryfoos, 1990; Dryfoos & Barkin, 2006):

1. *Intensive individualized attention.* In successful programs, high-risk adolescents are attached to a responsible adult, who gives the adolescent attention and deals with the adolescent's specific needs. This theme occurs in a number of programs. In a successful substance-abuse program, a student assistance counselor is available full-time for individual counseling and referral for treatment.

2. *Community-wide multiagency collaborative approaches.* The basic philosophy of community-wide programs is that a number of different programs and services have to be in place. In one successful substance-abuse program, a community-wide health promotion campaign has been implemented that uses local media and community education, in concert with a substance-abuse curriculum in the schools.

3. *Early identification and intervention.* Reaching younger children and their families before children develop problems, or at the beginning of their problems, is a successful strategy (Dodge & McCourt, 2010). One preschool program serves as an excellent model for the prevention of delinquency, pregnancy, substance abuse, and dropping out of school. Operated by the High/Scope Foundation in Ypsilanti, Michigan, the Perry Preschool has had a long-term positive impact on its students. This enrichment program, directed by David Weikart, serves disadvantaged African American children. They attend a high-quality, two-year preschool program and receive weekly home visits from program personnel. Based on official police records, by age 19, individuals who had attended the Perry Preschool program were less likely to have been arrested and reported fewer adult offenses than a control group did. The Perry Preschool students also were less likely to drop out of school, and teachers rated their social behavior as more competent than that of a control group who had not received the enriched preschool experience (High/Scope Resource, 2005).

How are problems interrelated in adolescence? Which components of programs have been successful in preventing or reducing adolescent problems?

Wardle, & Steptoe, 2009). The young adults' life satisfaction was positively related to not smoking, exercising regularly, using sun protection, eating fruit and limiting fat intake, but was not related to consuming alcohol and fiber intake.

Eating and Weight

In Chapters 5 and 7, we discussed aspects of overweight children's lives, and in Chapter 9 we examined the eating disorders of anorexia nervosa and bulimia nervosa in adolescence. Now, we turn our attention to obesity and the extensive preoccupation that many young adults have with dieting.

Obesity Obesity is a serious and pervasive health problem for many individuals (Howell, 2010; Schiff, 2011). The prevalence of obesity in U.S. adults 20 years of age and older increased from 19 percent in 1997 to 33 percent in 2006 (Centers for Disease Control and Prevention, 2008). In this survey, obesity was defined as having a body mass index (which takes into account height and weight) of 30 or more. The National Health and Nutrition Examination Survey (NHANES) also projected that 86 percent of Americans will be overweight or obese by 2030 if current weight trends continue (Beydoun & Wang, 2009).

Obesity is linked to increased risk of hypertension, diabetes, and cardiovascular disease (Granger & others, 2010; Wardlaw & Smith, 2011). For individuals who are 30 percent overweight, the probability of dying in middle adulthood increases by about 40 percent. Overweight and obesity also are associated with mental health problems. For example, a recent meta-analysis revealed that overweight women were more likely to be depressed than women who were not overweight, but no significant difference was found for men (de Wit & others, 2010).

Dieting Ironically, although obesity is on the rise, dieting has become an obsession with many Americans (Schiff, 2011; Thompson, Manore, & Vaughan, 2011). Although many Americans regularly embark on a diet, few are successful in keeping weight off long term (Saquib & others, 2009). A recent research review of the long-term outcomes of calorie-restricting diets revealed that overall one-third to two-thirds of dieters regain more weight than they lost on their diets (Mann & others, 2007). However, some individuals do lose weight and maintain the loss (Yancy & others, 2009). How often this occurs and whether some diet programs work better than others are still open questions.

What we do know about losing weight is that the most effective programs include exercise (Fahey, Insel, & Roth, 2011). A recent research review concluded that adults who engaged in diet-plus-exercise programs lost more weight than those who followed diet-only programs (Wu & others, 2009). A study of approximately 2,000 U.S. adults found that exercising 30 minutes a day, planning meals, and weighing themselves daily were the main strategies used by successful dieters compared with unsuccessful dieters (Kruger, Blanck, & Gillespie, 2006) (see Figure 11.2).

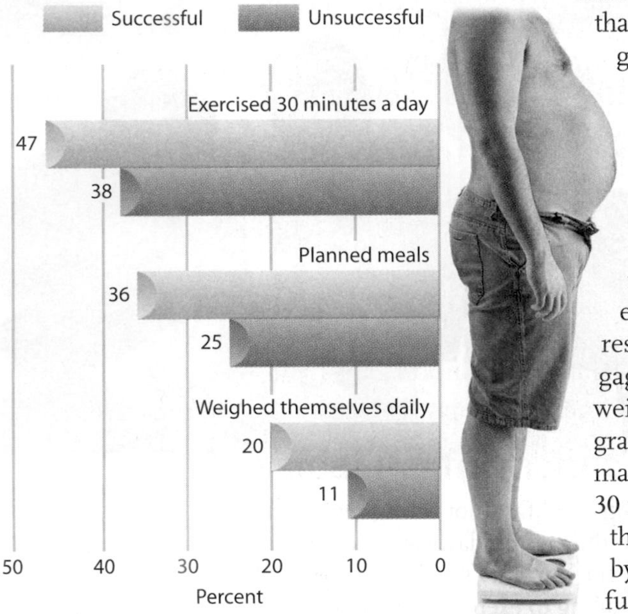

How Would You...?
As a health-care professional, how would you counsel young women of normal weight to accept their body image and set point for weight management?

How Would You...? As a health-care professional, how would you design a community education program to emphasize the importance of regular exercise for young adults?

Figure 11.2
Comparison of Strategies of Successful and Unsuccessful Dieters

Successful   Unsuccessful

Exercised 30 minutes a day
47
38

Planned meals
36
25

Weighed themselves daily
20
11

50 40 30 20 10 0
Percent

Regular Exercise

One of the main reasons that health experts want people to exercise is that it helps to prevent diseases, such as heart disease and diabetes (Hales, 2011;

Wardlaw & Smith, 2011). Many health experts recommend that young adults engage in 30 minutes or more of aerobic exercise a day, preferably every day. **Aerobic exercise** is sustained exercise—jogging, swimming, or cycling, for example—that stimulates heart and lung activity. Most health experts recommend that you raise your heart rate to at least 60 percent of your maximum heart rate. Only about one-fifth of adults, however, are active at these recommended levels of physical activity.

aerobic exercise Sustained exercise (such as jogging, swimming, or cycling) that stimulates heart and lung activity.

Researchers have found that exercise benefits not only physical health, but mental health as well (Donatelle, 2011; Shaw, Clark, & Wagenmakers, 2010). In particular, exercise improves self-concept and reduces anxiety and depression (Sylvia & others, 2009). Meta-analyses have shown that exercise can be as effective in reducing depression as psychotherapy (Richardson & others, 2005).

Substance Abuse

In Chapter 9, we explored substance abuse in adolescence. Fortunately, by the time individuals reach their mid-twenties, many have reduced their use of alcohol and drugs (Bachman & others, 2002). As in adolescence, male college students and young adults are more likely to take drugs than their female counterparts (Johnston & others, 2008). A recent study revealed that only 20 percent of college students reported that they abstain from drinking alcohol (Huang & others, 2009).

Heavy binge drinking often increases in college, and it can take its toll on students (Fields, 2010). Chronic binge drinking is more common among college men than women and students living away from home, especially in fraternity houses (Schulenberg & others, 2000).

In a national survey of drinking patterns on 140 campuses (Wechsler & others, 1994), almost half of the binge drinkers reported problems that included missing classes, sustaining physical injuries, experiencing troubles with police, and having unprotected sex. For example, binge-drinking college students were 11 times more likely to fall behind in school, 10 times more likely to drive after drinking, and twice as likely to have unprotected sex than college students who did not binge drink. Also, one study found that after an evening of binge drinking memory retrieval was significantly impaired during the alcohol hangover the next morning (Verster & others, 2002). A recent study revealed that only 20 percent of college students reported that they abstain from drinking alcohol (Huang & others, 2009).

Drinking alcohol before going out—called *pregaming*—has become common among college students. A recent study revealed that almost two-thirds of students on one campus had pregamed at least once in a two-week period (DeJong, DeRicco, & Schneider, 2010). Another recent study found that two-thirds of 18- to 24-year-old women on one college pregamed (Read, Merrill, & Bytschkow, 2010). Drinking games, in which the goal is to become intoxicated, also have become common on college campuses (Cameron & others, 2010; Ham & others, 2010). Higher levels of alcohol use have been consistently linked to higher rates of sexual risk taking, such as engaging in casual sex, sex without contraceptives, and sexual assaults (Lawyer & others, 2010; White & others, 2009).

A special concern is the increase in binge drinking by females during emerging adulthood (Davis & others, 2010; Smith & Berger, 2010). In a national longitudinal study, binge drinking by 19- to 22-year-old women increased from 28 percent in 1995 to 34 percent in 2007 (Johnston & others, 2008).

When does binge drinking peak during development? A longitudinal study revealed that binge drinking peaks at about 21 to 22 years of age and then declines through the remainder of the twenties (Bachman & others, 2002) (see Figure 11.3).

How Would You...?

As a social worker, how would you apply your understanding of binge drinking to develop a program to encourage responsible alcohol use on college campuses?

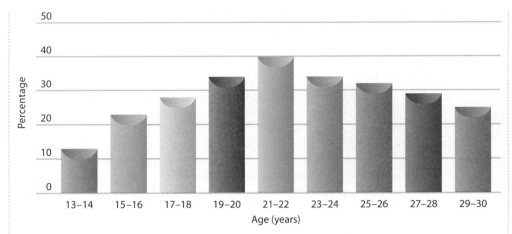

Figure 11.3 Binge Drinking in the Adolescence–Early Adulthood Transition
Note that the percentage of individuals engaging in binge drinking peaked at 21 or 22 years of age and then began to gradually decline through the remainder of the twenties. Binge drinking was defined as having five or more alcoholic drinks in a row in the past two weeks.

Sexuality

In Chapter 9, we explored how adolescents develop a sexual identity and become sexually active. What happens to their sexuality in adulthood?

Sexual Activity in Emerging Adulthood

At the beginning of emerging adulthood (age 18), surveys indicate that slightly more than 60 percent of individuals have experienced sexual intercourse, but by the end of emerging adulthood (age 25), most individuals have had sexual intercourse (Lefkowitz & Gillen, 2006). Also, the average age of marriage in the United States is currently 27 for males and 26 for females (Popenoe & Whitehead, 2006). Thus, emerging adulthood is a time during which most individuals are "both sexually active and unmarried" (Lefkowitz & Gillen, 2006, p. 235).

Patterns of heterosexual behavior for males and females in emerging adulthood include the following (Lefkowitz & Gillen, 2006): (1) Males have more casual sexual partners, and females report being more selective about their choice of a sexual partner. (2) Casual sex is more common in emerging adulthood than in young adulthood. One study indicated that 30 percent of emerging adults said they had "hooked up" (had casual sex) with someone and had sexual intercourse during college (Paul, McManus, & Hayes, 2000).

Sexual Orientation and Behavior

Obtaining accurate information about such a private activity as sexual behavior is not easy (Carroll, 2010). The best information we currently have comes from what is often referred to as the 1994 Sex in America survey. In this well-designed, comprehensive study of American adults' sexual patterns, Robert Michael and his colleagues (1994) interviewed more than 3,000 people from 18 to 59 years of age who were randomly selected, a sharp contrast from earlier samples that were based on unrepresentative groups of volunteers.

Heterosexual Attitudes and Behavior

Here are some of the key findings from the 1994 Sex in America survey:

- Americans tend to fall into three categories: One-third have sex twice a week or more, one-third a few times a month, and one-third a few times a year or not at all.

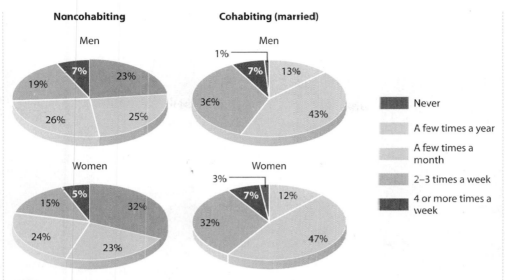

Figure 11.4 The Sex in America Survey

The percentages show noncohabiting and cohabiting (married) males' and females' responses to the question "How often have you had sex in the past year?" in a 1994 survey (Michael & others, 1994). *What was one feature of the Sex in America survey that made it superior to most surveys of sexual behavior?*

- Married (and cohabiting) couples have sex more often than noncohabiting couples (see Figure 11.4).

- Most Americans do not engage in kinky sexual acts. When asked about their favorite sexual acts, the vast majority (96 percent) said that vaginal sex was "very" or "somewhat" appealing. Oral sex was in third place, after an activity that many have not labeled a sexual act—watching a partner undress.

- Adultery is clearly the exception rather than the rule. Nearly 75 percent of the married men and 85 percent of the married women in the survey indicated that they had never been unfaithful.

- Men think about sex far more than women do—54 percent of the men said they thought about it every day or several times a day, whereas 67 percent of the women said they thought about it only a few times a week or a few times a month.

In sum, one of the most powerful messages in the 1994 survey was that Americans' sexual lives are more conservative than previously believed. Although 17 percent of the men and 3 percent of the women said they had had sex with at least 21 partners, the overall impression from the survey was that sexual behavior is ruled by marriage and monogamy for most Americans.

How extensive are gender differences in sexuality? A recent meta-analysis revealed that men reported having slightly more sexual experiences and more permissive attitudes than women for most aspects of sexuality (Peterson & Hyde, 2010). For the following factors, stronger differences were found: Men said that they engaged more in masturbation, pornography use, and casual sex, and had more permissive attitudes about casual sex than their female counterparts.

Given all the media and public attention to the negative aspects of sexuality—such as adolescent pregnancy, sexually transmitted infections, rape, and so on—it is important to underscore that research strongly supports the role of sexuality in well-being (Brody, 2010). For example, in a recent Swedish study frequency of sexual intercourse was strongly linked to life satisfaction for both women and men (Brody & Costa, 2009).

Sources of Sexual Orientation

Until the end of the nineteenth century, it was generally believed that people were either heterosexual or homosexual. Today, it is more accepted to view sexual

What likely determines an individual's sexual preference?

orientation not as an either/or proposition but as a continuum from exclusive male-female relations to exclusive same-sex relations (Crooks & Baur, 2011). Some individuals are also *bisexual,* being sexually attracted to people of both sexes.

In the Sex in America survey, 2.7 percent of the men and 1.3 percent of the women reported that they had had same-sex relations in the past year (Michael & others, 1994). Why are some individuals lesbian, gay, or bisexual (LGB) and others heterosexual? Speculation about this question has been extensive (Diamond, Fagundes, & Butterworth, 2011; Yarber, Sayed, & Strong, 2010).

All people, regardless of their sexual orientation, have similar physiological responses during sexual arousal and seem to be aroused by the same types of tactile stimulation. Investigators typically find no differences between LGBs and heterosexuals in a wide range of attitudes, behaviors, and adjustments (Peplau & Fingerhut, 2007).

Recently, researchers have explored the possible biological basis of same-sex relations. The results of hormone studies have been inconsistent (Gooren, 2006). If gay males are given male sex hormones (androgens), their sexual orientation doesn't change. Their sexual desire merely increases. A very early prenatal critical period might influence sexual orientation (James, 2005). In the second to fifth months after conception, exposure of the fetus to hormone levels characteristic of females might cause the individual (male or female) to become attracted to males (Ellis & Ames, 1987). If this critical-period hypothesis turns out to be correct, it would explain why clinicians have found that sexual orientation is difficult, if not impossible, to modify.

Researchers have also examined genetic influences on sexual orientation by studying twins. A recent Swedish study of almost 4,000 twins found that only about 35 percent of the variation in homosexual behavior in men and 19 percent in women were explained by genetic differences (Langstrom & others, 2010). This result suggests that although genes likely play a role in sexual orientation, they are not the only factor (King, 2011).

An individual's sexual orientation—same-sex, heterosexual, or bisexual—is most likely determined by a combination of genetic, hormonal, cognitive, and environmental factors (Hyde & DeLamater, 2011; King, 2011). Most experts on same-sex relations believe that no one factor alone causes sexual orientation, and that the relative weight of each factor can vary from one individual to the next.

Attitudes and Behavior of Lesbians and Gay Males

Many gender differences that appear in heterosexual relationships occur in same-sex relationships (Diamond, Fagundes, & Butterworth, 2011; Diamond & Savin-Williams,

How Would You...?
As a human development and family studies professional, what information would you include in a program designed to educate young adults about healthy sexuality and sexual relationships?

2009). For example, like heterosexual women, lesbians have fewer sexual partners than gays, and lesbians have less permissive attitudes about casual sex outside a primary relationship than gays (Peplau & Fingerhut, 2007).

According to psychologist Laura Brown (1989), lesbians and gays experience life as a minority in a dominant, majority culture. For lesbians and gays, developing a *bicultural identity* creates new ways of defining themselves. Brown believes that lesbians and gays adapt best when they don't define themselves in polarities, such as trying to live in an encapsulated lesbian or gay world completely divorced from the majority culture or completely accepting the dictates and bias of the majority culture.

sexually transmitted infections (STIs) Diseases that are contracted primarily through sex.

Sexually Transmitted Infections

Sexually transmitted infections (STIs) are diseases that are primarily contracted through sex—intercourse as well as oral-genital and anal-genital sex. STIs affect about one of every six U.S. adults (National Center for Health Statistics, 2010a). Among the most prevalent STIs are bacterial infections—such as gonorrhea, syphilis, and chlamydia—and STIs caused by viruses—such as AIDS (acquired immune deficiency syndrome), genital herpes, and genital warts. Figure 11.5 describes these sexually transmitted infections.

No single disease has had a greater impact on sexual behavior, or created more public fear in the last several decades, than infection with the human immunodeficiency virus (HIV) (Crooks & Baur, 2011). HIV is a virus that destroys the body's immune system. Once a person is infected with HIV, the virus breaks down and overpowers the immune system, which leads to AIDS. An individual sick with AIDS has such a weakened immune system that a common cold can be life-threatening.

STI	Description/cause	Incidence	Treatment
Gonorrhea	Commonly called the "drip" or "clap." Caused by the bacterium *Neisseria gonorrhoeae*. Spread by contact between infected moist membranes (genital, oral-genital, or anal-genital) of two individuals. Characterized by discharge from penis or vagina and painful urination. Can lead to infertility.	500,000 cases annually in U.S.	Penicillin, other antibiotics
Syphilis	Caused by the bacterium *Treponema pallidum*. Characterized by the appearance of a sore where syphilis entered the body. The sore can be on the external genitals, vagina, or anus. Later, a skin rash breaks out on palms of hands and bottom of feet. If not treated, can eventually lead to paralysis or even death.	100,000 cases annually in U.S.	Penicillin
Chlamydia	A common STI named for the bacterium *Chlamydia trachomatis*, an organism that spreads by sexual contact and infects the genital organs of both sexes. A special concern is that females with chlamydia may become infertile. It is recommended that adolescent and young adult females have an annual screening for this STI.	About 3 million people in U.S. annually.	Antibiotics
Genital herpes	Caused by a family of viruses with different strains. Involves an eruption of sores and blisters. Spread by sexual contact.	One of five U.S. adults	No known cure but antiviral medications can shorten outbreaks
AIDS	Caused by a virus, the human immunodeficiency virus (HIV), which destroys the body's immune system. Semen and blood are the main vehicles of transmission. Common symptoms include fevers, night sweats, weight loss, chronic fatigue, and swollen lymph nodes.	More than 300,000 cumulative cases of HIV virus in U.S. 25–34-year-olds; epidemic incidence in sub-Saharan countries	New treatments have slowed the progression from HIV to AIDS; no cure
Genital warts	Caused by the human papillomavirus, which does not always produce symptoms. Usually appear as small, hard painless bumps in the vaginal area, or around the anus. Very contagious. Certain high-risk types of this virus cause cervical cancer and other genital cancers. May recur despite treatment. A new HPV preventive vaccine, Gardasil, has been approved for girls and women 9–26 years of age.	About 5.5 million new cases annually; considered the most common STI in the U.S.	A topical drug, freezing, or surgery

Figure 11.5 Sexually Transmitted Infections

Through 2007, 580,146 cases of AIDS in 20- to 39-year-olds had been reported in the United States (National Center for Health Statistics, 2010b). In 2007, male-male sexual contact continued to be the most frequent AIDS transmission category (National Center for Health Statistics, 2010b). Because of education and the development of more effective drug treatments, deaths due to HIV/AIDS have begun to decline in the United States (National Center for Health Statistics, 2010b).

Globally, the total number of individuals living with HIV was 33 million in 2007 with 22 million of these individuals with HIV living in sub-Saharan Africa (UNAIDS, 2009). Approximately half of all new HIV infections around the world occur in the 15- to 24-year-old age category (Campbell, 2009).

What are some good strategies for protecting against HIV and other sexually transmitted infections? They include:

- *Knowing your and your partner's risk status.* Anyone who has had previous sexual activity with another person might have contracted an STI without being aware of it. Spend time getting to know a prospective partner before you have sex. Use this time to inform the other person of your STI status and inquire about your partner's. Remember that many people lie about their STI status.

- *Obtaining medical examinations.* Many experts recommend that couples who want to begin a sexual relationship should have a medical checkup to rule out STIs before they engage in sex. If cost is an issue, contact your campus health service or a public health clinic.

- *Having protected, not unprotected, sex.* When correctly used, latex condoms help to prevent many STIs from being transmitted. Condoms are most effective in preventing gonorrhea, syphilis, chlamydia, and HIV. They are less effective against the spread of herpes.

- *Not having sex with multiple partners.* One of the best predictors of getting an STI is having sex with multiple partners. Having more than one sex partner elevates the likelihood that you will encounter an infected partner.

Forcible Sexual Behavior and Sexual Harassment

Too often, sex involves the exercise of power. Here we briefly look at three of the problems that may result: two types of rape and sexual harassment.

Rape

Rape is forcible sexual intercourse with a person who does not give consent. Legal definitions of rape differ from state to state. For example, in some states, husbands are not prohibited from forcing their wives to have intercourse, although this has been challenged in several of those states.

Because victims may be reluctant to suffer the consequences of reporting rape, the actual number of incidences is not easily determined (Carroll, 2010). Rape occurs most often in large cities, where it has been reported that 8 of every 10,000 women 12 years and older are raped each year. Nearly 200,000 rapes are reported each year in the United States. Although most victims of rape are women, rape of men does occur (McLean, Balding, & White, 2005). Men in prisons are especially vulnerable to rape, usually by heterosexual males who use rape as a means of establishing their dominance and power.

Why does rape of women occur so often in the United States? Among the causes given are that males are socialized to be sexually aggressive, to regard women as inferior beings, and to view their own pleasure as the most important objective in sexual relations (Beech, Ward, & Fisher, 2006). Researchers have found that male rapists

What are some characteristics of acquaintance rape in college and universities?

share the following characteristics: aggression enhances their sense of power or masculinity; they are angry at women in general; and they want to hurt and humiliate their victims. A recent study revealed that a higher level of men's sexual narcissism (assessed by these factors: sexual exploitation, sexual entitlement, low sexual empathy, and sexual skill) was linked to a greater likelihood that they would engage in sexual aggression (Widman & McNulty, 2010).

date or acquaintance rape Coercive sexual activity directed at someone with whom the perpetrator is at least casually acquainted.

Rape is a traumatic experience for the victims and those close to them (Jordan, Campbell, & Follingshead, 2010). As victims strive to get their lives back to normal, they may experience depression, fear, anxiety, and increased substance use for months or years (Herrera & others, 2006). Sexual dysfunctions, such as reduced sexual desire and an inability to reach orgasm, occur in 50 percent of female rape victims (Sprei & Courtois, 1988). Recovery depends on the victim's coping abilities, psychological adjustments prior to the assault, and social support (White & Frabult, 2006). Parents, partner, and others close to the victim can provide important support for recovery, as can mental health professionals (Littleton 2010).

An increasing concern is **date or acquaintance rape**, which is coercive sexual activity directed at someone with whom the victim is at least casually acquainted (Bouffard & Bouffard, 2010; Carroll, 2010). By some estimates, one in three adolescent girls will be involved in a controlling, abusive relationship before she graduates from high school, and two-thirds of college freshman women report having been date raped or having experienced an attempted date rape at least once (Watts & Zimmerman, 2002). About two-thirds of college men admit that they fondle women against their will, and half admit to forcing sexual activity.

A number of colleges and universities describe the *red zone* as a period of time early in the first year of college when women are at especially high risk for unwanted sexual experiences. A recent study revealed that first-year women were more at risk for unwanted sexual experiences, especially early in the fall term, than second-year women (Kimble & others, 2008).

Sexual Harassment

Sexual harassment is a manifestation of power of one person over another. It takes many forms—from inappropriate sexual remarks and physical contact (patting, brushing against one's body) to blatant propositions and sexual assaults. Millions of women experience sexual harassment each year in work and educational settings (Best & others, 2010; Das, 2009). Sexual harassment of men by women also occurs but to a far lesser extent than sexual harassment of women by men.

In a survey of 2,000 college women, 62 percent reported that they had experienced sexual harassment while attending college (American Association of University Women, 2006). Most of the college women said that the sexual harassment involved noncontact forms such as crude jokes, remarks, and gestures. However, almost one-third said that the sexual harassment was physical in nature.

Sexual harassment can result in serious psychological consequences for the victim. A study of almost 1,500 college women revealed that when they had been sexually harassed they reported an increase in psychological distress, greater physical illness, and an increase in disordered eating (Huerta & others, 2006).

The elimination of such exploitation requires the improvement of work and academic environments. These types of improvements help to provide equal opportunities for people to be able to develop a career and obtain an education in a climate free of sexual harassment (Hunes & Davis, 2009).

How Would You...?
As an educator, how would you develop a sensitivity workshop in sexual harassment?

Cognitive Development

Are there changes in cognitive performance during these years? To explore the nature of cognition in early adulthood, we focus on issues related to cognitive stages and creative thinking.

Cognitive Stages

Are young adults more advanced in their thinking than adolescents are? Let's examine what Piaget and others have said about this intriguing question.

Piaget's View

Piaget concluded that an adolescent and an adult think qualitatively in the same way. That is, Piaget argued that at approximately 11 to 15 years of age, adolescents enter the formal operational stage, which is characterized by more logical, abstract, and idealistic thinking than the concrete operational thinking of 7- to 11-year-olds. Piaget did believe that young adults are more *quantitatively* advanced in their thinking in the sense that they have more knowledge than adolescents. He also believed, as do information-processing psychologists, that adults especially increase their knowledge

in a specific area, such as a physicist's understanding of physics or a financial analyst's knowledge about finance. According to Piaget, however, formal operational thought is the final stage in cognitive development, and it characterizes adults as well as adolescents.

Some developmentalists theorize it is not until adulthood that many individuals consolidate their formal operational thinking. That is, they may begin to plan and hypothesize about intellectual problems in adolescence, but they become more systematic and sophisticated at this as young adults. Nonetheless, even many adults do not think in formal operational ways at all (Kuhn, 2009).

What are some ways that young adults might think differently than adolescents?

How Would You...?
As an educator, how would you characterize the differences in the intellectual development of adolescents and adults? How would this distinction change the way you teach to these different populations?

Realistic and Pragmatic Thinking

Some developmentalists propose that as young adults move into the world of work, their way of thinking does change. One idea is that as they face the constraints of reality, which work promotes, their idealism decreases (Labouvie-Vief, 1986). A related change in thinking is that in early adulthood individuals often switch from acquiring knowledge to applying knowledge as they pursue success in their work (Schaie & Willis, 2000).

Reflective and Relativistic Thinking

William Perry (1999) also described changes in cognition that take place in early adulthood. He said that adolescents often view the world in terms of polarities—right/wrong, we/they, or good/bad. As youth age into adulthood, they gradually move away from this type of absolutist thinking as they become aware of the diverse opinions and multiple perspectives of others. Thus, in Perry's view, the absolutist, dualistic thinking of adolescence gives way to the reflective, relativistic thinking of adulthood. Other developmentalists also believe that reflective thinking is an important indicator of cognitive change in young adults (Fischer & Bidell, 2006).

Is There a Fifth, Postformal Stage?

Some theorists have pieced together cognitive changes in young adults and proposed a new stage of cognitive development, **postformal thought**, which is qualitatively different from Piaget's formal operational thought (Sinnott, 2003). Postformal thought involves understanding that the correct answer to a problem requires reflective thinking and can vary from one situation to another, and that the search for truth is often an ongoing, never-ending process (Kitchener, King, & DeLuca, 2006). Postformal thought also includes the belief that solutions to problems need to be realistic, and that emotions and subjective factors can influence thinking.

How strong is the evidence for a fifth, postformal stage of cognitive development? Researchers have found that young adults are more likely to engage in this postformal thinking than adolescents are (Commons & Bresette, 2006). But critics argue that research has yet to document that postformal thought is a qualitatively more advanced stage than formal operational thought.

Creativity

Early adulthood is a time of great creativity for some people. At the age of 30, Thomas Edison invented the phonograph, Hans Christian Andersen wrote his first volume of fairy tales, and Mozart composed *The Marriage of Figaro*. One early study of creativity found that individuals' most creative products were generated in their thirties, and that 80 percent of the most important creative contributions were completed by age 50 (Lehman, 1960). Even though a decline in creative contributions is often found in the fifties and later, the decline is not as great as commonly thought.

Any consideration of decline in creativity with age requires consideration of the field of creativity involved. In such fields as philosophy and history, older adults often show as much creativity as when they were in their thirties and forties. By contrast, in such fields as lyric poetry, abstract math, and theoretical physics, the peak of creativity is often reached in the twenties or thirties.

Can you make yourself more creative? Mihaly Csikszentmihalyi (1995) interviewed 90 leading figures in art, business, government, education, and science to learn how creativity works. He discovered that creative people regularly experience a state he calls *flow,* a heightened state of pleasure experienced when we are engaged in mental and physical challenges that absorb us. Csikszentmihalyi (2000) believes everyone is capable of achieving flow. Based on his interviews with some of the most creative people in the world, the first step toward a more creative life is cultivating your curiosity and interest. How can you do this?

- *Try to be surprised by something every day.* Maybe it is something you see, hear, or read about. Become absorbed in a lecture or a book. Be open to what the world is telling you. Life is a stream of experiences. Swim widely and deeply in it, and your life will be richer.

- *Try to surprise at least one person every day.* In a lot of things you do, you have to be predictable and patterned. Do something different for a change. Ask a question you normally would not ask. Invite someone to go to a show or a museum you never have visited.

- Write down each day what surprised you and how you surprised others. Most creative people keep a diary, notes, or lab records to ensure that their experience is not fleeting or forgotten. Start with a specific task. Each evening, record the most surprising event that occurred that day and your most surprising action. After a few days, reread your notes and reflect on your past experiences. After a few weeks, you might see a pattern of interest emerging in your notes, one that might suggest an area you can explore in greater depth.

- When something sparks your interest, follow it. Usually when something captures your attention, it is short lived—an idea, a song, a flower. Too often we are too busy to explore the idea, song, or flower further. Or we think these areas are none of our business because we are not experts about them. Yet the world is our business. We can't know which part of it is best suited to our interests until we make a serious effort to learn as much about as many aspects of it as possible.

- Wake up in the morning with a specific goal to look forward to. Creative people wake up eager to start the day. Why? Not necessarily because they are cheerful, enthusiastic types but because they know that there is something meaningful to accomplish each day, and they can't wait to get started.

- Spend time in settings that stimulate your creativity. In Csikszentmihalyi's (1995) research, he gave people an electronic pager and beeped them randomly at different times of the day. When he asked them how they felt, they reported the highest levels of creativity when walking, driving, or swimming. I (your author) do my most creative thinking when I'm jogging. These activities are semiautomatic in that they take a certain amount of attention while leaving some time free to make connections among ideas. Another setting in which highly creative people report coming up with novel ideas is the sort of half-asleep, half-awake state we are in when we are deeply relaxed or barely awake.

Mihaly Csikszentmihalyi, in the setting where he gets his most creative ideas. *When and where do you get your most creative thoughts?*

How Would You...?
As an educator, how would you use your understanding of creativity to become a more effective teacher?

Careers and Work

Earning a living, choosing an occupation, establishing a career, and developing in a career—these are important themes of early adulthood. Let's consider some of the factors that go into choosing a career and a job, and how work typically affects the lives of young adults.

Careers

What are some developmental changes young adults experience as they choose a career? How effectively are individuals finding a path to purpose today?

Developmental Changes

Many children have idealistic fantasies about what they want to be when they grow up. For example, many young children want to be superheroes, sports stars, or movie stars. In the high school years, they often have begun to think about careers on a somewhat less idealistic basis. In their late teens and early twenties, their career decision making has usually turned more serious as they explore different career possibilities and zero in on the career they want to enter. In college, this often means choosing a major or specialization that is designed to lead to work in a particular field. By their early and mid-twenties, many individuals have completed their education or training and started to enter a full-time occupation. From the mid-twenties through the remainder of early adulthood, individuals often seek to establish their emerging career in a particular field. They may work hard to move up the career ladder and improve their financial standing.

Phyllis Moen (2009a) recently described the *career mystique*, which includes ingrained cultural beliefs that engaging in hard work for long hours through adulthood will produce a path to status, security, and happiness. That is, many individuals have an ideal concept of a career path toward achieving the American dream of upward mobility through occupational ladders. However, the lockstep career mystique has never been a reality for many individuals, especially ethnic minority individuals, women, and poorly educated adults. Further, the career mystique has increasingly become a myth for many individuals in middle-income occupations as global outsourcing of jobs and the 2007–2009 recession have meant reduced job security for millions of Americans.

"Did you think the ladder of success would be straight up?"

© Joseph Farris/The New Yorker Collection/www.cartoonbank.com

Finding a Path to Purpose

In the book *The Path to Purpose: Helping Our Children Find Their Calling in Life*, William Damon (2008) explored how purpose is a missing ingredient in many adolescents' and emerging adults' achievement and career development. Too many youth drift and aimlessly go through their high school and college years, Damon says, engaging in behavior that places them at risk for not fulfilling their potential and not finding a life pursuit that energizes them.

In interviews with 12- to 22-year-olds, Damon found that only about 20 percent had a clear vision of where they want to go in life, what they want to achieve, and why. The largest percentage—about 60 percent—had engaged in some potentially purposeful activities, such as service learning or fruitful discussions with a career counselor—but they still did not have a real commitment or any reasonable plans for reaching their goals. And slightly more than 20 percent expressed no aspirations and in some instances said they didn't see any reason to have aspirations.

Damon concludes that most teachers and parents communicate the importance of such goals as studying hard and getting good grades, but rarely discuss the purpose of these goals and where they might lead young adults. Damon emphasizes that too often students focus only on short-term goals and don't explore the big, long-term picture of what they want to do with their life. These interview questions that Damon (2008, p. 135) has used in his research are good springboards for getting individuals to reflect on their purpose:

- What's most important to you in your life?
- Why do you care about those things?
- Do you have any long-term goals?
- Why are these goals important to you?

Hari Prabhakar (*in rear*) at a screening camp in India that he created as part of his Tribal India Health Foundation (www.tihf.org). As he made the transition from high school to college, Hari created the foundation to bring low-cost health care to rural areas in India. Juggling his roles as a student at Johns Hopkins University and the foundation's director, Hari spent about 15 hours a week leading Tribal India Health throughout his four undergraduate years.

CAREERS AND WORK

285

- What does it mean to have a good life?
- What does it mean to be a good person?
- If you were looking back on your life now, how would you like to be remembered?

Work

Let's explore these aspects of work: Its impact on people's lives, the role of work in college, the occupational outlook, unemployment, dual-earner couples, and diversity in the workplace.

The Impact of Work

Work defines people in fundamental ways (Blustein, 2008). It is an important influence on their financial standing, housing, the way they spend their time, where they live, their friendships, and their health (Hodson, 2009). Some people define their identity through their work. Work also creates a structure and rhythm to life that is often missed when individuals do not work for an extended period. When unable to work, many individuals experience emotional distress and low self-esteem.

Most individuals spend about one-third of their lives at work. In one survey, 35 percent of Americans worked 40 hours a week, but 18 percent worked 51 hours or more per week (Center for Survey Research at the University of Connecticut, 2000). Only 10 percent worked less than 30 hours a week.

An important consideration regarding work is how stressful it is (Fernandez & others, 2010). A recent national survey of U.S. adults revealed that 55 percent indicated they were less productive because of stress (American Psychological Association, 2007). In this study, 52 percent reported that they considered or made a career decision, such as looking for a new job, declining a promotion, or quitting a job, because of stress in the workplace. In this survey, main sources of stress included low salaries (44 percent), lack of advancement opportunities (42 percent), uncertain job expectations (40 percent), and long hours (39 percent).

Many adults have changing expectations about work, yet employers often aren't meeting their expectations (Grzywacz, 2009; Lavoie-Temple & others, 2010). For example, current policies and practices were designed for a single breadwinner (male) workforce and an industrial economy, making these policies and practices out of step with a workforce of women and men, and of single parent and dual earners. Many workers today want flexibility and greater control over the time and timing of their work, and yet most employers offer little flexibility, even though policies like flextime may be "on the books."

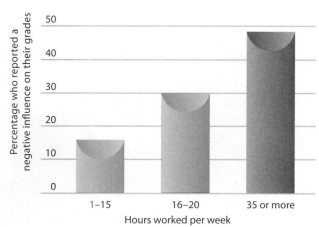

Figure 11.6 The Relation of Hours Worked Per Week in College to Grades

Among students working to pay for school expenses, 16 percent of those working 1 to 15 hours per week reported that working negatively influenced their grades (National Center for Education Statistics, 2002). Thirty percent of college students who worked 16 to 20 hours a week said the same, as did 48 percent who worked 35 hours or more per week.

Work During College

The percentage of full-time U.S. college students who were employed increased from 34 percent in 1970 to 46 percent in 2006 (down from a peak of 52 percent in 2000) (National Center for Education Statistics, 2008c). In this recent survey, 81 percent of part-time U.S. college students were employed.

Working can pay or help offset some costs of schooling, but working also can restrict students' opportunities to learn. For those who identified themselves primarily as students, one national study found that as the number of hours worked per week increased, their grades suffered (National Center for Education Statistics, 2002) (see Figure 11.6). Thus, college students need to carefully examine whether the number of hours they work is having a negative impact on their college success.

How Would You...?

As an educator, how would you advise a student who works a full-time job while taking college classes?

Of course, jobs also can contribute to your education. More than 1,000 colleges in the United States offer *cooperative (co-op) programs*, which are paid apprenticeships in a field that you are interested in pursuing. (You may not be permitted to participate in a co-op program until your junior year.) Other useful opportunities for working while going to college include internships and part-time or summer jobs relevant to your field of study. Participating in these work experiences can be a key factor in whether you land the job you want when you graduate.

Monitoring the Occupational Outlook

As you explore the type of work you are likely to enjoy and in which you can succeed, it is important to be knowledgeable about different fields and companies. Occupations may have many job openings one year but few in another year as economic conditions change. Thus, it is critical to keep up with the occupational outlook in various fields. An excellent source for doing this is the U.S. government's *Occupational Outlook Handbook, 2010–2011* (2010), which is revised every two years.

According to the 2010–2011 handbook, service industries, especially health services, professional and business services, and education are projected to account for the most new jobs in the next decade. Projected job growth varies widely by education requirements. Jobs that require a college degree are expected to grow the fastest. Most of the highest-paying occupations require a college degree.

"Uh-huh. Uh-huh. And for precisely how long were you a hunter-gatherer at I.B.M.?"

© Jack Ziegler/The New York Collection/www.cartoonbank.com

Unemployment

Unemployment produces stress regardless of whether the job loss is temporary, cyclical, or permanent (Perrucci & Perrucci, 2009; Roman, Cohen, & Forte, 2010). Banking financial problems and the recession toward the end of the first decade of the 21st century have produced very high unemployment rates, especially in the United States. Researchers have found that other factors affect unemployment as well: physical problems (such as heart attack and stroke), mental problems (such as depression and anxiety), marital difficulties, and homicide (Gallo & others, 2006). A 15-year longitudinal study of more than 24,000 adults found that life satisfaction dropped considerably following unemployment and increased after becoming reemployed but did not completely return to the same level of life

The economic recession that hit in 2007 resulted in millions of Americans losing their jobs, such as the individuals in line here waiting to apply for unemployment benefits in June 2009 in Chicago. *What are some of the potential negative outcomes of the stress caused by job loss?*

satisfaction previous to being unemployed (Lucas & others, 2004). Another study also revealed that immune system functioning declined with unemployment and increased with new employment (Cohen & others, 2007).

Stress comes not only from a loss of income and the resulting financial hardships but also from decreased self-esteem (Audhoe & others, 2010; Beutel & others, 2010). Individuals who cope best with unemployment have financial resources to rely on, often savings or the earnings of other family members. The support of understanding, adaptable family members also helps individuals to cope with unemployment. Job counseling and self-help groups can provide practical advice on job searching, résumé writing, and interviewing skills, and also can lend emotional support.

Dual-Earner Couples

Dual-earner couples may have special problems finding a balance between work and the rest of life (Eby, Maher, & Butts, 2010; Setterson & Ray, 2010). If both partners are working, who cleans up the house or calls the repairman or takes care of the other endless details involved in maintaining a home? If the couple has children, who is responsible for being sure that the children get to school or to piano practice, who writes the notes to approve field trips or meets the teacher or makes the dental appointments?

Although single-earner married families still make up a sizable minority of families, the two-earner couple has increased considerably in recent decades. As more U.S. women worked outside the home, the division of responsibility for work and family changed: (1) U.S. husbands are taking increased responsibility for maintaining the home; (2) U.S. women are taking increased responsibility for breadwinning; (3) U.S. men are showing greater interest in their families and parenting.

Many jobs have been designed for single earners, usually a male breadwinner, without regard for family responsibilities and the realities of people's actual lives. Consequently, many dual-earner couples engage in a range of adaptive strategies to coordinate their work and manage the family side of the work-family equation (Moen, 2009b). Researchers have found that even though couples may strive for gender equality in dual-earner families, gender inequalities still persist (Cunningham, 2009). For example, women still do not earn as much as men in the same jobs, and this inequity means that gender divisions in how much time each partner spends in paid work, homemaking, and caring for children continue. Thus, the decisions that dual-earner couples often make are in favor of men's greater earning power and women spending more time than men in homemaking and caring for children (Moen, 2009b).

Diversity in the Workplace

The workplace is becoming increasingly diverse (*Occupational Outlook Handbook, 2008–2009*). Whereas at one time few women were employed outside the home, in developed countries women have increasingly entered the labor force. A recent projection indicates that women's share of the U.S. labor force will increase faster than men's share through 2018 (*Occupational Outlook Handbook, 2010–2011*). In the United States, more than one-fourth of all lawyers, physicians, computer scientists, and chemists today are females.

Ethnic diversity also is increasing in the workplace in every developed country except France. In the United States, between 1980 and 2004, the percentage of

How has the diversity of the workplace changed in recent years?

Latinos and Asian Americans more than doubled in the workplace, a trend that is expected to continue (*Occupational Outlook Handbook, 2010–2011*). Latinos are projected to constitute a larger percentage of the labor force than African Americans by 2018, growing from 13 percent in 2006 to 17.6 percent in 2018 (*Occupational Outlook Handbook, 2010–2011*). The increasing diversity in the workplace requires a sensitivity to cultural differences, and the cultural values that workers bring to a job need to be recognized and appreciated (Fassinger, 2008).

Despite the increasing diversity in the workplace, women and ethnic minorities experience difficulty in breaking through the *glass ceiling*. This invisible barrier to career advancement prevents women and ethnic minorities from holding managerial or executive jobs regardless of their accomplishments and merits (Hynes & Davis, 2009).

Summary

The Transition from Adolescence to Adulthood

- Emerging adulthood, the time of transition from adolescence to adulthood, is characterized by experimentation and exploration.
- The transition from high school to college can involve both positive and negative features.

Physical Development

- Peak physical performance is often reached between 19 and 26 years of age. Then, toward the latter part of early adulthood, a detectable slowdown in physical performance is apparent for most individuals.
- Health problems in emerging and young adults may include obesity, a serious problem throughout the U.S. Binge drinking is a special problem among college students in the U.S., but by the mid-twenties alcohol and drug use often decreases.

Sexuality

- Patterns of sexual activity change during emerging adulthood.
- An individual's sexual preference likely stems from a combination of genetic, hormonal, cognitive, and environmental factors.
- Sexually transmitted infections, also called STIs, are contracted primarily through sexual contact.
- Rape and sexual harassment are special concerns for emerging and young adults.

Cognitive Development

- Some experts argue that the idealism of Piaget's formal operational stage declines in young adults and is replaced by more realistic, pragmatic thinking. Some experts have proposed a qualitatively different, fifth cognitive stage called postformal thought.
- Creativity peaks in adulthood, often in the forties, and then declines.

    Csikszentmihalyi proposed that the first step toward living a creative life is to cultivate curiosity and interest.

Careers and Work

- Thoughts about career choice for adolescents and young adults reflect developmental changes. Damon argues that too many individuals have difficulty finding a path to purpose today.
- Work defines people in fundamental ways and is a key aspect of their identity. Working during college can have a positive outcome, but it may also have a negative impact on grades. Jobs that require a college education will be the fastest growing and highest paying in the United States in the next decade.

    As the number of women working outside the home has increased, new work-related and family issues have arisen. Women and ethnic minorities, although a growing presence in the U.S. workplace, have had difficulty breaking through the glass ceiling.

Key Terms

romantic love Also called passionate love, or eros; romantic love has strong sexual and infatuation components and often predominates in the early period of a love relationship.

affectionate love In this type of love, also called companionate love, an individual desires to have the other person near and has a deep, caring affection for the other person.

have a best friend of the same sex (Blieszner, 2009). Many friendships are long lasting as 65 percent of U.S. adults have known their best friend for at least 10 years and only 15 percent have known their best friend for less than 5 years. Adulthood brings opportunities for new friendships; when individuals move to new locations, they may establish new friendships in their neighborhood or at work (Blieszner, 2009).

As in the childhood years, there are gender differences in adult friendship. Compared with men, women have more close friends and their friendships involve more self-disclosure and exchange of mutual support (Wood, 2012). Women are more likely to listen at length to what a friend has to say and be sympathetic, and women have been labeled "talking companions" because talk is so central to their relationships (Gouldner & Strong, 1987). Women's friendships tend to be characterized not only by depth but also by breadth: Women share many aspects of their experiences, thoughts, and feelings (Wood, 2012). A recent study revealed that in their early twenties, women showed more emotional intimacy with a closest friend than did men (Boden, Fischer, & Niehuis, 2010).

Romantic and Affectionate Love

Although friendship is included in some conceptualization of love, when we think about what love is, other types of love typically come to mind. In this section we explore two widely identified types of love: romantic love and affectionate love.

Romantic Love

Some friendships evolve into **romantic love**, which is also called passionate love, or eros. Romantic love has strong components of sexuality and infatuation, and as well-known love researcher Ellen Berscheid (2010) has found, it often predominates in the early part of a love relationship.

A complex intermingling of different emotions goes into romantic love—including passion, fear, anger, sexual desire, joy, and jealousy. Sexual desire is the most important ingredient of romantic love (Berscheid, 2010). Obviously, some of these emotions are a source of anguish, which can lead to other issues such as depression. One study found that a relationship between romantic lovers was more likely than a relationship between friends to be a cause of depression (Berscheid & Fei, 1977).

Affectionate Love

How Would You...?

As a health-care professional, how would you advise individuals who are concerned about their sexual functioning because their romantic relationship seems to be losing its spark?

Love is more than just passion. **Affectionate love**, also called *companionate love*, is the type of love that occurs when someone desires to have the other person near and has a deep, caring affection for the person.

The early stages of love have more romantic love ingredients—but as love matures, passion tends to give way to affection (Berscheid, 2010). Phillip Shaver (1986) proposed a developmental model of love in which the initial phase of romantic love is fueled by a mixture of sexual attraction and gratification, a reduced sense of loneliness, uncertainty about the security of developing another attachment, and excitement from exploring the novelty of another human being. With time, he says, sexual attraction wanes, attachment anxieties either lessen or produce conflict and withdrawal, novelty is replaced with familiarity, and lovers find themselves either securely attached in a deeply caring relationship or distressed—feeling bored, disappointed, lonely, or hostile, for example. In the latter case, one or both partners may eventually end the relationship and then move on to another relationship.

Consummate Love

So far we have discussed two forms of love: romantic (or passionate) and affectionate (or companionate). According to Robert J. Sternberg (1988; Sternberg & Sternberg, 2010), these are not the only forms of love. Sternberg proposed a triarchic theory of love in which love can be thought of as a triangle with three main dimensions—passion, intimacy, and commitment. Passion involves physical and sexual attraction to another. Intimacy relates to the emotional feelings of warmth, closeness, and sharing in a relationship. Commitment is the cognitive appraisal of the relationship and the intent to maintain the relationship even in the face of problems.

In Sternberg's theory, the strongest, fullest form of love is *consummate love*, which involves all three dimensions (see Figure 12.1). If passion is the only ingredient in a relationship (with intimacy and commitment low or absent), we are merely *infatuated*. An affair or a fling in which there is little intimacy and even less commitment is an example. A relationship marked by intimacy and commitment but low or lacking in passion is called *affectionate love*, a pattern often found among couples who have been married for many years. If passion and commitment are present but intimacy is not, Sternberg calls the relationship *fatuous love*, as when one person worships another from a distance. But if couples share all three dimensions— passion, intimacy, and commitment—they experience consummate love (Sternberg & Sternberg, 2010).

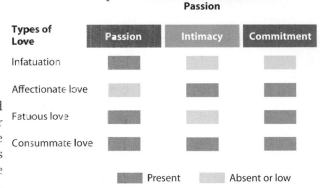

Figure 12.1 Sternberg's Triangle of Love
Sternberg identified three types of love: passion, intimacy, and commitment. Various combinations of these result in infatuation, affectionate love, fatuous love, and consummate love.

Adult Lifestyles

Adults today choose many lifestyles and form many types of families. One of the most striking social changes in recent decades is the decreased stigma attached to people who do not maintain what were long considered conventional families. They may choose to live alone, cohabit, marry, divorce, remarry, or live with someone of the same sex. Let's explore each of these lifestyles and how they affect adults.

Single Adults

Over a 30-year period, a dramatic rise in the percentage of single adults has occurred. From 1980 to 2006, there was a significant increase in the United States in single adults from 20 to 29 years of age (U.S. Census Bureau, 2007). In 1980, 64 percent of men in this age range said they were single, but by 2006 the percentage had increased to 73 percent, while the comparable percentages for women were 53 percent in 1980 and 62 percent in 2006.

Advantages of being single include having time to make decisions about one's life course, time to develop personal resources to meet goals, freedom to make autonomous decisions and pursue one's own schedule and interests, opportunities to explore new places and try out new things, and privacy. Common problems of single adults may include forming intimate relationships with other adults, confronting loneliness, and finding a niche in a society that is marriage-oriented (Koropeckyj-Cox, 2009).

Once adults reach the age of 30, there can be increasing pressure to settle down and get married. This is when many single adults make a conscious decision to marry or to remain single. A recent national survey revealed that a higher percentage of singles (58 percent) reported they experienced extreme stress in the past month than married (52 percent) and divorced individuals (48 percent) (American Psychological Association, 2007).

Cohabiting Adults

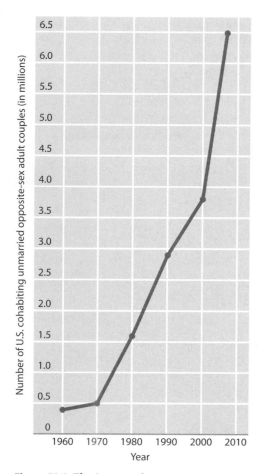

Figure 12.2 The Increase in Cohabitation in the United States Since 1970, there has been a dramatic increase in the number of unmarried adults living together in the United States.

Cohabitation refers to living together in a sexual relationship without being married. Cohabitation has undergone considerable changes in recent years (Goodwin, Mosher, & Chandra, 2010). As indicated in Figure 12.2, there has been a dramatic increase in the number of cohabiting U.S. couples since 1970 with more than 75 percent cohabiting prior to getting married (Popenoe, 2009). And the trend shows no sign of letting up—from 3.8 million cohabiting couples in 2000 to 6.5 million cohabiting couples in 2007. Cohabiting rates are even higher in some countries—in Sweden, for example, cohabitation before marriage is virtually universal (Stokes & Raley, 2009).

A number of couples view their cohabitation not as a precursor to marriage but as an ongoing lifestyle (Wilson & Stuchbury, 2010). These couples do not want the official aspects of marriage. In the United States, cohabiting arrangements tend to be short-lived, with one-third lasting less than a year (Hyde & DeLamater, 2011). Fewer than 1 out of 10 lasts five years. Of course, it is easier to dissolve a cohabitation relationship than to divorce.

Couples who cohabit face certain problems (Rhoades, Stanley, & Markman, 2009). Disapproval by parents and other family members can place emotional strain on the cohabiting couple. Some cohabiting couples have difficulty owning property jointly. Legal rights on the dissolution of the relationship are less certain than in a divorce. A recent study also revealed that cohabiting women experience an elevated risk of partner violence compared to married women (Brownridge, 2008).

If a couple lives together before they marry, does cohabiting help or harm their chances of later having a stable and happy marriage? The majority of studies have found lower rates of marital satisfaction and higher rates of divorce in couples who lived together before getting married (Whitehead & Popenoe, 2003). A recent meta-analysis found that individuals who had cohabited with a romantic partner were more likely to experience lower levels of marital quality and stability than their counterparts who had not cohabited (Jose, O'Leary, & Moyer, 2010).

What might explain the finding that cohabiting is linked with divorce more than not cohabiting? The most frequently given explanation is that the less traditional lifestyle of cohabitation may attract less conventional individuals who are not great believers in marriage in the first place (Whitehead & Popenoe, 2003). An alternative explanation is that the experience of cohabiting changes people's attitudes and habits in ways that increase their likelihood of divorce.

(a)

(b)

(c)

(a) In Scandinavian countries, cohabitation is popular; only a small percentage of 20- to 24-year-olds are married. (b) Islam stresses male honor and female purity. (c) Japanese young adults live at home longer with their parents before marrying than young adults in most other countries.

How Would You...?

As a psychologist, how would you counsel a couple deciding whether or not to cohabit before marriage?

Recent research has provided clarification of cohabitation outcomes. One meta-analysis found the negative link between cohabitation and marital instability did not hold up when only cohabitation with the eventual marital partner was examined, indicating that these cohabitors may attach more long-term positive meaning to living together (Jose, O'Leary, & Moyer, 2010). Another study also revealed that for first marriages, cohabiting with the spouse without first being engaged was linked to more negative interaction and a higher probability of divorce compared to cohabiting after engagement (Stanley & others, 2010). In contrast, premarital cohabitation prior to a second marriage placed couples at risk for divorce regardless of whether they were engaged or not.

Married Adults

Until about 1930, stable marriage was widely accepted as the endpoint of adult development. In the last 80 years, however, personal fulfillment both inside and outside marriage has emerged as a goal that competes with marital stability. The changing norm of male-female equality in marriage has produced marital relationships that are more fragile and intense than they were early in the 20th century (Trask & Koivur, 2007).

Marital Trends

In recent years, marriage rates in the United States have declined (Waite, 2009; National Vital Statistics Reports, 2010). Part of this decline is due to more adults remaining single for a longer period of time. In 2007, the U.S. average age for a first marriage climbed to 27.5 years for men and 25.6 years for women, higher than at any other point in history (U.S. Census Bureau, 2008). In 1980, the average age for a first marriage in the United States was 24 years for men and 21 years for women. In addition, the increase in cohabitation and a slight decline in the percentage of divorced individuals who remarry have contributed to the decline in marriage rates (Stokes & Raley, 2009).

Despite the decline in marriage rates, the United States is still a marrying society (Popenoe, 2009). More than 90 percent of U.S. women still marry at some point in their lives, although projections indicate that in the future this rate will drop into the 80 to 90 percent range (Popenoe, 2008). If women and men are going to marry, virtually all do so by the time they are 45 years of age (Popenoe, 2008).

Is there a best age to get married? Marriages in adolescence are more likely to end in divorce than marriages in adulthood (Waite, 2009). However, researchers have not been able to pin down a specific age or age span of several years in adulthood for getting married that is most likely to result in a successful marriage (Furstenberg, 2007).

How happy are people who do marry? The average duration of a marriage in the United States is currently just over nine years. As indicated in Figure 12.3, the

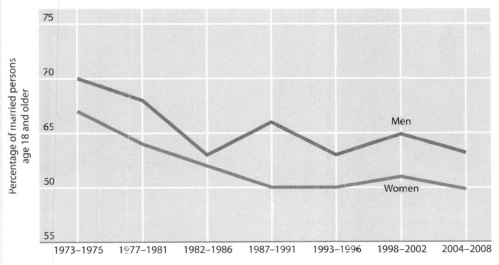

Figure 12.3 Percentage of Married Persons Age 18 and Older With "Very Happy" Marriages

percentage of married individuals in the United States who said their marriages were "very happy" declined from the 1970s through the early 1990s, but recently has begun to increase (Popenoe, 2009). Notice in Figure 12.3 that men consistently report being happier in their marriage than women.

The Benefits of a Good Marriage

Are there any benefits to having a good marriage? There are. Individuals who are happily married live longer, healthier lives than either divorced individuals or those who are unhappily married (Waite, 2009). A recent examination of U.S. adults 50 years and older also revealed that a lower portion of adult life spent in marriage was linked to an increased likelihood of dying at an earlier age (Henretta, 2010). Further, an unhappy marriage can shorten a person's life by an average of four years (Gove, Style, & Hughes, 1990).

What are the reasons for these benefits of a happy marriage? People in happy marriages likely feel less physically and emotionally stressed, which puts less wear and tear on a person's body. Such wear and tear can lead to numerous physical ailments, such as high blood pressure and heart disease, as well as psychological problems such as anxiety, depression, and substance abuse.

Divorced Adults

Divorce has become an epidemic in the United States (Hoelter, 2009). The number of divorced adults rose from 1.8 percent of the adult population in 1960, to 4.8 percent in 1980, and to 8.6 percent in 2007, but it declined from 2007 to 2009 (National Center for Vital Statistics, 2010; Popenoe, 2009).

Individuals in some groups have a higher incidence of divorce (Amato, 2010). Youthful marriage, low educational level, low income, not having a religious affiliation, having parents who are divorced, and having a baby before marriage are factors that are associated with increases in divorce (Hoelter, 2009). And these characteristics of one's partner increase the likelihood of divorce: alcoholism, psychological problems, domestic violence, infidelity, and inadequate division of household labor (Hoelter, 2009).

Earlier, we indicated that researchers have not been able to pin down a specific age that is the best time to marry so that the marriage is unlikely to end in a divorce. However, if a divorce is going to occur, it usually takes place early in a marriage; most occur in the fifth to tenth year of marriage (National Center for Health Statistics, 2000) (see Figure 12.4). This timing may reflect an effort by partners in troubled marriages to stay in the marriage and try to work things out. If after several years these efforts don't improve the relationship, they may then seek a divorce.

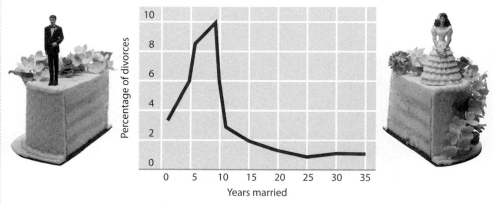

Figure 12.4 The Divorce Rate in Relation to Number of Years Married
Shown here is the percentage of divorces as a function of how long couples have been married. Notice that most divorces occur in the early years of marriage, peaking in the fifth to tenth years of marriage.

Remarried Adults

Adults who remarry usually do so rather quickly with approximately 50 percent remarrying within three years after they initially divorce (Sweeney, 2009, 2010). Men remarry sooner than women. Men with higher incomes are more likely to remarry than their counterparts with lower incomes. Remarriage occurs sooner for partners who initiate a divorce (especially in the first several years after divorce and for older women) than for those who do not initiate it (Sweeney, 2009, 2010).

Evidence on the benefits of remarriage for adults is mixed. Remarried families are more likely to be unstable and divorce is more likely to occur, especially in the first several years of the remarriage, compared to first-marriage families (Waite, 2009). Adults who get remarried have a lower level of mental health (higher rates of depression, for example) than adults in first marriages, but remarriage often improves the financial status of remarried adults, especially women (Waite, 2009). Researchers have found that the relationship in remarriages is more egalitarian and more likely to be characterized by shared decision making than the relationship in first marriages (Waite, 2009). Remarried wives also report that they have more influence on financial matters in their new family than do wives in first marriages (Waite, 2009).

Gay and Lesbian Adults

The legal and social context of marriage creates barriers to breaking up that do not usually exist for same-sex partners (Biblarz & Savci, 2010; Rostosky & others, 2010). But in other ways, researchers have found that gay and lesbian relationships are similar—in their satisfactions, loves, joys, and conflicts—to heterosexual relationships (Crooks & Baur, 2011). For example, like heterosexual couples, gay and lesbian couples need to find the balance of romantic love, affection, autonomy, and equality that is acceptable to both partners (Hope, 2009). An increasing number of gay and lesbian couples are creating families that include children.

There are a number of misconceptions about gay and lesbian couples (Diamond, Fagundes, & Butterworth, 2011). Contrary to stereotypes, one partner is masculine and the other feminine in only a small percentage of gay and lesbian couples. Only a small segment of the gay population has a large number of sexual partners, and this is uncommon among lesbians. Furthermore, researchers have found that gay and lesbian couples prefer long-term, committed relationships (Peplau & Fingerhut, 2007). About half of committed gay couples do have an open relationship that allows the possibility of sex (but not affectionate love) outside of the relationship. Lesbian couples usually do not have this open relationship.

Challenges in Marriage, Parenting, and Divorce

Whatever lifestyles young adults choose, they will bring certain challenges. Because many choose the lifestyle of marriage, we'll consider some of the challenges in marriage and how to make it work. We also examine some challenges in parenting and trends in childbearing. Given the statistics about divorce rates in the previous section, we'll then consider how to deal with divorce.

Making Marriage Work

John Gottman (1994, 2006; Gottman & Gottman, 2009; Gottman & Silver, 2000) uses many methods to analyze what makes marriages work. He interviews couples about the history of their marriage, their philosophy about marriage, and how they view their parents' marriages. He videotapes them talking to each other about how their day went and evaluates what they say about the good and bad times of their

What makes marriages work? What are the benefits of having a good marriage?

How Would You...?
As a human development and family studies professional, how would you counsel a newly married couple seeking advice on how to make their marriage work?

marriages. Gottman also uses physiological measures to chart their heart rate, blood flow, blood pressure, and immune functioning moment by moment. In addition, he checks back with the couples every year to see how their marriage is faring. Gottman's research represents the most extensive assessment of marital relationships available. Currently, he and his colleagues are following 700 couples in seven studies.

Among the principles Gottman has found that determine whether a marriage will work are:

- *Establishing love maps.* Individuals in successful marriages have personal insights and detailed maps of each other's life and world. They aren't psychological strangers. In good marriages, partners are willing to share their feelings with each other. They use these "love maps" to express not only their understanding of each other but also their fondness and admiration.

- *Nurturing fondness and admiration.* In successful marriages, partners sing each other's praises. More than 90 percent of the time, when couples put a positive spin on their marriage's history, the marriage is likely to have a positive future.

- *Turning toward each other instead of away.* In good marriages, spouses are adept at turning toward each other regularly. They see each other as friends. This friendship doesn't keep arguments from occurring, but it can prevent differences from overwhelming the relationship. In these good marriages, spouses respect each other and appreciate each other's point of view despite disagreements.

- *Letting your partner influence you.* Bad marriages often involve one spouse who is unwilling to share power with the other. Although power-mongering is more common in husbands, some wives also show this trait. A willingness to share power and to respect the other person's view is a prerequisite to compromising.

- *Creating shared meaning.* The more partners can speak candidly and respectfully with each other, the more likely they will create shared meaning in their marriage. This also includes sharing goals with one's spouse and working together to achieve each other's goals.

In a provocative book, *Marriage, a History: How Love Conquered Marriage,* Stephanie Coontz (2005) concluded that marriages in America today are fragile not because Americans have become self-centered and career-minded, but because expectations for marriage have become unrealistically high compared with previous generations. To make a marriage work, she emphasizes like Gottman that partners need to develop a deep friendship, show respect for each other, and embrace commitment.

Becoming a Parent

For many young adults, parental roles are well planned, coordinated with other roles in life, and developed with the individual's economic situation in mind. For others, the discovery that they are about to become parents is a startling surprise. In either event, the prospective parents may have mixed emotions and romantic illusions about having a child.

Parenting requires a number of interpersonal skills and imposes emotional demands, yet there is little in the way of formal education for this task. Most parents learn parenting practices from their own parents—some they accept, some they discard. Unfortunately, when parenting practices are passed on from one generation to the next, both desirable and undesirable practices are perpetuated. Adding to the reality of the task of parenting, husbands and wives may bring different parenting practices to the marriage (Huston & Holmes, 2004). The parents, then, may struggle with each other about which is a better way to interact with a child.

Parent educators seek to help individuals to become better parents. To read about the work of one parent educator, see "Careers in Life-Span Development."

CAREERS IN LIFE-SPAN DEVELOPMENT

Janis Keyser, Parent Educator

Janis Keyser is a parent educator and teaches in the Department of Early Childhood Education at Cabrillo College in California. In addition to teaching college classes and conducting parenting workshops, she has co-authored a book with Laura Davis (1997), *Becoming the Parent You Want to Be: A Sourcebook of Strategies for the First Five Years.*

Janis writes as an expert on the iVillage Web site (www. parentsplace.com). She also co-authors a nationally syndicated parenting column, "Growing Up, Growing Together." She is the mother of three, stepmother of five, grandmother of twelve, and great-grandmother of six.

Parent educators may have different educational backgrounds and occupational profiles. Janis Keyser has a background in early childhood education and, as just indicated, teaches at a college. Many parent educators have majored in areas such as child development as an undergraduate and/or taken a specialization of parenting and family courses in a master's or doctoral

Janis Keyser (right), conducting a parenting workshop.

degree program in human development and family studies, clinical psychology, counseling psychology, or social work. As part of, or in addition to, their work in colleges and clinical settings, they may conduct parent education groups and workshops.

As birth control has become common practice, many individuals consciously choose when they will have children and how many children they will rear. The number of one-child families is increasing, for example, and U.S. women overall are having fewer children. These childbearing results are creating several trends:

- By giving birth to fewer children, and reducing the demands of child care, women free up a significant portion of their life spans for other endeavors.

- As working women increase in number, they invest less actual time in the child's development.

- Men are apt to invest a greater amount of time in fathering.

- Parental care is often supplemented by institutional care (child care, for example).

As more women show an increased interest in developing a career, they are not only marrying later, but also having fewer children and having them later in life (Morgan, 2009). What are some of the advantages of having children early or late? Some of the advantages of having children early (in the twenties) are that the parents are likely to have more physical energy (for example, they can cope better with such matters as getting up in the middle of the night with infants and waiting up until adolescents come home at night); the mother is likely to have fewer medical problems with pregnancy and childbirth; and the parents may be less likely to build up expectations for their children, as do many couples who have waited many years to have children.

There are also advantages to having children later (in the thirties). The parents will have had more time to consider and achieve some of their goals in life, such as what they want from their family and career roles; the parents will be more mature and will be able to benefit from their life experiences to engage in more competent parenting; and the parents will be better established in their careers and have more income for child-rearing expenses.

Dealing With Divorce

If a marriage doesn't work, what happens after divorce? Psychologically, one of the most common characteristics of divorced adults is difficulty in trusting someone else in a romantic relationship. Following a divorce, though, people's lives can take diverse turns (Ahrons, 2007). For example, in one research study 20 percent of the divorced group became more competent and better adjusted following their divorce (Hetherington & Kelly, 2002).

Strategies for divorced adults include (Hetherington & Kelly, 2002):

What are some strategies for coping with divorce?

- Thinking of divorce as a chance to grow personally and to develop more positive relationships.

- Making decisions carefully. The consequences of your decision regarding work, lovers, and children may last a lifetime.

- Focusing more on the future than the past. Think about what is most important for you going forward in your life, set some challenging goals, and plan how to reach them.

- Using your strengths and resources to cope with difficulties.

- Not expecting to be successful and happy in everything you do. The path to a more enjoyable life will likely have a number of twists and turns, and moving forward will require considerable effort and resilience.

Gender, Communication, and Relationships

When Deborah Tannen (1990) analyzed the talk of women and men, she found that many wives complain about their husbands: "He doesn't listen to me anymore" and "He doesn't talk to me anymore." Lack of communication, though high on women's lists of reasons for divorce, is mentioned much less often by men.

Communication problems between men and women may come in part from differences in their preferred ways of communicating (Guerrero, Andersen, & Afifi, 2011; Wood, 2011). Tannen distinguishes two ways of communicating: rapport talk and report talk. **Rapport talk** is the language of conversation; it is a way of establishing connections and negotiating relationships. **Report talk** is talk that is designed to give information, which includes public speaking. According to Tannen, women enjoy rapport talk more than report talk, and men's lack of interest in rapport talk bothers many women. In contrast, men prefer to engage in report talk. Men hold center stage through such verbal performances as telling stories and jokes. They learn to use talk as a way of getting and keeping attention.

How extensive are the gender differences in communication? Research has yielded somewhat mixed results. Several studies do reveal some gender differences (Guerrero, Andersen, & Afifi, 2011). One study of a sampling of students' e-mails found that people could guess the writer's gender two-thirds of the time (Thompson & Murachver, 2001). Another study revealed that women make 63 percent of phone calls and, when talking to another woman, stay on the phone longer (7.2 minutes) than men do when talking with other men (4.6 minutes) (Smoreda & Licoppe, 2000). However, meta-analyses suggest that overall gender differences in communication are small for both children and adults (Hyde, 2005, 2007; Leaper & Smith, 2004). Further, a recent analysis revealed no gender differences in the average number of total words spoken by seven different samples of college men and women over 17 waking hours (Mehl & others, 2007).

A thorough recent study documented some gender differences in specific aspects of communication (Newman & others, 2008). In this study, women used words more for discussing people and what they were doing, as well as for communicating internal processes to others, including expression of doubts. By contrast, men used words more for external events, objects, and processes, including occupation, money, sports, and swearing. Contrary to popular stereotypes, men and women could not be distinguished in their reference to sexuality and anger.

How Would You...?
As a social worker, how would you educate a marital therapy group about the role of gender in communication and relationships?

Summary

Stability and Change from Childhood to Adulthood

- The first 20 years are important in predicting an adult's personality, but so are continuing experiences in the adult years. Attachment styles, for example, reflect childhood patterns and continue to influence relationships in adulthood. Adult attachments are categorized as secure, avoidant, or anxious. A secure attachment style is linked with positive aspects of relationships.

Love and Close Relationships

- Erikson theorized that intimacy versus isolation is the key developmental issue in early adulthood.

- Friendship plays an important role in adult development, especially in terms of emotional support.

- Romantic love, also called passionate love, includes passion, sexuality, and a mixture of emotions, not all of which are positive. Affectionate love, also called companionate love, usually becomes more important as relationships mature.

- Sternberg proposed a triarchic model of love: passion, intimacy, and commitment. If all three qualities are present, the result is consummate love.

Adult Lifestyles

- Being single has become an increasingly prominent lifestyle. Autonomy is one of its advantages. Challenges faced by single adults include intimacy, loneliness, and finding a positive identity in a marriage-oriented society.

- Cohabitation, an increasingly popular lifestyle, does not lead to greater marital happiness but is linked to possible negative consequences if a cohabiting couple marries.

- The age at which individuals marry in the U.S. is increasing. Though marriage rates have declined, a large percentage of Americans still marry. The benefits of marriage include better physical and mental health and a longer life.

- The U.S. divorce rate increased dramatically in the 20th century but began to decline in the 1980s.

- Divorce is complex and emotional.

- Stepfamilies are complex and adjustment is difficult. Evidence on the benefits of remarriage after divorce is mixed.

- One of the most striking research findings about gay and lesbian couples is how similar their relationships are to heterosexual couples' relationships.

Challenges in Marriage, Parenting, and Divorce

- Gottman's research indicates that in marriages that work, couples establish love maps, nurture fondness and admiration, turn toward each other, accept the influence of the partner, and create shared meaning.

The Nature of Middle Adulthood

Is midlife experienced the same way today as it was 100 years ago? How can middle adulthood be defined, and what are some of its main characteristics?

Changing Midlife

Many of today's 50-year-olds are in better shape, more alert, and more productive than their 40-year-old counterparts from a generation or two earlier. As more people lead healthier lifestyles and medical discoveries help to stave off the aging process, the boundaries of middle age are being pushed upward. It looks like middle age is starting later and lasting longer for increasing numbers of active, healthy, and productive people. A current saying is "60 is the new 40," implying that many 60-year-olds today are living a life that is as active, productive, and healthy as earlier generations did in their forties.

Questions such as, "To which age group do you belong?" and "How old do you feel?" reflect the concept of *age identity*. A consistent finding is that as adults become older their age identity is younger than their chronological age (Setterson & Trauten, 2009; Westerhof, 2009). One study found that almost half of the individuals 65 to 69 years of age considered themselves middle-aged (National Council on Aging, 2000), and another study found a similar pattern: Half of the 60- to 75-year-olds viewed themselves as being middle-aged (Lachman, Maier, & Budner, 2000). Also, some individuals consider the upper boundary of midlife as the age at which they make the transition from work to retirement.

When Carl Jung studied midlife transitions early in the 20th century, he referred to midlife as "the afternoon of life" (Jung, 1933). Midlife serves as an important preparation for late adulthood, "the evening of life" (Lachman, 2004, p. 306). But "midlife" came much earlier in Jung's time. In 1900 the average life expectancy was only 47 years of age; only 3 percent of the population lived past 65. Today, the average life expectancy is 78, and 12 percent of the U.S. population is older than 65. As a much greater percentage of the population lives to an older age, the midpoint of life and what constitutes middle age or middle adulthood are getting harder to pin down. Statistically, the middle of life today is about 39 years of age, but most 39-year-olds don't want to be called "middle-aged." What we think of as middle age comes later—anywhere from 40 or 45 to about 60 or 65 years of age. And as more people live longer, the 60 to 65 years upper boundary will likely be nudged upward.

How is midlife changing?

Compared to previous decades and centuries, an increasing percentage of the population is made up of middle-aged and older adults. In the past, the age structure of the population could be represented by a pyramid, with the largest percentage of the population in the childhood years. Today, the percentages of people at different ages in the life span are more similar, creating what is called the "rectangularization" of the age distribution (a vertical rectangle) (Himes, 2009a).

middle adulthood The developmental period beginning at approximately 40 years of age and extending to about 60 to 65 years of age.

Although middle adulthood has been a relatively neglected period of the human life span (except for pop psychology portrayals of the midlife crisis), life-span developmentalists are beginning to give more attention to this age period (Schaie, 2011; Willis & Martin, 2005). One reason for the increased attention is that the largest cohort in U.S. history is currently moving through the middle-age years. From 1990 to 2015, the middle-aged U.S. population is projected to increase from 47 million to 80 million, a 72 percent increase. Because of the size of the baby-boom cohort (recall from Chapter 1 that a *cohort* is a group of people born in a particular year or time period), the median age of the U.S. population will increase from 33 years in 1990 to 42 years in 2050. The baby boomers, born from 1946 to 1964, are of interest to developmentalists not only because of their increased numbers but also because they are the best-educated and most affluent cohort in history to pass through middle age (Willis & Martin, 2005).

Defining Middle Adulthood

Though the age boundaries are not set in stone, we will consider **middle adulthood** as the developmental period that begins at approximately 40 years of age and extends to about 60 to 65 years of age. For many people, middle adulthood is a time of declining physical skills and expanding responsibility; a period in which people become more conscious of the young-old polarity and the shrinking amount of time left in life; a point when individuals seek to transmit something meaningful to the next generation; and a time when people reach and maintain satisfaction in their careers. In sum, middle adulthood involves "balancing work and relationship responsibilities in the midst of the physical and psychological changes associated with aging" (Lachman, 2004, p. 305).

In midlife, as in other age periods, individuals make choices, selecting what to do, how to invest time and resources, and evaluating what aspects of their lives they need to change. In midlife, "a serious accident, loss, or illness" may be a "wake-up call" and produce "a major restructuring of time and a reassessment" of life's priorities (Lachman, 2004, p. 310).

As we mentioned earlier, for many increasingly healthy adults, middle age is lasting longer. Indeed, an increasing number of experts on middle adulthood describe the age period of 55 to 65 as *late midlife* (Deeg, 2005). Compared to earlier midlife, late midlife is more likely to be characterized by the death of a parent, the last child leaving the parental home, becoming a grandparent, the preparation for retirement, and in most cases actual retirement. Many people in this age range experience their first confrontation with health problems. Overall, then, although gains and losses may balance each other in early midlife, losses may begin to dominate gains for many individuals in late midlife (Baltes, Lindenberger, & Staudinger, 2006).

Keep in mind, though, that midlife is characterized by individual variations (Perrig-Chiello & Perren, 2005). As life-span expert Gilbert Brim (1992) commented, middle adulthood is full of changes, twists, and turns; the path is not fixed. People move in and out of states of success and failure.

What are the main characteristics of middle adulthood? What differentiates early and late midlife?

Physical Development

What physical changes accompany the change to middle adulthood? How healthy are middle-aged adults? How sexually active are middle-aged adults?

Physical Changes

How Would You...?
As a human development and family studies professional, how would you characterize the impact of the media in shaping middle-aged adults' expectations about their changing physical appearance?

Although everyone experiences some physical change due to aging in the middle adulthood years, the rates of this aging vary considerably from one individual to another. Genetic makeup and lifestyle factors play important roles in whether chronic disease will appear and when (Kaplan, Gurven, & Winking, 2009). Middle age is a window through which we can glimpse later life while there is still time to engage in prevention and to influence some of the course of aging (Lachman, 2004).

Visible Signs

One of the most visible signs of physical changes in middle adulthood is physical appearance. The first outwardly noticeable signs of aging usually are apparent by the forties or fifties. The skin begins to wrinkle and sag because of a loss of fat and collagen in underlying tissues (Datta & others, 2010). Small, localized areas of pigmentation in the skin produce aging spots, especially in areas that are exposed to sunlight, such as the hands and face. For most people, their hair becomes thinner and grayer. Fingernails and toenails develop ridges and become thicker and more brittle.

Since a youthful appearance is stressed in our culture, many individuals whose hair is graying, whose skin is wrinkling, whose bodies are sagging, and whose teeth are yellowing strive to make themselves look younger. Undergoing cosmetic surgery, dyeing hair, wearing wigs, enrolling in weight-reduction programs, participating in exercise regimens, and taking heavy doses of vitamins are common in middle age. Many baby boomers have shown a strong interest in plastic surgery and Botox, which may reflect their desire to take control of the aging process (Ascher & others, 2010; Wu, 2010).

Height and Weight

Individuals lose height in middle age. On average, from 30 to 50 years of age, men lose about 1/2 inch in height, then may lose another 3/4 inch from 50 to 70 years of age (Hoyer & Roodin, 2009). The height loss for women can be as much as 2 inches over a 50-year span from 25 to 75 years of age. Note that there are large variations in the extent to which individuals become shorter with aging. The decrease in height is due to bone loss in the vertebrae.

Although people in middle age may lose height, many gain weight. On average, body fat accounts for about 10 percent of body weight in adolescence; it makes up 20 percent or more in middle age. In a national survey, 29 percent of U.S. adults 40 to 59 years of age were classified as obese (Centers for Disease Control and Prevention, 2006). In Chapter 11, we saw that in this survey 22 percent of U.S. adults 20 to 39 years of age were classified as obese. Being overweight is a critical health problem in middle adulthood (Himes, 2009b; Wyn & Peckham, 2010). For example, obesity increases the probability that an individual will suffer a number of other ailments, among them hypertension (abnormally high blood pressure), diabetes, and digestive disorders (Bazzano & others, 2010; Bloomgarden, 2010). A large-scale study found that being overweight or obese in middle age increases an individual's risk of dying earlier (Adams & others, 2006).

Actor Sean Connery as a young adult in his twenties (*top*) and as a middle-aged adult in his fifties (*bottom*). *What are some of the most outwardly noticeable signs of aging in the middle adulthood years?*

How Would You...?
As a social worker, how would you apply the statistics on weight and health to promote healthier lifestyles for middle-aged adults?

Strength, Joints, and Bones

As we saw in Chapter 11, maximum physical strength often is attained in the twenties. The term *sarcopenia* is given to age-related loss of muscle mass and strength (Doran & others, 2009; Narici & Maffulli, 2010). The rate of muscle loss with age occurs at a rate of approximately 1 to 2 percent per year past the age of 50 (Marcell, 2003). A loss of strength especially occurs in the back and legs. Exercise can reduce the decline involved in sarcopenia (Park & others, 2010).

Peak functioning of the body's joints also usually occurs in the twenties. The cartilage that cushions the movement of bones and other connective tissues, such as tendons and ligaments, become less efficient in the middle-adult years, a time when many individuals experience joint stiffness and more difficulty in movement.

Maximum bone density occurs by the mid- to late thirties from which point there is a progressive loss of bone. The rate of this bone loss begins slowly but accelerates in the fifties (Ryan & Elahi, 2007). Women experience about twice the rate of bone loss as men. By the end of midlife, bones break more easily and heal more slowly (Neer & SWAN Investigators, 2010; Ritchie, 2010).

Vision and Hearing

Accommodation of the eye—the ability to focus and maintain an image on the retina—experiences its sharpest decline between 40 and 59 years of age. In particular, middle-aged individuals begin to have difficulty viewing close objects, which means that many individuals have to wear glasses with bifocal lenses, lenses with two sections to see items at different distances (Scheiber, 2006). Also, there is some evidence that the retina becomes less sensitive to low levels of illumination.

Hearing also can start to decline by the age of 40 (Roring, Hines, & Charness, 2007). Sensitivity to high pitches usually declines first. The ability to hear low-pitched sounds does not seem to decline much in middle adulthood, though. Men usually lose their sensitivity to high-pitched sounds sooner than women do. However, this gender difference might be due to men's greater exposure to noise in occupations such as mining, automobile work, and so on (Scialfa & Kline, 2007).

Cardiovascular System

Midlife is the time when high blood pressure and high cholesterol take many individuals by surprise (Lachman, 2004). The level of cholesterol in the blood increases through the adult years and in midlife begins to accumulate on the artery walls, increasing the risk of cardiovascular disease (Khera & Rader, 2010; Yetukuri & others, 2010). Blood pressure (hypertension), too, usually rises in the forties and fifties. At menopause, a woman's blood pressure rises sharply and usually remains above that of a man through life's later years (Taler, 2009).

Exercise, weight control, and a diet rich in fruits, vegetables, and whole grains can often help to stave off many cardiovascular problems in middle age (Natali & others, 2009; O'Donovan & others, 2010). For example, though heredity influences cholesterol levels, LDL (the bad cholesterol) can be reduced and HDL (the good cholesterol) increased by eating food that is very low in saturated fat and cholesterol and by exercising regularly (Kawano & others, 2009). A recent study of postmenopausal women found that 12 weeks of aerobic exercise training improved their cardiovascular functioning (O'Donnell, Kirwan, & Goodman, 2009).

Members of the Masai tribe in Kenya, Africa, can stay on a treadmill for a long time because of their active lives. Heart disease is extremely low in the Masai tribe, which also can be attributed to their energetic lifestyle.

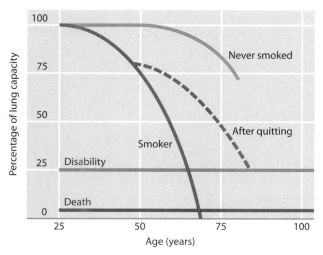

Figure 13.1 The Relation of Lung Capacity to Age and Cigarette Smoking

Lung capacity shows little change through middle age for individuals who have not smoked. However, smoking is linked with reduced lung capacity in middle-aged and older adults. When individuals stop smoking their lung capacity becomes greater than those who continue to smoke, but not as great as the lung capacity of individuals who have never smoked.

An increasing problem in middle age is *metabolic syndrome,* a condition characterized by hypertension, obesity, and insulin resistance. Metabolic syndrome often leads to the development of diabetes and cardiovascular disease (Cheung, 2010). A recent meta-analysis revealed that metabolic syndrome was an important risk factor for all-cause mortality (Hui, Liu, & Ho, 2010).

Lungs

There is little change in lung capacity through most of middle adulthood. However, at about the age of 55, the proteins in lung tissue become less elastic. This change, combined with a gradual stiffening of connective tissues in the chest wall, decreases the lungs' capacity to shuttle oxygen from the air people breathe to the blood in their veins. As shown in Figure 13.1, the lung capacity of individuals who are smokers drops precipitously in middle age, but if the individuals quit smoking their lung capacity improves, although not to the level of individuals who have never smoked.

Sleep

Some aspects of sleep become more problematic in middle age (McCrae & Dubyak, 2009). The total number of hours slept usually remains the same as in early adulthood, but beginning in the forties, wakeful periods are more frequent and there is less of the deepest type of sleep (stage 4). The amount of time spent lying awake in bed at night begins to increase in middle age, and this can produce a feeling of being less rested in the morning (Abbott, 2003). Sleep problems in middle-aged adults are more common in individuals who use a higher number of prescription and nonprescription drugs, are obese, have cardiovascular disease, or are depressed (Kaleth & others, 2007; Lopenen & others, 2010).

Health and Disease

In middle adulthood, the frequency of accidents declines, and individuals are less susceptible to colds and allergies than in childhood, adolescence, or early adulthood. Indeed, many individuals live through middle adulthood without having a disease or persistent health problem. For others, however, disease and persistent health problems become more common in middle adulthood than in earlier life stages.

Stress is increasingly being found to be a factor in disease (Kahana, Kahana, & Hammel, 2009). The cumulative effect of stress often takes a toll on the health of individuals by the time they reach middle age. Stress is linked to disease through both the immune system and cardiovascular disease (Bauer, Jeckel, & Luz, 2009; Ho & others, 2010).

Mortality Rates

Infectious disease was the main cause of death until the middle of the 20th century. As infectious disease rates declined and more individuals lived through middle age, chronic disorders increased. These are characterized by a slow onset and a long duration (Kelley-Moore, 2009).

In middle age, many deaths are caused by a single, readily identifiable condition, whereas in old age, death is more likely to result from the combined effects of several chronic conditions. For many years heart disease was the leading cause of death in middle adulthood, followed by cancer; however, in 2005 more individuals 45 to 64 years old in the United States died of cancer, followed by cardiovascular disease (National Center for Health Statistics, 2008). The gap between cancer as the leading cause of death widens as individuals age from 45 to 54 and 55 to 64 years of age (National Center for Health Statistics, 2008). Men have higher mortality rates than women for all the leading causes of death

climacteric The midlife transition in which fertility declines.

menopause The complete cessation of a woman's menstruation, which usually occurs in the late forties or early fifties.

Sexuality

What kinds of changes characterize the sexuality of women and men as they go through middle age? **Climacteric** is a term that is used to describe the midlife transition in which fertility declines. Let's explore the substantial differences in the climacteric of women and men during middle adulthood.

Menopause

Menopause is the time in middle age, usually in the late forties or early fifties, when a woman's menstrual periods completely cease. The average age at which women have their last period is 51 (Wise, 2006). However, there is large variation in the age at which menopause occurs—from 39 to 59 years of age. Later menopause is linked with increased risk of breast cancer (Mishra & others, 2009).

In menopause, production of estrogen by the ovaries declines dramatically, and this decline produces uncomfortable symptoms in some women—"hot flashes," nausea, fatigue, and rapid heartbeat, for example. Cross-cultural studies also reveal wide variations in the menopause experience (Anderson & Yoshizawa, 2007; Lerner-Geva & others, 2010). For example, hot flashes are uncommon in Mayan women (Beyene, 1986). Asian women report fewer hot flashes than women in Western societies (Payer, 1991). It is difficult to determine the extent to which these cross-cultural variations are due to genetic, dietary, reproductive, or cultural factors.

Menopause overall is not the negative experience for most women it was once thought to be (Weissmiller, 2009). Most women do not have severe physical or psychological problems related to menopause. However, the loss of fertility is an important marker for women—it means that they have to make final decisions about having children. Women in their thirties who have never had children sometimes speak about being "up against the biological clock" because they cannot postpone choices about having children much longer.

Until recently, hormone replacement therapy was often prescribed as treatment for unpleasant side effects of menopause. *Hormone replacement therapy (HRT)* augments the declining levels of reproductive hormone production by the ovaries (Nappi & Polatti, 2009; Studd, 2010). HRT can consist of various forms of estrogen, and usually a progestin. A study of HRT's effects was halted as evidence emerged that participants who were receiving HRT faced an increased risk of stroke (National Institutes of Health, 2004). Recent analyses also confirmed that combined estrogen and progestin hormone therapy poses an increased risk of cardiovascular disease (Toh & others, 2010). Studies have also revealed that coinciding with the decreased use of HRT is a related decline in the incidence of breast cancer (Dobson, 2009; Parkin, 2009).

The National Institutes of Health recommends that women with a uterus who are currently taking hormones should consult with their doctor to determine whether they should continue the treatment. If they are taking HRT for short-term relief of symptoms, the benefits may outweigh the risks. However, the evidence of risks associated with HRT suggests that long-term hormone therapy should be seriously reevaluated (Warren, 2007). Consequently, many middle-aged women are seeking alternatives to HRT such as regular exercise, dietary supplements, herbal remedies, relaxation therapy, acupuncture, and nonsteroidal medications (Holloway, 2010).

How Would You...?
As a human development and family studies professional, how would you counsel middle-aged women who voice the belief that hormone replacement therapy is necessary to "stay young"?

Researchers have found that almost 50 percent of Canadian and American women have occasional hot flashes, but only 1 in 7 Japanese women do (Lock, 1998). *What factors might account for these variations?*

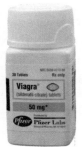

Hormonal Changes in Middle-Aged Men

Do men go through anything like the menopause that women experience? That is, is there a male menopause? During middle adulthood, most men do not lose their capacity to father children, although there usually is a modest decline in their sexual hormone level and activity. They experience hormonal changes in their fifties and sixties, but nothing like the dramatic drop in estrogen that women experience. Testosterone production begins to decline about 1 percent a year during middle adulthood, and sperm count usually shows a slow decline, but men do not lose their fertility in middle age. What has been referred to as "male menopause," then, probably has less to do with hormonal change than with the psychological adjustment men must make when they are faced with declining physical energy and with family and work pressures. Testosterone therapy has not been found to relieve such symptoms, suggesting that they are not induced by hormonal change.

The gradual decline in men's testosterone levels in middle age can reduce their sexual drive (Goel & others, 2009). Their erections are less full and less frequent, and men require more stimulation to achieve them. Researchers once attributed these changes to psychological factors, but increasingly they find that as many as 75 percent of the erectile dysfunctions in middle-aged men stem from physiological problems. Smoking, diabetes, hypertension, and elevated cholesterol levels are at fault in many erectile problems in middle-aged men (Corona & others, 2009; Heidelbaugh, 2010).

Treatment for men with erectile dysfunction has focused on the drug Viagra and on similar drugs, such as Levitra and Cialis (Althof & others, 2010; Sperling & others, 2010). Viagra works by allowing increased blood flow into the penis, which produces an erection. Its success rate is in the 60 to 85 percent range (Claes & others, 2010).

Sexual Attitudes and Behavior

Although the ability of men and women to function sexually shows little biological decline in middle adulthood, sexual activity usually occurs on a less frequent basis than in early adulthood (Burgess, 2004). Career interests, family matters, energy level, and routine may contribute to this decline (Avis & others, 2009).

In the Sex in America survey (described initially in Chapter 11), the frequency of having sex was greatest for individuals 25 to 29 years old (47 percent had sex twice a week or more) and dropped off for individuals in their fifties (23 percent of 50- to 59-year-old males said they had sex twice a week or more, while only 14 percent of the females in this age group reported this frequency) (Michael & others, 1994). Note, though, that the Sex in America survey may underestimate the frequency of sexual activity of middle-aged adults because the data were collected prior to the widespread use of erectile dysfunction drugs such as Viagra.

How does the pattern of sexual activity change when individuals become middle-aged?

Living with a spouse or partner makes all the difference in whether people engage in sexual activity, especially for women over 40 years of age. In one study conducted by the MacArthur Foundation, 95 percent of women in their forties with partners said that they have been sexually active in the last six months, compared with only 53 percent of those without partners (Brim, 1999). By their fifties, 88 percent of women living with a partner have been sexually active in the last six months, but only 37 percent of those who are neither married nor living with someone say they have had sex in the last six months.

A recent large-scale study of U.S. adults 40 to 80 years of age found that early ejaculation (26 percent) and erectile difficulties (22 percent) were the most common sexual problems of older men (Laumann & others, 2009). In this study, the most common sexual problems of women were lack of sexual interest (33 percent) and lubrication difficulties (21 percent).

How Would You...?
As a psychologist, how would you counsel a couple about the ways that the transition to middle adulthood might affect their sexual relationship?

Cognitive Development

crystallized intelligence Accumulated information and verbal skills, which increase in middle age, according to Horn.

fluid intelligence The ability to reason abstractly, which steadily declines from middle adulthood on, according to Horn.

We have seen that middle-aged adults may not see as well, run as fast, or be as healthy as they were in their twenties and thirties. We've also seen a decline in their sexual activity. What about their cognitive skills? Do they decline as we enter and move through middle adulthood? To answer this question we explore the possibility of cognitive changes in intelligence and information processing.

Intelligence

Our exploration of possible changes in intelligence in middle adulthood focuses on the concepts of fluid and crystallized intelligence, cohort effects, and the Seattle Longitudinal Study.

Fluid and Crystallized Intelligence

John Horn argues that some abilities begin to decline in middle age, whereas others increase (Horn & Donaldson, 1980). He argues that **crystallized intelligence**, an individual's accumulated information and verbal skills, continues to increase in middle adulthood whereas **fluid intelligence**, one's ability to reason abstractly, begins to decline in the middle adulthood years (see Figure 13.2).

Horn's data were collected in a cross-sectional manner. Remember from Chapter 1 that a cross-sectional study assesses individuals of different ages at the same point in time. For example, a cross-sectional study might assess the intelligence of different groups of 40-, 50-, and 60-year-olds in a single evaluation, such as in 1980. The 40-year-olds in the study would have been born in 1940 and the 60-year-olds in 1920—different eras that offered different economic and educational opportunities. The 60-year-olds likely had fewer educational opportunities as they grew up. Thus, if we find differences between 40- and 60-year-olds on intelligence tests when they are assessed cross-sectionally, these differences might be due to cohort effects related to educational differences rather than to age.

By contrast, remember from Chapter 1 that in a longitudinal study, the same individuals are studied over a period of time. Thus, a longitudinal study of intelligence in middle adulthood might consist of giving the same intelligence test to the same individuals when they are 40, then 50, and then 60 years of age. As we see next, whether data on intelligence are collected cross-sectionally or longitudinally can make a difference in what is found about changes in crystallized and fluid intelligence and about intellectual decline.

How Would You...?
As an educator, how would you explain how changes in fluid and crystallized intelligence might influence the way middle-aged adults learn?

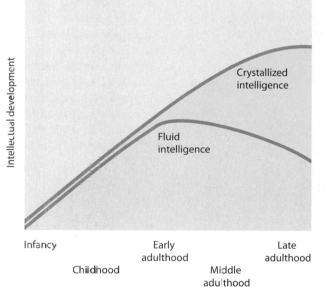

Figure 13.2 Fluid and Crystallized Intellectual Development Across the Life Span
According to Horn, crystallized intelligence (based on cumulative learning experiences) increases throughout the life span, but fluid intelligence (the ability to perceive and manipulate information) steadily declines from middle adulthood.

The Seattle Longitudinal Study

K. Warner Schaie (1996, 2005, 2010, 2011) is conducting an extensive study of intellectual abilities in the adulthood years. Five hundred individuals initially were tested in 1956. New waves of participants are added periodically. The main focus in the Seattle Longitudinal Study has been on individual change and stability in intelligence. The

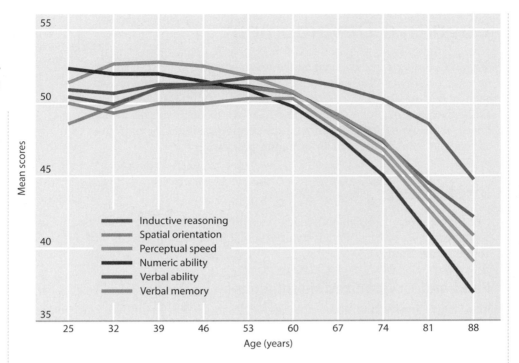

Figure 13.3 Longitudinal Changes in Six Intellectual Abilities from Age 25 to Age 88

main mental abilities tested are *verbal ability* (ability to understand ideas expressed in words); *verbal memory* (ability to encode and recall meaningful language units, such as a list of words); *numeric ability* (ability to perform simple mathematical computations such as addition, subtraction, and multiplication); *spatial orientation* (ability to visualize and mentally rotate stimuli in two- and three-dimensional space); *inductive reasoning* (ability to recognize and understand patterns and relationships in a problem and use this understanding to solve other instances of the problem); and *perceptual speed* (ability to quickly and accurately make simple discriminations in visual stimuli).

The highest level of functioning for four of the six intellectual abilities occurred in the middle adulthood years (Willis & Schaie, 2005) (see Figure 13.3). For both women and men, peak performance on verbal ability, verbal memory, inductive reasoning, and spatial orientation was attained in middle age. Only two of the six abilities—numeric ability and perceptual speed—showed a decline in middle age. Perceptual speed showed the earliest decline, actually beginning in early adulthood. Interestingly, in terms of John Horn's ideas that were discussed earlier, for the participants in the Seattle Longitudinal Study, middle age was a time of peak performance for some aspects of both crystallized intelligence (verbal ability) and fluid intelligence (spatial orientation and inductive reasoning).

Notice in Figure 13.3 that decline in functioning for most cognitive abilities began in the sixties, although the decline in verbal ability did not drop until the mid-seventies. From the mid-seventies through the late eighties, all cognitive abilities showed considerable decline.

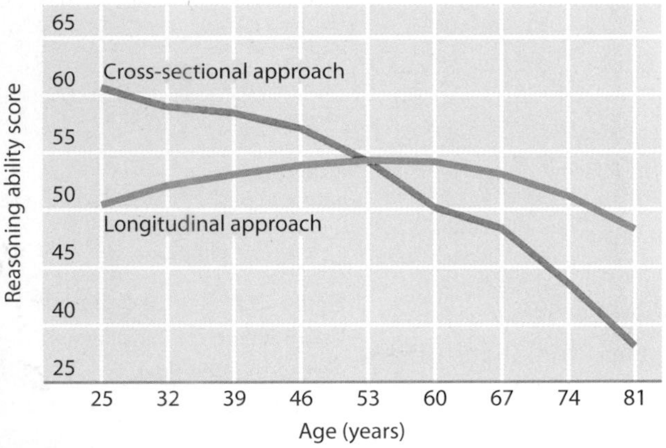

Figure 13.4 Cross-Sectional and Longitudinal Comparisons of Intellectual Change in Middle Adulthood

Why do you think reasoning ability peaks during middle adulthood?

When Schaie (1994) assessed intellectual abilities both cross-sectionally and longitudinally, he found decline more likely in the cross-sectional than in the longitudinal assessments. For example, as shown in Figure 13.4, when assessed cross-sectionally, inductive reasoning showed a consistent decline in the middle adulthood years. In contrast, when assessed longitudinally, inductive reasoning increased until toward the end of middle adulthood, when it began to show a slight decline. In Schaie's (2009, 2010, 2011) view, it is in middle adulthood, not early adulthood, that people reach a peak in their cognitive functioning for many intellectual skills.

Information Processing

As we saw in our discussion of theories of development (Chapter 1) and of cognitive development from infancy through adolescence (Chapters 3, 5, 7, and 9), the information-processing approach provides another way of examining cognitive abilities. Among the information-processing changes that take place in middle adulthood are those involved in speed of processing information, memory, and expertise.

Speed of Information Processing

As we saw in Schaie's (1996) Seattle Longitudinal Study, perceptual speed begins declining in early adulthood and continues to decline in middle adulthood. A common way to assess speed of information is through a reaction-time task, in which individuals simply press a button as soon as they see a light appear. Middle-aged adults are slower to push the button when the light appears than young adults are (Salthouse, 2009). However, keep in mind that the decline is not dramatic—under 1 second in most investigations.

Memory

In Schaie's (1994, 1996) Seattle Longitudinal Study, verbal memory peaked in the fifties. However, in some other studies, verbal memory has shown a decline in middle age, especially when assessed in cross-sectional studies (Salthouse, 2009). For example, when asked to remember lists of words, numbers, or meaningful prose, younger adults outperformed middle-aged adults (Salthouse & Skovronek, 1992). Although there still is some controversy about whether memory declines in the middle adulthood years, most experts conclude that it does decline, at least in late middle age (Hoyer & Roodin, 2009; Salthouse, 2009).

Aging and cognition expert Denise Park (2001) argues that starting in late middle age, more time is needed to learn new information. The slowdown in learning new information has been linked to changes in **working memory**, the mental "workbench" where individuals manipulate and assemble information when making decisions, solving problems, and comprehending written and spoken language (Baddeley, 2007). In this view, in late middle age, working memory capacity—the amount of information that can be immediately retrieved and used—becomes more limited.

Memory decline is more likely to occur when individuals don't use effective memory strategies, such as organization and imagery (Hoyer & Roodin, 2009). By organizing lists of phone numbers into different categories or imagining the phone numbers as representing different objects around the house, many people can improve their memory in middle adulthood.

Stephen J. Hawking is a world-renowned expert in physics and the author of the best-selling book *A Brief History of Time*. Hawking has a neurological disorder that prevents him from walking or talking. He communicates with the aid of a voice-equipped computer. *What distinguishes experts from novices?*

Expertise

Because it takes so long to attain, expertise often shows up more in the middle adulthood than in the early adulthood years (Kim & Hasher, 2005). Recall from Chapter 7 that *expertise* involves having extensive, highly organized knowledge and understanding of a particular domain.

leisure The pleasant times after work when individuals are free to pursue activities and interests of their own choosing.

Developing expertise and becoming an "expert" in a field usually is the result of many years of experience, learning, and effort.

Adults in middle age who have become experts in their fields are likely to do the following: rely on their accumulated experience to solve problems; process information automatically and analyze it more efficiently when solving a problem; devise better strategies and shortcuts to solving problems; and be more creative and flexible in solving problems.

Careers, Work, and Leisure

What are some issues that workers face in midlife? What role does leisure play in the lives of middle-aged adults?

Work in Midlife

The role of work, whether one works in a full-time career, at a part-time job, as a volunteer, or as a homemaker, is central during the middle years. Middle-aged

What characterizes work in middle adulthood?

adults may reach their peak in position and earnings. They may also be saddled with multiple financial burdens from rent or mortgage, child care, medical bills, home repairs, college tuition, loans to family members, or bills from nursing homes.

For many people, midlife is a time of evaluation, assessment, and reflection in terms of the work they do and want to do in the future (Moen, 2009). Among the work issues that some people face in midlife are recognizing limitations in career progress, deciding whether to change jobs or careers, deciding whether to rebalance family and work, and planning for retirement (Sterns & Huyck, 2001).

Career Challenges and Changes

How Would You...?
As a social worker, how would you advise middle-aged adults who are dissatisfied with their careers?

The current middle-aged worker faces several important challenges in the 21st century (Blossfeld, 2009). These include the globalization of work, rapid developments in information technologies, downsizing of organizations, early retirement, and concerns about pensions and health care.

Globalization has replaced what was once a primarily non-Latino White male workforce in the United States with employees of different ethnic and national backgrounds who have immigrated from different parts of the world. To improve profits, many companies are restructuring, downsizing, and outsourcing jobs. One of the outcomes of this is to offer incentives to middle-aged employees to retire early—in their fifties, or in some cases even forties, rather than their sixties.

The decline in defined-benefit pensions and increased uncertainty about the fate of health insurance are decreasing the sense of personal control for middle-aged workers. As a consequence, many are delaying retirement plans.

Some midlife career changes are self-motivated, others are the consequence of losing one's job (Moen, 2009). Some individuals in middle age decide that they don't want to do the same work they have been doing for the rest of their working lives (Hoyer & Roodin, 2009). One aspect of middle adulthood involves adjusting idealistic hopes to realistic possibilities in light of how much time individuals have before they retire and how fast they are reaching their occupational goals (Levinson, 1978). Individuals could become motivated to change jobs, if they perceive that they are behind schedule, if their goals are unrealistic, if they don't like the work they are doing, or if their job has become too stressful.

Leisure

As adults, not only must we learn how to work well, but we also need to learn how to relax and enjoy leisure (Gibson, 2009). **Leisure** refers to the pleasant times after work when individuals are free to pursue activities and interests of their own choosing—hobbies, sports, or reading, for example. In one analysis of research on what U.S. adults regret the most, not engaging in more leisure was one of the top six regrets (Roese & Summerville, 2005).

Leisure can be an especially important aspect of middle adulthood (Parkes, 2006). By middle adulthood, more money may be available to many individuals, and there may be more free time and paid vacations. In short, midlife changes may produce expanded opportunities for leisure. For many individuals, middle adulthood is the first time in their lives when they have the opportunity to follow their leisure-time interests.

Adults at midlife need to begin preparing psychologically for retirement. Developing constructive and fulfilling leisure activities in middle adulthood is an important part of this preparation (Gibson, 2009). If an adult develops leisure activities that can be continued into retirement, the transition from work to retirement can be less stressful.

How Would You...?
As a health-care professional, how would you explain the link between work and health to a patient?

Sigmund Freud once commented that the two things adults need to do well to adapt to society's demands are to work and to love. To his list we add "to play." In our fast-paced society, it is all too easy to get caught up in the frenzied, hectic pace of our achievement-oriented work world and ignore leisure and play. *Imagine your life as a middle-aged adult. What would be the ideal mix of work and leisure? What leisure activities do you want to enjoy as a middle-aged adult?*

Religion and Meaning in Life

What role does religion play in our development as adults? Is the meaning of life an important theme for many middle-aged adults?

Religion and Adult Lives

In the MacArthur Study of Midlife Development, more than 70 percent of U.S. middle-aged adults said they are religious and consider spirituality a major part of their lives (Brim, 1999). In thinking about religion and adult development, it is important to consider the role of individual differences. Religion is a powerful influence in some adults' lives, whereas it plays little or no role in others' lives (George, 2009; Sapp, 2010). In a longitudinal study of individuals from their early thirties through their late sixties/early seventies, a significant increase in spirituality occurred between late middle (mid-fifties/early sixties) and late adulthood (Wink & Dillon, 2002) (see Figure 13.5).

Females have consistently shown a stronger interest in religion than males have (Bijur & others, 1993). Compared with men, they participate more in both organized and personal forms of religion, are more likely to believe in a higher power or presence, and are more likely to feel that religion is an important dimension of their lives. In the longitudinal study just described, the spirituality of women increased more than men in the second half of life (Wink & Dillon, 2002).

What roles do religion and spirituality play in the lives of middle-aged adults?

Religion and Health

What might be some of the effects of religion on physical health? Some cults and religious sects encourage behaviors that are damaging to health, such as ignoring sound medical advice. For individuals in the religious mainstream, however, researchers are increasingly finding positive links between religion and physical health (Campbell, Yoon, & Johnstone, 2010; McCullough & Willoughby, 2009). Researchers have found that religious attendance is linked to a reduction in hypertension (Gillum & Ingram, 2007). Also, a number of studies have confirmed a positive association between religious participation and longevity (Oman & Thoresen, 2006).

Why might religion promote physical health? There are several possible answers (Hill & Butter, 1995). First, there are *lifestyle issues*—for example, religious individuals have lower drug use than their non-religious counterparts (Gartner, Larson, & Allen, 1991). Second are *social networks*—the degree to which individuals are connected to others affects their health. Well-connected individuals have fewer health problems (Hill & Pargament, 2003). Religious groups, meetings, and activities provide social connectedness for individuals. A third answer involves *coping with stress*—religion offers a source of comfort and support when individuals are confronted with stressful events. A recent study revealed that when religion was an important aspect of people's lives, they worried less and were less depressed (Rosmarin, Krumei, & Andersson, 2009).

Religious counselors often advise people about mental health and coping. To read about the work of one religious counselor, see "Careers in Life-Span Development."

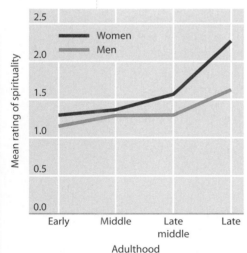

Figure 13.5 Level of Spirituality in Four Adult Age Periods

In a longitudinal study, the spirituality of individuals in four different adult age periods—early (thirties), middle (forties), late middle (mid-fifties/early sixties), and late (late sixties/early seventies) adulthood—was assessed (Wink & Dillon, 2002). Based on responses to open-ended questions in interviews, the spirituality of the individuals was coded on a 5-point scale, with 5 being the highest level of spirituality and 1 the lowest.

Gabriel Dy-Liacco, Pastoral Counselor

Gabriel Dy-Liacco is a pastoral counselor at the Pastoral Counseling and Consultation Centers of Greater Washington, D.C. He obtained his Ph.D. in pastoral counseling from Loyola College in Maryland and also has experience as a psychotherapist in such mental health settings as a substance abuse program, military family center, psychiatric clinic, and community mental health center. As a pastoral counselor, he works with adolescents and adults in the aspects of their life that they show the most concern about—psychological, spiritual, or the interface of both. Having lived in Peru, Japan, and the Philippines, he brings considerable multicultural experience to the counseling setting. Dr. Dy-Liacco also is a professor in the Graduate School of Psychology and Counseling at Regent University in the Washington, D.C., area.

Pastoral counselors, like Gabriel Dy-Liacco, are trained in both psychology and theology, which enables them to provide clients with psychological and spiritual guidance. Most pastoral counselors have an undergraduate degree and a master's or doctoral degree in theology and/or pastoral counseling. If they have only an advanced theology degree, they also must take a certain amount of pastoral counseling courses. Pastoral counselors usually work in such care settings as hospitals, nursing homes, rehabilitation facilities, psychiatric facilities, and correctional institutions.

Meaning in Life

Austrian psychiatrist Viktor Frankl's mother, father, brother, and wife died in the concentration camps and gas chambers in Auschwitz, Poland. Frankl survived the concentration camp and went on to write about meaning in life. In his book, *Man's Search for Meaning,* Frankl (1984) emphasized each person's uniqueness and the finiteness of life. He believed that examining the finiteness of our existence and the certainty of death adds meaning to life. If life were not finite, said Frankl, we could spend our life doing just about whatever we please because time would continue forever.

Frankl said that the three most distinct human qualities are spirituality, freedom, and responsibility. Spirituality, in his view, does not have a religious underpinning. Rather, it refers to a human being's uniqueness—to spirit, philosophy, and mind. Frankl proposed that people need to ask themselves such questions as why they exist, what they want from life, and what the meaning of their life is.

It is in middle adulthood that individuals begin to be faced with death more often, especially the deaths of parents and other older relatives. Also faced with less time in their life, many individuals in middle age begin to ask and evaluate the questions that Frankl proposed. And meaning-making coping is especially helpful in times of chronic stress and loss.

Researchers are increasingly studying the factors involved in a person's exploration of meaning in life and whether developing a sense of meaning in life is linked to positive developmental outcomes (Park, 2010). In research studies, many individuals state that religion played an important role in increasing their exploration of meaning in life (Krause, 2008, 2009). Studies also suggest that individuals who have found a sense of meaning in life are physically healthier and happier, and experience less depression, than their counterparts who report that they have not discovered meaning in life (Krause, 2009).

What characterizes the search for meaning in life?

Summary

The Nature of Middle Adulthood

- As more people live to an older age, what we think of as middle age is starting later and lasting longer.

- Middle age involves extensive individual variation. For most people, middle adulthood involves declining physical skills, expanding responsibility, being conscious of the young-old polarity, motivation to transmit something meaningful to the next generation, and reaching and maintaining career satisfaction. Increasingly, researchers are distinguishing between early and late midlife.

Physical Development

- The physical changes of midlife are usually gradual. Decline in a number of aspects of physical development occurs.

- In middle adulthood, the frequency of accidents declines and individuals are less susceptible to colds. Stress can be a factor in disease.

- Until recently, cardiovascular disease was the leading cause of death in middle age, but now cancer is the leading cause of death in this age group.

- Most women do not have serious physical or psychological problems related to menopause. Sexual behavior occurs less frequently in middle adulthood than early adulthood.

Cognitive Development

- Horn argued that crystallized intelligence continues to increase in middle adulthood, whereas fluid intelligence declines. Schaie found that declines in cognitive development are less likely to occur when longitudinal rather than cross-sectional studies are conducted. He also revealed that the highest level of a number of intellectual abilities occur in middle age.

- Working memory declines in late middle age. Memory is more likely to decline in middle age when individuals don't use effective memory strategies. Expertise often increases in the middle adulthood years.

Careers, Work, and Leisure

- Midlife is often a time to reflect on career progress and prepare for retirement.

- The current middle-aged worker faces a number of challenges.

- We not only need to learn to work well, but we also need to learn to enjoy leisure.

Religion and Meaning in Life

- The majority of middle-aged adults say that spirituality is a major part of their lives.

- In mainstream religions, religion is positively linked to physical health. Religion can play an important role in coping for some individuals.

- Many middle-aged individuals reflect on life's meaning.

Key Terms

Socioemotional Development in Middle Adulthood

14

Stories of Life-Span Development: Sarah and Wanda, Middle-Age Variations

Forty-five-year-old Sarah feels tired, depressed, and angry when she looks back on the way her life has gone. She became pregnant when she was 17 and married Ben, the baby's father. They stayed together for three years after their son was born, and then Ben left her for another woman. Sarah went to work as a salesclerk to make ends meet. Eight years later, she married Alan, who had two children of his own from a previous marriage. Sarah stopped working for several years to care for the children. Then, like Ben, Alan started going out on her. She found out about it from a

friend. Nevertheless, Sarah stayed with Alan for another year. Finally, he was gone so much that she could not take it anymore and decided to divorce him. Sarah went back to work again as a salesclerk; she has been in the same position for 16 years now. During those 16 years, she has dated a number of men, but the relationships never seemed to work out. Her son never finished high school and has drug problems. Her father died last year, and Sarah is trying to help her mother financially, although she can barely pay her own bills. Sarah looks in the mirror and does not like

what she sees. She sees her past as a shambles, and the future does not look rosy, either.

Forty-five-year-old Wanda feels energetic, happy, and satisfied. As a young woman, she graduated from college and worked for three years as a high school math teacher. She married Andy, who had just finished law school. One year later, they had their first child, Josh. Wanda stayed home with Josh for two years, and then returned to her job as a math teacher. Even during her pregnancy, Wanda stayed active and exercised regularly, playing tennis almost every

generativity Adults' desires to leave legacies of themselves to the next generation; the positive side of Erikson's generativity versus stagnation middle adulthood stage.

stagnation Sometimes called "self-absorption"—develops when individuals sense that they have done little or nothing for the next generation; the negative side of Erikson's generativity versus stagnation middle adulthood stage.

day. After her pregnancy, she kept up her exercise habits. Wanda and Andy had another child, Wendy. Now, as they move into their middle-age years, their children are both off to college, and Wanda and Andy are enjoying spending more time with each other. Last weekend they visited Josh at his college, and the weekend before they visited Wendy at her college. Wanda continued working as a high school math teacher until six years ago. She had developed computer skills as part of her job and taken some computer courses at a nearby college, doubling up during the summer months. She resigned her math teaching job and took a job with a computer company, where she has already worked her way into management. Wanda looks in the mirror and likes what she sees. She sees her past as enjoyable, although not without hills and valleys, and she looks to the future with zest and enthusiasm.

As with Sarah and Wanda, there are individual variations in the way people experience middle age. To begin the chapter, we examine personality theories and development in middle age, including ideas about individual variation. Then we turn our attention to how much individuals change or stay the same as they go through the adult years, and finally we explore a number of aspects of close relationships during the middle adulthood years.

Personality Theories and Development

What is the best way to conceptualize middle age? Is it a stage or a crisis? How extensively is middle age influenced by life events? Do middle-aged adults experience stress differently than young and older adults? Is personality linked with contexts such as the point in history in which individuals go through midlife, their culture, and their gender?

Stages of Adulthood

Adult stage theories have been plentiful, and they have contributed to the view that midlife brings a crisis in development. Two prominent theories that define stages of adult development are Erik Erikson's life-span view and Daniel Levinson's seasons of a man's life.

Erikson's Stage of Generativity Versus Stagnation

Erikson (1968) proposed that middle-aged adults face a significant issue—*generativity versus stagnation*, which is the name Erikson gave to the seventh stage in his life-span theory. **Generativity** encompasses adults' desire to leave legacies of themselves to the next generation. Through these legacies adults achieve a kind of immortality. By contrast, **stagnation** (sometimes called "self-absorption") develops when individuals sense that they have done little or nothing for the next generation.

Generative adults commit themselves to the continuation and improvement of society as a whole through their connection to the next generation. Generative adults develop a positive legacy of the self and then offer it as a gift to the next generation. Middle-aged adults can develop generativity in a number of ways (Kotre, 1984). Through biological generativity, adults have offspring. Through parental generativity, adults nurture and guide children. Through work generativity, adults develop skills that are passed down to others. And through cultural generativity, adults create, renovate, or conserve some aspect of culture that ultimately survives.

Through generativity, adults promote and guide the next generation by parenting, teaching, leading, and doing things that benefit the community (Pratt & others, 2008). One of the participants in a study of aging said: "From twenty to thirty I learned how to get along with my wife. From thirty to forty I learned

How Would You...? As an educator, how would you describe ways in which the profession of teaching might establish generativity for someone in middle adulthood?

How Would You...?

As a human development and family studies professional, how would you advise a middle-aged woman who never had children and now fears she has little opportunity to leave a legacy to the next generation?

how to be a success at my job, and at forty to fifty I worried less about myself and more about the children" (Vaillant, 2002, p. 114).

Does research support Erikson's theory that generativity is an important dimension of middle age? Yes, it does (McAdams, 2009; Pratt & others, 2008). In one study, Carol Ryff (1984) examined the views of women and men at different ages and found that middle-aged adults especially were concerned about generativity. In a longitudinal study of Smith College women, the desire for generativity increased as the participants aged from their thirties to their fifties (Stewart, Ostrove, & Helson, 2001). And in a recent study, generativity was strongly linked to middle-aged adults, positive social engagement in such contexts as family life and community activities (Cox & others, 2010).

Levinson's Seasons of a Man's Life

In *The Seasons of a Man's Life* (1978), clinical psychologist Daniel Levinson reported the results of extensive interviews with 40 middle-aged men. The interviews were conducted with hourly workers, business executives, academic biologists, and novelists. Levinson bolstered his conclusions with information from the biographies of famous men and the development of memorable characters in literature. Although Levinson's major interest focused on midlife change in men, he described a number of stages and transitions during the period from 17 to 65 years of age, as

Era of late adulthood: 60 to ?

Late adult transition: Age 60 to 65

Culminating life structure for middle adulthood: 55 to 60

Age 50 transition: 50 to 55

Entry life structure for middle adulthood: 45 to 50

Middle adult transition: Age 40 to 45

Culminating life structure for early adulthood: 33 to 40

Age 30 transition: 28 to 33

Entry life structure for early adulthood: 22 to 28

Early adult transition: Age 17 to 22

Figure 14.1 Levinson's Periods of Adult Development
According to Levinson, adulthood for men has three main stages, which are surrounded by transition periods. Specific tasks and challenges are associated with each stage.

shown in Figure 14.1. Levinson emphasizes that developmental tasks must be mastered at each stage.

At the end of one's teens, according to Levinson, a transition from dependence to independence should occur. This transition is marked by the formation of a dream—an image of the kind of life the youth wants to have, especially in terms of a career and marriage. Levinson sees the twenties as a *novice phase* of adult development. It is a time of reasonably free experimentation and of testing the dream in the real world. In early adulthood, the two major tasks to be mastered are exploring the possibilities for adult living and developing a stable life structure.

From about the ages of 28 to 33, the man goes through a transition period in which he must face the more serious question of determining his goals. During the thirties, he usually focuses on family and career development. In the later years of this period, he enters a phase of *Becoming One's Own Man* (or BOOM, as Levinson calls it). By age 40, he has reached a stable location in his career, has outgrown his earlier, more tenuous attempts at learning to become an adult, and now must look forward to the kind of life he will lead as a middle-aged adult.

According to Levinson, the transition to middle adulthood lasts about five years (ages 40 to 45) and requires the adult male to come to grips with four major conflicts that have existed in his life since adolescence: (1) being young versus being old, (2) being destructive versus being constructive, (3) being masculine versus being feminine, and (4) being attached to others versus being separated

contemporary life-events approach
An approach that emphasizes that how a life event influences the individual's development depends not only on the life event, but also on mediating factors, the individual's adaptation to the life event, the life-stage context, and the sociohistorical context.

from them. Seventy to 80 percent of the men Levinson interviewed found the midlife transition tumultuous and psychologically painful, as many aspects of their lives came into question. According to Levinson, the success of the midlife transition rests on how effectively the individual reduces the polarities and accepts each of them as an integral part of his being.

Because Levinson interviewed middle-aged males, we can consider the data about middle adulthood more valid than the data about early adulthood. When individuals are asked to remember information about earlier parts of their lives, they may distort and forget things. The original Levinson data included no females, although Levinson (1996) reported that his stages, transitions, and the crisis of middle age hold for females as well as males. Levinson's work included no statistical analysis. However, the quality and quantity of the Levinson biographies make them outstanding examples of the clinical tradition.

How Pervasive Are Midlife Crises?

Levinson (1978) views midlife as a crisis, believing that the middle-aged adult is suspended between the past and the future, trying to cope with this gap that threatens life's continuity. George Vaillant (1977) has a different view. Vaillant's study—called the "Grant Study"—involved men who were in their early thirties and in their late forties who initially had been interviewed as undergraduates at Harvard University. He concludes that just as adolescence is a time for detecting parental flaws and discovering the truth about childhood, the forties are a decade of reassessing and recording the truth about the adolescent and adulthood years. However, whereas Levinson sees midlife as a crisis, Vaillant maintains that only a minority of adults experience a midlife crisis.

Today, adult development experts are virtually unanimous in their belief that midlife crises have been exaggerated (Brim, Ryff, & Kessler, 2004; Lachman & Krantz, 2010). In sum, the stage theories place too much emphasis on crises in development, especially midlife crises. Also, there often is considerable individual variation in the way people experience the stages, a topic that we turn to next.

The Life-Events Approach

Age-related stages represent one major way to examine adult personality development. A second major way to conceptualize adult personality development is to focus on life events. In the early version of the life-events approach, life events were viewed as taxing circumstances for individuals, forcing them to change their personality (Holmes & Rahe, 1967). Such events as the death of a spouse, divorce, marriage, and so on were believed to involve varying degrees of stress, and therefore likely to influence the individual's development.

Today's life-events approach is more sophisticated. The **contemporary life-events approach** emphasizes that how life events influence the individual's development depends not only on the life event itself but also on mediating factors (physical health, family supports, for example), the individual's adaptation to the life event (appraisal of the threat, coping strategies, for example), the life-stage context, and the sociohistorical context (see Figure 14.2). For example, if individuals are in poor health and have little family support, life events are likely to be more stressful. Whatever the context or mediating variables, however, one individual may perceive a life event as highly stressful, whereas another individual may perceive the same event as a challenge.

Though the life-events approach is a valuable addition to understanding adult development, like other approaches to adult development, it has its drawbacks. One significant drawback is that the life-events approach places too much emphasis on change. Another drawback is that it may not be life's major events that are the primary sources of stress, but our daily experiences (O'Connor & others, 2009). Enduring a boring but tense job, staying in an unsatisfying marriage, or living in poverty do not show up on scales of major life events. Yet the everyday pounding we take from these living conditions can add up to a highly stressful life and eventually illness (McIntosh, Gillanders, & Rodgers, 2010).

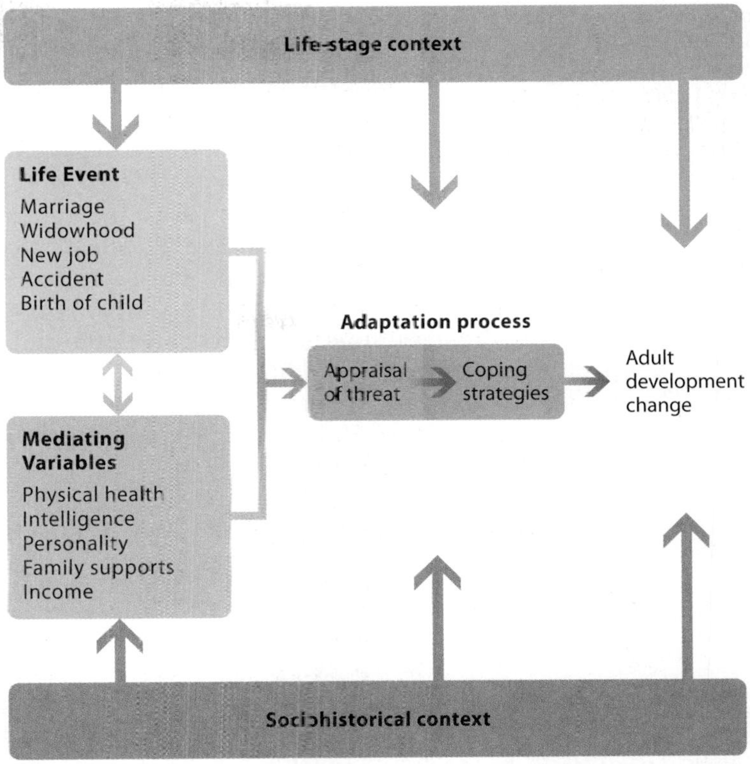

Stress and Personal Control in Midlife

As we have seen, there is conclusive evidence that midlife is not a time when a majority of adults experience a tumultuous crisis, and when they do experience a midlife crisis, it is often linked to stressful life events. Do middle-aged adults experience stress differently than young adults and older adults? One study using

How Would You...? As a health-care professional, how would you convince a company that it should sponsor a stress-reduction program for its middle-aged employees?

Figure 14.2 A Contemporary Life-Events Framework for Interpreting Adult Developmental Change

According to the contemporary life-events approach, the influence of a life event depends on the event itself, on mediating variables, on the life-stage and sociohistorical context, and on the individual's appraisal of the event and coping strategies.

daily diaries over a one-week period found that both young and middle-aged adults had more stressful days than older adults (Almeida & Horn, 2004). In this study, although young adults experienced daily stressors more frequently than middle-aged adults, middle-aged adults experienced more "overload" stressors that involved juggling too many activities at once.

To what extent do middle-aged adults perceive that they can control what happens to them? Researchers have found some aspects of personal control increase with age while others decrease (Lachman, 2006; Lachman & others, 2011). For example, middle-aged adults feel they have a greater sense of control over their finances, work, and marriage than younger adults but less control over their sex life and their children (Lachman & Firth, 2004; Lachman & Weaver, 1998).

Contexts of Midlife Development

The contemporary life-events approach (like Bronfenbrenner's theory, discussed in Chapter 1) highlights the importance of the complex setting of our lives—of everything from our income and family supports to our sociohistorical circumstances. Let's examine how two aspects of the contexts of life influence development during middle adulthood: historical contexts (cohort effects) and culture.

Historical Contexts (Cohort Effects)

Bernice Neugarten (1964) has been emphasizing the power of age group or cohort since the 1960s. Our values, attitudes, expectations, and behaviors are influenced by the period in which we live. For example, the group of individuals born during the difficult times of the Great Depression may have a different outlook on life than the group born during the optimistic 1950s, says Neugarten.

social clock The timetable according to which individuals are expected to accomplish life's tasks, such as getting married, having children, or establishing a career.

Neugarten (1986) argues that the social environment of a particular age group can alter its **social clock**—the timetable according to which individuals are expected to accomplish life's tasks, such as getting married, having children, or establishing themselves in a career. Social clocks provide guides for our lives; individuals whose lives are not synchronized with these social clocks find life to be more stressful than those who are on schedule, says Neugarten. She argues that today there is much less agreement than in the past on the right age or sequence for the occurrence of major life events such as having children or retiring.

Trying to tease out universal truths and patterns about adult development from one birth cohort is complicated because the findings may not apply to another birth cohort (Schaie, 2010, 2011). Most of the individuals studied by Levinson and Vaillant, for example, were born before and during the Great Depression. What was true for these individuals may not be true for today's 50-year-olds, born in the optimistic aftermath of World War II, or for the post-baby-boom generation as they approach the midlife transition. The midlife men in Levinson's and Vaillant's studies might have been burned out at a premature age rather than being representatives of a normal adult developmental pattern (Rossi, 1989).

Cultural Contexts

In many cultures, especially nonindustrialized cultures, the concept of middle age is not very clear or, in some cases, is absent. It is common in nonindustrialized societies to describe individuals as young or old, but not as middle-aged (Grambs, 1989). Some cultures have no words for "adolescent," "young adult," or "middle-aged adult," but they do have other categories they use.

What is middle age like for women in other cultures? It depends on the modernity of the culture and the culture's view of gender roles. Some anthropologists believe that when women become middle-aged in nonindustrialized societies they may experience certain advantages (Brown, 1985). First, they are often freed from cumbersome restrictions that were placed on them when they were younger. For example, in middle age they enjoy greater geographical mobility. Child care has ceased or can be delegated, and domestic chores are reduced. They may venture forth from the village for commercial opportunities, visit relatives living at a distance, and attend religious events. Second, with middle age a woman has the right to exercise authority over specified younger kin. Middle-aged women can extract labor from younger family members. The work of middle-aged women tends to be administrative, delegating tasks and making assignments to younger women. Middle-aged women also make important decisions for certain members of the younger generation: what a grandchild is to be named, who is ready to be initiated into adulthood, and who is eligible to marry whom. Third, middle-aged women may become eligible for special statuses, which may provide recognition beyond the household. These statuses include the vocations of midwife, curer, holy woman, and matchmaker.

Gusii dancers perform on World Habitat Day in Nairobi, Kenya. Movement from one status to another in the Gusii culture is due primarily to life events, not age. The Gusii do not have a clearly labeled midlife transition.

Stability and Change

Recall from Chapter 1 that questions about stability and change are an important issue in life-span development. One of the main ways that stability and change are assessed is through longitudinal studies that measure the same individuals at different points in their lives.

Longitudinal Studies

We examine three longitudinal studies to help us understand the extent to which there is stability or change in adult personality development: Costa and McCrae's Baltimore Study, the Berkeley Longitudinal Studies, and Vaillant's studies.

Big Five factors of personality
Openness to experience, conscientiousness, extraversion, agreeableness, and neuroticism (emotional stability).

Costa and McCrae's Baltimore Study

A major study of adult personality development continues to be conducted by Paul Costa and Robert McCrae (1998; McCrae & Costa, 2006). They focus on what are called the **Big Five factors of personality**, which are openness to experience, conscientiousness, extraversion, agreeableness, and neuroticism (emotional stability); they are described in Figure 14.3. (Notice that if you create an acronym from these factor names, you will get the word *OCEAN*.) These traits are sometimes referred to as the Big Five. A number of research studies point toward these factors as important dimensions of personality (McCrae & Costa, 2003).

Using their five-factor personality test, Costa and McCrae (1998, 2000) studied approximately a thousand college-educated men and women aged 20 to 96, assessing the same individuals over many years. Data collection began in the 1950s to the mid-1960s and is ongoing. Costa and McCrae concluded that considerable stability across the adult years occurs for the five personality factors.

A meta-analysis of the Big Five framework revealed more change across the adult years than Costa and McRae found. The meta-analysis of 87 longitudinal studies spanning 10 to 101 years of age indicated that (Roberts, Walton, & Viechtbauer, 2006):

- Results for extraversion were complex until it was subdivided into social dominance (assertiveness, dominance) and social vitality (talkativeness, sociability). Social dominance increased from adolescence through middle adulthood, social vitality increased in adolescence and then decreased in early and late adulthood.

- Agreeableness and conscientiousness increased in early and middle adulthood.

- Neuroticism decreased in early adulthood.

- Openness to experience increased in adolescence and early adulthood and then decreased in late adulthood.

In general, this study revealed that personality traits changed most during early adulthood.

Berkeley Longitudinal Studies

In the Berkeley Longitudinal Studies, more than 500 children and their parents were initially studied in the late 1920s and early 1930s. The book *Present and Past in Middle Life* (Eichorn & others, 1981) profiles these individuals as they became middle-aged. The results from early adolescence through a portion of midlife did

Openness	**C**onscientiousness	**E**xtraversion	**A**greeableness	**N**euroticism (emotional stability)
• Imaginative or practical	• Organized or disorganized	• Sociable or retiring	• Softhearted or ruthless	• Calm or anxious
• Interested in variety or routine	• Careful or careless	• Fun-loving or somber	• Trusting or suspicious	• Secure or insecure
• Independent or conforming	• Disciplined or impulsive	• Affectionate or reserved	• Helpful or uncooperative	• Self-satisfied or self-pitying

Figure 14.3 The Big Five Factors of Personality
Each of the broad supertraits encompasses more narrow traits and characteristics. Use the acronym OCEAN to remember the Big Five personality factors (openness, conscientiousness, extraversion, agreeableness, neuroticism).

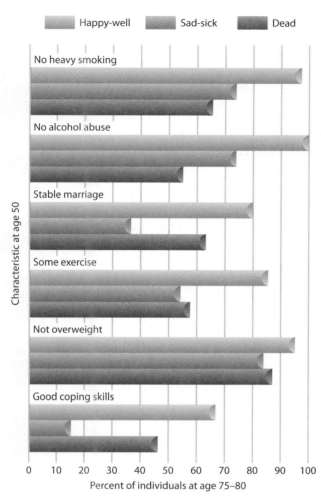

Figure 14.4 Links Between Characteristics at Age 50 and Health and Happiness at Age 75 to 80

In a longitudinal study, the characteristics shown above at age 50 were related to whether individuals were happy-well, sad-sick, or dead at age 75 to 80 (Vaillant, 2002).

not support either extreme in the debate over whether personality is characterized by stability or change. Some characteristics were more stable than others, however. The most stable characteristics were the degree to which individuals were intellectually oriented, self-confident, and open to new experiences. The characteristics that changed the most included the extent to which the individuals were nurturant or hostile and whether they had good self-control or not.

George Vaillant's Studies

Longitudinal studies by George Vaillant help us examine a somewhat different question than the studies described so far: Does personality at middle age predict what a person's life will be like in late adulthood? Vaillant (2002) has conducted three longitudinal studies of adult development and aging: (1) a sample of 268 socially advantaged Harvard graduates born about 1920 (called the Grant Study); (2) a sample of 456 socially disadvantaged inner-city men born about 1930; and (3) a sample of 90 middle-SES, intellectually gifted women born about 1910. These individuals have been assessed numerous times (in most cases, every two years), beginning in the 1920s to 1940s and continuing today for those still living. The main assessments involve extensive interviews with the participants, their parents, and teachers.

Vaillant categorized 75- to 80-year-olds as "happy-well," "sad-sick," and "dead." He used data collected from these individuals when they were 50 years of age to predict which categories they were likely to end up in at 75 to 80 years of age. Alcohol abuse and smoking at age 50 were the best predictors of which individuals would be dead at 75 to 80 years of age. Other factors at age 50 were linked with being in the "happy-well" category at 75 to 80 years of age: getting regular exercise, avoiding being overweight, being well-educated, having a stable marriage, being future-oriented, being thankful and forgiving, empathizing with others, being active with other people, and having good coping skills.

Wealth and income at age 50 were not linked with being in the "happy-well" category at 75 to 80 years of age. Generativity in middle age (defined in this study as "taking care of the next generation") was more strongly related than intimacy to whether individuals would have an enduring and happy marriage at 75 to 80 years of age (Vaillant, 2002).

The results for one of Vaillant's studies, the Grant Study of Harvard men, are shown in Figure 14.4. Note that when individuals at 50 years of age were not heavy smokers, did not abuse alcohol, had a stable marriage, exercised, maintained a normal weight, and had good coping skills, they were more likely to be alive and happy at 75 to 80 years of age.

Conclusions

What can be concluded about stability and change in personality development during the adult years? Avshalom Caspi and Brent Roberts (2001) concluded that

How Would You...?
As a health-care professional, how would you use the results of Vaillant's research to advise a middle-aged adult patient who abuses alcohol and smokes?

the evidence does not support the view that personality traits become completely fixed at a certain age in adulthood. However, they argue that change is typically limited, and in some cases the changes in personality are small. They also say that age is positively related to stability and that stability peaks in the fifties and sixties. That is, people show greater stability in their personality when they reach midlife than when they were younger adults. These findings support what is called a **cumulative personality model** of development, which states that with time and age, people become more adept at interacting with their environment in ways that promote the stability of personality.

This does not mean that change is absent throughout midlife. Ample evidence shows that social contexts, new experiences, and sociohistorical changes can affect personality development (Mroczek, Spiro, & Griffin, 2006). However, Caspi and Roberts (2001) concluded that as people get older, stability increasingly outweighs change.

In general, changes in personality traits across adulthood also occur in a positive direction. Over time, "people become more confident, warm, responsible, and calm" (Roberts & Mroczek, 2008, p. 33). Such positive changes equate with becoming more socially mature.

In sum, recent research contradicts the old view that stability in personality begins to set in at about 30 years of age (McAdams & Olson, 2010; Roberts, Wood, & Caspi, 2008). Although there are some consistent developmental changes in the personality traits of large numbers of people, at the individual level people can show unique patterns of personality traits—and these patterns often reflect life experiences related to themes of their particular developmental period (Roberts & Mroczek, 2008). For example, researchers have found that individuals who are in a stable marriage and on a solid career track become more socially dominant, conscientious, and emotionally stable as they go through early adulthood (Roberts & Wood, 2006). And, for some of these individuals, there is greater change in their personality traits than for other individuals (McAdams & Olson, 2010; Roberts & others, 2009).

Close Relationships

There is a consensus among middle-aged Americans that a major component of well-being involves positive relationships with others, especially parents, spouse, and offspring (Lachman, 2004). To begin our examination of midlife relationships, let's explore love and marriage in middle-aged adults.

Love and Marriage at Midlife

Remember from Chapter 12 that two major forms of love are romantic love and affectionate love. The fires of romantic love are strong in early adulthood. Affectionate, or companionate, love increases during middle adulthood. That is, physical attraction, romance, and passion are more important in new relationships, especially those begun in early adulthood. Security, loyalty, and mutual emotional interest become more important as relationships mature, especially in middle adulthood.

A recent study revealed that marital satisfaction increased in middle age (Gorchoff, John, & Helson, 2008). Even some marriages that were difficult and rocky during early adulthood turn out to be better adjusted during middle adulthood. Although the partners may have lived through a great deal of turmoil, they eventually discover a deep and solid foundation on which to anchor their relationship. In middle adulthood, the partners may have fewer financial worries, less housework and chores, and more time with each other. Middle-aged partners are more likely to view their marriage as positive if they engage in mutual activities.

Most individuals in midlife who are married voice considerable satisfaction with being married. In a large-scale study of individuals in middle adulthood, 72 percent of those who were married said their marriage was either "excellent" or "very good" (Brim, 1999). Possibly by middle age, many of the worst marriages already have dissolved. However, a recent study revealed that married and partnered middle-aged adults were more likely to rate their relationships as more ambivalent or indifferent than their late adulthood counterparts (Windsor & Butterworth, 2010).

Divorce in middle adulthood may be more positive in some ways, more negative in others, than divorce in early adulthood (Pudrovska, 2009). On the one hand, for mature individuals, the perils of divorce can be fewer and less intense than for younger individuals. They have more resources, and they can use this time as an opportunity to simplify their lives by disposing of possessions, such as a large home, which they no longer need. Their children are adults and may be able to cope with their parents' divorce more effectively. The partners may have gained a better understanding of themselves and may be searching for changes that could include the end to an unhappy marriage.

On the other hand, the emotional and time commitment to marriage that has existed for so many years may not be lightly given up. Many midlife individuals perceive a divorce as failing in the best years of their lives. The divorcer might see the situation as an escape from an untenable relationship, but the divorced partner usually sees it as betrayal, the ending of a relationship that had been built up over many years and that involved a great deal of commitment and trust.

A survey by AARP (2004) of 1,148 40- to 79-year-olds who were divorced at least once in their forties, fifties, or sixties found that staying married because of their children was by far the main reason many people took so long to become divorced. Despite the worry and stress involved in going through a divorce, three in four of the divorcees said they had made the right decision to dissolve their marriage and reported a positive outlook on life. Sixty-six percent of the divorced women said they initiated the divorce compared with only 41 percent of the divorced men. The divorced women were much more afraid of having financial problems (44 percent) than the divorced men (11 percent).

Following are the main reasons the middle-aged and older adults cited for their divorce:

Main Causes for Women

1. Verbal, physical, or emotional abuse (23 percent)
2. Alcohol or drug abuse (18 percent)
3. Cheating (17 percent)

Main Causes for Men

1. No obvious problems, just fell out of love (17 percent)
2. Cheating (14 percent)
3. Different values, lifestyles (14 percent)

What characterizes marriage in middle adulthood?

How Would You...?
As a social worker, how would you describe the different reasons for divorce between young and middle-aged adults?

The Empty Nest and Its Refilling

An important event in a family is the launching of a child into adult life. Parents face new adjustments as a result of the child's absence. Students usually think that their parents suffer from their absence. In fact, parents who live vicariously through their children might experience the **empty nest syndrome**, which includes a decline in marital satisfaction after children leave the home. For most parents, however, marital satisfaction does not decline after children have left home. Rather, for most parents marital satisfaction increases during the years after child rearing (Fingerman & Baker, 2006). With their children gone, marital partners have time to pursue careers and other interests and more time for each other. A recent study

Doonesbury

BY GARRY TRUDEAU

revealed that the transition to an empty nest increased marital satisfaction and this increase was linked to an increase in the quality of time—but not the quantity of time—spent with partners (Gorchoff, John, & Helson, 2003).

In today's uncertain economic climate, the refilling of the empty nest is becoming a common occurrence as adult children return to live at home after several years of college, after graduating from college, or to save money after taking a full-time job (Merril 2009). Young adults also may move back in with their parents after an unsuccessful career or a divorce. And some individuals don't leave home at all until their middle to late twenties because they cannot financially support themselves. Numerous labels have been applied to these young adults who return to their parents' homes to live, including "boomerang kids" and "B2B" (or Back-to-Bedroom) (Furman. 2005).

The middle generation has always provided support for the younger generation, even after the nest is bare. Through loans and monetary gifts for education, and through emotional support, the middle generation has helped the younger generation. Adult children appreciate the financial and emotional support their parents provide them at a time when they often feel considerable stress about their career, work, and lifestyle. And parents feel good that they can provide this support.

However, as with most family living arrangements, there are both pluses and minuses when adult children return to live at home. One of the most common complaints voiced by both adult children and their parents is a loss of privacy. The adult children complain that their parents restrict their independence, cramp their sex lives, reduce their rock music listening, and treat them as children rather than adults. Parents often complain that their quiet home has become noisy, that they stay up late worrying when their adult children will come home, that meals are difficult to plan because of conflicting

schedules, that their relationship as a married couple has been invaded, and that they have to shoulder too much responsibility for their adult children. In sum, when adult children return home to live, a disequilibrium in family life is created, which requires considerable adaptation on the part of parents and their adult children.

When adult children ask to return home to live, parents and their adult children should agree on the conditions and expectations beforehand. For example, they might discuss and agree on whether young adults will pay rent, wash their own clothes, cook their own meals, do any household chores, pay their phone bills, come and go as they please, be sexually active or drink alcohol at home, and so on. If these conditions aren't negotiated at the beginning, conflict often results because the expectations of parents and young adult children will likely be violated.

How Would You...?

As a psychologist, how would you counsel parents of adult children who return to live at home for a few years following their college?

What are some strategies that can help parents and their young adult children get along better?

Sibling Relationships and Friendships

Sibling relationships persist over the entire life span for most adults (Dunn, 2007). Eighty-five percent of today's adults have at least one living sibling. Sibling relationships in adulthood may be extremely close, apathetic, or highly rivalrous (Bedford, 2009). The majority of sibling relationships in adulthood are close (Cicirelli, 2009). Those siblings who are psychologically close to each other in adulthood tended to be that way in childhood. It is rare for sibling closeness to develop for the first time in adulthood (Dunn, 1984). A recent study revealed that adult siblings often provide practical and emotional support to each other (Voorpostel & Blieszner, 2008). Another study revealed that men who had poor sibling relationships in childhood were more likely to develop depression by age 50 than men who had more positive sibling relationships as children (Waldinger, Vaillant, & Orav, 2007).

Friendships continue to be important in middle adulthood just as they were in early adulthood (Antonucci, 1989). It takes time to develop intimate friendships, so friendships that have endured over the adult years are often deeper than those that have just been formed in middle adulthood.

Grandparenting

The increase in longevity is influencing the nature of grandparenting (Szinovacz, 2009). In 1900 only 4 percent of 10-year-old children had four living grandparents, but in 2000 that figure had risen to more than 40 percent. And in 1990 only about 20 percent of children at 30 years of age had living grandparents, a figure that is projected to increase to 80 percent in 2020 (Hagestad & Uhlenberg, 2007). Further increases in longevity are likely to support this trend in the future, although the current trend in delaying childbearing is likely to undermine it (Szinovacz, 2009).

Grandparent Roles

Grandparents play important roles in the lives of many grandchildren (Oberlander, Black, & Starr, 2007). Many adults become grandparents for the first time during middle age. Researchers have consistently found that grandmothers have more contact with grandchildren than do grandfathers (Watson, Randolph, & Lyons, 2005). Perhaps women tend to define their role as grandmothers as part of their responsibility for maintaining ties between family members across generations. Men may have fewer expectations about the grandfather role and see it as more voluntary.

What are some grandparents' roles and styles?

Three prominent meanings are attached to being a grandparent (Neugarten & Weinstein, 1964). For some older adults, being a grandparent is a source of biological reward and continuity. For others, being a grandparent is a source of emotional self-fulfillment, generating feelings of companionship and satisfaction that may have been missing in earlier adult-child relationships. And for yet others, being a grandparent is a remote role.

The grandparent role may have different functions in different families, in different ethnic groups and cultures, and in different situations (Szinovacz, 2009). For example, in one study of White, African American, and Mexican American grandparents and grandchildren, the Mexican American grandparents saw their grandchildren more frequently, provided more support for the grandchildren and their parents, and had more satisfying relationships with their grandchildren (Bengtson, 1985). And in a study of three generations of families in Chicago, grandmothers had closer relationships with their children and grandchildren and gave more personal advice than grandfathers did (Hagestad, 1985).

The Changing Profile of Grandparents

An increasing number of U.S. grandchildren live with their grandparents (Silverstein, 2009). In 1980, 2.3 million grandchildren lived with their grandparents, but in 2005 that figure had reached 6.1 million (U.S. Census Bureau, 2006). Divorce, adolescent pregnancies, and drug use by parents are the main reasons that grandparents are thrust back into the "parenting" role they thought they had shed. A recent study revealed that grandparent involvement was linked with better adjustment when it occurred in single-parent and stepparent families than in two-parent biological families (Attar-Schwartz & others, 2009).

Grandparents who are full-time caregivers for grandchildren are at elevated risk for health problems, depression, and stress (Silverstein 2009). Caring for grandchildren is linked with these problems in part because full-time grandparent caregivers are often characterized by low-income, minority status and by not being married (Minkler & Fuller-Thompson, 2005). Grandparents who are part-time caregivers are less likely to have the negative health portrait that full-time grandparent caregivers have. In a recent study of part-time grandparent caregivers, few negative effects on grandparents were found (Hughes & others, 2007).

As divorce and remarriage have become more common, a special concern of grandparents is visitation privileges with their grandchildren. In the last 10 to 15 years, more states have passed laws giving grandparents the right to petition a court for visitation privileges with their grandchildren, even if a parent objects. Whether such forced visitation rights for grandparents are in the child's best interest is still being debated.

How Would You...?

As a human development and family studies professional, how would you educate parents about the mutual benefits of having grandparents actively involved in their children's lives?

Intergenerational Relationships

Family is important to most people. When 21,000 adults aged 40 to 79 in 21 countries were asked, "When you think of who you are, you think mainly of _____," 63 percent said "family," 9 percent said "religion," and 8 percent said "work" (HSBC Insurance, 2007). In this study, in all 21 countries, middle-aged and older adults expressed a strong feeling of responsibility between generations in their family, with the strongest intergenerational ties indicated in Saudi Arabia, India, and Turkey. More than 80 percent of the middle-aged and older adults reported that adults have a duty to care for their parents (and parents-in-law) in time of need later in life.

Adults in midlife play important roles in the lives of the young and the old (Birditt & others, 2010; Martini & Busseri, 2010). Middle-aged adults share their experience and transmit values to the younger generation. They may be launching children and experiencing the empty nest, adjusting to having grown children return home, or becoming grandparents. They also may be giving or receiving financial assistance, caring for a widowed or sick parent, or adapting to being the oldest generation after both parents have died.

Middle-aged adults have been described as the "sandwich," "squeezed," or "overload" generation because of the responsibilities they have for their adolescent and young adult children on the one hand and their aging parents on the other (Etaugh & Bridges, 2010; Pudrovska, 2009). These simultaneous pressures from adolescents or young adult children and aging parents may contribute to stress in middle adulthood. Many middle-aged adults experience considerable stress when their parents become very ill and die. One survey found that when adults enter midlife, 41 percent have both parents alive but that 77 percent leave midlife

Middle-aged and older adults around the world show a strong sense of family responsibility. A recent study of middle-aged and older adults in 21 countries revealed the strongest intergenerational ties in Saudi Arabia.

with no parents alive (Bumpass & Aquilino, 1994). A recent study revealed that middle-aged parents are more likely to provide support to their grown children than to their parents (Fingerman & others, 2010). When middle-aged adults' parents have a disability, their support for their aging parents increases.

A valuable service that adult children can perform is to coordinate and monitor services for an aging parent who becomes disabled. This might involve locating a nursing home and monitoring its quality, procuring medical services, arranging public service assistance, and handling finances. In some cases, adult children provide direct assistance with daily living, including such activities as eating, bathing, and dressing. Even less severely impaired older adults may need help with shopping, housework, transportation, home maintenance, and bill paying.

In most cases researchers have found that relationships between aging parents and their children are usually characterized by ambivalence (Birditt, Fingerman, & Zarit, 2010; Davey & others, 2009; Fingerman & others, 2008). Perceptions include love, reciprocal help, and shared values on the positive side and isolation, family conflicts and problems, abuse, neglect, and caregiver stress on the negative side.

With each new generation, personality characteristics, attitudes, and values are replicated or changed. As older family members die, their biological, intellectual, emotional, and personal legacies are carried on in the next generation. Their children become the oldest generation and their grandchildren the second generation. As adult children become middle-aged, they often develop more positive perceptions of their parents (Field, 1999). Both similarity and dissimilarity across generations are found. For example, similarity between parents and an adult child is most noticeable in religion and politics, least in gender roles, lifestyle, and work orientation.

The following studies provide further evidence of the importance of intergenerational relationships in development:

- The motivation of adult children to provide social support to their older parents was linked with earlier family experiences (Silverstein & others, 2002). Children who spent more time in shared activities with their parents and were given more financial support by them earlier in their lives provided more support to their parents when they became older.

- Adult children of divorce who were classified as securely attached were less likely to divorce in the early years of their marriage than their insecurely attached counterparts (Crowell, Treboux, & Brockmeyer, 2009).

- Parents who smoked early and often, and persisted in becoming regular smokers, were more likely to have adolescents who became smokers (Chassin & others, 2008).

How Would You...?
As a health-care professional, how would you advise a family contemplating the potential challenges of having a middle-aged family member take on primary responsibility for the daily care of a chronically ill parent?

Gender differences also characterize intergenerational relationships (Etaugh & Bridges, 2010) Women have an especially important role in connecting family relationships across generations. Women's relationships across generations are typically closer than other family bonds (Merrill, 2009). In one study, mothers and their daughters had much closer relationships during their adult years than mothers and sons, fathers and daughters, and fathers and sons (Rossi, 1989). Also in this study, married men were more involved with their wives' kin than with their own. And maternal grandmothers and maternal aunts were cited twice as often as their counterparts on the paternal side of the family as the most important or loved relative. Also, a recent study revealed that mothers' intergenerational ties were more influential for grandparent-grandchild relationships than fathers' (Monserud, 2008).

Summary

Personality Theories and Development

- Erikson says that the seventh stage of the human life span, generativity versus stagnation, occurs in middle adulthood. Levinson concluded that a majority of Americans, especially men, experience a midlife crisis. Research, though, indicates that midlife crises are not pervasive.

- In the contemporary version of the life-events approach, how life events influence the individual's development depends not only on the life event but also on mediating factors, adaptation to the event, the life-stage context, and the sociohistorical context.

- Young and middle-aged adults experience more stressful days than do older adults, and as adults become older, they report less control over some areas of their lives and more control over other areas.

- Neugarten argues that the social environment of a particular cohort can alter its social clock. Many cultures do not have a clear concept of middle age.

Stability and Change

- In Costa and McCrae's Baltimore Study, the big five personality factors showed considerable stability. In the Berkeley Longitudinal Studies, the extremes in the stability-change argument were not supported. George Vaillant's research revealed links between a number of characteristics at age 50 and health and well-being at 75 to 80 years of age.

- Some researchers suggest that stability peaks in the fifties and sixties, others say that it begins to stabilize at about 30, and still others argue that limited personality changes continue during midlife.

Close Relationships

- Affectionate love increases in midlife for many individuals.

- Rather than decreasing marital satisfaction as once thought, the empty nest increases it for most parents. An increasing number of young adults are returning home to live with their middle-aged parents.

- Sibling relationships continue throughout life, and friendships continue to be important in middle age.

- Depending on the family's culture and situation, grandparents assume different roles. The profile of grandparents is changing.

- Family members usually maintain contact across generations. The middle-aged generation plays an important role in linking generations.

Key Terms

generativity 322
stagnation 322
contemporary life-events
  approach 324

social clock 326
Big Five factors of
  personality 327

cumulative personality
  model 329

empty nest
  syndrome 330

15 Physical and Cognitive Development in Late Adulthood

Stories of Life-Span Development: Learning to Age Successfully

Jonathan Swift said, "No wise man ever wished to be younger." Without a doubt, a 70-year-old body does not work as well as it once did. It is also true that an individual's fear of aging is often greater than need be. As more individuals live to a ripe and active old age, our image of aging is changing. While on the average a 75-year-old's joints should be stiffening, people can practice not to be average. For example, a 75-year-old man might choose to train for and run a marathon; an 80-year-old

woman whose capacity for work is undiminished might choose to make and sell children's toys.

Consider 85-year-old Sadie Halperin, who has been working out for 11 months at a rehabilitation center for the aged in Boston. She lifts weights and rides a stationary bike. She says that before she started working out, about everything she did—shopping, cooking, walking—was a major struggle. Sadie says she always felt wobbly and held on to a wall when she walked. Now she walks down the

center of the hallways and reports that she feels wonderful. Initially she could lift only 15 pounds with both legs; now she lifts 30 pounds. At first she could bench-press only 20 pounds; now she bench-presses 50 pounds. Sadie's exercise routine has increased her muscle strength and helps her to battle osteoporosis by slowing the calcium loss from her bones, which can lead to deadly fractures (Ubell, 1992).

The story of Sadie Halperin's physical development and well-being in late

Eighty-five-year-old Sadie Halperin engaging in her exercise routine.

adulthood raises some truly fascinating questions about life-span development, which we explore in this chapter. They include: Why do we age, and what, if anything, can we do to delay the aging process? What chance do you have of living to be 100? How does the body change in old age? How well do older adults function cognitively? What roles do work and retirement play in older adults' lives?

Longevity, Biological Aging, and Physical Development

What do we really know about longevity? What are the current biological theories about why we age? How does our brain change during this part of our life span? What happens to us physically? Does our sexuality change?

Longevity

The United States is no longer a youthful society. As more individuals are living past age 65, the proportion of individuals at different ages has become increasingly similar. Indeed, the concept of a period called "late adulthood," beginning in the sixties or seventies and lasting until death, is a recent one. Before the 20th century, most individuals died before they reached 65.

Life Span and Life Expectancy

Since the beginning of recorded history, **life span**, the maximum number of years an individual can live, has remained at approximately 120 to 125 years of age. But since 1900 improvements in medicine, nutrition, exercise, and lifestyle have increased our life expectancy an average of 31 additional years.

Recall from Chapter 1 that **life expectancy** is the number of years that the average person born in a particular year will probably live. Sixty-five-year-olds in the United States today can expect to live an average of 18 more years (20 for females, 16 for males). The average life expectancy of individuals born today in the United States is 78 years (National Center for Health Statistics, 2009).

Differences in Life Expectancy

How does the United States fare in life expectancy, compared with other countries around the world? We do considerably better than some, a little worse than some others (Powell, 2009). Japan has the highest life expectancy at birth today (82 years) (Guillot, 2009).

Today, the overall life expectancy for females is 80.7 years of age, for males 75.4 years of age (National Center for Health Statistics, 2009). Beginning in the mid-thirties, females outnumber males; this gap widens during the remainder of the adult years. By the time adults are 75 years of age, more than 61 percent of the population is female; for those 85 and over, the figure is almost 70 percent female. Why can women expect to live longer than men? Social factors such as health attitudes, habits, lifestyles, and occupation are probably important (Saint Onge, 2009). In fact, men are more likely than women to die from the leading causes of death in the United States, such as cancer of the respiratory system,

evolutionary theory of aging The view that natural selection has not eliminated many harmful conditions and nonadaptive characteristics in older adults.

cellular clock theory Leonard Hayflick's theory that the maximum number of times that human cells can divide is about 75 to 80. As we age, our cells become increasingly less capable of dividing.

motor vehicle accidents, cirrhosis of the liver, emphysema, and coronary heart disease (Yoshida & others, 2006). These causes of death are associated with lifestyle. For example, the sex difference in deaths due to lung cancer and emphysema occurs because men are heavier smokers than women.

The sex difference in longevity also is influenced by biological factors (Guillot, 2009; Oksuzyan & others, 2008). In virtually all species, females outlive males. Women have more resistance to infections and degenerative diseases (Candore & others, 2006). For example, the female's estrogen production helps to protect her from arteriosclerosis (hardening of the arteries). And the additional X chromosome that women carry in comparison to men may be associated with the production of more antibodies to fight off disease.

Centenarians

In the United States, there were only 15,000 centenarians in 1980, a number that had risen to 55,000 in 2008. It is projected that this number will reach more than 800,000 by 2050. Many people expect that "the older you get, the sicker you get." However, researchers are finding that is not true for some centenarians (Kutner, 2009). A study of 93 centenarians revealed that despite some physical limitations, they had a low rate of age-associated diseases and most had good mental health (Selim & others, 2005).

What chance do you have of living to be 100? Genes play an important role in surviving to an extreme old age (Bostock, Solza, & Whalley, 2009). As we saw in Chapter 2, the search for longevity genes has recently intensified (Hinks & others, 2009). But there are also other factors at work such as family history, health (weight, diet, smoking, and exercise), education, personality, and lifestyle (Barbieri & others, 2009).

Biological Theories of Aging

Even if we stay remarkably healthy, we begin to age at some point. Four biological theories provide intriguing explanations of why we age: evolutionary, cellular clock, free-radical, and hormonal stress.

Evolutionary Theory

In the **evolutionary theory of aging**, natural selection has not eliminated many harmful conditions and nonadaptive characteristics in older adults (Austad, 2009; Kittas, 2010). Why? Because natural selection is linked to reproductive fitness, which only is present in the earlier part of adulthood. For example, consider Alzheimer disease, an irreversible brain disorder, which does not appear until the late middle adulthood or late adulthood years. In evolutionary theory, possibly if Alzheimer disease occurred earlier in development, it may have been eliminated many centuries ago.

Cellular Clock Theory

Cellular clock theory is Leonard Hayflick's (1977) theory that cells can divide a maximum of about 75 to 80 times and that, as we age, our cells become less capable of dividing. Hayflick found that cells extracted from adults in their fifties to seventies divided fewer than 75 to 80 times. Based on the ways cells divide, Hayflick places the upper limit of the human life-span potential at about 120 to 125 years of age.

In the last decade, scientists have tried to fill in a gap in cellular clock theory (Sahin & Daphino, 2010; Zou & others, 2009). Hayflick did not know why cells die. The answer may lie at the tips of chromosomes, at *telomeres,* which are DNA sequences that cap chromosomes (Davoli, Denchi, & de Lange, 2010; Osterhage & Friedman, 2009). Each time a cell divides, the telomeres become shorter and shorter (see Figure 15.1). After about 70 or 80 replications, the telomeres are dramatically reduced, and the cell no longer can reproduce. A recent study revealed that healthy centenarians had longer telomeres than unhealthy centenarians (Terry & others, 2008).

Figure 15.1 Telomeres and Aging
The photograph shows actual telomeres lighting up the tips of chromosomes. Each time a cell divides, the telomeres become shorter and shorter, until eventually they can no longer reproduce.

Injecting the enzyme *telomerase* into human cells grown in the laboratory can substantially extend the life of the cells beyond the approximately 70 to 80 normal cell divisions (Aubert & Lansdorp, 2008). However, telomerase is present in approximately 85 percent of cancerous cells and thus may not produce healthy life extension of cells (Fakhoury, Nimmo, & Autexier, 2007). To capitalize on the high presence of telomerase in cancerous cells, researchers currently are investigating gene therapies that inhibit telomerase and lead to the death of cancerous cells while keeping healthy cells alive (Effros, 2009).

free-radical theory A theory of aging that states that people age because inside their cells normal metabolism produces unstable oxygen molecules known as free radicals. These molecules ricochet around inside cells, damaging DNA and other cellular structures.

hormonal stress theory The theory that aging in the body's hormonal system can lower resilience to stress and increase the likelihood of disease.

Free-Radical Theory

A third theory of aging is **free-radical theory**, which states that people age because when cells metabolize energy, the by-products include unstable oxygen molecules known as *free radicals*. The free radicals ricochet around the cells, damaging DNA and other cellular structures (Afanas'ev, 2009). The damage can lead to a range of disorders, including cancer and arthritis (Farooqui & Farooqui, 2009).

Hormonal Stress Theory

Cellular clock and free radical theories attempt to explain aging at the cellular level. In contrast, **hormonal stress theory** argues that aging in the body's hormonal system can lower resistance to stress and increase the likelihood of disease. Normally, when people experience stressors, the body responds by releasing certain hormones. As people age, the hormones stimulated by stress remain at elevated levels longer than when people were younger (Simm & others, 2008). These prolonged, elevated levels of stress-related hormones are associated with increased risks for many diseases, including cardiovascular disease, cancer, diabetes, and hypertension (Epel, 2009; Wolkowitz & others, 2010).

Recently, a variation of hormonal stress theory has emphasized the contribution of a decline in immune system functioning with aging (Walston & others, 2009). Aging contributes to immune system deficits that give rise to infectious diseases in older adults (Bauer, Jeckel, & Luz, 2009). The extended duration of stress and diminished restorative processes in older adults may accelerate the effects of aging on immunity.

Which of these biological theories best explains aging? That question has not yet been answered. It might turn out that more than one or all of these biological processes contribute to aging.

The Aging Brain

How does the brain change during late adulthood? Does it retain plasticity? Here we examine how the brain shrinks and slows but still has considerable adaptive ability.

The Shrinking, Slowing Brain

On average, the brain loses 5 to 10 percent of its weight between the ages of 20 and 90. Brain volume also decreases (Bondare, 2007). One study found that the volume of the brain was 15 percent less in older adults than younger adults (Shan & others, 2005). Scientists are not sure why these changes occur but think that they might result from a decrease in dendritic connections or damage to the

cataracts Involve a thickening of the lens of the eye that causes vision to become cloudy, opaque, and distorted.

glaucoma Damage to the optic nerve because of the pressure created by a buildup of fluid in the eye.

macular degeneration A disease that involves deterioration of the macula of the retina, which corresponds to the focal center of the visual field.

shorter when we get older. As we saw in Chapter 13, both men and women become shorter in late adulthood because of bone loss in their vertebrae (Hoyer & Roodin, 2009).

Our weight usually drops after we reach 60 years of age. This likely occurs because we lose muscle, which also gives our bodies a "sagging" look (Evans, 2010).

Older adults move slower than young adults, and this slowing occurs for many types of movement with a wide range of difficulty (Sakuma & Yamaguchi, 2010). A recent study revealed that obesity was linked to mobility limitation in older adults (Houston & others, 2009).

Exercise and appropriate weight lifting can help to reduce the decrease in muscle mass and improve the older person's body appearance (Peterson & others, 2009; Venturelli & others, 2010). And a recent study revealed that it's not just physical exercise that is linked to preserving older adults' motor functions; in this study, engaging in social activities protected against loss of motor abilities (Buchman & others, 2009).

Sensory Development

Seeing, hearing, and other aspects of sensory functioning are linked with our ability to perform everyday activities, and they decline in older adults (Cimarolli, 2009; Wood & others, 2010).

Vision In late adulthood, the decline in vision that began for most adults in early or middle adulthood becomes more pronounced (Dillon & others, 2010; Sharts-Hopko, 2009). The eye does not adapt as quickly when moving from a well-lighted place to one of semidarkness. The tolerance for glare also diminishes. The area of the visual field becomes smaller, and it's possible that events that occur away from the center of the visual field might not be detected (Scialfa & Kline, 2007). All these changes may make night driving especially difficult (Babizhayev, Minasyan, & Richer, 2009; Wood & others, 2010).

Recent research has shown that sensory decline in older adults is linked to a decline in cognitive functioning. One study of individuals in their seventies revealed that visual decline was related to slower speed of processing information, which in turn was associated with greater cognitive decline (Clay & others, 2009).

Color vision also may decline as a result of the yellowing of the lens of the eye (Scheiber, 2006). As a result, older adults may have trouble accurately matching closely related colors such as navy socks and black socks.

Depth perception typically declines in late adulthood, which can make it difficult for the older adult to determine how close or far away or how high or low something is (Bian & Anderson, 2009). A decline in depth perception can make steps or street curbs difficult to manage.

Three diseases that can impair the vision of older adults are cataracts, glaucoma, and macular degeneration:

- **Cataracts** involve a thickening of the lens of the eye that causes vision to become cloudy, opaque, and distorted. By age 70, approximately 30 percent of individuals experience a partial loss of vision due to cataracts. Initially, cataracts can be treated by glasses; if they worsen, a simple surgical procedure can remove them (Chung & others, 2009).

- **Glaucoma** involves damage to the optic nerve because of the pressure created by a buildup of fluid in the eye (Fechtner & others, 2010). Approximately 1 percent of individuals in their seventies and 10 percent of those in their nineties have glaucoma, which can be treated with eyedrops. If left untreated, glaucoma can ultimately destroy a person's vision (Musch & others, 2009).

- **Macular degeneration** is a disease that involves deterioration of the *macula* of the retina, which corresponds to the focal center of the visual field. Individuals with macular degeneration may have relatively normal peripheral vision but be unable to see clearly what is right in front of them (Ghosh & others,

How Would You...?
As a health-care professional, how would you respond to an older adult who shows signs of impaired vision but denies, or is unaware of, the problem?

2010; Rovner & others, 2009) (see Figure 15.3). It affects 1 in 25 individuals from age 66 to 74 and 1 in 6 of those age 75 and older. Macular degeneration is difficult to treat and thus is a leading cause of blindness in older adults (Wang & others, 2009).

Hearing For hearing as for vision, it is important to determine the degree of decline in the aging adult (Dillon & others, 2010). The decline in vision and hearing is much greater in individuals 75 years and older than in individuals aged 65 to 74 (Charness & Bosman, 1992). Hearing impairment usually does not become much of an impediment until late adulthood, usually due to degeneration of the *cochlea*, the primary neural receptor for hearing in the inner ear (Adams, 2009). Even in late adulthood, some, but not all, hearing problems can be corrected by hearing aids (Cook & Hawkins, 2006). Wearing two hearing aids that are balanced to correct the hearing loss in each ear separately can sometimes help hearing-impaired adults.

Figure 15.3 Macular Degeneration
This simulation of the effect of macular degeneration shows how individuals with this eye disease can see their peripheral field of vision but can't clearly see what is in their central visual field.

How Would You...?
As an educator, how would you structure your classroom and class activities to accommodate the sensory decline of older adult students?

Smell and Taste Most older adults lose some of their sense of smell or taste, or both (Murphy, 2009). These losses often begin around 60 years of age (Hawkes, 2006). A majority of individuals 80 years of age and older experience a significant reduction in smell (Lafreiere & Mann, 2009). Researchers have found that older adults show a greater decline in their sense of smell than in their taste (Schiffman, 2007). Smell and taste decline less in healthy older adults than in their less healthy counterparts.

Touch and Pain Changes in touch and pain are also associated with aging (Gagliese, 2009; Schmader & others, 2010). For most older adults, a decline in touch sensitivity is not problematic (Hoyer & Roodin, 2009). Older adults are less sensitive to pain and suffer from it less than younger adults (Harkins, Price, & Martinelli, 1986). Although decreased sensitivity to pain can help older adults cope with disease and injury, it can also mask injury and illness that need to be treated.

The Circulatory System and Lungs

Consistent blood pressures above 120/80 should be treated to reduce the risk of heart attack, stroke, or kidney disease (Krakoff, 2008). A rise in blood pressure with age can be linked with illness, obesity, stiffening of blood vessels, stress, or lack of exercise (Shizukuda, Plummer, & Harrelson, 2010). The longer any of these factors persist, the worse the individual's blood pressure gets (Miura & others, 2009). Various drugs, a healthy diet, and exercise can reduce the risk of cardiovascular disease in older adults (Coke & Fletcher, 2010; Hedberg & others, 2009). One recent study revealed that among a number of factors, exercise capacity and walking were the best predictors of whether individuals' death would involve cardiovascular problems (Reibis & others, 2010).

Lung capacity drops 40 percent between the age of 20 and 80, even without disease (Fozard, 1992). Lungs lose elasticity, the chest shrinks, and the diaphragm weakens (Simpson & others, 2005). The good news, though, is that older adults can improve lung functioning with diaphragm-strengthening exercises.

Sexuality

In the absence of two circumstances—disease and the belief that old people are or should be asexual—sexuality can be lifelong (Bain, 2010; Woloski-Wruble & others, 2010). Aging, however, does induce some changes in human sexual performance, more so in the male than in the female (Bauman, 2008).

Orgasm becomes less frequent in males with age, occurring in every second to third attempt rather than every time. More direct stimulation usually is needed to produce an erection. From age 65 to 80, approximately one out of four men have serious problems getting and/or keeping erections, and after 80 years of age the percentage rises to one out of two men (Butler & Lewis, 2002).

A recent study revealed that many older adults are sexually active as long as they are healthy (Lindau & others, 2007). Sexual activity did decline through the later years of life: 73 percent of 57- to 64-year-olds, 53 percent of 65- to 74-year-olds, and 26 percent 75- to 85-year-olds reported that they were sexually active. Even in the sexually active oldest group (75 to 85), more than 50 percent said they still have sex at least two to three times a month. Also, a recent large-scale study of individuals 57 to 85 years of age revealed that sexual activity, a good quality sexual life, and interest in sex were positively related to the health of middle-aged and older adults (Lindau & Gavrilova, 2010). In this study, men lost more years of sexually active life due to poor health than women did.

What are some characteristics of sexuality in older adults? How does sexuality change as older adults go through the late adulthood period?

How Would You...? As a social worker, how would you advise couples in late adulthood who are concerned that they will no longer be able to have a satisfying sexual relationship due to their age?

Health

What types of health problems do adults have in late adulthood, and what can be done to maintain or improve their health and ability to function in everyday life?

Health Problems

As we age, the probability increases that we will have some disease or illness. The majority of adults still alive at 80 years of age or older are likely to have some type of impairment. Chronic diseases (those with a slow onset and a long duration) are rare in early adulthood, increase in middle adulthood, and become more common in late adulthood.

Arthritis is the most common chronic disorder in late adulthood, followed by hypertension. Older women have a higher incidence of arthritis and hypertension and are more likely to have visual problems, but are less likely to have hearing problems, than older men are.

Low income is also strongly related to health problems in late adulthood (Ferraro, 2006; Yang & Lee, 2010). Approximately three times as many poor as non-poor older adults report that chronic disorders limit their activities. One study also revealed that frailty increased for low-income older adults regardless of their ethnicity (Szanton & others, 2010).

Causes of Death in Older Adults

Nearly 60 percent of U.S. adults age 65 to 74 die of cancer or cardiovascular disease (National Center for Health Statistics, 2008). As we saw in Chapter 13, Physical

What are the most common chronic conditions in late adulthood?

and Cognitive Development in Middle Adulthood, cancer recently replaced cardiovascular disease as the leading cause of death in U.S. middle-aged adults. The same realignment of causes of death has also occurred in 65- to 74-year olds, with cancer now the leading cause of death in this age group (National Center for Health Statistics, 2010). The decline in cardiovascular disease in middle-aged and older adults is due to improved drugs, a decrease in smoking, better diet, and an increase in exercise. However, in the 75-to-84 and 85-and-over age groups, cardiovascular disease is still the leading cause of death (National Center for Health Statistics, 2010), and the older a person is, the more likely the person will die of cardiovascular disease (National Center for Health Statistics, 2010).

Arthritis

Arthritis is an inflammation of the joints accompanied by pain, stiffness, and movement problems. This incurable disorder can affect hips, knees, ankles, fingers, and vertebrae. Individuals with arthritis often experience difficulty moving about and performing routine daily activities. Arthritis is especially prevalent in older adults (Villeneuve & Haraoui, 2010). Recent studies document the benefits of exercise in older adults with arthritis (de Jong & others, 2009; Metsios & others, 2010). For example, a high-intensity, 16-week strength training program significantly increased the strength and reduced the pain of arthritis patients (Flint-Wagner & others, 2009).

Osteoporosis

Normal aging brings some loss of bone tissue, but for some individuals loss of bone tissue can become severe. **Osteoporosis** involves an extensive loss of bone tissue. Osteoporosis is the main reason many older adults walk with a marked stoop (Ishikawa & others, 2009). Women are especially vulnerable to osteoporosis, the leading cause of broken bones in women (Bessette & others, 2009). Approximately 80 percent of osteoporosis cases in the United States occur in females, 20 percent in males. Almost two-thirds of all women over the age of 60 are affected by osteoporosis. It is more common in non-Latina White, thin, and small-framed women.

Osteoporosis is related to deficiencies in calcium, vitamin D, estrogen, and lack of exercise (Bonjour & others, 2009; Dionyssiotis & others, 2010). A program of regular exercise also has the potential to reduce osteoporosis (Iwamoto & others, 2009).

Accidents

Accidents are the sixth leading cause of death among older adults (National Center for Health Statistics, 2010). Falls are the leading cause of injury deaths among adults who are age 65 and older (National Center for Health Statistics, 2010). Each year, approximately 200,000 adults over the age of 65 (most of them women) fracture a hip in a fall. Half of these older adults die within 12 months, frequently from pneumonia. A recent study revealed that participation in an exercise class once a week for three years reduced the fall risk and the number of falling incidents in older adults who were at high risk for falling (Yokoya, Demura, & Sato, 2009).

How Would You...?
As a health-care professional, how would you educate older adults on the range of chronic diseases that are common for this age group?

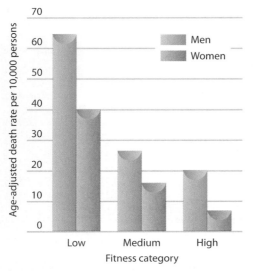

Figure 15.4 Physical Fitness and Mortality
In this study of middle-aged and older adults, being moderately fit or highly fit meant that individuals were less likely to die over a period of eight years than their less fit (sedentary) counterparts (Blair & others, 1989).

Exercise, Nutrition, and Weight

Although we may be in the evening of our lives in late adulthood, we are not meant to live out our remaining years passively. Everything we know about older adults suggests they are healthier and happier the more active they are. Can regular exercise lead to a healthier late adulthood and increase longevity? How does eating a calorie-restricted diet and controlling weight also contribute?

Exercise

In one study, exercise literally meant a difference in life or death for middle-aged and older adults (Blair, 1990). More than 10,000 men and women were divided into categories of low fitness, medium fitness, and high fitness (Blair & others, 1989). Then they were studied over a period of eight years. As shown in Figure 15.4, sedentary participants (low fitness) were more than twice as likely to die during the eight-year time span of the study than those who were moderately fit and more than three times as likely to die as those who were highly fit. The positive effects of being physically fit occurred for both men and women in this study. Also, a recent study of more than 11,000 women found that low cardiorespiratory fitness was a significant predictor of all-cause mortality (Farrell & others, 2010).

Gerontologists increasingly recommend strength training in addition to aerobic activity and stretching for older adults. Resistance exercise can preserve and possibly increase muscle mass in older adults (Williamson & others, 2010). A recent meta-analysis revealed that resistance training—especially high intensity training—was effective in improving older adults' strength and is a viable strategy for reducing muscular weakness associated with aging (Peterson & others, 2010).

Exercise is an excellent way to maintain health, and researchers continue to document its positive effects in older adults (Desai, Grossberg, & Chibnall, 2010; Erickson & others, 2009). Exercise helps people to live independent lives with dignity in late adulthood. At age 80, 90, and even 100, exercise can help prevent older adults from falling down or even being institutionalized (Maimoun & others, 2010; Peterson & others, 2009). And exercise increases the information processing skills of older adults (Marks, Katz, & Smith, 2009; Williamson & others, 2009).

Exercise is linked to increased longevity. A recent study also revealed that systolic blood pressure during exercise was linked to an increase in long-term survival of 75-year-olds (Hedberg & others, 2009). Energy expenditure during exercise of at least 1,000 kcal/week reduces mortality by about 30 percent, while 2,000 kcal/week reduces mortality by about 50 percent (Lee & Skerrett, 2001).

Nutrition and Weight

Scientists have accumulated considerable evidence that caloric restriction (CR) in laboratory animals (in most cases rats) can increase the animals' life span (Minor & others, 2010). Animals fed diets restricted in calories, although adequate in protein, vitamins, and minerals, live as much as 40 percent longer than animals given unlimited access to food (Jolly, 2005). And chronic problems such as kidney disease appear at a later age (Fernandez, 2008). CR also delays biochemical alterations such as the age-related rise in cholesterol and triglycerides observed in both humans and animals (Fontana, 2009). And recent research indicates that CR may provide neuroprotection for an aging central nervous system (Contestabile, 2009; Opalach & others, 2010) (see Figure 15.5). For example, a recent study revealed that following CR for three months, the verbal memory of older adults improved (Witte & others, 2009).

No one knows for certain how CR works to increase the life span of animals. Some scientists say that CR might lower the level of free radicals and reduce oxidative stress in cells. Others argue that CR might trigger a state of emergency called "survival mode" in which the body eliminates all unnecessary functions to focus only on staying alive.

Whether similar very low calorie diets can stretch the human life span is not known (Blagosklonny, 2010). In some instances the animals in these studies ate 40 percent less than normal. In humans, a typical level of calorie restriction involves a 30 percent decrease, which translates into about 1,120 calories a day for the average woman and 1,540 for the average man.

Leaner adults, especially women, do live longer, healthier lives (Wandell, Carlsson, & Theobold, 2009). In one study of 19,297 Harvard alumni, those weighing the least were less likely to die over the three decades studied.

Health Treatment

About 3 percent of adults age 65 and older in the United States reside in a nursing home at some point in time. As older adults age, however, their probability of being in a nursing home or other extended-care facility increases. Twenty-three percent of adults aged 85 and older live in nursing homes or other extended-care facilities.

The quality of nursing homes and other extended-care facilities for older adults varies enormously and is a source of continuing national concern (Eskildsen & Price, 2009). More than one-third are seriously deficient. They fail federally mandated inspections because they do not meet the minimum standards for physicians, pharmacists, and various rehabilitation specialists (occupational and physical therapists). Further concerns focus on the patient's right to privacy, access to medical information, safety, and lifestyle freedom within the individual's range of mental and physical capabilities.

Because of the inadequate quality and the escalating costs of many nursing homes, many specialists in the health problems of the aged stress that home health care, elder-care centers, and preventive medicine clinics are good alternatives (Katz & others, 2009). They are potentially less expensive than hospitals and nursing homes. They also are less likely to engender the feelings of depersonalization and dependency that occur so often in residents of institutions. Currently, there is an increased demand for but shortage of home care workers because of the increase in population of older adults and their preference to stay out of nursing homes (Moos, 2007).

In a classic study, Judith Rodin and Ellen Langer (1977) found that an important factor related to health, and even survival, in a nursing home is the patient's

Figure 15.5 Calorie Restriction in Monkeys
Shown here are two monkeys at the Wisconsin Primate Research Center. Both are 24 years old. The monkey in the top photograph was raised on a calorie-restricted diet, while the monkey in the bottom photograph was raised on a normal diet. Notice that the monkey on the calorie-restricted diet looks younger; he also has lower glucose and insulin levels. The monkey raised on a normal diet has higher triglycerides and more oxidative damage to his cells.

How Would You...?
As a psychologist, how would you structure the environment of a nursing home to produce maximum health and psychological benefits for the residents?

divided attention Concentrating on more than one activity at the same time.

sustained attention The state of readiness to detect and respond to small changes occurring at random times in the environment.

episodic memory The retention of information about the where and when of life's happenings.

semantic memory A person's knowledge about the world—including a person's fields of expertise, general academic knowledge of the sort learned in school, and "everyday knowledge."

simple tasks involving searching for a feature, such as determining whether a target item is present on a computer screen, age differences are minimal when individuals are given sufficient practice.

Divided attention involves concentrating on more than one activity at the same time. When the two competing tasks are reasonably easy, age differences among adults are minimal or nonexistent. However, the more difficult the competing tasks are, the less effectively older adults divide attention than younger adults (Bucur & Madden, 2007).

Sustained attention is the state of readiness to detect and respond to small changes occurring at random times in the environment. Sometimes sustained attention is referred to as *vigilance*. Researchers have found that older adults perform as well as middle-aged and younger adults on measures of sustained attention (Berardi, Parasuraman, & Haxby, 2001).

Memory

Memory does change during aging, but not all types of memory change with age in the same way (Barba, Attali, & La Corte, 2010; Bialystok & Craik, 2010; Ornstein & Light, 2010). The main dimensions of memory and aging that have been studied include episodic memory and semantic memory, cognitive resources (such as working memory and perceptual speed), explicit and implicit memory, and noncognitive factors such as health, education, and socioeconomic factors.

Episodic and Semantic Memory Episodic memory is the retention of information about the where and when of life's happenings. For example, what were you doing when you heard that the World Trade Center was attacked on 9/11/2001, or what did you eat for breakfast this morning?

Younger adults have better episodic memory than older adults have (Cansino, 2009). Also, older adults think that they can remember older events better than more recent events. However, researchers consistently have found that the older the memory, the less accurate it is in older adults (Smith, 1996).

Semantic memory is a person's knowledge about the world. It includes a person's fields of expertise, general academic knowledge of the sort learned in school, and "everyday knowledge" about the meanings of words, important places, and common things. Older adults do often take longer to retrieve semantic information, but usually they can ultimately retrieve it. However, the ability to retrieve very specific information (such as names) usually declines in older adults (Luo & Craik, 2008). For the most part, episodic memory declines more than semantic memory in older adults (Yoon, Cole, & Lee, 2009).

Cognitive Resources: Working Memory and Perceptual Speed Two important cognitive resource mechanisms are working memory and perceptual speed. Recall from Chapter 13 that *working memory* is closely linked to short-term memory but places more emphasis on memory as a place for mental work (Baddeley, 2007). Researchers have found declines in working memory during the late adulthood years (Delaloye & others, 2009). Explanation of the decline in working memory in older adults focuses on their less efficient inhibition in preventing irrelevant information from entering working memory and their increased distractibility (Lustig & Hasher, 2010; Rowe, Hasher, & Turcotte, 2010).

Perceptual speed is another cognitive resource that has been studied by researchers on aging. Perceptual speed is the amount of time it takes to perform simple perceptual-motor tasks such as how long it takes to decide whether pairs of two-digit or two-letter strings are the same, or how long it takes someone to step on the brakes when the car directly ahead stops. Perceptual speed shows considerable decline in late adulthood, and it is strongly linked with decline in working memory (Salthouse, 2009).

Explicit and Implicit Memory Researchers also have found that aging is linked with changes in explicit memory (Hoyer & Roodin, 2009). Explicit memory is memory of facts and experiences that individuals consciously know and can state. Explicit memory also is sometimes called *declarative memory*. Examples of explicit memory include recounting the events of a movie you have seen or being at a grocery store and remembering what you wanted to buy. Implicit memory is memory without conscious recollection; it involves skills and routine procedures that are automatically performed, such as driving a car or typing on a computer keyboard, without having to consciously think about it.

Implicit memory is less likely to be adversely affected by aging than explicit memory (Howard & others, 2008). Thus, older adults are more likely to forget what items they wanted to buy at a grocery store than they are to forget how to drive a car. Their perceptual speed might be slower in driving the car, but they remember how to do it.

Noncognitive Factors Health, education, and socioeconomic status (SES) can influence an older adult's performance on memory tasks (Lachman & others, 2010; Noble & others, 2010). Although such noncognitive factors as good health are associated with less memory decline in older adults, they do not eliminate memory decline. A recent study revealed that older adults with less education had lower cognitive abilities than those with more education (Lachman & others, 2010). However, for older adults with less education, frequently engaging in cognitive activities improved their episodic memory.

Conclusions About Memory and Aging Some, but not all, aspects of memory decline in older adults (Healey & Hasher, 2009). The decline occurs primarily in episodic and working memory, not in semantic memory or implicit memory. A decline in perceptual speed is associated with memory decline (Salthouse, 2009). Successful aging does not mean eliminating memory decline, but does mean reducing it and adapting to it.

Wisdom

Does wisdom, like good wine, improve with age? What is this thing we call "wisdom"? Wisdom is expert knowledge about the practical aspects of life that permits excellent judgment about important matters. This practical knowledge involves exceptional insight into human development and life matters, good judgment, and an understanding of how to cope with difficult life problems. Thus, wisdom, more than standard conceptions of intelligence, focuses on life's pragmatic concerns and human conditions (Bluck & Barron, 2009; Karelitz, Jarvin, & Sternberg, 2011). A recent study revealed that older adults engaged in superior reasoning about social conflicts than young or middle-aged adults (Grossman & others, 2010). Older adults' superior reasoning included taking multiple perspectives, allowing for compromise, and recognizing the limits of their knowledge.

In regard to wisdom, Paul Baltes and his colleagues (2006) have found the following. (1) High levels of wisdom are rare. Few people, including older adults, attain a high level of wisdom. That only a small percentage of adults show

Older adults might not be as quick with their thoughts or behavior as younger people, but wisdom may be an entirely different matter. This older man shares the wisdom of his experience with a classroom of children. *How is wisdom described by life-span developmentalists?*

total worth of his or her life might be negative (despair).

Life review is prominent in Erikson's final stage of integrity versus despair. Life review involves looking back at one's life experiences, evaluating them, interpreting them, and often reinterpreting them (George, 2010; Robitaille & others, 2010). Distinguished aging researcher Robert Butler (2007) argues that the life review is set in motion by looking forward to death. Sometimes the life review proceeds quietly; at other times it is intense, requiring considerable work to achieve some sense of personality integration. The life review may be observed initially in stray and insignificant thoughts about oneself and one's life history. These thoughts may continue to emerge in brief intermittent spurts or become essentially continuous.

When older adults engage in a life review, they may reevaluate previous experiences and their meaning, often with revision or expanded understanding taking place. This reorganization of the past may provide a more valid picture for the individual, providing new and significant meaning to one's life (Stinson & Kirk, 2006).

activity theory The theory that the more active and involved older adults are, the more likely they are to be satisfied with their lives.

socioemotional selectivity theory The theory that older adults become more selective about their social networks. Because they place a high value on emotional satisfaction, older adults often spend more time with familiar individuals with whom they have had rewarding relationships.

One aspect of life review involves identifying and reflecting not only on the positive aspects of one's life but also on regrets as part of developing a mature wisdom and self-understanding (Choi & Jun, 2009). The hope is that by examining not only the positive aspects of one's life, but also what an individual has regretted doing, a more accurate vision of the complexity of one's life and possibly increased life satisfaction will be attained (King & Hicks, 2007). A recent study revealed that for low-income older adults, regrets about education, careers, and marriage were common, but the intensity of regrets was greater for finance/money, family conflict and children's problems, loss and grief, and health (Choi & Jun, 2009). Common indications of pride involved children and parenting, careers, volunteering/informal caregiving, having a long/strong marriage, and personal growth.

What characterizes a life review in late adulthood?

Some clinicians use *reminiscence therapy* with their older clients. Reminiscence therapy involves discussing past activities and experiences with another individual or group. The therapy may include the use of photographs, familiar items, and video/audio recordings (Peng & others, 2009). Researchers have found that reminiscence therapy improves the mood of older adults (Fiske, Wetherell, & Gatz, 2009). For example, a recent study of institutionalized older adults found that reminiscence therapy increased their life satisfaction and decreased their depression and loneliness (Chiang & others, 2010). Also, a recent study revealed that a life-review course, "Looking for Meaning," reduced the depressive symptoms of middle-aged and older adults (Pot & others, 2010).

How Would You...?

As a psychologist, how would you explain to an older adult the benefits of engaging in a life review?

Activity Theory

Activity theory states that the more active and involved older adults are, the more likely they are to be satisfied with their lives. Researchers have found strong support for activity theory, beginning in the 1960s and continuing into the 21st century (Neugarten, Havighurst, & Tobin, 1968; Riebe & others, 2005). These researchers have found that when older adults are active, energetic, and productive, they age more successfully and are happier than if they disengage from society.

Activity theory suggests that many individuals will achieve greater life satisfaction if they continue their middle-adulthood roles into late adulthood. If these roles are stripped from them (as in early retirement), it is important for them to find substitute roles that keep them active and involved.

Socioemotional Selectivity Theory

Socioemotional selectivity theory states that older adults become more selective about their social networks. Because they place a high value on emotional satisfaction, older adults spend more time with familiar individuals with whom they have had rewarding relationships. Developed by Laura Carstensen (1998, 2006, 2008), this theory argues that older adults deliberately withdraw from social contact with individuals peripheral to their lives while they maintain or increase contact with close friends and family members with whom they have had enjoyable relationships. This selective narrowing of social interaction maximizes positive emotional experiences and minimizes emotional risks as individuals become older.

Laura Carstensen. Her theory of socioemctional selectivity is gaining recognition as an important theory.

selective optimization with compensation theory The theory that successful aging is related to three main factors: selection, optimization, and compensation.

Socioemotional selectivity theory challenges the stereotype that the majority of older adults are in emotional despair because of their social isolation (Charles & Carstensen, 2010; Scheibe & Carstensen, 2010). Rather, older adults consciously choose to decrease the total number of their social contacts in favor of spending increasing time in emotionally rewarding moments with friends and family. That is, they systematically hone their social networks so that available social partners satisfy their emotional needs.

Is there research evidence to support life-span differences in the composition of social networks? Researchers have found that older adults have far smaller social networks than younger adults (Charles & Carstensen, 2010).

Socioemotional selectivity theory also focuses on the types of goals that individuals are motivated to achieve (Charles & Carstensen, 2010). It states that two important classes of goals are (1) knowledge-related and (2) emotion-related (Mikels & others, 2010). This theory emphasizes that the trajectory of motivation for knowledge-related goals starts relatively high in the early years of life, peaking in adolescence and early adulthood and then declining in middle and late adulthood. The emotion trajectory is high during infancy and early childhood, declines from middle childhood through early adulthood, and increases in middle and late adulthood.

Researchers have found that across diverse samples (Norwegians, Catholic nuns, African Americans, Chinese Americans, and European Americans) older adults report better control of their emotions and fewer negative emotions than younger adults (Mroczek, 2001; Scheibe & Carstensen, 2010). Compared with younger adults, the emotional life of older adults is on a more even keel with fewer highs and lows (Charles & Carstensen, 2010; Samanez-Larkin & Carstensen, 2011). It may be that although older adults have less extreme joy, they have more contentment, especially when they are connected in positive ways with friends and family.

How Would You...?
As a health-care professional, how would you assess whether an older adult's limited social contacts signal unhealthy social isolation or healthy socioemotional selectivity?

Selective Optimization With Compensation Theory

Selective optimization with compensation theory states that successful aging is linked with three main factors: selection, optimization, and compensation (SOC). The theory describes how people can produce new resources and allocate them effectively to the tasks they want to master (Baltes, Lindenberger, & Staudinger, 2006; Freund & Lamb, 2011; Staudinger & Jacobs, 2011). *Selection* is based on the concept that older adults have a reduced capacity and loss of functioning, which require a reduction in performance in most life domains. *Optimization* suggests that it is possible to maintain performance in some areas through continued practice and the use of new technologies. *Compensation* becomes relevant when life tasks require a level of capacity beyond the current level of the older adult's performance potential. Older adults especially need to compensate in circumstances with high mental or physical demands, such as when thinking about and memorizing new material very fast, reacting quickly when driving a car, or running fast. When older adults develop an illness, the need for compensation is obvious.

In the view of Paul Baltes and his colleagues (2006), the selection of domains and life priorities is an important aspect of development. Life goals and personal life investments likely vary across the life course for most people. For many individuals, it is not just the sheer attainment of goals, but rather the attainment of *meaningful* goals, that makes life satisfying. In one cross-sectional study, the personal life investments of 25- to 105-year-olds were assessed (Staudinger, 1996)

12 percent of the population. The health-care needs of older adults are reflected in Medicare, the program that provides health-care insurance to adults over 65 under the Social Security system (Fu & others, 2010).

A special concern is that while many of the health problems of older adults are chronic rather than acute, the medical system is still based on a "cure" rather than a "care" model. Chronic illness is long-term, often lifelong, and requires long-term, if not life-term, management (Harris, Pan, & Mukhtar, 2010).

Eldercare Eldercare is the physical and emotional caretaking of older members of the family, whether that care is day-to-day physical assistance or responsibility for arranging and overseeing such care. An important issue involving eldercare is how it can best be provided (Beverly & others, 2010; Nabe-Nielsen & others, 2009). Before so many women entered the workforce, they often served as caretakers for the elderly. Now with so many women working outside the home, there is a question of who will replace them as caregivers. An added problem is that many caregivers are in their sixties, and many of them are ill themselves. They may find it especially stressful to be responsible for the care of relatives who are in their eighties or nineties.

Technology

The Internet plays an increasingly important role in access to information and communication for adults as well as youth (Cresci, Yarandi, & Morrell, 2010; Rosenberg & others, 2009). How well are older adults keeping up with changes in technology? Older adults are less likely to have a computer in their home and less likely to use the Internet than younger adults, but older adults are the fastest-growing segment of Internet users (Czaja & others, 2006). Older adults log more time on the Internet (an average of 8.3 hours per week), visit more Web sites, and spend

Are older adults keeping up with changes in technology?

more money on the Internet than their younger adult counterparts. They are especially interested in learning to use e-mail and going online for health information (Westlake & others, 2007). Increasing numbers of older adults use e-mail to communicate with relatives. And a recent study found that frequent computer use was linked to higher performance on cognitive tasks in older adults (Tun & Lachman, 2010). As with children and younger adults, cautions about the accuracy of information—in areas such as health care—on the Internet need to always be kept in mind (Cutler, 2009).

Families and Social Relationships

Are the close relationships of older adults different from those of younger adults? What are the lifestyles of older adults like? What characterizes the relationships of older adult parents and their adult children? What do friendships and social networks contribute to the lives of older adults? How might older adults' altruism and volunteerism contribute to positive outcomes?

Lifestyle Diversity

The lifestyles of older adults are changing (Blieszner & Bedford, 2011; Carr & Moorman, 2011). Formerly, the later years of life were likely to consist of marriage for men and widowhood for women. With demographic shifts toward marital dissolution characterized by divorce, one-third of adults can now expect to marry, divorce, and remarry during their lifetime. Let's now explore some of the diverse lifestyles of older adults, beginning with those who are married or partnered.

What are some characteristics of marriage in late adulthood?

Married Older Adults

In 2009, 56 percent of U.S. adults over 65 years of age were married (U.S. Census Bureau, 2010). Individuals who are in a marriage or a partnership in late adulthood are usually happier, are less distressed, and live longer than those who are single (Peek, 2009). One study found that older adults were more satisfied with their marriages than were young and middle-aged adults (Bookwala & Jacobs, 2004). Indeed, the majority of older adults evaluate their marriages as happy or very happy (Huyck, 1995). A recent study of octogenerians revealed that marital satisfaction helped to protect their happiness from daily fluctuations in perceived health (Waldinger & Schulz, 2010). Also, a longitudinal study of adults 75 years of age and older revealed that individuals who were married were less likely to die across a span of seven years (Rasulo, Christensen, & Tomassini, 2005).

Divorced and Remarried Older Adults

In 2008, 13 percent of women and 10 percent of men 65 years and older in the United States were divorced or separated (U.S. Census Bureau, 2010). Many of these individuals were divorced or separated before they entered late adulthood (Carr & Pudrovska, 2011). The majority of divorced older adults are women, due to their greater longevity, and men are more likely to remarry, thus removing themselves from the pool of divorced older adults (Peek, 2009). Divorce is far less common in older adults than younger adults likely reflecting cohort effects rather than age effects since divorce was somewhat rare when current cohorts of older adults were young (Peek, 2009).

There are social, financial, and physical consequences of divorce for older adults (Carr & Pudrovska, 2011). Divorce can weaken kinship ties when it occurs in later life, especially in the case of older men. Divorced older women are less likely to have adequate financial resources than married older women, and as earlier in adulthood, divorce is linked to more health problems in older adults (Bennett, 2006).

Rising divorce rates, increased longevity, and better health have led to an increase in remarriage by older adults (Ganong & Coleman, 2006). What happens when an older adult wants to remarry or does remarry? Researchers have found that some older adults perceive negative social pressure about their decision to remarry (McKain, 1972). These negative sanctions range from raised eyebrows to rejection by adult children (Ganong & Coleman, 2006). However, the majority of adult children support the decision of their older adult parents to remarry.

Adult children can be personally impacted by remarriage between older adults. Researchers have found that remarried parents and stepparents provide less support to adult stepchildren than parents in first marriages (White, 1994).

Cohabiting Older Adults

An increasing number of older adults cohabit. In the middle of the 20th century, hardly any older adults cohabited. Today, approximately 3 percent of older adults cohabit, but that percentage is expected to increase as baby boomers with their less traditional values about love, sex, and relationships enter late adulthood. In many cases, the cohabiting is more for companionship than for love. In other cases, for example, when one partner faces the potential for expensive care, a couple may decide

How Would You...?
As a psychologist, how would you assist older adults in coping with the unique challenges faced by divorcées at this age?

to maintain their assets separately and thus not marry. One study found that older adults who cohabited had a more positive, stable relationship than younger adults who cohabited, although cohabiting older adults were less likely to have plans to marry their partner than younger ones (King & Scott, 2005). Other research also has revealed that middle-aged and older adult cohabiting men and women reported higher levels of depression than their married counterparts (Brown, Bulanda, & Lee, 2005).

Older Adult Parents and Their Adult Children

Approximately 80 percent of older adults have living children, many of whom are middle-aged. About 10 percent of older adults have children who are 65 years or older. Adult children are an important part of the aging parent's social network. Researchers have found that older adults with children have more contacts with relatives than those without children (Johnson & Troll, 1992).

Increasingly, diversity characterizes older adult parents and their adult children. Divorce, cohabitation, and nonmarital childbearing are more common in the history of older adults today than in the past (Carr & Pudrovska, 2011).

Gender plays an important role in relationships involving older adult parents and their children (Ward-Griffin & others, 2007). Adult daughters rather than adult sons are more likely to be involved in the lives of aging parents. For example, adult daughters are three times more likely than are adult sons to give parents assistance with daily living activities (Dwyer & Coward, 1991).

A valuable task that adult children can perform is to coordinate and monitor services for an aging parent (or relative) who becomes disabled (Silverstein, 2009). This might involve locating a nursing home and monitoring its quality, procuring medical services, arranging public service assistance, and handling finances. In some cases, adult children provide direct assistance with daily living, including such activities as eating, bathing, and dressing. Even less severely impaired older adults may need help with shopping, housework, transportation, home maintenance, and bill paying.

Friendship

How Would You...?
As a human development and family studies professional, how would you characterize the importance of friendships for older adults?

In early adulthood, friendship networks expand as new social connections are made away from home. In late adulthood, new friendships are less likely to be forged, although some adults do seek out new friendships, especially following the death of a spouse (Zettel-Watson & Rook, 2009).

Aging expert Laura Carstensen (2006) concluded that people choose close friends over new friends as they grow older. And as long as they have several close people in their network, they seem content, says Carstensen.

In one study of 128 married older adults, women were more depressed than men if they did not have a best friend, and women who did have a friend reported lower levels of depression (Antonucci, Lansford, & Akiyama, 2001). Similarly, women who did not have a best friend were less satisfied with life than women who did have a best friend. And a longitudinal study of adults 75 years of age and older revealed that individuals with close ties with friends were less likely to die across a seven-year age span (Rasulo, Christensen, & Tomassini, 2005). The findings were stronger for women than men.

Social Support and Social Integration

Social support and social integration play important roles in the physical and mental health of older adults (Antonucci & others, 2011). In the *social convoy* model of social relations, individuals go through life embedded in a personal network of individuals to whom they give, and from whom they receive, social support (Antonucci, Birditt, & Kalinauskas, 2009; Antonucci & others, 2011). Social support can help individuals of all ages cope more effectively (Griffiths & others, 2007). For older adults, social support is related to their physical and mental health (Cheng, Lee, & Chow, 2010). It is linked with a reduction in symptoms of disease, with the ability to meet one's own health-care needs, and mortality (Rook & others, 2007). Social support also decreases the probability that an older adult will be institutionalized and is associated with a lower incidence of depression (Cacioppo & others, 2006).

Social integration also plays an important role in the lives of many older adults (Antonucci & others, 2011). Remember from our earlier discussion of socioemotional selectivity theory that many older adults choose to have fewer peripheral social contacts and more emotionally positive contacts with friends and family (Charles & Carstensen, 2010). Thus, a decrease in the overall social activity of many older adults may reflect their greater interest in spending more time in the small circle of friends and families where they are less likely to have negative emotional experiences. A low level of social integration is linked with poorer health and earlier death in older adults (Koropeckyj-Cox, 2009). A recent study found that loneliness predicted increased blood pressure four years later in middle-aged and older adults (Hawkley & others, 2010).

What role does social support play in the health of older adults?

Researchers have found that older adults tend to report being less lonely than younger adults and less lonely than would be expected based on their circumstances (Schnittker, 2007). Their reports of feeling less lonely than younger adults likely reflect their more selective social networks and greater acceptance of loneliness in their lives (Koropeckyj-Cox, 2009).

Altruism and Volunteerism

A common perception is that older adults need to be given help rather than give help themselves. However, a recent study found that older adults perceived their well-being as better when they provided social support to others than when they received, except when received from a spouse or sibling (Thomas, 2010). And a 12-year longitudinal study revealed that older adults who had persistently low or declining feelings of usefulness to others had an increased risk of earlier death (Gruenewald & others, 2009). Further, researchers recently have found that when older adults engage in altruistic behavior and volunteering, they benefit from these activities (Morrow-Howell, 2010). For example, one study revealed that volunteering was linked to less frailty in older adults (Jung & others, 2010). A recent analysis concluded that rates of volunteering do not decline significantly until the mid-seventies, and older adults commit more hours than younger volunteers (Morrow-Howell, 2010). Older adults are also more likely than any other age group to volunteer more than 100 hours annually (Burr, 2009).

How Would You...?
As an educator, how would you persuade the school board to sponsor a volunteer program to bring older adults into the school system to work with elementary students?

Researchers also have found that volunteering as an older adult is associated with a number of positive outcomes (Burr, 2009). For example, a study of 2,000 older adults in Japan revealed that those who gave more assistance to others had

Ninety-eight-year-old volunteer Iva Broadus plays cards with 10-year-old DeAngela Williams in Dallas, Texas. Iva recently was recognized as the oldest volunteer in the Big Sister program in the United States. Iva says that card-playing helps to keep her memory and thinking skills good and can help DeAngela's as well.

better physical health than their elderly counterparts who gave less assistance (Krause & others, 1999). Among the reasons for the positive outcomes of volunteering are its provision of constructive activities and productive roles, social integration, and enhanced meaningfulness (Tan & others, 2007).

Ethnicity, Gender, and Culture

How is ethnicity linked to aging? Do gender roles change in late adulthood? What are some of the social aspects of aging in different cultures?

Ethnicity

Of special concern are ethnic minority older adults, especially African Americans and Latinos, who are overrepresented in poverty statistics (Kingson & Bartholomew, 2009). Comparative information about African Americans, Latinos, and non-Latino Whites indicates a possible double jeopardy for elderly ethnic minority individuals. They face problems related to *both* ageism and racism (Ciol & others, 2008). They also are more likely to have a history of less education, unemployment, worse housing conditions, and shorter life expectancies than their older White counterparts.

Despite the stress and discrimination older ethnic minority individuals face, many of these older adults have developed coping mechanisms that allow them to survive in the dominant White world. Extension of family networks helps older minority group individuals cope with the bare essentials of living and gives them a sense of being loved (Karasik & Hamon, 2007). Churches in African American and Latino communities provide avenues for meaningful social participation, feelings of power, and a sense of internal satisfaction (Hill & others, 2005). To read about one individual who is providing help for aging minorities, see "Careers in Life-Span Development."

CAREERS IN LIFE-SPAN DEVELOPMENT

Norma Thomas, Social Work Professor and Administrator

Dr. Norma Thomas has worked for more than three decades in the field of aging. She obtained her undergraduate degree in social work from Pennsylvania State University and her doctoral degree in social work from the University of Pennsylvania. Thomas' activities are varied. Earlier in her career, as a social work practitioner, she provided services to older adults of color in an effort to improve their lives. She currently is a professor and academic administrator at Widener University in Chester, Pennsylvania, a fellow of the Institute of Aging at the University of Pennsylvania, and the chief executive officer and co-founder of the Center on Ethnic and Minority Aging (CEMA). CEMA was formed to provide research, consultation, training, and services to benefit aging individuals of color, their families, and their communities. Thomas has created numerous community service events that benefit older adults of color, especially African Americans and Latinos. She has also been a consultant to various national, regional, and state agencies in her effort to improve the lives of aging adults of color.

Norma Thomas.

Gender

Do our gender roles change when we become older adults? Some developmentalists believe there is decreasing femininity in women and decreasing masculinity in men when they reach the late adulthood years (Gutmann, 1975). The evidence suggests that older men do become more feminine—nurturant, sensitive, and so on—but it appears that older women do not necessarily become more masculine—assertive, dominant, and so on (Turner, 1982). Keep in mind that cohort effects are especially important to consider in areas such as gender roles. As sociohistorical changes take place and are assessed more frequently in life-span investigations, what were once perceived to be age effects may turn out to be cohort effects (Schaie, 2007).

A possible double jeopardy also faces many women—the burden of *both* ageism and sexism (Calisanti, 2009). The poverty rate for older adult females is almost double that of older adult males.

Not only is it important to be concerned about older women's double jeopardy of ageism and sexism, but special attention also needs to be devoted to female ethnic minority older adults (Leitheit-Limson & Levy, 2009). They face what could be described as triple jeopardy—ageism, sexism, and racism.

Culture

What factors are associated with whether older adults are accorded a position of high status in a culture? Six factors are most likely to predict high status for older adults in a culture (Sangree, 1989):

- Older persons have valuable knowledge.

- Older persons control key family/community resources.

- Older persons are permitted to engage in useful and valued functions as long as possible.

A special concern is the stress faced by older African American women, many of whom view religion as a source of strength to help them cope. *What are some other characteristics of being female, ethnic, and old?*

- Age-related role changes involve greater responsibility, authority, and advisory capacity.

- The extended family is a common family arrangement in the culture, and the older person is integrated into the extended family.

- In general, respect for older adults is greater in collectivistic cultures (such as China and Japan) than in individualistic cultures (such as the United States). However, some researchers are finding that this collectivistic/individualistic difference in respect for older adults is not as strong as it used to be and that, in some cases, older adults in individualistic cultures receive considerable respect (Antonucci, Vandewater, & Lansford, 2000).

Cultures vary in the prestige they give to older adults. In the Navajo culture, older adults are especially treated with respect because of their wisdom and extensive life experiences. *What are some other factors that are linked with respect for older adults in a culture?*

Successful Aging

For too long, the positive dimensions of late adulthood were ignored (Depp & Jeste, 2010; Stirling, 2011). Throughout this book, we have called attention to the positive aspects of aging. In fact, examining the positive aspects of aging is an important trend in life-span development and is likely to benefit future generations of older adults (Charles & Carstensen, 2010; Depp & Jeste, 2010). There are many robust, healthy older adults. With a proper diet, an active lifestyle, mental stimulation and flexibility, positive coping skills, good social relationships and support, and the absence of disease, many abilities can be maintained or in some

Defining Death and Life/Death Issues

Is there one point in the process of dying that is *the* point at which death takes place, or is death a more gradual process? What are some decisions individuals can make about life, death, and health care?

Determining Death

Twenty-five years ago, determining if someone was dead was simpler than it is today. The end of certain biological functions—such as breathing and blood pressure, and the rigidity of the body (rigor mortis)—were considered to be clear signs of death. In the past several decades, defining death has become more complex (Zamperetti & Bellomo, 2009).

Brain death is a neurological definition of death, which states that a person is brain dead when all electrical activity of the brain has ceased for a specified period of time. A flat EEG (electroencephalogram) recording for a specified period of time is one criterion of brain death. The higher portions of the brain often die sooner than the lower portions. Because the brain's lower portions monitor heartbeat and respiration, individuals whose higher brain areas have died may continue breathing and have a heartbeat. The definition of brain death currently followed by most physicians includes the death of both the higher cortical functions and the lower brain stem functions (Truog, 2008).

Some medical experts argue that the criteria for death should include only higher cortical functioning. If the cortical death definition were adopted, then physicians could claim a person is dead who has no cortical functioning, even though the lower brain stem is functioning. Supporters of the cortical death policy argue that the functions we associate with being human, such as intelligence and personality, are located in the higher cortical part of the brain. They believe that when these functions are lost, the "human being" is no longer alive.

How Would You...? As a health-care professional, how would you explain "brain death" to the family of an individual who has suffered a severe head injury in an automobile accident?

Decisions Regarding Life, Death, and Health Care

In cases of catastrophic illness or accidents, patients might not be able to respond adequately to participate in decisions about their medical care. To prepare for this situation, some individuals make choices earlier.

Natural Death Act and Advance Directive

For many patients in a coma, it has not been clear what their wishes regarding termination of treatment might be if they still were conscious. Recognizing that terminally ill patients might prefer to die rather than linger in a painful or vegetative state, the organization "Choice in Dying" created the living will. This document is designed to be filled in while the individual can still think clearly; it expresses the person's desires regarding extraordinary medical procedures that might be used to sustain life when the medical situation becomes hopeless (Henrikson, 2010; Racine & others, 2010).

Physicians' concerns over malpractice suits and the efforts of people who support the living will concept have produced natural death legislation in many states. For example, California's Natural Death Act permits individuals who have been diagnosed by two physicians as terminally ill to sign an *advance directive,* which states that life-sustaining procedures shall not be used to prolong their lives when death is imminent. An advance directive must be signed while the individual still is able to think clearly (Westphal & McKee, 2009).

How Would You...? As a social worker, how would you explain to terminally ill clients the advantages of preparing a living will?

Euthanasia

Euthanasia ("easy death") is the act of painlessly ending the lives of individuals who are suffering from an incurable disease or severe disability. Sometimes euthanasia is called "mercy killing." Distinctions are made between two types of euthanasia: passive and active. **Passive euthanasia** occurs when a person is allowed to die by withholding available treatment such as withdrawing a life-sustaining device. For example, this might involve turning off a respirator or a heart-lung machine. **Active euthanasia** occurs when death is deliberately induced, as when a lethal dose of a drug is injected. A recent Dutch study of almost 7,000 dying persons revealed that only 7 percent requested passive or active euthanasia, and of those who requested, approximately one-third of the requests were granted (Onwuteaka-Philipsen & others, 2010).

Technological advances in life-support devices raise the issue of quality of life. Nowhere was this more apparent than in the highly publicized case of Terri Schiavo, who suffered severe brain damage related to cardiac arrest and a lack of oxygen to the brain (Givens & Mitchell, 2009). She went into a coma and spent 15 years in a vegetative state. Across the 15 years, whether passive euthanasia should be implemented, or whether she should be kept in the vegetative state with the hope that her condition might change for the better, was debated between family members and eventually at a number of levels in the judicial system. At one point toward the end of her life in early spring 2005, a judge ordered her feeding tube be removed. However, subsequent appeals led to its reinsertion twice. The feeding tube was removed a third and final time on March 18, 2005, and she died 13 days later. Withholding the life-support system allowed Terri Schiavo to die from passive euthanasia.

Should individuals like Terri Schiavo be kept alive in a vegetative state? The trend is toward acceptance of passive euthanasia in the case of terminally ill patients (Truog, 2008). However, a recent study revealed that family members were reluctant to have their relatives disconnected from a ventilator but rather wanted an escalation of treatment for them (Sviri & others, 2009). In this study, most of the individuals said that in similar circumstances they would not want to be chronically ventilated or resuscitated.

The most widely publicized cases of active euthanasia involve "assisted suicide." Jack Kevorkian, a Michigan physician, has assisted a number of terminally ill patients in ending their lives. After a series of trials, Kevorkian was convicted in the state of Michigan of second-degree murder and served eight years in prison.

Active euthanasia is a crime in most countries and in all states in the United States except in two states—Oregon and Washington. In 1994, the state of Oregon passed the Death with Dignity Act, which allows active euthanasia. Through 2001, 91 individuals were known to have died by active euthanasia in Oregon. In January 2006, the U.S. Supreme Court upheld Oregon's active euthanasia law. Active euthanasia is legal in the Netherlands, Belgium, Luxembourg, and Uruguay (Smets & others, 2010; Watson, 2009).

Needed: Better Care for Dying Individuals

Too often, death in America is lonely, prolonged, and painful. Scientific advances sometimes have made dying harder by delaying the inevitable. Also, even though painkillers are available, too many people experience severe pain during the last days and months of life (Alonso-Babarro & others, 2010; Cassell & Rich, 2010). Many health-care professionals have not been trained to provide adequate end-of-life care or to understand its importance.

How Would You...?
As a psychologist, how would you counsel the family of a brain-dead patient on the topic of euthanasia when there is no living will or advance directive for guidance?

Terri Schiavo (*right*) shown with her mother in an undated photo. *What issues did the Terri Schiavo case raise?*

DEFINING DEATH AND LIFE/DEATH ISSUES

375

hospice A program committed to making the end of life as free from pain, anxiety, and depression as possible. The goals of hospice contrast with those of a hospital, which are to cure disease and prolong life.

palliative care Emphasized in hospice care; involves reducing pain and suffering and helping individuals die with dignity.

Care providers are increasingly interested in helping individuals experience a "good death" (Goodie & McGlory, 2010; Ott, 2010; Toledo-Pereyra, 2010). One view is that a good death involves physical comfort, support from loved ones, acceptance, and appropriate medical care. For some individuals, a good death involves accepting one's impending death and not feeling like a burden to others (Carr, 2009).

Hospice is a program committed to making the end of life as free from pain, anxiety, and depression as possible (Berry, 2010). Whereas a hospital's goals are to cure illness and prolong life, hospice care emphasizes **palliative care**, which involves reducing pain and suffering and helping individuals die with dignity (Bruera & others, 2010; Chan & Webster, 2010). Hospice-care professionals work together to treat the dying person's symptoms, make the individual as comfortable as possible, show interest in the person and the person's family, and help them all cope with death (Ireland, 2010; Kahana, Kahana, & Wykle, 2010).

Today more hospice programs are home-based, a blend of institutional and home care designed to humanize the end-of-life experience for the dying person. To read about the work of a home hospice nurse, see "Careers in Life-Span Development."

How Would You...?
As a human development and family studies professional, how would you advocate for a terminally ill person's desire for hospice care?

CAREERS IN LIFE-SPAN DEVELOPMENT

Kathy McLaughlin, Home Hospice Nurse

Kathy McLaughlin is a home hospice nurse in Alexandria, Virginia. She provides care for individuals with terminal cancer, Alzheimer disease, and other diseases. There currently is a shortage of home hospice nurses in the United States.

Kathy says that she has seen too many people dying in pain, away from home, hooked up to needless machines. In her work as a home hospice nurse, she comments, "I know I'm making a difference. I just feel privileged to get the chance to meet this person who is not going to be around much longer. I want to enjoy the moment with this person. And I want them to enjoy the moment. They have great stories. They are better than novels" (McLaughlin, 2003, p. 1).

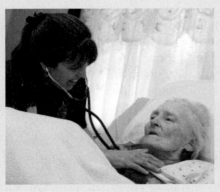

Kathy McLaughlin checks the vital signs of Kathryn Francis, 86, who is in an advanced stage of Alzheimer disease.

Hospice nurses, like Kathy McLaughlin, care for terminally ill patients and seek to make their remaining days in life as pain-free and comfortable as possible. They typically spend several hours a day in the terminally ill patient's home, serving not just as a medical caregiver but also as an emotional caregiver. Hospice nurses usually coordinate the patient's care through an advising physician.

Hospice nurses must be registered nurses (RNs) plus be certified as a hospice worker. Educational requirements are an undergraduate degree in nursing; some hospice nurses also have graduate degrees in nursing. To be a certified hospice nurse requires a current license as an RN, a minimum of two years of experience as an RN in hospice-nursing settings, and passing an exam administered by the National Board for the Certification of Hospice Nurses.

Death and Sociohistorical, Cultural Contexts

Today in the United States, the deaths of older adults account for approximately two-thirds of the 2 million deaths that occur each year. Thus, what we know about death, dying, and grieving mainly is based on information about older adults. Youthful death is far less common. When, where, and how people die have changed historically in the United States. Also, attitudes toward death vary across cultures.

Changing Historical Circumstances

We have already described one of the historical changes involving death—the increasing complexity of determining when someone is truly dead. Another historical change involves the age group in which death most often strikes. Two hundred years ago, almost one of every two children died before the age of 10, and one parent died before children grew up. Today, death occurs most often among older adults (Carr, 2009). In the United States, life expectancy has increased from 47 years for a person born in 1900 to 78 years for someone born today (U.S. Census Bureau, 2008). In 1900, most people died at home, cared for by their family. As our population has aged and become more mobile, more older adults die apart from their families (Carr, 2009). In the United States today, more than 80 percent of all deaths occur in institutions or hospitals. The care of a dying older person has shifted away from the family and minimized our exposure to death and its painful surroundings.

Death in Different Cultures

Cultural variations characterize the experience of death and attitudes about death (Bruce, 2007). Individuals are more conscious of death in times of war, famine, and plague.

Most societies throughout history have had philosophical or religious beliefs about death, and most societies have a ritual that deals with death (see Figure 17.1). Death may be seen as a punishment for one's sins, an act of atonement, or a judgment of a just God. For some, death means loneliness; for others, death is a quest for happiness. For still others, death represents redemption, a relief from the trials and tribulations of the earthly world. Some embrace death and welcome it; others abhor and fear it. For those who welcome it, death may be seen as the fitting end to a fulfilled life. From this perspective, how we depart from earth is influenced by how we have lived.

Figure 17.1 A Ritual Associated With Death
Family memorial day at the national cemetery in Seoul, South Korea.

In most societies, death is not viewed as the end of existence—though the biological body has died, the spirit is believed to live on (Hedayat, 2006). This religious perspective is favored by most Americans as well. Cultural variations in attitudes toward death include belief in reincarnation, which is an important aspect of the Hindu and Buddhist religions. In the Gond culture of India, death is believed to be caused by magic and demons.

In many ways, we in the United States are death avoiders and death deniers (Norouzieh, 2005). This denial can take many forms the tendency of the funeral industry to gloss over death and fashion lifelike qualities in the dead; the persistent search for a "fountain of youth"; the rejection and isolation of the aged, who may remind us of death; and the medical community's emphasis on prolonging biological life rather than on diminishing human suffering.

Facing One's Own Death

Most dying individuals want an opportunity to make some decisions regarding their own life and death (Kastenbaum, 2007). Some individuals want to complete unfinished business; they want time to resolve problems and conflicts and to put their affairs in order (Emanuel, Bennett, & Richardson, 2007). Might there be a sequence of stages we go through as we face death?

denial and isolation Kübler-Ross'
first stage of dying, in which the
dying person denies that she or he
is really going to die.

anger Kübler-Ross' second stage of
dying, in which the dying person's
denial often gives way to anger,
resentment, rage, and envy.

bargaining Kübler-Ross' third stage
of dying, in which the dying person
develops the hope that death can
somehow be postponed.

depression Kübler-Ross' fourth
stage of dying, in which the dying
person comes to accept the certainty
of her or his death. A period of
depression or preparatory grief
may appear.

acceptance Kübler-Ross' fifth stage
of dying, in which the dying person
develops a sense of peace, an
acceptance of her or his fate, and, in
many cases, a desire to be left alone.

Kübler-Ross' Stages of Dying

Elisabeth Kübler-Ross (1969) divided the behavior and thinking of dying persons into five stages: denial and isolation, anger, bargaining, depression, and acceptance.

Denial and isolation is Kübler-Ross' first stage of dying, in which the person denies that death is really going to take place. The person may say, "No, it can't be me. It's not possible." This is a common reaction to terminal illness. However, denial is usually only a temporary defense. It is eventually replaced with increased awareness when the person is confronted with such matters as financial considerations, unfinished business, and worry about surviving family members.

Anger is Kübler-Ross' second stage of dying, in which the dying person recognizes that denial can no longer be maintained. Denial often gives way to anger, resentment, rage, and envy. The dying person's question is "Why me?" At this point, the person becomes increasingly difficult to care for as anger may become displaced and projected onto physicians, nurses, family members, and even God. The realization of loss is great, and those who symbolize life, energy, and competent functioning are especially salient targets of the dying person's resentment and jealousy.

Bargaining is Kübler-Ross' third stage of dying, in which the person develops the hope that death can somehow be postponed or delayed. Some persons enter into a bargaining or negotiation—often with God—as they try to delay their death. Psychologically, the person is saying, "Yes, me, but . . ." In exchange for a few more days, weeks, or months of life, the person promises to lead a reformed life dedicated to God or to the service of others.

Depression is Kübler-Ross' fourth stage of dying, in which the dying person comes to accept the certainty of death. At this point, a period of depression or preparatory grief may appear. The dying person may become silent, refuse visitors, and spend much of the time crying or grieving. This behavior is normal and is an effort to disconnect the self from love objects. Attempts to cheer up the dying person at this stage should be discouraged, says Kübler-Ross, because the dying person has a need to contemplate impending death.

Acceptance is Kübler-Ross' fifth stage of dying, in which the person develops a sense of peace, an acceptance of one's fate, and in many cases, a desire to be left alone. In this stage, feelings and physical pain may be virtually absent. Kübler-Ross describes this fifth stage as the end of the dying struggle, the final resting stage before death. A summary of Kübler-Ross' dying stages is presented in Figure 17.2.

What is the current evaluation of Kübler-Ross' approach? According to Robert Kastenbaum (2007), there are some problems with Kübler-Ross' approach. For example, the existence of the five-stage sequence has not been demonstrated by either Kübler-Ross or independent research. Also, the stage interpretation neglected the patients' situations, including relationship support, specific effects of illness, family obligations, and institutional climate in which they were interviewed. However, Kübler-Ross' pioneering efforts were important in calling attention to those who are attempting to cope with life-threatening illnesses. She did much to encourage attention to the quality of life for dying persons and their families.

How Would You...?
As a psychologist, how would you prepare a dying individual for the emotional and psychological stages they may go through as they approach death?

378

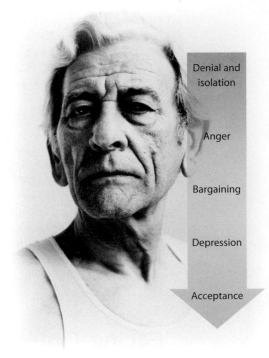

Figure 17.2 Kübler-Ross' Stages of Dying

According to Elisabeth Kübler-Ross, we go through five stages of dying: denial and isolation, anger, bargaining, depression, and acceptance. *Does everyone go through these stages, or go through them in the same order? Explain.*

Dc individuals become more spiritual as they get closer to death? A recent study of more than 100 patients with advanced congestive heart failure who were studied at two times six months apart found that as the patents perceived they were closer to death, they became more spiritual (Park, 2009).

Perceived Control and Denial

Perceived control may work as an adaptive strategy for some older adults who face death. When individuals are led to believe they can influence and control events—such as prolonging their lives—they may become more alert and cheerful. Remember from Chapter 15 that giving nursing home residents options for control improved their attitudes and increased their longevity (Rodin & Langer, 1977).

Denial also may be a fruitful way for some individuals to approach death. It can be adaptive or maladaptive. Denial can be used to avoid the destructive impact of shock by delaying the necessity of dealing with one's death. Denial can insulate the individual from having to cope with intense feelings of anger and hurt; however, if denial keeps us from having a life-saving operation, it clearly is maladaptive. Denial is neither good nor bad; its adaptive qualities need to be evaluated on an individual basis.

How Would You...?

As a human development and family studies professional, how would you advise family members to empower dying loved ones to feel they have more control over the end of their lives?

Coping With the Death of Someone Else

Loss can come in many forms in our lives—divorce, a pet's death, loss of a job, loss of a limb—but no loss is greater than that which comes through the death of someone we love and care for—a parent, sibling, spouse, relative, or friend. In the ratings of life's stresses that require the most adjustment, death of a spouse is given the highest number. How should we communicate with a dying individual? How does grieving help us cope with the death of someone we love? How do we make sense of the world when a loved one has passed away? What are the effects on someone after losing a life partner? And what are some forms of mourning and funeral rites?

Communicating With a Dying Person

Most psychologists believe that it is best for dying individuals to know that they are dying, and that significant others know they are dying, so they can interact and communicate with each other on the basis of this mutual knowledge (Banja, 2005). What are some of the advantages of this open awareness for the dying individual? First, dying individuals can close their lives in accord with their own ideas about proper dying. Second, they may be able to complete some plans and projects, can make arrangements for survivors, and can participate in decisions about a funeral and burial. Third, dying individuals have the opportunity to reminisce, to converse with others who have been important in their life, and to end life conscious of what life has been like. And fourth, dying individuals have more understanding of what is happening within their bodies and what the medical staff is doing to them (Kalish, 1981).

In addition to keeping communication open, what are some suggestions for conversing with a dying individual? Some experts believe that conversation should not focus on mental pathology or preparation for death but should focus on strengths of the individual and preparation for the remainder of life. Because external accomplishments are not possible, communication should be directed more at internal growth. Keep in mind also that important support for a dying

for them. Such deaths often are accompanied by post-traumatic stress disorder (PTSD) symptoms, such as intrusive thoughts, flashbacks, nightmares, sleep disturbance, problems in concentrating, and others. The death of a child can be especially devastating and extremely difficult for parents (Edwards & others, 2009).

individual may come not only from mental health professionals, but also from nurses, physicians, a spouse, or intimate friends (DeSpelder & Strickland, 2005).

Effective strategies for communicating with a dying person in-

These restaurant workers, who lost their jobs on 9/11/01, have made a bittersweet return with a New York restaurant they call their own. Colors, named for the many nationalities and ethnic groups among its owners, is believed to be the city's first cooperative restaurant. World-famous restaurant Windows on the World was destroyed and 73 workers killed when the Twin Towers were destroyed by terrorists. The former Windows survivors at the new venture will split 60 percent of the profits between themselves and the rest will be given to a fund to open other cooperative restaurants.

Making Sense of the World

One beneficial aspect of grieving is that it stimulates many individuals to try to make sense of their world (Carr, 2009; Furnes & Dysik, 2010). A common occurrence is to go over again and again all of the events that led up to the death. In the days and weeks after the death, the closest family members share experiences with each other, sometimes reminiscing over family experiences.

When a death is caused by an accident or a disaster, the effort to make sense of it is pursued more vigorously. As added pieces of news come trickling in, they are integrated into the puzzle. The bereaved want to put the death into a perspective that they can understand—divine intervention, a curse from a neighboring tribe, a logical sequence of cause and effect, or whatever it may be. A study of more than 1,000 college students found that making sense was an important factor in their grieving of a violent loss by accident, homicide, or suicide (Currier, Holland, & Neimeyer, 2006).

Losing a Life Partner

In 2008 in the United States, 14 percent of men and 42 percent of women aged 65 and older were widowed (Administration on Aging, 2009). Those left behind after the death of an intimate partner often suffer profound grief and often endure financial loss, loneliness, increased physical illness, and psychological disorders, including depression. How surviving spouses cope varies considerably (Park, 2009). In a study that included data from 3 years predeath to 18 months postdeath, nearly half of surviving spouses experienced low levels of distress consistently over the 4½ years (Bonanno, Wortman, & Nesse, 2004). In another study, widowed individuals were more likely to increase their religious and spiritual beliefs following the death of a spouse, and this increase was linked with a lower level of grief (Brown & others, 2004).

How surviving spouses cope varies considerably. A 6-year longitudinal study of individuals 80+ years of age found that the loss of a spouse, especially in men, was related to a lower level of life satisfaction over time (Berg & others, 2009). Another study concluded that chronic grief was more likely to characterize bereaved spouses who were highly dependent on their spouse (Ott & others, 2007). And another study revealed that finding meaning in the death of a spouse was linked to a lower level of anger during bereavement (Kim, 2009).

Many widows are lonely. The poorer and less educated they are, the lonelier they tend to be. The bereaved are also at increased risk for many health problems (Elwert & Christakis, 2008; Mechakra-Tahiri & others, 2010).

For either widows or widowers, social support helps them adjust to the death of a spouse (Bennett, 2009). The Widow-to-Widow program, begun in the 1960s, provides support for newly widowed women. Volunteer widows reach out to other widows, introducing them to others who may have similar problems, leading group discussions, and organizing social activities. The program has been adopted by the American Association of Retired Persons and disseminated throughout the

How Would You...?
As a social worker, how would you help a widow or widower to connect with a support group to deal with the death of a loved one?

United States as the Widowed Person's Service. The model has since been adopted by numerous community organizations to provide support for those going through a difficult transition.

Forms of Mourning

One decision facing the bereaved is what to do with the body. In the United States, in 2006, approximately two-thirds of corpses were disposed of by burial, the remaining one-third by cremation—a significant increase from 15 percent in

Remembrance at a Jewish cemetery. *What are some regional and cultural variations in the rituals that follow the loss of a loved one?*

1985 (Cremation Association of North America, 2008). Cremation is more popular in the Pacific region of the United States, less popular in the South. Cremation also is more popular in Canada than in the United States and most popular of all in Japan and many other Asian countries. In the United States, the trend is away from public funerals and displaying the dead body in an open casket and toward private funerals followed by a memorial ceremony (Callahan, 2009).

The funeral industry has been the source of controversy in recent years. Funeral directors and their supporters argue that the funeral provides a form of closure to the relationship with the deceased, especially when there is an open casket. Their critics claim that funeral directors are just trying to make money and that embalming is grotesque. One way to avoid being exploited during bereavement is to purchase funeral arrangements in advance.

The family and the community have important roles in mourning in some cultures. Two of those cultures are the Amish and traditional Judaism (Worthington, 1989). The Amish are a conservative group with approximately 80,000 members in the United States, Ontario, and several small settlements in South and Central America. The Amish live in a family-oriented society in which family and community support are essential for survival. Today, they live at the same unhurried pace as that of their ancestors, using horses instead of cars and facing death with the same steadfast faith as their forebears. At the time of death, close neighbors assume the responsibility of notifying others of the death. The Amish community handles virtually all aspects of the funeral.

The funeral service is held in a barn in warmer months and in a house during colder months. Calm acceptance of death, influenced by a deep religious faith, is an integral part of the Amish culture. Following the funeral, a high level of support is given to the bereaved family for at least a year. Visits to the family, special scrapbooks and handmade items for the family, new work projects started for the widow, and quilting days that combine fellowship and productivity are among the supports given to the bereaved family.

We have arrived at the end of this book. Our study of the human life span has been long and complex. You have read about many physical, cognitive, and socioemotional changes that take place from conception through death. This is a good time to reflect on what you have learned. Which theories, studies, and ideas were especially interesting to you? What did you learn about your own development?

I hope this book and course have been a window to the life span of the human species and a window to your own personal journey in life. I wish you all the best in the remaining years of your journey through the human life span.

John W. Santrock

Summary

Defining Death and Life/Death Issues

- Most physicians today agree that the higher and lower portions of the brain must stop functioning in order for an individual to be considered *brain dead*.

- Decisions regarding life, death, and health care can involve a number of circumstances and issues, and individuals can use a living will to make these choices while they can still think clearly. Hospice care emphasizes reducing pain and suffering rather than prolonging life.

Death and Sociohistorical, Cultural Contexts

- Over the years, when, where, and why people die have changed. Throughout history, most societies have had philosophical or religious beliefs about death, and most societies have rituals that deal with death.

- The United States has been described as a death-denying and death-avoiding culture.

Facing One's Own Death

- Kübler-Ross proposed five stages of facing death, and although her view has been criticized, her efforts were important in calling attention to the experience of coping with life-threatening illness.

- Perceived control over events and denial may work together as an adaptive orientation for a dying individual.

Coping With the Death of Someone Else

- Most psychologists recommend an open communication system with someone who is dying and their significant others.

- Grief is multidimensional and in some cases may last for years. Prolonged grief and disenfranchised grief are especially challenging.

- The grieving process may stimulate individuals to strive to make sense out of the world.

- Usually the most difficult loss is the death of a spouse. The bereaved are at increased risk for health problems.

- Forms of mourning vary across cultures.

Key Terms

brain death 374
euthanasia 375
passive euthanasia 375
active euthanasia 375

hospice 376
palliative care 376
denial and
    isolation 378

anger 378
bargaining 378
depression 378
acceptance 378

grief 380
prolonged grief 381

Glossary

A

A-not-B error Also called A$\overline{\text{B}}$ error, the term used to describe the tendency of infants to reach where an object was located earlier rather than where the object was last hidden.

acceptance Kübler-Ross' fifth stage of dying, in which the dying person develops a sense of peace, an acceptance of her or his fate, and, in many cases, a desire to be left alone.

accommodation Piagetian concept of adjusting schemes to fit new information and experiences.

active euthanasia Death induced deliberately, as by injecting a lethal dose of a drug.

activity theory The theory that the more active and involved older adults are, the more likely they are to be satisfied with their lives.

adolescent egocentrism The heightened self-consciousness of adolescents.

adoption study A study in which investigators seek to discover whether, in behavior and psychological characteristics, adopted children are more like their adoptive parents, who provided a home environment, or more like their biological parents, who contributed their heredity. Another form of the adoption study is to compare adoptive and biological siblings.

aerobic exercise Sustained exercise (such as jogging, swimming, or cycling) that stimulates heart and lung activity.

affectionate love In this type of love, also called companionate love, an individual desires to have the other person near and has a deep, caring affection for the other person.

ageism Prejudice against other people because of their age, especially prejudice against older adults.

Alzheimer disease A progressive, irreversible brain disorder characterized by a gradual deterioration of memory, reasoning, language, and eventually physical function.

amygdala The region of the brain that is the seat of emotions.

androgyny The presence of positive masculine and feminine characteristics in the same individual.

anger Kübler-Ross' second stage of dying, in which the dying person's denial often gives way to anger, resentment, rage, and envy.

anger cry A cry similar to the basic cry, with more excess air forced through the vocal cords.

animism The belief that inanimate objects have lifelike qualities and are capable of action.

anorexia nervosa An eating disorder that involves the relentless pursuit of thinness through starvation.

anxious attachment style An attachment style that describes adults who demand closeness, are less trusting, and are more emotional, jealous, and possessive.

Apgar Scale A widely used assessment of the newborn's health at 1 and 5 minutes after birth.

arthritis Inflammation of the joints that is accompanied by pain, stiffness, and movement problems; especially common in older adults.

assimilation Piagetian concept of using existing schemes to deal with new information or experiences.

attachment A close emotional bond between two people.

attention The focusing of mental resources on select information.

attention deficit hyperactivity disorder (ADHD) A disability in which children consistently show one or more of the following characteristics: (1) inattention, (2) hyperactivity, and (3) impulsivity.

authoritarian parenting A restrictive punitive style in which parents exhort the child to follow their directions and to respect work and effort. The authoritarian parent places firm limits and controls on the child and allows little verbal exchange. Authoritarian parenting is associated with children's social incompetence.

authoritative parenting A parenting style in which parents encourage their children to be independent but still place limits and controls on their actions. Extensive verbal give-and-take is allowed, and parents are warm and nurturant toward the child. Authoritative parenting is associated with children's social competence.

autism spectrum disorders (ASD) Also called pervasive developmental disorders, they range from the severe disorder labeled autistic disorder to the milder disorder called Asperger syndrome. These disorders are characterized by problems in social interaction, verbal and nonverbal communication, and repetitive behaviors.

autonomous morality The second stage of moral development in Piaget's theory, displayed by older children (about 10 years of age and older). The child becomes aware that rules and laws are created by people and, in judging an action, one should consider the actor's intentions as well as the consequences.

average children Children who receive an average number of both positive and negative nominations from their peers.

avoidant attachment style An attachment style that describes adults who are hesitant about getting involved in romantic relationships and once in a relationship tend to distance themselves from their partner.

bargaining Kübler-Ross' third stage of dying, in which the dying person develops the hope that death can somehow be postponed.

basic cry A rhythmic pattern usually consisting of a cry, a briefer silence, a shorter inspiratory whistle that is higher pitched than the main cry, and then a brief rest before the next cry.

behavioral and social cognitive theories Theories that hold that development can be described in terms of the behaviors learned through interactions with the environment.

behavior genetics The field that seeks to discover the influence of heredity and environment on individual differences in human traits and development.

big five factors of personality Openness to experience, conscientiousness, extraversion, agreeableness, and neuroticism (emotional stability).

biological processes Changes in an individual's physical nature.

brain death A neurological definition of death. A person is brain dead when all electrical activity of the brain has ceased for a specified period of time. A flat EEG recording is one criterion of brain death.

Bronfenbrenner's ecological theory Bronfenbrenner's environmental systems theory that focuses on five environmental systems: microsystem, mesosystem, exosystem, macrosystem, and chronosystem.

bulimia nervosa An eating disorder in which the individual consistently follows a binge-and-purge pattern.

C

care perspective The moral perspective of Carol Gilligan, which views people in terms of their connectedness with others and emphasizes interpersonal communication, relationships with others, and concern for others.

case study An in-depth examination of an individual.

cataracts Involve a thickening of the lens of the eye that causes vision to become cloudy, opaque, and distorted.

cellular clock theory Leonard Hayflick's theory that the maximum number of times that human cells can divide is about 75 to 80. As we age, our cells become increasingly less capable of dividing.

centration The focusing of attention on one characteristic to the exclusion of all others.

cephalocaudal pattern The sequence in which the earliest growth always occurs at the top—the head—with physical growth in size, weight, and feature differentiation gradually working from top to bottom.

child-centered kindergarten Education that involves the whole child by considering both the child's physical, cognitive, and socioemotional development and the child's needs, interests, and learning styles.

child-directed speech Language spoken in a higher pitch than normal with simple words and sentences.

chromosomes Threadlike structures made up of deoxyribonucleic acid, or DNA.

climacteric The midlife transition in which fertility declines.

clique A small group that ranges from 2 to about 12 individuals, averaging about 5 to 6 individuals, and can form because adolescents engage in similar activities.

cognitive processes Changes in an individual's thought, intelligence, and language.

cohort effects Effects that are due to a subject's time of birth or generation but not age.

commitment Marcia's term for the part of identity development in which adolescents show a personal investment in forming an identity.

conservation In Piaget's theory, awareness that altering an object's or a substance's appearance does not change its basic properties.

constructive play Play that combines sensorimotor and repetitive activity with symbolic representation of ideas. Constructive play occurs when children engage in self-regulated creation or construction of a product or a problem solution.

constructivist approach A learner-centered approach that emphasizes the importance of individuals actively constructing their knowledge and understanding with guidance from the teacher.

contemporary life-events approach An approach that emphasizes that how a life event influences the individual's development depends not only on the life event, but also on mediating factors, the individual's adaptation to the life event, the life-stage context, and the sociohistorical context.

context The setting in which development occurs that is influenced by historical, economic, social, and cultural factors.

continuity-discontinuity issue The debate about the extent to which development involves gradual, cumulative change (continuity) or distinct stages (discontinuity).

controversial children Children who are frequently nominated both as someone's best friend and as being disliked.

conventional reasoning The second, or intermediate, level in Kohlberg's theory of moral development. At this level, individuals abide by certain standards, but they are the standards of others, such as parents or the laws of society.

convergent thinking Thinking that produces one correct answer and is characteristic of the kind of thinking tested by standardized intelligence tests.

core knowledge approach States that infants are born with domain-specific innate knowledge systems.

corpus callosum The location where fibers connect the brain's left and right hemispheres.

correlational research The goal is to describe the strength of the relation between two or more events or characteristics.

correlation coefficient A number based on statistical analysis that is used to describe the degree of association between two variables.

creative thinking The ability to think in novel and unusual ways and to come up with unique solutions to problems.

crisis Marcia's term for a period of identity development during which the adolescent is exploring alternatives.

critical thinking Thinking reflectively and productively, as well as evaluating the evidence.

cross-cultural studies Comparisons of one culture with one or more other cultures. These provide information about the degree to which children's development is similar, or universal, across cultures, and to the degree to which it is culture-specific.

cross-sectional approach A research strategy in which individuals of different ages are compared at one time.

crowd A larger group structure than a clique, a crowd is usually formed based on reputation, and members may or may not spend much time together.

crystallized intelligence Accumulated information and verbal skills, which increase in middle age, according to Horn.

cultural-familial retardation Retardation characterized by no evidence of organic brain damage but the individual's IQ generally is between 50 and 70.

culture The behavior patterns, beliefs, and all other products of a group that are passed on from generation to generation.

culture-fair tests Tests of intelligence that are designed to be free of cultural bias.

cumulative personality model States that with time and age, people become more adept at interacting with their environment in ways that promote the stability of personality.

D

date or acquaintance rape Coercive sexual activity directed at someone with whom the perpetrator is at least casually acquainted.

deferred imitation Imitation that occurs after a delay of hours or days.

dementia A global term for any neurological disorder in which the primary symptoms involve a deterioration of mental functioning.

denial and isolation Kübler-Ross' first stage of dying, in which the dying person denies that she or he is really going to die.

depression Kübler-Ross' fourth stage of dying, in which the dying person comes to accept the certainty of her or his death. A period of depression or preparatory grief may appear.

development The pattern of movement or change that starts at conception and continues through the human life span.

developmentally appropriate practice (DAP) Education that focuses on the typical developmental patterns of children (age appropriateness) and the uniqueness of each child (individual appropriateness).

difficult child A child who tends to react negatively and cry frequently, who engages in irregular daily routines, and who is slow to accept new experiences.

direct instruction approach A structured, teacher-centered approach that is characterized by teacher direction and control, high teacher expectations for students' progress, maximum time spent by students on learning tasks, and efforts by the teacher to keep negative affect to a minimum.

dishabituation Recovery of a habituated response after a change in stimulation.

divergent thinking Thinking that produces many answers to the same question and is characteristic of creativity.

divided attention Concentrating on more than one activity at the same time.

DNA A complex molecule with a double helix shape that contains genetic information.

Down syndrome A chromosomally transmitted form of mental retardation, caused by the presence of an extra copy of chromosome 21.

dynamic systems theory The perspective on motor development that seeks to explain how motor behaviors are assembled for perceiving and acting.

E

easy child A child who is generally in a positive mood, who quickly establishes regular routines in infancy, and who adapts easily to new experiences.

eclectic theoretical orientation An approach that selects and uses whatever is considered the best in many theories.

ecological view The view that perception functions to bring organisms in contact with the environment and to increase adaptation.

egocentrism The inability to distinguish between one's own perspective and someone else's (salient feature of the first substage of preoperational thought).

elaboration An important strategy that involves engaging in more extensive processing of information.

eldercare Physical and emotional caretaking for older members of the family, whether by giving day-to-day physical assistance or by being responsible for overseeing such care.

embryonic period The period of prenatal development that occurs two to eight weeks after conception. During the embryonic period, the rate of cell differentiation intensifies, support systems for the cells form, and organs appear.

emerging adulthood The transition from adolescence to adulthood (approximately 18 to 25 years of age) that involves experimentation and exploration.

emotion Feeling, or affect, that occurs when a person is in a state or interaction that is important to them. Emotion is characterized by behavior that reflects (expresses) the pleasantness or unpleasantness of the state a person is in or the transactions being experienced.

empty nest syndrome A term used to indicate a decrease in marital satisfaction after children leave home.

epigenetic view Emphasizes that development is the result of an ongoing, bidirectional interchange between heredity and environment.

episodic memory The retention of information about the where and when of life's happenings.

equilibration A mechanism that Piaget proposed to explain how children shift from one stage of thought to the next.

Erikson's theory A psychoanalytic theory in which eight stages of psychosocial development unfold throughout the human life span. Each stage consists of a unique developmental task that confronts individuals with a crisis that must be faced.

ethnic identity An enduring, basic aspect of the self that includes a sense of membership in an ethnic group and the attitudes and feelings related to that membership.

ethnicity A range of characteristics rooted in cultural heritage, including nationality, race, religion, and language.

ethology An approach that stresses that behavior is strongly influenced by biology, tied to evolution, and characterized by critical or sensitive periods.

euthanasia The act of painlessly ending the lives of persons who are suffering from incurable diseases or severe disabilities; sometimes called "mercy killing."

evolutionary psychology Emphasizes the importance of adaptation, reproduction, and "survival of the fittest" in shaping behavior.

evolutionary theory of aging The view that natural selection has not eliminated many harmful conditions and nonadaptive characteristics in older adults.

executive attention Involves action planning, allocating attention to goals,

error detection and compensation, monitoring progress on tasks, and dealing with novel or difficult circumstances.

experiment A carefully regulated procedure in which one or more of the factors believed to influence the behavior being studied is manipulated and all other factors are held constant. Experimental research permits the determination of cause.

explicit memory Memory of facts and experiences that individuals consciously know and can state.

F

fetal alcohol spectrum disorders (FASD) A cluster of abnormalities that appears in the offspring of mothers who drink alcohol heavily during pregnancy.

fetal period The prenatal period of development that begins two months after conception and lasts for seven months, on the average.

fine motor skills Motor skills that involve finely tuned movements, such as finger dexterity.

fluid intelligence The ability to reason abstractly, which steadily declines from middle adulthood on, according to Horn.

free-radical theory A theory of aging that states that people age because inside their cells normal metabolism produces unstable oxygen molecules known as free radicals. These molecules ricochet around inside cells, damaging DNA and other cellular structures.

fuzzy trace theory States that memory is best understood by considering two types of memory representations: (1) verbatim memory trace and (2) gist. In this theory, older children's better memory is attributed to the fuzzy traces created by extracting the gist of information.

G

games Activities engaged in for pleasure that include rules and often competition with one or more individuals.

gender The psychological and sociocultural dimensions of being female or male.

gender identity The sense of being male or female, which most children acquire by the time they are 3 years old.

gender roles Sets of expectations that prescribe how females or males should think, act, and feel.

gender schema theory The theory that gender typing emerges as children gradually develop gender schemas of what is gender-appropriate and gender-inappropriate in their culture.

gender stereotypes Broad categories that reflect our impressions and beliefs about females and males.

generativity Adults' desires to leave legacies of themselves to the next generation; the positive side of Erikson's generativity versus stagnation middle adulthood stage.

genes Units of hereditary information composed of DNA. Genes direct cells to reproduce themselves and manufacture the proteins that maintain life.

gene x environment (g x e) interaction The interaction of a specified measured variation in DNA and a specific measured aspect of the environment.

genotype A person's genetic heritage; the actual genetic material.

germinal period The period of prenatal development that takes place in the first two weeks after conception. It includes the creation of the zygote, continued cell division, and the attachment of the zygote to the uterine wall.

gifted Having above-average intelligence (an IQ of 130 or higher) and/or superior talent for something.

glaucoma Damage to the optic nerve because of the pressure created by a buildup of fluid in the eye.

gonads The sex glands—the testes in males and the ovaries in females.

goodness of fit Refers to the match between a child's temperament and the environmental demands with which the child must cope.

grief The emotional numbness, disbelief, separation anxiety, despair, sadness, and loneliness that accompany the loss of someone we love.

gross motor skills Motor skills that involve large-muscle activities, such as walking.

H

habituation Decreased responsiveness to a stimulus after repeated presentations of the stimulus.

heteronomous morality Kohlberg's first stage in preconventional reasoning in which moral thinking is tied to punishment.

heteronomous morality The first stage of moral development in Piaget's theory, occurring from approximately 4 to 7 years of age. Justice and rules are conceived of as unchangeable properties of the world, removed from the control of people.

hormonal stress theory The theory that aging in the body's hormonal system can lower resilience to stress and increase the likelihood of disease.

hormones Powerful chemical substances secreted by the endocrine glands and carried through the body by the bloodstream.

hospice A program committed to making the end of life as free from pain, anxiety, and depression as possible. The goals of hospice contrast with those of a hospital, which are to cure disease and prolong life.

hypothalamus A structure in the higher portion of the brain that monitors eating and sex.

hypotheses Assertions or predictions, often derived from theories, that can be tested.

hypothetical-deductive reasoning Piaget's formal operational concept that adolescents have the cognitive ability to develop hypotheses, or best guesses, about ways to solve problems, such as an algebraic equation.

I

identity achievement Marcia's term for adolescents who have undergone a crisis and have made a commitment.

identity diffusion Marcia's term for adolescents who have not yet experienced a crisis (explored meaningful alternatives) or made any commitments.

identity foreclosure Marcia's term for adolescents who have made a commitment but have not experienced a crisis.

identity moratorium Marcia's term for adolescents who are in the midst of a crisis, but their commitments are either absent or vaguely defined.

imaginary audience Involves adolescents' belief that others are as interested in them as they themselves are; attention-getting behavior motivated by a desire to be noticed, visible, and "on stage."

immanent justice The concept that, if a rule is broken, punishment will be meted out immediately.

implicit memory Memory without conscious recollection; involves skills and routine procedures that are automatically performed.

inclusion Educating a child with special education needs full-time in the regular classroom.

individualism, instrumental purpose, and exchange The second Kohlberg stage of moral development. At this stage, individuals pursue their own interests but also let others do the same.

individualized education plan (IEP) A written statement that spells out a program tailored to a child with a disability.

indulgent parenting A style of parenting in which parents are highly involved with their children but place few demands or controls on them. Indulgent parenting is associated with children's social incompetence, especially a lack of self-control.

infinite generativity The ability to produce an endless number of meaningful sentences using a finite set of words and rules.

information-processing theory A theory that emphasizes that individuals manipulate information, monitor it, and strategize about it. The processes of memory and thinking are central.

insecure avoidant babies Babies that show insecurity by avoiding the mother.

insecure disorganized babies Babies that show insecurity by being disorganized and disoriented.

insecure resistant babies Babies that often cling to the caregiver, then resist her by fighting against the closeness, perhaps by kicking or pushing away.

integrity versus despair Erikson's eighth and final stage of development, which individuals experience in late adulthood. This involves reflecting on the past and either piecing together a positive review or concluding that one's life has not been well spent.

intelligence Problem-solving skills and the ability to learn from, and adapt to, the experiences of everyday life.

intelligence quotient (IQ) A person's mental age divided by chronological age, multiplied by 100.

intermodal perception The ability to relate and integrate information from two or more sensory modalities, such as vision and hearing.

intuitive thought substage Piaget's second substage of preoperational thought, in which children begin to use primitive reasoning and want to know the answers to all sorts of questions (between about 4 and 7 years of age).

J

joint attention Process that occurs when individuals focus on the same object and an ability to track another's behavior is present, one individual directs another's attention, and reciprocal interaction is present.

justice perspective A moral perspective that focuses on the rights of the individual; individuals independently make moral decisions.

juvenile delinquent An adolescent who breaks the law or engages in behavior that is considered illegal.

L

laboratory A controlled setting.

language A form of communication, whether spoken, written, or signed, that is based on a system of symbols. Language consists of the words used by a community and the rules for varying and combining them.

language acquisition device (LAD) Chomsky's term that describes a biological endowment enabling the child to detect the features and rules of language, including phonology, syntax, and semantics.

lateralization Specialization of function in one hemisphere of the cerebral cortex or the other.

learning disability Describes a child who has difficulty in learning that involves understanding or using spoken or written language, and the difficulty can appear in listening, thinking, reading, writing, and spelling. A learning disability also may involve difficulty in doing mathematics. To be classified as a learning disability, the learning problem is not primarily the result of visual, hearing, or motor disabilities; mental retardation; emotional disorders; or due to environmental, cultural, or economic disadvantage.

least restrictive environment (LRE) The concept that a child with a disability must be educated in a setting that is as similar as possible to the one in which children who do not have a disability are educated.

leisure The pleasant times after work when individuals are free to pursue activities and interests of their own choosing.

life expectancy The number of years that will probably be lived by the average person born in a particular year.

life span The upper boundary of life, the maximum number of years an individual can live. The maximum life span of human beings is about 120 to 125 years of age.

life-span perspective The perspective that development is lifelong, multidimensional, multidirectional, plastic, multidisciplinary, and contextual; involves growth, maintenance, and regulation; and is constructed through biological, sociocultural, and individual factors working together.

longitudinal approach A research strategy in which the same individuals are studied over a period of time, usually several years or more.

long-term memory A relatively permanent type of memory that holds huge amounts of information for a long period of time.

M

macular degeneration A disease that involves deterioration of the macula of the retina, which corresponds to the focal center of the visual field.

major depression A mood disorder in which the individual is deeply unhappy, demoralized, self-derogatory, and bored. The person does not feel well, loses stamina easily, has poor appetite, and is listless and unmotivated. Major depression is so widespread that it has been called the "common cold" of psychological disorders.

meiosis A specialized form of cell division that occurs to form eggs and sperm (or gametes).

memory A central feature of cognitive development, pertaining to all situations in which an individual retains information over time.

menarche A girl's first menstruation.

menopause The complete cessation of a woman's menstruation, which usually occurs in the late forties or early fifties.

mental age (MA) Binet's measure of an individual's level of mental development, compared with that of others.

mental retardation A condition of limited mental ability in which an individual has a low IQ, usually below 70 on a traditional test of intelligence, and has difficulty adapting to everyday life.

metacognition Cognition about cognition, or knowing about knowing.

metalinguistic awareness Refers to knowledge about language, such as knowing what a preposition is or the ability to discuss the sounds of a language.

middle adulthood The developmental period beginning at approximately 40 years of age and extending to about 60 to 65 years of age.

mindset The cognitive view that individuals develop for themselves.

mitosis Cellular reproduction in which the cell's nucleus duplicates itself with two new cells being formed, each containing the same DNA as the parent cell, arranged in the same 23 pairs of chromosomes.

Montessori approach An educational philosophy in which children are given considerable freedom and spontaneity in choosing activities and are allowed to move from one activity to another as they desire.

moral development Development that involves thoughts, feelings, and actions regarding rules and conventions about what people should do in their interactions with other people.

morphology Units of meaning involved in word formation.

mutual interpersonal expectations, relationships, and interpersonal conformity Kohlberg's third stage of moral development. At this stage, individuals value trust, caring, and loyalty to others as a basis of moral judgments.

myelination The process by which the axons are covered and insulated with a layer of fat cells, which increases the speed at which information travels through the nervous system.

N

natural childbirth A childbirth method in which no drugs are given to relieve pain or assist in the birth process. The mother and her partner are taught to use breathing methods and relaxation techniques during delivery.

naturalistic observation Observation that occurs in a real-world setting without an attempt to manipulate the situation.

nature-nurture issue The debate about the extent to which development is influenced by nature and by nurture. Nature refers to an organism's biological inheritance, nurture to its environmental experiences.

neglected children Children who are infrequently nominated as a best friend but are not disliked by their peers.

neglectful parenting A style of parenting in which the parent is very uninvolved in the child's life; it is associated with children's social incompetence, especially a lack of self-control.

neo-Piagetians Developmentalists who have elaborated on Piaget's theory, giving more emphasis to how children use attention, memory, and strategies to process information.

neurons Nerve cells, which handle information processing at the cellular level in the brain.

nonnormative life events Unusual occurrences that have a major impact on a person's life. The occurrence, pattern, and sequence of these events are not applicable to many individuals.

normal distribution A symmetrical distribution with most scores falling in the middle of the possible range of scores and few scores appearing toward the extremes of the range.

normative age-graded influences Biological and environmental influences that are similar for individuals in a particular age group.

normative history-graded influences Biological and environmental influences that are associated with history. These influences are common to people of a particular generation.

O

object permanence The Piagetian term for understanding that objects and events continue to exist, even when they cannot directly be seen, heard, or touched.

operations In Piaget's theory, internalized reversible sets of actions that allow children to do mentally what they formerly did physically.

organic retardation Mental retardation that involves some physical damage and is caused by a genetic disorder or brain damage.

organization Piaget's concept of grouping isolated behaviors and thoughts into a higher-order, more smoothly functioning cognitive system.

osteoporosis A chronic condition that involves an extensive loss of bone tissue and is the main reason many older adults walk with a marked stoop. Women are especially vulnerable to osteoporosis.

P

pain cry A sudden appearance of loud crying without preliminary moaning, followed by breath holding.

palliative care Emphasized in hospice care; involves reducing pain and suffering and helping individuals die with dignity.

Parkinson disease A chronic, progressive disease characterized by muscle tremors, slowing of movement, and partial facial paralysis.

passive euthanasia The withholding of available treatments, such as life-sustaining devices, allowing the person to die.

perception The interpretation of what is sensed.

personal fable The part of adolescent egocentrism that involves an adolescent's sense of uniqueness and invincibility (or invulnerability).

phenotype The way an individual's genotype is expressed in observed and measurable characteristics.

phonics approach The idea that reading instruction should teach the basic rules for translating written symbols into sounds.

phonology The sound system of a language, including the sounds used and how they may be combined.

Piaget's theory The theory that children construct their understanding of the world and go through four stages of cognitive development.

pituitary gland An important endocrine gland that controls growth and regulates other glands, including the gonads.

popular children Children who are frequently nominated as a best friend and are rarely disliked by their peers.

postconventional reasoning The highest level in Kohlberg's theory of moral development. At this level, the individual recognizes alternative moral courses, explores the options, and then decides on a personal moral code.

postformal thought A form of thought that is qualitatively different from Piaget's formal operational thought. It involves understanding that the correct answer to a problem can require reflective thinking, that the correct answer can vary from one situation to another, and that the search for truth is often an ongoing, never-ending process. It also involves the belief that solutions to problems need to be realistic, and that emotions and subjective factors can influence thinking.

postpartum period The period after childbirth when the mother adjusts, both physically and psychologically, to the process of childbirth. This period lasts for about six weeks or until her body has completed its adjustment and returned to a near prepregnant state.

practice play Play that involves repetition of behavior when new skills are being learned or when physical or mental mastery and coordination of skills are required for games or sports.

pragmatics The appropriate use of language in different contexts.

preconventional reasoning The lowest level in Kohlberg's theory of moral development. The individual's moral reasoning is controlled primarily by external rewards and punishment.

preoperational stage Piaget's second stage, lasting from about 2 to 7 years of age, during which children begin to represent the world with words, images, and drawings, and symbolic thought goes beyond simple connections of sensory information and physical action; stable concepts are formed, mental reasoning emerges, egocentrism is present, and magical beliefs are constructed.

prepared childbirth Developed by French obstetrician Ferdinand Lamaze, this childbirth strategy is similar to natural childbirth but includes a special breathing technique to control pushing in the final stages of labor and a more detailed anatomy and physiology course.

pretense/symbolic play Play in which the child transforms the physical environment into a symbol.

Project Head Start A government-funded program that is designed to provide children from low-income families the opportunity to acquire the skills and experiences important for school success.

prolonged grief Grief that involves enduring despair and is still unresolved over an extended period of time.

proximodistal pattern The sequence in which growth starts at the center of the body and moves toward the extremities.

psychoanalytic theories Theories that hold that development depends primarily on the unconscious mind and is heavily couched in emotion, that behavior is merely a surface characteristic, that it is important to analyze the symbolic meanings of

behavior, and that early experiences are important in development.

psychoanalytic theory of gender A theory deriving from Freud's view that the preschool child develops a sexual attraction to the opposite-sex parent, by approximately 5 or 6 years of age renounces this attraction because of anxious feelings, and subsequently identifies with the same-sex parent, unconsciously adopting the same-sex parent's characteristics.

puberty A period of rapid physical and sexual maturation that occurs mainly during early adolescence.

R

rape Forcible sexual intercourse with a person who does not consent to it.

rapport talk The language of conversation; it is a way of establishing connections and negotiating relationships.

reciprocal socialization Socialization that is bidirectional; children socialize parents, just as parents socialize children.

reflexive smile A smile that does not occur in response to external stimuli. It appears during the first month after birth, usually during sleep.

rejected children Children who are infrequently nominated as a best friend and are actively disliked by their peers.

report talk Talk that is designed to give information and includes public speaking.

rite of passage A ceremony or ritual that marks an individual's transition from one status to another. Most rites of passage focus on the transition to adult status.

romantic love Also called passionate love, or eros; romantic love has strong sexual and infatuation components and often predominates in the early period of a love relationship.

S

scaffolding Parents time interactions so that infants experience turn-taking with the parents.

schemes In Piaget's theory, actions or mental representations that organize knowledge.

secure attachment style An attachment style that describes adults who have positive views of relationships, find it easy to get close to others, and are not overly concerned or stressed out about their romantic relationships.

securely attached babies Babies that use the caregiver as a secure base from which to explore the environment.

selective attention Focusing on a specific aspect of experience that is relevant while ignoring others that are irrelevant.

selective optimization with compensation theory The theory that successful aging is related to three main factors: selection, optimization, and compensation.

self-concept Domain-specific evaluations of the self.

self-efficacy The belief that one can master a situation and produce favorable outcomes.

self-esteem The global evaluative dimension of the self. Self-esteem is also referred to as self-worth or self-image.

self-understanding The child's cognitive representation of self, the substance and content of the child's self-conceptions.

semantic memory A person's knowledge about the world—including a person's fields of expertise, general academic knowledge of the sort learned in school, and "everyday knowledge."

semantics The meaning of words and sentences.

sensation The product of the interaction between information and the sensory receptors—the eyes, ears, tongue, nostrils, and skin.

sensorimotor play Behavior engaged in by infants to derive pleasure from exercising their existing sensorimotor schemes.

sensorimotor stage The first of Piaget's stages, which lasts from birth to about 2 years of age; infants construct an understanding of the world by coordinating sensory experiences with motoric actions.

separation protest An infant's distressed crying when the caregiver leaves.

seriation The concrete operation that involves ordering stimuli along a quantitative dimension (such as length).

service learning A form of education that promotes social responsibility and service to the community.

sexually transmitted infections (STIs) Infections contracted primarily through sexual contact, including oral-genital and anal-genital contact.

short-term memory The memory component in which individuals retain information for up to 30 seconds, assuming there is no rehearsal of the information.

slow-to-warm-up child A child who has a low activity level, is somewhat negative, and displays a low intensity of mood.

social clock The timetable according to which individuals are expected to accomplish life's tasks, such as getting married, having children, or establishing a career.

social cognitive theory The theory that behavior, environment, and person/cognitive factors are important in understanding development.

social cognitive theory of gender A theory that emphasizes that children's gender development occurs through the observation and imitation of gender behavior and through the rewards and punishments children experience for gender-appropriate and gender-inappropriate behavior.

social constructivist approach An approach that emphasizes the social contexts of learning and that knowledge is mutually built and constructed. Vygotsky's theory reflects this approach.

social contract or utility and individual rights The fifth Kohlberg stage. At this stage, individuals reason that values, rights, and principles undergird or transcend the law.

social play Play that involves social interactions with peers.

social policy A national government's course of action designed to promote the welfare of its citizens.

social referencing "Reading" emotional cues in others to help determine how to act in a particular situation.

social role theory A theory that gender differences result from the contrasting roles of men and women.

social smile A smile in response to an external stimulus, which, early in development, typically is a face.

social systems morality The fourth stage in Kohlberg's theory of moral development. Moral judgments are based on understanding the social order, law, justice, and duty.

socioeconomic status (SES) Refers to the conceptual grouping of people with similar occupational, educational, and economic characteristics.

socioemotional processes Changes in an individual's relationships with other people, emotions, and personality.

socioemotional selectivity theory The theory that older adults become more selective about their social networks. Because they place a high value on emotional satisfaction, older adults often spend more time with familiar individuals with whom they have had rewarding relationships.

stability-change issue The debate about the degree to which early traits and characteristics persist through life or change.

stagnation Sometimes called "self-absorption"—develops when individuals sense that they have done little or nothing for the next generation; the negative side of Erikson's generativity versus stagnation middle adulthood stage.

standardized test A test that is given with uniform procedures for administration and scoring.

stranger anxiety An infant's fear and wariness of strangers; it tends to appear in the second half of the first year of life.

Strange Situation An observational measure of infant attachment that requires the infant to move through a series of introductions, separations, and reunions with the caregiver and an adult stranger in a prescribed order.

strategies Consist of deliberate mental activities to improve the processing of information.

sudden infant death syndrome (SIDS) A condition that occurs when an infant stops breathing, usually during the night, and suddenly dies without an apparent cause.

sustained attention The state of readiness to detect and respond to small changes occurring at random times in the environment.

symbolic function substage Piaget's first substage of preoperational thought, in which the child gains the ability to mentally represent an object that is not present (between about 2 and 4 years of age).

syntax The ways words are combined to form acceptable phrases and sentences.

T

telegraphic speech The use of short and precise words without grammatical markers such as articles, auxiliary verbs, and other connectives.

temperament An individual's behavioral style and characteristic way of emotionally responding.

teratogen Any agent that can potentially cause a birth defect or negatively alter cognitive and behavioral outcomes.

theory A coherent set of ideas that helps to explain data and to make predictions.

theory of mind Refers to the awareness of one's own mental processes and the mental processes of others.

thinking Manipulating and transforming information in memory.

top-dog phenomenon The circumstance of moving from the top position in elementary school to the lowest position in middle or junior high school.

transitivity The ability to logically combine relations to understand certain conclusions.

triarchic theory of intelligence Sternberg's theory that intelligence consists of analytical intelligence, creative intelligence, and practical intelligence.

twin study A study in which the behavioral similarity of identical twins is compared with the behavioral similarity of fraternal twins.

U

universal ethical principles The sixth and highest stage in Kohlberg's theory of moral development. Individuals develop a moral standard based on universal human rights.

V

visual preference method A method used to determine whether infants can distinguish one stimulus from another by measuring the length of time they attend to different stimuli.

Vygotsky's theory A sociocultural cognitive theory that emphasizes how culture and social interaction guide cognitive development.

W

whole-language approach An approach to reading instruction based on the idea that instruction should parallel children's natural language learning. Reading materials should be whole and meaningful.

wisdom Expert knowledge about the practical aspects of life that permits excellent judgment about important matters.

working memory Closely related to short-term memory but places more emphasis on mental work. Working memory is like a mental "work-bench" where individuals can manipulate and assemble information when making decisions, solving problems, and comprehending written and spoken language.

Z

zone of proximal development (ZPD) Vygotsky's term for tasks too difficult for children to master alone but that can be mastered with assistance.

References

A

Aalsma, M. C., Tong, Y., Wiehe, S. E., & Tu, W. (2010). The impact of delinquency on young adult sex risk behaviors and sexually transmitted infections. *Journal of Adolescent Health, 46,* 17–24.

AAP. (2000). Changing concepts of sudden infant death syndrome. *Pediatrics, 105,* 650–656.

AARP. (2004). *The divorce experience: A study of divorce at midlife and beyond.* Washington, DC: AARP.

Abbott, A. (2003). Restless nights, listless days. *Nature, 425,* 896–898.

ABC News. (2005, December 12). Larry Page and Sergey Brin. Available at http://abcnews.go.com?Entertainment/12/8/05

Abellan van Kan, G., Holland, Y., Nourhashemi, F., Coley, N., Andrieu, S., & Vellas, B. (2009). Cardiovascular disease risk factors and progression of Alzheimer's disease. *Dementia and Geriatric Cognitive Disorders, 27,* 240–246.

Abruscato, J. A., & DeRosa, D. A. (2010). *Teaching children science: A discovery approach* (7th ed.). Boston: Allyn & Bacon.

Accornero, V. H., Anthony, J. C., Morrow, C. E., Xue, L., & Bandstra, E. S. (2006). Prenatal cocaine exposure: An examination of childhood externalizing and internalizing behavior problems at age 7 years. *Epidemiology, Psychiatry, and Society, 15,* 20–29.

Ackerman, J. P., Riggins, T., & Black, M. M. (2010). A review of the effects of prenatal cocaine exposure among school-aged children. *Pediatrics, 125,* 554–565.

Adams, J. C. (2009). Immunocytochemical traits of type IV fibrocytes and their possible relation to cochlear function and pathology. *Journal of the Association for Research in Otolaryngology, 10,* 369–382.

Adams, K. F., Schatzkin, A., Harris, T. B., Kipnis, V., Mouw, T., Ballard-Barbash, R., & others. (2006). Overweight, obesity, & mortality in a large prospective cohort of persons 50 to 71 years old. *New England Journal of Medicine, 355,* 763–768.

Administration for Children & Families. (2008). *Statistical Fact Sheet Fiscal Year 2008.* Washington, DC: Author.

Administration on Aging. (2009). *A profile of older Americans: 2009.* Washington, DC: U.S. Department of Health and Human Services.

Adolph, K. E. (1997). Learning in the development of infant locomotion. *Monographs of the Society for Research in Child Development, 62*(3, Serial No. 251).

Adolph, K. E. (2010). Perceptual learning. Retrieved January 10, 2010, from http://www.psych.nyu.edu/adolph/research1.php

Adolph, K. E., & Berger, S. E. (2005). Physical and motor development. In M. H. Bornstein & M. E. Lamb (Eds.), *Developmental psychology* (5th ed.). Mahwah, NJ: Erlbaum.

Adolph, K. E., Eppler, M. A., & Joh, A. S. (2010, in press). Infants' perception of affordances of slopes under low and high friction conditions. *Journal of Experimental Psychology: Human Perception and Performance.*

Adolph, K. E., & Joh, A. S. (2009). Multiple learning mechanisms in the development of action. In A. Needham & A. Woodward (Eds.), *Learning and the infant mind.* New York: Oxford University Press.

Adolph, K. E., Karasik, L. B., & Tamis-LeMonda, C. S. (2010). Moving between cultures: Cross-cultural research on motor development. In M. Bornstein & L. R. Cote (Ed.), *Handbook of cross-cultural developmental science, Vol. 1, Domains of development across cultures.* Clifton, NJ: Psychology Press.

Afanas'ev, I. (2009). Superoxide and nitric oxide in senescence and aging. *Frontiers in Bioscience, 14,* 3899–3912.

Agency for Healthcare Research and Quality. (2007). *Evidence report/Technology assessment: Number 153: Breastfeeding and maternal and health outcomes in developed countries.* Rockville, MD: U.S. Department of Health and Human Services.

Agras, W. S., & others. (2004). Report of the National Institutes of Health workshop on overcoming barriers to treatment research in anorexia nervosa. *International Journal of Eating Disorders, 35,* 509–521.

Ahrons, C. (2007). Introduction to the special issue on divorce and its aftermath. *Family Process, 46,* 3–6.

Ainsworth, M. D. S. (1979). Infant-mother attachment. *American Psychologist, 34,* 932–937.

Akbari, A., & others. (2010, in press). Parity and breastfeeding are preventive measures against breast cancer in Iranian women. *Breast Cancer.*

Akhtar, N., & Herold, K. (2008). Pragmatic development. In M. M. Haith & J. B. Benson (Eds.), *Encyclopedia of infant and early childhood development.* Oxford, UK: Elsevier.

Alberts, E., Elkind, D., & Ginsberg, S. (2007). The personal fable and risk taking in early adolescence. *Journal of Youth and Adolescence, 36,* 71–76.

Alcaro, S., & others. (2010). Simple choline esters as potential anti-Alzheimer agents. *Current Pharmaceutical Design, 16,* 692–697.

Aldwin, C. M., Yancura, L. A., & Boeninger, D. K. (2011). Coping across the life span. In R. M. Lerner, W. F. Overton, A. M. Freund, & M. E. Lamb (Eds.), *Handbook of life-span development.* New York: Wiley.

Allemand, M., Zimprich, D., & Hendriks, A. A. J. (2008). Age differences in five personality domains across the life span. *Developmental Psychology, 44,* 758–770.

Allen, J. P., & Miga, E. M. (2010, in press). Attachment in adolescence: A move to the level of emotion regulation. *Journal of Social and Personal Relationships.*

Allen, J. P., & others. (2009, April). *Portrait of the secure teen as an adult.* Paper presented at the meeting of the Society for Research in Child Development, Denver.

Allen, M., Svetaz, M. V., Hardeman, R., & Resnick, M. D. (2008, February). *What research tells us about parenting practices and their relationship to youth sexual behavior.* Campaign to Prevent Teen and Unplanned Pregnancy. Retrieved December 2, 2008, from http://www.TheNationalCampaign.org

Almeida, D., & Horn, M. (2004). Is daily life more stressful during middle adulthood? In G. Brim, C., Ryff, & R. Kessler (Eds.), *How healthy we are: A national study of well-being in midlife.* Chicago: University of Chicago Press.

Alonso-Babarro, A., Varela-Cerdeira, M. A., Rodriguez-Barrientos, R., & Bruera, E. (2010, in press). At-home palliative sedation for end-of-life cancer patients. *Palliative Medicine.*

Althof, S. E., Rubio-Aurioles, E., Kingsberg, S., Zeigler, H., Wong, D. G., & Burns, P. (2010, in press). Impact of tadalafil once daily in men with erectile dysfunction—including a report of the partner's evaluation. *Urology.*

Alvarez, A., & del Rio, P. (2007). Inside and outside the zone of proximal development: An eco-functional reading of Vygotsky. In H. Daniels, J. Wertsch, & M. Cole (Eds.), *The Cambridge companion to Vygotsky.* New York: Cambridge University Press.

Alzheimer's Association. (2010). 2010 Alzheimer's disease facts and figures. *Alzheimer's and Dementia, 6,* 158–194.

Amato, P. R. (2006). Marital discord, divorce, and children's well-being: Results from a 20-year longitudinal study of two generations. In A. Clarke-Stewart & J. Dunn (Eds.), *Families count.* New York: Cambridge University Press.

Amato, P. R. (2010, in press). Research on divorce: Continuing trends and new developments. *Journal of Marriage and the Family.*

Amato, P. R., & Dorius, C. (2011). Fathers, children, and divorce. In M. E. Lamb (Ed.), *The role of the father in child development* (5th ed.). New York: Wiley.

Amed, S., Daneman, D., Mahmud, F. H., & Hamilton, J. (2010). Type 2 diabetes in children and adolescents. *Expert Review of Cardiovascular Therapy, 8,* 393–406.

American Academy of Pediatrics (AAP). Work Group on Breastfeeding (1997). Breastfeeding and the use of human milk. *Pediatrics, 100,* 1035–1039.

American Association of University Women. (2006). *Drawing the line: Sexual harassment on campus.* Washington, DC: American Association of University Women.

American Psychological Association. (2003). *Psychology: Scientific problem solvers.* Washington, DC: American Psychological Association.

American Psychological Association. (2007). *Stress in America.* Washington, DC: American Psychological Association.

Amos, D., & Johnson, S. P. (2011, in press). Building object knowledge from perceptual input. In B. Hood & L. Santos (Eds.), *The origins of object knowledge.* New York: Oxford University Press.

Amsterdam, B. K. (1968). *Mirror behavior in children under two years of age.* Unpublished doctoral dissertation, University of North Carolina, Chapel Hill.

Anderman, E. M., & Anderman, L. H. (2010). *Classroom motivation.* Upper Saddle River, NJ: Prentice Hall.

Anderson, B. M., & others. (2009). Examination of associations of genes in the serotonin system to autism. *Neurogenetics, 10,* 209–216.

Anderson, C. A., Gentile, D. A., & Buckley, K. E. (2007). *Violent video game effects on children and adolescents.* New York: Oxford University Press.

Anderson, D. J., & Yoshizawa, T. (2007). Cross-cultural comparisons of the health-related quality of life in Australian and Japanese women: The Australian and Japanese Midlife Women's Health study. *Menopause, 35,* 18–38.

Anderson, E., Greene, S. M., Hetherington, E. M., & Clingempeel, W. G. (1999). The dynamics of parental remarriage. In H. M. Hetherington (Ed.), *Coping with divorce, single parenting, and remarriage.* Mahwah, NJ: Erlbaum.

Anderson, K., & Harwood, J. (2009). Cultural images, later life. In D. Carr (Ed.), *Encyclopedia of the life course and human development.* Boston: Gale Cengage.

Angel, L., Fay, S., Bourazzaoui, B., Granion, L., & Isingrini, M. (2009). Neural correlates of cued recall to young and older adults: An event-related potential study, *Neuroreport, 20,* 75–79.

Antonucci, T. C. (1989). Understanding adult social relationships. In K. Kreppner & R. M. Lerner (Eds.), *Family systems and life-span development.* Hillsdale, NJ: Erlbaum.

Antonucci, T. C., Birditt, K. S., & Akiyama, H. (2009). Convoys of social relationships: An interdisciplinary approach. In V. L. Bengtson, D. Gans, N. M. Putney, & M. Silverstein (Eds.), *Handbook of theories of aging* (2nd ed.). New York: Springer.

Antonucci, T. C., Fiori, K. L., Birditt, K., & Jackey, L. M. H. (2011). Convoys of social relations: Integrating life-span and life-course perspectives. In R. M. Lerner, M. E. Lamb, & A. M. Freund (Eds.), *Handbook of life-span development* (Vol. 2). New York: Wiley.

Antonucci, T. C., Lansford, J. E., & Akiyama, H. (2001). The impact of positive and negative aspects of marital relationships and friendships on the well-being of older adults. In J. P. Reinhardt (Ed.), *Negative and positive support*. Mahwah, NJ: Erlbaum.

Antonucci, T. C., Vandewater, E. A., & Lansford, J. E. (2000). Adulthood and aging: Social processes and development. In A. Kazdin (Ed.), *Encyclopedia of psychology*. Washington, DC, and New York: American Psychological Association and Oxford University Press.

Appleton, J. V., & Stanley, N. (2009). Editorial: Childhood outcomes. *Child Abuse Review, 18,* 1–5.

Arendas, K., Qui, Q., & Gruslin, A. (2008). Obesity in pregnancy: Preconceptual to postpartum consequences. *Journal of Obstetrics and Gynecology Canada, 30,* 477–488.

Arenkiel, B. R. (2010, in press). Adult neurogenesis supports short-term olfactory memory. *Journal of Neurophysiology.*

Ariceli, G., Castro, J., Cesena, J., & Toro, J. (2005). Anorexia nervosa in male adolescents: Body image, eating attitudes, and psychological traits. *Journal of Adolescent Health, 36,* 221–226.

Ariza, E. N. W., & Lapp, S. I. (2011). *Literacy, language, and culture*. Boston: Allyn & Bacon.

Arnett, J. J. (2004). *Emerging adulthood*. New York: Oxford University Press.

Arnett, J. J. (2006). Emerging adulthood: Understanding the new way of coming of age. In J. J. Arnett & J. L. Tanner (Eds.), *Emerging adults in America*. Washington, DC: American Psychological Association.

Arnett, J. J. (2010). *Adolescence and emerging adulthood* (4th ed.). Upper Saddle River, NJ: Pearson.

Aronson, E. (1986, August). *Teaching students things they think they already know about: The case of prejudice and desegregation*. Paper presented at the meeting of the American Psychological Association, Washington, DC.

Arterberry, M. E. (2008). Perceptual development. In M. M. Haith & J. B. Benson (Eds.), *Handbook of infant and early childhood development*. New York: Elsevier.

Ascher, B., & others. (2010, in press). International consensus recommendations on the aesthetic usage of botulinum toxin type a (Speywood Unit)—part I: upper facial wrinkles. *Journal of the European Academy of Dermatology.*

Asghar-Ali, A., & Braun, U. K. (2009). Depression in geriatric patients. *Minerva Medico, 100,* 105–113.

Ashcraft, M. H., & Radvansky, G. A. (2010). *Cognition* (5th ed.). Upper Saddle River, NJ: Pearson.

Aslin, R. N. (2009). The role of learning in cognitive development. In A. Woodward & A. Needham (Eds.), *Learning and the infant mind*. New York: Oxford University Press.

Aslin, R. N. (2010, in press). Perceptual constraints on implicit memory to visual features: Statistical learning in infants. In L. Oakes, C. Cashon, M. Casasola, & D. Rakison (Eds.), *Infant perception and cognition*. New York: Oxford University Press.

Aslin, R. N., Jusczyk, P. W., & Pisoni, D. B. (1998). Speech and auditory processing during infancy: Constraints on and precursors to language. In W. Damon (Ed.), *Handbook of child psychology* (5th ed., Vol. 2). New York: Wiley.

Aslin, R. N., & Lathrop, A. L. (2008). Visual perception. In M. Haith & J. Benson (Eds.), *Handbook of infant and early childhood development*. London: Elsevier.

Attar-Schwartz, S., Tan, J. P., Buchanan, A., Flouri, E., & Griggs, J. (2009). Grandparenting and adolescent development in two-parent biological, lone-parent, and stepfamilies. *Journal of Family Psychology, 23,* 67–75.

Aubert, G., & Lansdorp, P. M. (2008). Telomeres and aging. *Physiological Review, 88,* 557–579.

Audhoe, S. S., Hoving, J. L., Sluiter, J. K., & Frings-Dresen, M. H. (2010). Vocational interventions for unemployed: Effects on work participation and mental distress. A systematic review. *Journal of Occupational Rehabilitation, 20,* 1–13.

Austad, S. N. (2009). Making sense of biological theories of aging. In V. L. Bengtson, D. Gans, N. M. Putney, & M. Silverstein (Eds.), *Handbook of theories of aging* (2nd ed.). New York: Springer.

Avis, N. E., Brockwell, S., Randolph, J. F., Shen, S., Cain, V. S., Orly, M., & others. (2009). Longitudinal changes in sexual functioning as women transition through menopause: Results from the Study of Women's Health Across the Nation. *Menopause, 16* (3), 442–452.

Aylott, M. (2006). The neonatal energy triangle. Part I: Metabolic adaptation. *Pediatric Nursing, 18,* 38–42.

B

Babbie, E. R. (2011). *The basics of social research* (5th ed.). Boston: Cengage.

Babizhayev, M. A, Minasyan, H., & Richer, S. P. (2009) Cataract halos: A driving hazard in aging populations: Implications of the Halometer DG test for assessment of intraocular light scatter. *Applied Ergonomics, 40,* 545–553.

Bachman, J. G., O'Malley, P. M., Schulenberg, J., Johnston, L. D., Bryant, A. L., & Merline, A. C. (2002). *The decline of substance abuse in young adulthood*. Mahwah, NJ: Erlbaum.

Bachman, J. G., O'Malley, P. M., Schulenberg, J. E., Johnston L. D., Freedman-Doan, P., & Messersmith, E. E. (2008). *The education–drug use connection*. New York: Psychology Press.

Baddeley, A. (2007). *Working memory, thought, and action*. New York: Oxford University Press.

Bahali, K., Akcan, R., Tahiroglu, A. Y., & Avci, A. (2010, in press). Child sexual abuse: Seven years into practice. *Journal of Forensic Science.*

Bahrick, L. E., & Hollich, G. (2008). Intermodal perception. In M. M. Haith & J. B. Benson (Eds.), *Encyclopedia of infant and early childhood development*. Oxford, UK: Elsevier.

Baillargeon, R. (2004). The acquisition of physical knowledge in infancy: A summary in eight lessons. In U. Goswami (Ed.), *Blackwell handbook of childhood cognitive development*. Malden, MA: Blackwell.

Baillargeon, R., Wu, D., Yuan, S., Li, J., & Luo, Y. (2009). Young infants' expectations about self-propelled objects. In B. Hood & L. Santos (Eds.), *The origins of object knowledge*. Oxford, UK: Oxford University Press.

Bain, J. (2010, in press). Testosterone and the aging male: To treat or not to treat? *Maturitas*.

Bakeman, R., & Brown, J. V. (1980). Early interaction: Consequences for social and mental development at three years. *Child Development, 51,* 437–447.

Baker, L. D., & others. (2010). Effects of aerobic exercise on mild cognitive impairment: A controlled trial. *Archives of Neurology, 67,* 71–79.

Bakersman-Kranenburg, M. J., & van IJzendoorn, M. H. (2009). The first 10,000 adult attachment interviews: Distributions of adult attachment representations in clinical and non-clinical groups. *Attachment and Human Development, 11,* 223–263.

Bakken, J. P., & Brown, B. B. (2010). Adolescent secretive behavior: African American and Hmong adolescents' strategies and justifications for managing parents' knowledge about peers. *Journal of Research on Adolescence, 20,* 359–388.

Balaji, P., Dhillon, P., & Russell, I. F. (2009). Low-dose epidural top up for emergency cesarean delivery: A randomized comparison of levobupivacaine versus lidocaine/epinephrine/fentanyl. *International Journal of Obstetric Anesthesia, 18,* 335–341.

Balchin, L., & Steer, P. J. (2007). Race, prematurity, and immaturity. *Early Human Development, 83,* 749–754.

Balsano, A., Theokas, C., & Bobek, D. L. (2009). A shared commitment to youth: The integration of theory, research, and policy. In R. M. Lerner & L. Steinberg (Eds.), *Handbook of adolescent psychology* (3rd ed.). New York: Wiley.

Baltes, P. B. (1987). Theoretical propositions of life-span developmental psychology: On the dynamics between growth and decline. *Developmental Psychology, 23,* 611–626.

Baltes, P. B. (2003). On the incomplete architecture of human ontogeny: Selection, optimization, and compensation as foundation of developmental theory. In U. M. Staudinger & U. Lindenberger (Eds.), *Understanding human development*. Boston: Kluwer.

Baltes, P. B. (2006). *Facing our limits: The very old and the future of aging*. Unpublished manuscript, Max Planck Institute, Berlin.

Baltes, P. B., Lindenberger, U., & Staudinger, U. (2006). Life span theory in developmental psychology. In W. Damon & R. Lerner (Eds.), *Handbook of child psychology* (6th ed.). New York: Wiley.

Baltes, P. B., Reuter-Lorenz, P., & Rösler, F. (Eds.). (2006). *Lifespan development and the brain*. New York: Cambridge University Press.

Baltes, P. B., & Smith, J. (2003). New frontiers in the future of aging: From successful aging of the young to the dilemmas of the fourth age. *Gerontology, 49,* 123–135.

Bandura, A. (1986). *Social foundations of thought and action: A social cognitive theory*. Englewood Cliffs, NJ: Prentice Hall.

Bandura, A. (1998, August). *Swimming against the mainstream: Accentuating the positive aspects of humanity*. Paper presented at the meeting of the American Psychological Association, San Francisco.

Bandura, A. (2001). Social cognitive theory. *Annual Review of Psychology*. Palo Alto, CA: Annual Reviews.

Bandura, A. (2004, May). *Toward a psychology of human agency*. Paper presented at the meeting of the American Psychological Society, Chicago.

Bandura, A. (2006). Toward a psychology of human agency. *Perspectives on Psychological Science, 1,* 164–180.

Bandura, A. (2009a). Self-efficacy. In S. Clegg & J. Bailey (Eds.), *International encyclopedia of organizational studies*. Thousand Oaks, CA: Sage.

Bandura, A. (2009b). Social and policy impact of social cognitive theory. In M. Mark, S. Donaldson, & B. Campbell (Eds.), *Social psychology and program/policy evaluation*. New York: Guilford.

Bandura, A. (2009c). Social and policy impact of social cognitive theory. In M. Mark, S. Donaldson, & B. Campell (Eds.), *Social psychology and program/policy evaluation*. New York: Guilford.

Bandura, A. (2010a). Self-efficacy. In D. Matsumoto (Ed.), *Cambridge dictionary of psychology*. New York: Cambridge University Press.

Bandura, A. (2010b). Observational learning. In D. Matsumoto (Ed.), *Cambridge dictionary of psychology*. New York: Cambridge University Press.

Bangdiwala, S. I., & others. (2010, in press). NIH consensus development conference draft statement on vaginal birth after cesarean: New insights. *NIH Consensus Statements and Scientific Statements*.

Banja, J. (2005). Talking to the dying. *Case Manager, 16,* 37–39.

Banks, J. A. (Ed.). (2010). *The Routledge international companion to multicultural education*. New York: Routledge.

Banks, M. S., & Salapatek, P. (1983). Infant visual perception. In P. H. Mussen (Ed.), *Handbook of child psychology* (4th ed., Vol. 2). New York: Wiley.

Bapat, S. A., Krishnan, A., Ghanate, A. D., Kusumbe, A. P., & Kaira, R. S. (2010, in press). Gene expression: Protein interaction systems network modeling identifies transformation-associated molecules and pathways in ovarian cancer. *Cancer Research*.

Barajas, R. G., Philipsen, N., & Brooks-Gunn, J. (2008). Cognitive and emotional outcomes for children living in poverty. In D. R. Crane & T. B. Heaton (Eds.), *Handbook of families and poverty*. Thousand Oaks, CA: Sage.

Barba, G. D., Attali, E., & La Corte, V. (2010, in press). Confabulation in healthy aging is related to interference of overlearned, semantically similar information on episodic memory recall. *Journal of Clinical and Experimental Neuropsychology*.

Barbarin, O. A., & Miller, K. (2009). Developmental science and early education: An introduction. In O. A. Barbarin & B. H. Wasik (Eds.), *Handbook of child development and early education*. New York: Guilford.

Barbieri, M., Boccardi, V., Papa, M., & Paolisso, G. (2009). Metabolic journey to healthy longevity. *Hormone Research, 71*(Suppl. 1), S24–S27.

Barker, R., & Wright, H. F. (1951). *One boy's day*. New York: Harper & Row.

Barnett, W. S., & others. (2006). Educational effectiveness of the Tools of the Mind curriculum: A randomized trial. New Brunswick, NJ: National Institute of Early Education Research, Rutgers University.

Barta, E., & Drugan, A. (2010). Glucose transfer from mother to fetus—a theoretical study. *Journal of Theoretical Biology, 263*, 295–302.

Bashir, M., & Holroyd, S. (2010). Caring for the elderly female psychiatric patient. *Psychiatric Clinics of North America, 33*, 475–485.

Bates, J. E. (2008). Unpublished review of J. W. Santrock's *Children* (11th ed.). New York: McGraw-Hill.

Bates, J. E., Schermerhorn, A. C., & Goodnight, J. A. (2011, in press). In R. M. Lerner, M. E. Lamb, & A. M. Freund (Eds.), *Handbook of life-span development* (Vol. 2). New York: Wiley.

Bauer, J., & others. (2010). Comparative transcriptional profiling identifies takeout as a gene that regulates life span. *Aging, 2*, 298–310.

Bauer, M. E., Jeckel, C. M., & Luz, C. (2009). The role of stress factors during aging of the immune system. *Annals of the New York Academy of Sciences, 1153*, 139–152.

Bauer, P. J. (2009a). Learning and memory: Like a horse and carriage. In A. Woodward & A. Needham (Eds.), *Learning and the infant mind*. New York: Oxford University Press.

Bauer, P. J. (2009b). Neurodevelopmental changes in infancy and beyond: Implications for learning and memory. In O. A. Barbarin & B. H. Wasik (Eds.), *Handbook of child development and early education*. New York: Guilford.

Bauer, P. J., Wenner, J. A., Dropik, P. I., & Wewerka, S. S. (2000). Parameters of remembering and forgetting in the transition from infancy to early childhood. *Monographs of the Society for Research in Child Development, 65*(4, Serial No. 263).

Bauman, W. P. (2008). Sexuality in later life. In R. Jacoby, C. Oppenheimer, T. Dening, & A. Thomas (Eds.), *Oxford textbook of old age psychiatry*. Oxford, UK: Oxford University Press.

Baumeister, R. F., Campbell, J. D., Krueger, J. I., & Vohs, K. D. (2003). Does high self-esteem cause better performance, interpersonal success, happiness, or healthier lifestyles? *Psychological Science in the Public Interest, 4*(1), 1–44.

Baumrind, D. (1971). Current patterns of parental authority. *Developmental Psychology Monographs, 4*(1, Pt. 2).

Bava, S., & others. (2010, in press). Longitudinal characterization of white matter maturation during adolescence. *Brain Research*.

Bayraktar, M. R., Ozerol, I. H., Gucluer, N., & Celik, O. (2010). Prevalence and antibiotic susceptibility of *Mycoplasma hominis* and *Ureaplasma urealyticum* in pregnant women. *International Journal of Infectious Diseases, 14*, e90–e95.

Baysinger, C. L. (2010). Imaging during pregnancy. *Anesthesia and Analgesia, 110*, 863–867.

Bazzano, L. A., & others. (2010). Body mass index and risk of stroke among Chinese men and women. *Annals of Neurology, 67*, 11–20.

Bearman, S. K., Presnall, K., Martinez, E., & Stice, E. (2006). The skinny on body dissatisfaction: A longitudinal study of adolescent girls and boys. *Journal of Youth and Adolescence, 35*, 217–229.

Beaty, J. J. (2009). *50 early childhood literacy strategies* (2nd ed.). Boston: Allyn & Bacon.

Beaty, J. J., & Pratt, L. (2011). *Early literacy in preschool and kindergarten* (3rd ed.). Boston: Allyn & Bacon.

Beck, C. T. (2006). Postpartum depression: It isn't just the blues. *American Journal of Nursing, 106*, 40–50.

Bedford, V. H. (2009). Sibling relationships: Adulthood. In D. Carr (Ed.), *Encyclopedia of the life course and human development*. Boston: Gale Cengage.

Bednar, R. L., Wells, M. G., & Peterson, S. R. (1995). *Self-esteem* (2nd ed.). Washington, DC: American Psychological Association.

Beech, A. R., Ward, T., & Fisher, D. (2006). The identification of sexual and violent motivations in men who assault women: Implications for treatment. *Journal of Interpersonal Violence, 21*, 1635–1653.

Beets, M. W., & Foley, J. T. (2008). Association of father involvement and neighborhood quality with kindergarteners' physical activity: A multilevel structural equation model. *American Journal of Health Promotion, 22*, 195–203.

Beghetto, R. A., & Kaufman, J. C. (Eds.). (2011). *Nurturing creativity in the classroom*. New York: Cambridge University Press.

Bell, M. A., Greene, D. R., & Wolfe, C. D. (2010). Psychobiological mechanisms of cognition-emotion integration in early development. In S. D. Calkins & M. A. Bell (Eds.), *Child development at the intersection of cognition and emotion*. New York: Psychology Press.

Belsky, J. (1981). Early human experience: A family perspective. *Developmental Psychology, 17*, 3–23.

Bem, S. L. (1977). On the utility of alternative procedures for assessing psychological androgyny. *Journal of Consulting and Clinical Psychology, 45*, 196–205.

Bender, H. L., Allen, J. P., McElhaney, K. B., Antonishak, J., Moore, C. M., Kello, H. O., & Davis, S. M. (2007). Use of harsh physical discipline and developmental outcomes in adolescence. *Development and Psychopathology, 19*, 227–242.

Bendersky, M., & Sullivan, M. W. (2007). Basic methods in infant research. In A. Slater & M. Lewis (Eds.), *Introduction to infant development* (2nd ed.). New York: Oxford University Press.

Benenson, J. F., Apostolaris, N. H., & Parnass, J. (1997). Age and sex differences in dyadic and group interaction. *Developmental Psychology, 33*, 538–543.

Bengtson, V. L. (1985). Diversity and symbolism in grandparental roles. In V. L. Bengtson & J. Robertson (Eds.), *Grandparenthood*. Newbury Park, CA: Sage.

Bennett, C. I. (2011). *Perspectives on human differences*. Boston: Allyn & Bacon.

Bennett, K. M. (2006). Does marital status and marital status change predict physical health in older adults? *Psychological Medicine, 36*, 1313–1320.

Bennett, K. M. (2009). Widowhood. In D. Carr (Ed.), *Encyclopedia of the life course and human development*. Boston: Gale Cengage.

Bennett, T., Szatmari, P., Bryson, S., Volden, J., Zwaigenbaum, L., Vaccarella, L., et al. (2008). Differentiating autism and Asperger syndrome on the basis of language delay or impairment. *Journal of Autism and Developmental Disorders, 38*, 616–625.

Benninghoven, D., Tetsch, N., Kunzendorf, S., & Jantschek, G. (2007). Body image in patients with eating disorders and their mothers, and the role of family functioning. *Comprehensive Psychiatry, 48*, 118–123.

Benoit, D., Coolbear, J., & Crawford, A. (2008). Abuse, neglect, and maltreatment of infants. In M. M. Haith & J. B. Benson (Eds.), *Encyclopedia of infant and early childhood development*. Oxford, UK: Elsevier.

Benson, L., Baer, H. J., & Kaelber, D. C. (2009). Trends in the diagnosis of overweight and obesity in children and adolescents: 1999–2007. *Pediatrics, 123*, e153–e158.

Berardi, A., Parasuraman, R., & Haxby, J. V. (2001). Overall vigilance and sustained attention decrements in healthy aging. *Experimental Aging Research, 27*, 19–39.

Berg, A. I., Hoffman, L., Hassing, L. B., McClearn, G. E., & Johansson, B. (2009). What matters, and what matters most, for change in life satisfaction in the oldest old? A study over 6 years among individuals 80+. *Aging and Mental Health, 13*, 191–201.

Bergen, D. (1988). Stages of play development. In D. Bergen (Ed.), *Play as a medium for learning and development*. Portsmouth, NH: Heinemann.

Berghella, V., Baxter, J. K., & Chauhan, S. P. (2008). Evidence-based labor and delivery management. *American Journal of Obstetrics and Gynecology, 199*, 445–454.

Berk, L. E. (1994). Why children talk to themselves. *Scientific American, 271*(5), 78–83.

Berk, L. E., & Spuhl, S. T. (1995). Maternal interaction, private speech, and task performance in preschool children. *Early Childhood Research Quarterly, 10*, 145–169.

Berko, J. (1958). The child's learning of English morphology. *Word, 14*, 150–177.

Berko Gleason, J. (2003). Unpublished review of J. W. Santrock's *Life-span development* (9th ed.). New York: McGraw-Hill.

Berko Gleason, J. (2009). The development of language: An overview. In J. Berko Gleason & N. B. Ratner (Ed.), *The development of language* (7th ed.). Boston: Allyn & Bacon.

Berko Gleason, J., & Ratner, N. B. (Eds.). (2009). *The development of language* (7th ed.). Boston: Allyn & Bacon.

Berlin, C. M., Paul, I. M., & Vesell, E. S. (2009). Safety issues of maternal drug therapy during breastfeeding. *Clinical Pharmacology and Therapeutics, 85*, 20–22.

Berlyne, D. E. (1960). *Conflict, arousal, and curiosity*. New York: McGraw-Hill.

Berndt, T. J., & Perry, T. B. (1990). Distinctive features and effects of early adolescent friendships. In R. Montemayor (Ed.), *Advances in adolescent research*. Greenwich, CT: JAI Press.

Berninger, V. W. (2006). Learning disabilities. In W. Damon & R. Lerner (Eds.), *Handbook of child psychology* (6th ed.). New York: Wiley.

Berry, J. L. (2010). Hospice and heart disease: Missed opportunities. *Journal of Pain and Palliative Care Pharmacotherapy, 24*, 23–26.

Berscheid, E. (2010). Love in the fourth dimension. *Annual Review of Psychology* (Vol. 61). Palo Alto, CA: Annual Reviews.

Berscheid, E., & Fei, J. (1977). Sexual jealousy and romantic love. In G. Clinton & G. Smith (Eds.), *Sexual jealousy*. Englewood Cliffs, NJ: Prentice Hall.

Bertenthal, B. I. (2008). Perception and action. In M. M. Haith & J. B. Benson (Eds.), *Infant and early childhood development*. Oxford, UK: Elsevier.

Bertenthal, B. I., Longo, M. R., & Kenny, S. (2007). Phenomenal permanence and the development of predictive tracking in infancy. *Child Development, 78*, 350–363.

Bessette, L., Jean, S., Davison, K. S., Roy, S., Ste-Marie, L. G., & Brown, J. P. (2009). Factors influencing the treatment of osteoporosis following fragility fracture. *Osteoporosis International, 20*, 1911–1919.

Best, C. L., Smith, D. W., Raymond, J. R., Greenberg, R. S., & Crouch, R. K. (2010). Preventing and responding to complaints of sexual harassment in an academic health center: A 10-year review from the Medical University of South Carolina. *Academic Medicine, 85*, 721–727.

Best, D. L. (2010). Gender. In M. H. Bornstein (Ed.), *Handbook of cultural developmental science*. New York: Psychology Press.

Bethell, J., & Roades, A. E. (2008). Adolescent depression and emergency department use: The roles of suicidality and deliberate self-harm. *Current Psychiatry Reports, 10*, 53–59.

Bettens, K., Sleegers, K., & Van Broeckhoven, C. (2010, in press). Current status on Alzheimer disease molecular genetics: From past, to present, to future. *Human Molecular Genetics*.

Beutel, M. E., Glaesmer, H., Wiltink, J., Marian, H., & Brahler, E. (2010). Life satisfaction, anxiety, depression, and resilience across the life span of men. *Aging Male, 13,* 32–39.

Beverly, C., Burger, S. G., Maas, M. L., & Specht, J. K. (2010). Aging issues: Nursing imperatives for healthcare reform. *Nursing Administration Quarterly, 34,* 95–109.

Beydoun, M. A., & Wang, Y. (2009). Gender-ethnic disparity in BMI and waist circumference distribution shifts in U.S. adults. *Obesity, 17,* 169–176.

Beyene Y. (1986). Cultural significance and physiological manifestations of menopause: A biocultural analysis. *Culture, Medicine and Psychiatry, 10,* 47–71.

Bialystok, E. (1997). Effects of bilingualism and biliteracy on children's emerging concepts of print. *Developmental Psychology, 33,* 429–440.

Bialystok, E. (2001). *Bilingualism in development: Language, literacy, and cognition.* New York: Cambridge University Press.

Bialystok, E. (2007). Acquisition of literacy in preschool children: A framework for research. *Language Learning, 57,* 45–77.

Bialystok, E., & Craik, F. I. M. (2010). Structure and process in life-span cognitive development. In R. M. Lerner & W. F. Overton (Eds.), *Handbook of life-span development* (Vol. 1). New York: Wiley.

Bian, Z., & Anderson, G. J. (2008). Aging and the perceptual organization of 3-D scenes. *Psychology and Aging, 23,* 342–352.

Biblarz, T. J., & Savci, E. (2010, in press). Lesbian, gay, bisexual, and transgender families. *Journal of Marriage and the Family.*

Bickham, D. S. (2009). Media and technology use, childhood and adolescence. In D. Carr (Ed.), *Encyclopedia of the life course and human development.* Gale Cengage.

Bigelow, A. E., & others. (2010). Maternal sensitivity throughout infancy: Continuity and its relation to attachment security. *Infant Behavior and Development, 33,* 50–60.

Biggs, B. K., & Vernberg, E. M. (2010). Future directions. In E. M. Vernberg & B. K. Biggs (Eds.), *Preventing and treating bullying and victimization.* New York: Oxford University Press.

Bijur, P. E., Wallston, K. A., Smith, C. A., Lifrak, S., & Friedman, S. B. (1993, August). *Gender differences in turning to religion for coping.* Paper presented at the meeting of the American Psychological Association, Toronto.

Birditt, K. S., Fingerman, K. L., & Zarit, S. H. (2010). Adult children's problems and successes: Implications for intergenerational ambivalence. *Journals of Gerontology B: Psychological Sciences and Social Sciences. 65B,* 145–153.

Birditt, K. S., Miller, L. M., Fingerman, K. L., & Lefkowitz, E. S. (2010, in press). Tensions in the parent and adult child relationship: Links to solidarity and ambivalence. *Psychology and Aging.*

Birman, B. F., Le Floch, K. C., Klekotka, A., Ludwig, M., Taylor, J., Walters, K., & others. (2007). *State and local implementation of the "No Child Left Behind Act." Volume II—Teacher quality under "NCLB": Interim report.* Jessup, MD: U.S. Department of Education.

Biro, M. M., Huang, B., Morrison, J. A., Horn, P. S., & Daniels, S. R. (2010). Body mass index and waist-to-height changes during teen years in girls are influenced by childhood body mass index. *Journal of Adolescent Health, 46,* 245–250.

Birren, J. E. (2002). Unpublished review of J. W. Santrock's *Life-span development,* 9th ed. (New York: McGraw-Hill).

Birren, J. E., Woods, A. M., & Williams, M. V. (1980). Behavioral slowing with age: Causes, organization, & consequences. In J. W. Poon (Ed.), *Aging in the 1980s: Psychological issues.* Washington, DC: American Psychological Association.

Bjorklund, D. F., & Pellegrini, A. D. (2002). The origins of human nature. New York: Oxford University Press.

Black, M. M., & Hurley, K. M. (2007). Helping children develop healthy eating habits. In R. E. Tremblay, R. G. Barr, R. D. Peters, & M. Boivin (Eds.), *Encyclopedia on early childhood development.* Retrieved March 19, 2008, from www.child-encyclopedia.com/documents/Black-HurleyANGxp_rev-Eating.pdf

Black, M. M., Hurley, K. M., Oberlander, S. E., Hager, E. R., McGill, A. E., White, N. T., & others. (2009). Participants' comments on changes in the revised special supplemental nutrition program for women, infants, and children food packages: The Maryland food preference study. *Journal of the American Dietetic Association, 109,* 116–123.

Black, M. M., & Lozoff, B. (2008). Nutrition and diet. In M. M. Haith & J. B. Benson (Eds.), *Encyclopedia of infant and early childhood development.* Oxford, UK: Elsevier.

Blackwell, L. S., & Dweck, C. S. (2008). *The motivational impact of a computer-based program that teaches how the brain changes with learning.* Unpublished manuscript. Department of Psychology, Stanford University, Palo Alto, CA.

Blackwell, L. S., Trzesniewski, K. H., & Dweck, C. S. (2007). Implicit theories of intelligence predict achievement across an adolescent tradition: A longitudinal study and an intervention. *Child Development, 78,* 246–263.

Blagosklonny, M. V. (2010). Calorie restriction: Decelerating mTOR-driven aging from cells to organisms (including humans). *Cell Cycle, 9,* 683–688.

Blair, C. (2010). Fluid cognitive abilities and general intelligence. In R. M. Lerner & W. F. Overton (Eds.), *Handbook of life-span development* (Vol. 1). New York: Wiley.

Blair, M., & Somerville, S. C. (2009). The importance of differentiation in young children's acquisition of expertise. *Cognition, 112,* 259–280.

Blair, S. N. (1990). *Personal communication.* Dallas: Cooper Aerobics Center.

Blair, S. N., Kohl, H. W., Paffenbarger, R. S., Clark, D. G., Cooper, K. H., & Gibbons, L. W. (1989). Physical fitness and all-cause mortality: A prospective study of healthy men and women. *Journal of the American Medical Association, 262,* 2395–2401.

Blake, J. S. (2011). *Nutrition and you.* Upper Saddle River, NJ: Pearson.

Blakemore, J. E. O., Berenbaum, S. A., & Liben, L. S. (2009). *Gender development.* New York: Psychology Press.

Blieszner, R. (2009). Friendship, adulthood. In D. Carr (Ed.), *Encyclopedia of the life course and human development.* Boston: Gale Cengage.

Blieszner, R., & Bedford, V. H. (Eds.). (2011, forthcoming). *Handbook of aging and the family.* Santa Barbara, CA: Praeger.

Blood-Siegfried, J., & Rende, E. K. (2010). The long-term effects of prenatal nicotine exposure on neurologic development. *Journal of Midwifery and Women's Health, 55,* 143–152.

Bloom, B. (1985). *Developing talent in young people.* New York: Ballantine.

Bloom, L., Lifter, K., & Broughton, J. (1985). The convergence of early cognition and language in the second year of life: Problems in conceptualization and measurement. In M. Barrett (Ed.), *Single word speech.* London: Wiley.

Bloomgarden, Z. T. (2010). Gestational diabetes mellitus and obesity. *Diabetes Care, 33,* e60–e65.

Blossfeld, H-P. (2009). Globalization. In D. Carr (Ed.), *Encyclopedia of the life course and human development.* Boston: Gale Cengage.

Bluck, S., & Baron, J. M. (2009). Wisdom. In D. Carr (Ed.), *Encyclopedia of the life course and human development.* Boston: Gale Cengage.

Blustein, D. L. (2008). The role of work in psychological health and well-being. *American Psychologist, 63,* 228–240.

Boden, J. S., Fischer, J. L., & Niehuis, S. (2010). Predicting marital adjustment from young adults' initial levels of and changes in emotional intimacy over time: A 25-year longitudinal study. *Journal of Adult Development, 17,* 121–134.

Bodrova, E., & Leong, D. J. (2007). *Tools of the mind* (2nd ed.). Geneva, Switzerland: International Bureau of Education, UNESCO.

Boelen, P. A., & Prigerson, H. G. (2007). The influence of symptoms of prolonged grief disorder, depression, and anxiety on quality of life among bereaved adults: A prospective study. *European Archives of Psychiatry and Clinical Neuroscience, 259,* 442–452.

Bohlin, G., & Hagekull, B. (1993). Stranger wariness and sociability in the early years. *Infant Behavior and Development, 16,* 53–67.

Boldo, E., & others. (2010). Health impact assessment of environmental tobacco smoke in European children: Sudden infant death syndrome and asthma episodes. *Public Health Reports.*

Bolte, G., Fromme, H., & the GME Study Group. (2009). Socioeconomic determinants of children's environmental tobacco smoke exposure and family's home smoking policy. *European Journal of Public Health, 19,* 52–58.

Bonanno, G. A., Wortman, C. B., & Nesse, R. M. (2004). Prospective patterns of resilience and maladjustment during widowhood. *Psychology and Aging, 19,* 260–271.

Bonda, D. J., & others. (2010, in press). Oxidative stress in Alzheimer's disease: A possibility for prevention. *Neuropharmacology.*

Bondare, W. (2007). Brain and central nervous system. In J. E. Birren (Ed.), *Encyclopedia of gerontology* (2nd ed.). San Diego: Academic Press.

Bonjour, J. P., Gueguen, L., Palacios, C., Shearer, M. J., & Weaver, C. M. (2009). Minerals and vitamins in bone health: The potential value of dietary enhancement. *British Journal of Nutrition, 101,* 1581–1596.

Bonney, C., & Sternberg, R. J. (2011). Learning to think critically. In P. A. Alexander & R. E. Mayer (Eds.), *Handbook of research on learning and instruction.* New York: Routledge.

Bookwala, J., & Jacobs, J. (2004). Age, marital processes, and depressed affect. *The Gerontologist, 44,* 328–338.

Booth, A. (2006). Object function and categorization in infancy: Two mechanisms of facilitation. *Infancy, 10,* 145–169.

Booth, M. (2002). Arab adolescents facing the future: Enduring ideas and pressures to change. In B. B. Brown, R. W. Larson, & T. S. Saraswathi (Eds.), *The world's youth.* New York: Cambridge University Press.

Borich, G. D. (2011). *Effective teaching methods* (7th ed.). Allyn & Bacon.

Bornstein, M. H., & Lansford, J. (2010). Parenting. In M. H. Bornstein (Ed.), *Handbook of cultural developmental science.* New York: Psychology Press.

Boron, J. B., Willis, S. L., & Schaie, K. W. (2007). Cognitive training gain as a predictor of mental status. *Journals of Gerontology: Psychological Sciences and Social Sciences, 62B,* P45–P52.

Bortfeld, H., Fava, E., & Boas, D. A. (2009). Identifying cortical lateralization of speech processing in infants using near-infrared spectroscopy. *Developmental Neuropsychology, 34,* 52–65.

Bostock, C. V., Soiza, R. L., & Whalley, L. J. (2009). Genetic determinants of aging processes and diseases in later life. *Maturitas, 62,* 225–229.

Bouchard, T. J., Lykken, D. T., McGue, M., Segal, N. L., & Tellegen, A. (1990). Source of human psychological differences: The Minnesota Study of Twins Reared Apart. *Science, 250,* 223–228.

Bouffard, L. A., & Bouffard, J. A. (2010, in press). Understanding men's perceptions of risks and rewards in a date rape scenario. *International Journal of Offender Therapy and Comparative Criminology.*

Bowlby, J. (1969). *Attachment and loss* (Vol. 1). London: Hogarth Press.

Bowlby, J. (1989). *Secure and insecure attachment.* New York: Basic Books.

Bowman, N. A. (2010). The development of psychological well-being among first-year college students. *Journal of College Student Development, 51*, 180–200.

Brainerd, C. J., & Reyna, V. F. (2004). Fuzzy trace theory and memory development. *Developmental Review, 24*, 396–439.

Brams, H., Mao, A. R., & Doyle, R. L. (2009). Onset of efficacy of long-lasting psychostimulants in pediatric attention-deficit/hyperactivity disorder. *Postgraduate Medicine, 120*, 69–88.

Brand, S., & others. (2010). High exercise levels are related to favorable sleep patterns and psychological functioning in adolescents: A comparison of athletes and controls. *Journal of Adolescent Health, 46*, 133–141.

Brandon, P. D. (2009). Poverty, childhood, and adolescence. In D. Carr (Ed.), *Encyclopedia of the life course and human development*. Boston: Gale Cengage.

Bransford, J., & others. (2006). Learning theories in education. In P. A. Alexander & P. H. Winne (Eds.), *Handbook of educational psychology* (2nd ed.). Mahwah, NJ: Erlbaum.

Bredekamp, S. (2011). *Effective practices in early childhood education*. Upper Saddle River, NJ: Merrill.

Brendgen, R. M. (2009). Aggression, childhood and adolescence. In D. Carr (Ed.), *Encyclopedia of the life course and human development*. Boston: Gale Cengage.

Brengden, M., Lamarche, V., Wanner, B., & Vitaro, F. (2010). Links between friendship relations and early adolescents' trajectories of depressed mood. *Developmental Psychology, 46*, 491–501.

Brenner, J. G., & others. (2010, in press). Two- and 8-month-old infants' cross-modal perception of dynamic auditory-visual spatial co-location. *Child Development*.

Brent, R. L. (2009). Saving lives and changing family histories: Appropriate counseling of pregnant women and men and women of reproductive age concerning the risk of diagnostic radiation exposure during and before pregnancy. *American Journal of Obstetrics and Gynecology, 200*, 4–24.

Bretherton, I., Stolberg, U., & Kreye, M. (1981). Engaging strangers in proximal interaction: Infants' social initiative. *Developmental Psychology, 17*, 746–755.

Bril, B. (1999). Dires sur l'enfant selon les cultures. Etat des lieux et perspectives. In B. Brill, P. R. Dasen, C. Sabatier, & B. Krewer (Eds.), *Propossur l'enfant et l'adolescent. Quels enfants pour quelles cultures?* Paris: L'Harmattan.

Brim, G. (1992, December 7). Commentary, *Newsweek*, p. 52.

Brim, G., Ryff, C. D., & Kessler, R. (Eds.). (2004). *How healthy we are: A national study of well-being in midlife*. Chicago: University of Chicago Press.

Brim, O. (1999). *The MacArthur Foundation study of midlife development*. Vero Beach, FL: MacArthur Foundation.

Britton, J. R., Britton, H. L., & Gronwaldt, V. (2006). Breastfeeding, sensitivity, and attachment. *Pediatrics, 118*, e1436–e1443.

Brockmeyer, S., Treboux, D., & Crowell, J. A. (2005, April). *Parental divorce and adult children's attachment status and marital relationships*. Paper presented at the meeting of the Society for Research in Child Development, Atlanta.

Brody, N. (2000). Intelligence. In A. Kazdin (Ed.), *Encyclopedia of psychology*. Washington, DC, & New York: American Psychological Association and Oxford University Press.

Brody, N. (2007). Does education influence intelligence? In P. C. Kyllonen, R. D. Roberts, & L. Stankov (Eds.), *Extending intelligence*. Mahwah, NJ: Erlbaum.

Brody, R. M., & Costa, R. M. (2009). Satisfaction (sexual, life, relationship, and mental health) is associated directly with penile-vaginal intercourse, but inversely related to other sexual behavior frequencies. *Journal of Sexual Medicine, 6*, 1947–1955.

Brody, S. (2010). The relative health benefits of different sexual activities. *Journal of Sexual Medicine, 7*, 1336–1361.

Bronfenbrenner, U. (1986). Ecology of the family as a context for human development: Research perspectives. *Developmental Psychology, 22*, 723–742.

Bronfenbrenner, U. (2004). *Making human beings human*. Thousand Oaks, CA: Sage.

Bronfenbrenner, U., & Morris, P. A. (2006). The ecology of developmental processes. In W. Damon & R. Lerner (Eds.), *Handbook of child psychology* (6th ed.). New York: Wiley.

Bronstein, P. (2006). The family environment: Where gender role socialization begins. In J. Worell & C. D. Goodheart (Eds.), *Handbook of girls' and women's psychological health*. New York: Oxford University Press.

Brook, J. S., Brook, D. W., Gordon, A. S., Whiteman, M., & Cohen, P. (1990). The psychological etiology of adolescent drug use: A family interactional approach. *Genetic Psychology Monographs, 116*(2).

Brooker, R. (2011). *Biology* (2nd ed.). New York: McGraw-Hill.

Brooks, J. G., & Brooks, M. G. (2001). *The case for constructivist classrooms* (2nd ed.). Upper Saddle River, NJ: Prentice Hall.

Brooks-Gunn, J. (2003). Do you believe in magic?: What we can expect from early childhood programs. *Social Policy Report, Society for Research in Child Development, XVII* (No. 1), 1–13.

Brooks-Gunn, J., & Warren, M. P. (1989). The psychological significance of secondary sexual characteristics in 9- to 11-year-old girls. *Child Development, 59*, 161–169.

Brown, B. B., & Larson, J. (2009). Informal peer groups in middle childhood and adolescence. In R. L. Lerner & L. Steinberg (Eds.), *Handbook of adolescent psychology* (3rd ed.). New York: Wiley.

Brown, B. B., & Larson, J. (2009). Peer relationships in adolescence. In R. L. Lerner & L. Steinberg (Eds.), *Handbook of adolescent psychology* (3rd ed.). New York: Wiley.

Brown, B. B., & Larson, R. W. (2002). The kaleidoscope of adolescence: Experiences of the world's youth at the beginning of the 21st century. In B. B. Brown, R. W. Larson, & T. S. Saraswathi (Eds.), *The world's youth*. New York: Cambridge University Press.

Brown, J. K. (1985). Introduction. In J. K. Brown & V. Kerns (Eds.), *In her prime: A new view of middle-aged women*. South Hadley, MA: Bergin & Garvey.

Brown, L. S. (1989). New voices, new visions: Toward a lesbian/gay paradigm for psychology. *Psychology of Women Quarterly, 13*, 445–458.

Brown, R. (1958). *Words and things*. Glencoe, IL: Free Press.

Brown, R. (1973). *A first language: The early stages*. Cambridge, MA: Harvard University Press.

Brown, S. L., Bulanda, J. R., & Lee, G. R. (2005). The significance of nonmarital cohabitation: Marital status and mental health benefits among middle-aged and older adults. *Journals of Gerontology B: Psychological Sciences and Social Sciences, 60*, S21–S29.

Brown, S. L., Nesse, R. M., House, J. S., & Utz, R. L. (2004). Religion and emotional compensation: Results from a prospective study of widowhood. *Personality and Social Psychology Bulletin, 30*, 1165–1174.

Brown, T. N., & Lesane-Brown, C. L. (2009). Socialization, race. In D. Carr (Ed.), *Encyclopedia of the life course and human development*. Boston: Gale Cengage.

Brown, W. H., Pfeiffer, K. A., McIver, K. L., Dowda, M., Addy, C. L., & Pate, R. R. (2009). Social and environmental factors associated with preschoolers' nonsedentary physical activity. *Child Development, 80*, 45–58.

Brownell, C., Nichols, S., Svetlova, M., Zerwas, S., & Ramani, G. (2010). The head bone's connected to the neck bone: When do toddlers represent their own body topography? *Child Development, 81*, 797–810.

Brownell, C. A., Ramani, G. B., & Zerwas, S. (2006). Becoming a social partner with peers: Cooperation and social understanding in one and two-year-olds. *Child Development, 77*, 803–821.

Brownridge, D. A., (2008). The elevated risk for violence against cohabiting women: A comparison of three nationally representative surveys of Canada. *Violence Against Women, 14*, 809–832.

Bruce, A. (2007). Time(lessness): Buddhist perspectives and end-of-life. *Nursing Philosophy, 8*, 151–157.

Bruck, M., & Ceci, S. J. (1999). The suggestibility of children's memory. *Annual Review of Psychology, 50*, 419–439.

Bruck, M., Ceci, S. J., & Hembrooke, H. (1998). Reliability and credibility of young children's reports: From research to policy and Practice. *American Psychologist, 53*(2), 136–151.

Bruera, E., & others. (2010). AAHPM position paper: Requirements for the successful development of academic palliative care programs. *Journal of Pain and Symptom Management, 39*, 743–745.

Bruine de Bruin, W., Parker, A., & Fischhoff, B. (2007). Can adolescents predict significant events in their lives? *Journal of Adolescent Health, 41*, 208–210.

Brune, C. W., & Woodward, A. L. (2007). Social cognition and social responsiveness in 10-month-old infants. *Journal of Cognition and Development, 2*, 3–27.

Brunstein Klomek, A., Marrocco, F., Kleinman, M., Schofeld, I. S., & Gould, M. S. (2007). Bullying, depression, and suicidality in adolescents. *Journal of the American Academy of Child and Adolescent Psychiatry, 46*, 40–49.

Bryant, J. A. (Ed.). (2007). *The children's television community*. Mahwah, NJ: Erlbaum.

Bryant, J. B. (2009). Language in social contexts: Communicative competence in the preschool years. In J. Berko Gleason & N. Ratner (Eds.), *The development of language* (7th ed.). Boston: Allyn & Bacon.

Buchman, A. S., Boyle, P. A., Wilson, R. S., Fleischman, D. A., Leurgans, S., & Bennett, D. A. (2009). Association between late-life social activity and motor decline in older adults. *Archives of Internal Medicine, 169*, 1139–1146.

Buckner, J. C., Mezzacappa, E., & Beardslee, W. R. (2009). Self-regulation and its relations to adaptive functioning in low income youths. *American Journal of Orthopsychiatry, 79*, 19–30.

Bucur, B., & Madden, D. J. (2007). Information processing/cognition. In J. E. Birren (Ed.)., *Encyclopedia of gerontology* (2nd ed.). San Diego: Academic Press.

Buglass, E. (2010). Grief and bereavement theories. *Nursing Standard, 24*, 44–47.

Buhrmester, D. (1998). Need fulfillment, interpersonal competence, and the developmental contexts of early adolescent friendship. In W. M. Bukowski & A. F. Newcomb (Eds.), *The company they keep: Friendship in childhood and adolescence:* New York: Cambridge University Press.

Buhrmester, D., & Chong, C. M. (2009). Friendship in adolescence. In H. Reis & S. Sprecher (Eds.), *Encyclopedia of human relationships*. Thousand Oaks, CA: Sage.

Bukowski, R., & others. (2008, January). *Folic acid and preterm birth*. Paper presented at the meeting of the Society for Maternal-Fetal Medicine, Dallas.

Bulik, C. M., Berkman, N. D., Brownley, K. A., Sedway, J. A., & Lohr, K. N. (2007). Anorexia nervosa treatment: A systematic review of randomized controlled trials. *International Journal of Eating Disorders, 40*, 310–320.

Bullock, M., & Lutkenhaus, P. (1990). Who am I? Self-understanding in toddlers. *Merrill-Palmer Quarterly, 36*, 217–238.

Bumpas, M. F., Crouter, A. C., & McHale, S. M. (2001). Parental autonomy granting during adolescence: Gender differences in context. *Developmental Psychology, 37*, 163–173.

Bumpass, L., & Aquilino, W. (1994). *A social map of midlife: Family and work over the middle life course.*

Center for Demography & Ecology, University of Wisconsin, Madison, WI.

Burgess, E. O. (2004). Sexuality in midlife and later life couples. In J. H. Harvey & A. Wetzel (Eds.), *The handbook of sexuality in close relationships*. Mahwah, NJ: Erlbaum.

Burgess-Champoux, T. L., Larson, N., Neumark-Sztainer, D., Hannan, P. J., & Story, M. (2009). Are family meal patterns associated with overall diet quality during the transition from early to middle adolescence? *Journal of Nutrition Education and Behavior, 41,* 79–86.

Burr, J. (2009). Volunteering, later life. In D. Carr (Ed.), *Encyclopedia of the life course and human development*. Boston: Gale Cengage.

Bursuck, W. D., & Damer, M. (2011). *Teaching reading to students who are at-risk or have disabilities* (2nd Ed.). Upper Saddle River, NJ: Merrill.

Buss, D. M. (2008). *Evolutionary Psychology* (3rd ed.). Boston: Allyn Bacon.

Buss, D. M. (2011, in press). *Evolutionary psychology* (4th ed.). Boston: Allyn & Bacon.

Busse, E. W., & Blazer, D. G. (1996). *The American Psychiatric Press textbook of geriatric psychiatry* (2nd ed.). Washington, DC: American Psychiatric Press.

Bussey, K., & Bandura A. (1999). Social cognitive theory of gender development and differentiation. *Psychological Review, 106,* 676–713.

Butcher, K., Sallis, J. F., Mayer, J. A. & Woodruff, S. (2008). Correlates of physical activity guideline compliance for adolescents in 100 U.S. cities. *Journal of Adolescent Health, 42,* 360–368.

Butler, R. N. (2007). Life review. In J. E. Birren (Ed.), *Encyclopedia of gerontology* (2nd ed.). San Diego: Academic Press.

Butler, R. N., & Lewis, M. (2002). *The new love and sex after 60.* New York: Ballantine.

Butz, A. M., & others. (2010, in press). Household smoking behavior: Effects of indoor air quality and health of urban children with asthma. *Maternal and Child Health Journal.*

Buzwell, S., & Rosenthal, D. (1996). Constructing a sexual self: Adolescents' sexual self-perceptions and sexual risk-taking. *Journal of Research on Adolescence, 6,* 489–513.

C

Cabeza, R. (2002). Hemispheric asymmetry reduction in older adults: The HAROLD model. *Psychology and Aging, 17,* 85–100.

Cabrera, N., Hutchens, R., & Peters, H. E. (Eds.). (2006). *From welfare to childcare.* Mahwah, NJ: Erlbaum.

Cacioppo, J. T., Hughes, M. E., Waite, L. J., Hawkley, L. C., & Thisted, R. A. (2006). Loneliness as a specific risk factor for depressive symptoms: Cross-sectional and longitudinal analyses. *Psychology and Aging, 21,* 140–151.

Calisanti, T. (2009). Theorizing feminist gerontology, sexuality, and beyond: An intersectional approach. In V. L. Bengtson, D. Gans, N. M. Putney, & M. Silverstein (Eds.), *Handbook of theories of aging* (2nd ed.). New York: Springer.

Callahan, D. (2009). Death, mourning, and medical practice. *Perspectives in Biological Medicine, 52,* 103–115.

Callan, J. E. (2001). Gender development: Psychoanalytic perspectives. In J. Worrel (Ed.), *Encyclopedia of women and gender.* San Diego: Academic Press.

Cameron, J. M., Heidelberg, N., Simmons, L., Lyle, S. B., Kathakali, M-V., & Correia, C. (2010). Drinking game participation among undergraduate students attending National Alcohol Screening Day. *Journal of American College Health, 58,* 499–506.

Campbell, C. A. (2009). AIDS. In D. Carr (Ed.), *Encyclopedia of the life course and human development.* Boston: Gale Cengage.

Campbell, J. D., Yoon, D. P., & Johnstone, B. (2010). Determining relationship between physical health and spiritual experience, religious practices, and congregational support in a heterogeneous sample. *Journal of Religion and Health, 49,* 3–17.

Campbell, L., Campbell, B., & Dickinson, D. (2004). *Teaching and learning through multiple intelligence* (3rd ed.). Boston: Allyn & Bacon.

Campos, J. J. (2005). Unpublished review of J. W. Santrock's *Life-span development* (11th ed.). New York: McGraw-Hill.

Campos, J. J. (2009). Unpublished review of J. W. Santrock's *Life-span development* (13th ed.). New York: McGraw-Hill.

Candore, G., & others. (2006). Immunogenetics, gender, and longevity. *Annals of the New York Academy of Sciences, 1089,* 516–537.

Canfield, J., & Hansen, M. V. (1995). *A second helping of chicken soup for the soul.* Deerfield Beach, FL: Health Communications.

Cansino, S. (2009). Episodic memory decay along the adult lifespan: A review of behavioral and neurophysiological evidence. *International Journal of Psychophysiology, 71,* 64–69.

Carbonell, O. A., Alzte, G., Bustamante, M. R., & Quiceno, J. (2002). Maternal caregiving and infant security in two cultures. *Developmental Psychology, 38,* 67–78.

Carli, L. L., & Eagly, A. H. (2011, in press). Gender and leadership. In D. Collinson & others (Eds.), *Sage handbook of leadership.* Thousand Oaks, CA: Sage.

Carnegie Council on Adolescent Development. (1989). *Turning points: Preparing American youth for the twenty-first century.* New York: Carnegie Foundation.

Carpendale, J. I. M., & Chandler, M. J. (1996). On the distinction between false belief understanding and subscribing to an interpretive theory of mind. *Child Development, 67,* 1686–1706.

Carpendale, J. I. M., & Lewis, C. (2011). The development of social understanding: A relational perspective. In R. M. Lerner, W. F. Overton, A. M. Freund, & M. E. Lamb (Eds.), *Handbook of life-span development.* New York: Wiley.

Carr, D. (2009). Death and dying. In D. Carr (Ed.), *Encyclopedia of the* *life course and human development.* Boston: Gale Cengage.

Carr, D., & Moorman, S. (2011, in press). Social relationships and aging. In R. A. Setterson & J. Angel (Eds.), *Handbook of sociology of aging.* New York: Springer.

Carr, D., & Pudrovska, T. (2011, in press). Divorce and widowhood in later life. In R. Blieszner & V. H. Bedford (Eds.), *Handbook of aging and the family.* Santa Barbara, CA: Praeger.

Carroll, J. L. (2010). *Sexuality now* (3rd ed.). Boston: Cengage.

Carkskadon, M. A. (2005). Sleep and circadian rhythms in children and adolescents: Relevance for athletic performance of young people. *Clinical Sports Medicine, 24,* 319–328.

Carskadon, M. A. (2006, March). *Too little, too late: Sleep bioregulatory processes across adolescence.* Paper presented at the meeting of the Society for Research on Adolescence, San Francisco.

Carstensen, L. L. (1998). A life-span approach to social motivation. In J. Heckhausen & C. Dweck (Eds.), *Motivation and self-regulation across the life span.* New York: Cambridge University Press.

Carstensen, L. L. (2006). The influence of a sense of time on human development. *Science, 312,* 1913–1915.

Carstensen, L. L. (2008, May). *Long life in the 21st century.* Paper presented at the meeting of the Association of Psychological Science, Chicago.

Carter, A. R., & others. (2010). Resting interhemispheric functional magnetic resonance imaging connectivity predicts performance after stroke. *Annals of Neurology, 67,* 365–375.

Carter, N., Prater, M. A., & Dyches, T. T. (2009). *What every teacher should know about: Adaptations and accommodations for students with mild to moderate disabilities.* Upper Saddle River, NJ: Prentice Hall.

Case, R., & Mueller, M. P. (2001). Differentiation, integration, and covariance mapping as fundamental processes in cognitive and neurological growth. In J. L. McClelland & R. S. Siegler (Eds.), *Mechanisms*

of cognitive development. Mahwah, NJ: Erlbaum.

Casey, P. H. (2008). Growth of low birth weight preterm children. *Seminars in Perinatology, 32,* 20–27.

Caspers, K. M., Paraiso, S., Yucuis, R., Troutman, B., Arndt, S., & Philibert, R. (2009). Association between the serotonin transporter polymorphism (5-HTTLPR) and adult unresolved attachment. *Developmental Psychology, 45,* 64–76.

Caspi, A., & Roberts, B. W. (2001). Personality development across the life course: The argument for change and continuity. *Psychological Inquiry, 12,* 49–66.

Caspi, A., Sugden, K., Moffitt, T. E., Taylor, A., Craig, I., Harrington, H., & others. (2003). Influence of life stress on depression: Moderation by a polymorphism in the 5-HTT gene. *Science, 301,* 386–389.

Cassell, E. J., & Rich, B. A. (2010, in press). Intractable end-of-life suffering and the ethics of palliative sedation. *Pain Medicine.*

Cassidy, J. (2008). The nature of the child's ties. In J. Cassidy & P. R. Shaver (Eds.), *Handbook of attachment* (2nd ed.). New York: Guilford.

Caughey, A. B., Hopkins, L. M., & Norton, M. E. (2006). Chorionic villus sampling compared with amniocentesis and the difference in the rate of pregnancy loss. *Obstetrics and Gynecology, 108,* 612–616.

Cavanagh, S. E. (2009). Puberty. In D. Carr (Ed.), *Encyclopedia of the life course and human development.* Boston: Gale Cengage.

Cavazos-Rehg, P. A., & others. (2010a). Understanding adolescent parenthood from a multisystemic perspective. *Journal of Adolescent Health, 46,* 525–531.

Cavazos-Rehg, P. A., & others. (2010b, in press). Associations between multiple pregnancies and health risk behaviors among U.S. adolescents. *Journal of Adolescent Health.*

Ceci, S. J., & Gilstrap, L. L. (2000). Determinants of intelligence:

Schooling and intelligence. In A. Kazdin (Ed.), *Encyclopedia of psychology.* Washington, DC, & New York: American Psychological Association and Oxford University Press.

Ceci, S. J., Kulkofsky, S., Klemfuss, J. Z., Sweeney, C. D., & Bruck, M. (2007). Unwarranted assumptions about children's testimonial accuracy. *Annual Review of Clinical Psychology, 3,* 311–328.

Center for Science in the Public Interest. (2008). *Obesity on the kids' menu at top chains.* Retrieved October 24, 2008, from http://www.cspinet.org/new/200808041.html

Center for Survey Research at the University of Connecticut. (2000). *Hours on the job.* Storrs: University of Connecticut, Center for Survey Research.

Centers for Disease Control and Prevention. (2006). *Health United States 2006.* Atlanta: Centers for Disease Control and Prevention.

Centers for Disease Control and Prevention. (2007). *Autism and developmental disabilities monitoring (ADDM) network.* Atlanta: Author.

Centers for Disease Control and Prevention. (2008). *Youth Risk Behavior Survey.* Atlanta: Centers for Disease Control and Prevention.

Centers for Disease Control and Prevention. (2011). *Body mass index for children and teens.* Atlanta: Centers for Disease Control and Prevention.

Chambers, B., Cheung, A. C. K., & Slavin, R. F. (2006). Effective preschool programs for children at risk of school failure: A best-evidence synthesis. In B. Spodek & O. N. Saracho (Eds.), *Handbook of research on the education of young children.* Mahwah, NJ: Erlbaum.

Chan, R., & Webster, J. (2010). End-of-life care pathways for improving outcomes in caring for the dying. *Cochrane Database of Systematic Reviews,* (1), CD008006.

Chang, J. S. (2009). Parental smoking and childhood leukemia. *Methods in Molecular Biology, 472,* 103–137.

Chang, M. Y., Chen, C. H., & Huang, K. F. (2006). A comparison of massage effects on labor pain using the

McGill Pain Questionnaire. *Journal of Nursing Research, 14,* 190–197.

Chao, R. (2001). Extending research on the consequences of parenting style for Chinese Americans and European Americans. *Child Development, 72,* 1832–1843.

Chao, R. (2005, April). *The importance of Guan in describing control of immigrant Chinese.* Paper presented at the meeting of the Society for Research in Child Development, Atlanta.

Chao, R. (2007, March). *Research with Asian Americans: Looking back and moving forward.* Paper presented at the meeting of the Society for Research in Child Development, Boston.

Chao, R., & Tseng, V. (2002). Parenting of Asians. In M. H. Bornstein, *Handbook of parenting* (2nd ed., Vol. 4). Mahwah: NJ: Erlbaum.

Charles, S. T., & Carstensen, L. L. (2010). Social and emotional aging. *Annual Review of Psychology* (Vol. 61). Palo Alto, CA: Annual Reviews.

Charlton, R. A., Barrick, T. R., Lawes, N. C., Markus, H. S., & Morris, R. G. (2010). White matter pathways associated with working memory in normal aging. *Cortex, 46,* 474–489.

Charness, N., & Bosman, E. A. (1992). Human factors and aging. In F. I. M. Craik & T. A. Salthouse (Eds.), *The handbook of aging and cognition.* Hillsdale, NJ: Erlbaum.

Chassin, L., Presson, C., Seo, D. C., Sherman, S. J., Macy, J., Wirth, R. J., & others. (2008). Multiple trajectories of cigarette smoking and the intergenerational transmission of smoking: A multigenerational, longitudinal study of a midwestern community sample. *Health Psychology, 27,* 819–828.

Chaudhuri, J. H., & Williams, P. H. (1999, April). *The contribution of infant temperament and parent emotional availability to toddler attachment.* Paper presented at the meeting of the Society for Research in Child Development, Albuquerque.

Chedraui, P. (2008). Pregnancy among young adolescents: Trends, risk factors, and maternal-perinatal outcome. *Journal of Perinatal Medicine, 36,* 256–259.

Chen, C., & Stevenson, H. W. (1989). Homework: A cross-cultural examination. *Child Development, 60,* 551–560.

Chen, G., & others. (2010, in press). Role of osteopontin in synovial Th 17 differentiation in rheumatoid arthritis. *Arthritis and Rheumatism.*

Chen, M. Y., Liou, Y. M., & Wu, J. Y. (2008). The relationship between TV/computer time and adolescents' health-promoting behavior: A secondary data analysis. *Journal of Nursing Research, 16,* 75–85.

Chen, X., & others. (2009). Interactions of IL-12A and IL-12B polymorphisms on the risk of cervical cancer in Chinese women. *Clinical Cancer Research, 15,* 400–405.

Chen, X., Hastings, P. D., Rubin, K. H., Chen, H., Cen, G., & Stewart, S. L. (1998). Child-rearing attitudes and behavioral inhibition in Chinese and Canadian toddlers: A cross-cultural study. *Developmental Psychology, 34,* 677–686.

Cheng, S. T., Lee, C. K., & Chow, P. K. (2010, in press). Social support and psychological well-being of nursing home residents in Hong Kong. *International Geriatrics.*

Cherlin, A. J., & Furstenberg, F. F. (1994). Stepfamilies in the United States: A reconsideration. In J. Blake & J. Hagen (Eds.), *Annual review of sociology.* Palo Alto, CA: Annual Reviews.

Chess, S., & Thomas, A. (1977). Temperamental individuality from childhood to adolescence. *Journal of Child Psychiatry, 16,* 218–226.

Cheung, B. M. (2010). The hypertension-diabetes continuum. *Journal of Cardiovascular Pharmacology, 55,* 333–339.

Chew, W., Osseck, J., Raygor, D., Eldridge-Houser, J., & Cox, C. (2010). Developmental assets: Profile of youth in a juvenile justice facility. *Journal of School Health, 80,* 66–72.

Chi, M. T. (1978). Knowledge structures and memory development. In R. S. Siegler (Ed.), *Children's thinking: What develops?* Hillsdale, NJ: Erlbaum.

Chiambretto, P., Moroni, L., Guarnerio, C., Bertolotti, G., & Prigerson, H. G. (2010). Prolonged grief and depression in caregivers of patients in vegetative state. *Brain Injury, 24,* 581–588.

Chiang, K. J., & others. (2010). The effects of reminiscence therapy on psychological well-being, depression, and loneliness among the institutionalized aged. *International Journal of Geriatric Psychiatry, 25,* 380–388.

Chida, Y., & Steptoe, A. (2008). Positive psychological well-being and mortality: A quantitative review of prospective observational studies. *Psychosomatic Medicine, 70,* 741–756.

Child Trends. (2006, April). *Fast facts at a glance.* Washington, DC: Author.

Childstats.gov. (2009). Retrieved November 16, 2009, from http://www.childstats.gov/americaschildren/index3.asp

Choi, N. G., & Jun, J. (2009). Life regrets and pride among low-income older adults: Relationships with depressive symptoms, current life stressors, and coping resources. *Aging and Mental Health, 13,* 213–225.

Chomsky, N. (1957). *Syntactic structures.* The Hague: Mouton.

Christenson, S. L., & Thurlow, M. L. (2004). School dropouts: Prevention considerations, interventions, and challenges. *Current Directions in Psychological Science, 13,* 36–39.

Christie, J., Enz, B. J., & Vukelich, C. (2011). *Teaching language and literacy* (4th ed.). Boston: Allyn & Bacon.

Chung, S. A., & others. (2009). Change in ocular alignment after topical anesthetic cataract surgery. *Graefes's Archive for Clinical and Experimental Ophthalmology, 247,* 1269–1272.

Chung-Hall, J., & Chen, X. (2010, in press). Aggressive and prosocial peer group functioning: Effects of children's social, school, and psychological adjustment. *Social Development.*

Cicchetti, D. (2011, in press). Developmental psychopathology. In R. M. Lerner, M. E. Lamb, & A. M. Freund (Eds.), *Handbook of life-span development* (Vol. 2). New York: Wiley.

Cicchetti, D., & Toth, S. L. (2011). Child maltreatment: The research imperative and the exploration of results to clinical contexts. In B. Lester & J. D. Sparrow (Eds.), *Nurturing children and families.* New York: Wiley.

Cicchetti, D., Toth, S. L., Nilsen, W. J., & Manly, J. T. (2010, in press). What do we know and why does it matter? The dissemination of evidence-based interventions for child maltreatment. In H. R. Schaffer & K. Durkin (Eds.), *Blackwell Handbook of Developmental Psychology in Action.* Oxford: Blackwell.

Cichetti, D., Toth, S. L., & Rogusch, F. A. (2006). *A prevention program for child maltreatment.* Unpublished manuscript, University of Rochester, Rochester, NY.

Cicirelli, V. (2009). Sibling relationships, later life. In D. Carr (Ed.), *Encyclopedia of the life course and human development.* Boston: Gale Cengage.

Cignini, P., & others. (2010, in press). The role of ultrasonography in the diagnosis of fetal isolated complete agenesis of the corpus callosum: A long-term prospective study. *Journal of Maternal-Fetal and Neonatal Medicine.*

Cillessen, A. H. N. (2009). Sociometric methods. In K. H. Rubin, W. M. Bukowski, & B. Laursen (Eds.), *Handbook of peer interactions, relationships, and groups.* New York: Guilford.

Cimarolli, V. R. (2009). Sensory impairments. In D. Carr (Ed.), *Encyclopedia of the life course and human development.* Gale Cengage.

Ciol, M. A., Shumway-Cook, A., Hoffman, J. M., Yorkston, K. M., Dudgeon, B. J., & Chan, L. (2008). Minority disparities in disability between Medicare beneficiaries. *Journal of the American Geriatrics Society, 56,* 444–453.

Claes, H. I., & others. (2010, in press). Understanding the effects of sildenafil treatment on erection maintenance and erection hardness. *Journal of Sexual Medicine.*

Clark, B. (2008). *Growing up gifted* (7th ed.). Upper Saddle River, NJ: Prentice Hall.

Clark, E. (1993). *The lexicon in acquisition.* New York: Cambridge University Press.

Clark, E. V. (2009). What shapes children's language? Child-directed speech and the process of acquisition. In V. C. M. Gathercole (Ed.), *Routes to language: Essays in honor of Melissa Bowerman.* New York: Psychology Press.

Clarke-Stewart, A. K., & Miner, J. L. (2008). Child and day care, effects of. In M. M. Haith & J. B. Benson (Eds.), *Encyclopedia of infant and early childhood development.* Oxford, UK: Elsevier.

Clay, O. J., & others. (2009). Visual function and cognitive speed of processing mediate age-related decline in memory span and fluid intelligence. *Journal of Aging and Health, 21,* 547–566.

Clearfield, M. W., Diedrich, F. J., Smith, L. B., & Thelen, E. (2006). Young infants reach correctly in A-not-B tasks: On the development of stability and perseveration. *Infant Behavior and Development, 29,* 435–444.

Clifton, R. K., Morrongiello, B. A., Kulig, J. W., & Dowd, J. M. (1981). Developmental changes in auditory localization in infancy. In R. N. Aslin, J. R. Alberts, & M. R. Petersen (Eds.), *Development of perception* (Vol. 1). Orlando, FL: Academic Press.

Clifton, R. K., Muir, D. W., Ashmead, D. H., & Clarkson, M. G. (1993). Is visually guided reaching in early infancy a myth? *Child Development, 64,* 1099–1110.

Cluett, E. R., & Burns, E. (2009). Immersion in water in labour and birth. *Cochrane Database of Systematic Reviews,* CD000111.

Cohen, F., Kemeny, M. E., Zegans, L. S., Johnson, P., Kearney, K. A., & Stites, D. P. (2007). Immune function declines with unemployment and recovers after stressor termination. *Psychosomatic Medicine, 69,* 225–234.

Cohen, P., Kasen, S., Chen, H., Hartmark, C., & Gordan, K. (2003). Variations in patterns of developmental transitions in the emerging adulthood period. *Developmental Psychology, 39,* 657–669.

Coie, J. (2004). The impact of negative social experiences on the development of antisocial behavior. In J. B. Kupersmidt & K. A. Dodge (Eds.), *Children's peer relations: From development to intervention.* Washington, DC: American Psychological Association.

Coke, L. A., & Fletcher, G. F. (2010). Exercise and the cardiac patient—success is just steps away. *Journal of Cardiovascular Nursing, 25,* 238–240.

Coker, T. R., & others. (2010). Improving access to and utilization of adolescent preventive health care: The perspectives of adolescents and their parents. *Journal of Adolescent Health, 47,* 133–142.

Colby, A., Kohlberg, L., Gibbs, J., & Lieberman, M. (1983). A longitudinal study of moral judgment. *Monographs of the Society of Research in Child Development* (Serial No. 201).

Colcombe, S. J., Erickson, K. I., Scalf, P. E., Kim, J. S., Prakash, R., McAuely, E., & others. (2006). Aerobic exercise training increases brain volume in aging humans. *Journals of Gerontology: Medical Sciences, 61A,* 1166–1170.

Cole, M., & Cagigas, X. E. (2010). Cognition. In M. Bornstein (Ed.), *Handbook of cultural developmental science.* New York: Psychology Press.

Cole, P. M., Dennis, T. A., Smith-Simon, K. E., & Cohen, L. H. (2009). Preschoolers' emotion regulation strategy understanding: Relations with emotion socialization and child self-regulation. *Social Development, 18,* 324–352.

Cole, P. M., & Tan, P. Z. (2007). Emotion socialization from a cultural perspective. In J. E. Grusec & P. D. Hastings (Eds.), *Handbook of socialization.* New York: Guilford.

Coleman, P. D. (1986, August). *Regulation of dendritic extent: Human aging brain and Alzheimer's disease.* Paper presented at the meeting of the American Psychology Association, Washington, DC.

Coleman-Phox, K., Odouli, R., & Li, D. K. (2008). Use of a fan during sleep and the risk of sudden infant death syndrome. *Archives of Pediatric and Adolescent Medicine, 162,* 963–968.

Collins, W. A., & van Dulmen, M. (2006). The significance of middle childhood peer competence for work and relationships in early childhood. In A. C. Huston & M. N. Ripke (Eds.), *Developmental contexts in middle childhood.* New York: Cambridge University Press.

Colombo, J. (2007, March). *The developmental course of attention.* Paper presented at the meeting of the Society for Research in Child Development, Boston.

Colombo, J., Kapa, L., & Curtendale, L. (2010, in press). Varieties of attention in infancy. In L. Oakes, C. Cashon, M. Casasola, & D. Rakison (Eds.), *Infant perception and cognition.* New York: Oxford University Press.

Coltrane, S. L., Parke, R. D., Schofield, T. J., Tsuha, S. J., Chavez, M., & Lio, S. (2008). Mexican American families and poverty. In D. R. Crane & T. B. Heaton (Eds.), *Handbook of families and poverty.* Thousand Oaks, CA: Sage.

Combs, M. (2010). *Readers and writers in the primary grades.* Boston: Allyn & Bacon.

Comer, J. (1988). Educating poor minority children. *Scientific American, 259,* 42–48.

Comer, J. (2004). *Leave no child behind.* New Haven, CT: Yale University Press.

Comer, J. (2006). Child development: The under-weighted aspect of intelligence. In P. C. Kyllonen, R. D. Roberts, & L. Stankov (Eds.), *Extending intelligence.* Mahwah, NJ: Erlbaum.

Comer, J. (2010). Comer School Development Program. In J. Meece & J. Eccles (Eds.), *Handbook of research on schools, schooling, and human development.* New York: Routledge.

Commoner, B. (2002). Unraveling the DNA myth: The spurious foundation of genetic engineering. *Harper's Magazine, 304,* 39–47.

Commons, M. L., & Bresette, L. M. (2006). Illuminating major creative scientific innovators with postformal stages. In C. Hoare (Ed.), *Handbook of adult development and learning.* New York: Oxford University Press.

Connolly, J. A., & McIssac, C. (2009). Romantic relationships in adolescence. In R. M. Lerner & L. Steinberg (Eds.), *Handbook of adolescent psychology* (3rd ed.). New York: Wiley.

Conradt, E., & Ablow, J. (2010, in press). Infant physiological response to the still-face paradigm: Contributions of maternal sensitivity and infants' early regulatory behavior. *Infant Behavior and Development.*

Constantine, N. A. (2008). Editorial: Converging evidence leaves policy behind: Sex education in the United States. *Journal of Adolescent Health, 42,* 324–326.

Contestabile, A. (2009). Benefits of caloric restriction on brain aging and related pathological states: Understanding mechanisms to devise novel therapies. *Current Medicinal Chemistry, 16,* 350–361.

Cook, J. A., & Hawkins, D. B. (2006). Hearing loss and hearing aid treatment options. *Mayo Clinic Proceedings, 81,* 234–237.

Cooksey, E. C. (2009). Sexual activity, adolescent. In D. Carr (Ed.), *Encyclopedia of the life course and human development.* Boston: Gale Cengage.

Coonrod, D. V., & others. (2008). The clinical context of preconception care: Immunizations as part of preconception care. *American Journal of Gynecology, 199*(6, Suppl. 2), S290–S295.

Coontz, S. (2005). *Marriage, history.* New York: Penguin.

Coplan, R. J., & Arbeau, K. A. (2009). Peer interactions and play in early childhood. In K. H. Rubin, W. M. Bukowski, & B. Laursen (Eds.), *Handbook of peer interactions, relationships, and groups.* New York: Guilford.

Cordier, S. (2008). Evidence for a role of paternal exposure in developmental toxicity. *Basic and Clinical Pharmacology and Toxicology, 102,* 176–181.

Corona, G., & others. (2009). The age-related decline of testosterone is associated with different specific symptoms and signs in patients with sexual dysfunction. *International Journal of Andrology, 32,* 720–728.

Cosmides, L. (2011). Evolutionary psychology. *Annual Review of Psychology* (Vol. 62). Palo Alto, CA: Sage.

Costa, P. T., & McCrae, R. R. (1998). Personality assessment. In H. S. Friedman (Ed.), *Encyclopedia of mental health* (Vol. 3). San Diego: Academic Press.

Costa, P. T., & McCrae, R. R. (2000). Contemporary personality psychology. In C. E. Coffey & J. L. Cummings (Eds.), *Textbook of geriatric neuropsychiatry.* Washington, DC: American Psychiatric Press.

Coté, J. E. (2009). Identity formation and self development in adolescence. In R. M. Lerner & L. Steinberg (Eds.), *Handbook of adolescent psychology* (3rd ed.). New York: Wiley.

Courage, M. L., Edison, S. C., & Howe, M. L. (2004). Variability in the early development of visual self-recognition. *Infant Behavior and Development, 27,* 509–532.

Cousineau, T. M., Goldstein, M., & Franco, D. L. (2005). A collaborative approach to nutrition education for college students. *Journal of American College Health, 53,* 79–84.

Cowan, P., & Cowan, C. (2000). *When partners become parents: The big life change for couples.* Mahwah, NJ: Erlbaum.

Cowan, P., & Cowan, C. (2009). How working with couples fosters children's development. In M. S. Schulz, P. K., Kerig, M. K. Pruett, & R. D. Parke (Eds.), *Feathering the nest.* Washington, DC: American Psychological Association.

Cowan, P., Cowan, C., Ablow, J., Johnson, V. K., & Measelle, J. (2005). *The family context of parenting in children's adaptation to elementary school.* Mahwah, NJ: Erlbaum.

Cox, K. S., Wilt, J., Olson, B., & McAdams, D. P. (2010). Generativity, the Big Five, and psychosocial adaptation in midlife adults. *Journal of Personality, 78,* 1185–1208.

Cozzi, B., & others. (2010, in press). Ontogenesis and migration of metallothonein I/II-containing glial cells in the human telencephalon during the second trimester. *Brain Research*.

Crawford, D., & others. (2010). The longitudinal influence of home and neighborhood environments on children's body mass index and physical activity over 5 years: The CLAN study. *International Journal of Obesity*.

Cremation Association of North America. (2008). *Fact sheet*. Milwaukee, WI: Author.

Cresci, M. K., Yarandi, H. N., & Morrell, R. W. (2010). The digital divide and urban older adults. *Computers, Informatics, Nursing, 28,* 88–94.

Crick, N. R., Murray-Close, D., Marks, P. E. L., & Mohajeri-Nelson, N. (2009). Aggression and peer relationships in school-age children: Relational and physical aggression in group and dyadic contexts. In K. H. Rubin, W. M. Bukowski, & B. Laursen (Eds.), *Handbook of peer interactions, relationships, and groups*. New York: Guilford.

Crissey, S. R. (2009). Dating and romantic relationships, childhood and adolescence. In D. Carr (Ed.), *Encyclopedia of the life course and human development*. Boston: Gale Cengage.

Crockenberg, S. B. (1986). Are temperamental differences in babies associated with predictable differences in caregiving? In J. V. Lerner & R. M. Lerner (Eds.), *Temperament and social interaction during infancy and childhood*. San Francisco: Jossey-Bass.

Crooks, R. L., & Baur, K. (2011). *Our sexuality* (11th ed.). Boston: Cengage.

Crosnoe, R., Riegle-Crumb, C., Field, S., Frank, K., & Muller, C. (2008). Peer group contexts of girls' and boys' academic experiences. *Child Development, 79,* 139–155.

Crosslin, D. R., & others. (2009). Genetic effects in the leukotriene biosynthesis pathway and association with atherosclerosis. *Human Genetics, 125*(2), 217–229.

Croucher, E. (2010). Comments on shaken baby syndrome. *Nursing for Women's Health, 14,* 9–10.

Crouter, A. C. (2006). Mothers and fathers at work. In A. Clarke-Stewart & J. Dunn (Eds.), *Families count*. New York: Cambridge University Press.

Crowell, J. A., Treboux, D., & Brockmeyer, S. (2009). Parental divorce and adult children's attachment representations and marital status. *Attachment and human development, 11,* 87–101.

Crowley, K., Callahan, M. A., Tenenbaum, H. R., & Allen, E. (2001). Parents explain more to boys than to girls during shared scientific thinking. *Psychological Science, 12,* 258–261.

Csikszentmihalyi, M. (1995). *Creativity*. New York: HarperCollins.

Csikszentmihalyi, M. (2000). Creativity: An overview. In A. Kazdin (Ed.), *Encyclopedia of psychology*. Washington, DC, & New York: American Psychological Association and Oxford University Press.

Cuevas, K. D., & Silver, D. R., Brooten, D., Youngblut, J. M., & Bobo, C. M. (2005). The cost of prematurity: Hospital charges at birth and frequency of rehospitalization and acute care visits over the first year of life: A comparison of gestational age and birth weight. *American Journal of Nursing, 105,* 56–64.

Cummings, E. M., & Davies, P. T. (2010). *Marital conflict and children: An emotional security perspective*. New York: Guilford.

Cummings, E. M., & Merrilees, C. E. (2009). Identifying the dynamic processes underlying links between marital conflict and child adjustment. In M. S. Schulz, P. K. Kerig, M. K. Pruett, & R. D. Parke (Eds.), *Feathering the nest*. Washington, DC: American Psychological Association.

Cunningham, M. (2004). Old is a three-letter word. *Geriatric Nursing, 25,* 277–260.

Cunningham, M. (2009). Housework. In D. Carr (Ed.), *Encyclopedia of the life course and human development*. Boston: Gale Cengage.

Cunningham, P. M. (2009). *What really matters in vocabulary*. Boston: Allyn & Bacon.

Cunningham, P. M., & Alllington, R. L. (2010). *Classrooms that work: They can all read and write* (5th Ed.). Boston: Allyn & Bacon.

Curran, K., DuCette, J., Eisenstein, J., & Hyman, I. A. (2001, August). *Statistical analysis of the cross-cultural data: The third year*. Paper presented at the meeting of the American Psychological Association, San Francisco, CA.

Currie, C., & others. (2008). *Inequalities in young people's health: HBSC international report from the 2005/2006 survey*. Geneva, Switzerland: World Health Organization.

Currier, J. M., Holland, J. M., & Neimeyer, R. A. (2006). Sensemaking, grief, and the experience of violent loss: Toward a mediational model. *Death Studies, 30,* 403–428.

Cutler, S. J. (2009). Media and technology use, later life. In D. Carr (Ed.), *Encyclopedia of the life course and human development*. Boston: Gale Cengage.

Czaja, S. J., Charness, N., Fisk, A. D., Hertzog, C., Nair, S. N., Rogers, W. A., & others. (2006). Factors predicting the use of technology: Findings from the Center for Research and Education on Aging and Technology (CREATE). *Psychology and Aging, 21,* 333–352.

D

da Fonseca, E. B., Bittar, R. E., Damiao, R., & Zugiab, M. (2009). Prematurity prevention: The role of progesterone. *Current Opinion in Obstetrics and Gynecology, 21,* 142–147.

Dahl, R. E. (2004). Adolescent brain development: A period of vulnerabilities and opportunities. *Annals of the New York Academy of Sciences, 1021,* 1–22.

Dale, P., & Goodman, J. (2004). Commonality and differences in vocabulary growth. In M. Tomasello & D. I. Slobin (Eds.), *Beyond nature-nurture*. Mahwah, NJ: Erlbaum.

Dalen, K., Bruaroy, S., Wentzel-Larsen, T., & Laegreid, L. M. (2009). Cognitive functioning in children prenatally exposed to alcohol and psychotropic drugs. *Neuropediatrics, 40,* 162–167.

Daley, A. J., Macarthur, C., & Winter, H. (2007). The role of exercise in treating postpartum depression: A review of the literature. *Journal of Midwifery & Women's Health, 52,* 56–62.

Daltro, P., & others. (2010). Congenital chest malformations: A multimodality approach with emphasis on fetal MRI imaging. *Radiographics, 30,* 385–395.

Damon, W. (2008). *The path to purpose.* New York: Free Press.

Daniels, H. (2011, in press). Vygotsky and psychology. In R. M. Lerner & W. F. Overton (Eds.), *Handbook of life-span development.* New York: Wiley.

Darwin, C. (1859). *On the origin of species.* London: John Murray.

Das, A. (2009). Sexual harassment at work in the United States. *Archives of Sexual Behavior, 38,* 909–921.

Datta, H. S., Mitra, S. K., Paramesh, R., & Patwardhan, B. (2010, in press). Theories and management of aging: Modern and ayurveda perspectives. *Evidence-Based Complementary and Alternative Medicine.*

Davey, A., Tucker, C. J., Fingerman, K. L., & Savia, J. (2009). Variability in representations of past relationships with parents. *Journals of Gerontology: Social Sciences, 64,* 125–136.

Davies, J., & Brember, I. (1999). Reading and mathematics attainments and self-esteem in years 2 and 6—an eight-year cross-sectional study. *Educational Studies, 25,* 145–157.

Davioli, T., Denchi, E. L., & de Lange, T. (2010). Persistent telomere damage induces bypass of mitosis and tetraploidy. *Cell, 141,* 81–93.

Davis-Kean, P. E., Jager, J., & Collins, W. A. (2010). The self in action: An emerging link between self-beliefs and behaviors in middle childhood. *Child Development, 3,* 184–188.

Davis, B. E., Moon, R. Y., Sachs, M. C., & Ottolini, M. C. (1998). Effects of sleep position on infant motor development. *Pediatrics, 102,* 1135–1140.

Davis, C. L., Tomporowski, P. D., Boyle, C. A., Waller, J. L., Miller, P. H., Nagieri, J. A., & Gregoski, M. (2007). Effects of aerobic exercise on overweight children's cognitive functioning: A randomized controlled trial. *Research Quarterly for Exercise and Sport, 75,* 510–519.

Davis, K. E., Norris, J., Hessler, D. M., Zawacki, T., Morrison, D. M., & George, W. H. (2010). College women's decision making: Cognitive mediation of alcohol expectancy effects. *Journal of American College Health, 58,* 481–488.

Davis, L., & Keyser, J. (1997). *Becoming the parent you want to be: A sourcebook of strategies for the first five years.* New York: Broadway.

Day, N. L., Goldschmidt, L., & Thomas, C. A. (2006). Prenatal marijuana exposure contributes to the prediction of marijuana use at age 14. *Addiction, 101,* 1313–1322.

Deary, I. J., Johnson, W., & Starr, J. M. (2010). Are processing speed tasks biomarkers of aging? *Psychology and Aging, 25,* 219–228.

de Haan, M., & Gunnar, M. R. (Eds.). (2009). *Handbook of developmental social neuroscience.* New York: Guilford.

de Hevia, M. D., & Spelke, E. S. (2010, in press). Number-space mapping in human infants. *Psychological Science.*

de Wit, L., & others. (2010). Depression and obesity: A meta-analysis of community-based studies. *Psychiatry Research, 178,* 230–235.

DeCasper, A. J., & Spence, M. J. (1986). Prenatal maternal speech influences newborn's perception of speech sounds. *Infant Behavior and Development, 9,* 133–150.

Deeg, D. J. H. (2005). The development of physical and mental health from late midlife to early old age. In S. L. Willis & M. Martin (Eds.), *Middle adulthood.* Thousand Oaks, CA: Sage.

DeJong, W., DeRicco, B., & Schneider, S. K. (2010). Pregaming: An exploratory study of strategic drinking by college students in Pennsylvania. *Journal of American College Health, 58,* 307–316.

de Jong, Z., & others. (2009). Long-term follow-up of a high-intensity exercise program in patients with rheumatoid arthritis. *Clinical Rheumatology, 28,* 663–671.

Delaloye, C., & others. (2009). The contribution of aging to the understanding of the dimensionality of executive function. *Archives of Gerontology and Geriatrics, 49,* e51–e59.

Delisle, T. T., Werch, C. E., Wong, A. H., Bian, H., & Weiler, R. (2010). Relationship between frequency and intensity of physical activity and health behaviors of adolescents. *Journal of School Health, 80,* 134–140.

DeLoache, J. S. (2004). Early development of the understanding and use of symbolic artifacts. In U. Goswami (Ed.), *Blackwell handbook of childhood cognitive development.* Malden, MA: Blackwell.

DeLoache, J. S., & Ganea, P. A. (2009). Symbol-based learning in infancy. In A. Woodward & A. Needham (Eds.), *Learning and the infant mind.* New York: Oxford University Press.

Dempster, F. N. (1981). Memory span: Sources of individual and developmental differences. *Psychological Bulletin, 80,* 63–100.

Denham, S. A., Bassett, H. H., & Wyatt, T. (2007). The socialization of emotional competence. In J. E. Grusec & P. D. Hastings (Eds.), *Handbook of socialization.* New York: Guilford.

Dennis, N. A., & Cabeza, R. (2010, in press). Age-related differentiation of learning systems: An fMRI study of implicit and explicit learning. *Neurobiology of Aging.*

Depp, C., & Jeste, D. V. (2010). Successful aging. *Annual Review of Clinical Psychology* (Vol. 6). Palo Alto, CA: Annual Reviews.

Desai, A. K., Grossberg, G. T., & Chibnall, J. T. (2010). Healthy brain aging: A road map. *Clinics in Geriatric Medicine, 26,* 1–16.

DeSpelder, L. A., & Strickland, A. L. (2005). *The last dance: Encountering death and dying* (6th ed., rev. update). Mountain View, CA: Mayfield.

Diamond, A. (1985). Development of the ability to use recall to guide action, as indicated by infants' performance on AB. *Child Development, 56,* 866–883.

Diamond, A. (2009). The interplay of biology and the environment broadly defined. *Developmental Psychology, 45,* 1–8.

Diamond, A., Barnett, W. S., Thomas, J., & Munro, S. (2007). Preschool program improves cognitive control. *Science, 318,* 1387–1388.

Diamond, A., Casey, B. J., & Munakata, Y. (2011, in press). *Developmental cognitive neuroscience.* New York: Oxford University Press.

Diamond, L. M., Fagundes, C. P., & Butterworth, M. R. (2011). Intimate relationships across the life span. In R. M. Lerner, A. Freund, & M. Lamb (Eds.), *Handbook of life-span development* (Vol. 2). New York: Wiley.

Diamond, L. M., & Savin-Williams, R. (2009). Adolescent sexuality. In R. M. Lerner & L. Steinberg (Eds.), *Handbook of adolescent psychology* (3rd ed.). New York: Wiley.

Di Bona, D., & others. (2010). Immune-inflammatory responses and oxidative stress in Alzheimer's disease: Therapeutic implications. *Current Pharmaceutical Design, 16,* 684–691.

Diego, M. A., Field, T., & Hernandez-Reif, M. (2008). Temperature increases in preterm infants during massage therapy. *Infant Behavior and Development, 31,* 149–152.

Diego, M. A., Field, T., Hernandez-Reif, M., Schanberg, S., Kuhn, C., & Gonzales-Quintero, V. H. (2009). Prenatal depression restricts fetal growth. *Early Human Development, 85,* 65–70.

Dietz, L. J., Jennings, K. D., Kelley, S. A., & Marshal, M. (2009). Maternal depression, paternal psychopathology, and toddlers' behavior problems. *Journal of Clinical Child and Adolescent Psychology, 38,* 48–61.

Dillon, C. F., Gu, Q., Hoffman, H. J., & Ko, C. W. (2010). Vision, hearing, balance, and sensory impairment in Americans aged 70 years and over: United States, 1999–2006. *NCHS Data Brief, 31,* 1–8.

Dionyssiotis, Y. (2010). Management of osteoporotic vertebral fractures. *International Journal of General Medicine, 3,* 167–171.

Dishion, T. J., & Piehler, T. F. (2009). Deviant by design: Peer contagion in development, interventions, and schools. In K. H. Rubin, W. M. Bukowski, & B. Laursen (Eds.), *Handbook of peer interactions, relationships, and groups.* New York: Guilford.

Dobson, R. (2009). Breast cancer incidence falls as women give up HRT. *British Medical Journal, 338,* 791.

Dodge, K. A. (1983). Behavioral antecedents of peer social status. *Child Development, 54,* 1386–1399.

Dodge, K. A. (2010, in press). Social information processing models of aggressive behavior. In M. Mikulincer & P. R. Shaver (Eds.), *Understanding and reducing aggression, violence, and their consequences.* Washington, DC: American Psychological Association.

Dodge, K. A., & McCourt, S. N. (2010). Translating models of antisocial behavioral development into efficacious intervention policy to prevent adolescent violence. *Developmental Psychobiology, 52,* 277–285.

Doherty, M. (2008). *Theory of mind.* Philadelphia: Psychology Press.

Donatelle, R. J. (2011). *Health* (9th ed.). Upper Saddle River, NJ: Pearson.

Doran, P., Donoghue, P., O'Connell, K., Gannon, J., & Ohlendieck, K. (2009). Proteomics of skeletal muscle aging. *Proteomics, 9,* 989–1003.

Doty, R. L., & Shah, M. (2008). Taste and smell. In M. M. Haith & J. B. Benson (Eds.), *Encyclopedia of infant and early childhood development.* Oxford, UK: Elsevier.

Dozier, M., Stovall-McClough, K. C., & Albus, K. E. (2009). Attachment and psychopathology in adulthood. In J. Cassidy & P. R. Shaver (Eds.), *Handbook of attachment* (2nd ed.). New York: Guilford.

Drake, M. (2008). Developing resilient children: After 100 years of Montessori education. *Montessori Life, 20*(2), 28–31.

Drummond, R. J., & Jones, K. D. (2010). *Assessment procedures* (7th ed.). Upper Saddle River, NJ: Pearson.

Dryfoos, J. G. (1990). *Adolescence at risk: Prevalence or prevention.* New York: Oxford University Press.

Dryfoos, J. G., & Barkin, C. (2006). *Adolescence: Growing up in America today.* New York: Oxford University Press.

Duck, S. (2011, in press). *Rethinking relationships.* Thousand Oaks, CA: Sage.

Duncan, R. E., & Sawyer, S. S. (2010). Editorial: Respecting adolescents' autonomy (as long as they make the right choice). *Journal of Adolescent Health, 47,* 113–114.

Dunkel Schetter, C. (2011, in press). Psychological science in the study of pregnancy and birth. *Annual Review of Psychology,* Vol. 62. Palo Alto, CA: Annual Reviews.

Dunlop, S. M., & Romer, D. (2010). Adolescent and young adult crash risk: Sensation seeking, substance use propensity, and substance use behaviors. *Journal of Adolescent Health, 46,* 90–92.

Dunn, J. (1984). Sibling studies and the developmental impact of critical incidents. In P. B. Baltes & O. G. Brim (Eds.), *Life-span development and behavior* (Vol. 6). Orlando, FL: Academic Press.

Dunn, J. (2007). Siblings and socialization. In J. E. Grusec & P. D. Hastings (Eds.), *Handbook of socialization.* New York: Guilford.

Dunn, J., & Kendrick, C. (1982). *Siblings.* Cambridge, MA: Harvard University Press.

Dupre, M. E., & Meadows, S. O. (2007). Disaggregating the effects of marital trajectories on health. *Journal of Family Issues, 28,* 623–652.

Durrant, J. E. (2008). Physical punishment, culture, and rights: Current issues for professionals. *Journal of Developmental and Behavioral Pediatrics, 29,* 55–66.

Durston, S. (2010). Imaging genetics in ADHD. *NeuroImage.*

Durston, S., Davidson, M. C., Tottenham, N. T., Galvan, A., Spicer, J., Fossella, J. A., & Casey, B. J. (2006). A shift from diffuse to focal cortical activity with development. *Developmental Science, 9,* 1–8.

Dweck, C. S. (2006). *Mindset.* New York: Random House.

Dweck, C. S., & Master, A. (2009). Self-theories and motivation: Students' beliefs about intelligence. In K. R. Wentzel & A. Wigfield (Eds.), *Handbook of motivation at school.* New York: Routledge.

Dworkin, S. L., & Santelli, J. (2007). Do abstinence-plus interventions reduce sexual risk behavior among youth? *PLoS Medicine, 4,* 1437–1439.

Dwyer, J. W., & Coward, R. T (1991). A multivariate comparison of the involvement of adult sons versus daughters in the care of impaired parents. *Journals of Gerontology B: Psychological Sciences and Social Sciences, 46,* S259–S269.

Dwyer, T., & Ponsonby, A. L. (2009). Sudden infant death syndrome and prone sleeping position. *Annals of Epidemiology, 19,* 245–249.

E

Eagly, A. H. (2001). Social role theory of sex differences and similarities. In J. Worrell (Ed.), *Encyclopedia of women and gender.* San Diego: Academic Press.

Eagly, A. H. (2009). Gender roles. In J. Levine & M. Hogg (Eds.), *Encyclopedia of group processes and intergroup relations.* Thousand Oaks, CA: Sage.

Eagly, A. H., & Crowley, M. (1986). Gender and helping: A meta-analytic review of the social psychological literature. *Psychological Bulletin, 108,* 233–256.

Eagly, A. H., & Steffen, V. J. (1986). Gender and aggressive behavior: A meta-analytic review of the social psychological literature. *Psychological Bulletin, 100,* 309–330.

Eagly, A. H., & Wood, W. (2011, in press). Gender roles in a biosocial world. In P. van Lange, A. Kruglanski, & E. T. Higgins (Eds.), *Handbook of theories in social psychology.* Thousand Oaks, CA: Sage.

East, P. (2009). Adolescent relationships with siblings. In R. M. Lerner & L. Steinberg (Eds.), *Handbook of adolescent psychology* (3rd ed.). New York: Wiley.

Eaton, D. K., & others. (2006). Youth risk behavior surveillance—United States, 2005. *MMWR Surveillance Summary, 55,* 1–108.

Eaton, D. K., & others. (2008, June 6). Youth risk surveillance—United States 2007. *MMWR, 57,* 1–131.

Eby, J. W., Herrell, A. L., & Jordan, M. L. (2011). *Teaching in elementary school: A reflective approach* (6th ed.). Boston: Allyn & Bacon.

Eby, L. T., Maher, C. P., & Butts, M. M. (2010). The intersection of work and family life: The role of affect. *Annual Review of Psychology* (Vol. 61). Palo Alto, CA: Annual Reviews.

Eccles, J. S. (2007). Families, schools, and developing achievement-related motivations and engagement. In J. E. Grusec & P. D. Hastings (Eds.), *Handbook of socialization.* New York: Guilford.

Eccles, J. S., & Roeser, R. W. (2009). Schools, academic motivation, and stage-environment fit. In R. M. Lerner & L. Steinberg (Eds.), *Handbook of adolescent psychology* (3rd ed.). New York: Wiley.

Eccles, J., & Roeser, R. (2010). Schools as a context for development. In J. Meece & J. Eccles (Eds.), *Handbook of research on schools, schooling, and human development.* New York: Routledge.

Eckenrode, J., & others. (2010). Long-term effects of prenatal and infancy nurse home visitation on the life course of youths: 19-year follow-up of a randomized trial. *Archives of Pediatric and Adolescent Medicine, 164,* 9–15.

Eckerman, C., & Whitehead, H. (1999). How toddler peers generate coordinated action: A cross-cultural exploration. *Early Education & Development, 10,* 241–266.

Eden, T. (2010, in press). Etiology of childhood leukemia. *Cancer Treatment Reviews.*

Educational Testing Service. (1992, February). *Cross-national comparisons of 9–13 year olds' science and math achievement.* Princeton, NJ: Educational Testing Service.

Edwards, S., McCreanor, T., Ormsby, M., Tuwhangal, N., & Tipene-Leach, D. (2009). Maori men and the grief of SIDS. *Death Studies, 33,* 130–152.

Edwardson, C. L., & Gorely, T. (2010). Activity-related parenting practices and children's objectively measured physical activity. *Pediatric Exercise Science, 22,* 105–113.

Effros, R. B. (2009). Kleemeier Award lecture 2008—the canary in the coal mine: Telomeres and human healthspan. *Journals of Gerontology A: Biological Sciences and Medical Sciences, 64A,* 511–515.

Eichorn, D. H., Clausen, J. A., Haan, N., Honzik, M. P., & Mussen, P. H. (Eds.). (1981). *Present and past in middle life.* New York: Academic Press.

Eiferman, R. R. (1971). Social play in childhood. In R. Herron & B. Sutton-Smith (Eds.), *Child's play.* New York: Wiley.

Eisenberg, N., Fabes, R. A., & Spinrad, T. L. (2006). Prosocial development. In W. Damon & R. Lerner (Eds.), *Handbook of child psychology* (6th ed.). New York: Wiley.

Eisenberg, N., Morris, A. S., McDaniel, B., & Spinrad, T. L. (2009). Moral cognitions and prosocial responding in adolescence. In R. M. Lerner & L. Steinberg (Eds.), *Handbook of adolescent psychology* (3rd ed). New York: Wiley.

Eisenberg, N., Spinrad, T. L., & Eggum, N. D. (2010). Emotion-related self-regulation and its relation to children's maladjustment. *Annual Review of Psychology* (Vol. 61). Palo Alto, CA: Annual Reviews.

Eisenberg, N., Spinrad, T. L., & Smith, C. L. (2004). Emotion-related regulation: Its conceptualization, relations to social functioning, and socialization. In P. Philippot & R. S. Feldman (Eds.), *The regulation of emotion.* Mahwah, NJ: Erlbaum.

Eklund, J. M., Kerr, M., & Stattin, H. (2010). Romantic relationships and delinquent behavior in adolescence: The moderating role of delinquency propensity. *Journal of Adolescence, 33,* 377–386.

El-Fishawy, P., & State, M. W. (2010). The genetics of autism: Key issues, recent findings and clinical implications. *Psychiatric Clinics of North America, 33,* 83–95.

Eliasieh, K., Liets, L. C., & Chalupa, L. M. (2007). Cellular reorganization in the human retina during normal aging. *Investigative Ophthalmology and Visual Science, 48,* 2824–2830.

Elkind, D. (1976). *Child development and education: A Piagetian perspective.* New York: Oxford University Press.

Elliott, A. F., Burgio, L. D., & Decoster, J. (2010). Enhancing caregiver health: Findings from the resources for enhancing Alzheimer's caregiver health II intervention. *Journal of the American Geriatrics Society, 58,* 30–37.

Ellis, L., & Ames, M. A. (1987). Neurohormonal functioning and sexual orientation. *Psychological Bulletin, 101,* 233–258.

Elwert, F., & Christakis, N. A. (2008). The effect of widowhood on mortality by the causes of death of both spouses. *American Journal of Public Health, 98,* 2092–2098.

Emanuel, L., Bennett, K., & Richardson, V. E. (2007). The dying role. *Journal of Palliative Medicine, 10,* 159–168.

Emde, R. N., Gaensbauer, T. G., & Harmon, R. J. (1976). Emotional expression in infancy: A biobehavioral study. *Psychological Issues: Monograph Series,* 10(37).

Emre, M., & others. (2010, in press). Drug profile: Transdermal rivastigmine patch in the treatment of Alzheimer disease. *CNS Neuroscience and Therapeutics.*

Engle, J. M., & McElwain, N. L. (2010, in press). Parental reactions to toddlers' negative emotions and child negative emotionality as correlates of problem behavior at the age of three. *Social Development.*

Ensor, R., Spencer, D., & Hughes, C. (2010, in press). "You feel sad?" Emotional understanding mediates the effects of verbal ability and mother-child mutuality on prosocial behaviors: Findings from 2 to 4 years. *Social Development.*

Entwisle, D. D., Alexander, K., & Olson, L. (2010). The long reach of socioeconomic status in education. In J. Meece & J. Eccles (Eds.), *Handbook of research on schools, schooling, and human development.* New York: Routledge.

Epel, E. S. (2009). Psychological and metabolic stress: A recipe for accelerated cellular aging. *Hormones, 8,* 7–22.

Ericsson, K. A., Krampe, R., & Tesch-Romer, C. (1993). The role of deliberate practice in the acquisition of expert performance. *Psychological Review, 100,* 363–406.

Erickson, K. I., & Kramer A. F. (2009). Aerobic exercise effects on cognitive and neural plasticity in older adults. *British Journal of Sports Medicine, 43,* 22–24.

Erickson, K. I., & others. (2009). Aerobic fitness is associated with hippocampal volume in elderly humans. *Hippocampus, 19,* 1030–1039.

Erickson, K. I., Prakash, R. S., Voss, M. W., Chaddock, L., Hu, L., Morris, K. S., & others. (2009). Aerobic fitness is associated with hippocampal volume in elderly humans. *Hippocampus, 19,* 1030–1039.

Erikson, E. H. (1950). *Childhood and society.* New York: W. W. Norton.

Erikson, E. H. (1968). *Identity: Youth and crisis.* New York: W. W. Norton.

Eriksson, U. J. (2009). Congenital malformations in diabetic pregnancy. *Seminar in Fetal and Neonatal Medicine.*

Escobar-Chaves, S. L., & Anderson, C. A. (2008). Media and risky behavior. *Future of Children,* 18(1), 147–180.

Eskildsen, M., & Price, T. (2009). Nursing home care in the USA. *Geriatrics and Gerontology, 9,* 1–16.

Etaugh, C., & Bridges, J. S. (2010). *Women's lives* (2nd ed.). Boston: Allyn & Bacon.

Evans, G. W., & English, G. W. (2002). The environment of poverty. *Child Development, 73,* 1238–1248.

Evans, W. J. (2010). Skeletal muscle loss: Cachexia, sarcopenia, and inactivity. *American Journal of Clinical Nutrition, 91,* S1123–S1127.

F

Fabiano, G. A., Pelham, W. E., Coles, E. K., Gnagy, E. M., Chronis-Tuscano, A., & O'Connor, B. C. (2009). A meta-analysis of behavioral treatments for attention deficit/hyperactivity disorder. *Clinical Psychology Review, 29,* 129–140.

Fagot, B. I., Rodgers, C. S., & Leinbach, M. D. (2000). Theories of gender socialization. In T. Eckes & H. M. Trautner (Eds.), *The developmental social psychology of gender.* Mahwah, NJ: Erlbaum.

Fahey, T. D., Insel, P. M., & Roth, W. T. (2011). *Fit and well* (9th ed.). New York: McGraw-Hill.

Fairweather, E., & Cramond, B. (2011). Infusing creative and critical thinking into the classroom. In R. A. Beghetto & J. C. Kaufman (Eds.), *Nurturing creativitiy in the classroom.* New York: Cambridge University Press.

Fakhoury, J., Nimmo, G. A., & Autexier, C. (2007). Harnessing telomerase in cancer therapeutics. *Anti-cancer Agents in Medicinal Chemistry, 7,* 475–483.

Falbo, T., & Poston, D. L. (1993). The academic personality, and physical outcomes of only children in China. *Child Development, 64,* 18–35.

Fanconi, M., & Lips, U. (2010, in press). Shaken baby syndrome in Switzerland: Results of a prospective follow-up study, 2002–2007. *European Journal of Pediatrics.*

Fantz, R. L. (1963). Pattern vision in newborn infants. *Science, 140,* 286–297.

Faraone, S. V., & Mick, E. (2010). Molecular genetics of attention deficit hyperactivity disorder. *Psychiatric Clinics of North America, 33,* 159–180.

Farin, A., Liu, C. Y., Langmoen, I. A., & Apuzzo, M. L. (2009). The biological restoration of central nervous system architecture and function: Part 2—emergence of the realization of adult neurogenesis. *Neurosurgery, 64,* 581–600.

Farooqui, T., & Farooqui, A. A. (2009). Aging: An important factor for the pathogenesis of neurodegenerative diseases. *Mechanisms of Aging and Development, 130,* 203–215.

Farrell, S. W., Fitzgerald, S. J., McAuley, P., & Barlow, C. E. (2010, in press). Cardiorespiratory fitness, adiposity, and all-cause mortality in women. *Medicine and Science in Sports Exercise.*

Farrington, D. P. (2009). Conduct disorder, aggression, and delinquency. In R. M. Lerner & L. Steinberg (Eds.), *Handbook of adolescent psychology* (3rd ed.). New York: Wiley.

Fasig, L. (2000). Toddlers' understanding of ownership: Implications for self-concept development. *Social Development, 9,* 370–382.

Fassinger, R. E. (2008). Workplace diversity and public policy. *American Psychologist, 63,* 252–268.

Fearon, R. P., & others. (2010). The significance of insecure attachment and disorganization in the development of children's externalizing behavior: A meta-analytic study. *Child Development, 81,* 435–456.

Fechtner, R. D., & others. (2010, in press). Prevalence of ocular surface complaints in patients with glaucoma using topical intraocular pressure-lowering medications. *Cornea.*

Feeney, B. C., & Thrush, R. L. (2010). Relationship influences on exploration in adulthood: The characteristics and function of a secure base. *Journal of Personality and Social Psychology, 98,* 57–66.

Feeney, J. A. (2008). Adult romantic attachment: Developments in the study of couple relationships. In J. Cassidy & P. R. Shaver (Eds.), *Handbook of attachment* (2nd ed.). New York: Guilford.

Feeney, S., Moravcik, E., Nolte, S., & Christensen, D. (2010). *California version of who am I in the lives of children?* (8th ed.). Upper Saddle River, NJ: Prentice Hall.

Feldman, D. C. (2007). Career mobility and career stability among older workers. In K. S. Shultz & G. A. Adams (Eds.), *Aging and work in the 21st century.* Mahwah, NJ: Erlbaum.

Feldman, H. D. (2001, April). Contemporary developmental theories and the concept of talent. Paper presented at the meeting of the Society for Research in Child Development, Minneapolis.

Feldman, S. S., Turner, R., & Araujo, K. (1999). Interpersonal context as an influence on sexual timetables of youths: Gender and ethnic effects. *Journal of Research on Adolescence, 9,* 25–52.

Feng, Y., Caiping, M., Li, C., Can, R., Feichao, X., Li, Z., & Zhice, X. (2010). Fetal and offspring arrhythmia following exposure to nicotine during pregnancy. *Journal of Applied Toxicology, 30,* 53–58.

Ferguson, D. M., Harwood, L. J., & Shannon, F. T. (1987). Breastfeeding and subsequent social adjustment in 6- to 8-year-old children. *Journal of Child Psychology and Psychiatry, 28,* 378–386.

Fernandez, G. (2008). Progress in nutritional immunology. *Immunologic Research, 40,* 244–261.

Fernandez, I. D., Su, H., Winters, P. C., & Liang, H. (2010). Association of workplace chronic and acute stressors with employee weight status: Data from worksites in turmoil. *Journal of Occupational and Environmental Medicine, 52*(Suppl. 1), S34–S41.

Ferraro, K. F. (2006). Health and aging. In R. H. Binstock & L. K. George (Eds.), *Handbook of aging and the social sciences* (6th ed.). San Diego: Academic Press.

Field, D. (1999). A cross-cultural perspective on continuity and change in social relations in old age: Introduction on a special issue. *International Journal of Aging and Human Development, 48,* 257–262.

Field, T. M. (2001). Massage therapy facilitates weight gain in preterm infants. *Current Directions in Psychological Science, 10,* 51–55.

Field, T. M. (2007). *The amazing infant.* Malden, MA: Blackwell.

Field, T. M. (2010). Postpartum depression effects on early interactions, parenting, and safety practices: A review. *Infant Behavior and Development, 33,* 1–6.

Field, T. M., Diego, M., & Hernandez-Reif, M. (2008). Prematurity and potential predictors. *International Journal of Neuroscience, 118,* 277–289.

Field, T. M., Diego, M., & Hernandez-Reif, M. (2010, in press). Preterm infant massage therapy research: A review. *Infant Behavior and Development.*

Field, T. M., Figueiredo, B., Hernandez-Reif, M., Diego, M., Deeds, O., & Ascencio, A. (2008). Massage therapy reduces pain in pregnant women, alleviates prenatal depression in both parents and improves their relationships. *Journal of Bodywork and Movement Therapies, 12,* 146–150.

Field, T. M., Grizzle, N., Scafidi, F., & Schanberg, S. (1996). Massage and relaxation therapies' effects on depressed adolescent mothers. *Adolescence, 31,* 903–911.

Field, T. M., Hernandez-Reif, M., Diego, M., Feijo, L., Vera, Y., & Gil, K. (2004). Massage therapy by parents improves early growth and development. *Infant Behavior & Development, 27,* 435–442.

Field, T. M., Schanberg, S. M., Scafidi, F., Bauer, C. R., Vega-Lahr, N., Garcia, R., & others. (1986). Tactile/kinesthetic stimulation effects on preterm neonates. *Pediatrics, 77,* 654–658.

Fields, R. (2010). *Drugs in perspective* (7th ed.). New York: McGraw-Hill.

Fiese, B. H., & Winter, M. A. (2008). Family influence. In M. M. Haith & J. B. Benson (Eds.), *Encyclopedia of infant and early childhood development.* Oxford, UK: Elsevier.

Finch, C. E. (2009). The neurobiology of middle-age has arrived. *Neurobiology of Aging, 30,* 515–520.

Finger, B., Hans, S. L., Bernstein, V. J., & Cox, S. M. (2009). Parent relationship quality and infant-mother attachment. *Attachment and Human Development, 11,* 285–306.

Fingerman, K. L., & Baker, B. (2006). Socioemotional aspects of aging. In J. Wilmouth & K. Ferraro (Eds.), *Perspectives in Gerontology* (3rd ed.). New York: Springer.

Fingerman, K. L., Pitzer, L. M., Chan, W., Birditt, K., Franks, M. M., & Zarit, S. (2010, in press). Who gets what and why? Help middle-aged adults provide to parents and grown children. *Journals of Gerontology B: Psychological Sciences and Social Sciences.*

Fingerman, K. L., Pitzer, L. M., Lefkowitz, E. S., Birditt, K. S., & Mroczek, D. (2008). Ambivalent relationship qualities between adults and their parents: Implications for both parties' well-being. *Journals of Gerontology B: Psychological Sciences and Social Sciences, 63,* 362–371.

Fischer, K. W., & Bidell, T. R. (2006). Dynamic development of action, thought, and emotion. In W. Damon & R. M. Lerner (Eds.), *Handbook of child psychology: Theoretical models of human development* (6th ed.). New York: Wiley.

Fischhoff, B., de Bruin, W., Parker, A. M., Millstein, S. G., & Halpern-Felsher, B. L. (2010). Adolescents' perceived risk of dying. *Journal of Adolescent Health, 56,* 265–269.

Fisher, C. B. (2009). *Decoding the ethics code* (2nd ed.). Thousand Oaks, CA: Sage.

Fiske, A., Wetherell, J. L., & Gatz, M. (2009). Depression in older adults. *Annual Review of Clinical Psychology* (Vol. 5). Palo Alto, CA: Annual Reviews.

Fivush, R. (1993). Developmental perspectives on autobiographical recall. In G. S. Goodman & B. Bottoms (Eds.), *Child victims and child witnesses: Understanding and improving testimony.* New York: Guilford.

Fivush, R. (2011). The development of autobiographical memory. *Annual Review of Psychology* (Vol. 62). Palo Alto, CA: Annual Reviews.

Flavell, J. H. (2004). Theory of mind development: Retrospect and prospect. *Merrill-Palmer Quarterly, 50,* 274–290.

Flavell, J. H., Friedrichs, A., & Hoyt, J. (1970). Developmental changes in memorization processes. *Cognitive Psychology, 1,* 324–340.

Flavell, J. H., Green, F. L., & Flavell, E. R. (1995). The development of children's knowledge about attentional focus. *Developmental Psychology, 31,* 706–712.

Flavell, J. H., Green, F. L., & Flavell, E. R. (2000). Development of

children's awareness of their own thoughts. *Journal of Cognition and Development, 7,* 97–112.

Fletcher, G. J., & Kerr, P. S. (2010). Through the eyes of love: Reality and illusion in intimate relationships. *Psychological Bulletin, 136,* 627–658.

Flint-Wagner, H. G., & others. (2009). Assessment of a sixteen-week training program on strength, pain, and function in rheumatoid arthritis patients. *Journal of Clinical Rheumatology, 15,* 165–171.

Flom, R., & Pick, A. D. (2003). Verbal encouragement and joint attention in 18-month-old infants. *Infant Behavior and Development, 26,* 121–134.

Florent-Bechard, S., & others. (2009). The essential role of lipids in Alzheimer's disease. *Biochimie, 91,* 804–809.

Florsheim, P., Moore, D., & Edgington, C. (2003). Romantic relationships among pregnant and parenting adolescents. In P. Florsheim (Ed.), *Adolescent romantic relations and sexual behavior.* Mahwah, NJ: Erlbaum.

Flouri, E., & Buchanan, A. (2004). Early father's and mother's involvement and child's later educational outcomes. *British Journal of Educational Psychology, 74,* 141–153.

Flynn, J. R. (1999). Searching for justice: The discovery of IQ gains over time. *American Psychologist, 54,* 5–20.

Flynn, J. R. (2007). The history of the American mind in the 20th century: A scenario to explain IQ gains over time and a case for the relevance of *g.* In P. C. Kyllonen, R. D. Roberts, & L. Stankov (Eds.), *Extending intelligence.* Mahwah, NJ: Erlbaum.

Fogelholm, M. (2008). How physical activity can work? *International Journal of Pediatric Obesity, 3,* (Suppl. 1), S10–S14.

Folari, L. (2011). *Foundations and best practices in early childhood education* (2nd ed.). Upper Saddle River, NJ: Merrill.

Food & Nutrition Service. (2009). *The new look of the women, infants, and children (WIC) program.* Retrieved

January 21, 2009, from http://www.health.state.ny.us/prevention/nutrition/wic/the_new_look_of_wic.htm

Fontana, L. (2009). The scientific basis of caloric restriction leading to longer life. *Current Opinion in Gastroenterology, 25,* 144–150.

Forster, M. B., & Merz, R. D. (2007). Risk of selected birth defects with prenatal illicit drug use, Hawaii, 1986–2002. *Journal of Toxicology and Environmental Health, 70,* 7–18.

Fox, B. J. (2010). *Phonics and structural analysis for the teacher of reading* (10th ed.). Boston: Allyn & Bacon.

Fox, E., & Alexander, P. A. (2011). Learning to read. In P. A. Alexander & R. E. Mayer (Eds.), *Handbook of research on learning and instruction.* New York: Routledge.

Fox, M. K., Pac, S., Devaney, B., & Jankowski, L. (2004). Feeding infants and toddlers study: What foods are infants and toddlers eating? *American Dietetic Association Journal, 104*(Suppl.), S22–S30.

Fox, S. E., Levitt, P., & Nelson, C. A. (2010). How the timing and quality of early experiences influence the development of brain architecture. *Child Development, 81,* 28–40.

Fozard, J. L. (1992, December 6). Commentary in "We can age successfully." *Parade Magazine,* pp. 14–15.

Fraiberg, S. (1959). *The magic years.* New York: Scribner.

Franchak, J. M., Kretch, K. S., Soska, K. C., Babcock, J. S., & Adolph, K. E. (2010, in press). Head-mounted eye-tracking of infants' natural interactions: A new method. *Proceedings of the 2010 Symposium on Eye-Tracking Research & Applications,* Austin, TX.

Francis, J., Fraser, G., & Marcia, J. E. (1989). *Cognitive and experimental factors in moratorium-achievement (MAMA) cycles.* Unpublished manuscript, Department of Psychology, Simon Fraser University, Burnaby, British Columbia.

Frankl, V. (1984). *Man's search for meaning.* New York: Basic Books.

Frederikse, M., Lu, A., Aylward, E., Barta, P., Sharma, T., & Pearlson, G. (2000). Sex differences in inferior lobule volume in schizophrenia. *American Journal of Psychiatry, 157,* 422–427.

Freud, S. (1917). *A general introduction to psychoanalysis.* New York: Washington Square Press.

Freund, A. M., & Lamb, M. E. (2011). Introduction: Social and emotional development across the life span. In R. M. Lerner, W. F. Overton, A. M. Freund, & M. E. Lamb (Eds.), *Handbook of life-span development.* New York: Wiley.

Fricker-Gates, R. A., & Gates, M. A. (2010). Stem cell–derived dopamine neurons for brain repair in Parkinson's disease. *Regenerative Medicine, 5,* 267–278.

Friedman, S. L., Melhuish, E., & Hill, C. (2009). Childcare research at the dawn of a new millennium: An update. In G. Brenner & T. Wachs (Eds.), *Wiley-Blackwell handbook of infant development.* New York: Wiley.

Friend, M. (2011). *Special education* (3rd ed.). Upper Saddle River, NJ: Merrill.

Frisco, M. L. (2009). Obesity, childhood and adolescence. In D. Carr (Ed.), *Encyclopedia of the life course and human development.* Boston: Gale Cengage.

Fritsch, T., McClendon, M. J., Smyth, K. A., Lerner, A. J., Friedland, R. P., & Larson, J. D. (2007). Cognitive functioning in healthy aging: The role of reserve and lifestyle factors early in life. *Gerontologist, 47,* 307–322.

Frost, J. J., Darroch, J. E., & Ramez, L. (2008). Improving contraceptive use in the United States. *Issues Brief (Alan Guttmacher Institute), 1,* 1–8.

Fry, B. G. (2009). Mining genomes to identify toxins. *Annual Review of Genomics and Human Genetics* (Vol. 10). Palo Alto, CA: Annual Reviews.

Fu, A. Z., Tang, A. S., Wang, N., Du, D. T., & Jiang, J. Z. (2010, in press). Effect of Medicare Part D on potentially inappropriate medication use by older adults. *Journal of the American Geriatrics Society.*

Fujisawa, Y., Miyashita, M., Nakajima, S., Ito, M., Kato, M., & Kim, Y. (2010, in press). Prevalence and determinants of complicated grief in general population. *Journal of Affective Disorders.*

Fuligni, A., Hughes, D. L., & Way, N. (2009). Ethnicity and immigration. In R. M. Lerner & L. Steinberg (Eds.), *Handbook of adolescent psychology* (3rd ed.). New York: Wiley.

Furman, E. (2005). *Boomerang nation.* New York: Fireside.

Furman, W., Low, S., & Ho, M. J. (2009). Romantic experience and psychosocial adjustment in middle adolescence. *Journal of Clinical Child and Adolescent Psychology, 38,* 75–90.

Furnes, B., & Dysvik, E. (2010). Dealing with grief related to loss by death and chronic pain: An integrated theoretical framework. Part 1. *Patient Preference and Adherence, 4,* 135–140.

Furstenberg, F. F. (2007). The future of marriage. In A. S. Skolnick & J. H. Skolnick (Eds.), *Family in transition* (14th ed.). Boston: Allyn & Bacon.

Furth, H. G., & Wachs, H. (1975). *Thinking goes to school.* New York: Oxford University Press.

G

Gagliese, L. (2009). Pain and aging: The emergence of a new subfield of pain research. *Journal of Pain, 10,* 343–353.

Galasko, D., & Montine, T. J. (2010). Biomarkers of oxidative damage and inflammation in Alzheimer's disease. *Biomarkers in Medicine, 4,* 27–36.

Galimberti, D., & Scarpini, E. (2010). Treatment of Alzheimer's disease: Symptomatic and disease-modifying approaches. *Current Aging Science, 3,* 46–56.

Galindo, C., & Durham, R. E. (2009). Immigration, childhood, and adolescence. In D. Carr (Ed.), *Encyclopedia of the life course and human development.* Boston: Gale Cengage.

Gallo, W. T., Bradley, E. H., Dubin, J. A., Jones, R. N., Falba, T. A., Teng, H. M., & others. (2006). The persistence of depressive symptoms in older workers who experience involuntary job loss: Results from the health and retirement survey. *Journals of Gerontology B: Psychological Sciences and Social Sciences, 61,* S221–S228.

Galloway, J. C., & Thelen, E. (2004). Feet first: Object exploration in young infants. *Infant Behavior & Development, 27,* 107–112.

Galotti, K. M. (2010). *Cognitive development.* Thousand Oaks, CA: Sage.

Ganong, L., & Coleman, M. (2006). Obligations to stepparents acquired in later life: Relationship quality and acuity of needs. *Journals of Gerontology B: Psychological Sciences and Social Sciences, 61,* 580–588.

Ganong, L., Coleman, M., & Hans, J. (2006). Divorce as prelude to stepfamily living and the consequences of re-divorce. In M. A. Fine & J. H. Harvey (Eds.), *Handbook of divorce and relationship dissolution.* Mahwah, NJ: Erlbaum.

Gao, L. L., Chan, S. W., & Mao, Q. (2009). Depression, perceived stress, and social support among first-time Chinese mothers and fathers in the postpartum period. *Research in Nursing and Health, 32,* 50–58.

Gardner, D. S., Hosking, J., Metcalf, B. S., An, J., Voss, L. D., & Wilkin, T. J. (2009). Contribution of early weight gain to childhood overweight and metabolic health: A longitudinal study (EarlyBird 36). *Pediatrics, 123,* e67–e73.

Gardner, H. (1983). *Frames of mind.* New York: Basic Books.

Gardner, H. (1993). *Multiple intelligences.* New York: Basic Books.

Gardner, H. (2002). The pursuit of excellence through education. In M. Ferrari (Ed.), *Learning from extraordinary minds.* Mahwah, NJ: Erlbaum.

Garenne, M. (2010). Urbanization and child health in resource poor settings with special reference to under-five mortality in Africa. *Archives of Disease in Childhood, 95,* 464–468.

Garofalo, R. (2010). Cytokines in human milk. *Journal of Pediatrics, 156*(Suppl. 2), S36–S40.

Gartner, J., Larson, D. B., & Allen, G. D. (1991). Religious commitment and mental health: A review of the empirical literature. *Journal of Psychology and Theology, 19,* 6–25.

Gartstein, M. A., Peleg, Y., Young, B. N., & Slobodskaya, H. R. (2009). Infant temperament in Russia, United States of America, and Israel: Differences and similarities between Russian-speaking families. *Child Psychiatry and Human Development, 40,* 241–256.

Garvey, C. (2000). *Play* (enlarged ed.). Cambridge, MA: Harvard University Press.

Gates, W. (1998, July 20). Charity begins when I'm ready (interview). *Fortune magazine.*

Gathercole, V. C., & Hoff, E. (2010). Input and the acquisition of language: Three questions. In E. Hoff & M. Shatz (Eds.), *Blackwell handbook of language development* (2nd ed.). New York: Wiley.

Gathwala, G., Singh, B., & Balhara, B. (2008). KMC facilitates baby attachment in low birth weight infants. *Indian Journal of Pediatrics, 75,* 43–47.

Gatz, M., Reynolds, C. A., Fratiglioni, L., Johansson, B., Mortimer, J. A., Berg, S., & others. (2006). Role of genes and environments for explaining Alzheimer's disease. *Archives of General Psychiatry, 63,* 168–174.

Gaudernack, L. C., Forbord, S., & Hole, E. (2006). Acupuncture administered after spontaneous rupture of membranes at term significantly reduces the length of birth and use of oxytocin. *Acta Obstetricia et Gynecologica Scandinavica, 85,* 1348–1353.

Gauvain, M., & Parke, R. D. (2010). Socialization. In M. H. Bornstein (Ed.), *Handbook of cultural developmental science.* New York: Psychology Press.

Ge, X., & Natusaki, M. N. (2010). In search of explanations for early puberty timing effects on developmental psychopathology. *Current Directions in Psychological Science, 18,* 327–331.

Gee, C. L., & Heyman, G. D. (2007). Children's evaluations of other people's self-descriptions. *Social Development, 16,* 800–818.

Gelman, R. (1969). Conservation acquisition: A problem of learning to attend to relevant attributes. *Journal of Experimental Child Psychology, 7,* 67–87.

Gelman, S. A. (2009). Learning from others: Children's construction of concepts. *Annual Review of Psychology, 60.* Palo Alto, CA: Annual Reviews.

Gelman, S. A., & Kalish, C. W. (2006). Conceptual development. In W. Damon & R. Lerner (Eds.), *Handbook of child psychology* (6th ed.). New York: Wiley.

Gennetian, L. A., & Miller, C. (2002). Children and welfare reform: A view from an experimental welfare reform program in Minnesota. *Child Development, 73,* 601–620.

Genovesi, S., & others. (2010, in press). Hypertension, prehypertension, and transient elevated blood pressure in children: Association with weight excess and waist circumference. *American Journal of Hypertension.*

Gentile, D. A., Mathieson, L. C., & Crick, N. R. (2010, in press). Media violence associations with the form and function of aggression among elementary school children. *Social Development.*

Genuis, S. J. (2009). Nowhere to hide: Chemical intoxicants in the unborn child. *Reproductive Toxicology, 28,* 115–116.

George, L. K. (2009). Religious and spirituality, later life. In D. Carr (Ed.), *Encyclopedia of the life course and human development.* Boston: Gale Cengage.

George, L. K. (2010). Still happy after all these years: Research frontiers on subjective well-being in later life. *Journals of Gerontology B: Psychological Sciences and Social Sciences, 65B,* 331–339.

Gershoff, E. T. (2002). Corporal punishment by parents and associated child behaviors and experiences: A meta-analysis and theoretical review. *Psychological Bulletin, 128,* 539–579.

Ghazarian, S. R., & Roche, K. M. (2010). Social support and low-income, urban mothers: Longitudinal associations with adolescent delinquency. *Journal of Youth and Adolescence, 39,* 1097–1108.

Ghetti, S., & Alexander, K. W. (2004). "If it happened, I would remember it": Strategic use of event memorability in the rejection of false autobiographical events. *Child Development, 75,* 542–561.

Ghosh, S., & others. (2010, in press). Prospective randomized comparative study of macular thickness following phacoemulsification and manual small incision cataract surgery. *Acta Ophthalmologica.*

Ghosh, S., Feingold, E., Chakaborty, S., & Dey, S. K. (2010, in press). Telomere length is associated with types of chromosome 21 nondisjunction: A new insight into the maternal age effect on Down syndrome birth. *Human Genetics.*

Gibbons, R. D., Hedeker, D., & DuToit, S. (2010). Advance in analysis of longitudinal data. *Annual Review of Clinical Psychology* (Vol. 6). Palo Alto, CA: Annual Reviews.

Gibbs, J. C. (2010). *Moral development and reality: Beyond the theories of Kohlberg and Hoffman* (2nd ed.). Boston: Allyn & Bacon.

Gibbs, J. C., Bassinger, K. S., Grime, R. L., & Snarey, J. R. (2007). Moral judgment across cultures: Revisiting Kohlberg's universality claims. *Developmental Review, 27,* 443–500.

Gibson, E. J. (1969). *Principles of perceptual learning and development.* New York: Appleton-Century-Crofts.

Gibson, E. J. (1989). Exploratory behavior in the development of perceiving, acting, and the acquiring of knowledge. *Annual Review of Psychology, 39.* Palo Alto, CA: Annual Reviews.

Gibson, E. J. (2001). *Perceiving the affordances.* Mahwah, NJ: Erlbaum.

Gibson, E. J., & Walk, R. D. (1960). The "visual cliff." *Scientific American, 202,* 64–71.

Gibson, H. J. (2009). Leisure and travel, adulthood. In D. Carr (Ed.), *Encyclopedia of the life course and human development.* Boston: Gale Cengage.

Gibson, J. J. (1966). *The senses considered as perceptual systems.* Boston: Houghton Mifflin.

Gibson, J. J. (1979). *The ecological approach to visual perception*. Boston: Houghton Mifflin.

Giedd, J. N. (2008). The teen brain: Insights from neuroimaging. *Journal of Adolescent Health, 42*, 335–343.

Gilbert, S. J., Meusese, J. D., Towgood, K. J., Frith, C. D., & Burgess, P. W. (2009). Abnormal functional specialization within medial prefrontal cortex in high-functioning autism: A multi-voxel similarity analysis.

Gilligan, C. (1982). *In a different voice*. Cambridge, MA: Harvard University Press.

Gilligan, C. (1996). The centrality of relationships in psychological development: A puzzle, some evidence, and a theory. In G. G. Noam & K. W. Fischer (Eds.), *Development and vulnerability in close relationships*. Hillsdale, NJ: Erlbaum.

Gillum, R. F., & Ingram, D. D. (2007). Frequency of attendance at religious services, hypertension, and blood pressure: The third National Health and Nutrition Examination Survey. *Psychosomatic Medicine, 68*, 382–385.

Gil-Mohapel, J., Simpson, J. M., Titerness, A. K., & Christie, B. R. (2010). Characterization of the neurogenesis quiet zone in the rodent brain: Effects of age and exercise. *European Journal of Neuroscience, 31*, 797–807.

Girls, Inc. (1991). *Truth, trusting, and technology: New research on preventing adolescent pregnancy*. Indianapolis: Author.

Givens, J. L., & Mitchell, J. L. (2009). Concerns about end-of-life care and support for euthanasia. *Journal of Pain and Symptom Management, 38*, 167–173.

Glaser, B., Shelton, K. H., & van den Bree, B. M. (2010). The moderating role of close friends in the relationship between conduct problems and adolescent substance use. *Journal of Adolescent Health, 47*, 35–42.

Glei, D. A. (1999). Measuring contraceptive use patterns among teenage and adult women. *Family Planning Perspectives, 31*, 73–80.

Gluck, M. E., Venti, C. A., Lindsay, R. S., Knowler, W. C., Salbe, A. D., & Krakoff, J. (2009). Maternal influence, not diabetic intrauterine environment, predicts children's energy intake. *Obesity, 17*, 772–777.

Goel, A., Sinha, R. J., Dalela, D., Sankhwar, S., & Singh, V. (2009). Andropause in Indian men: A preliminary cross-sectional study. *Urology Journal, 6*, 40–46.

Gogtay, N., & Thompson, P. M. (2010). Mapping gray matter development: Implications for typical development and vulnerability to psychopathology. *Brain and Cognition, 72*, 6–15.

Goldberg, W. A., & Lucas-Thompson, R. (2008). Maternal and paternal employment, effects of. In M. M. Haith & J. B. Benson (Eds.), *Encyclopedia of infant and early childhood development*. Oxford, UK: Elsevier.

Goldenberg, R. L., & Culhane, J. F. (2007). Low birth weight in the United States. *American Journal of Clinical Nutrition, 85*(Suppl.), S584–S590.

Goldfield, B. A., & Snow, C. A. (2009). Individual differences in language development. In J. Berko Gleason & N. Ratner (Eds.), *The development of language* (7th ed.). Boston: Allyn & Bacon.

Goldin-Meadow, S. A. (2010, in press). Creating and learning language by hand. In M. A. Gernsbacher, R. W. Pew, L. Hough, & J. R. Pomerantz (Eds.), *Psychology and the real world: Essays illustrating fundamental contributions to society*. New York: Worth.

Goldman, N., Giel, D. A., Lin, Y. H., & Weinstein, M. (2010). The serotonin transporter polymorphism (5-HTTLPR): Allelic variation and its link with depressive symptoms. *Depression and Anxiety, 27*, 260–269.

Goldschmidt, L., Richardson, G. A., Willford, J., & Day, N. L. (2008). Prenatal marijuana exposure and intelligence test performance at age 6. *Journal of the American Academy of Child and Adolescent Psychiatry, 47*, 254–263.

Goldsmith, B., Borrison, R. S., Vanderwerker, L. C., & Prigerson, H. G. (2008). Elevated rates of prolonged grief disorder in African Americans. *Death Studies, 32*, 352–365.

Goldsmith, D. F. (2007). Challenging children's negative internal working models. In D. Oppenheim & D. F. Goldsmith (Eds.), *Attachment theory in clinical work with children*. New York: Guilford.

Goldsmith, H. H. (2011, in press). Human development: Biological and genetic processes. *Annual Review of Psychology* (Vol. 62). Palo Alto, CA: Annual Reviews.

Goldstein, M. H., King, A. P., & West, M. J. (2003). Social interaction shapes babbling: Testing parallels between birdsong and speech. *Proceedings of the National Academy of Sciences, 100*(13), 8030–8035.

Golombok, S., & Tasker, F. (2010). Gay fathers. In M. E. Lamb (Ed.), *The role of the father in child development* (5th ed.). New York: Wiley.

Gong, X., & others. (2009). An investigation of ribosomal protein L10 gene in autism spectrum disorders. *BMC Medical Genetics, 10*, 7.

Goodie, J. A., & McGlory, G. (2010). Compassionate care: A focus on dying well. *Nursing, 40*, 12–14.

Goodnow, J. (2010). Culture. In M. H. Bornstein (Ed.), *Handbook of cultural developmental science*. New York: Psychology Press.

Goodwin, P. Y., Mosher, W. D., & Chandra, A. (2010). Marriage and cohabitation in the United States: A statistical portrait based on cycle 6 (2002) of the National Survey of Family Growth. *Vital Health Statistics, 23*, 1–45.

Gooren, L. (2006). The biology of human psychosexual differentiation. *Hormones and Behavior, 50*, 589–601.

Gorchoff, S. M., John, O. P., & Helson, R. (2008). Contextualizing change in marital satisfaction during middle age: An 18-year longitudinal study. *Psychological Science, 19*, 1194–1200.

Gore, K. (2009). Socialization, gender. In D. Carr (Ed.), *Encyclopedia of the life course and human development*. Boston: Gale Cengage.

Gosselin, J. (2010). Individual and family factors related to psychosocial adjustment in stepmother families with adolescents. *Journal of Divorce and Remarriage, 51,* 108–123.

Gottlieb, G. (2007). Probabilistic epigenesis. *Developmental Science, 10,* 1–11.

Gottman, J. M. (1994). *What predicts divorce?* Mahwah, NJ: Erlbaum.

Gottman, J. M. (2006, April, 29). Secrets of long term love. *New Scientist, 2549,* 40.

Gottman, J. M. (2009). *Research on parenting.* Retrieved December 9, 2009, from http://www.gottman.com/parenting/research

Gottman, J. M., & DeClaire, J. (1997). *The heart of parenting: Raising an emotionally intelligent child.* New York: Simon & Schuster.

Gottman, J. M., & Gottman, J. S. (2009). Gottman method of couple therapy. In A. S. Gurman (Ed.), *Clinical handbook of couple therapy* (4th ed.). New York: Guilford.

Gottman, J. M., Gottman, J. S., & Shapiro, A. (2009). A new couples approach to interventions for the transition to parenthood. In M. S. Schulz, P. K. Kerig, M. K. Pruett, & R. D. Parke (Eds.), *Feathering the nest.* Washington, DC: American Psychological Association.

Gottman, J. M., & Parker, J. G. (Eds.). (1987). *Conversations of friends.* New York: Cambridge University Press.

Gottman, J. M., & Silver, N. (2000). *The seven principles for making marriages work.* New York: Crown.

Gould, S. J. (1981). *The mismeasure of man.* New York: W. W. Norton.

Gouldner, H., & Strong, M. M. (1987). *Speaking of friendship.* New York: Greenwood Press.

Gove, W. R., Style, C. B., & Hughes, M. (1990). The effect of marriage on the well-being of adults: A theoretical analysis. *Journal of Health and Social Behavior, 24,* 122–131.

Graber, J. A., Brooks-Gunn, J., & Warren, M. P. (2006). Pubertal effects on adjustment in girls: Moving from demonstrating effects to identifying pathways. *Journal of Youth and Adolescence, 35,* 391–401.

Graber, J. A., & Sontag, L. M. (2009). Internalizing problems during adolescence. In R. M. Lerner & L. Steinberg (Eds.), *Handbook of adolescent psychology* (3rd ed.). New York: Wiley.

Grady, C. L., Springer, M. V., Hongwanishkul, D., McIntosh, A. R., & Winocur, G. (2006). Age-related changes in brain activity across the adult lifespan. *Journal of Cognitive Neuroscience, 18,* 227–241.

Grafenhain, M., Behne, T., Carpenter, M., & Tomasello, M. (2009). Young children's understanding of joint commitments. *Developmental Psychology, 45,* 1430–1443.

Graham, G. M., Holt/Hale, S., & Parker, M. A. (2010). *Children moving.* New York: McGraw-Hill.

Grambs, J. D. (1989). *Women over forty* (rev. ed.). New York: Springer.

Granger, D. N., Rodrigues, S. F., Yildirim, A., & Senchenkova, E. Y. (2010). Microvascular responses to cardiovascular risk factors. *Microcirculation, 17,* 192–205.

Grant, J. (1993). *The state of the world's children.* New York: UNICEF and Oxford University Press.

Grant, N., Wardle, J., & Steptoe, A. (2009). The relationship between life satisfaction and health behavior: A cross-cultural analysis of young adults. *International Journal of Behavioral Medicine, 16,* 259–268.

Graven, S. (2006). Sleep and brain development. *Clinical Perinatology, 33,* 693–706.

Graziano, A. M., & Raulin, M. L. (2010). *Research methods* (7th ed.). Boston: Allyn & Bacon.

Greve, W., & Bjorklund, D. F. (2009). The nestor effect: Extending evolutionary developmental psychology to a lifespan perspective. *Developmental Review, 29,* 163–179.

Griffiths, L. J., Hawkins, S. S., Cole, T. J., & Dezateux, C. (2010, in press). Risk factors for rapid weight gain in preschool children: Findings from a UK-wide prospective study. *International Journal of Obesity.*

Griffiths, R., Horsfall, J., Moore, M., Lane D., Kroon, V., & Langdon, R. (2007). Assessment of health, well-being, and social connections: A survey of women living in western Sydney. *International Journal of Nursing Practice, 13,* 3–13.

Grigorenko, E. (2000). Heritability and intelligence. In R. J. Sternberg (Ed.), *Handbook of intelligence.* New York: Cambridge University Press.

Grigorenko, E. L., & Takanishi, R. (Eds.). (2010). *Immigration, diversity, and education.* New York: Routledge.

Grolnick, W. S., Bridges, L. J., & Connell, J. P. (1996). Emotion regulation in two-year-olds: Strategies and emotional expression in four contexts. *Child Development, 67,* 928–941.

Grossman, I., & others. (2010). Reasoning about social conflicts improves into old age. *Proceedings of the National Academy of Sciences USA, 107,* 7246–7250.

Gruenewald, T. L., Karlamangia, A. S., Greendale, G. A., Singer, B. H., & Seeman, T. E. (2009). Increased mortality risk in older adults with persistently low or declining feelings of usefulness to other. *Journal of Aging and Health, 21,* 398–425.

Grusec, J. E. (2009). Unpublished review of J. W. Santrock's *Child Development* (13th ed.). New York: McGraw-Hill.

Grusec, J. E. (2011). Socialization processes in the family: Social and emotional development. *Annual Review of Psychology* (Vol. 62). Palo Alto, CA: Annual Reviews.

Grusec, J. E., & Davidov, M. (2007). Socialization in the family: The roles of parents. In J. E. Grusec & P. D. Hastings (Eds.), *Handbook of socialization.* New York: Guilford.

Grzywacz, J. G. (2009). Work-family conflict. In D. Carr (Ed.), *Encyclopedia of the life course and human development.* Boston: Gale Cengage.

Guerra, N. G., & Williams, K. R. (2010). Implementing bullying prevention in diverse settings: Geographic, economic, and cultural influences. In E. M. Vernberg & B. K. Biggs (Eds.), *Preventing and treating bullying and victimization*. New York: Oxford University Press.

Guerrero, L. K., Andersen, P. A., & Afifi, W. A. (2011). *Close encounters: Communication in relationships* (3rd ed.). Thousand Oaks, CA: Sage.

Guilford, J. P. (1967). *The structure of intellect*. New York: McGraw-Hill.

Guillot, M. (2009). Life expectancy. In D. Carr (Ed.), *Encyclopedia of the life course and human development*. Gale Cengage.

Gumbo, F. Z., & others. (2010). Rising mother-to-child HIV transmission in a resource-limited breastfeeding population. *Tropical Doctor, 40*, 70–73.

Gunderson, E. P., Rifas-Shiman, S. L., Oken, E., Rich-Edwards, J. W., Kleinman, K. P., Taveras, E. M., & others. (2008). Association of fewer hours of sleep at 6 months postpartum with substantial weight retention at 1 year postpartum. *American Journal of Epidemiology, 167*, 178–187.

Gunnar, M. R., Malone, S., & Fisch, R. O. (1987). The psychobiology of stress and coping in the human neonate: Studies of the adrenocortical activity in response to stress in the first week of life. In T. Field, P. McCabe, & N. Scheiderman (Eds.), *Stress and coping*. Hillsdale, NJ: Erlbaum.

Gunnar, M. R., & Quevado, K. (2007). The neurobiology of stress and development. *Annual Review of Psychology* (Vol. 58). Palo Alto, CA: Annual Reviews.

Guo, G., & Tillman, K. H. (2009). Trajectories of depressive symptoms, dopamine D2 and D4 receptors, family socioeconomic status, and social support in adolescence and young adulthood. *Psychiatric Genetics, 19*, 14–26.

Gur, R. C., Mozley, L. H., Mozley, P. D., Resnick, S. M., Karp, J. S., Alavi, A., & others. (1995). Sex differences in regional cerebral glucose metabolism during a resting state. *Science, 267*, 528–531.

Gurwitch, R. H., Silovksy, J. F., Schultz, S., Kees, M., & Burlingame, S. (2001). *Reactions and guidelines for children following trauma, disaster*. Norman, OK: Department of Pediatrics, University of Oklahoma Health Sciences Center.

Gustafsson, J-E. (2007). Schooling and intelligence: Effects of track of study on level and profile of cognitive abilities. In P. C. Kyllonen, R. D. Roberts, & L. Stankov (Eds.), *Extending intelligence*. Mahwah, NJ: Erlbaum.

Gutmann, D. L. (1975). Parenthood: A key to the comparative study of the life cycle. In N. Datan & L. Ginsberg (Eds.), *Life-span developmental psychology: Normative life crises*. New York: Academic Press.

H

Hackney, M. E., & Earhart, G. M. (2010a). Effects of dance on balance and gait in severe Parkinson disease: A case study. *Disability and Rehabilitation, 32*, 679–684.

Hackney, M. E., & Earhart, G. M. (2010b). Effects of dance on gait and balance in Parkinson's disease: A comparison of partnered and nonpartnered dance movement. *Neurorehabilitation and Neural Repair, 24*, 384–392.

Hadwin, J., & Perner, J. (1991). Pleased and surprised: Children's cognitive theory of emotion. *British Journal of Developmental Psychology, 9*, 215–234.

Hagen, J. W., & Lamb-Parker, F. G. (2008). Head Start. In M. M. Haith & J. B. Benson (Eds.), *Encyclopedia of infant and early childhood development*. Oxford, UK: Elsevier.

Hagestad, G. O. (1985). Continuity and connectedness. In V. L. Bengtson (Ed.), *Grandparenthood*. Beverly Hills, CA: Sage.

Hagestad, G. O., & Uhlenberg, P. (2007). The impact of demographic changes on relations between age groups and generations: A comparative perspective. In K. W. Schaie & P. Uhlenberg (Eds.), *Demographic changes and the well-being of older persons*. New York: Springer.

Hagg, T. (2009). From neurotransmitters to neurotrophic factors to neurogenesis. *Neuroscientist, 15*, 20–27.

Hahn, D. B., Payne, W. A., & Lucas, E. B. (2011). *Focus on health* (10th ed.). New York: McGraw-Hill.

Hahn, W. K. (1987). Cerebral lateralization of function: From infancy through childhood. *Psychological Bulletin, 101*, 376–392.

Hakuta, K. (2001, April 5). *Key policy milestones and directions in the education of English language learners*. Paper prepared for the Rockefeller Foundation Symposium, Leveraging change: An emerging framework for educational equity, Washington, DC.

Hakuta, K. (2005, April). *Bilingualism at the intersection of research and public policy*. Paper presented at the meeting of the Society for Research on Child Development, Atlanta.

Hakuta, K., Butler, Y. G., & Witt, D. (2001). *How long does it take English learners to attain proficiency?* Berkeley, CA: The University of California Linguistic Minority Research Institute Policy Report 2000–2001.

Hales, D. (2011). *An invitation to health* (14th ed.). Boston: Cengage.

Halford, G. S., & Andrews, G. (2011). Information-processing models of cognitive development. In U. Goswami (Eds.), *Wiley-Blackwell handbook of childhood cognitive development* (2nd ed.). New York: Wiley.

Hall, C. B., Lipton, R. B., Sliwinski, M., Katz, M. J., Derby, C. A., & Verghese, J. (2009). Cognitive activities delay onset of memory decline in persons who develop dementia. *Neurology, 73*, 356–361.

Hall, G. N. (2010). *Multicultural psychology* (2nd ed.). Upper Saddle River, NJ: Prentice Hall.

Hall, G. S. (1904). *Adolescence* (Vols. 1 & 2). Englewood Cliffs, NJ: Prentice Hall.

Hall, L. (2009). *Autism spectrum disorders: From therapy to practice*. Boston: Allyn & Bacon.

Hallahan, D. P., Kauffman, J. M., & Pullen, P. C. (2009). *Exceptional learners* (11th ed.). Boston: Allyn & Bacon.

Halpern, D. F., Benbow, C. P., Geary, D. C., Gur, R. C., Hyde, J. S., & Gernsbacher, M. A. (2007). The science of sex differences in science and mathematics. *Psychological Science in the Public Interest, 8,* 1–51.

Ham, L. S., & others. (2010). No fear, just relax and play: Social anxiety, alcohol expectancies, and drinking games among college students. *Journal of American College Health, 58,* 473–479.

Hamilton, B. E., Martin, J. A., & Ventura, J. A. (2010, April). Births: Preliminary data for 2008. *National Vital Statistics Reports, Vol. 58* (No. 16). Hyattsville, MD: National Center for Health Statistics.

Hammen, C. (2009). Adolescent depression: Stressful interpersonal contexts and risk for recurrence. *Current Directions in Psychological Science, 18,* 200–204.

Han, W-J. (2009). Maternal employment. In D. Carr (Ed.), *Encyclopedia of the life course and human development.* Boston: Gale Cengage.

Hannish, L. D., & Guerra, N. G. (2004). Aggressive victims, passive victims, and bullies: Developmental continuity or developmental change? *Merrill-Palmer Quarterly, 50,* 17–38.

Harakeh, Z., Scholte, R. H. J., Vermulst, A. A., de Vries, H., & Engles, R. C. (2010). The relations between parents' smoking, general parenting, parental smoking communication, and adolescents' smoking. *Journal of Research on Adolescence, 20,* 140–165.

Hardy, M. (2006). Older workers. In R. H. Binstock & L. K. George (Eds.), *Handbook of aging and the social sciences* (6th ed.). San Diego: Academic Press.

Harkins, S. W., Price, D. D., & Martinelli, M. (1986). Effects of age on pain perception. *Journal of Gerontology, 41,* 58–63.

Harkness, S., & Super, E. M. (1995). Culture and parenting. In M. H. Bornstein (Ed.), *Handbook of parenting* (Vol. 3). Hillsdale, NJ: Erlbaum.

Harlow, H. F. (1958). The nature of love. *American Psychologist, 13,* 673–685.

Harris, C. D., Pan, L., & Mukhtar, Q. (2010, in press). Changes in receiving preventive care services among U.S. adults with diabetes, 1997–2007. *Preventing Chronic Disease.*

Harris, G., Thomas, A., & Booth, D. A. (1990). Development of salt taste in infancy. *Developmental Psychology, 26,* 534–538.

Harris, K. M., Gorden-Larsen, P., Chantala, K., & Udry, J. R. (2006). Longitudinal trends in race/ethnic disparities in leading health indicators from adolescence to young adulthood. *Archives of Pediatric and Adolescent Medicine, 160,* 74–81.

Harris, P. L. (2000). *The work of the imagination.* Oxford University Press.

Harris, P. L. (2006). Social cognition. In W. Damon & R. Lerner (Eds.), *Handbook of child psychology* (6th ed.). New York: Wiley.

Hart, B., & Risley, T. R. (1995). *Meaningful differences.* Baltimore, MD: Paul Brookes.

Hart, C. H., Yang, C., Charlesworth, R., & Burts, D. C. (2003, April). *Early childhood teachers' curriculum beliefs, classroom practices, and children's outcomes: What are the connections?* Paper presented at the biennial meeting of the Society for Research in Child Development, Tampa, FL.

Hart, D., & Karmel, M. P. (1996). Self-awareness and self-knowledge in humans, great apes, and monkeys. In A. Russori, K. Bard, & S. Parker (Eds.), *Reaching into thought.* New York: Cambridge University Press.

Hart, D., Matsuba, M. K., & Atkins, R. (2008). The moral and civic effects of learning to serve. In L. Nucci & D. Narvaez (Eds.), *Handbook of moral and character education.* Clifton, NJ: Psychology Press.

Hart, K. A. (2007). The aging workforce: Implications for health care organizations. *Nursing Economics, 25,* 101–102.

Harter, S. (2006). The self. In W. Damon & R. Lerner (Eds.), *Handbook of child psychology* (6th ed.). New York: Wiley.

Hartley, A. (2006). Changing role of the speed of processing construct in the cognitive psychology of human aging. In J. E. Birren & K. W. Schaie (Eds.), *Handbook of the psychology of aging* (6th ed). San Diego: Academic Press.

Hartshorne, H., & May, M. S. (1928–1938). *Moral studies in the nature of character: Studies in the nature of character.* New York: Macmillan.

Hartup, W. W. (1983). The peer system. In P. H. Mussen (Ed.), *Handbook of child psychology* (4th ed., Vol. 4). New York: Wiley.

Hartup, W. W. (1996). The company they keep—friendships and their development significance. *Child Development, 67,* 1–13.

Hartup, W. W. (2009). Critical issues and theoretical viewpoints. In K. H. Rubin, W. M. Bukowski, & B. Laursen (Eds.), *Handbook of peer interactions, relationships, and groups.* New York: Guilford.

Hattery, A. J., & Smith, E. (2007). *African American families.* Thousand Oaks, CA: Sage.

Hauksdottir, A., Steineck, G., Furst, C. J., & Valdimarsdottir, U. (2010, in press). Long-term harm of low preparedness for a wife's death from cancer—a population-based study of widowers 4–5 years after the loss. *American Journal of Epidemiology.*

Hawkes, C. (2006). Olfaction in neurodegenerative disorder. *Advances in Otorhinolaryngology, 63,* 133–151.

Hawkley, L. C., Thisted, R. A., Masi, C. M., & Cacioppo, J. T. (2010). Loneliness predicts increased blood pressure: 5-year cross-lagged analyses in middle-aged and older adults. *Psychology and Aging, 25,* 132–141.

Hayflick, L. (1977). The cellular basis for biological aging. In C. E. Finch & L. Hayflick (Eds.), *Handbook of the biology of aging.* New York: Van Nostrand.

Hazan, C., & Shaver, P. R. (1987). Romantic love conceptualized as an attachment process. *Journal of Personality and Social Psychology, 52,* 522–524.

Healey, M. K., & Hasher, L. (2009). Limitations to the deficit attenuation hypothesis: Aging and decision making. *Journal of Consumer Psychology*, 19, 17–22.

Health Management Resources. (2001). *Child health and fitness.* Boston: Author.

Hedayat, K. (2006). When the spirit leaves: Childhood death, grieving, and bereavement in Islam. *Journal of Palliative Medicine*, 9, 1282–1291.

Hedberg, P., Ohrvik, J., Lonnberg, I., & Nilsson, G. (2009). Augmented blood pressure response to exercise is associated with improved long-term survival in older people. *Heart*, 95, 1072–1078.

Heidelbaugh, J. J. (2010). Management of erectile dysfunction. *American Family Physician*, 81, 305–312.

Heimann, M., Strid, K., Smith, L., Tjus, T., Ulvund, S. E., & Meltzoff, A. N. (2006). Exploring the relation between memory, gestural communication, and the emergence of language in infancy: A longitudinal study. *Infant and Child Development*, 15, 233–249.

Helzner, E. P., & others. (2009). Contribution of vascular risk factors to the progression of Alzheimer disease. *Archives of Neurology*, 66, 343–348.

Hendrick, J., & Weissman, P. (2010). *The whole child: Developmental education for the early years* (9th ed.). Upper Saddle River, NJ: Prentice Hall.

Hendry, C. (2009). Incarceration and the tasks of grief: A narrative review. *Journal of Advanced Nursing*, 65, 270–278.

Hennesey, B. A. (2011). Intrinsic motivation and creativity: Have we come full circle? In R. A. Beghetto & J. C. Kaufman (Eds.), *Nurturing creativity in the classroom.* New York: Cambridge University Press.

Henniger, M. L. (2009). *Teaching young children* (4th ed.). Upper Saddle River, NJ: Prentice Hall.

Henretta, J. C. (2010, in press). Lifetime marital history and mortality after age 50. *Journal of Aging and Health.*

Henriksen, T. B., Hjollund, N. H., Jensen, T. K., Bonde, J. P., Andersson, A. M., Kolstad, H., & others. (2004). Alcohol consumption at the time of conception and spontaneous abortion. *American Journal of Epidemiology*, 160, 661–667.

Henrikson, C. A. (2010). Advance directives and surrogate decision making before death. *New England Journal of Medicine*, 363, 296.

Hentz, K., & Fields, J. (2009). Sex education/abstinence education. In D. Carr (Ed.), *Encyclopedia of the life course and human development.* Boston: Gale Cengage.

Hermann-Giddens, M. E. (2007). The decline in the age of menarche in the United States: Should we be concerned? *Journal of Adolescent Health*, 40, 201–203.

Herrera, S. G., & Murry, K. G. (2011). *Mastering ESL and bilingual methods* (2nd ed.). Boston: Allyn & Bacon.

Herrera, V. M., Koss, M. P., Bailey, J., Yuan, N. P., & Lichter, E. L. (2006). Survivors of male violence. In J. Worell & C. D. Goodheart (Eds.), *Handbook of girls' and women's psychological health.* New York: Oxford University Press.

Hertzog, C., Kramer, A. F., Wilson, R. S., & Lindenberger, U. (2009). Enrichment effects on adult cognitive development. *Psychological Perspectives in the Public Interest*, 9, 1–65.

Hetherington, E. M. (1989). Coping with family transitions: Winners, losers, and survivors. *Child Development*, 60, 1–14.

Hetherington, E. M. (2006). The influence of conflict, marital problem solving, and parenting on children's adjustment in nondivorced, divorced, and remarried families. In A. Clarke-Stewart & J. Dunn (Eds.), *Families count.* New York: Cambridge University Press.

Hetherington, E. M., & Kelly, J. (2002). *For better or for worse: Divorce reconsidered.* New York: Norton.

Hetherington, E. M., & Stanley-Hagan, M. (2002). Parenting in divorced and remarried families. In M. H. Bornstein (Ed.), *Handbook of parenting* (2nd ed., Vol. 3). Mahwah, NJ: Erlbaum.

Hewlett, B. S. (1991). *Intimate fathers: The nature and context of Aka Pygmy.* Ann Arbor: University of Michigan Press.

Hewlett, B. S. (2000). Culture, history and sex: Anthropological perspectives on father involvement. *Marriage and Family Review*, 29, 324–340.

Hewlett, B. S., & MacFarlan, S. J. (2010). Fathers' roles in hunter-gatherer and other small-scale cultures. In M. E. Lamb (Ed.), *The role of the father in child development* (5th ed.). New York: Wiley.

Hick, P., & Thomas, G. (Eds.). (2009). *Inclusion and diversity in education.* Thousand Oaks, CA: Sage.

Higginbotham, B., Skogrand, L., & Torres, E. (2010). Stepfamily education: Perceived benefits for children. *Journal of Divorce and Remarriage*, 1, 36–49.

High/Scope Resource. (2005, spring). The High/Scope Perry Preschool Study and the man who began it. *High/Scope Resource.* Ypsilanti, MI: High/Scope Press.

Highfield, R. (2008, April 30). *Harvard's baby brain research lab.* Retrieved on January 24, 2009, from www.telegraph.co.uk/ scienceandtechnology/science/ sciencenews/3341166/Harvards

Higo, M., & Williamson, J. B. (2009). Retirement. In D. Carr (Ed.), *Encyclopedia of the life course and human development.* Boston: Gale Cengage.

Hill, C. R., & Stafford, F. P. (1980). Parental care of children: Time diary estimate of quantity, predictability, and variety. *Journal of Human Resources*, 75, 219–239.

Hill, P. C., & Butter, E. M. (1995). The role of religion in promoting physical health. *Journal of Psychology and Christianity*, 14, 141–155.

Hill, P. C., & Pargament, K. I. (2003). Advances in conceptualization and measurement of religion and spirituality: Implications for physical and mental health research. *American Psychologist*, 58, 64–74.

Hill, T. D., Angel, J. L., Ellison, C. G., & Angel, R. J. (2005). Religious attendance and mortality: An 8-year follow-up of older Mexican Americans. *Journals of Gerontology B: Psychological Sciences and Social Sciences, 60,* S102–S109.

Hillman, C. H., Buck, S. M., Themanson, J. R., Pontifex, M. B., & Castelli, D. M. (2009). Aerobic fitness and cognitive development: Event-related brain potential and task performance indices of executive control in preadolescent children. *Developmental Psychology, 45,* 114–129.

Himes, C. L. (2009a). Age structure. In D. Carr (Ed.), *Encyclopedia of the life course and human development.* Boston: Gale Cengage.

Himes, C. (2009b). Obesity. In D. Carr (Ed.), *Encyclopedia of the life course and human development.* Boston: Gale Cengage.

Hindman, A. H., Skibbek, L. E., Miller, A., & Zimmerman, M. (2010). Ecological contexts and early learning: Contributions of child, family, and classroom factors during Head Start to literacy and mathematics growth through first grade. *Early Childhood Research Quarterly, 25,* 235–250.

Hines, M. (2011). Gendered behavior across the life span. In R. M. Lerner, A. Freund, & M. Lamb (Eds.), *Handbook of life-span development* (Vol. 2). New York: Wiley.

Hinks, A., & others. (2009). Identification of a novel susceptibility locus for juvenile idiopathic arthritis by genome-wide association analysis. *Arthritis and Rheumatism, 60,* 258–263.

Hipwell, A. E., Keenan, K., Loeber, R., & Battista, D. (2010). Early predictors of intimate sexual behaviors in an urban sample of young girls. *Developmental Psychology, 46,* 366–378.

Hirsch, B. J., & Rapkin, B. D. (1987). The transition to junior high school: A longitudinal study of self-esteem, psychological symptomatology, school life, and social support. *Child Development, 58,* 1235–1243.

Ho, J., & Birman, D. (2010). Acculturation gaps in Vietnamese immigrant families: Impact on family

relationships. *International Journal of Intercultural Relations, 34,* 22–23.

Ho, R. C., Neo, L. F., Chua, A. N., Cheak, A. A., & Mak, A. (2010). Research on psychoneuroimmunology: Does stress influence immunity and cause coronary artery disease? *Annals of the Academy of Medicine, Singapore, 39,* 191–196.

Hockenberry, M. (2010). *Wong's essentials of pediatric nursing* (8th ed.). New York: Elsevier.

Hockenberry, M., & Wilson, D. (2009). *Wong's essentials of pediatric nursing.* Oxford, UK: Elsevier.

Hodson, R. (2009). Employment. In D. Carr (Ed.), *Encyclopedia of the life course and human development.* Boston: Gale Cengage.

Hoeksema, E., & others. (2010, in press). Enhanced neural activity in frontal and cerebellar circuits after cognitive training in children with attention deficit hyperactivity disorder. *Human Brain Mapping.*

Hoekstra, R., Happe, F., Baron-Cohen, S., & Ronald, A. (2010, in press). Limited genetic covariance between autistic traits and intelligence: Findings from a longitudinal twin study. *American Journal of Medical Genetics B: Neuropsychiatric Genetics.*

Hoelter, L. (2009). Divorce and separation. In D. Carr (Ed.), *Encyclopedia of the life course and human development.* Boston: Gale Cengage.

Hofer, A., Siedentopf, C. M., Ischebeck, A., Rettenbacher, M. A., Verius, M., Felber, S., & Fleischbacker, W. (2007). Sex differences in brain activation patterns during processing of positively and negatively balanced emotional stimuli. *Psychological Medicine, 37,* 109–119.

Hoff, E., Laursen, B., & Tardit, T. (2002). Socioeconomic status and parenting. In M. H. Bornstein (Ed.), *Handbook of parenting* (2nd ed.). Mahwah, NJ: Erlbaum.

Hoffman, E., & Ewen, D. (2007). Supporting families, nurturing young children. *CLASP Policy Brief No. 9,* 1–11.

Holliday, J. C., Rothwell, H. A., & Moore, L. A. R. (2010). The relative

importance of different measures of peer smoking on adolescent smoking behavior: Cross-sectional and longitudinal analysis of a large British cohort. *Journal of Adolescent Health, 47,* 58–66.

Hollier, L., & Wendel, G. (2008). Third trimester antiviral prophylaxis for preventing maternal genital herpes simplex virus (HSV) recurrences and neonatal infection. *Cochrane Database of Systematic Reviews, 1,* CD004946.

Holloway, D. (2010). Clinical update on hormone replacement therapy. *British Journal of Nursing, 19,* 498–504.

Holmes, T. H., & Rahe, R. H. (1967). The social readjustment scale. *Journal of Psychosomatic Research, 11,* 213–218.

Holter, A. C., & Narvaez, D. (2009). Moral development and education. In D. Carr (Ed.), *Encyclopedia of the life course and human development.* Boston: Gale Cengage.

Holzman, L. (2009). *Vygotsky at work and play.* Oxford, UK: Routledge.

Hope, D. A. (2009). Contemporary perspectives on lesbian, gay, and bisexual identities: Introduction. *Nebraska Symposium on Motivation, 54,* 1–4.

Horn, J. L., & Donaldson, G. (1980). Cognitive development II: Adulthood development of human abilities. In O. G. Brim & S-J. Kagan (Eds.), *Constancy and change in human development.* Cambridge, MA: Harvard University Press.

Hornickel, J., Skoe, E., & Kraus, N. (2008). Subcortical laterality of speech encoding. *Audiology and Neuro-Otology, 14,* 198–207.

Horowitz, F. D. (2009). Introduction: A developmental understanding of giftedness and talent. In F. D. Horowitz, R. F. Subotnik, & D. J. Matthews (Eds.), *The development of giftedness and talent across the life span.* Washington, DC: American Psychological Association.

Houston, D. K., & others. (2009). Overweight and obesity over the adult life course and incident mobility limitation in older adults: The health, aging, and body composition study. *American Journal of Epidemiology, 169,* 927–936.

Howard, D. V., Howard, J. H., Dennis, N. A., LaVine, S., & Valentino, K. (2008). Aging and implicit learning of an invariant association. *Journals of Gerontology B: Psychological Sciences and Social Sciences, 63,* P100–P105.

Howe, M. J. A., Davidson, J. W., Moore, D. G., & Sloboda, J. A. (1995). Are there early childhood signs of musical ability? *Psychology of Music, 23,* 162–176.

Howell, D. (2010, in press). Trends in the prevalence of obesity and overweight in English adults by age and birth cohort, 1991–2006. *Public Health and Nutrition.*

Howell, D. C. (2010). *Statistical methods for psychology* (7th ed.). Boston: Cengage.

Howes, C. (2009). Friendship in early childhood. In K. H. Rubin, W. M. Bukowski, & B. Laursen (Eds.), *Handbook of peer interactions, relationships, and groups.* New York: Guilford.

Howland, R. H. (2010, in press). Drug therapies for cognitive impairment and dementia. *Journal of Psychosocial Nursing and Mental Health Services.*

Howlin, P., Magiati, I., & Charman, T. (2009). Systematic review of early intensive behavioral interventions with autism. *American Journal on Intellectual and Developmental Disabilities, 114,* 23–41.

Hoyer, W. J., & Roodin, P. A. (2009). *Adult development and aging* (6th ed.). New York: McGraw-Hill.

Hrabosky, J. I., Masheb, R. M., White, M. A., & Grilo, C. M. (2007). Overvaluation of shape and weight in binge eating disorder. *Journal of Consulting and Clinical Psychology, 75,* 175–180.

HSBC Insurance. (2007). *The future of retirement.* London: HSBC.

Huang, J-H., DeJong, W., Towvim, L. G., & Schneider, S. K. (2009). Sociodemographic and psychobehavioral characteristics of U.S. college students who abstain from alcohol. *Journal of American College Health, 57,* 395–410.

Huda, S. S., Brodie, L. E., & Sattar, N. (2010). Obesity in pregnancy: Prevalence and metabolic consequences. *Seminars in pregnancy: Prevalence and metabolic consequences, 15,* 70–76.

Huerta, M., Cortina, L. M., Pang, J. S., Torges, C. M., & Magley, V. J. (2006). Sex and power in the academy: Modeling sexual harassment in the lives of college women. *Personality and Social Psychology Bulletin, 32,* 616–628.

Huesmann, L. R., Dubow, E. F., Eron, L. D., & Boxer, P. (2006). Middle childhood family-contextual and personal factors as predictors of adult outcomes. In A. C. Huston & M. N. Ripke (Eds.), *Developmental contexts in middle childhood: Bridges to adolescence and adulthood.* New York: Cambridge University Press.

Huesmann, L. R., Moise-Titus, S., Podolski, C., & Eron, L. D. (2003). Longitudinal relations between children's exposure to TV violence and their aggressive and violent behavior in young adulthoods 1971–1992. *Developmental Psychology, 39,* 201–221.

Hughes, M. E., Wake, L. J., LaPierre, T. A., & Luo, Y. (2007). All in the family: The impact of caring for grandchildren on grandparents' health. *Journals of Gerontology B: Psychological Sciences and Social Sciences, 62,* S108–S119.

Hughes, T. F. (2010). Promotion of cognitive health through cognitive activity in the aging population. *Aging and Health, 6,* 111–121.

Hui, W. S., Liu, Z., & Ho, S. C. (2010, in press). Metabolic syndrome and all-cause mortality: A meta-analysis of prospective cohort studies. *European Journal of Epidemiology.*

Hunes, K., & Davis, K. D. (2009). Gender in the workplace. In D. Carr (Ed.), *Encyclopedia of the life course and human development.* Boston: Gale Cengage.

Hurt, H., Brodsky, N. L., Roth, H., Malmud, R., & Giannetta, J. M. (2005). School performance of children with gestational cocaine exposure. *Neurotoxicology and Teratology, 27,* 203–211.

Huston, A. C., & Bentley, A. C. (2010). Human development in societal context. *Annual Review of Psychology* (Vol. 61). Palo Alto, CA: Annual Reviews.

Huston, A. C., & Ripke, N. N. (2006). Experiences in middle and late childhood and children's development. In A. C. Huston & M. N. Ripke (Eds.), *Developmental contexts in middle childhood.* New York: Cambridge University Press.

Huston, T. L., & Holmes, E. K. (2004). Becoming parents. In A. L. Vangelisti (Ed.), *Handbook of family communication.* Mahwah, NJ: Erlbaum.

Huttenlocher, P. R., & Dabholkar, A. S. (1997). Regional differences in synaptogenesis in human cerebral cortex. *Journal of Comparative Neurology, 37*(2), 167–178.

Huyck, M. H. (1995). Marriage and close relationships of the marital kind. In R. Blieszner & V. H. Bedford (Eds.), *Handbook of aging and the family.* Westport, CT: Greenwood Press.

Hyde, J. S. (2005). The gender similarities hypothesis. *American Psychologist, 60,* 581–592.

Hyde, J. S. (2007). *Half the human experience* (7th ed.). Boston: Houghton Mifflin.

Hyde, J. S., & DeLamater, J. D. (2011). *Understanding human sexuality* (11th ed.). New York: McGraw-Hill.

Hyde, J. S., Lindberg, S. M., Linn, M. C., Ellis, A. B., & Williams, C. C. (2008). Gender similarities characterize math performance. *Science, 321,* 494–495.

Hynes, K., & Davis, K. D. (2009). Gender in the work place. In D. Carr (Eds.). *Encyclopedia of the life course and human development.* Boston: Cengage.

Hyson, M. C., Copple, C., & Jones, J. (2006). Early childhood development and education. In W. Damon & R. Lerner (Eds.), *Handbook of child psychology* (6th ed.). New York: Wiley.

IJzerman, M. J., Renzenbrink, G. J., & Geurts, A. C. (2009). Neuromuscular stimulation after stroke: From technology to clinical development. *Expert Reviews of Neurotherapeutics, 9,* 541–552.

International Montessori Council. (2006). Much of their success on prime-time television. Available at http://www.Montessori.org/enews/barbara_walters.html

Ip, S., Chung, M., Raman, G., Chew, P., Magula, N., Devine, D., & others. (2009). Breastfeeding and maternal and infant health outcomes in developed countries. *Evidence Report/Technology Assessment, 153,* 1–86.

Ip, S., Chung, M., Raman, G., Trikaliinos, T. A., & Lau, J. (2009). A summary of the Agency for Healthcare Research and Quality's evidence report on breastfeeding in developed countries. *Breastfeeding Medicine,* 4(Suppl. 2), S17–S30.

Ireland, J. (2010). Palliative care: A case study and reflections on some spiritual issues. *British Journal of Nursing, 19,* 237–240.

Irvine, S. H., & Berry, J. W. (Eds.). (2010, in press). *Human abilities in cultural context.* New York: Cambridge University Press.

Ise, E., & Schulte-Korne, G. (2010, in press). Spelling deficits in dyslexia: Evaluation of an orthographic spelling training. *Annals of Dyslexia.*

Ishikawa, Y., & others. (2009). Spinal curvature and postural balance in patients with osteoporosis. *Osteoporosis International, 20,* 2049–2053.

Iwamoto, J., Sato, Y., Takeda, T., & Matsumoto, H. (2009). Role of sport and exercise in the maintenance of female bone health. *Journal of Bone and Mineral Metabolism, 27,* 530–537.

Iwasa, H., Masul, Y., Gondo, Y., Inagaki, H., Kawaal, C., & Suzuki, T. (2008). Personality and all-cause mortality among older adults dwelling in a Japanese community: A five-year population-based prospective cohort study. *American Journal of Geriatric Psychiatry, 16,* 399–405.

Izard, V., & Spelke, E. S. (2010, in press). Development of sensitivity of geometry in visual forms. *Human Evolution.*

Jabr, Z. (2010). *English language learners.* Upper Saddle River, NJ: Prentice Hall.

Jackson, J. J., & others. (2009). Not all conscientiousness scales change alike: A multimethod, multisample study of age differences in the facets of conscientiousness. *Journal of Personality and Social Psychology, 96,* 446–459.

Jackson, S. L. (2011). *Research methods* (2nd ed.). Boston: Cengage.

Jacobs, J. M., Hammerman-Rozenberg, R., Cohen, A., & Stressman, J. (2008). Reading daily predicts reduced mortality among men from a cohort of community-dwelling 70-year-olds. *Journals of Gerontology B: Psychological Sciences and Social Sciences, 63,* S73–S80.

Jaeggi, S. M., Berman, M. G., & Jonides, J. (2009). Training attentional processes. *Trends in Cognitive Science, 37,* 644–654.

Jafar, T. H. (2009). Children, obesity, and high blood pressure: Asian populations at high risk. *American Journal of Hypertension, 22,* 6–7.

Jaffee, S., & Hyde, J. S. (2000). Gender differences in moral orientation: A meta-analysis. *Psychological Bulletin, 126,* 703–726.

Jago, R., Froberg, K., Cooper, A. R., Eiberg, S., & Andersen, L. B. (2010). Three-year changes in fitness and adiposity are independently associated with cardiovascular risk factors among young Danish children. *Journal of Physical Activity and Health, 7,* 37–44.

Jahromi, L. B., Putnam, S. P., & Stifter, C. A. (2004). Maternal regulation of infant reactivity from 2 to 6 months. *Developmental Psychology, 40,* 477–487.

Jalongo, M. R. (2011). *Early childhood language arts* (5th ed.). Boston: Allyn & Bacon.

James, A. H., Brancazio, L. R., & Price, T. (2008). Aspirin and reproductive outcomes. *Obstetrical and Gynecological Survey, 63,* 49–57.

James, W. (1890/1950). *The principles of psychology.* New York: Dover.

Jansen, J., de Weerth, C., & Riksen-Walraven, J. M. (2008). Breastfeeding and the mother-infant relationship—a review. *Developmental Review, 28,* 503–521.

Janssen, I., Katzmarzyk, P. T., Boyce, W. F., Vereecken, C., Mulvihill, C., Roberts, C., Currie, C., & Pickett, W. (2005). Comparison of overweight and obesity prevalence in school-aged youth from 34 countries and their relationships with physical activity and dietary patterns. *Obesity Reviews, 6,* 123–132.

Jenni, O. G., & Carskadon, M. A. (2007). Sleep behavior and sleep regulation from infancy through adolescence: Normative aspects. In O. G. Jenni & M. A. Carskadon (Eds.), *Sleep medicine clinics: Sleep in children and adolescents.* Philadelphia: W. B. Saunders.

Jessberger, S., & Gage, F. H. (2008). Stem-cell-associated structural and functional plasticity in the aging hippocampus. *Psychology and Aging, 23,* 684–691.

Jessor, R., Turbin, M. S., & Costa, F. M. (2010, in press). Predicting developmental change in healthy eating and regular exercise among adolescents in China and the United States: The role of psychosocial behavioral protection and risk. *Journal of Research on Adolescence.*

Ji, B. T., Shu, X. O., Linet, M. S., Zheng, W., Wacholde, S., Gao, Y. T., & others. (1997). Paternal cigarette smoking and the risk of childhood cancer among offspring of non-smoking mothers. *Journal of the National Cancer Institute, 89,* 238–244.

Jiao, S., Ji, G., & Jing, Q. (1996). Cognitive development of Chinese urban only children and children with siblings. *Child Development, 67,* 387–395.

Johnson, C. C., Filion, F., Campbell-Yeo, M., Goulet, C., Bell, L., McNaughton, K., & Bryon, J. (2009). Enhanced kangaroo care for heel lance in preterm neonates: A crossover trial. *Journal of Perinatology, 29,* 51–56.

Johnson, C. L., & Troll, L. E. (1992). Family functioning in late life. *Journals of Gerontology, 47,* S66–S72.

Johnson, G. B., & Losos, J. (2010). *The living world* (6th ed.). New York: McGraw-Hill.

Johnson, J. A., Musial, D. L., Hall, G. E., & Gollnick, D. M. (2011). *Foundations of American education in a changing world* (15th ed.). Upper Saddle River, NJ: Merrill.

Johnson, J. G., Zhang, B. Greer, J. A., & Prigerson, H. G. (2007). Parental control, partner dependency, and complicated grief among widowed adults in the community. *Journal of Nervous and Mental Disease, 195,* 26–30.

Johnson, J. S., & Newport, E. L. (1991). Critical period effects on universal properties of language: The status of subjacency in the acquisition of a second language. *Cognition, 39,* 215–258.

Johnson, M. (2008, April 30). Commentary in R. Highfield's *Harvard's baby brain research lab.* Retrieved on January 24, 2008, from http://www.telegraph.co.uk/scienceandtechnology/science/sciencenews/3341166/Harvards

Johnson, M. H. (2010). Understanding the social world: A developmental neuroscience approach. In S. D. Calkins & M. A. Bell (Eds.), *Child development at the intersection of emotion and cognition.* Washington, DC: American Psychological Association.

Johnson, M. H., Grossmann, T., & Cohen-Kadosh, K. (2009). Mapping functional brain development: Building a social brain through interactive specialization. *Developmental Psychology, 45,* 151–159.

Johnson, S. P. (2010a, in press). A constructivist view of object perception in infancy. To appear in L. M. Oakes, C. H. Cashon, M. Casasola, & D. H. Rakison (Eds.), *Early perceptual and cognitive development.* New York: Oxford University Press.

Johnson, S. P. (2010b). Perceptual completion in infancy. In S. P. Johnson (Ed.), *Neoconstructivism: The new science of cognitive development.* New York: Oxford University Press.

Johnson, S. P. (Ed.). (2010c). *Neoconstructivism: The new science of cognitive development.* New York: Oxford University Press.

Johnston, L. D., O'Malley, P. M., Bachman, J. G., & Schulenberg, J. E. (2008). *Monitoring the future: National survey results on drug use, 1975–2007* (Vol. 2: College students and adults ages 19–45). Washington, DC: National Institute of Drug Abuse.

Johnston, L. D., O'Malley, P. M., Bachman, J. G., & Schulenberg, J. E. (2009). *Monitoring the future national results on adolescent drug use: Overview of key findings, 2008.* Bethesda, MD: National Institute on Drug Abuse.

Johnston, L. D., O'Malley, P. M., Bachman, J. G., & Schulenberg, J. E. (2010). *Monitoring the Future: National results on adolescent drug use 2009.* Bethesda, MD: National Institute on Drug Abuse.

Jokela, M., & others. (2010). From midlife to early old age: Health trajectories associated with retirement. *Epidemiology, 21,* 284–290.

Jolly, C. A. (2005). Diet manipulation and prevention of aging, cancer, and autoimmune disease. *Current Opinions in Clinical Nutrition and Metabolic Care, 8,* 382–387.

Jones, M. C. (1965). Psychological correlates of somatic development. *Child Development, 36,* 899–911.

Jordan, C. E., Campbell, R., & Follingstad, D. (2010). Violence and women's mental health: The impact of physical, sexual, and psychological aggression. *Annual Review of Clinical Psychology* (Vol. 6). Palo Alto, CA: Annual Reviews.

Jose, A., O'Leary, K. D., & Moyer, A. (2010). Does premarital cohabitation predict subsequent marital stability and marital quality? A meta-analysis. *Journal of Marriage and the Family, 72,* 105–116.

Joseph, J. (2006). *The missing gene.* New York: Algora.

Joyner, K. (2009). Transition to parenthood. In D. Carr (Ed.), *Encyclopedia of the life course and human development.* Boston: Gale Cengage.

Juang, L., & Syad, M. (2010, in press). Family cultural socialization practices and ethnic identity in college-going emerging adults. *Journal of Adolescence.*

Jung, C. (1933). *Modern man in search of a soul.* New York: Harcourt Brace.

Jung, Y., Gruenewald, T. L., Seeman, T. E., & Sarkkisian, C. A. (2010). Productive activities and development of frailty in older adults. *Journals of Gerontology B: Psychological Sciences and Social Sciences, 65B,* 256–261.

Jylhava, J., & others. (2009). Genetics of C-reactive protein and complement factor H have an epistatic effect on carotid artery compliance: The Cardiovascular Risk in Young Finns Study. *Clinical and Experimental Immunology, 155,* 53–58.

K

Kaatsch, P. (2010, in press). Epidemiology of childhood cancer. *Cancer Treatment Reviews.*

Kagan, J. (1987). Perspectives on infancy. In J. D. Osofsky (Ed.), *Handbook on infant development* (2nd ed.). New York: Wiley.

Kagan, J. (2002). Behavioral inhibition as a temperamental category. In R. J. Davidson, K. R. Scherer, & H. H. Goldsmith (Eds.), *Handbook of affective sciences.* New York: Oxford University Press.

Kagan, J. (2010). Emotions and temperament. In M. H. Bornstein (Ed.), *Handbook of cultural developmental science.* New York: Psychology Press.

Kagan, J. J., Kearsley, R. B., & Zelazo, P. R. (1978). *Infancy: Its place in human development.* Cambridge, MA: Harvard University Press.

Kagan, S. H. (2008). Faculty profile, University of Pennsylvania School of Nursing. Retrieved January 5 from http://www.nursing.upenn.edu/faculty/profile.asp

Kahana, A., Kahana, B., & Hammel, R. (2009). Stress in later life. In D. Carr (Ed.), *Encyclopedia of the life course and human development*. Boston: Cengage.

Kahana, E., Kahana, B., & Wykle, M. (2010). "Care-getting": A conceptual model of marshalling support near the end of life. *Current Aging Science, 3*, 71–78.

Kahn, J. A., Huang, B., Gillman, M. W., Field, A. E., Austin, S. B., Colditz, G. A., & Frazier, A. L. (2008). Patterns and determinants of physical activity in U.S. adolescents. *Journal of Adolescent Health, 42*, 369–377.

Kail, R. V. (2007). Longitudinal evidence that increases in processing speed and working memory enhance children's reasoning. *Psychological Science, 18*, 312–313.

Kalder, M., Knoblauch, K., Hrgovic, I., & Munstedt, K. (2010, in press). Use of complementary and alternative medicine during pregnancy and delivery. *Archives of Gynecology and Obstetrics.*

Kaleth, A. S., Chittenden, T. W., Hawkins, B. J., Hargens, T. A., Guill, S. G., Zedalis, D., & others. (2007). Unique cardiopulmonary exercise test responses in overweight middle-aged adults with obstructive sleep apnea. *Sleep Medicine, 8*, 160–168.

Kalish, R. A. (1981). *Death, grief, and caring relationships.* Monterey, CA: Brooks/Cole.

Kao, G., & Turney, K. (2010). Adolescents and schooling: Differences by race, ethnicity, and immigrant status. In D. P. Swanson, M. C. Edwards, & M. B. Spencer (Eds.), *Adolescence: Development in a global era.* San Diego: Academic Press.

Kaplan, H., Gurven, M., & Winking, J. (2009). An evolutionary theory of human life span: Embodied capital and the human adaptive complex. In V. L. Bengtson, D. Gans, N. M. Putney, & M. Silverstein (Eds.), *Handbook of theories of aging* (2nd ed.). New York: Springer.

Kaplan, H. B. (2009). Self-esteem. In D. Carr (Ed.), *Encyclopedia of the life course and human development.* Boston: Gale Cengage.

Kar, N. (2009). Psychological impact of disasters on children: Review of assessment and interventions. *World Journal of Pediatrics, 5*, 5–11.

Karasik, R. J., & Hamon, R. R. (2007). Cultural diversity and aging families. In B. S. Trask & R. R. Hamon (Eds.), *Cultural diversity and families.* Thousand Oaks, CA: Sage.

Karelitz, T. M., Jarvin, L., & Sternberg, R. J. (2011, in press). The meaning of wisdom and its development throughout life. In R. M. Lerner & W. F. Overton (Eds.), *Handbook of life-span development* (Vol. 1). New York: Wiley.

Karniol, R., Grosz, E., & Schorr, I. (2003). Caring, gender-role orientation, and volunteering. *Sex Roles, 49*, 11–19.

Karoly, L. A., & Bigelow, J. H. (2005). *The Economics of Investing in Universal Preschool Education in California.* Santa Monica, CA: RAND Corporation.

Karreman, A., van Tuijl, C., van Aken, M. A., & Dekovic, M. (2008). Parenting, coparenting, and effortful control in preschoolers. *Journal of Family Psychology, 22*, 30–40.

Kasari, C., & Lawton, K. (2010). New directions in behavioral treatment of autism spectrum disorders. *Current Opinion in Neurology, 23*, 137–143.

Kastenbaum, R. J. (2007). *Death, society, and human experience* (9th ed.). Boston: Allyn & Bacon.

Katz, L. (1999). Curriculum disputes in early childhood education. *ERIC Clearinghouse on Elementary and Early Childhood Education,* Document EDO-PS-99-13.

Katz, P. R., Karuza, J., Intrator, O., & Mor, V. (2009). Nursing home physician specialists: A response to the workforce crisis in long-term care. *Annals of Internal Medicine, 150*, 411–413.

Kauffman, J. M., McGee, K., & Brigham, M. (2004). Enabling or disabling? Observations on changes in special education. *Phi Delta Kappan, 85*, 613–620.

Kavsek, M. (2009). The perception of subjective contours and neon color spreading figures in young infants. *Attention, Perception, and Psychophysics, 71*, 412–420.

Kawano, M., Shono, N., Youshimura, T., Yamaguchi, M., Hirano, T., & Hisatomi, A. (2009). Improved cardio-respiratory fitness correlates with changes in the number and size of small dense LSD: Randomized controlled trial with exercise training and dietary instruction. *Internal Medicine, 48*, 25–32.

Keating, D. P. (1990). Adolescent thinking. In S. S. Feldman & G. R. Elliott (Eds.), *At the threshold: The developing adolescent.* Cambridge, MA: Harvard University Press.

Keers, R., & others. (2010, in press). Interaction between serotonin transporter gene variants and life events predicts response to antidepressants in the GENDEP project. *Pharmacogenetics.*

Keijsers, L., & Laird, R. D. (2010). Introduction to special issue: Careful conversations: Adolescents managing their parents' access to information. *Journal of Adolescence, 33*, 255–359.

Keister, L. A., & Destro, L. M. (2009). Wealth. In D. Carr (Ed.), *Encyclopedia of the life course and human development.* Boston: Gale Cengage.

Keller, A., Ford, L., & Meacham, J. (1978). Dimensions of self-concept in preschool children. *Developmental Psychology, 14*, 483–489.

Kelley-Moore, J. (2009). Chronic illness, adulthood and later life. In D. Carr (Ed.), *Encyclopedia of the life course and human development.* Boston: Gale Cengage.

Kelly, J. P., Borchert, J., & Teller, D. Y. (1997). The development of chromatic and achromatic sensitivity in infancy as tested with the sweep VEP. *Vision Research, 37*, 2057–2072.

Kelsey, S. G., Laditka, S. B., & Laditka, J. N. (2010, in press). Caregiver perspectives on transitions in assisted living and memory care. *American Journal of Alzheimer's Disease and Other Dementias.*

Kennedy, M. A. (2009). Child abuse. In D. Carr (Ed.), *Encyclopedia* of the life course and human development. Boston: Gale Cengage.

Kennell, J. H. (2006). Randomized controlled trial of skin-to-skin contact from birth versus conventional incubator for physiological stabilization in 1200 g to 2199 g newborns. *Acta Paediatrica (Sweden), 95*, 15–16.

Kennell, J. H., & McGrath, S. K. (1999). Commentary: Practical and humanistic lessons from the third world for perinatal caregivers everywhere. *Birth, 26*, 9–10.

Kersting, A., & Kroker, K. (2010). Prolonged grief as a distinct disorder, specifically affecting female health. *Archives of Women's Mental Health, 13*, 27–28.

Khabour, O. F., & Barnawi, J. M. (2010, in press). Association of longevity with IL-10 1082 G/A and TNF-alpha-308 G/A polymorphisms. *International Journal of Immunogenetics.*

Khera, A. V., & Radar, D. J. (2010). Future therapeutic directions in reverse cholesterol transport. *Current Atherosclerosis Reports, 12*, 73–81.

Kim, G., Walden, T. A., & Knieps, L. J. (2010). Impact and characteristics of positive and fearful emotional messages during infant social referencing. *Infant Behavior and Development, 33*, 189–195.

Kim, H., & Johnson, S. P. (2011, in press). Infant perception. In B. Goldstein (Ed.), *The origins of object knowledge.* New York: Oxford University Press.

Kim, J. H., Kwon, T. H., Koh, S. B., & Park, J. Y. (2010). Parkinsonism-hyperpyrexia syndrome after deep brain stimulation surgery: Case report. *Neurosurgery, 66*, E1029.

Kim, K. H. (2010, May). Unpublished data. School of Education, College of William & Mary, Williamsburg, VA.

Kim, S., & Hasher, L. (2005). The attraction effect in decision making: Superior performance by older adults. *Quarterly Journal of Experimental Psychology, 58A*, 120–133.

Kim, S. H. (2009). The influence of finding meaning and worldview of accepting death on anger among

bereaved older spouses. *Aging and Mental Health, 13*, 38–45.

Kim, T. A., Gordes, K. L., & Alon, G. (2010). Utilization of physical therapy in home health care under the prospective payment system. *Journal of Geriatric Physical Therapy, 33*, 2–9.

Kimble, M., Neacsiu, A. D., Flack, W. F., & Horner, J. (2008). Risk of unwanted sex for college women: Evidence for a red zone. *Journal of American College Health, 57*, 331–338.

King, L. A. (2011). *Psychology* (2nd ed.). New York: McGraw-Hill.

King, L. A., & Hicks, J. A. (2007). Whatever happened to "What might have been?" Regrets, happiness, and maturity. *American Psychologist, 62*, 625–636.

King, V., & Scott, M. E. (2005). A comparison of cohabiting relationships among older and younger adults. *Journal of Marriage and the Family, 67*, 271–285.

Kingson, E. R., & Bartholomew, J. (2009). Social Security. In D. Carr (Ed.), *Encyclopedia of the life course and human development.* Boston: Gale Cengage.

Kini, S., Morrell, D., Thong, K. J., Kopakaki, A., Hillier, S., & Irvine, D. S. (2010). Lack of impact of semen quality on fertilization in assisted conception. *Scottish Medicine, 55*, 20–23.

Kinney, H. C., Richerson, G. B., Dymecki, S. M., Darnall, R. A., & Nattie, E. E. (2009). The brainstem and serotonin in sudden infant death syndrome. *Annual Review of Pathology, 4*, 517–550.

Kirby, D., Laris, B. A., & Rollier, L. A. (2007). Sex and HIV education programs: Their impact on sexual behaviors of young people throughout the world. *Journal of Adolescent Health, 40*, 206–217.

Kisilevsky, B. S., & others. (2009). Fetal sensitivity to properties of maternal speech and language. *Infant Behavior and Development, 32*, 59–71.

Kistler, M., Rodgers, K. B., Power, T., Austin, E. W., & Hill, L. G. (2010, in press). Adolescents and music media: Toward an involvement-mediational model of

consumption and self-concept. *Journal of Research on Adolescence.*

Kistner, J. A., David-Ferdon, C. F., Repper, K. K., & Joiner, T. E. (2006). Bias and accuracy of children's perceptions of peer acceptance: Prospective associations with depressive symptoms. *Journal of Abnormal Child Psychology, 34*, 349–361.

Kitayama, S. (2011, in press). Psychology and culture: Cross-country or regional comparisons. *Annual Review of Psychology* (Vol. 62). Palo Alto, CA: Annual Reviews.

Kitchener, K. S., King, P. M., & DeLuca, S. (2006). The development of reflective judgment in adulthood. In C. Hoare (Ed.), *Handbook of adult development and learning.* New York: Oxford University Press.

Kitsantas, P., & Gaffney, K. F. (2010). Racial/ethnic disparities in infant mortality. *Journal of Perinatal Medicine, 38*, 87–94.

Kittas, A. (2010, in press). Evolution of the rate of biological aging using a phenotype based computational model. *Journal of Theoretical Biology.*

Klaczynski, P. A., & Narasimham, G. (1998). Development of scientific reasoning biases: Cognitive versus ego-protective explanations. *Developmental Psychology, 34*, 175–187.

Klaus, M., & Kennell, H. H. (1976). *Maternal-infant bonding.* St. Louis: Mosby.

Klima, C., Norr, K., Conderheld, S., & Handler, A. (2009). Introduction of Centering Pregnancy in a public health clinic. *Journal of Midwifery and Women's Health, 54*, 27–34.

Klingenberg, C. P., & others. (2010, in press). Prenatal alcohol exposure alters the patterns of facial asymmetry. *Alcohol.*

Klingman, A. (2006). Children and war trauma. In W. Damon & R. Lerner (Eds.), *Handbook of child psychology* (6th ed.). New York: Wiley.

Klug, W. S., Cummings, M. R., Spencer, C., & Palladino, M. A. (2010). *Essentials of genetics* (7th ed.). Upper Saddle River, NJ: Benjamin Cummings.

Knopik, V. S. (2009). Maternal smoking during pregnancy and child outcomes: Real or spurious? *Developmental Neuropsychology, 34*, 1–36.

Knox, M. (2010). On hitting children: A review of corporal punishment in the United States. *Journal of Pediatric Health Care, 24*, 103–107.

Koenig, H. G., & Blazer, D. G. (1996). Depression. In J. E. Birren (Ed.), *Encyclopedia of gerontology* (Vol. 1). San Diego: Academic Press.

Kohen, D. E., Lerenthal, T., Dahinten, V. S., & McIntosh, C. N. (2008). Neighborhood disadvantage: Pathways of effects for young children. *Child Development, 79*, 156–169.

Kohlberg, L. (1958). *The development to modes of moral thinking and choice in the years 10 to 16.* Unpublished doctoral dissertation, University of Chicago.

Kohlberg, L. (1986). A current statement of some theoretical issues. In S. Modgil & C. Modgil (Eds.), *Lawrence Kohlberg.* Philadelphia: Falmer.

Kohler, P. K., Manhart, L. E., & Lafferty, W. E. (2008). Abstinence-only and comprehensive sex education and the initiation of sexual activity and teen pregnancy. *Journal of Adolescent Health, 42*, 344–351.

Kolling, T., Goertz, C., Stefanie, F., & Knopf, M. (2010). Memory development through the second year: Overall developmental pattern, individual differences, and developmental trajectories. *Infant Behavior and Development, 33*, 159–167.

Kopp, C. B. (2011). Socio-emotional development in the early years. *Annual Review of Psychology* (Vol. 62). Palo Alto, CA: Annual Reviews.

Koppelman, K., & Goodhart, L. (2011). *Understanding human differences* (3rd ed.). Boston: Allyn & Bacon.

Korat, O. (2009). The effect of maternal teaching talk on children's emergent literacy as a function of type of activity and maternal education level. *Journal of Applied Developmental Psychology, 30*, 34–42.

Koropeckyj-Cox, T. (2009). Loneliness, later life. In D. Carr (Ed.), *Encyclopedia of the life course and human development.* Boston: Gale Cengage.

Koropeckyj-Cox, T. (2009). Singlehood. In D. Carr (Ed.), *Encyclopedia of the life course and human development.* Boston: Gale Cengage.

Kostelnik, M. J., Soderman, A. K., & Whiren, A. P. (2011). *Developmentally appropriate curricula* (5th ed.). Upper Saddle River, NJ: Merrill.

Kotre, J. (1984). *Outliving the self: Generativity and the interpretation of lives.* Baltimore: Johns Hopkins University Press.

Kottak, C. P. (2009). *Cultural anthropology* (13th ed.). New York: McGraw-Hill.

Kozol, J. (2005). *The shame of the nation.* New York: Crown.

Krakoff, L. R. (2008). Older patients need better guidelines for optimal treatment of high blood pressure: 1 size fits few. *Hypertension, 51*, 817–818.

Kramer, A. F., & Morrow, D. (2010, in press). Cognitive training and expertise. In D. Park & N. Schwartz (Eds.), *Cognitive aging: A primer.* New York: Psychology Press.

Kramer, L. (2006, July 10). Commentary in "How your siblings make you who you are" by Kluger, J. *Time,* pp. 46–55.

Kramer, L., & Perozynski, L. (1999). Parental beliefs about managing sibling conflict. *Developmental Psychology, 35*, 489–499.

Kramer, L., & Radey, C. (1997). Improving sibling relationships among young children: A social skills training model. *Family Relations, 46*, 237–246.

Krause, N. (2008). The social foundations of religious meaning in life. *Research on Aging, 30*(4), 395–427.

Krause, N. (2009). Deriving a sense of meaning in late life. In V. L. Bengtson, D. Gans, N. M. Putney, & M. Silverstein (Eds.), *Handbook of theories of aging.* New York: Springer.

Krause, N., Ingersoll-Dayton, B., Liang, J., & Sugisawa, H. (1999). Religion, social behavior, and health among the Japanese elderly. *Journal of Health and Social Behavior, 40*, 405–421.

Kreutzer, M., Leonard, C., & Flavell, J. H. (1975). An interview study of children's knowledge about memory. *Monographs of the Society for Research in Child Development, 40* (1, Serial No. 159).

Kriemler, S., & others. (2010, in press). Effect of school based physical activity program (KISS) on fitness and adiposity in primary schoolchildren: Cluster randomized controlled trial. *British Medical Journal.*

Kroger, J., Martinussen, M., & Marcia, J. E. (2010, in press). Identity change during adolescence and young adulthood: A meta-analysis. *Journal of Adolescence.*

Krueger, J. I., Vohs, K. D., & Baumeister, R. F. (2008). Is the allure of self-esteem a mirage after all? *American Psychologist, 63*, 64.

Krueger, P. M., & Chang, V. W. (2008). Being poor and coping with stress: Health behaviors and the risk of death. *American Journal of Public Health, 98*, 889–896.

Kruger, J., Blanck, M. H., & Gillespie, C. (2006). Dietary and physical activity behaviors among adults successful at weight loss management. *International Journal of Behavioral Nutrition and Physical Activity, 3*, 17.

Kübler-Ross, E. (1969). *On death and dying.* New York: Macmillan.

Kuebli, J. (1994, March). Young children's understanding of everyday emotions. *Young Children,* pp. 36–48.

Kuhl, P. K. (2000). A new view of language acquisition. *Proceedings of the National Academy of Science, 97*(22), 11850–11857.

Kuhl, P. K. (2009). Linking infant speech perception to language acquisition: Phonetic learning predicts language growth. In J. Colombo, P. McCardle, & L. Freund (Eds.), *Infant pathways to language.* New York: Psychology Press.

Kuhn, D. (2009). Adolescent thinking. In R. M. Lerner & L. Steinberg (Eds.), *Handbook of adolescent psychology* (3rd ed.). New York: Wiley.

Kuhn, D. (2011, in press). What is scientific thinking and how does it develop? In R. M. Lerner & W. F. Overton (Eds.), *Handbook of life-span development.* New York: Wiley.

Kulkofsky, S., & Klemfuss, J. Z. (2008). What the stories children tell can tell about their memory: Narrative skill and young children's suggestibility. *Developmental Psychology, 44,* 1442–1456.

Kutner, N. (2009). Centenarians. In D. Carr (Ed.), *Encyclopedia of the life course and human development.* Boston: Gale Cengage.

L

Labouvie-Vief, G. (1986, August). *Modes of knowing and life-span cognition.* Paper presented at the meeting of the American Psychological Association, Washington, DC.

Labouvie-Vief, G. (2006). Emerging structures of adult thought. In J. J. Arnett & J. L. Tanner (Eds.), *Emerging adults in America.* Washington, DC: American Psychological Association.

Lachman, M., Neupert, S., & Agrigoroaei, S. (2011, in press). The relevance of a sense of control for health and aging. In K. W. Schaie & S. L. Willis (Eds.), *Handbook of the psychology of aging* (7th ed.). New York: Elsevier.

Lachman, M. E. (2004). Development in midlife. *Annual Review of Psychology, 55.* Palo Alto, CA: Annual Reviews.

Lachman, M. E. (2006). Perceived control over aging-related declines. *Current Directions in Psychological Science, 15,* 282–286.

Lachman, M. E., Agrigoroaei, S., Murphy, C., & Tun, P. A. (2010). Frequent cognitive activity compensates for education differences in episodic memory. *American Journal of Geriatric Psychiatry, 18,* 4–10.

Lachman, M. E., & Firth, K. (2004). The adaptive value of feeling in control in midlife. In G. O. Brim, C. D. Ryff, & R. C. Kessler (Eds.), *How healthy are we? A national study of well-being at midlife.* Chicago: University of Chicago Press.

Lachman, M. E., & Kranz, E. (2010). The midlife crisis. In I. Wiener & E. Craighead (Eds.), *The Corsini encyclopedia of psychology* (4th ed.). New York: Wiley.

Lachman, M. E., Maier, H., & Budner, R. (2000). *A portrait of midlife.* Unpublished manuscript, Brandeis University, Waltham, MA.

Lachman, M. E., & Weaver, S. L. (1998). Sociodemographic variations in the sense of control by domain: Findings from the MacArthur Study of Midlife. *Psychology and Aging, 13,* 553–562.

Laflin, M. T., Wang, J., & Barry, M. (2008). A longitudinal study of adolescent transition from virgin to nonvirgin status. *Journal of Adolescent Health, 42,* 228–236.

Lafreiere, D., & Mann, N. (2009). Anosmia: Loss of smell in the elderly. *Otolaryngologic Clinics of North America, 42,* 123–131.

Lahey, B. B., Van Hulle, C. A., D'Onofrio, B. M., Rodgers, J. L., & Waldman, I. D. (2008). Is parental knowledge of their adolescent offspring's whereabouts and peer associations spuriously associated with offspring delinquency? *Journal of Abnormal Child Psychology, 36,* 807–823.

Laible, D., & Thompson, R. A. (2007). Early socialization: A relationship perspective. In J. E. Grusec & P. D. Hastings (Eds.), *Handbook of socialization.* New York: Guilford.

Lamb, M. E. (1986). *The father's role: Applied perspectives.* New York: Wiley.

Lamb, M. E. (1994). Infant care practices and the application of knowledge. In C. B. Fisher & R. M. Lerner (Eds.), *Applied developmental psychology.* New York: McGraw-Hill.

Lamb, M. E. (2000). The history of research on father involvement: An overview. *Marriage and Family Review, 29,* 23–42.

Lamb, M. E. (2005). Attachments, social networks, and developmental contexts. *Human Development, 48,* 108–112.

Lamb, M. E. (2010). How do fathers influence children's development? In M. E. Lamb (Ed.), *The role of the father in child development* (5th ed.). New York: Wiley.

Lamb, M. E., Bornstein, M. H., & Teti, D. M. (2002). *Development in infancy* (4th ed.). Mahwah, NJ: Erlbaum.

Lamb, M. M., & others. (2010). Early-life predictors of higher body mass index in healthy children. *Annals of Nutrition & Metabolism, 56,* 16–22.

Lane, H. (1976). *The wild boy of Aveyron.* Cambridge, MA: Harvard University Press.

Lane, R. M., & He, Y. (2009). Emerging hypotheses regarding the influences of butyrylcholinesterase-K variant, APOE epsilon4, and hyperhomocysteinemia in neurodegenerative dementias. *Medical Hypotheses, 73,* 230–250.

Langston, W. (2011). *Research methods laboratory manual for psychology* (3rd ed.). Boston: Cengage.

Langstrom, N., Rahman, Q., Carlstrom, E., & Lichtenstein, P. (2010). Genetic and environmental effects on same-sex behavior: A population study of twins in Sweden. *Archives of Sexual Behavior, 39,* 75–80.

Lansford, J. E. (2009). Parental divorce and children's adjustment. *Perspectives on Psychological Science, 4,* 140–152.

Lansford, J. E., Yu, T., Erath, S. A., Pettit, G. S., Bates, J. E., & Dodge, K. A. (2010, in press). Developmental precursors of number of sexual partners from ages 16 to 22. *Journal of Research on Adolescence.*

Larson, N. J., & others. (2008). Fruit and vegetable intake correlates during the transition to young adulthood. *American Journal of Preventive Medicine, 35,* 33–37.

Larson, R., Wilson, S., & Rickman, A. (2009). Globalization, societal change, and adolescence across the world. In R. M. Lerner & L. Steinberg (Eds.), *Handbook of adolescent psychology* (3rd ed.). New York: Wiley.

La Rue, A. (2010). Healthy brain aging: Role of cognitive reserve, cognitive stimulation, and cognitive exercises. *Clinics in Geriatric Medicine, 26,* 99–111.

Larzelere, R. E., & Kuhn, B. R. (2005). Comparing child outcomes of physical punishment and alternative disciplinary tactics: A meta-analysis. *Clinical Child and Family Psychology Review, 8,* 1–37.

Laumann, E. O., Glasser, D. B., Neves, R. C., & Moreira, E. D.

Loehlin, J. C. (2010, in press). Is there an active gene-environment correlation in adolescent drinking behavior? *Behavior Genetics.*

Loehlin, J. C., Horn, J. M., & Ernst, J. L. (2007). Genetic and environmental influences on adult life outcomes: Evidence from the Texas adoption project. *Behavior Genetics, 37,* 463–476.

Logsdon, M. C., Wisner, K., & Hanusa, B. H. (2009). Does maternal role functioning improve with antidepressant treatment in women with postpartum depression? *Journal of Women's Health, 18,* 85–90.

Lopenen, M., Hublin, C., Kalimo, R., Manttari, M., & Tenkanen, L. (2010). Joint effect of self-reported sleep problems and three components of the metabolic syndrome on risk of coronary heart disease. *Journal of Psychosomatic Research, 68,* 149–158.

Lorenz, K. Z. (1965). *Evolution and the modification of behavior.* Chicago: University of Press.

Loukas, A., Roalson, L. A., & Herrera, D. E. (2010). School connectedness buffers the effects of negative family relations and poor effortful control on early adolescent conduct problems. *Journal of Research on Adolescence, 20,* 13–22.

Lowdermilk, D. L., Perry, S. E., & Cashion, M. C. (2011). *Maternity Nursing* (8th ed.). New York: Elsevier.

Lu, L. H., & others. (2009). Effects of prenatal methamphetamine exposure on verbal memory revealed with functional magnetic resonance imaging. *Journal of Developmental and Behavioral Pediatrics, 30,* 185–192.

Lucas, P. J., McIntosh, K., Petticrew, M., Roberts, H., & Shiell, A. (2008). Financial benefits for child health and well-being in low income or socially disadvantaged families in developed world countries. *Cochrane Database of Systematic Reviews, 16,* CD006358.

Lucas, R. E., Clark, A. E., Yannis, G., & Diener, E. (2004). Unemployment alters the setpoint for life satisfaction. *Psychological Science, 15,* 8–13.

Luders, E., Narr, K. L., Thompson, P. M., Rex, D. E., Jancke, L., Steinmetz, H., & Toga, A. W. (2004). Gender differences in cortical complexity. *Nature Neuroscience, 1,* 799–800.

Lumpkin, A. (2011). *Introduction to physical education, exercise science, and sport studies* (8th ed.). New York: McGraw-Hill.

Lund, D. A., Utz, R., Caserta, M. S., & De Vries, B. (2009). Humor, laughter, and happiness in the lives of recently bereaved spouses. *Omega, 58,* 87–105.

Luo, L., & Craik, F. I. M. (2008). Aging and memory: A cognitive approach. *Canadian Journal of Psychology, 53,* 346–353.

Luria, A., & Herzog, E. (1985, April). *Gender segregation across and within settings.* Paper presented at the biennial meeting of the Society for Research in Child Development, Toronto.

Lustig, C., & Hasher, L. (2010, in press). Interference. In R. Schulz, L. Noelker, K. Rockwood, & R. Sprott (Eds.), *Encyclopedia of aging* (4th Ed.). New York: Springer Publishing.

Lyon, T. D., & Flavell, J. H. (1993). Young children's understanding of forgetting over time. *Child Development, 64,* 789–800.

M

Maccoby, E. E. (1984). Middle childhood in the context of the family. In *Development during middle childhood.* Washington, DC: National Academy Press.

Maccoby, E. E. (1998). *The two sexes: Growing up apart, coming together.* Cambridge, MA: Harvard University Press.

Maccoby, E. E. (2002). Gender and group processes. *Current Directions in Psychological Science, 11,* 54–58.

Maccoby, E. E., & Martin, J. A. (1983). Socialization in the context of the family: Parent-child interaction. In P. H. Mussen (Ed.), *Handbook of child psychology* (4th ed., Vol. 4). New York: Wiley.

MacFarlane, J. A. (1975). Olfaction in the development of social preferences in the human neonate. In *Parent-infant interaction.* Ciba Foundation Symposium No. 33. Amsterdam: Elsevier.

MacGeorge, E. L. (2003). Gender differences in attributions and emotions in helping contexts. *Sex Roles, 48,* 175–182.

Maciejewski, P. K., Zhang, B., Block, S. D., & Prigerson, H. G. (2007). An empirical examination of the stage theory of grief. *Journal of the American Medical Association, 297,* 716–723.

Madden, D. J., Gottlob, L. R., Denny, L. L., Turkington, T. G., Provenzale, J. M., Hawk, T. C., & others. (1999). Aging and recognition memory: Changes in regional cerebral blood flow associated with components of reaction time distributions. *Journal of Cognitive Neuroscience, II,* 511–520.

Mader, S. S. (2011). *Biology* (13th ed.). New York: McGraw-Hill.

Madkour, A. S., Farhat, T., Halpern, C. T., Godeu, E., & Gabhainn, S. N. (2010, in press). Early adolescent sexual initiation as a problem behavior: A comparative study of five nations. *Journal of Adolescent Health.*

Madole, K. L., Oakes, L. M., & Rakison, D. H. (2010, in press). Information processing approaches to infants' developing representations of dynamic features. In L. Oakes, C. Cashon, M. Casasola, & D. Rakison (Eds.), *Infant perception and cognition.* New York: Oxford University Press.

Maimoun, L., & Sultan, C. (2010, in press). Effects of physical activity on bone remodeling. *Metabolism.*

Malamitsi-Puchner, A., & Boutsikou, T. (2006). Adolescent pregnancy and perinatal outcome. *Pediatric Endocrinology Review, 3*(Suppl. 1), 170–171.

Malizia, B. A., Hacker, M. R., & Penzias, A. S. (2009). Cumulative live-birth rates after in vitro fertilization. *New England Journal of Medicine, 360,* 236–243.

Mandara, J. (2006). The impact of family functioning on African American males' academic achievement: A review and clarification of the empirical literature. *Teachers College Record, 108,* 206–233.

Mandler, J. (2000). Unpublished review of J. W. Santrock's *Life-span development* (8th ed.). New York: McGraw-Hill.

Mandler, J. M. (2004). *The foundations of the mind: Origins of conceptual thought*. New York: Oxford University Press.

Mandler, J. M. (2006). *Jean Mandler*. Retrieved January 15, 2006, from http://cogsci.ucsd.edu/~jean/

Mandler, J. M. (2009). Conceptual categorization. In D. H. Rakison & L. M. Oakes (Eds.), *Early category and concept development*. New York: Oxford University Press.

Mandler, J. M., & McDonough, L. (1993). Concept formation in infancy. *Cognitive Development, 8*, 291–318.

Mann, T., Tomiyama, A. J., Westling, E., Lew, A-M., Samuels, B., & Chatman, J. (2007). Medicare's search for effective obesity treatments. *American Psychologist, 62*, 220–233.

Manton, K. G., Lowrimore, G. R., Ullian, A. D., Gu, X., & Tolley, H. D. (2007). From the cover: Labor force participation and human capital increases in an aging population and implications for U.S. research investment. *Proceedings of the National Academy of Sciences USA, 104*, 10802–10807.

Marcdante, K., Kliegman, R. M., & Behrman, R. E. (2011). *Nelson's essentials of pediatrics* (6th ed.). New York: Elsevier.

Marcell, J. J. (2003). Sarcopenia: Causes, consequences, and preventions. *Journals of Gerontology A: Biological and Medical Sciences*, M911–M916.

Marcia, J. E. (1980). Ego identity development. In J. Adelson (Ed.), *Handbook of adolescent psychology*. New York: Wiley.

Marcia, J. E. (1994). The empirical study of ego identity. In H. A. Bosma, T. L. G. Graafsma, H. D. Grotevant, & D. J. De Levita (Eds.), *Identity and development*. Newbury Park, CA: Sage.

Marcia, J. E. (2002). Identity and psychosocial development in adulthood. *Identity: An International Journal of Theory and Research, 2*, 7–28.

Margarett, J. A., & Deshpande-Kamat, N. (2009). Cognitive functioning and decline. In D. Carr (Ed.), *Encyclopedia of the life course and human development*. Boston: Gale Cengage.

Marion, M. C. (2010). *Introduction to early childhood education*. Upper Saddle River, NJ: Prentice Hall.

Marlatt, M. W., Lucassen, P. J. & van Pragg, H. (2010, in press). Comparison of neurogenic effects of fluoxetine, duloxetine, and running in mice. *Brain Research*.

Marret, S., & others. (2010). Prenatal low-dose aspirin and neurobehavioral outcomes of children born very preterm. *Pediatrics, 125*, e29–e34.

Marsh, H., Ellis, L., & Craven, R. (2002). How do preschool children feel about themselves? Unraveling measurement and multidimensional self-concept structure. *Developmental Psychology, 38*, 376–393.

Martin, C. L., & Ruble, D. N. (2010). Patterns of gender development. *Annual Review of Psychology* (Vol. 61). Palo Alto, CA: Annual Reviews.

Martin, J. A., Hamilton, B. E., Menacker, F., Sutton, P. D., & Matthews, T. J. (2005, November 15). Preliminary births for 2004: Infant and maternal health. *Health E-Stats*. Atlanta: National Center for Health Statistics.

Martin, L. R., Friedman, H. S., & Schwartz, J. E. (2007). Personality and mortality risk across the life span: The importance of conscientiousness as a biopsychosocial attribute. *Health Psychology, 26*, 428–436.

Martinez, M. E. (2010). *Learning and cognition*. Upper Saddle River, NJ: Merrill.

Martini, T. S., & Busseri, M. A. (2010). Emotion regulation strategies and goals as predictors of older mothers' and daughters' helping-related subjective well-being. *Psychology and Aging, 25*, 48–59.

Mascolo, M. F., & Fischer, K. (2007). The co-development of self and sociomoral emotions during the toddler years. In C. A. Brownell & C. B. Kopp (Eds.), *Transitions in early development*. New York: Guilford.

Mason, W. A., Hitchings, J. E., & Spoth, R. L. (2007). Emergence of delinquency and depressed mood throughout adolescence as predictors of late adolescent problem substance use. *Psychology of Addictive Behaviors, 21*, 13–24.

Masten, A. S., Obradovic, J., & Burt, K. B. (2006). Resilience in emerging adulthood: Developmental perspectives on continuity and transformation. In J. J. Arnett & J. L. Tanner (Eds.), *Emerging adults in America*. Washington, DC: American Psychological Association.

Matlin, M. W. (2008). *The psychology of women* (6th ed.). Belmont, CA: Wadsworth.

Matthews, D. J. (2009). Developmental transitions in giftedness and talent: Childhood into adolescence. In F. D. Horowitz, R. F. Subotnik, & D. J. Matthews (Eds.), *The development of giftedness and talent across the life span*. Washington, DC: American Psychological Association.

Mattson, S., & Smith, J. E. (2011). *Core curriculum for maternal-newborn nursing* (4th ed.). New York: Elsevier.

Maurya, D. K., Sundaram, C. S., & Bhargava, P. (2009). Proteome profile of the mature rat olfactory bulb. *Proteomics, 9*, 2593–2599.

Maxim, G. W. (2010). *Dynamic social studies for constructive classrooms* (9th ed.). Boston: Allyn & Bacon.

Mayer, K. D., & Zhang, L. (2009). Short- and long-term effects of cocaine abuse during pregnancy on heart development. *Therapeutic Advances in Cardiovascular Disease, 3*, 7–16.

Mayer, R. E. (2008). *Curriculum and instruction* (2nd ed.). Upper Saddle River, NJ: Prentice Hall.

Mayo Clinic. (2009). *Pregnancy week by week*. Retrieved on October 1, 2009, from www.mayoclinic.com/health/pregnancy-nutrition/PR00109

McAdams, D. P. (2009). *The person* (5th ed.). New York: Wiley.

McAdams, D. P., & Cox, K. S. (2011). Self and identity across the life span. In R. M. Lerner, A. Freund, & M. Lamb (Eds.), *Handbook of life-span development* (Vol. 2). New York: Wiley.

McAdams, D. P., & Olson, B. D. (2010). Personality development:

Continuity and change over the life course. *Annual Review of Psychology* (Vol. 61). Palo Alto, CA: Annual Reviews.

McCartney, K. (2003, July 16). Interview with Kathleen McCartney in A. Bucuvalas, "Child care and behavior." *HGSE News.* Cambridge, MA: Harvard Graduate School of Education.

McCartney, K., Dearing, E., Taylor, B. A., & Bub, K. L. (2007). Quality child care supports the achievement of low-income children: Direct and indirect pathways through caregiving and the home environment. *Journal of Applied Developmental Psychology, 28,* 411–426.

McClellan, M. D. (2004, February 9). Captain Fantastic: The interview. *Celtic Nation,* pp. 1–9.

McCombs, B. (2010). Learner-centered practices: Providing the context for positive learner development, motivation, and achievement. In J. Meece & J. Eccles (Eds.), *Handbook of schools, schooling, and human development.* New York: Routledge.

McCrae, C., & Dubyak, P. (2009). Sleep patterns and behavior. In D. Carr (Ed.), *Encyclopedia of the life course and human development.* Boston: Gale Cengage.

McCrae, R. R., & Costa, P. T. (2003). *Personality in adulthood* (2nd ed.). New York: Guilford.

McCrae, R. R., & Costa, P. T. (2006). Cross-cultural perspectives on adult personality trait development. In D. K. Mroczek & T. D. Little (Eds.), *Handbook of personality development.* Mahwah, NJ: Erlbaum.

McCullough, M. E., & Willoughby, B. L. (2009). Religion, self-regulation, and self-control: Associations, explanations, and implications. *Psychological Bulletin, 135,* 69–93.

McDonald, S. D., & others. (2010). Preterm birth and low birth weight among in vitro fertilization twins: A systematic review and meta-analyses. *European Journal of Obstetrics, Gynecology, and Reproductive Biology, 148,* 105–113.

McElhaney, K. B., Allen, J. P., Stephenson, J. C., & Hare, A. L. (2009). Attachment and autonomy during adolescence. In R. M. Lerner & L. Steinberg (Eds.), *Handbook of adolescent psychology.* New York: Wiley.

McGarry, J., Kim, H., Sheng, X., Egger, M., & Baksh, L. (2009). Postpartum depression and help-seeking behavior. *Journal of Midwifery and Women's Health, 54,* 50–56.

McHale, J., & Sullivan, M. (2008). Family systems. In M. Hersen & A. Gross (Eds.), *Handbook of Clinical Psychology, Volume II: Children and Adolescents.* New York: Wiley.

McIntosh, E., Gillanders, D., & Rodgers, S. (2010). Rumination, goal linking, daily hassles, and life events in major depression. *Clinical Psychology and Psychotherapy, 17,* 33–43.

McKain, W. C. (1972). A new look at older marriages. *The Family Coordinator, 21,* 61–69.

McLaughlin, K. (2003, December 30). Commentary in K. Painter, "Nurse dispenses dignity for dying." *USA Today,* Section D, pp. 1–2.

McLean, I. A., Balding, V., & White, C. (2005). Further aspects of male-on-male rape and sexual assault in greater Manchester. *Medical Science and Law, 45,* 225–232.

McLoyd, V. C., Kaplan, R., Purtell, K. M., Bagley, E., Hardaway, C. R., & Smalls, C. (2009). Poverty and socioeconomic disadvantage in adolescence. In R. M. Lerner & L. Steinberg (Eds.), *Handbook of adolescent psychology* (3rd ed.). New York: Wiley.

McMillan, J. H., & Wergin, J. F. (2010). *Understanding and evaluating educational research* (4th ed.). Upper Saddle River, NJ: Pearson.

McMurran, M., Jinks, M., Howells, K., & Howard, R. C. (2010). Alcohol-related violence defined by ultimate goals: A qualitative analysis of the features of three different types of violence by intoxicated young male offenders. *Aggressive Behavior, 36,* 67–79.

McMurray, R. G., Harrell, J. S., Creighton, D., Wang, Z., & Bangdiwala, S. I. (2008). Influence of physical activity on change in weight status as children become adolescents. *International Journal of Pediatric Obesity, 3,* 69–77.

McWilliams, L. A., & Bailey, S. J. (2010). Associations between adult attachment ratings and health conditions: Evidence from the National Comorbidity Survey replication. *Health Psychology, 29,* 446–453.

Meade, C. S., Kershaw, T. S., & Ickovics, J. R. (2008). The intergenerational cycle of teenage motherhood: An ecological approach. *Health Psychology, 27,* 419–429.

Mechakra-Tahiri, S. D., Zunzunegui, M. V., Preville, M., & Dube, M. (2010). Gender, social relationships and depressive disorders in adults aged 65 and over in Quebec. *Chronic Diseases in Canada, 30,* 56–65.

Meerlo, P., Sgoifo, A., & Suchecki, D. (2008). Restricted and disrupted sleep: Effects on autonomic function, neuroendocrine stress systems, and stress responsivity. *Sleep Medicine Review, 12*(3), 197–210.

Mehl, M. R., Vazire, S., Ramirez-Esparza, N., Slatcher, R. B., & Pennebaker, J. W. (2007). Are women really more talkative than men? *Science, 317,* 82.

Meltzi, G., & Ely, R. (2009). Language development in the school years. In J. B. Gleason & N. Ratner (Eds.), *The development of language* (7th ed.). Boston: Allyn & Bacon.

Meltzoff, A. N. (1988). Infant imitation and memory: Nine-month-old infants in immediate and deferred tests. *Child Development, 59,* 217–225.

Meltzoff, A. N. (2004). Imitation as a mechanism of social cognition: Origins of empathy, theory of mind, and the representation of action. In U. Goswami (Ed.), *Blackwell handbook of childhood cognitive development.* Malden, MA: Blackwell.

Meltzoff, A. N. (2005). Imitation. In B. Hopkins (Ed.), *Cambridge encyclopedia of child development.* Cambridge: Cambridge University Press.

Meltzoff, A. N. (2007). Infants' causal learning. In A. Gopnik & L. Schulz (Eds.), *Casual learning.* New York: Oxford University Press.

Meltzoff, A. N., & Brooks, R. (2009). Social cognition and language: The role of gaze following in early word learning. In J.

Colombo, P. McCardle, & L. Freund (Eds.), *Infant pathways to language.* Clifton, NJ: Psychology Press.

Menn, L., & Stoel-Gammon, C. (2009). Phonological development: Learning sounds and patterns. In J. Berko Gleason & N. Ratner (Eds.), *The development of language* (7th ed.). Boston: Allyn & Bacon.

Menon, M., Tobin, D. D., Corby, B. C., Menon, M., Hodges, E. V. E., & Perry, D. G. (2007). The developmental costs of high self-esteem in aggressive children. *Child Development, 78,* 1627–1639.

Meredith, N. V. (1978). Research between 1960 and 1970 on the standing height of young children in different parts of the world. In H. W. Reece & L. P. Lipsitt (Eds.), *Advances in child development and behavior* (Vol. 12). New York: Academic Press.

Merrill, D. M. (2009). Parent-child relationships: Later-life. In D. Carr (Ed.), *Encyclopedia of the life course and human development.* Boston: Gale Cengage.

Messinger, D. (2008). Smiling. In M. M. Haith & J. B. Benson (Eds.), *Encyclopedia of infant and early childhood development.* Oxford, UK: Elsevier.

Metsios, G. S., & others. (2010). Vascular function and inflammation in rheumatoid arthritis: The role of physical activity. *Open Cardiovascular Medicine Journal, 4,* 89–96.

Meyer, S. L., Wieble, C. M., & Woeber, K. (2010). Perceptions and practice of waterbirth: A survey of Georgia midwives. *Journal of Midwifery and Women's Health, 55,* 55–59.

Meyers, J. (2010, April 1). Suicides open eyes to bullying. *Dallas Morning News,* pp. 1A–2A.

Miano, S., & others. (2009). Development of NREM sleep instability-continuity (cyclic alternating pattern) in healthy term infants aged 1 to 4 months. *Sleep, 32,* 83–90.

Mibugua Gitau, G., Liversedge, H., Goffey, D., Hawton, A., Liversedge, N., & Taylor, M. (2009). The influence of maternal age on the outcomes of pregnancy complicated by bleeding at less than 12 weeks. *Acta Obstetricia et Gynecologica Scandinavica, 88,* 116–118.

Michael, R. T., Gagnon, J. H., Laumann, E. O., & Kolata, G. (1994). *Sex in America.* Boston: Little, Brown.

Mikami, A. Y., & others. (2010). Adolescent peer relationships and behavior problems predict young adults' communication on social networking websites. *Developmental Psychology, 46,* 46–56.

Mikels, J. A., Lockenhoff, C. E., Maglio, S. J., Carstensen, L. L., Goldstein, M. K., & Garber, A. M. (2010). Following your heart or your head: Focusing on emotions versus information differentially influences the decisions of younger and older adults. *Journal of Experimental Psychology Applied, 16,* 87–95.

Miller, P., & Plant, M. (2010). Parental guidance about drinking: Relationship with teenage psychoactive drug use. *Journal of Adolescence, 33,* 55–68.

Miller, P. H. (2011, in press). Piaget's theory: Past, present, and future. In U. Goswami (Ed.), *Wiley-Blackwell handbook of childhood cognitive development.* New York: Wiley.

Mills, D., & Mills, C. (2000). *Hungarian kindergarten curriculum translation.* London: Mills Production.

Milot, T., Ethier, L. S., St-Laurent, D., & Provost, M. A. (2010, in press). The role of trauma symptoms in the development of behavioral problems in maltreated preschoolers. *Child Abuse and Neglect.*

Minde, K., & Zelkowitz, P. (2008). Premature babies. In M. M. Haith & J. B. Benson (Eds.), *Encyclopedia of infancy and early childhood development.* Oxford, UK: Elsevier.

Minkler, M., & Fuller-Thompson, E. (2005). African American grandparents raising grandchildren: A national study using the Census 2000 American Community Survey. *Journals of Gerontology B: Psychological Sciences and Social Sciences, 60,* S82–S92.

Minnesota Family Investment Program. (2009). *Longitudinal study of early MFIP recipients.* Retrieved on January 12, 2009, from http://www.dhs.state.mn.us/main/idcplg?IdcService=GET_DYNAMIC_CONVERSION&

Minor, R. K., Allarad, J. S., Younts, C. M., Ward, T. M., & de Cabo, R. (2010, in press). Dietary interventions to extend life span and health span based on calorie restriction. *Journals of Gerontology A: Biological Sciences and Medical Sciences.*

Mischel, W. (2004). Toward an integrative science of the person. *Annual Review of Psychology* (Vol. 55). Palo Alto, CA: Annual Reviews.

Mishra, G. D., Cooper, R., Tom, S. E., & Kuh, D. (2009). Early life circumstances and their impact on menarche and menopause. *Women's Health, 5,* 175–190.

Mitchell, E. A. (2009). What is the mechanism of SIDS? Clues from epidemiology. *Developmental Psychology, 51,* 215–222.

Mitchell, K. J., Finkelhor, D., Jones, L. M., & Wolak, J. (2010). Use of social networking sites in online sex crimes against minors: An examination of national incidence and means of utilization. *Journal of Adolescent Health, 47,* 183–190.

Mitchell, M. L., & Jolley, J. M. (2010). *Research design explained* (7th ed.). Boston: Cengage.

Miura, K., & others. (2009). Four blood pressure indexes and the risk of stroke and myocardial infarction in Japanese men and women: A meta-analysis of 16 cohort studies. *Circulation, 119,* 1892–1898.

Miura, Y., Yasuda, K., Yamamoto, K., Kopike, M., Nishida, Y., & Kobayashi, K. (2007). Inhibition of Alzheimer amyloid aggregation with sulfated glycopolymers. *Biomacromolecules, 8,* 2129–2134.

MMWR. (2006, June 9). Youth risk behavior surveillance—United States 2005, Vol. 255. Atlanta: Centers for Disease Control and Prevention.

Modell, J. H. (2010, in press). Prevention of needless deaths from drowning. *Southern Medical Journal.*

Moen, P. (2007). Unpublished review of J. W. Santrock's *Life-span development* (12th ed.). New York: McGraw-Hill.

Moen, P. (2009a). Careers. In D. Carr (Ed.), *Encyclopedia of the* life course and human development. Boston: Gale Cengage.

Moen, P. (2009b). Dual-career couples. In D. Carr (Ed.), *Encyclopedia of the life course and human development*. Boston: Gale Cengage.

Moen, P., & Spencer, D. (2006). Converging divergences in age, gender, health, and well-being. In R. H. Binstock & L. K. George (Eds.), *Handbook of aging and the social sciences* (6th ed.). San Diego: Academic Press.

Moise, K. J. (2005). Fetal RhD typing with free DNA in maternal plasma. *American Journal of Obstetrics and Gynecology, 192,* 663–665.

Moleti, C. A. (2009). Trends and controversies in labor induction. *MCN The American Journal of Maternal and Child Nursing, 34,* 40–47.

Monserud, M. A. (2008). Intergenerational relationships and affectual solidarity between grandparents and young adults. *Journal of Marriage and the Family, 70,* 182–195.

Moody, H. R. (2009). *Aging* (6th ed.). Thousand Oaks, CA: Sage.

Moore, D. (2001). *The dependent gene.* W.H. Freeman.

Moos, B. (2007, July 4). Who'll care for aging boomers? *Dallas Morning News,* A1–2.

Moran, S., & Gardner, H. (2007). Hill, skill, and will: Executive function from a multiple intelligences perspective. In L. Meltzer (Ed.), *Executive function in education*. New York: Guilford.

Morgan, S. P. (2009). Childbearing. In D. Carr (Ed.), *Encyclopedia of the life course and human development.* Boston: Gale Cengage.

Morra, S., Gobbo, C., Marini, Z., & Sheese, R. (2008). *Cognitive development: Neo-Piagetian perspectives.* Mahwah, NJ: Erlbaum.

Morrison, G. S. (2011). *Fundamentals of early childhood education* (6th ed.). Upper Saddle River, NJ: Merrill.

Morrissey, T. W. (2009). Multiple child-care arrangements and young children's behavioral outcomes. *Child Development, 80,* 59–76.

Morrow, L. (2009). *Literacy development in the early years.* Boston: Allyn & Bacon.

Morrow-Howell, N. (2010, in press). Volunteering in later life: Research frontiers. *Journals of Gerontology B: Psychological Sciences and Social Sciences, 65B.*

Mroczek, D. K. (2001). Age and emotion in adulthood. *Current Directions in Psychological Science, 10,* 87–90.

Mroczek, D. K., Spiro, A., & Griffin, P. W. (2006). Personality and aging. In J. E. Birren & K. W. Schaie (Eds.), *Handbook of the psychology of aging* (6th ed.). San Diego: Academic Press.

Murphy, C. (2009). The chemical senses and nutrition in older adults. *Journal of Nutrition for the Elderly, 27,* 247–265.

Murphy-Hoefer, R., Alder, S., & Higbee, C. (2004). Perceptions about cigarette smoking and risks among college students. *Nicotine and Tobacco Research, 63*(Suppl. 3), S371–S374.

Murray, J. P., & Murray, A. D. (2008). Television: Uses and effects. In M. M. Haith & J. B. Benson (Eds.), *Encyclopedia of infant and early childhood development*. Oxford, UK: Elsevier.

Murray, S. S., & McKinney, E. L. (2010). *Foundations of maternal-newborn and women's health* (5th ed.). New York: Elsevier.

Musch, D. C., & others. (2009). Visual field progression in the Collaborative Initial Glaucoma Treatment Study: The impact of treatment and other baseline factors. *Ophthalmology, 116,* 200–207.

Mussen, P. H., Honzik, M., & Eichorn, D. (2002). Early adult antecedents of life satisfaction at age 70. *Journal of Gerontology, 37,* 316–322.

Mustelin, L., Silventoinen, K., Pietilainen, K., Rissanen, A., & Kaprio, J. (2009). Physical activity reduces the influence of genetic effects on BMI and waist circumference: A study of young adult twins. *International Journal of Obesity, 33,* 29–36.

Myers, D. G. (2010). *Psychology* (9th ed.). New York: Worth.

Myerson, J., Rank, M. R., Raines, F. Q., & Schnitzler, M. A. (1998). Race and general cognitive ability: The myth of diminishing returns in education. *Psychological Science, 9,* 139–142.

N

Nabe-Nielsen, K., & others. (2009). Differences between day and noonday workers in exposure to physical and psychological work factors in the Danish eldercare sector. *Scandinavian Journal of Work, Environment, and Health, 35,* 48–55.

Nader, P., O'Brien, M., Houts, R., Bradley, R., Belsky, J., Corsnoe, R., Friedman, S., Mei, Z., & Susman, E. J. (2006). Identifying risk for obesity in early childhood. *Pediatrics, 118,* e594–e601.

Nader, P. R., Bradley, R. H., Houts, R. M., McRitchie, S. L., & O'Brian, M. (2008). Moderate-to-vigorous physical activity from 9 to 15 years. *Journal of the American Medical Association, 300,* 295–305.

NAEYC. (2009). *Developmentally appropriate practice in early childhood programs serving children from birth through age 8*. Washington, DC: NAEYC.

Najman, J. M., Hayatbakhsh, M. R., Heron, M. A., Bor, W., O'Callaghan, M. J., & Williams, G. M. (2009). The impact of episodic and chronic poverty on child cognitive development. *Journal of Pediatrics, 154,* 284–289.

Nakamoto, J., & Schwartz, D. (2010). Is peer victimization associated with academic achievement? A meta-analytic review. *Social Development, 19,* 221–242.

Nansel, T. R., Overpeck, M., Pilla, R., Ruan, W., Simons-Morton, B., & Scheidt, P. (2001). Bullying behaviors among U.S. youth. *Journal of the American Medical Association, 285,* 2094–2100.

Napierski-Pranel, M. (2009). Eating disorders. In D. Carr (Ed.), *Encyclopedia of the life course and human development*. Boston: Gale Cengage.

Narici, M. V., & Maffulli, N. (2010, in press). Sarcopenia: Characteristics, mechanisms, and functional significance. *British Medical Bulletin.*

Natali, A., Pucci, G., Boldrini, B., & Schillaci, G. (2009). Metabolic syndrome: At the crossroads of cardiorenal risk. *Journal of Nephrology, 22*, 29–38.

National Assessment of Educational Progress. (2005). *The nation's report card: 2005.* Washington, DC: National Center for Education Statistics.

National Assessment of Educational Progress. (2007). *The nation's report card: 2007.* Washington, DC: U.S. Department of Education.

National Association for Sport and Physical Education. (2002). *Active Start: A Statement of Physical Activity Guidelines for Children Birth to Five Years.* Reston, VA: National Association for Sport and Physical Education Publications.

National Cancer Institute. (2008a). *Cancer trends progress report.* Retrieved January 15, 2008, from http://progressreport.cancer.gov/highlights.asp

National Cancer Institute. (2008b). *Acute lymphoblastic leukemia in children.* Retrieved January 15, 2008, from www.cancer.gov/cancertopics/factsheet/ALLinchildren

National Center for Education Statistics. (2002). *Work during college.* Washington, DC: U.S. Office of Education.

National Center for Education Statistics. (2008a). *The condition of education 2008.* Washington, DC: U.S. Department of Education.

National Center for Education Statistics. (2008b). *School dropout rates.* Washington, DC: U.S. Department of Education.

National Center for Education Statistics. (2008c). *Work during college.* Washington, DC: U.S. Office of Education.

National Center for Health Statistics. (2000). *Health United States, 2000, with adolescent health chartbook.* Bethesda, MD: U.S. Department of Health and Human Services.

National Center for Health Statistics. (2008a). *Death by age and selected causes: 2005. National Vital Statistics Report: Final data for 2005, 56,* No. 10, Table 114.

National Center for Health Statistics. (2008b). *Table 115: Deaths and*

death rates by leading causes of death and age: 2005. Atlanta: Centers for Disease Control and Prevention.

National Center for Health Statistics. (2009a). *Health United States.* Atlanta: Centers for Disease Control and Prevention.

National Center for Health Statistics. (2009b, January 7). *Public Release Statement: Preterm births rise 36 percent since early 1980s.* Atlanta: Centers for Disease Control and Prevention.

National Center for Health Statistics. (2010a). *Sexually transmitted infections.* Atlanta: Centers for Disease Control and Prevention.

National Center for Health Statistics. (2010b). *AIDS.* Atlanta: Centers for Disease Control and Prevention.

National Center for Health Statistics. (2010c). *Health United States 2010.* Atlanta Centers for Disease Control and Prevention.

National Clearinghouse on Child Abuse and Neglect. (2004). *What is child abuse and neglect?* Washington, DC: U.S. Department of Health and Human Services.

National Council on Aging. (2000, March). *Myths and realities survey results.* Washington, DC: Author.

National Institute of Mental Health. (2008). *Autism spectrum disorders (pervasive developmental disorders).* Retrieved January 6, 2008, from http://www.nimh.nih.gov/Publical/autism.cfm

National Institutes of Health. (2004). *Women's Health Initiative Hormone Therapy Study.* Bethesda, MD: National Institutes of Health.

National Sleep Foundation. (2006). *2006 Sleep in America poll.* Washington, DC: Author.

National Sleep Foundation. (2007). *Sleep in America poll 2007.* Washington, DC: Author.

National Vital Statistics. (2010). Births, marriages, divorces, deaths: Provisional data for November 2009. *National Vital Statistics Reports, 58* (23), 1–5.

National Vital Statistics Reports. (2008, June 11). Table 7. Deaths and death rates for the 10 leading causes of death in specified age

groups: United States, preliminary 2006. *National Vital Statistics Reports, 56,* No. 16, p. 30.

Neal, A. R. (2009). Autism. In D. Carr (Ed.), *Encyclopedia of the life course and human development.* Boston: Gale Cengage.

Needham, A. (2009). Learning in infants' object perception, object-directed action, and tool use. In A. Needham & A. Woodward (Eds.), *Learning and the infant mind.* New York: Oxford University Press.

Needham, A. Barrett, T., & Peterman, K. (2002). A pick-me-up for infants' exploratory skills: Early simulated experiences reaching for objects using "sticky mittens" enhances young infants' object exploration skills. *Infant Behavior and Development, 25,* 279–295.

Neer, R. M., & SWAN Investigators. (2010). Bone loss across menopausal transition. *Annals of the New York Academy of Sciences, 1192,* 66–71.

Nelson, C. A. (2003). Neural development and lifelong plasticity. In R. M. Lerner, F. Jacobs, & D. Wertlieb (Eds.), *Handbook of applied developmental science* (Vol. 1). Thousand Oaks, CA: Sage.

Nelson, C. A. (2008). Unpublished review of J. W. Santrock's *Topical life-span development* (5th ed.). New York: McGraw-Hill.

Nelson, C. A. (2011). Brain development and behavior. In A. M. Rudolph, C. Rudolph, L. First, G. Lister, & A. A. Gersohon (Eds.), *Rudolph's Pediatrics* (22nd ed.). New York: McGraw-Hill.

Nelson, L. J., Padilla-Walker, L. M., Carroll, J. S., Madsen, S. D., Barry, C. M., & Badger, S. (2007). "If you want me to treat you like an adult, start acting like one!" Comparing the criteria that emerging adults and their parents have for adulthood. *Journal of Family Psychology, 21,* 665–674.

Neugarten, B. L. (1964). *Personality in middle and late life.* New York: Atherton.

Neugarten, B. L. (1986). The aging society. In A. Pifer & L. Bronte (Eds.), *Our aging society: Paradox and promise.* New York: W. W. Norton.

Neugarten, B. L., Havighurst, R. J., & Tobin, S. S. (1968). Personality and patterns of aging. In B. L. Neugarten (Ed.), *Middle age and aging*. Chicago: University of Chicago Press.

Neugarten, B. L., & Weinstein, K. K. (1964). The changing American grandparent. *Journal of Marriage and the Family, 26*, 199–204.

Neville, H. J. (2006). Different profiles of plasticity within human cognition. In Y. Munakata & M. H. Johnson (Eds.), *Attention and Performance XXI: Processes of change in brain and cognitive development*. Oxford, UK: Oxford University Press.

New, R. (2007). Reggio Emilia as cultural activity theory in practice. *Theory into Practice, 46*, 5–13.

Newcombe, N. (2008). The development of implicit and explicit memory. In N. Cowan & M. Courage (Eds.), *The development of memory in childhood*. Philadelphia: Psychology Press.

Newman, M. L., Groom, C. J., Handelman, L. D., & Pennebaker, J. W. (2008). *Discourse Processes, 45*, 211–246.

Newton, A. W., & Vandeven, A. M. (2010). Child abuse and neglect: A worldwide concern. *Current Opinion in Pediatrics, 22*, 226–233.

NICHD. (2010). *SIDS facts*. Retrieved January 8, 2010, from http://www.nichd.nih/gov/sids

NICHD Early Child Care Network. (2001). Nonmaternal care and family factors in early development: An overview of the NICHD study of Early Child Care. *Journal of Applied Developmental Psychology, 22*, 457–492.

NICHD Early Child Care Network. (2002). Structure→Process→Outcome: Direct and indirect effects of child care quality on young children's development. *Psychological Science, 13*, 199–206.

NICHD Early Child Care Network. (2003). Does amount of time spent in child care predict socioemotional adjustment during the transition to kindergarten? *Child Development, 74*, 976–1005.

NICHD Early Child Care Network. (2004). Type of child care and children's development at 54 months. *Early Childhood Research Quarterly, 19*, 203–230.

NICHD Early Child Care Network. (2005). *Child care and development*. New York: Guilford.

NICHD Early Child Care Research Network. (2005). Predicting individual differences in attention, memory, and planning in first graders from experiences at home, child care, and school. *Developmental Psychology, 41*, 99–114.

NICHD Early Child Care Research Network. (2006). Infant-mother attachment classification: Risk and protection in relation to changing maternal caregiving quality. *Developmental Psychology, 42*, 38–58.

NICHD Early Child Care Research Network. (2009). Family-peer linkages: The meditational role of attentional processes. *Social Development, 18*, 875–895.

Nieto, S. (2010). Multicultural education in the United States: Historical realities, ongoing challenges, and transformative possibilities. In J. A. Banks (Ed.), *The Routledge international companion to multicultural education*. New York: Routledge.

Nisbett, R. (2003). *The geography of thought*. New York: Free Press.

Nitko, A. J., & Brookhart, S. M. (2011). *Educational assessment of students* (6th ed.). Boston: Allyn & Bacon.

Noble, J. M., & others. (2010). Association of C-reactive protein with cognitive impairment. *Archives of Neurology, 67*, 87–92.

Noftle, E. E., & Fleeson, W. (2010). Age differences in big five factor behavior averages and variabilities across the adult life span: Moving beyond retrospective, global summary accounts of personality. *Psychology and Aging, 25*, 95–107.

Nolen-Hoeksema, S. (2011, in press). *Abnormal psychology* (5th ed.). New York: McGraw-Hill.

Nomoto, M., & others. (2009). Inter- and intra-individual variation in L-dopa pharmacokinetics in the treatment of Parkinson's disease. *Parkinsonism and Related Disorders, 15*(Suppl. 1), S21–S24.

Norman, J. E., & others. (2009). Progesterone for the prevention of preterm birth in twin pregnancy (STOPPIT): A randomized, double-blind, placebo-controlled study and meta-analysis. *Lancet, 373*, 2034–2040.

Norouzieh, K. (2005). Case management of the dying child. *Case Manager, 36*, 54–57.

Nottelmann, E. D., Susman, E. J., Blue, J. H., Inoff-Germain, G., Dorn, L. D., Loriaux, D. L., Cutler, G. B., & Chrousos, G. P. (1987). Gonadal and adrenal hormone correlates of adjustment in early adolescence. In R. M. Lerner & T. T. Foch (Eds.), *Biological-psychological interactions in early adolescence*. Hillsdale, NJ: Erlbaum.

Nrugham, L., Holen, A., & Sund, A. M. (2010). Associations between attempted suicide, life events, depressive symptoms, and resilience in adolescents and young adults. *Journal of Nervous and Mental Disease, 198*, 131–136.

Nucci, L. (2006). Education for moral development. In M. Killen & J. Smetana (Eds.), *Handbook of moral development*. Mahwah, NJ: Erlbaum.

Nyaronga, D., & Wickrama, K. A. S. (2009). Health behaviors, childhood and adolescence. In D. Carr (Ed.), *Encyclopedia of the life course and human development*. Boston: Gale Cengage.

Nyqvist, K. H., & others. (2010, in press). Towards universal kangaroo mother care: Recommendations and report from the 1 European conference and 7 international workshops on Kangaroo care. *Acta Pediatrica*.

O

O'Brien, J. M., & Lewis, D. F. (2009). Progestins for the prevention of spontaneous preterm birth: Review and implications of recent studies. *Journal of Reproductive Medicine, 54*, 73–87.

O'Brien, M., & Moss, P. (2010). Fathers, work, and family policies in Europe. In M. E. Lamb (Ed.), *The role of the father in child development* (5th ed.). New York: Wiley.

O'Bryant, S. E., & others. (2009). Brain-derived neurotrophic factor levels in Alzheimer's disease. *Journal of Alzheimer's Disease, 17,* 337–341.

O'Connor, A. B., & Roy, C. (2008). Electric power plant emissions and public health. *American Journal of Nursing, 108,* 62–70.

O'Connor, D. B., Conner, M., Jones, F., McMillan, B., & Ferguson, E. (2009). Exploring the benefits of conscientiousness: An investigation of the role of daily stressors and health benefits. *Annals of Behavioral Medicine, 37,* 184–196.

O'Donnell, E., Kirwan, L. D., & Goodman, J. M. (2009). Aerobic exercise training in healthy postmenopausal women: Effects of hormone therapy. *Menopause, 16,* 770–776.

O'Donovan, G., & others. (2010). The ABC of physical activity for health: A consensus statement from the British Association of Sport and Exercise Science. *Journal of Sports Sciences, 28,* 573–591.

Oakes, L. M., Cashon, C., Casasola, M., & Rakison, D. (2010, in press). *Infant perception and cognition.* New York: Oxford University Press.

Oates, J., & Abraham, S. (2010). *Llewellyn-Jones fundamentals of obstetrics and gynecology* (9th ed.). New York: Elsevier.

Obenauer, S., & Maestre, L. A. (2008). Fetal MRI of lung hypoplasia: Imaging findings. *Clinical Imaging, 32,* 48–50.

Oberlander, S. E., Black, M. M., & Starr, R. H. (2007). African American adolescent mothers and grandmothers: A multigenerational approach to parenting. *American Journal of Community Psychology, 39,* 37–46.

Occupational Outlook Handbook. (2010–2011). Washington, DC: U.S. Department of Labor.

Offer, D., Ostrov E., Howard, K. I., & Atkinson, R. (1988). *The teenage world: Adolescents' self-image in ten countries.* New York: Plenum.

Ogden, C. L., Carroll, M. D., & Flegal, K. M. (2008). High body mass index for age among U.S. children and adolescents, 2003–2006.

Journal of the American Medical Association, 299, 2401–2405.

Oksuzyan, A., Juel, K., Vaupel, J. W., & Christensen, K. (2008). Men: good health and high mortality. Sex differences in health and aging. *Aging: Clinical and Experimental Research, 20,* 91–102.

Oladokun, R. E., Brown, B. J., & Osinusi, K. (2010, in press). Infant-feeding pattern of HIV-positive women in a prevention of mother-to-child transmissions (PMTCT) program. *AIDS Care.*

Oldehinkel, A. J., Ormel, J., Veenstra, R., De Winter, A., & Verhulst, F. C. (2008). Parental divorce and off-spring depressive symptoms: Dutch developmental trends during early adolescence. *Journal of Marriage and the Family, 70,* 284–293.

Olds, D. L., & others. (2004). Effects of home visits by paraprofessionals and nurses: Age four follow-up of a randomized trial. *Pediatrics, 114,* 1560–1568.

Olds, D. L., & others. (2007). Effects of nurse home visiting on maternal and child functioning: Age-9 follow-up of a randomized trial. *Pediatrics, 120,* e832–e845.

Oliver, S. R., & others. (2010, in press). Increased oxidative stress and altered substrate metabolism in obese children. *International Journal of Pediatric Obesity.*

Olweus, D. (2003). Prevalence estimation of school bullying with the Olweus bully/victim questionnaire. *Aggressive Behavior, 29* (3), 239–269.

Oman, D., & Thoresen, C. E. (2006). Do religion and spirituality influence health? In R. F. Paloutzian & C. L. Park (Eds.), *Handbook of the psychology of religion and spirituality.* New York: Guilford.

Onwuteaka-Philipsen, B. D., Rurup, M. L., Pasman, H. R., & van der Heide, A. (2010). The last phase of life: Who requests and who receives euthanasia or physician-assisted suicide? *Medical Care, 48,* 596–603.

Opalach, K., Rangaraju, S., Madorsky, I., Leeuwenburgh, C., & Notterpek, L. (2010). Lifelong calorie restriction alleviates age-related oxidative

damage on peripheral nerves. *Rejuvenation Research, 13,* 65–74.

Ornstein, P. A., Coffman, J. L., & Grammer, J. K. (2009). Learning to remember. In O. A. Barbarin & B. H. Wasik (Eds.), *Handbook of child development and early education.* New York: Guilford.

Ornstein, P. A., Coffman, J. L., Grammer, J. K., San Souci, P. P., & McCall, L. E. (2010). Linking the classroom context and the development of children's memory skills. In J. Meece & J. Eccles (Eds.), *Handbook of research on schools, schooling, and human development.* New York: Routledge.

Ornstein, P. A., & Light, L. L. (2011). Memory development across the life span. In R. M. Lerner & W. F. Overton (Eds.), *Handbook of life-span development* (Vol. 1). New York: Wiley.

Osofsky, J. D. (Ed.). (2007). *Young children and trauma.* New York: Guilford.

Osterhage, J. L., & Friedman, K. L. (2009). Chromosome end maintenance by telomerase. *Journal of Biological Chemistry, 284,* 16061–16065.

Ostfeld, B. M., Esposito, L., Perl, H., & Hegyi, T. (2010). Concurrent risks in sudden infant death syndrome. *Pediatrics, 125,* 447–453.

Ott, B. B. (2010). Progress in ethical decision making in the care of the dying. *Dimensions of Critical Care Nursing, 29,* 73–80.

Ott, C. H., Lueger, R. J., Kelber, S. T., & Prigerson, H. G. (2007). Spousal bereavement in older adults: Common, resilient, and chronic grief with defining characteristics. *Journal of Nervous and Mental Disease, 195,* 332–341.

Otto, B. W. (2010). *Language development in early childhood* (3rd ed.). Upper Saddle River, NJ: Prentice Hall.

Ozer, E. M., & Irwin, C. (2009). Adolescent and youth adult health: From basic health status to clinical interventions. In R. M. Lerner & L. Steinberg (Eds.), *Handbook of adolescent psychology* (3rd ed.). New York: Wiley.

P

Pahwa, R., & Lyons, K. E. (2010). Early diagnosis of Parkinson's disease: Recommendations from diagnostic clinical guidelines. *American Journal of Managed Care, 16*(Suppl.), S94–S99.

Palmore, E. B. (2004). Research note: Ageism in Canada and the United States. *Journal of Cross Cultural Gerontology, 19,* 41–46.

Pan, B. A., & Uccelli, P. (2009). Semantic development. In J. Berko Gleason & N. Ratner (Eds.), *The development of language* (7th ed.). Boston: Allyn & Bacon.

Panigrahy, A., Borzaga, M., & Blumi, S. (2010). Basic principles and concepts underlying recent advances in magnetic resonance imaging of the developing brain. *Seminars in Perinatology, 34,* 3–19.

Paquette, J., & others. (2010, in press). Risk of autoimmune diabetes in APECED: Association with short alleles of the 5'insulin VNTR. *Genes and Immunity.*

Parade, S. H., Leerkes, E. M., & Blankson, A. N. (2010). Attachment to parents, social anxiety, and close relationships of female students over the transition to college. *Journal of Youth and Adolescence, 39,* 127–137.

Paradis, J. (2010). Second language acquisition in childhood. In E. Hoff & M. Shatz (Eds.), *Blackwell handbook of language development.* New York: Wiley.

Pardo, J. V., & others. (2007). Where the brain grows old: Decline in anterior cingulate and medial prefrontal function with normal aging. *Neuroimage, 35,* 1231–1237.

Parens, E., & Johnston, J. (2009). Facts, values, and attention-deficit hyperactivity disorder (ADHD): An update on the controversies. *Child and Adolescent Psychiatry and Mental Health, 3,* 1.

Paris, S. G., & Paris, A. H. (2006). Assessments of early reading. In W. Damon & R. Lerner (Eds.), *Handbook of child psychology* (6th ed.). New York: Wiley.

Park, C. L. (2009). Meaning making in cancer survivorship. In P. T. P. Wong (Ed.), *The human quest for meaning* (2nd ed.). New York: Psychology Press.

Park, C. L. (2010). Making sense of the meaning literature: An integrative review of meaning making and its effects on adjustment to stressful life events. *Psychological Bulletin.*

Park, D. (2001). Commentary in Restak, R. *The secret life of the brain.* Washington, DC: Joseph Henry Press.

Park, D. C., & Goh, J. (2010, in press). Healthy aging: A neurocognitive perspective. In J. Cacioppo & G. Bentson (Eds.), *Handbook of cognitive neuroscience.* New York: Oxford.

Park, D. C., & Gutchess, A. H. (2005). Long-term memory and aging: A cognitive neuroscience perspective. In R. Cabeza, L. Nyberg, & D. Park (Eds.), *Cognitive neuroscience of aging: Linking cognitive and cerebral aging.* New York: Oxford University Press.

Park, D. C., & Reuter-Lorenz, P. (2009). The adaptive brain: Aging and neurocognitive scaffolding. *Annual Review of Psychology* (Vol. 60). Palo Alto, CA: Annual Reviews.

Park, H., Park, S., Shephard, R. J., & Aoyagi, Y. (2010, in press). Year-long physical activity and sarcopenia in older adults: The Nakanojo Study. *European Journal of Applied Physiology.*

Park, M. J., Paul Mulye, T., Adams, S. H., Brindis, C. D., & Irwin, C. E. (2006). The health status of young adults in the United States. *Journal of Adolescent Health, 39,* 305–317.

Parkay, F. W., & Stanford, B. H. (2010). *Becoming a teacher* (8th ed.). Upper Saddle River, NJ: Prentice Hall.

Parke, R. D., & Buriel, R. (2006). Socialization in the family: Ethnic and ecological perspectives. In W. Damon & R. Lerner (Eds.), *Handbook of child psychology* (6th ed.). New York: Wiley.

Parke, R. D., & Clarke-Stewart, A. K. (2011). *Social development.* New York: Wiley.

Parke, R. D., Leidy, M. S., Schofield, T. J., Miller, M. A., & Morris, K. L. (2008). Socialization. In M. M. Haith & J. B. Benson (Eds.), *Encyclopedia of infant and early childhood development.* Oxford, UK: Elsevier.

Parkes, A., Wight, D., Henderson, M., Stephenson, J., & Strange, V. (2009). Contraceptive method at first intercourse and subsequent pregnancy risk: Findings from a secondary analysis of 16-year-old girls from the RIPPLE and SHARE studies. *Journal of Adolescent Health, 44,* 55–63.

Parkes, K. R. (2006). Physical activity and self-rated health: Interactive effects of activity in work and leisure domains. *British Journal of Health Psychology, 11,* 533–550.

Parkin, D. M. (2009). Is the recent fall in incidence of post-menopausal breast cancer in UK related to changes in use of hormone replacement therapy? *European Journal of Cancer, 45,* 1649–1653.

Parnes, H. S., & Sommers, D. G. (1994). Shunning retirement: Work experiences of men in their seventies and early eighties. *Journal of Gerontology, 49,* S117–S124.

Parten, M. B. (1933). Social play among preschool children. *Journal of Abnormal and Social Psychology, 27,* 243–269.

Pasley, K., & Moorefield, B. S. (2004). Stepfamilies. In M. Coleman & L. Ganong (Eds.), *Handbook of contemporary families.* Thousand Oaks, CA: Sage.

Pasquini, E. S., Corriveau, K. H., Koenig, M., & Harris, P. L. (2007). Preschoolers monitor the relative accuracy of informants. *Developmental Psychology, 43,* 1216–1226.

Patrick, M. E., Abar, C., & Maggs, J. L. (2009). Drinking, adolescent. In D. Carr (Ed.), *Encyclopedia of the life course and human development.* Boston: Gale Cengage.

Patterson, C. J. (2009). Lesbian and gay parents and their children: A social science perspective. *Nebraska Symposium on Motivation, 54,* 142–182.

Patterson, C. J., & Farr, R. H. (2010, in press). Children of gay and lesbian parents: Reflections on the research-policy interface. In H. R.

Schaffer & Durkin, K. (Eds.), *Blackwell handbook of developmental psychology in action*. London: Blackwell.

Patterson, C. J., & Wainright, J. L. (2010, in press). Adolescents with same-sex parents: Findings from the National Longitudinal Study of Adolescent Health. In D. Brodzinsky, A. Pertman, & D. Kunz (Eds.), *Lesbian and gay adoption: A new American reality*. New York: Oxford University Press.

Paul, E. L., McManus, B., & Hayes, A. (2000). "Hookups": Characteristics and correlates of college students' spontaneous and anonymous sexual experiences. *Journal of Sexual Research, 37*, 76–88.

Paulhus, D. L. (2008). Birth order. In M. M. Haith & J. B. Benson (Eds.), *Encyclopedia of infant and early childhood development*. Oxford, UK: Elsevier.

Paus, T. (2009). Brain development. In R. M. Lerner & L. Steinberg (Eds.), *Handbook of adolescent psychology* (3rd ed.). New York: Wiley.

Paus, T., Toro, R., Leonard, G., Lerner, J. V., Lerner, R. M., Perron, M., & others. (2007). Morphological properties of the action-observation cortical network in adolescents with low and high resistance to peer influence. *Social Neuroscience, 3*(3), 303–316.

Paxson, C., Donahue, E., Orleans, C. T., & Grisso, J. A. (2006). Introducing the issue. *Future of Children, 16* (No. 1), 3–17.

Payer, L. (1991). The menopause in various cultures. In H. Burger & Boulet (Eds.), *A portrait of the menopause*. Park Ridge, NJ: Parthenon.

Pedersen, S., Vitaro, F., Barker, E. D., & Borge, A. I. H. (2007). The timing of middle childhood peer rejection and friendship: Linking early behavior to early adolescent adjustment. *Child Development, 78*, 1037–1051.

Peek, M. K. (2009). Marriage in later life. In D. Carr (Ed.), *Encyclopedia of the life course and human development*. Boston: Gale Cengage.

Pellicano, E. (2010). Individual differences in executive function and central coherence predict developmental changes in theory of mind in autism. *Developmental Psychology, 46*, 530–544.

Peng, X. D., Huang, C. Q., Chen, L. J., & Lu, Z. C. (2009). Cognitive behavioral therapy and reminiscence techniques for the treatment of depression in the elderly: A systematic review. *Journal of International Medical Research, 37*, 975–982.

Pennington, B. F., & others. (2009). Gene x environment interactions in reading disability and attention-deficit/hyperactivity disorder. *Developmental Psychology, 45*, 77–89.

Peplau, L. A., & Fingerhut, A. (2007). The close relationships of lesbians and gay men. *Annual Review of Psychology* (Vol. 58). Palo Alto, CA: Annual Reviews.

Perrig-Chiello, P., & Perren, S. (2005). The impact of past transitions on well-being in middle age. In S. L. Willis & M. Martin (Eds.), *Middle adulthood*. Thousand Oaks, CA: Sage.

Perrucci, C. C., & Perrucci, R. (2009). Unemployment. In D. Carr (Ed.), *Encyclopedia of the life course and human development*. Boston: Gale Cengage.

Perry, W. G. (1999). *Forms of ethical and intellectual development in the college years: A scheme*. San Francisco: Jossey Bass.

Peskin, H. (1967). Pubertal onset and ego functioning. *Journal of Abnormal Psychology, 72*, 1–15.

Peterson, C. C., Garnett, M., Kelly, A., & Attwood, T. (2009). Everyday social and conversation applications of theory-of-mind understanding by children with autism-spectrum disorders or typical development. *European Child and Adolescent Psychiatry, 18*, 105–115.

Peterson, J. L., & Hyde, J. S. (2010). A meta-analytic review of research on gender differences in sexuality, 1973–2007. *Psychological Bulletin, 136*, 21–38.

Peterson, M. D., Rhea, M. R., Sen, A., & Gordon, P. M. (2010, in press). Resistance exercise for muscular strength in older adults: A meta-analysis. *Aging Research Reviews*.

Peterson, M. J., & others. (2009). Physical activity as a preventive factor for frailty: The Health, Aging, and Body Composition Study. *Journals of Gerontology A: Biological Sciences and Medical Sciences, 64*, 61–68.

Philipsen, N. M., Johnson, A. D., & Brooks-Gunn, J. (2009). Poverty, effects on social and emotional development. *International Encyclopedia of Education*. Oxford, UK: Elsevier.

Phillips, D. A., & Lowenstein, A. (2011). Early care, education, and development. *Annual Review of Psychology* (Vol. 62). Palo Alto, CA: Annual Reviews.

Phillips, L. H., & Andres, P. (2010). The cognitive neuroscience of aging: New findings on compensation and connectivity. *Cortex, 46*, 421–424.

Phinney, J. S. (2008). Bridging identities and disciplines: Advances and challenges in understanding multiple identities. In M. Azmitia, M. Syed, & K. Radmacher (Eds.), *The intersections of personal and social identities: New Directions for Child and Adolescent Development, 120*, 97–109.

Phinney, J. S., & Ong, A. D. (2007). Ethnic identity in immigrant families. In J. E. Lansford, K. Deater-Deckard, & M. H. Bornstein (Eds.), *Immigrant families in contemporary society*. New York: Guilford.

Piaget, J. (1932). *The moral judgment of the child*. New York. Harcourt Brace Jovanovich.

Piaget, J. (1952). *The origins of intelligence in children* (M. Cook, Trans.). New York: International Universities Press.

Piaget, J. (1954). *The construction of reality in the child*. New York: Basic Books.

Piaget, J. (1962). *Play, dreams, and imitation*. New York: W. W. Norton.

Piaget, J., & Inhelder, B. (1969). *The child's conception of space* (F. J. Langdon & J. L. Lunger, Trans.). New York: W. W. Norton.

Pihlajamaki, M., Jauhialinen, A. M., & Soininen, H. (2009). Structural and functional fMRI in mild cognitive impairment. *Current Alzheimer Research, 6*, 179–185.

Pinette, M., Wax, J. & Wilson, E. (2004). The risks of underwater birth. *American Journal of Obstetrics & Gynecology, 190,* 1211–1215.

Pipp, S. L., Fischer, K. W., & Jennings, S. L. (1987). The acquisition of self *and* mother knowledge in infancy. *Developmental Psychology, 23,* 86–96.

Piruccello, L. M. (2010, in press). Preventing adolescent suicide. *Journal of Psychosocial Nursing and Mental Health Services.*

Pitkänen, T., Lyrra, A. L., & Pulkkinen, L. (2005). Age of onset of drinking and the use of alcohol in adulthood: A follow-up study from age 8–42 for females and males. *Addiction, 100,* 652–661.

Plomin, R., DeFries, J. C., McClearn, G. E., & McGuffin, P. (2009). *Behavioral genetics* (5th ed.). New York: Worth.

Plucker, J. (2010, July 19). Commentary in P. Bronson & A. Merryman, The creativity crisis. *Newsweek,* 45–46.

Pluess, M., & Belsky, J. (2009). Differential susceptibility to rearing experience: The case of child care. *Journal of Child Psychology and Psychiatry, 50,* 390–404.

Pollack, S., & others. (2010). Neurodevelopmental effects of early deprivation in postinstitutionalized children, *Child Development, 81,* 224–236.

Pollack, W. (1999). *Real boys.* New York: Owl Books.

Popenoe, D. (2008). *Cohabitation, marriage, and child well-being: A cross-national perspective.* Piscataway, NJ: The National Marriage Project, Rutgers University.

Popenoe, D. (2009). *The state of our unions 2008. Updates of social indicators: Tables and charts.* Piscataway, NJ: The National Marriage Project.

Popenoe, D., & Whitehead, B. D. (2006). *The state of our unions 2006.* New Brunswick, NJ: The National Marriage Project, Rutgers University.

Popham, W. J. (2011). *Classroom assessment* (6th ed.). Boston: Allyn & Bacon.

Posner, M. I., & Rothbart, M. K. (2007). *Educating the human brain.*

Washington, DC: American Psychological Association.

Pot, A. M., & others. (2010, in press). The impact of life review on depression in older adults: A randomized controlled trial. *International Psychogeriatrics.*

Powell, J. L. (2009). Global aging. In D. Carr (Ed.), *Encyclopedia of the life course and human development.* Boston: Gale Cengage.

Prabhakar, H. (2007). Hopkins interactive guest blog: The public health experience at Johns Hopkins. Retrieved January 31, 2008, from http://hopkins.typepad.com/guest/2007/03/the_public_heal.html

Prakash, R. S., Snook, E. M., Motl, R. W, & Kramer, A. F. (2010). Aerobic fitness is associated with gray matter volume and white matter integrity in multiple sclerosis. *Brain Research, 1341,* 41–51.

Pratt, M. W., Norris, J. E., Cressman, K., Lawford, H., & Hebblethwaite, S. (2008). Parents' stories of grandparenting concerns in the three-generational family: Generativity, optimism, and forgiveness. *Journal of Personality, 76,* 581–604.

Pratt, M. W., Norris, J. E., Hebblethwaite, S., & Arnold, M. O. (2008). International transmission of values: Family generality and adolescents' narratives of parent and grandparent value teaching. *Journal of Personality, 76,* 171–198.

Pressley, M. (2007). Achieving best practices. In L. B. Bambrell, L. M. Morrow, & M. Pressley (Eds.), *Best practices in literacy instruction.* New York: Guilford.

Pressley, M. (2007). An interview with Michael Pressley by Terri Flowerday and Michael Shaughnessy. *Educational Psychology Review, 19,* 1–12.

Prinstein, M. J., Boivan, M., & Bukowski, W. M. (2009). Peer reputations and psychological adjustment. In K. H. Rubin, W. M. Bukowski, & B. Laursen (Eds.), *Handbook of peer interactions, relationships, and groups.* New York: Guilford.

Prinstein, M. J., & Dodge, K. A. (2010). Current issues in peer influence research. In M. J.

Prinstein & K. A. Dodge (Eds.), *Understanding peer influence in children and adolescents.* New York: Guilford.

Prinstein, M. J., Rancourt, D., Guerry, J. D., & Browne, C. B. (2009). Peer reputations and psychological adjustment. In K. H. Rubin, W. M. Bukowksi, & B. Laursen (Eds.), *Handbook of peer interactions, relationships, and groups.* New York: Guilford.

Prinz, R. J., Sanders, M. R., Shapiro, C. J., Witaker, D. J., & Lutzker, J. R. (2009). Population-based prevention of child maltreatment: The U.S. Triple P System Population Trial. *Prevention Science, 10,* 1–12.

Pudrovska, T. (2009). Midlife crises and transitions. In D. Carr (Ed.), *Encyclopedia of the life course and human development.* Boston: Gale Cengage.

Pujazaon-Zazik, M., & Park, M. J. (2010). To tweet, or not to tweet: Gender differences and potential positive and negative health outcomes of adolescents' social internet use. *American Journal of Men's Health, 4,* 77–85.

Puma, M., & others. (2010). *Head Start impact study. Final report.* Washington, DC: Administration for Children & Families.

Putallaz, M., Grimes, C. L., Foster, K. J., Kupersmidt, J. B., Clie, J. D., & Dearing, K. (2007). Overt and relational aggression and victimization: Multiple perspectives within the school setting. *Journal of School Psychology, 45,* 523–547.

Putnam, S. P., Sanson, A. V., & Rothbart, M. K. (2002). Child temperament and parenting. In M. H. Bornstein (Ed.), *Handbook of parenting* (2nd ed.). Mahwah, NJ: Erlbaum.

Puzzanchera, C., & Sickmund, M. (2008, July). *Juvenile court statistics 2005.* Pittsburgh: National Center for Juvenile Justice.

Q

Quinn, P. C. (2011). Born to categorize. In U. Goswami (Ed.), *Wiley-Blackwell handbook of childhood cognitive development* (2nd ed.). New York: Wiley.

Quinn, P. C., Doran, M. M., Reiss, J. E., & Hoffman, J. E. (2009). Time course of visual attention in infant categorization of cats versus dogs: Evidence for a head bias as revealed through eye tracking. *Child Development, 80*, 151–161.

Quinn, P. C., Doran, M. M., Reiss, J. E., & Hoffman, J. E. (2010). Neural markers of subordinate-level categorization in 6- to 7-month-old infants. *Developmental Science, 13*, 499–507.

Quinn, P. C., & Eimas, P. D. (1996). Perceptual cues that permit categorical differentiation of animal species by infants. *Journal of Experimental Child Psychology, 63*, 189–211.

R

Racine, E., Karczewska, M., Seidler, M., Amaram, R., & Illes, J. (2010). How the public responded to the Schiavo controversy: Evidence from letters to editors. *Journal of Medical Ethics, 36*, 571–573.

Rafii, M. S., & Aisen, P. S. (2009). Recent developments in Alzheimer's disease therapeutics. *BMC Medicine, 7*, 7.

Raghuveer, G. (2010, in press). Lifetime cardiovascular risk of childhood obesity. *American Journal of Clinical Nutrition.*

Raikes, H., Pan, B. A., Luze, G., Tamis-LeMonda, C. S., Brooks-Gunn, J., Constantine, J., & others. (2006). Mother-child bookreading in low-income families: Correlates and outcomes during the first three years of life. *Child Development, 77*, 924–953.

Raikes, H. A., & Thompson, R. A. (2009). Attachment security and parenting quality predict children's problem-solving, attributions, and loneliness with peers. *Attachment and Human Development, 10*, 319–344.

Ramsey-Rennels, J. L., & Langlois, J. H. (2007). How infants perceive and process faces. In A. Slater & M. Lewis (Eds.), *Introduction to infant development* (2nd ed.). Malden, MA: Blackwell.

Rasmussen, M. M., & Clemmensen, D. (2010). Folic acid supplementation in pregnant women. *Danish Medical Bulletin, 57*, A4134.

Rasulo, D., Christensen, K., & Tomasini, C. (2005). The influence of social relations on mortality in later life: A study on elderly Danish twins. *Gerontologist, 45*, 601–608.

Rathunde, K., & Csikszentmihalyi, M. (2006). The developing person: An experiential perspective. In W. Damon & R. Lerner (Eds.), *Handbook of child psychology* (6th ed.). New York: Wiley.

Raven, P. H. (2011). *Biology* (9th ed.). New York: McGraw-Hill.

Rawlins, W. K. (2009). *The compass of friendship*. Thousand Oaks, CA: Sage.

Raz, N., Ghisletta, P., Rodrique, K. M., Kennedy, K. M., & Lindenberger, U. (2010, in press). Trajectories of brain imaging in middle-aged and older adults: Regional and individual differences. *Neuroimage.*

Read, J. P., Merrill, J. E., & Bytschkow, K. (2010). Before the party starts: Risk factors and reasons for "pregaming" in college students. *Journal of American College Health, 58*, 461–472.

Reese, E., Sparks, A., & Leyva, D. (2010). A review of parent interventions for preschool children's language and emergent literacy. *Journal of Early Childhood Literacy, 10*, 97–117.

Reeve, C. L., & Charles, J. E. (2008). Survey of opinions on the primacy of g and social consequences of ability testing: A comparison of expert and non-expert views. *Intelligence, 36*, 631–688.

Regalado, M., Sareen, H., Inkelas, M., Wissow, L. S., & Halfon, N. (2004). Parents' discipline of young children: Results from the National Survey of Early Childhood Health. *Pediatrics, 113*, 1952–1958.

Regev, R. H., Lusky, A., Dolfin, T., Litmanovitz, L., Arnon, S., Reichman, B., & others. (2003). Excess mortality and morbidity among small-for-gestational-age premature infants: A population based study. *Journal of Pediatrics, 143*, 186–191.

Reibis, R. K., Treszi, A., Wegscheider, K., Ehrlich, B., Dissmann, R., & Voller, H. (2010). Exercise capacity is the most powerful predictor of 2-year mortality in patients with left ventricular systolic dysfunction. *Herz, 35*, 104–110.

Reichstadt, L., Depp, C. A., Palinkas, L. A., Folsom, D. P., & Jeste, D. V. (2007). Building blocks of successful aging: A focus group study of older adults' perceived contributors to successful aging. *American Journal of Geriatric Psychiatry, 15*, 194–201.

Reiman, E. M., Langbaum, J. B., & Tariot, P. N. (2010). Alzheimer's prevention initiative: A proposal to evaluate presymptomatic treatments as quickly as possible. *Biomarkers in Medicine, 4*, 3–14.

Reuter-Lorenz, P., & Park, D. C. (2010, in press). Human neuroscience and the aging mind: A new look at old problems. *Journals of Gerontology B: Psychological Sciences and Social Sciences.*

Rey-Lopez, J. P., Vicente-Rodriguez, G., Biosca, M., & Moreno, L. A. (2008). Sedentary behavior and obesity development in children and adolescents. *Nutrition, Metabolism, and Cardiovascular Diseases, 18*, 242–251.

Reyna, V. F., & Rivers, S. E. (2008). Current theories of risk and rational decision making. *Developmental Review, 28*, 1–11.

Reynolds, F. (2010, in press). The effects of maternal labour analgesia on the fetus. *Best Practices & Research. Clinical Obstetrics & Gynaecology.*

Rhoades, G. K., Stanley, S. M., & Markman, H. J. (2009). The pre-engagement cohabitation effect: A replication and extension of previous findings. *Journal of Family Psychology, 23*, 107–111.

Rholes, W. S., & Simpson, J. A. (2007). Introduction: New directions and emerging issues in adult attachment. In W. S. Rholes & J. A. Simpson (Eds.), *Adult attachment*. New York: Guilford.

Richards, J. E. (2010, in press). Infant attention, arousal, and the brain. In L. Oakes, C. Cashon, M. Casasola,

around the world. *Psychology Today*, 71–76.

Smets, T., & others. (2010). Euthanasia in patients dying at home in Belgium: Interview study on adherence to legal standards. *British Journal of General Practice, 60*, e163-e170.

Smith, A. D. (1996). Memory. In J. E. Birren (Ed.), *Encyclopedia of gerontology*. San Diego: Academic Press.

Smith, A. D. (2007). Memory. In J. E. Birren (Ed.), *Encyclopedia of gerontology* (2nd ed.). San Diego: Academic Press.

Smith, J. B. (2009). High school organization. In D. Carr (Ed.), *Encyclopedia of the life course and human development*. Boston: Gale Cengage.

Smith, L. E., & Howard, K. S. (2008). Continuity of paternal social support and depressive symptoms among new mothers. *Journal of Family Psychology, 22*, 763–773.

Smith, L. M., Chang, L., Yonekura, M. L., Gilbride, K., Kuo, J., Poland, R. E., & others. (2001). Brain proton magnetic resonance spectroscopy and imaging in children exposed to cocaine in utero. *Pediatrics, 107*, 227.

Smith, M. A., & Berger, J. B. (2010). Women's ways of drinking: College women, high-risk alcohol use, and negative consequences. *Journal of College Student Development, 51*, 35–49.

Smith, N. G., Tarakeshwr, N., Hansen, N. B., Kochman, A., & Sikkema, K. J. (2009). Coping mediates outcome following a randomized group intervention for HIV-positive bereaved individuals. *Journal of Clinical Psychology, 65*, 319–325.

Smith, R. A., & Davis, S. F. (2010). *The psychologist as detective* (5th ed.). Upper Saddle River, NJ: Prentice Hall.

Smith, R. L., Rose, A. J., & Schwartz-Mette, R. A. (2010). Relational and overt aggression in childhood and adolescence: Clarifying mean-level gender differences and associations with peer acceptance. *Social Development, 19*, 243–269.

Smoreda, Z., & Licoppe, C. (2000). Gender-specific use of the domestic telephone. *Social Psychology Quarterly, 63*, 238–252.

Snarey, J. (1987, June). A question of morality. *Psychology Today*, pp. 6–8.

Snow, C. E., & Yang, J. Y. (2006). Becoming bilingual, biliterate, and bicultural. In W. Damon & R. Lerner (Eds.), *Handbook of child psychology* (6th ed.). New York: Wiley.

Snowdon, A. W., Hussein, A., High, L., Millar-Polgar, J., Patriack, L., & Ahmed, E. (2008). The effectiveness of a multimedia intervention on parents' knowledge and use of vehicle safety systems for children. *Journal of Pediatric Nursing, 23*, 126–139.

Snowdon, D. A. (2002). *Aging with grace: What the Nun Study teaches us about leading longer, healthier, and more meaningful lives*. New York: Bantam.

Snowdon, D. A. (2003). Healthy aging and dementia: Findings from the Nun Study. *Annals of Internal Medicine, 139*, 450–454.

Snowling, M. J., & Gobel, S. M. (2011). Reading development and dyslexia. In U. Goswami (Ed.), *Wiley-Blackwell handbook of childhood cognitive development* (2nd ed.). New York: Wiley.

Sokol, B. W., Snjezana, H., & Muller, U. (2010). Social understanding and self-regulation. In B. Sokol, U. Muller, J. Carpendale, A. Young, & G. Iarocci (Eds.), *Self- and social regulation*. New York: Oxford University Press.

Sophian, C. (1985). Perseveration and infants' search: A comparison of two- and three-location tasks. *Developmental Psychology, 21*, 187–194.

Sorte, J., Daeschel, I., & Amador, C. (2011). *Nutrition, health, and wellness*. Upper Saddle River, NJ: Prentice Hall.

Soska, K. C., Adolph, K. E., & Johnson, S. P. (2010). Systems in development: Motor skills acquisition facilitates 3D object completion. *Developmental Psychology, 46*, 129–138.

Spangler, G., Johann, M., Ronai, Z., & Zimmermann, P. (2009). Genetic and environmental influences on attachment disorganization. *Journal of Child Psychology and Psychiatry, 50*, 952–961.

Sparks, D. L., Hunsaker, J. G., Scheff, S. W., Kryscio, R. J., Henson, H., & Markesbery, W. R. (1990). Cortical senile plaques in coronary artery disease, aging, and Alzheimer's disease. *Neurobiology of Aging, 11*, 601–607.

Spelke, E. S. (2004). Core knowledge. In N. Kanwisher & J. Duncan (Eds.), *Attention and performance: Functional neuroimaging of visual cognition* (Vol. 20). Oxford, UK: Oxford University Press.

Spelke, E. S., & Kinzler, K. D. (2009). Innateness, learning and rationality. *Cognitive Development Perspectives, 3*, 96–98.

Spelke, E. S., & Owsley, C. J. (1979). Intermodal exploration and knowledge in infancy. *Infant Behavior and Development, 2*, 13–28.

Spence, A. P. (1989). *Biology of human aging*. Englewood Cliffs, NJ: Prentice Hall.

Spence, J. T., & Helmreich, R. (1978). *Masculinity and femininity: Their psychological dimensions*. Austin: University of Texas Press.

Sperling, H., Debruyne, F., Boermans, A., Beneke, M., Ulbrich, E., & Ewald, S. (2010, in press). The POTENT I randomized trial: Efficacy and safety of an orodispersible vardenafil formulation of the treatment of erectile dysfunction. *Journal of Sexual Medicine*.

Sprei, J. E., & Courtois, C. A. (1988). The treatment of women's sexual dysfunctions arising from sexual assault. In R. A. Brown & J. R. Fields (Eds.), *Treatment of sexual problems in individual and group therapy*. Great Neck, NY: PMA.

Spring, J. (2010). *Deculturalization and the struggle for equality* (6th ed.). New York: McGraw-Hill.

Srabstein, J. C., McCarter, R. J., Shao, C., & Huang, Z. J. (2006). Morbidities associated with bullying behaviors in adolescents: School based study of American adolescents. *International Journal of Adolescent Medicine and Health, 18*, 587–596.

Sroufe, L. A., Coffino, B., & Carlson, E. A. (2010). Conceptualizing the role of early experience: Lessons from the

Minnesota Longitudinal Study. *Developmental Review, 30,* 36–51.

Sroufe, L. A., Egeland, B., Carlson, E., & Collins, W. A. (2005a). The place of early attachment in developmental context. In K. E. Grossman, K. Krossman, & E. Waters (Eds.), *The power of longitudinal attachment research: From infancy and childhood to adulthood.* New York: Guilford.

Sroufe, L. A., Waters, E., & Matas, L. (1974). Contextual determinants of infant affectional response. In M. Lewis & L. Rosenblum (Eds.), *Origins of fear.* New York: Wiley.

Stager, L. (2009–2010). Supporting women during labor and birth. *Midwifery Today with International Midwife, 23,* 12–15.

Stake, R. E. (2010). *Qualitative research.* New York: Guilford.

Stangor, C. (2011). *Research methods for the behavioral sciences* (4th ed.). Boston: Cengage.

Stanley, S. M., Rhoades, G. K., Amato, P. R., Markman, H. J., & Johnson, C. A. (2010). The timing of cohabitation and engagement: Impact on first and second marriages. *Journal of Marriage and the Family, 72,* 906–918.

Starr, C. (2011). *Biology* (8th ed.). Boston: Cengage.

Starr, L. R., & Davila, J. (2009). Clarifying co-rumination: Associations with internalizing symptoms and romantic involvement among adolescent girls. *Journal of Adolescence, 32,* 19–37.

Staudinger, U. M. (1996). Psychologische Produktivität und Selbstenfaltung im Alter. In M. M. Baltes & L. Montada (Eds.), *Produktives Leben im Alter.* Hamburg: Campus.

Staudinger, U. M., & Gluck, J. (2011). Psychological wisdom research. *Annual Review of Psychology* (Vol. 62). Palo Alto, CA: Annual Reviews.

Staudinger, U. M., & Jacobs, C. B. (2011). Life-span perspectives on positive personality development in adulthood and old age. In R. M. Lerner, W. F. Overton, A. M. Freund, & M. E. Lamb (Eds.), *Handbook of life-span development.* New York: Wiley.

Steel, A. J., & Sutcliffe, A. (2010). Long-term health implications for children conceived by IVF/ICSI. *Human Fertility, 12,* 21–27.

Steele, J., Waters, E., Crowell, J., & Treboux, D. (1998, June). *Self-report measures of attachment: Secure bonds to other attachment measures and attachment theory.* Paper presented at the meeting of the International Society for the Study of Personal Relationships, Saratoga Springs, NY.

Steelman, L. C., & Koch, P. R. (2009). Sibling relationships, childhood, and adolescence. In D. Carr (Ed.), *Encyclopedia of the life course and human development.* Boston: Gale Cengage.

Steinberg, L. (2008). A social neuroscience perspective on adolescent risk-taking. *Developmental Review, 28,* 78–106.

Steinberg, L. (2009). Adolescent development and juvenile justice. *Annual Review of Clinical Psychology* (Vol. 5). Palo Alto, CA: Annual Reviews.

Steinberg, L. D., & Silk, J. S. (2002). Parenting adolescents. In M. Bornstein (Ed.), *Handbook of parenting* (2nd ed., Vol. 1). Mahwah, NJ: Erlbaum.

Steiner, J. E. (1979). Human facial expressions in response to taste and smell stimulation. In H. Reese & L. Lipsitt (Eds.), *Advances in child development and behavior, 13,* 257–295.

Steinhausen, H. C., Blattmann, B., & Pfund, F. (2007). Developmental outcome in children with intrauterine exposure to substances. *European Addiction Research, 13,* 94–100.

Steming, C. (2008). Centering Pregnancy: Group prenatal care. *Creative Nursing, 14,* 182–183.

Stern, D. N. (2010). A new look at parent-infant interaction: Infant arousal dynamics. In B. Lester & J. D. Sparrow (Eds.), *Nurturing children and families: Building on the legacy of T. Berry Brazelton.* New York: Wiley.

Sternberg, K., & Sternberg, R. J. (2010, in press). Love. In H. Pashler (Ed.), *Encyclopedia of the mind.* Thousand Oaks, CA: Sage.

Sternberg, R. J. (1986). *Intelligence applied.* San Diego: Harcourt Brace Jovanovich.

Sternberg, R. J. (1988). *The triangle of love.* New York: Basic Books.

Sternberg, R. J. (2004). Individual differences in cognitive development. In U. Goswami (Ed.), *Blackwell handbook of childhood cognitive development.* Malden, MA: Blackwell.

Sternberg, R. J. (2008). The triarchic theory of successful intelligence. In N. Salkind (Ed.), *Encyclopedia of educational psychology.* Thousand Oaks, CA: Sage.

Sternberg, R. J. (2009). *Cognitive psychology* (5th ed.). Belmont, CA: Wadsworth.

Sternberg, R. J. (2010a, in press). Intelligence. In B. McGaw, P. Peterson, & E. Baker (Eds.), *The international encyclopedia of education* (3rd ed.). New York: Elsevier.

Sternberg, R. J. (2010b, in press). The triarchic theory of successful intelligence. In B. Kerr (Ed.), *Encyclopedia of giftedness, creativity, and talent.* Thousand Oaks, CA: Sage.

Sternberg, R. J. (2011a, in press). Individual differences in cognitive development. In U. Goswami (Ed.), *Blackwell handbook of childhood cognitive development.* Malden, MA: Blackwell.

Sternberg, R. J. (2011b, in press). Intelligence. In B. McGaw, P. Peterson, & E. Baker (Eds.), *International encyclopedia of education* (3rd ed.). New York: Elsevier.

Sternberg, R. J. (2011c, in press). Intelligence in cultural context. In M. Gelfand, C-Y Chiu, & Y-Y Hong (Eds.), *Advances in cultures and psychology* (Vol. 2). New York: Oxford University Press.

Sternberg, R. J. (2011d). Teaching for creativity. In R. A. Beghetto & J. C. Kaufman (Eds.), *Nurturing creativity in the classroom.* New York: Cambridge University Press.

Sternberg, R. J., Jarvin, I., & Grigorenko, E. L. (2011, in press). *Explorations of the nature of giftedness.* New York: Cambridge University Press.

Wentzel, K. R., & Asher, S. R. (1995). The academic lives of neglected, rejected, popular, and controversial children. *Child Development, 66*, 754–763.

Wentzel, K. R., Barry, C. M., & Caldwell, K. A. (2004). Friendships in middle school: Influences on motivation and school adjustment. *Journal of Educational Psychology, 96*, 195–203.

Wertsch, J. V. (2007). Mediation. In H. Daniels, J. Wertsch, & M. Cole (Eds.), *The Cambridge companion to Vygotsky.* New York: Cambridge University Press.

Westerhof, G. J. (2009). Age identity. In D. Carr (Ed.), *Encyclopedia of the life course and human development.* Boston: Gale Cengage.

Westlake, C., Evangelista, L. S., Stromberg, A., Ter-Galstanyan, A., Vazirani, S., & Dracup, K. (2007). Evaluation of a web-based education and counseling pilot for older heart failure patients. *Progress in Cardiovascular Nursing, 22*, 20–26.

Weston, M. J. (2010). Magnetic resonance imaging in fetal medicine: A pictorial review of current and developing indications. *Postgraduate Medicine Journal, 86*, 42–51.

Westphal, D. M., & McKee, S. A. (2009). End-of-life decision making in the intensive care unit: Physician and nurse perspectives. *American Journal of Medical Quality, 24*, 222–228.

Wheeler, S. B. (2010, in press). Effects of self-esteem and academic performance on adolescent decision-making: An examination of early sexual intercourse and illegal substance abuse. *Journal of Adolescent Health.*

White, B., Frederiksen, J., & Collins, A. (2010). The interplay of scientific inquiry and metacogniton: More than a marriage of convenience. In D. J. Hacker, J. Dunlosky, & A. C. Graesser (Eds.), *Handbook of metacognition and education.* New York: Psychology Press.

White, H. R., Fleming, C. B., Catalano, R. F., & Bailey, J. A. (2009). Prospective associations among alcohol use–related sexual enhancement expectancies, sex after alcohol use, and casual sex. *Psychology of Addictive Behaviors, 23*, 702–707.

White, J. W. (2001). Aggression and gender. In J. Worell (Ed.), *Encyclopedia of gender and women.* San Diego: Academic Press.

White, J. W., & Frabutt, J. M. (2006). Violence against girls and women. In J. Worell & C. D. Goodheart (Eds.), *Handbook of girls' and women's psychological health.* New York: Oxford University Press.

White, L. (1994). Stepfamilies over the life course: Social support. In A. Booth & J. Dunne (Eds.), *Stepfamilies: Who benefits and who does not.* Hillsdale, NJ: Erlbaum.

Whitehead, B. D., & Popenoe, D. (2003). *The state of our unions.* Piscataway, NJ: The National Marriage Project, Rutgers University.

Wick, P., & others. (2010). Barrier capacity of the human placenta for nanosized materials. *Environmental Health Perspectives, 118*, 432–436.

Wickham, S. (2009). *Midwifery: Best practice.* London: Elsevier.

Wider, C., Foroud, T., & Wszolek, Z. K. (2010). Clinical implications of gene discovery in Parkinson's disease and Parkinsonism. *Movement Disorders, 25*(Suppl. 1), S15–S20.

Widman, L., & McNulty, J. K. (2010). Sexual narcissism and the perpetration of sexual aggression. *Archives of Sexual Behavior, 39*, 926–939.

Wiesner, M., & Ittel, A. (2002). Relations of pubertal timing and depressing symptoms to substance use in early adolescence. *Journal of Early Adolescence, 22*, 5–23.

Wight, G., Cummings, J. R., Karlamangia, A. S., & Aneshensei, C. S. (2009). Urban neighborhood context and change in depressive symptoms in late life. *Journals of Gerontology B: Psychological Sciences and Social Sciences, 64*, 247–251.

Williams, D., & Happe, F. (2010). Representing intentions in self and others: Studies of autism and typical development. *Developmental Science, 13*, 307–319.

Williamson, D. L, Raue, U., Slivka, D. R., & Trappe, S. (2010). Resistance exercise, skeletal muscle FOXO3A, and 85-year-old women. *Journals of Gerontology A: Biological Sciences and Medical Sciences, 65A*, 335–343.

Williamson, J. D., & others. (2009). Changes in cognitive function in a randomized trial of physical activity: Results of the Lifestyle Interventions and Independence for Elders Pilot Study. *Journals of Gerontology A: Biological Sciences and Medical Sciences, 64*, 688–694.

Willis, S. L., & Martin, M. (2005). Preface. In S. L. Willis & M. Martin (Eds.), *Middle adulthood.* Thousand Oaks, CA: Sage.

Willis, S. L., & Schaie, K. W. (1986) Training the elderly on the ability factors of spatial orientation and inductive reasoning. *Psychology and Aging, 1*, 239–247.

Willis, S. L., & Schaie, K. W. (1994). Assessing everyday competence in the elderly. In C. Fisher & R. Lerner (Eds.), *Applied developmental psychology.* Hillsdale, NJ: Erlbaum.

Willis, S. L., & Schaie, K. W. (2005). Cognitive trajectories in midlife and cognitive functioning in old age. In S. K. Willis & M. Martin (Eds.), *Middle adulthood.* Thousand Oaks, CA: Sage.

Wilson, B., & Stuchbury, R. (2010). Do partnerships last? Comparing marriage and cohabitation using longitudinal census data. *Population Trends, 139*, 37–63.

Wilson, B. J. (2008). Media and children's aggression, fear, and altruism. *Future of Children, 18*(1), 87–118.

Wilson, D. R. (2010). Breastfeeding: A women's issue. *Beginnings, 30*, 6–9.

Wilson, M. N. (2008). Poor fathers' involvement in the lives of their children. In D. R. Crane & T. B. Heaton (Eds.), *Handbook of families and poverty.* Thousand Oaks, CA: Sage.

Windle, W. F. (1940). *Physiology of the fetus.* Philadelphia: W. B. Saunders.

Windsor, T. D., & Butterworth, P. (2010). Supportive, aversive, ambivalent, and indifferent partner evaluations in midlife and young-old adulthood. *Journals of Gerontology B: Psychological Sciences and Social Sciences, 65B,* 287–295.

Wink, P., & Dillon, M. (2002). Spiritual development across the adult life course: Findings from a longitudinal study. *Journal of Adult Development, 9,* 79–94.

Winne, P. H., & Nesbit, J. C. (2010). The psychology of academic achievement. *Annual Review of Psychology* (Vol. 61). Palo Alto, CA: Annual Reviews.

Winner, E. (1996). *Gifted children: Myths and realities.* New York: Basic Books.

Winner, E. (2009). Toward broadening our understanding of giftedness: The spatial domain. In F.D. Horowitz, R.F. Subotnik, & D.J. Matthews (Eds.), *The development of giftedness and talent across the life span.* Washington, DC: American Psychological Association.

Winsler, A., Carlton, M. P., & Barry, M. J. (2000). Age-related changes in preschool children's systematic use of private speech in a natural setting. *Journal of Child Language, 27,* 665–687.

Wise, P. M. (2006). Aging of the female reproductive system. In E. J. Masoro & S. N. Austad (Eds.), *Handbook of the biology of aging* (6th ed.). San Diego: Academic Press.

Witkin, H. A., Mednick, S. A., Schulsinger, R., Bakkestrom, E., Christiansen, K. O., Goodenbough, D. R., & others. (1976). Criminality in XYY and XXY men. *Science, 193,* 547–555.

Witte, A. V., Fobker, M., Gellner, R., Knecht, S., & Fioel, A. (2009). Caloric restriction improves memory in elderly humans. *Proceedings of the National Academy of Sciences U.S.A., 106,* 1255–1260.

Wittig, S. L., & Spatz, D. L. (2008). Induced lactation: Gaining a better understanding. *MCN. Journal of Maternal Child Nursing, 33,* 76–81.

Wittmeier, K. D., Mollar, R. C., & Kriellaars, D. J. (2008). Physical activity intensity and risk of overweight and adiposity in children. *Obesity, 16,* 415–420.

Witvliet, M., & others. (2010). Peer group affiliation in children: The role of perceived popularity, likeability, and behavioral similarity in bullying. *Social Development, 19,* 285–303.

Woelders, L. C. S., Larsen, J. K., Scholte, R., Cillessen, T, & Engles, R. C. M. E. (2010, in press). Friendship group influences on body dissatisfaction and dieting among adolescent girls: A prospective study. *Journal of Adolescent Health.*

Wolak, J., Mitchell, K., & Finkelhor, D. (2007). Unwanted and wanted exposure to online pornography in a national sample of youth Internet users. *Pediatrics, 119,* 247–257.

Wolfson, A. R. (2010). Adolescents and emerging adults' sleep patterns: New developments. *Journal of Adolescent Health, 46,* 97–99.

Wolkowitz, O. M., Epel, E. S. Reus, V. I., & Mellon, S. H. (2010). Depression gets old fast: Do stress and depression accelerate cell aging? *Depression and Anxiety, 27,* 327–338.

Woloski-Wruble, A. C., Oliel, Y., Leefsman, M., & Hochner-Celnikier, C. (2010, in press). Sexual activities, sexual and life satisfaction, and successful aging in women. *Journal of Sexual Medicine.*

Wood, L. D. (2010). Clinical review and treatment of select adverse effects of dopamine receptor agonists in Parkinson's disease. *Drugs and Aging, 27,* 295–310.

Wood, J., Chaparro, A., Carberry, T., & Chu, B. S. (2010). Effect of simulated visual impairment on nighttime driving performance. *Optometry and Vision Science.*

Wood, J. T. (2011). *Communication mosaics* (6th ed.). Boston: Cengage.

Wood, J. T. (2012, in press). *Communication in our lives* (6th ed.). Boston: Cengage.

Woodward, A. L., & Markman, E. M. (1998). Early word learning. In D. Kuhn & R. S. Siegler (Eds.), *Handbook of child psychology* (5th ed., Vol. 2). New York: Wiley.

World Health Organization. (2000, February 2). *Adolescent health behavior in 28 countries.* Geneva, Switzerland: World Health Organization.

Worthington, E. L. (1989). Religious faith across the life span: Implications for counseling and research. *Counseling Psychologist, 17,* 555–612.

Worthman, C. M. (2010). Survival and health. In M. H. Bornstein (Ed.), *Handbook of cultural developmental science.* New York: Psychology Press.

Wright, R. O., & Christiani, D. (2010, in press). Gene-environment interaction and children's health and development. *Current Opinion in Pediatrics.*

Wu, T., Gao, X., Chen, M., & van Dam, R. M. (2009). Long-term effectiveness of diet-plus-exercise interventions vs. diet-only interventions for weight loss: A meta-analysis. *Obesity, 10,* 313–323.

Wu, W. T. (2010). Botox facial slimming/facial sculpting: The role of botulinum toxin-A in the treatment of hypertrophic masseteric muscle and parotid enlargement to narrow the lower facial width. *Facial Plastic Surgery Units of North America, 18,* 133–140.

Wyn, R., & Peckham, E. (2010). Health and health care access among California women ages 50–64. *Policy Brief: UCLA Center for Health Policy Research,* (PB 2010–1), 1–8.

X

Xue, F., Holzman, C., Rahbar, M. H., Trosko, K., & Fischer, L. (2007). Maternal fish consumption, mercury levels, and risk of preterm delivery. *Environmental Health Perspectives, 115,* 42–47.

Y

Yancy, W. S., Almirall, D., Maciejewski, M. L., Kolotkin, R. L., McDuffie, J. R., & Westman, E. C. (2009). Effects of two weight-loss diets on health-related quality of life. *Quality of Life Research, 18,* 281–289.

Yang, Y., & Lee, L. C. (2010). Dynamics and heterogeneity in the process of human frailty and aging: Evidence from the U.S. older adult population. *Journals of Gerontology B: Psychological Sciences and Social Sciences, 65B,* 246–255.

Yarber, W., Sayad, B., & Strong, B. (2010). *Human Sexuality* (7th ed.). New York: McGraw-Hill.

Yazdy, M. M., Liu, S., Mitchell, A. A., & Werler, N. M. (2010). Maternal dietary glycemic intake and the risk of neural tube defects. *American Journal of Epidemiology, 171,* 407–414.

Yell, M. L., & Drasgow, E. (2009). *What every teacher should know about No Child Left Behind* (2nd ed.). Upper Saddle River, NJ: Prentice Hall.

Yetukuri, L., & others. (2010, in press). Composition and lipid spatial distribution of high density lipoprotein particles in subjects with low and high HDL-cholesterol. *Journal of Lipid Research.*

Yokoya, T., Demura, S., & Sato, S. (2009). Three-year follow-up of the fall risk and physical function characteristics of the elderly participating in a community exercise class. *Journal of Physiological Anthropology, 28,* 55–62.

Yolton, K., & others. (2010). Associations between secondhand smoke exposure and sleep patterns in children. *Pediatrics, 125,* e261–e268.

Yoon, C., Cole, C. A., & Lee, M. P. (2009). Consumer decision making and aging: Current knowledge and future directions. *Journal of Consumer Psychology, 19,* 2–16.

Yoshida, S., Kozu, T., Gotoda, T., & Saito, D. (2006). Detection and treatment of early cancer in high-risk populations. *Best Practice and Research: Clinical Gastroenterology, 20,* 745–765.

Young, K. T. (1990). American conceptions of infant development from 1955 to 1984: What the experts are telling parents. *Child Development, 61,* 17–28.

Z

Zaff, J. F., Hart, D., Flanagan, C. A., Youniss, J., & Levine, P. (2011, in press). Developing civic engagement within a civic context. In R. M. Lerner, M. E. Lamb, & A. M. Freund (Eds.), *Handbook of life-span development* (Vol. 2). New York: Wiley.

Zamperetti, N., & Bellomo, R. (2009). Total brain failure: A new contribution to the President's Council on Bioethics to the definition of death according to the neurological standard. *Intensive Care Medicine, 35,* 1673–1677.

Zayas, L., Gulbas, L. E., Fedoravivicus, N., & Cabassa, L. J. (2010, in press). Patterns of distress, precipitating events, and reflections on suicide attempts by young Latinas. *Social Science & Medicine.*

Zeifman, D., & Hazan, C. (2008). Pair bonds as attachments: Reevaluating the evidence. In J. Cassidy & P. R. Shaver (Eds.), *Handbook of attachment* (2nd ed.). New York: Guilford.

Zelazo, P. D., & Lee, W. S. C. (2010). Brain development: An overview. In R. M. Lerner & W. F. Overton (Eds.), *Handbook of life-span development* (Vol. 1). New York: Wiley.

Zeskind, P. S., Klein, L., & Marshall, T. R. (1992). Adults' perceptions of experimental modifications of durations and expiratory sounds in infant crying. *Developmental Psychology, 28,* 1153–1162.

Zettel-Watson, L., & Rook, K. S. (2009). Friendship, later life. In D. Carr (Ed.), *Encyclopedia of the life course and human development.* Boston: Gale Cengage.

Zhang, L-F., & Sternberg, R. J. (2011, in press). Learning in cross-cultural perspective. In T. Husen & T. N. Postlethwaite (Eds.), *International encyclopedia of education* (3rd ed.). New York: Elsevier.

Zhou, M., & others. (2010). Forebrain over expression of CK1delta leads to down-regulation of dopamine receptors and altered locomotor activity reminiscent of ADHD. *Proceedings of the National Academy of Sciences, 107,* 4401–4406.

Zhu, D., Kang, Q., Huang, P. Y., He, T. C., & Xie, P. (2009). Neurogenesis-related genes expression profiling of mouse fibroblastic stem cell inducted by Wnt scaling. *Neural Research, 31,* 200–203.

Zhu, D. C., Zacks, R. T., & Slade, J. M. (2010). Brain activation during interference resolution in young and older adults: An fMRI study. *Neuroimage, 50,* 810–817.

Zielinski, D. S. (2009). Child maltreatment and adult socioeconomic well-being. *Child Abuse and Neglect, 33,* 666–678.

Zigler, E. F., Gilliam, W. S., & Jones, S. M. (2006). *A vision for universal preschool education.* New York: Cambridge University Press.

Zigler, E. F., & Styfco, S. J. (1994). Head Start: Criticisms in a constructive context. *American Psychologist, 49,* 127–132.

Zigler, E. F., & Styfco, S. J. (2010). *The hidden history of Head Start.* New York: Oxford University Press.

Zimmer-Gembeck, M. J., & Helfand, M. (2008). Ten years of longitudinal research on U.S. adolescent sexual behavior: Developmental correlates of sexual intercourse, and the importance of age, gender, and ethnic background. *Developmental Review, 28,* 153–224.

Zisook, S., & others. (2010). Bereavement, complicated grief, and DSM, part 1: Depression. *Journal of Clinical Psychiatry, 71,* 955–956.

Zou, L., & others. (2010). Proliferation, migration, and neuronal differentiation of the endogenous neural progenitors in hippocampus after fimbria fornix transection. *International Journal of Neuroscience, 120,* 192–200.

Zou, Y., Misri, S., Shay, J. W., Pandita, T. K., & Wright, W. E. (2009). Altered states of telomere deprotection and the two-stage mechanism of replicative aging. *Molecular and Cellular Biology, 29,* 2390–2397.

Zuckoff, A., Shear, K., Frank, E., Daley, D. C., Seligman, K., & Silowash, R. (2006). Treating complicated grief and substance use disorders: A pilot study. *Journal of Substance Abuse and Treatment, 30,* 205–211.

Credits

Photo Credits

Chapter 1
Opener: © Julie Habel/Corbis; p. 2 (top left): © Seanna O'Sullivan; (bottom left): WBBM-TV/AFP/Getty Images; (top right): © AP Wide World Photos; (bottom right): Photograph of Alice Walker, Alice Walker Papers, Manuscript, Archives and Rare Book Library, Emory University; p. 3: © Image Source/Getty Images; p. 5: FEMA Photo/Andrea Booher; p. 6: Courtesy of Luis Vargas; p. 7: © Nancy Agostini; p. 8: Naser Siddique/UNICEF Bangladesh; p. 12 (left): KAREN PULFER FOCHT/The Commercial Appeal/Landov; p. 12 (right): Getty Images; p. 16: © Bettmann/Corbis; p. 17 (left to right): © Stockbyte/Getty Images; © BananaStock/PunchStock; image100/Corbis; © RF/Corbis; p. 18 (top): © Yves de Braine/Black Star/Stock Photo; p. 18 (bottom): A.R. Lauria/Dr. Michael Cole, Laboratory of Human Cognition, University of California, San Diego; p. 19: Courtesy Albert Bandura, Stanford University; p. 21: Time & Life Pictures/Getty Images; p. 22: Courtesy of Urie Bronfenbrenner; p. 26: © Digital Vision/PunchStock; p. 29 (left): George Grantham Bain Collection, Library of Congress, Reproduction Number #LC-USZ62-63966; (right): Jamie Grill/Blend Images/Corbis; p. 30: (left to right): © Brand X Pictures/PunchStock; © Digital Vision; Laurence Mouton/Photoalto/PictureQuest; © Stockbyte; Getty Images/SW Productions; © Blue Moon Stock/Alamy Images; Doug Menuez/Getty Images; Ryan McVay Getty Images

Chapter 2
p. 32: © Alamy Images; p. 33: © Enrico Ferorelli Enterprises; p. 34: © 1996 PhotoDisc, Inc./Getty Images; p. 35: © David Wilkie; p. 37: © Custom Medical Stock Photo; p. 40: © James Shaffer/PhotoEdit; p. 41: Courtesy of Jillian Ranson; p. 42: Courtesy of Holly Ishmael; p. 43: © RF/Corbis; p. 45: © Science Source/Photo Researchers; p. 48: © Lennart Nilsson/Albert Bonniers Forlag AB/A Child Is Born, Dell Publishing Company; p. 49: © Lennart Nilsson/Albert Bonniers Forlag AB/A Child Is Born, Dell Publishing Company;

p. 50: © Larry Berman; p. 52: Courtesy of Ann Streissguth; p. 53: © Joan Chiasson; p. 55: © Betty Press/Woodfin Camp & Associates; p. 56: Ryan Pyle/Ryan Pyle/Corbis; p. 57 (top): © Sharon Schindler Rising, Centering Pregnancy Program; p. 57 (bottom): © Jonathan Nourok/Getty Images; p. 58: © RF/Corbis; p. 59: © Dr. Holly Beckwith; p. 61: Paul Schreck, Photographer, Wellspan Health System; p. 62: © Marc Asnin/CORBIS SABA; p. 63: Courtesy of Dr. Tiffany Field; p. 65: Howard Grey/Getty Images

Chapter 3
p. 67: Trinette Reed/Brand X Pictures/JupiterImages; p. 68 (left): © Wendy Stone/Corbis; (right): © Dave Bartruff/Corbis; p. 70: ER Productions/Getty Images; p. 72 (top): © David Grugin Productions, Inc. Reprinted by permission; p. 72 (bottom): Image courtesy of Dana Boatman, Ph.D., Department of Neurology, Johns Hopkins University, reprinted with permission from *The Secret Life of the Brain*, Joseph Henry Press; p. 73: Jamie Grill/Getty Images; p. 74 (top): Blend Images/Getty Images; (bottom): © Stockbyte/PictureQuest; p. 75: Courtesy Dr. T. Berry Brazelton and Brazelton Touchpoints Center; p. 76: Courtesy of Esther Thelan; p. 78: Courtesy Dr. Karen Adolph, New York University; p. 79 (left to right): © Barbara Penoyar/Getty Images; © Digital Vision/Getty Images; © Image Source/Alamy; Titus/Getty Images; © Digital Vision; BananaStock/PictureQuest; Corbis/PictureQuest; © Brand X Pictures/PunchStock; p. 80: Courtesy Amy Needham, Duke University; p. 81: Adapted from "The Origin of Form and Perception" by R.L. Fantz; p. 82 (top): Photo from Karen Adolph's laboratory at New York University; p. 82 (bottom): Kevin Peterson/Getty Images/Simulation by Vischeck; p. 84: © Mark Richards/PhotoEdit; p. 85: From D. Rosenstein and H. Oster "Differential Facial Responses to Four Basic Tastes in Newborns," *Child Development*, Vol. 59, 1988. © Society for Research in Child Development, Inc.; p. 86: Anthony Cain/Flickr/Getty Images; p. 88: © Doug Goodman/Photo Researchers;

p. 89: © Radius Images/Corbis; p. 90: Courtesy of Dr. Carolyn Rovee-Collier; p. 91 (top): © Stockbyte/Getty Images; (bottom): © Andrew Meltzoff; p. 93: From Jean Mandler, University of California, San Diego. Reprinted by permission of Oxford University Press, Inc.; p. 94: © 2003 University of Washington, Institute for Learning and Brain Sciences (I-LABS); p. 96: © ABPL Image Library/Animals Animals/Earth Scenes; p. 98: © Digital Vision/Getty Images; p. 99: Mark Hall/Taxi/Getty Images

Chapter 4
p. 101: © Rick Gomez/Corbis; p. 102: Jose Luis Pelaez Inc./Getty Images; p. 103 (left to right): © BananaStock/PictureQuest; The McGraw-Hill Companies, Inc./Jill Braaten, photographer; David Sacks/Getty Images; © Getty Images; p. 104: © 2007 Getty Images, Inc.; p. 110: © BananaStock/PictureQuest; p. 111: Courtesy Celia A. Brownell, University of Pittsburgh; p. 112: © Martin Rogers/Stock Boston; p. 113: © Camille Tokerud/Getty Images; p. 114: © Penny Tweedie/Stone/Getty Images; p. 116: Photodisc/Getty Images; p. 117: Courtesy of Dr. Barry Hewlett; p. 118: © Schwartzwald Lawrence/Corbis; p. 119: Courtesy of Wanda Mitchell

Chapter 5
p. 122: © Rubberball/PictureQuest; p. 123 (top): Ruby Washington/The New York Times/Redux Pictures; p. 123 (bottom): DK Stock/Robert Glenn/Getty Images; p. 126: Pixtal Images/photolibrary; p. 128: © AP Wide World Photos; p. 131: © Michael Newman/PhotoEdit; p. 132: Jose Luis Pelaez Inc./Blend Images/Getty Images; p. 134 (left): A.R. Lauria/Dr. Michael Cole, Laboratory of Human Cognition, University of California, San Diego; (right): © Bettmann/Corbis; p. 136: © BananaStock/PunchStock; p. 137: © 2005 JAMESKAMP.com; p. 142: Michael Grecco/Hulton Archive/Getty Images; p. 144: Courtesy of Yolanda Garcia

Chapter 6
p. 148: A. Chederros/Getty Images; p. 150 (top): © Kevin Dodge/Corbis; (bottom): © RF/Corbis; p. 152: © Image Source/PunchStock; p. 153: © Yves De

Chapter 17

p. 373: Dennis Stock/Magnum Photos; p. 375: © Handout Courtesy of the Schiavo Family/Corbis; p. 376: © USA Today, photographer Tim Dillon; p. 377: © Patrick Ward/Stock Boston, Inc.; p. 378: Tim Hall/Getty Images; p. 380: Stockbroker/photolibrary; p. 381: © Digital Vision; p. 382: Thomas Hinton/Splash News/Newscom; p. 383: © Robert Mulder/Godong/Corbis

Text and Line Art Credits

Figure 1.9: Kopp, Claire B. and Krakow, Joanne B. *The Child: Development in the Social Context*, p. 648. Copyright © 1982 Pearson Education. Reprinted by permission of Pearson Education, Inc., Upper Saddle River, New Jersey.

Figure 2.1: From John Santrock, *A Topical Approach to Life-Span Development*, 2nd ed. Copyright © 2005 The McGraw-Hill Companies, Inc. Reproduced with permission by The McGraw-Hill Companies.

Figure 2.2: From John Santrock, *Psychology*, 7th ed. Copyright © 2003 The McGraw-Hill Companies, Inc. Reproduced with permission by The McGraw-Hill Companies.

Figure 2.9: From John Santrock, *Child Development*, 10th ed. Copyright © 2004 The McGraw-Hill Companies, Inc. Reproduced with permission by The McGraw-Hill Companies.

Figure 3.1: From John Santrock, *Children*, 9th ed. Copyright © 2007 The McGraw-Hill Companies, Inc. Reproduced with permission by The McGraw-Hill Companies.

Figure 3.3: From John Santrock, *Child Development*, 10th ed. Copyright © 2004 The McGraw-Hill Companies, Inc. Reproduced with permission by The McGraw-Hill Companies.

Figure 3.5: From John Santrock, *A Topical Approach to Life-Span Development*. Copyright ©2002 The McGraw-Hill Companies, Inc. Reproduced with permission by The McGraw-Hill Companies.

Figure 3.7: From John Santrock, *Children*, 5th ed. Copyright © 1997 The McGraw-Hill Companies, Inc. Reproduced with permission by The McGraw-Hill Companies.

Figure 3.20: From *Learning and the Infant Mind* edited by Woodward and Needham (2009). Table 1, p. 12. © 2005 by Amanda Woodward and Amy Needham. By permission of Oxford University Press, Inc.

Figure 3.23: From John Santrock *Children*, 9th ed. Copyright © 2007 The McGraw-Hill Companies, Inc. Reproduced with permission by The McGraw-Hill Companies.

Figure 3.24: From John Santrock, *Children*, 9th ed. Copyright © 2007 The McGraw-Hill Companies, Inc. Reproduced with permission by The McGraw-Hill Companies.

Figure 3.25: From John Santrock, *Child Development*, 10th ed. Copyright © 2004 The McGraw-Hill Companies, Inc. Reproduced with permission by The McGraw-Hill Companies.

Figure 4.4: From John Santrock, *Life-Span Development*, 4th ed. Copyright © 1992 The McGraw-Hill Companies, Inc. Reproduced with permission by The McGraw-Hill Companies.

Figure 4.7: From Jay Belsky, "Early Human Experiences: A Family Perspective," in *Developmental Psychology*, Vol. 17, pp. 3–25. Copyright © 1981 by the American Psychological Association.

Figure 4.9: Reprinted from *Encyclopedia of Infant and Early Childhood Development*, Vol. 1, A. Clarke-Steward and J.L. Miner, "Child and Day Care, Effects of," p. 269 Copyright © 2008 with permission from Elsevier.

Figure 5.1: From John Santrock, *Children*, 9th ed. Copyright © 2007 The McGraw-Hill Companies, Inc. Reproduced with permission by The McGraw-Hill Companies.

Figure 5.2: From *Well Being* by M H. Bornstein et al. (eds.). Copyright 2003 by Taylor & Francis Group, LLC—Books. Reproduced with permission of Taylor & Francis Group LLC—Books in the format Textbook via Copyright Clearance Center.

Figure 5.3: From John Santrock, *Psychology*, 7th ed. Copyright © 2003 The McGraw-Hill Companies, Inc. Reproduced with permission by The McGraw-Hill Companies.

Figure 5.10: Courtesy of Jean Berko Gleason.

Ch. 5, p. 141: (The devl and the babe ghoste) From Jean Berko Gleason, *The Development of Language*, 3/e. Published by Allyn and Bacon, Boston MA. Reprinted with permission by Maryanne Wolf, Ph.D., Tufts University.

Ch. 6, pp. 148–149: Text excerpts from Craig Lesley *Burning Fence: A Western Memoir of Fatherhood*, pp. 8–10, St. Martin's Press. Copyright © 2005 Craig Lesley.

Reprinted by permission from St. Martin's Press, LLC.

Figure 6.1: From John Santrock, *Child Development*, 10th ed. Copyright © 2004 The McGraw-Hill Companies, Inc. Reproduced with permission by The McGraw-Hill Companies.

Figure 6.3: From John Santrock, *Life-Span Development*, 13th ed. Copyright © 2011 The McGraw-Hill Companies, Inc. Reproduced with permission by The McGraw-Hill Companies.

Figure 7.2: From John Santrock, *Children*, 9th ed. Copyright © 2007 The McGraw-Hill Companies, Inc. Reproduced with permission by The McGraw-Hill Companies.

Figure 7.10: From "The Rise in IQ Scores from 1932 to 1997" from "The Increase in IQ Scores from 1932 to 1997" by Ulric Neisser. Reprinted by permission.

Figure 8.2: From Colby et al., "A Longitudinal Study of Moral Judgment," *Monographs of the Society for Research in Child Development*, Serial No. 201. Reprinted with permission by Blackwell Publishing, Ltd.

Figure 8.3: Reproduced by special permission of the Publisher, Mind Garden, Inc., www.mindgarden.com from the Bem Sex Role Inventory by Sandra Bem. Copyright © 1978, 1981 by Consulting Psychologists Press, Inc. Further reproduction is prohibited without the Publisher's written consent.

Figure 8.5: From Stevenson, Lee, & Stigler, 1986, Figure 6. "Mathematics Achievement of Chinese, Japanese and American Children," *Science*, Vol. 231, pp. 693–699. Reprinted with permission from AAAS.

Figure 10.3: From John Santrock, *Child Development*, 11th ed. Copyright © 2007 The McGraw-Hill Companies, Inc. Reproduced with permission by The McGraw-Hill Companies.

Figure 11.1: Reprinted from *Journal of Adolescent Health* 39, Park et al., "The Health Status of Young Adults . . ." pp. 305–317. Elsevier Science. Copyright 2006, with permission from Elsevier.

Figure 11.2: Centers for Disease Control and Prevention (2006). Based on data collected in the 2005 National Health Interview Study.

Figure 11.4: From *Sex in America* by Robert T. Michael, John H. Gagnon, Edward O. Laumann, and Gina Kolata. Copyright © 1994 by CSG Enterprises,

Name Index

Subject Index

SUBJECT INDEX